MW01054341

Additional Praise for
Implementing Enterprise Risk Management

"Educators the world over seeking to make the management of risk an integral part of management degrees have had great difficulties in providing their students with a definitive ERM text for their course. The Standards and associated Handbooks helped, but until the arrival of *Implementing Enterprise Risk Management: Case Studies and Best Practices*, there has been no text to enlighten students on the application of an effective program to manage risk across an enterprise so that objectives are maximized and threats minimized. Fraser, Simkins, and Narvaez have combined with a group of contributors that represent the cream of risk practitioners, to provide the reader with a clear and concise journey through the management of risk within a wide range of organizations and industries. The knowledge, skills, and experience in the management of risk contained within the covers of this book are second to none. It will provide a much needed resource to students and practitioners for many years to come and should become a well-used reference on the desk of every manager of risk."
>   —Kevin W. Knight AM, chairman, ISO/TC 262—Risk Management

"The authors—Fraser, Simkins, and Narvaez—have done an invaluable service to advance the science of enterprise risk management by collecting an extensive number of wonderful case studies that describe innovative risk management practices in a diverse set of companies around the world. This book should be an extremely valuable source of knowledge for anyone interested in the emerging and evolving field of risk management."
>   —Robert S. Kaplan, senior fellow, Marvin Bower Professor of Leadership
>   Development, emeritus, Harvard University

"Lessons learned from case studies and best practices represent an efficient way to gain practical insights on the implementation of ERM. *Implementing Enterprise Risk Management* provides such insights from a robust collection of ERM programs across public companies and private organizations. I commend the editors and contributors for making a significant contribution to ERM by sharing their experiences."
>   —James Lam, president, James Lam & Associates; director and Risk Oversight
>   Committee chairman, E*TRADE Financial Corporation;
>   author, *Enterprise Risk Management—From Incentives to Controls*

"For those who still think that enterprise risk management is just a fad, the varied examples of practical value-generating uses contained in this book should dispel any doubt that the discipline is here to stay! The broad collection of practices is insightful for students, academics, and executives, as well as seasoned risk management professionals."
>   —Carol Fox, ARM, director of Strategic and Enterprise Risk Practice, RIMS

"Managing risk across the enterprise is the new frontier of business management. Doing so effectively, in my view, will be the single most important differentiating factor for many enterprises in the twenty-first century. *Implementing Enterprise Risk Management: Case Studies and Best Practices* is an innovative and important addition to the literature and contains a wealth of insight in this critical area. This book's integration of theory with hands-on, real-world lessons in managing enterprise risk provides an opportunity for its readers to gain insight and understanding that could otherwise be acquired only through many years of hard-earned experience.

I highly recommend this book for use by executives, line managers, risk managers, and business students alike."

—Douglas F. Prawitt, professor of Accounting at Brigham Young University, and Committee of Sponsoring Organizations (COSO) Executive Board member

"The real beauty of and value in this book is its case study focus and the wide variety of firms profiled and writers' perspectives shared. This will provide readers with a wealth of details and views that will help them chart an ERM journey of their own that is more likely to fit the specific and typically customized ERM needs of the firms for whom they toil."

—Chris Mandel, senior vice president, Strategic Solutions for Sedgwick; former president of the Risk Management Society and the 2004 Risk Manager of the Year

"*Implementing Enterprise Risk Management* looks at many industries through excellent case studies, providing a real-world base for its recommendations and an important reminder that ERM is valuable in many industries. I highly recommend this text."

—Russell Walker, Clinical associate professor, Kellogg School of Management; author of *Winning with Risk Management*

"The body of knowledge in *Implementing Enterprise Risk Management* continues to develop as business educators and leaders confront a complex and rapidly changing environment. This book provides a valuable resource for academics and practitioners in this dynamic area."

—Mark L. Frigo, director, Strategic Risk Management Lab, Kellstadt Graduate School of Business, DePaul University

"The management of enterprise risk is one of the most vexatious problems confronting boards and executives worldwide. This is why this latest book by Fraser, Simkins, and Narvaez is a much needed and highly refreshing approach to the subject. The editors have managed to assemble an impressive list of contributors who, through a series of fascinating real-life case studies, adroitly help educate readers to better understand and deal with the myriad of risks that can assault, seriously maim, and/or kill an organization. This is a 'how to' book written with the 'risk management problem solver' in mind. It provides the link that has been missing for effectively teaching ERM at the university and executive education levels and it is an exceptional achievement by true risk management advocates."

—Dr. Chris Bart, FCPA, founder and lead faculty, The Directors College of Canada

"The Institute of Risk Management welcomes the publication of this highly practical text which should be of great interest to our students and members around the world. *Implementing Enterprise Risk Management* brings together a fine collection of detailed case studies from organizations of varying sizes and working in different sectors, all seeking to enhance their business performance by managing their risks more effectively, from the boardroom to the shop floor. This book makes a valuable contribution to the body of knowledge of what works that will benefit the development of the risk profession."

—Carolyn Williams, technical director, Institute of Risk Management

IMPLEMENTING ENTERPRISE RISK MANAGEMENT

The *Robert W. Kolb Series in Finance* provides a comprehensive view of the field of finance in all of its variety and complexity. The series is projected to include approximately 65 volumes covering all major topics and specializations in finance, ranging from investments, to corporate finance, to financial institutions. Each volume in the *Kolb Series in Finance* consists of new articles especially written for the volume.

Each volume is edited by a specialist in a particular area of finance, who develops the volume outline and commissions articles by the world's experts in that particular field of finance. Each volume includes an editor's introduction and approximately thirty articles to fully describe the current state of financial research and practice in a particular area of finance.

The essays in each volume are intended for practicing finance professionals, graduate students, and advanced undergraduate students. The goal of each volume is to encapsulate the current state of knowledge in a particular area of finance so that the reader can quickly achieve a mastery of that special area of finance.

IMPLEMENTING ENTERPRISE RISK MANAGEMENT

Case Studies and Best Practices

Editors

John R.S. Fraser
Betty J. Simkins
Kristina Narvaez

The Robert W. Kolb Series in Finance

WILEY

Cover Design: Wiley
Cover Image: © iStock.com/clauiad

Copyright © 2015 by John R.S. Fraser, Betty J. Simkins, Kristina Narvaev. All rights reserved.

Published by John Wiley & Sons, Inc., Hoboken, New Jersey.
Published simultaneously in Canada.

No part of this publication may be reproduced, stored in a retrieval system, or transmitted in any form or by any means, electronic, mechanical, photocopying, recording, scanning, or otherwise, except as permitted under Section 107 or 108 of the 1976 United States Copyright Act, without either the prior written permission of the Publisher, or authorization through payment of the appropriate per-copy fee to the Copyright Clearance Center, Inc., 222 Rosewood Drive, Danvers, MA 01923, (978) 750-8400, fax (978) 646-8600, or on the Web at www.copyright.com. Requests to the Publisher for permission should be addressed to the Permissions Department, John Wiley & Sons, Inc., 111 River Street, Hoboken, NJ 07030, (201) 748-6011, fax (201) 748-6008, or online at http://www.wiley.com/go/permissions.

Limit of Liability/Disclaimer of Warranty: While the publisher and author have used their best efforts in preparing this book, they make no representations or warranties with respect to the accuracy or completeness of the contents of this book and specifically disclaim any implied warranties of merchantability or fitness for a particular purpose. No warranty may be created or extended by sales representatives or written sales materials. The advice and strategies contained herein may not be suitable for your situation. You should consult with a professional where appropriate. Neither the publisher nor author shall be liable for any loss of profit or any other commercial damages, including but not limited to special, incidental, consequential, or other damages.

For general information on our other products and services or for technical support, please contact our Customer Care Department within the United States at (800) 762-2974, outside the United States at (317) 572-3993 or fax (317) 572-4002.

Wiley publishes in a variety of print and electronic formats and by print-on-demand. Some material included with standard print versions of this book may not be included in e-books or in print-on-demand. If this book refers to media such as a CD or DVD that is not included in the version you purchased, you may download this material at http://booksupport.wiley.com. For more information about Wiley products, visit www.wiley.com.

Library of Congress Cataloging-in-Publication Data:

ISBN 978-1-118-69196-0 (Hardcover)
ISBN 978-1-118-74576-2 (ePDF)
ISBN 978-1-118-74618-9 (ePub)

10 9 8 7 6 5 4 3 2 1

To Wendy, my wonderful wife and my inspiration, and to my parents who instilled in me a lifelong thirst for learning.

—John Fraser

To my husband (Russell) and our family: sons and daughters-in-law (Luke & Stephanie and Walt & Lauren), daughter and son-in-law (Susan & Jason), and our youngest daughter (April). Thank you for your love, support, and encouragement!

—Betty Simkins

I would like to thank my husband and four children for supporting me on my journey of writing two chapters and co-editing this book. I would also like to thank the Risk and Insurance Management Society for supporting me during my educational years and providing great workshops and conferences on enterprise risk management.

—Kristina Narvaez

Contents

Foreword

Enterprise Risk Management is an evolving discipline focused on a complex and still imperfectly-understood subject. In such a situation, science is advanced best by collecting data from multiple, independent sites. A rich set of observations educates the field's scholars and practitioners and provides the foundation for them to develop descriptive and normative theories as well as codified best practices about the subject.

The authors—Fraser, Simkins, and Narvaez—have done an invaluable service to advance the science of enterprise risk management by collecting an extensive number of wonderful case studies that describe innovative risk management practices in a diverse set of companies around the world. This book should be an extremely valuable source of knowledge for anyone interested in the emerging and evolving field of risk management. We should be grateful to the editors and to each chapter author for expanding the body of knowledge for risk management professionals and academics.

Robert S. Kaplan
Senior Fellow, Marvin Bower Professor
of Leadership Development, Emeritus
Harvard University

CHAPTER 1

Enterprise Risk Management Case Studies

An Introduction and Overview

JOHN R.S. FRASER
Senior Vice President, Internal Audit, and former Chief Risk Officer, Hydro One
Networks Inc.

BETTY J. SIMKINS
Williams Companies Chair of Business and Professor of Finance, Oklahoma State
University

KRISTINA NARVAEZ
President and Owner of ERM Strategies, LLC

> Businesses, business schools, regulators, and the public are now scrambling to
> catch up with the emerging field of enterprise risk management.
> —Robert Kaplan (quote from Foreword in Fraser and Simkins, 2010)

> Most executives with MBA degrees were not taught ERM. In fact, there are only
> a few universities that teach ERM. So some business school graduates are strong
> in finance, marketing, and management theory, but they are limited in terms of
> critical thinking, business acumen, and risk analysis skills.
> —Paul Walker[1]

THE EVOLUTION OF ENTERPRISE RISK MANAGEMENT

Over the past two decades enterprise risk management (ERM) has evolved
from concepts and visions of how risks should be addressed to a methodology that is becoming entrenched in modern management and is now
increasingly expected by those in oversight roles (e.g., governing bodies and
regulators). As Felix Kloman describes in his chapter "A Brief History of Risk Management," published in Fraser and Simkins (2010), many of the concepts go back
a very long time and many of the so-called newly discovered techniques can be

referenced to the earlier writings and practices described by Kloman. However, it is only from around the mid-1990s that the concept of giving a name to managing risks in a holistic way across the many operating silos of an enterprise started to take hold. In the 1990s, terms such as *integrated risk management* and *enterprise-wide risk management* were also used. Many thought leaders, for example, those who created ISO 31000,[2] believe that the term *risk management* is all that is needed to describe good risk management; however, many others believe that the latter term is often used to describe risk management at the lower levels of the organization and does not necessarily capture the concepts of enterprise-level approaches to risk. As a result, the term ERM is used throughout this book.

As ERM continues to evolve there is still much discussion and confusion over exactly what it is and how it should be achieved. It is important to realize that it is still evolving and may take many more years before it is fully codified and practiced in a consistent way. In fact, there is a grave danger now of believing that there is only one way of doing ERM. This is probably a mistake by regulators who have too eagerly seized some of these concepts and are trying to impose them when the methods are not fully understood, and in some cases the requirements are unlikely to produce the desired results. As Fraser and Simkins (2010) noted in their first book on ERM: "While regulatory interest can force ERM into companies, if not done well, it can become another box-ticking exercise that adds little value."[3]

The leading and most commonly agreed[4] guideline to holistic risk management is ISO 31000. However, it should be mentioned that in the United States the COSO 2004 Enterprise Risk Management–Integrated Framework has been the dominant framework used to date. Many organizations are currently adopting one or the other of these frameworks and then customizing them to their own context.

WHY THE NEED FOR A BOOK WITH ERM CASE STUDIES?

Following the success of the earlier *Enterprise Risk Management: Today's Leading Research and Best Practices for Tomorrow's Executives* by Fraser and Simkins (2010), we found through our own teaching experiences, and by talking to others, that there was an urgent need for a university-level textbook of ERM case studies to help educate executives, risk practitioners, academics, and students alike about the evolving methodology. As a result, Fraser and Simkins, together with Kristina Narvaez, approached many of the leading ERM specialists to write case studies for this book.

Surveys have also shown that there is a dire need for more case studies on ERM (see Fraser, Schoening-Thiessen, and Simkins 2008). Additionally, surveys of risk executives report that business risk is increasing due to new technologies, faster rate of change, increases in regulatory risk, and more (PWC 2014). As Paul Walker of St. John's University points out in the opening quote of the 2014 American Productivity & Quality Center (APQC) report on ERM, "Most executives with MBA degrees were not taught ERM. In fact, there are only a few universities that teach ERM. So some business school graduates are strong in finance, marketing, and management theory, but they are limited in terms of critical thinking, business acumen, and risk analysis skills." Learning Centered Teaching (LCT), as discussed in Chapter 2, is an ideal way to achieve this. Using LCT and the case study approach, students actively participate in the learning process through constructive reflective reasoning, critical thinking and analysis, and discussion of key issues. This is the first book to provide such a broad coverage of case studies on ERM.

The case studies that follow are from some of the leading academics and practitioners of enterprise risk management. While many of the cases are about real-life situations, there are also those that, while based on real-life experiences, have had names changed to maintain confidentiality or are composites of several situations. We are deeply indebted to the authors and to the organizations that agreed so kindly to share their stories to help benefit future generations of ERM practitioners. In addition, we have added several chapters where we feel the fundamentals of these specialized techniques (e.g., VaR) deserve to be understood by ERM students and practitioners. Each case study provides opportunities for executives, risk practitioners, and students to explore what went well, what could have been done differently, and what lessons are to be learned.

Teachers of ERM will find a wealth of material to use in demonstrating ERM principles to students. These can be used for term papers or class discussions, and the approaches can be contrasted to emphasize different contexts that may require customized approaches. This book introduces the reader to a wide range of concepts and techniques for managing risks in a holistic way, by correctly identifying risks and prioritizing the appropriate responses. It offers a broad overview of the various types of ERM techniques, the role of the board of directors, risk tolerances, profiles, workshops, and allocation of resources, while focusing on the principles that determine business success.

Practitioners interested in implementing ERM, enhancing their knowledge on the subject, or wishing to mature their ERM program, will find this book an absolute must resource to have. Case studies are one of the best ways to learn more on this topic.

This book is a companion to *Enterprise Risk Management: Today's Leading Research and Best Practices for Tomorrow's Executives* (Fraser and Simkins 2010). Together, these two books can create a curriculum of study for business students and risk practitioners who desire to have a better understanding of the world of enterprise risk management and where it is heading in the future. Boards and senior leadership teams in progressive organizations are now engaging in building ERM into their scenario-planning and decision-making processes. These forward-looking organizations are also integrating ERM into the business-planning process with resource allocation and investment decisions. At the business unit level, ERM is being used to measure the performance of risk-taking activities of employees.

As these case studies demonstrate, ERM is a continuous improvement process and takes time to evolve. As can be gleaned from these case studies, most firms that have taken the ERM journey started with a basic ERM language, risk identification, and risk-assessment process and then moved down the road to broaden their programs to include risk treatments, monitoring, and reporting processes. The ultimate goal of ERM is to have it embedded into the risk culture of the organization and drive the decision-making process to make more sound business decisions.

SUMMARY OF THE BOOK CHAPTERS

As mentioned earlier, the purpose of this book is to provide case studies on ERM in order to educate executives, risk practitioners, academics, and students alike about this evolving methodology. To achieve this goal, the book is organized into the following sections:

Part I: Overview and Insights for Teaching ERM
Part II: ERM Implementation at Leading Organizations
Part III: Linking ERM to Strategy and Strategic Risk Management
Part IV: Specialized Aspects of Risk Management
Part V: Mini-Cases on ERM and Risk
Part VI: Other Case Studies

Brief descriptions of the contributors and the chapters are provided next.

PART I: OVERVIEW AND INSIGHTS FOR TEACHING ERM

The first two chapters provide an overview of ERM and guidance on ERM education. As we have pointed out, education on ERM is crucial and more universities need to offer courses in this area. Our conversations with many ERM educators and consultants highlight how extremely challenging it is to achieve excellence in ERM education.

Chapter 2, "An Innovative Method to Teaching Enterprise Risk Management: A Learner-Centered Teaching Approach," offers insights and suggestions on teaching ERM. This chapter covers the concept of flipping the classroom with learner-centered teaching (LCT), distinguishes it from traditional lectures, and describes how it can be used in teaching ERM. The LCT approach emphasizes active student participation and collaboration on in-class activities such as case studies versus the traditional lecture approach. This chapter provides several examples as to how LCT can be applied in teaching ERM, utilizing Fraser and Simkins' (2010) book. David R. Lange and Betty J. Simkins, both experienced ERM educators, team together to write this chapter. David Lange, DBA, is an Auburn University Montgomery (AUM) Distinguished Research and Teaching Professor of Finance. He has received many prestigious awards for both research and teaching from the University and from several academic associations. He has taught many courses in the area of risk management and has consulted in a significant number of individual and class insurance–related cases in both state and federal court. Betty Simkins, PhD, the Williams Companies Chair of Business and Professor of Finance at Oklahoma State University, is coeditor of this book.

PART II: ERM IMPLEMENTATION AT LEADING ORGANIZATIONS

Part II is a collection of ERM case studies that give examples of how ERM was developed and applied in major organizations around the world. Note that there is no perfect ERM case study and the objective is for readers to assess what they believe was successful or not so successful about these ERM programs.

The first case study in this book describes ERM at Mars, Inc. Larry Warner, who is the former corporate risk manager at Mars, Inc. and now is president of Warner Risk Group, describes the ERM program at the company in Chapter 3. Mars is a global food company and one of the largest privately held corporations in the United States. It has more than 72,000 associates and annual net sales in excess of $33 billion across six business segments—Petcare, Chocolate, Wrigley, Food, Drinks, and Symbioscience. Its brands include Pedigree, Royal Canin, M&M's, Snickers, Extra, Skittles, Uncle Ben's, and Flavia. With such complex business operations, Mars recognized the importance of providing its managers with a tool to knowledgably and comfortably take risk in order to achieve its long-term goals. Mars business units use its award-winning process to test their annual operating plan and thereby increase the probability of achieving these objectives.

The case study in Chapter 4 entitled "Value and Risk: ERM in Statoil" was written by Alf Alviniussen, who is the former Group Treasurer and Senior Vice President of Norsk Hydro ASA, Oslo, Norway, and Håkan Jankensgård who holds a PhD in risk management from Lund University, Sweden. Håkan is also a former risk manager of Norsk Hydro. In this case study, the authors discuss ERM at Statoil, one of the top oil and gas companies in the world, located in Norway. In Statoil, understanding and managing risk is today considered a core value of the company, which is written into the corporate directives and widely communicated to employees. ERM is thoroughly embedded in the organization's work processes, and its risk committee has managed the transition from a "silo"-mentality to promoting Statoil's best interests in areas where risk needs to be considered.

Chapter 5, called "ERM in Practice at University of California Health Systems," is written by their former Chief Risk Officer (CRO), Grace Crickette, who is now the Senior Vice President and Chief Risk and Compliance Officer of AAA Northern California, Nevada, and Utah. The University of California's (UC) Health System is comprised of numerous clinical operations, including five medical centers that support the clinical teaching programs for the university's medical and health science school and handle more than three million patient visits each year. ERM plays an important role at the UC Health System and assists the organization in assessing and responding to all risks (operational, clinical, business, accreditation, and regulatory) that affect the achievement of the strategic and financial objectives of the UC Health System.

The descriptive case study in Chapter 6, written by Dr. Mark Frigo from DePaul University and Hans Læssøe, the Strategic Risk Manager of the LEGO Group, provides a great example of integrating risk management in strategy development and strategy execution at the LEGO Group, which is based on an initiative started in late 2006 and led by co-author Hans Læssøe. The LEGO methodology is also part of the continuing work of the Strategic Risk Management Lab at DePaul University, which is identifying and developing leading practices in integrating risk management with strategy development and execution.

United Grain Growers (UGG), a conservative 100-year-old Winnipeg, Canada-based grain handler and distributor of farm supplies, was an ERM pioneer. Chapter 7 called "Turning the Organizational Pyramid Upside Down: Ten Years of Evolution in Enterprise Risk Management at United Grain Growers" analyzes the ERM program at United Grain Growers 15 years later. When UGG announced that it had implemented a new integrated risk-financing program in 1999, it received a great deal of attention in the financial press. CFO magazine hailed the UGG program as "the deal of the decade." *The Economist* characterized it as a "revolutionary advance in corporate finance," and Harvard University created a UGG case study. While most outside attention focused on the direct financial benefits of implementing the program (protection of cash flow, the reduced risk-capital required, and a 20 percent increase in stock price), scant attention was given to the less tangible and therefore less measurable issues of governance, leadership, and corporate culture—the conditions that enabled such innovation. It was a combination of a collaborative leadership open to new ideas, a culture of controlled risk taking, and active risk oversight by the board that produced a strategic approach to UGG's risk management process. This chapter is written by John Bugalla, who is the principal of ermINSIGHTS.

John Hargreaves has written Chapter 8 titled "Housing Association Case Study of ERM in a Changing Marketplace." He has a mathematics degree from Cambridge University and six years strategy consultancy experience at KPMG. This case study features four real-life charitable housing associations in England and Wales, each with a different strategy and risk environment. Simple yet practical tools to assist in risk identification and prioritization are also presented. This case study has two main aims. The first is to help develop an understanding of the importance of ERM in a charitable context, showing that modern charities are often very active organizations that face significant risks. Second, the case aims to illustrate the need for a close relationship between risk assessment and strategy development, particularly in sectors where objectives are defined in social as well as economic terms. Each of the four cases has a different perspective and challenges the student or practitioner to identify and assess the risk and develop possible risk treatments for each.

Chapter 9, "Lessons from the Academy: ERM Implementation in the University Setting," was written by Anne E. Lundquist. She is pursuing a PhD in the Educational Leadership program at Western Michigan University with a concentration in Higher Education Administration. This chapter explores the unique aspects of the University of Washington's (UW) risk environment, including how leadership, goal-setting, planning, and decision-making differ from the for-profit sector. The lack of risk management regulatory requirements, combined with cultural and environmental differences, helps explain why there are a limited number of fully evolved ERM programs at colleges and universities. The second half of the chapter explores the decision to adopt and implement ERM at UW, including a description of early decisions, a timeline of how the program evolved, a discussion of the ERM framework, and examples of some of the tools used in the risk management process. It traces the evolution of the UW program as well as demonstrates decisions that administrators made to tailor ERM to fit the decentralized culture of a university.

The case study in Chapter 10, "Developing Accountability in Risk Management: The British Columbia Lottery Corporation Case Study," demonstrates how ERM was successfully implemented in a Canadian public sector organization over a 10-year period. Jacquetta Goy, author of this chapter, was the Senior Manager, Risk Advisory Services at British Columbia Lottery Corporation and was responsible for establishing and developing the ERM program. Currently, Jacquetta is the Director of Risk Management at Thompson Rivers University, Canada. This case study focuses on initiation, early development, and sustainment of the ERM program, highlighting some of the barriers and enablers that affected implementation. This case study includes a focus on developing risk profiles; the role of risk managers, champions, and committees; and the development of effective risk evaluation tools. The approach to ERM has evolved from informal conversations supported by an external assessment, through a period of high-level corporate focus supported by a dedicated group of champions using voting technology to an embedded approach, where risk assessment is incorporated into both operational practice and planning.

Chapter 11, "Starting from Scratch: The Evolution of ERM at the Workers Compensation Fund," describes the evolution of a formal ERM program at a midsize property casualty insurance carrier. This chapter is authored by Dan Hair, the CRO of the Workers Compensation Fund. In this chapter, the motivations of executive management and the board of directors in taking existing strategic risk management discussions to a higher level are reviewed. The step-by-step actions taken by the company to develop the ERM program are explained in chronological order. External resources used are also commented upon. The chapter concludes with a discussion of striking an ongoing balance between program rigor, documentation, and business needs.

Chapter 12, "Measuring Performance at Intuit: A Value-Added Component in ERM Programs," shows how Intuit, maker of Quicken, QuickBooks, and Turbo-Tax, is committed to creating new and easier ways for consumers and businesses to tackle life's financial chores, giving them more time to live their lives and run their businesses. This case study shows how Intuit, a global company, is exposed to a wide range of customer-related and operational risks. Understanding the risk landscape enables Intuit to formulate and execute strategies to address potential pitfalls and opportunities. The author, Janet Nasburg, is Chief Risk Officer at Intuit. Janet is responsible for driving Intuit's ERM capability, ensuring that the company appropriately balances opportunities and risks to achieve optimal business results. Before Intuit, Janet spent 16 years in various finance roles at Visa, and has more than 30 years of risk management and finance experience.

Chapter 13 describes TD Bank's ERM program and how it has been developed to reinforce the risk culture and ensure that all stakeholders have a common understanding of how risks are addressed within the organization. This is achieved by identifying the risks to TD Bank's business strategy and operations, determining the types of risk it is prepared to take, establishing policies and practices to govern risks, and following an ERM framework to manage those risks. This chapter is co-authored by Paul Cunha and Kristina Narvaez. Paul Cunha is Vice President, Enterprise Risk Management at TD Bank. During his career at TD Bank, he has spent time in risk management, internal audit, retail banking, commercial banking, and corporate and investment banking. Kristina Narvaez is the president and owner of ERM Strategies, LLC, and is co-editor of this book.

PART III: LINKING ERM TO STRATEGY AND STRATEGIC RISK MANAGEMENT

Part III of this book demonstrates the link between ERM and strategy in what is now being called strategic risk management (SRM). SRM represents an important evolution in enterprise risk management, shifting from a reactive approach to a proactive approach in dealing with the large spectrum of risks across the organization. These case studies view their risk-taking activities in a strategic way, not only to protect the organization's value and assets, but also to be able to capture new value that is in alignment with the strategic goals of the organization.

Zurich Insurance Group, the case study in Chapter 14, demonstrates the link between ERM and strategy. Zurich is a global insurance carrier and is exposed to a wide range of risks. Zurich recognizes that taking the right risks is a necessary part of growing and protecting shareholder value. It is careful not to miss valuable market opportunities that could attract the best talent and investor capital, but must also balance the growth opportunities with the reality that it is operating in a complex world economy. This chapter is co-authored by Linda Conrad, Director of Strategic Business Risk Management at Zurich and Kristina Narvaez, president and owner of ERM Strategies, LLC and co-editor of this book. Linda leads a global team responsible for delivering tactical solutions to Zurich and to its customers on strategic issues such as business resilience, supply chain risk, ERM, risk culture, and total risk profiling.

Chapter 15, "Embedding ERM into Strategic Planning at the City of Edmonton," is written by Ken Baker, who is their ERM Program Manager. This study examines the process used by the City of Edmonton in Alberta, Canada, to establish its strategic ERM model. After examining several existing frameworks, the City decided on a framework based on the ISO 31000 risk management standard, but customized to suit the City's needs. During the process, administration had to weigh factors common to any large organization, as well as those specific to governments in general and municipalities in particular. The chronicling of this process may assist those in similar organizations to more successfully implement their own ERM and SRM programs.

Chapter 16 describes a brief history of the evolution of enterprise risk management and describes a new and innovative approach (value mapping) to measuring the potential value by taking risks. This chapter also provides a model for incorporating the ERM process into strategic planning. John Bugalla, Principal of ermINSIGHTS and author of Chapter 7, and James Kallman, a finance professor at St. Edward's University, co-author this chapter. John's experience includes 30 years in the risk management profession serving as Managing Director of Marsh & McLennan, Inc., Willis Group, Plc., and Aon Corp., before founding ermINSIGHTS. James teaches courses in finance, statistics, and risk management.

PART IV: SPECIALIZED ASPECTS OF RISK MANAGEMENT

Part IV of the book captures unique aspects of ERM so that the reader can learn about the many broad applications, including insights into managing specific types of risk. This part starts with a case study in Chapter 17 of the challenges of risk management within a typical police department. This case is followed by eight additional chapters addressing other intriguing aspects of risk management.

Andrew Graham reveals the complex and challenging aspects of risk management in Chapter 17, "Developing a Strategic Risk Plan for the Hope City Police Service." This fictional case study was developed based on many years of teaching risk management to police forces. The setting is a medium-sized but growing city that is facing many issues, including changes in demographics, traffic issues, budgetary challenges, and so on. The student is required to act as a consultant who has been hired by the chief of police to assist him in briefing the Police Services Board and the mayor in understanding the most critical risks to their objective of having a best-in-class police service for their citizens. Andrew Graham researches, teaches, and writes on public-sector management, financial management, integrated risk management, and governance at Queen's University School of Policy Studies, Canada, as well as a variety of international and Canadian venues. Andrew had an extensive career in Canada's criminal justice system and has taught and worked with police services and police boards and commissioners in a variety of ways for the past 10 years.

Chapter 18, "Blue Wood Chocolates," is designed to facilitate discussion of the implementation of an ERM framework, corporate governance issues, and commodity risk management. The situation that this fictional company faces is typical of many midsize companies that have performed satisfactorily in the past but are exposed, often unknowingly, to major potential risks and do not have the internal governance and risk management structures to identify, quantify, and manage such risks adequately. In particular, this case illustrates commodity and foreign currency exposures, and challenges the student to investigate the specifics of hedging such positions. Rick Nason, PhD, CFA, and Stephen McPhie, CA, coauthored this chapter. Rick is an associate professor of finance at Dalhousie University, Canada, and is also a founding partner of RSD Solutions, a risk management consultancy firm. His coauthor, Stephen McPhie, CA, is a partner of RSD Solutions Inc. and has also held various positions in the United States, Canada, and the United Kingdom with a major Canadian bank.

Foreign exchange (FX) risk management is one of the greatest financial risks a company faces when expanding globally. Chapter 19, "Kilgore Custom Milling," illuminates the myriad of issues that arise when hedging FX risk, such as faced by a midsize original equipment manufacturer (OEM) operating in the automobile industry. Kilgore Custom Milling (a fictional company) needs to develop a hedging strategy to manage its foreign exchange risk for a new contract and decide what type of derivatives to use, what size of hedge to implement, and how the company's financial risk management fits in with its overall ERM process. Rick Nason and Stephen McPhie, coauthors of Chapter 18, team together again to explore the complex and challenging issues that many companies face with FX risk.

ERM is currently of very high interest to companies operating in the Middle East, an area that presents unique challenges for implementation. Alexander Larsen captures this scenario in Chapter 20, "Implementing Risk Management within Middle Eastern Oil and Gas Companies." This case study is based on real-life examples of Middle Eastern oil and gas companies and captures the challenges of implementing risk management in the Middle East. Alexander Larsen holds a degree in risk management from Glasgow Caledonian University and is a Fellow of the Institute of Risk Management. He has over 10 years of experience across a wide range of sectors, including oil and gas, construction, utilities, finance, and the public sector. Alexander has considerable expertise in training and working with organizations to develop, enhance, and embed their ERM.

Public safety organizations are increasingly adopting sophisticated enterprise governance and risk management techniques as a means of managing their programs and expenditures. Root cause analysis can provide these agencies with detailed insights into the problems and issues they face, and provide them with the information they need to make informed decisions on risk management. Chapter 21, "The Role of Root Cause Analysis in Public Safety ERM Programs," explores these issues by presenting six common root cause analysis techniques that are applied in a public safety or law enforcement environment. The chapter author, Andrew Bent, is a practicing risk manager with a large Canadian integrated energy company and was previously in charge of ERM for one of Canada's largest municipal police services.

Chapter 22, "JAA Inc.—A Case Study in Creating Value from Uncertainty: Best Practices in Managing Risk," provides extensive details about ERM implementation in a fictional international organization and discusses topics including governance structure, the processes, and the various tools used. The case is built on the principles and guidance of ISO 31000 and the implementation guidance created by The Australian and New Zealand Hand Book HB 436. This case emphasizes the roles of the heads of the internal audit function and the risk management function. The three coauthors of this chapter have extensive experience in risk management. Julian du Plessis, Head of Internal Audit at AVBOB Mutual Assurance Society, South Africa, has over eight years of financial sector experience. Arnold Schanfield is a Principal with Schanfield Risk Management Advisors LLC, and is an internal audit and risk professional with diversified industry expertise. Alpaslan Menevse is currently the Risk Officer at Sekerbank T.A.S., which has in excess of 310 branches in Turkey. He has 28 years of experience in information systems, both as an academic and as a practitioner.

A book on ERM case studies is not complete without some coverage of risk management failures. One of the most famous failures involving operational risk is discussed in Chapter 23, "Control Complacency: Rogue Trading at Société Générale." In January 2008, Société Générale uncovered €49 billion of unauthorized equity positions at its Paris head office, which cost €4.9 billion to unwind. Using an interactive format, this case study analyzes the origins, actors, causes, and consequences of this notorious control breakdown and derives risk management lessons from it in the areas of corporate governance, controls, compliance, systems, technology, and reputation risk. The author, Steve Lindo, Principal, SRL Advisory Services, has many years of experience in ERM and provides a thorough and fascinating coverage of this disaster.

Value at risk (VaR) is one of the most widely used techniques to measure financial risks, particularly in the area of investment portfolios. However, it is a technique that has not been fully understood by many risk managers. In Chapter 24, "The Role of VaR in Enterprise Risk Management: Calculating Value at Risk for Portfolios Held by the Vane Mallory Investment Bank," VaR is described along with its underlying assumptions, advantages, and disadvantages. Several examples for single assets are detailed for both the dollar and percentage VaR estimation methods. The main focus of this case study is a tutorial on calculating VaR for portfolios of assets using the covariance approach utilized in portfolio theory. Allissa A. Lee coauthored this case study with Betty J. Simkins. Allissa is an assistant professor of finance in the College of Business Administration at Georgia Southern University. She has published several academic articles and also worked in the mortgage industry for MidFirst Bank. Betty, coeditor of this book, is the

Williams Companies Chair of Business and Professor of Finance at Oklahoma State University.

Chapter 25, "Uses of Efficient Frontier Analysis in Strategic Risk Management," covers an advanced analytical technique, efficient frontier analysis (EFA), where complex property and casualty risk profiles are being considered. This chapter provides insights into risk portfolio volatility, pricing, and insurance layering efficiency using EFA and is applied to a risk portfolio that presents catastrophic loss potential within the context of strategic risk management. This chapter's coauthors are Ward Ching, who is Vice President, Risk Management Operations, at Safeway Inc., and Loren Nickel, who is Regional Director and Actuary, Actuarial and Analytics Practice, at Aon Global Risk Consulting. Both authors have extensive experience in property and casuality risk management and share their expertise in this specialized topic of ERM.

PART V: MINI-CASES ON ERM AND RISK

Mini-cases are a very powerful and highly useful resource in teaching ERM and can be easily utilized in short time periods such as a one-hour class segment. This part fills this gap in the education literature on ERM and includes six fictional mini-cases that have been developed by leading risk practitioners who draw from the wealth of their experiences in various applications of risk management.

Chapter 26, "Bim Consultants Inc.," is based on a real event in which a company was faced with an important strategic acquisition decision. All names and data have been changed for confidentially reasons. The purpose of the case is to illustrate the complexity of making strategic decisions and how greed and ego can cause a firm to change strategy that may put the business at risk. The author, John Fraser, Senior Vice President, Internal Audit, and former Chief Risk Officer of Hydro One Networks Inc., is also coeditor of this book. Fraser is currently an adjunct professor at York University, Canada, and a member of the faculty of the Directors College. He is a recognized authority on ERM and has written extensively on the topic.

Chapter 27, "Nerds Galore," is based on a fictitious small services company that appears to be on the verge of a major downturn. The focus of the case study is human resources–related risks, and the exercise is to conduct a risk assessment to aid in making the decision on whether to proceed with a major human resources strategy. This case study could be used as the basis for an actual risk workshop simulation with students role-playing various positions on the management team. Rob Quail, the author of this case study, draws on his extensive experience as Director of ERM at Hydro One Networks Inc., and provides an excellent mini-case to illuminate ERM applications.

Can a company have a successful ERM program that does not involve a key function, such as the legal department? And if not willing to participate, how do you convince this department to commit to ERM? The reader is challenged with tackling this crucial issue in Chapter 28, "The Reluctant General Counsel." This mini-case is about the implementation of ERM at a software company and illustrates the challenges faced when the general counsel of the company has reservations and is not willing to support the implementation. The author, Norman Marks, CPA, CRMA, has been chief audit executive of major global corporations for over 20 years, and is highly regarded in the global profession of internal auditing. Furthermore, he is a prolific blogger about internal audit, risk management, governance, and compliance.

Chapter 29, "Transforming Risk Management at Akawini Copper," describes how the approach to managing risk can be transformed and enhanced in a company. The case study is based on a hypothetical mining company, Akawini Copper, that has recently been acquired by an international concern. It draws on the practical concepts of ISO 31000 to show how a weak approach to risk management can be enhanced to be more robust and comprehensive by following a logical framework and transformation plan. The author, Grant Purdy, has worked in risk management for more than 35 years, across a wide range of industries and in more than 25 countries. Grant is coauthor of the 2004 version of AS/NZS 4360 and also of AS/NZS 5050, a standard for managing disruption-related risk, and has also written many risk management handbooks and guides.

Richard Leblanc, PhD, who is a governance lawyer, certified management consultant, and Associate Professor of Law, Governance, and Ethics at York University, draws on his extensive experience in board of director effectiveness when writing Chapter 30, "Alleged Corruption at Chessfield: Corporate Governance and the Risk Oversight Role of the Board of Directors." Richard has advised regulators on corporate governance guidelines, and, as part of his external professional activities, has served as an external board evaluator and governance adviser for many companies, as well as in an expert witness capacity in litigation concerning corporate governance reforms. This case deals with the inner workings of a large organization's board of directors, including allegations of alleged corruption and self-dealing, and provides the reader with a captivating application of risk management shortcomings in governance and internal controls.

Diana Del Bel Belluz, president and founder of Risk Wise, Inc., draws on her experience in operational risk when writing Chapter 31, "Operational Risk Management Case Study: Bon Boulangerie." This mini-case provides the opportunity for students to discuss and present their knowledge of operational risk. It describes the challenges and opportunities faced by a fictional bakery business in a small city. The bakery's owner has decided to expand the business for greater rewards, but in doing so is faced with a number of operational challenges. Additional information on the steps of operational risk management is available in Chapter 16 in Fraser and Simkins (2010). Diana has many years of consulting experience in ERM, and advances the practice of ERM through her thought leadership as an educator, conference organizer, speaker, and author of ERM resources.

PART VI: OTHER CASE STUDIES

Many risk management lessons can be learned from the financial crisis of 2008, and we begin this part with a chapter addressing this topic: Chapter 32, "Constructive Dialogue and ERM: Lessons from the Financial Crisis." In this chapter, Tom Stanton eloquently examines the critical distinctive factors between successful and unsuccessful firms in the crisis and refers to the presence or absence of these factors as constructive dialogue. Successful firms managed to create productive and constructive tension between those in the firm who wanted to do deals or offer certain financial products and services and those who were responsible for limiting risk exposures. Instead of simply deciding to do a deal or not, successful firms considered ways to hedge risks or otherwise reduce exposure from doing the deal. Thomas H. Stanton is a Fellow of the Center for Advanced Governmental Studies at Johns Hopkins University, a director of the Association of Federal Enterprise Risk Management, a former director of the National Academy of Public Administration, and a former member of the federal Senior Executive Service.

An important objective in this book is to provide global coverage about ERM by including insightful applications in various countries. Poland, after the transition into the free market economy in 1989, became open to knowledge and transfer of the best practices from around the world. Chapter 33, "Challenges and Obstacles of ERM Implementation in Poland," draws on years of research, both formal and informal, and documents the country's first approaches to ERM implementation. The successes, challenges, and weaknesses are described and provide a valuable lesson for other countries, regions, or even organizations in how they might go about implementing ERM. Two experts on ERM implementation in Poland teamed together to write this chapter. Zbigniew Krysiak, PhD, is an associate professor of finance at the Warsaw School of Economics in Poland. He is the author or coauthor of more than 100 publications, intended both for practitioners and for the academic community, concerning finance, risk management, financial engineering, and banking. His coauthor, Sławomir Pijanowski, PhD, is president of the POL-RISK Risk Management Association in Poland, where he is responsible for development of good risk management practices for the Polish market. He is coauthor of the Polish book titled *Risk Management for Sustainable Business* published by the Polish Ministry of the Economy and has many other accomplishments in the area of risk management.

Chapter 34 entitled "Turning Crisis into Opportunity: Building an ERM Program at General Motors" was written by leaders of ERM at GM—Marc Robinson, Lisa Smith, and Brian Thelen. This case study chronicles the ground-up implementation of ERM at General Motors Company (GM), starting in 2010 after it emerged from bankruptcy. While GM recognizes that its ERM is a work in progress, there have been important successes both in improving the management of risk and making better business decisions. Critical to these successes has been a clear strategic vision on adding value for the business leaders that are the true risk owners, unique decision tools such as game theory, and a continuous improvement mindset, including robust lessons learned. The study describes the lessons learned during implementation and some of the unique approaches, tools, and techniques that GM has employed. Examples of senior management reporting are also included.

The last case study in the book is also extremely insightful because it provides an excellent example of an ERM application at a company in Asia. The authors demonstrate in Chapter 35 how Astro, a Malaysia-based media company, uses ERM to grow through international acquisitions, and how it implements enterprise risk management not only to ensure sound risk management by its foreign subsidiaries and joint ventures, but also to make better risk/return decisions on its portfolio of direct investments. Both authors are authorities on ERM implementation globally. Ghislain Giroux Dufort is President of Baldwin Risk Strategies Inc., a consulting firm advising boards of directors and management teams on risk governance and ERM and has over 25 years of experience. Patrick Adam Kanagaratnam Abdullah is the Vice President of ERM for Astro Overseas Limited

(AOL), Malaysia. He specializes in the implementation of ERM practices across AOL's investments and has over 21 years of experience in various areas of risk management.

CONCLUSION

As outlined above, the case studies and specialized topic chapters in this book present an impressive coverage of new information on enterprise risk management, and all chapters are written by leading ERM experts globally. To our knowledge, this is the first book to be published that provides such comprehensive coverage of ERM case studies. We hope you find this book a valuable resource in your education and/or implementation of ERM. We welcome your comments and suggestions. Answers to the end-of-chapter questions and detailed teaching notes to most cases are available to instructors at www.wiley.com.

NOTES

1. See the 2014 American Productivity & Quality Center Report.
2. ISO 31000 was issued by the International Standards Organization in 2009. For a description refer to Chapter 7 of Fraser/Simkins by John Shortreed.
3. Fraser/Simkins, 15.
4. ISO 31000 has been agreed to by about 25 major countries of the international community as the guideline for risk management.

REFERENCES

American Productivity & Quality Center (APQC). 2014. APQC Report. www.apqc.org/.

Fraser, John, and Betty J. Simkins, eds. 2010. *Enterprise Risk Management: Today's Leading Research and Best Practices for Tomorrow's Executives.* Hoboken, NJ: John Wiley & Sons.

Fraser, John, Karen Schoening-Thiessen, and Betty J. Simkins. 2008. "Who Reads What Most Often? A Survey of Enterprise Risk Management Literature Read by Risk Executives." *Journal of Applied Finance* 18:1 (Spring/Summer).

PWC (PricewaterhouseCoopers). 2014. *Risk in Review: Re-Evaluating How Your Company Addresses Risk.* www.pwc.com/us/en/risk-assurance-services/publications/risk-in-review-transformation-management.jhtml.

ABOUT THE EDITORS

John R.S. Fraser is the Senior Vice-President, Internal Audit, and former Chief Risk Officer of Hydro One Networks Inc., Canada, one of North America's largest electricity transmission and distribution companies. He is a Fellow of the Institute of Chartered Accountants of Ontario, a Fellow of the Association of Chartered Certified Accountants (U.K.), a Certified Internal Auditor, and a Certified Information Systems Auditor. He has over 30 years of experience in the risk and control field mostly in the financial services sector, including areas such as finance, fraud, derivatives, safety, environmental, computers, and operations. He is a member of the Faculty at the Directors College for the Strategic Risk Oversight Program, and has developed and teaches a master's degree course entitled Enterprise Risk

Management in the Masters in Financial Accountability Program at York University where he is an adjunct professor. He is a recognized authority on enterprise risk management and has co-authored several academic papers on ERM. He is co-editor of a best-selling university textbook released in 2010, *Enterprise Risk Management: Today's Leading Research and Best Practices for Tomorrow's Executives.*

Betty J. Simkins, PhD, is Williams Companies Chair of Business and Professor of Finance at Oklahoma State University. Betty received her PhD from Case Western Reserve University. She has had more than 50 publications in academic finance journals. She has won awards for her teaching, research, and outreach, including the top awards at Oklahoma States University: Regents Distinguished Research Award and Outreach Excellence Award. Her primary areas of research are risk management, energy finance, and corporate governance. Betty serves on the editorial boards of nine academic journals, including the *Journal of Banking and Finance;* is past coeditor of the *Journal of Applied Finance;* and is past president of the Eastern Finance Association. She also serves on the Executive Advisory Committee of the Conference Board of Canada's Strategic Risk Council. In addition to this book, she has published two others: *Energy Finance and Economics: Analysis and Valuation, Risk Management and the Future of Energy* and *Enterprise Risk Management: Today's Leading Research and Best Practices for Tomorrow's Executives* (co-edited with John Fraser). Prior to entering academia, she worked in the corporate world for ConocoPhillips and Williams Companies. She conducts executive education courses for companies globally.

Kristina Narvaez is the president and owner of ERM Strategies, LLC (www.erm-strategies.com), which offers ERM research and training to organizations on various ERM-related topics. She graduated from the University of Utah in environmental risk management and then received her MBA from Westminster College. She is a two-time Spencer Education Foundation Graduate Scholar from the Risk and Insurance Management Society and has published more than 25 articles relating to enterprise risk management and board risk governance. She has given many presentations to various risk management associations on topics of ERM. She is an adjunct professor at Brigham Young University, teaching a business strategy course for undergraduates.

PART I

Overview and Insights for Teaching ERM

CHAPTER 2

An Innovative Method to Teaching Enterprise Risk Management

A Learner-Centered Teaching Approach

DAVID R. LANGE
Distinguished Research and Teaching Professor of Finance, Auburn University
Montgomery

BETTY J. SIMKINS
Williams Companies Chair of Business and Professor of Finance, Oklahoma State
University

Learner-centered teaching (LCT), commonly referred to as "flipping the classroom" (Shibley and Wilson 2012), is an alternative to the traditional teacher lecture (TL). With LCT, students actively participate in the pedagogical process and take increased responsibility for learning through constructive reflective reasoning. Where with TL content is covered, content in LCT is used as a "means to learning" (Weimer 2002). LCT is ideally suited for content provided in lists, tables, charts, and exhibits, and particularly so if these are in the form of topic overviews, flowcharts, or summaries. The case method espouses similar student-engaged learning processes by promoting critical thinking and analysis, creating discussion of conflicting issues and requiring a decision (Bean 2011). LCT amplifies and broadens student learning from cases. Hence, the case studies in this book are ideal for teaching enterprise risk management (ERM) using LCT.

The chapter is presented in three sections. The first section clarifies the concept of flipping the classroom with LCT, distinguishing LCT from a TL, and *why* the growing LCT movement should be joined. The second section considers the *what*, Weimer's (2002) *Learner Centered Teaching* "Five Key Changes to Practice," a definitive paradigm for changing pedagogy to LCT from a TL. A final section, the appendix, provides examples of *how*, using content to utilize LCT in an enterprise risk management (ERM) course at Auburn University Montgomery. The examples are from *Enterprise Risk Management: Today's Leading Research and Best Practices for Tomorrow's Executives* (Fraser and Simkins 2010), which opportunely provides ERM content in the supporting formats. The LCT examples are provided in

Exhibit 2.1   TL versus LCT

Bloom (1956)	Anderson and Krathwohl (2001)	Expanded
• Knowledge	• Remember: *Recognize, recall*	• *Memorize, recollect, retain*
• Comprehension	• Understand: *Interpret, explain*	• *Comprehend, realize, apprehend*
• Application	• Apply: *Calculate, solve*	• *Compute, estimate, determine*
• Analysis	• Analyze: *Distinguish, relate*	• *Examine, explore, study, associate*
• Evaluation	• Evaluate: *Critique, test*	• *Assess, appraise, review, comment*
• Synthesis	• Create: *Hypothesize, devise*	• *Speculate, theorize, postulate, offer, imagine, assume, suggest*

contrast to TL approaches, and include learning notes expanding the *how* of examples.

LEARNER-CENTERED TEACHING: THE *WHY*

Flipping the classroom refers to Bloom's Cognitive Learning Taxonomy (1956), a commonly accepted identification of levels of learning (Anderson and Krathwohl 2001; Bean 2011; Shibley and Wilson 2012), and thus an easily identifiable model with which to distinguish LCT from TL. Exhibit 2.1 has inverted Bloom's taxonomy to illustrate flipping the classroom. In a TL, the teacher normally progresses through the taxonomy starting with imparting knowledge:

- Knowledge: covering content with PowerPoint presentations, lecturers, and so on
- Comprehension: offering alternative descriptions and definitions, followed by a question of "What does this mean in your own words?"
- Application: solving problems step-by-step, demonstrating necessary calculations, and solving homework problems replicating calculations
- Analysis: comparing and explaining results from different problems
- Evaluation: questioning validity of assumptions, processes, and textbook sections on weaknesses in the model
- Synthesis: concluding with summaries and overviews

We may recognize the TL approach from our own experience or through classroom observation of peers.

To further illustrate the levels of learning, Anderson and Krathwohl's (2001) revision of Bloom's taxonomy is included in the center column of Exhibit 2.1. The third column contains an expanded list of active learning for additional clarification.

Learner-Centered Teaching

In LCT, content is used as a means to learning (Weimer 2002). Envision a learning process in which students compute a financial problem, examine different points of view, review and comment on an article, or postulate explanations for survey results. The knowledge (content) is discovered and used by the students in the learning process. Content in LCT is used as a means to learning (Weimer 2002), not presented and covered as in the context of a TL. In effect, as the examples will demonstrate, LCT enters Bloom's Cognitive Learning Taxonomy through the higher levels of application, analysis, evaluation, and synthesis.

Why LCT?

A primary explanation for education moving toward LCT is based on learning research that supports "more active, inductive instruction" (Smart, Witt, and Scott 2012). Increased student engagement, strengthened team-based skills, personalized student guidance, focused classroom discussion, and faculty freedom are several benefits of the growing LCT pedagogical adoption (Millard 2012). In a review of pedagogical literature with courses adopting LCT, Wright (2011, p. 96) found college teachers believe "a more effective learning environment" was provided, and "students tended to respond positively." A smaller study by Wohlfarth et al. (2008) acknowledged the need for further research and offered strong qualitative student support of LCT's importance in assisting learning.

There are several other reasons why LCT should be adopted. In a paper applying 29 components to benchmark the degree of LCT implementation, Blumberg and Pontiggia (2011) note the importance of LCT in their institutions' faculty development workshops, the implications for assessments and accreditation, and potential student admission promotional material. Yang (2010, p. 80) offers a globalization justification to adopt LCT, the need to "encourage students to actively participate in the discussion, and the need for students to fully express their views," even if it is counter to student cultural behavior.

Poor teaching experience with the TL is another supporting reason for LCT. The prepared TL covering knowledge, with students attempting to retain and simultaneously comprehend key points, may appear more as a sermon, speech, homily, or oration. Instructors, from their own experience or through classroom observation of peers, may relate to the "picture of somewhat lifeless students sitting passively in classrooms, with glazed eyes, some struggling to stay awake in dimmed classrooms as an instructor shared key concepts … using slides" (Smart, Witt, and Scott 2012, p. 393).

The educational goal is to engage students to become active versus passive learners by promoting critical thinking and "emphasizing inquiry" (Bean 2011, p. 38). LCT's flipped classrooms focus on *critique*, *assess*, *hypothesize*, and *speculate*, the higher levels of Bloom's Cognitive Learning Taxonomy. The base levels of knowledge and understanding may be assigned before class (Shibley and Wilson 2012).

FIVE KEY CHANGES TO PRACTICE THE *WHAT*

Weimer's *Learner Centered Teaching* (2002) "Five Key Changes to Practice" is a definitive paradigm for changing pedagogy to LCT. This section describes each of these "Five Key Changes to Practice," which are:

1. The Balance of Power
2. The Function of Content

3. The Role of the Teacher
4. The Responsibility for Learning
5. Evaluation Purpose and Process

Consideration of the five steps with each of the LCT ERM examples paradoxically resembles the TL approach. Therefore, instructors are encouraged to appraise their current pedagogy and associate the respective LCT changes to practice with their course. To assist your movement to LCT, Weimer's (2002) Part Two, "Implementing the Learner-Centered Approach," includes discussions of responding to resistance from students and faculty, taking a developmental approach in converting students from passive to active learners, and making LCT work based on principles of successful instructional improvement. Appendixes in Weimer (2002) offer suggestions for the syllabus and learning log (Appendix A), handouts for developing learning skills (B), and a recommended reading list (C). Blumberg (2009) provides an extensive step-by-step guide to adopting LCT.

The Balance of Power

The LCT classroom is more democratic than the TL, where sequencing, content, and information flow are one-way: professor to student. With LCT, students actively participate in the learning process and are likely to alter its direction by connecting to prior tangential or experiential knowledge. Generally, the teacher retains the responsibility for selecting the course content, learning goals, and itinerary, though even these may include student input. Regardless, with LCT, the learning path taken, the direction of course discussion, and practical examples are at the very least influenced, and more likely chosen, by the student; thus "power is shared" (Weimer 2002).

LCT often includes case studies, small group discussions or assignments, and/or designating a student to be a group discussion leader on a rotating basis. Power sharing is not easy for teachers accustomed to a TL approach. But LCT power sharing has several benefits. Students are more active, engaged, interested, and motivated, and less passive and disconnected (Weimer 2002, p. 31). It is easier for a student to hide in a class of 30, 50, or 100 than in a group of five students. It should be noted that the student discussion leader is equally asked to "share the power," and there are potential "tough spots for running a risk management workshop"—nonparticipation and dominators (Fraser and Simkins 2010, p. 169).

The Function of Content

With LCT, content is used in the learning process, not covered in the context of the TL. This does not infer that the content, base knowledge, is not covered. It simply means that students do not first memorize the base knowledge for later recall. Instead, students constructively examine, explore, review, and assess content. It is extremely interesting to see students strongly arguing for the most important step in an ERM process even when there may not actually be a hierarchy. Creating and defending an argument for the most important step, what risk stands out, or what is the most challenging step requires a cognitive reasoning process and a subtle incorporation of base knowledge and linkage to previously learned material—the

LCT version of content coverage. With LCT, the content learning process "develops learning skills" and "promotes self-awareness of learning," and students "experience it firsthand" (Weimer 2002, p. 51–52).

The amount of content covered is a possible concern for those more inclined toward a TL. However, contrary to expectations, experience suggests that more content is covered, not less, as students explore and assess content versus memorization.

As shown in the Appendix, Example #10, Chapter 18: "Managing Financial Risk," is a good illustration of more coverage. The TL approach gives an example of the trade-offs, costs, and benefits of hedging with futures contracts, often starting with a simple natural hedge. Here, the student records the respective payoffs to long and short positions when prices change. Students memorize the transactions and expect to replicate the steps with different numbers, and maybe even a different futures contract for a challenging TL course. With LCT, students first view a short video about futures markets (www.cmegroup.com/), and then review the listing of available futures contracts, selected quotes, and specifications. LCT scenarios in which futures contracts could be applied quite often begin with weather futures, as students' curiosity is awakened when they imagine rain, snow, and tornadoes, not the TL farmer and cereal producer with corn futures. With LCT, students first suggest, appraise, and associate scenarios with futures contracts, and then calculate payoffs given the contract specifications. As noted previously, the LCT teacher needs to be prepared to assist with any futures calculation.

A second example in the Appendix of expanded content is Example #13, Chapter 23: "Academic Research on Enterprise Risk Management." In a TL course, students would memorize the articles and the findings of each, with the goal of restating the findings on an exam. With LCT, *critiquing*, *appraising*, and *theorizing* often lead to discussions of *hypotheses*. For example, why is there an expected relationship between ERM and "organizational slack" or "asset opacity" (Fraser and Simkins 2010, p. 426)? This level of hypothetical discussion is considerably beyond "Who found what?"

The Role of the Teacher

Perhaps the most difficult change in moving to LCT for a teacher accustomed to the TL is that lectures are replaced with individual student learning, small group discussions, or other group activities. The teacher's role is that of a moderator, tour guide, and/or facilitator of learning. This role is a necessary part of LCT, not an option; the teacher "must move aside, often and regularly" (Weimer 2002, p. 74).

Serving as guide extends to after groups (or individuals) report their *suggestions, hypotheses, comments, explorations,* or *computations*. It is very tempting to return to the TL, the "sage on the stage," with corrections, conclusions, or examples. A moderator or facilitator would ask: Was your group in agreement? What issues did you differ on? What do you believe is the lesson here, the point to be learned? Does anyone else have a different solution or computation?

Granted, the teacher's workload may be more, not less. We often prepare, or receive with the textbook, a series of very structured lecture slides, "talking PowerPoints," demonstrating what and how much we know about the topic. Our thorough, insightful, wise lecture is interrupted only by the proverbial unanswered inquiries of: Does anyone have any questions? Is this clear? Do you understand?

It is quite another task to be able to guide constructive explorative reasoning and learning. It is not that LCT is without structure; it is that the LCT learning structure is flexible, fluctuating, adjustable, and often unpredictable. Weimer (2002, pp. 83–91) offers the following seven principles:

1. Teachers do learning tasks less.
2. Teachers do less telling; students do more discovering.
3. Teachers do more design work.
4. Faculty do more modeling.
5. Faculty do more to get students learning from and with each other.
6. Faculty work to create climates for learning.
7. Faculty do more with feedback.

The "Useful Facilitation Tips" for running a risk management workshop (Fraser and Simkins 2010, p. 169) may serve a dual purpose as student content and LCT advice:

- *Inquire.* Ask open-ended questions, such as "Why?" Ask participants to speak not just on behalf of themselves but about what they think others might be thinking. Ask for the contrary view: "What are some of the arguments against this?" Ask for evidence: "How do you know?"
- *Restate.* Summarize or paraphrase what you have just heard. Summarize the key points and then ask someone to add to them or comment on them or contradict them.
- *Provoke.* State extreme views that you might have heard or imagined on the subject under discussion. Encourage healthy debate.
- *Use silence.* After asking a question that gets no immediate response, it is extremely tempting to fill the silence by talking more or restating the question. Don't. Wait through the silence. If you wait long enough, someone will speak.
- *Get out of the way.* If a good animated discussion starts to happen that is directly on topic and there is available time, try to "blend in with the furniture." Walk to the side of the room or sit down. Let the students run with it. Wait for the discussion to peter out or drift off topic before again making your presence felt.
- *Don't overexplain.* The authors' experience is that the more participation (and less explanation or lecturing) there is in a workshop agenda, the more engaged the participants will be. Avoid lengthy descriptions of the steps to be taken or the underlying theory. Tell them the bare bones of what they need to do for the next step in the process, and then let them learn by doing.

The Responsibility for Learning

Teachers remain responsible for creating a learning environment, but students take responsibility for learning (Weimer 2002). Many of the example questions, exercises, and activities provided in the appendix were created by students in the

ERM course. Students on a rotating basis provide discussion questions and serve as small group moderators. Student small group moderators are encouraged to have every student engage in the discussion process, limiting individual students who may try to dominate, and motivating timid students. Engaged students accept the linkage between their actions and learning. Misbehavior is better corrected by peers who see that learning is being prevented than by teacher retribution.

Students are also responsible for contributing to course content, further engaging their interest and ownership of the responsibility for learning. For example, in the Appendix, the tornado incident at the truck yard in LCT Example #6, Chapter 13: "Quantitative Risk Assessment in ERM," was found by a student. The student was delighted to share the discovered risk example, as other students accepted a challenge to find additional videos of the incident or similar catastrophic events. The whistle-blowing websites and information in LCT Example #12, Chapter 20: "Legal Risk Post-SOX and the Subprime Fiasco," were also found by students. The content served as a basis for spirited group discussions on whistle-blowing. Consider the benefit of 30 students searching and exploring the web for current content versus the teacher presenting a few selected sites in a TL. Avoid the classic student statement, "That seems like a good example, but I cannot quite relate to it. It was before I was born."

Evaluation Purpose and Process

It reasonably follows that LCT also results in a change in evaluation procedures, essentially orienting the evaluation process to promote learning. LCT does not reduce the importance of evaluations and the structural value of course grades. LCT does alter the focus of evaluations to learning, as grades do not necessarily reflect the desired higher-level learning, especially if exams only measure recall and rote memorization of base knowledge.

It is not a straightforward change for evaluations to emphasize learning. Accordingly, Weimer (2002) considers the opportunities in greater detail:

- As a foundation to reduce the stakes and stress of the exam, provide review sessions, make sure exams reflect covered content, offer multiple opportunities, or have exams taken as a group.
- For papers, suggest appropriate paper topics, and clearly state academic coverage expectations.
- Develop participation through both self and peer assessment.
- Utilize review sessions at the end of classes and prior to exams as learning exercises, allowing groups to summarize important content and topics that are expected to be on the exam.
- Avoid returning to the TL in the review, however tempting and accidentally reverted to it may be.
- Continue LCT into the postexam review by encouraging students to support answers they argue are correct, citing content or their reasoning process. How often, when a student states that answer C seems to be correct, we respond with "Sorry, B is the only correct answer." Imagine the different response of "Why do you think C is correct?" Place the emphasis on learning, and we may sometimes discover that answer C may also be correct.

CONCLUSION

Overall, movement toward LCT may not be as large a pedagogical change as one may be concerned about, and case study teaching is a type of LCT. The goals of the TL generally rely on Bloom's (1956) original taxonomy or Anderson and Krathwohl's (2001) meta cognitive revision—striving for evaluation and synthesis. Programs to improve critical thinking and active learning through writing (Bean 2011) also cite Bloom's taxonomy. So the TL and LCT approaches both have the desired educational cognitive learning theory goals of evaluation and synthesis.

Top-down instruction and hands-on methods of learning have been around for some time, emphasizing *why*, *what*, and then *how*. This pedagogy has included preparing students for learning, activating relevant knowledge, gaining students' attention, aids to understanding, promoting meaningful processing, and directing and maintaining attention (Steinberg 1991). In essence, when evaluation and synthesis are achieved, students know the *why* and the *what*, which leads to *how*. Knowing only *how*, including knowledge, comprehension, and application, does not necessarily lead to evaluation and synthesis.

If we want to increase student engagement, strengthen team skills, and use content for learning rather than covering content for recall, LCT offers pedagogical advantages over the TL.

We want students to *examine, explore, study, associate, assess, appraise, review, comment, speculate, theorize, postulate, offer, imagine, assume, suggest,* and *hypothesize.* Observing student success is extremely rewarding and encouraging, good reasons to create a learner-centered environment versus a teacher-dominated lecture.

QUESTIONS

1. Which of Maryellen Weimer's classic *Learner Centered Teaching* (2002), "Five Key Changes to Practice" do you feel is the most important and/or challenging? Why?
   (a) The Balance of Power
   (b) The Function of Content
   (c) The Role of the Teacher
   (d) The Responsibility for Learning
   (e) Evaluation Purpose and Process
2. Given the importance of globalization, how would you approach adopting LCT even if it is counter to your student's cultural behavior?
3. What techniques and/or guidelines do you envision to change your role as a teacher, to "step out of the way" of learning and serve as a moderator, not a "sage on the stage" or lecturer?
4. How do you plan to introduce and orient your students to LCT? Do you have specific concerns about student response and their acceptance of responsibility for learning?

APPENDIX: LCT ERM EXAMPLES FROM THE *HOW*

This appendix provides several LCT examples along with the related TL alternatives for an ERM course that has been conducted at Auburn University Montgomery (Alabama) since 2010. All examples and page number references apply to *Enterprise Risk Management: Today's Leading Research and Best Practices for Tomorrow's Executives*, co-edited by John Fraser and Betty J. Simkins (2010). Learning notes (LN) include pedagogical suggestions and course experiences. The following LCT examples are generally small group discussions, but LCT often includes reading assignments or problems that may be done prior to the actual class meeting (Shibley and Wilson 2012). In each example, TL begins with the traditional teacher lecture on the topic (such as using PowerPoint slides to speak to the students and cover the material, etc.). LCT starts with the students.

While reviewing the examples, imagine the possible implications of Weimer's (2002) "Five Key Changes to Practice" described in this chapter where the process has been flipped. Most importantly, notice how content is covered but not in a traditional lecture context where the teacher presents the information. Rather, content is used as a means of learning. Additional examples of LCT for business communication courses are contained in Smart, Witt, and Scott (2012). Wright (2011) offers an insightful pedagogical literature review of Weimer's "Five Key Changes to Practice."

Example #1. Chapter 2: A Brief History of Risk Management

TL: Risk management "spans the millennia of human history" (page 19).
      Cover the list of significant milestones in a series of PowerPoint slides and explain the contribution of each to the development of ERM.

LCT: *Review* the List of Contributions (pages 22–27) and *suggest* the three most significant milestones in the development of ERM.
      Comment on why your group chose these milestones.
      Was the group generally in agreement? If not, what were the other selected milestones?

LN: Groups generally differ on the top three milestones, usually based on different themes: economic events, creation of professional organizations, contributions and development of risk management theory, or possibly legislative actions.
      The list of significant milestones small group exercise provides an early and substantial insight into LCT. Rather than *memorize*, *recall*, and *explain*, the students are asked to *review*, *suggest*, and *comment*—all higher levels of Bloom's Cognitive Learning Taxonomy. It is most rewarding to see students argue about the top three, supporting their choices by associating or assessing the impact of milestones on the development of risk management. There may not even be a top three, and even if there is, the teacher has a postgroup selection opportunity to guide the discussion or note the differences in theme the groups selected.

Example #2. Chapter 3: ERM and Its Role in Strategic Planning and Strategy Execution

TL: *Cover* the List of 11 Tenets of the Return-Driven Framework (pages 37–38).
LCT: *Appraise* the list of risk categories for the greatest risk (pages 41–42).
      • Shareholder value risk
      • Financial reporting risk
      • Governance risk

- Customer and market risk
- Operations risk
- Innovation risk
- Brand risk
- Partnering risk
- Supply chain risk
- Employee engagement risk
- Research and development (R&D) risk
- Communication risk

LN: The textbook presentation states that "the framework encourages think-ing about these risk categories" (page 41). With LCT, students should be encouraged to do so, and in the learning process incorporate the 11 tenets.

TL: A "genuine asset" is ... (page 38).
LCT: *Create* a list of "genuine assets" for a company of your choice.
LN: A simple *create* exercise includes *recognize*, *apprehend*, and *determine*. The teacher may facilitate clarifications and corrections by guiding subsequent classroom discussion in *examining*, *critiquing*, and *exploring* the different lists of "genuine assets."

Example #3. Chapter 5: Becoming the Lamp Bearer—The Emerging Roles of the Chief Risk Officer

TL: The chief risk officer has four major roles: (1) compliance champion, (2) modeling expert, (3) strategic controller, and (4) strategic adviser. In the first role ... (pages 75–81).
LCT: *Reviewing* Exhibit 5.1 (page 80), *distinguish* the roles of strategic controller and adviser.
        Postulate which role of the chief risk officer is the most important.
LN: Postulating requires memorization, comprehension, distinguishing, and appraisal.

Example #4. Chapter 8: Identifying and Communicating Key Risk Indicators

TL: Key risk indicators are an ERM tool that ... (page 129).
LCT: *Distinguish* key risk indicators from key performance indicators.
        Suggest the key risk indicator practical applications that are most impor-tant to achieve the organizational strategy of the company you work for, a company chosen by your group, or the university.
LN: The facilitator role is often needed on this topic, as key risk indicators may be confused with or closely aligned with key performance indicators.

Example #5. Chapter 11: How to Prepare a Risk Profile

TL: The Risk Map is a graphic representation of a Risk Profile and in this case contains eight risks (page 173). The first risk is ...

There are eight steps to create a Risk Profile (pages 177–186).

Step 1: Schedule interviews and gather background information.

Step 2: Prepare the interview tools.

Step 3: Summarize the interview findings.

Step 4: Summarize the risk ratings and trends.

Step 5: Draft the Top 10 Risk Profile.

Step 6: Review the Draft Risk Profile.

Step 7: Communicate the Risk Profile with the board or a board committee.

Step 8: Track the results.

LCT: *Appraise* the benefit of a Risk Profile and Risk Map.

Suggest which step is the most challenging in preparing a Risk Profile.

Comment on why your group selected this step.

Create a Top 10 Risk Profile for the company you work for, your university, or your school.

Example #6. Chapter 13: Quantitative Risk Assessment in ERM

TL: This chapter discusses risk assessment and risk quantification ... (page 219).

LCT: *Explore* information related to the Schneider Truck Yard Tornado Damage in Dallas, Texas, on April 3, 2012. This results in a large number of videos and news stories.

Assess where this event would be placed in a Risk Map. *Comment* on how the event may be viewed in a statistical analysis. Now *speculate* on your reaction if you have just received a phone call stating, "All of the trailers and tractors in your Dallas Hub have been destroyed."

See Exhibit 13.3 of Fraser and Simkins (2010, p. 224).

LN: The video of tractor trailers flying through the air is striking. This is a learning opportunity to consider the ERM of "tail events" and "known unknowns."

Example #7. Chapter 14: Market Risk Management/Credit Risk Management

TL: Looking at the Taxonomy of Market Risk and Credit Risk (page 240):

The first market risk is .... The next one is .... The third one is ....

The first credit risk is .... The next one is .... The third one is ....

LCT: *Distinguish* between market risk and credit risk.

Reviewing the different types of risk, *assess* which risk is most striking and noteworthy. *Comment* on why your group chose this risk.

Example #8. Chapter 16: Operational Risk Management

TL: This chapter illustrates the answers to fundamental questions, including (page 280):

- What is operational risk? Why should you care about it?
- Is risk all bad?

- How do you assess operational risks, particularly in a dynamic business environment?
- Why do you need to define risk tolerance for aligned decision making?
- What can you do to manage operational risk?
- How do you encourage a culture of risk management at the operational level?
- How do you align operational risk management with enterprise risk management?

First, let's answer the question of "What is operational risk?"

LCT: Using Exhibit 16.2, The Bow Tie Model (page 291), provide an *analysis* of a current news event. This is reprinted as Exhibit 2.2 in this chapter.

LN: The current news event may be any risk event, from explosions to traffic wrecks, bankruptcies to product recalls, flood damage to tornado damage, information leaks to software failures. The *analysis* answers the questions, and the *content* is used as a means to learning.

TL: "The 5 Whys is a question-asking method that can be used to explore the cause-and-effect relationships underlying a particular risk event or problem" (page 294).

LCT: Continue your current news event *analysis* by *exploring* with at least five whys.

LN: There are always current risk events in the news, most of which can be searched for, often including videos. As an example, a recent class chose a wreck between a church bus and a truck on an expressway. At first, it appeared that the group's risk event selection was a direct adoption of the textbook example—a fatal accident (page 294).

However, the student-engaged whys expanded quickly, as follows:

Why did the wreck occur? Bus crossed median of expressway after tire blew out.

Why did the tire blow out? Poor bus maintenance, bad tire, debris on roadway.

Why was there poor bus maintenance? Expenses limited by budget.

Why was the driver not able to control the bus? Young, inexperienced volunteer.

Why was the driver an inexperienced volunteer? Previous older, experienced driver quit driving given his age. Newer driver only needs to pass commercial driver's license (CDL) exam and drives no more than twice per week, rarely on the expressway.

Why did the bus cross the median? No safety barrier in place.

Why was there no safety barrier in place? State had added several hundred miles of wire or concrete median barrier, but this section of expressway had lower priority based on wreck history. Why wasn't topology and shallow median considered? Engineering expertise more expensive.

Why were individuals seriously injured? Lack of personal restraints.

Why were there no personal restraints? Not required, expensive option.

Why are personal costs not given greater weight in budgeting?

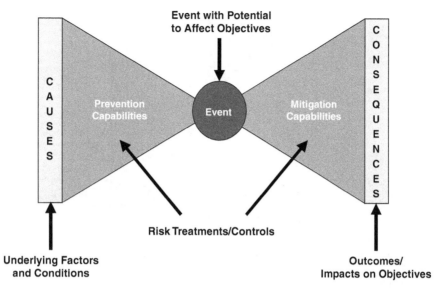

Exhibit 2.2   The Bow Tie Model

Example #9. Chapter 17: Types of Risk

TL: "Distinguishing between beta and alpha risk can be difficult" (page 304).
Beta risk is …. Alpha risk is ….

LCT: *Reviewing* Exhibit 17.1, Value Implications of Risk Appetite Change, *distinguish* between beta and alpha risk. This is reprinted as Exhibit 2.3 in this chapter.

LN: *Distinguishing* requires *recognizing*, *comprehending*, and *determining*. Definition *recall* does not. Difficult material may necessitate additional teacher facilitation and at the same time offer another student learning opportunity for discovery.

Example #10. Chapter 18: Managing Financial Risk

TL: *Cover* Exhibit 18.1, Examples of Contracts Traded on Major U.S. Futures Exchanges (page 322).
Cover cases on currency risk, interest rate risk, and commodity price risk (page 323–325).
Identify financial question of "Does Hedging Affect Firm Value?" (page 327).

LCT: *Explore* the available futures contracts on www.cmegroup.com:
- Agriculture
- Energy
- Equity index
- Foreign exchange (FX)
- Interest rates
- Metals
- Options

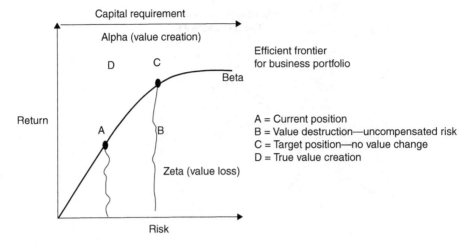

Exhibit 2.3   Value Implications of Risk Appetite Changes

- Over-the-counter (OTC) market
- Real estate
- Weather

Select a specific futures contract of interest to your group under Products & Trading, Products (for example, EUR/USD under FX).

Review the quotes and the contract specifications for your selected futures contract.

Suggest a scenario where your selected futures contract could be *applied.*

Critique the financial issue of "Does Hedging Affect Firm Value?"

LN: Students are engaged by *explore, review, suggest,* and *apply* versus covering three examples they have already read. Note that the teacher may need to facilitate the *estimation* of the selected futures contract's payoff, which may be any of those available, not just the three prepared text examples. Every class to date has had at least one group select a weather futures contract. *Content* is used in the learning process.

Example #11. Chapter 19: Bank Capital Regulation and Enterprise Risk Management

TL: Economic capital is …

Cover Exhibit 19.4 (page 344). This is reprinted as Exhibit 2.4 in this chapter.

LCT: *Distinguish* minimum capital requirements from economic capital.

Assess the impact of a "black swan" event on the expected loss and confidence level.

Appraise the effect of Asset Price Liquidity under a Panic, Exhibit 17.6 (page 312), on the expected loss.

Offer an economic outcome scenario that includes the black swan event and panic.

LN: This obviously refers to the subprime crisis (pages 89–90, 346, 351, 360–361), economic crisis (page 32), and Troubled Asset Relief Program (TARP)

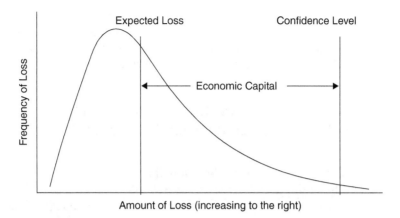

Exhibit 2.4 Economic Capital

Source: Robert L. Burns, "Economic Capital and the Assessment of Capital Adequacy," *Supervisory Insights,* Federal Deposit Insurance Corporation, Winter 2004.

(pages 11 and 303), along with related topics discussed elsewhere. The intent is to not repeat (*cover*) the knowledge, but rather to build on (*use*) the knowledge the students are likely to have already seen, if not experienced.

Example #12. Chapter 20: Legal Risk Post-SOX and the Subprime Fiasco

TL: Whistle-blower protection is … (pages 357–358, 363).

LCT: *Assume* you find yourself in a position to be a whistle-blower.
        Speculate as to the trade-offs involved if you're the whistle-blower.

LN: *Google* "whistle-blowers SOX." In other areas of ERM, students, especially working MBAs, may be able to provide examples of loss experiences, mitigation efforts, and risk management. To avoid overly personal discussion, whistle-blowing may be better approached by referring to publicly available information and examples.
        Discussion of successful and unsuccessful whistle-blowing protection under SOX is very enlightening and productive, while avoiding overly personal disclosure.

Example #13. Chapter 23: Academic Research on Enterprise Risk Management

TL: The first article is …; it found … (pages 422–438).

LCT: *Critique* the article(s) your group was assigned.
        Appraise the article(s) and survey findings.
        Theorize about one or more of the findings.

LN: Reading the findings of the academic research is a *recall*, *memorization*, and possible *comprehension* learning activity. *Creating* a *hypothesis* or *theory* as to why growing firms, for example, are more likely to appoint a CRO (page 427) leads to an inductive learning discussion.

Example #14. Chapter 10: How to Plan and Run a Risk Management Workshop; Chapter 22: Who Reads What Most Often?

TL: *Cover* respective chapters without any link.

LCT: *Review* the findings on the use of consultants in Chapter 22 (page 394). *Imagine* your group is an ERM consulting firm. *Suggest* techniques, approaches, and tools that could be used to respond to the survey results in Chapter 22.

LN: This is an example of one of many instances where topic coverage can be linked to further group discussion.

REFERENCES

Anderson, Lorin W., and David R. Krathwohl, eds. 2001. *A Taxonomy for Learning, Teaching, and Assessing—A Revision of Bloom's Taxonomy of Educational Objectives*. New York: Longman Press.

Bean, John C. 2011. *Engaging Ideas: The Professor's Guide to Integrating Writing, Critical Thinking and Active Learning in the Classroom*. 2nd ed. San Francisco: Jossey-Bass, A Wiley Imprint.

Bloom, Benjamin S. 1956. *Taxonomy of Educational Objectives: The Classification of Educational Goals*. New York: David McKay.

Blumberg, Phyllis. 2009. *Developing Learner-Centered Teaching: A Practical Guide for Faculty*. San Francisco: Jossey-Bass, A Wiley Imprint.

Blumberg, Phyllis, and Laura Pontiggia. 2011. "Benchmarking the Degree of Implementation of Learner-Centered Teaching Approaches." *Innovative Higher Education* 36 (November), 189–202.

Fraser, John, and Betty J. Simkins, eds. 2010. *Enterprise Risk Management: Today's Leading Research and Best Practices for Tomorrow's Executives*. Robert W. Kolb Series in Finance. Hoboken, NJ: John Wiley & Sons.

Millard, Elizabeth. 2012. "5 Reasons FLIPPED Classrooms Work." *University Business* 15:11 (December), 26–29.

Shibley, Ivan A., Jr., and Timothy D. Wilson. 2012. "The Flipped Classroom: Rethinking the Way You Teach." Magna Online Seminars, Magna Publications, August 23.

Smart, Karl L., Christine Witt, and James P. Scott. 2012. "Toward Learner-Centered Teaching: An Inductive Approach." *Business Communication Quarterly* 75:4, 392–403.

Steinberg, Esther R. 1991. *Computer-Assisted Instruction: A Synthesis of Theory, Practice and Technology*. Hillsdale, NJ: Lawrence Erlbaum Associates.

Weimer, Maryellen. 2002. *Learner Centered Teaching*. San Francisco: Jossey-Bass, A Wiley Imprint.

Wohlfarth, DeDe, with Graduate Students Daniel Sheras, Jessica L. Bennett, Bethany Simon, Jody H. Pimental, and Laura E. Gabel. 2008. "Student Perceptions of Learner-Centered Teaching." *Insight: A Journal of Scholarly Teaching* 3, 67–74.

Wright, Gloria Brown. 2011. "Student-Centered Learning in Higher Education." *International Journal of Teaching and Learning in Higher Education* 23:3, 92–97, www.isetl.org/ijtlhe/.

Yang, Xiaomei. 2010. "The Globalization and Localization of 'Learner-Centered' Strategy for an International Horizon." *Asian Social Science* 6:9, 78–81.

ABOUT THE CONTRIBUTORS

David R. Lange, DBA (University of Kentucky), is an Auburn University Montgomery (AUM) Distinguished Research and Teaching Professor of Finance. He has received many prestigious awards for both research and teaching from the University and from several academic associations. In 2012, he received the Academy of Economics and Finance (AEF) Fellow Award in recognition of extraordinary contributions and achievements to the AEF's mission of advancing teaching, research, and service. David was the Lowder-Weil Professor and Chair of the Applied Life Insurance Education and Research Program, and a frequent presenter in the AEF Teacher Training Program. He has taught classes in commercial risk management and insurance, enterprise risk management, financial valuation, and investments and portfolio management. He has also consulted in a significant number of individual and class insurance-related cases in both state and federal court. Professionally, David has served as the Eastern Finance Association executive director and VP-finance, as well as program chair and president for both the Academy of Financial Services and the Academy of Economics and Finance.

Betty J. Simkins, PhD, is Williams Companies Chair of Business and Professor of Finance at Oklahoma State University. Betty received her PhD from Case Western Reserve University. She has had more than 50 publications in academic finance journals. She has won awards for her teaching, research, and outreach, including the top awards at Oklahoma State University: the Regents Distinguished Research Award and the Outreach Excellence Award. Her primary areas of research are risk management, energy finance, and corporate governance. She serves on the editorial boards of nine academic journals, including the *Journal of Banking and Finance*; is past co-editor of the *Journal of Applied Finance*; and is past president of the Eastern Finance Association. She also serves on the Executive Advisory Committee of the Conference Board of Canada's Strategic Risk Council. In addition to this book, she has published two others: *Energy Finance and Economics: Analysis and Valuation, Risk Management and the Future of Energy* and *Enterprise Risk Management: Today's Leading Research and Best Practices for Tomorrow's Executives*. Prior to entering academia, she worked in the corporate world for ConocoPhillips and Williams Companies. She conducts executive education courses for companies globally.

PART II

ERM Implementation at Leading Organizations

CHAPTER 3

ERM at Mars, Incorporated

ERM for Strategy and Operations

LARRY WARNER
President, Warner Risk Group

This case study outlines the development of Mars, Incorporated's Enterprise Risk Management (ERM) program, from its initial phases in early 2003 through the spring of 2012. The views expressed in this case study are those of the author, and may not be those of Mars, Incorporated (Mars). Additionally, as with any ERM program, Mars' program has continued to evolve since 2012.

Throughout this case study, I have used first names for a number of key individuals who contributed to the success of program. (Please note all names have been changed.) In speaking with other ERM practitioners, such early adopters of an ERM program typically help contribute to an ERM program's development, evolution, and success. In this case study they helped spread and embed the process in their business units and in other units as they took on new roles. Most of the major improvements in the evolution of this program resulted from working with these individuals to address the needs of their business units. By identifying these players' involvement in the early stages of the program and their subsequent roles, the case study reader should gain an understanding of the importance of and the need to cultivate relationships with these early adopters.

MARS' ERM HISTORY

In essence, Mars' ERM program began with the company's inception by Forrest Mars.[1] Historically, the leadership at Mars had a serious commitment to risk management. ERM represented one natural evolution from these practices.

In conjunction with the transition to nonfamily management in the early 2000s, the corporation established challenging growth, earnings, and cost targets. In order to achieve these objectives, the company undertook a number of key initiatives to ensure the achievement of these objectives. ERM became one of these.

In 2002, Roger, the CFO at the time, and I sat down and discussed how an ERM program might help better manage the business. We recognized that we lacked the experience to implement such a program on our own, and asked two of our existing service providers with ERM practices to make proposals as to how they might assist us in this project. As Roger put it, "We need someone to transfer knowledge to Larry."

One vendor pushed for a Committee of Sponsoring Organizations (COSO) structure. The other suggested we develop a program that leveraged Mars' unique strengths. As a large, privately held, decentralized company, we agreed that the latter better met our needs.

At this point, we decided that we wanted to develop ERM and not what one might call an "enterprise compliance management" (ECM) program. This represented a critical decision in Mars' ERM development.

To kick things off, we took a risk management survey of the 15 or so managers on Mars' global management team. We spent a couple of hours personally completing the survey with David, who was to become the president of Mars at the beginning of 2003. This was a critical move in the development of the program, as we gained an understanding of his views on risk management and how we might develop the ERM program.

Following the survey, we recognized the need to gain an even broader understanding of how the associates (Mars does not have employees) in the business viewed risk. We decided to conduct risk assessment workshops for a function (Service & Finance), geography (Canada), and product group (European Sugar). Working with our consultants, we selected a gap analysis methodology. In gap analysis, you evaluate the inherent risk (impact and likelihood) with limited controls (e.g., buying commodities at spot cost as opposed to with futures contracts) against management effectiveness.

We had the first workshop with the global finance team during our corporate meetings in the summer of 2003. The ERM team had a major win during this session. At the time, Mars was undertaking a substantial investment. During the session, the consensus of the group was that we, Mars, had undertaken a too aggressive time frame to be successful. By the next day, the corporation announced a change in the rollout of the project.

During the session, the CFOs of Europe and the United States both commented on how beneficial this workshop had been. This was critical for two reasons. First, it generated buy-in from additional senior management. Second, the CFO of Europe, Oscar, would soon be named the new CFO of Mars upon Roger's retirement.

We began calling discoveries like the one in the global finance team's workshop the "known unknowns," because many of the participants knew and/or were concerned about the issue before the meeting; however, it had never risen to such a level that it was formally brought forward to the group. We developed a scenario that explained such discoveries and how they could help the business. For example, two management team members have dinner after work. They discuss an issue that concerns them; however, for some reason this issue does not arise during team meetings, perhaps because they do not believe they have adequate expertise to challenge the group's thinking, or one team member was so passionate about the issue that everyone else deferred. Over the years, we found that these "known unknowns" frequently held the key to a business's success. In training workshop facilitators, we held identifying known unknowns as a major key to successful workshops.

In Canada, the general manager asked us to help his team evaluate their newly finalized strategy and provide an additional day of action planning based on our findings. While the workshop did not turn up any major known unknowns, the participants felt the process enabled them to evaluate properly the risks with their strategy and make enhancements that would increase the likelihood of success.

Our final assessment with European Sugar had a major win, as it delayed a major product launch. The workshop identified key doubts in the potential success of the new product and its distinct format. The product team was tasked to return to the next management team meeting to address the issues identified in the risk assessment.

The participants in all three workshops deemed them successful and provided senior management with positive feedback. The ERM team also had major learnings. First, the workshops revealed a common risk aversion among most associates. To enable the company to grow faster, senior management knew that units had to take on more risk. Based on the initial success of our risk assessments, senior management felt that ERM would be one tool to enhance growth.

The second major discovery revolved around the workshops themselves. To determine management effectiveness, we had asked participants to base their anonymous votes on limited controls (e.g., buying commodities at spot as opposed to with futures contracts). Universally, we received push-back, as the company had a control mind-set as one of its basic tenets. As such, the importance of control had become ingrained within all associates over many years.

Failure and Retrenchment

Based on the success of our three pilot workshops, we received the go-ahead to develop a full-scale ERM process. In early 2004, we put together a multifunctional, global team, supported by our consultant, to develop an ERM program. Over the next five months, we held monthly meetings to rough out a program. Three of the regional presidents acted as our advisers.

In June we presented our program, including a unit to pilot its implementation, to the Mars management team. At the end of the presentation, David, Mars' president, looked at us and stated that this looked like a major software transition, and we had done that once and were not going through that again. The rest of the management team agreed. David looked at me and said, "Larry, I know you can scare people when it comes to risk. I want you to take your team and develop a process that will generate a risk discussion mentality for the units. I want you to work with several of our larger units—China, Russia, Australia, and Europe." He asked us to begin in China in three weeks and build the process around our annual operating planning process.

I believe it is important to note here that ERM is an evolutionary process. I believe that having our first approach rejected ultimately led to our successful development of a more practical, less complex approach. Looking back, I doubt that our initial approach would have worked at Mars due to its complexity.

PHASE 2—SUCCESS

There were three components of the proposal that were well received, which we kept with minor revisions and additions. First, our basic tenets for development still existed, but we now had better clarity. Senior management clearly sought:

- A methodology to determine what is actually achievable by business units in the context of corporate performance objectives
- To improve alignment and accountability around the pursuit and execution of each business unit's goals and objectives
- To foster a risk discussion mentality among business unit management teams
- A mechanism that enables managers to knowledgably and comfortably take risks in order to achieve growth goals that exceed overall market growth
- A tool to objectively track performance

Our original mission statement remained: "The objective of ERM is to provide the company with a proven, sustainable framework to proactively understand and deal with complex business risks, both tangible and intangible, existing and emerging, across the entire organization." This statement became the guideline against which we evaluated the development and evolution of the program.

Senior management also agreed with the major principles for the design of an ERM process:

- Create value.
- Leverage the company's unique strengths.
- Work with existing organizational structure.
- View risk as opportunity.
- Encourage alignment and accountability.

While these represented great tenets to develop a program, we basically were where we had begun six months before, working with a clean slate.

While "create value" seems obvious, we did not know where this would take us as we began building a new program following our unsuccessful initial attempt. However, we had better clarity regarding senior management's view of what was needed. Understanding and meeting the needs of senior management provided the keystone for the development of our program.

From the company's perspective, "unique strengths" meant privately held and decentralized. Senior management similarly made working within an existing organizational structure equally straightforward. They wanted the ERM team to build the ERM process into the annual operating plan without adding any staff. We were to use regional Service & Finance Staff Officers to assist us.

Based on our findings of risk aversion in our initial workshops, we knew that viewing risk as an opportunity meant a cultural shift. Finally, we understood that encouraging alignment and accountability meant a process that enabled unit management teams to align and agree to the objectives they could legitimately achieve within the constraints of the risks identified in the ERM process. We found that these two things went hand in hand. By developing alignment around the risks to a unit's operating plan and the optimal risk treatments, the ERM process would enable business units (BUs) to take on more risk to enhance their opportunities and capabilities for growth.

On the Monday three weeks after our presentation to the management team, our consultant, his two assistants, and I were blankly looking at each other across a table in a meeting room in the China office outside of Beijing. We had no idea what we should do. We decided interviewing everyone on the China management team might generate some ideas.

Based on the unit's 2005 operating plan and these interviews, we developed a template that we thought captured their input. Each sheet reflected an initiative of the operating plan (e.g., grow Brand X 5 percent in 2005 and deliver operating plan profit). The template looked quite simple. It had a header for the objective with a block for a score next to it and two columns underneath—risks on the left and risk treatments on the right. (We initially used the term *mitigation*; however, at an ERM conference, one of the audience members pointed out that mitigation did not coincide with our stated objectives. Instead risk *treatment* better reflected "viewing risk as an opportunity.") We spent several days filling the templates with the risk and risk treatments, which the business unit managers had identified with their 10 key initiatives for 2005.

We provided the templates and additional background in a preread package to allow the participants to prepare in advance of the workshop.

We started the workshop by having the management team force rank the initiatives from 1 to 10 (or the total number of initiatives which they had). We compiled the results and projected them onto the screen, discussing the differences and/or alignment among the votes. We then asked them to agree or change the prioritization, thereby beginning the alignment process. (This became the initial item in all future workshops.) Understanding the differences in rankings led the participants to understand others' views of importance, and in some cases gain a better understanding of the actual operating plan objectives.

We took the initiative voted as the top priority and began the workshop. We reviewed the definition of the initiative, and the management team edited and aligned behind the final definition. We then validated and added risks and then risk treatments. When we, the facilitators, sensed we had captured the major risks and risk treatments, we moved to an anonymous vote on the probability of successfully achieving the objectives, using a scale of 1 to 9, with 1 representing 10 percent or less, 2 representing 20 percent, and 9 representing 90 percent or more. Voters would take into consideration the things they could control, their unit's capabilities and resources, potential competitor activities, and so on.

When the votes appeared on the screen, we found them generally spread across a range of 4 to 5 on the scale (e.g., 3, 4, 5, 6, and 7). As facilitators, we led a discussion as to why someone might vote a 3 and others a 7. We found that having the lower-voting participants lay out their reasoning led to better discussions. The higher-voting team members would attempt to address the concerns raised by the lower-voting participants. Over time the facilitators could sense alignment in the room and have the participants take a second anonymous vote. The second vote's results generally aligned around two numbers or were centered on one number with one or two outliers above and below the center vote.

The first workshop went exceedingly well. We then headed to Australia for our second workshop. This was a critical test for two reasons. First, one of the Mars regional presidents, who advised us throughout the initial ERM development process, participated. Second, our senior consultant had to go back to the United

States, so his two assistants were to help me build and facilitate the workshop—one as a co-facilitator and the other as the editor of the workshop templates and operator of the voting technology and workshop. Here again we had a successful workshop.

Our next workshop took place in Russia. We had several major learnings from this workshop. First, when you have a very strong and charismatic general manager (GM), it is important for the facilitators to ensure that the entire management team participates. To this end, we pulled the GM aside and requested that he withhold his comments to the end. We would go to him to wrap things up. It became a common practice for facilitators to ask GMs to "work with us" to ensure that all team members participated, and to allow the GMs to wrap up with comments before the final vote. It was a way for facilitators to better control the process and to make sure the known unknowns became visible.

At one point the GM stopped the session and stated, "This process helps you focus on what's important." This became a mantra of our ERM process.

As Russia had gone through several currency issues in the 10 years the unit had been in operation, the GM and CFO asked for us to build a template of how it could effectively handle a currency crisis. We did as requested, and the management team felt they identified the actions they needed to take in the event of such an occurrence.

This activity may seem minor, but it highlights two key points that ultimately contributed to the ERM program's success. First, business units have unique needs and frequently need help in maximizing the use of ERM. By ensuring that the program had some flexibility, units were more likely to leverage its benefits. Second, we learned to constantly try new things. Many of our evolutionary improvements to the process resulted from requests or suggestions from individual units.

Our final workshop in the 2004 pilot took place with a subgroup of the European management team. Known to only a few key members of this team and a few senior managers at the corporate level, Mars had begun the initial phases of a major project. The Regional Staff Officer of Service & Finance (S&F) lobbied the Regional President of Europe to have our new ERM process validate their work. Here again we tried a new activity with them in the workshop. This enabled them to identify the low, high, and most likely outcome of their key objectives, based on an analysis of the risk involved. While this activity was helpful, they advised us that the template that we had used in the other workshops proved the most beneficial to them.

Based on the success of this workshop, the Regional President of Europe asked us to perform three workshops, one in each of the countries that would be participating in the project.

During the interview process in one of the countries, it became clear to us that they had not progressed to the point needed to launch their project. We advised the European management team of this. The general managers of the two units in this country were not only greatly appreciative but also became two of the biggest advocates of ERM in each role they subsequently held within the business.

The participants in all three countries found this process better enabled them to prepare for implementation. They identified critical risks and solutions that enabled them to successfully achieve their objectives.

Ben, the new Regional S&F Staff Officer from Europe, cofacilitated each of these workshops with me. (Through this work, Ben became a major supporter of

ERM as he progressed to become the CFO of the company's largest segment.) As the program developed, several of our earliest participants in the program (facilitators and management team members) became our biggest advocates. This acted to increase the "pull" of the program through the business as opposed to corporate needing to "push" it through.

GLOBAL ROLLOUT

Based on the feedback from the workshops and the support of the two regional presidents, the next phase was to move forward with a global rollout of the ERM program.

For 2005, we targeted 17 units for workshops to assess the risks of their 2006 Operating Plans. China, Australia, Russia, and virtually every general manager from the seven units in the European project asked to be included in the rollout.

Here again our design principles were reaffirmed. Management believed the process created value, helped units become less risk averse (view risk as an opportunity), and encouraged alignment and accountability among the participants. Our remit to work within the annual operating plan reaffirmed "work within an existing organizational structure."

Many companies would find their planning process similar to Mars. Business units begin developing their annual plans nine to 12 months before January 1, based on their long-term strategies within the context of the broader segment and corporate strategies. They receive input from their segment management teams. Mars has six segments: Chocolate, Drinks, Food, Petcare, Symbioscience, and Wrigley. Late in the year they present their plan to management. ERM represents one component of their presentations.

For the rollout, the ERM team developed formalized interview templates. Although we always interviewed the GM first, the team began to have joint interviews with the GM and S&F head (CFO), who acts as the GM's copilot. We found that these joint interviews provided much more detail and reduced the number of other business unit (BU) team members we had to interview. The workshops were time consuming to build, each taking approximately one person-week, or more for larger, more complex units. Any time savings proved beneficial, as the team had very limited resources. It also represented an evolutionary step in our process.

The ERM team entered the process with only three facilitators skilled in our new process—our consultants (Bill and Greg) and me. As we wanted to internalize the process, we had to train an adequate number of internal facilitators. Optimally, two facilitators would run a workshop with one operator, the person responsible for operating the voting technology, updating the templates as we spoke, and keeping notes.

These ERM workshops require atypical facilitation skills. A facilitator needs a great deal of knowledge of the business, good facilitation skills, and the ability to challenge participants. We found over time that some people, recognized as good facilitators for most activities, proved ineffective in ERM workshops as they lacked the ability to aggressively challenge the management teams from an operational or strategic perspective.

Oscar instructed both regional and functional S&F staff officers, who reported to him, to support us. (Regional S&F staff officers support the Mars CFO in the region, while functional staff officers oversee specific functions—e.g., Treasury,

Risk, Control, Strategy, etc.) Oscar directed the regional S&F staff to help us sched-ule the sessions and to act as our cofacilitators in their regions. Several nonregional S&F staff officers and George, who worked for me, were also to be trained and act as facilitators. All of these associates had the requisite skill set to be effective in the ERM workshops. The use of S&F staff officers to assist us reaffirmed both "work within an existing organizational structure" and "leverage unique strengths."

We kicked off the rollout the first two weeks of August, conducting workshops at our three U.S. units—Food, Snackfood, and Petcare. All three were successful and we identified serious risks or (better said) opportunities for each plan. We trained George and Elizabeth (the Staff Officer of Strategy) during the Food and Snackfood workshops.

The votes at U.S. Petcare revealed a lack of alignment around the probability of success of several key initiatives to their plan. The GM complained that the team had just spent two weeks, including an off-site planning session, making major additions and revisions to the plan, but no one had raised the issue, which arose during the workshop; however, we pointed out that the intent of the ERM process was to identify these issues prior to the implementation of the operating plan. This would enable units to address these issues in time to increase the likelihood of success.

The following week, Elizabeth ran the Mexican workshop, training the regional staff officer and Jim, her direct report. In the meantime, I went to Asia for the China, Japan, and three Australian workshops. In Asia, the point of early supporters played a key role in our success. Mars China had found great value in our initial workshop and began to use the program as a key component of its operational and strategic planning process.

The new general manager in Japan had participated in the pilot workshop in Canada and in the UK project workshop as one of the GMs. He was keen to use ERM as a tool to help his team reinforce their growth and market position.

In Australia, we began the following week with our Snackfood unit. It was the first day on the job for the general manager, who was new to Mars. He felt the workshop proved quite beneficial as not only did he become familiar with his direct reports, but he gained an understanding of the issues confronting the busi-ness, which he felt would have otherwise taken months to learn.

In Australia, we had a major learning: We needed a process to ensure follow-up on issues identified during the workshops. John, the CFO for Australia with operational responsibility for the petcare unit, noted that in his preparation for the workshop he reviewed the output from the prior year. The team had actually identified their major risk for 2005 and the treatments to address this issue. Unfor-tunately, they had not used the prior year's solutions, and had not met their targets for the issue. John became one of the biggest advocates and supporters of ERM as he moved on to CFO of the Russia unit and then U.S. Chocolate.

REPORTING

Ultimately we conducted 18 unit workshops, one for our quant group, and a cor-porate one. At the end of the process we reviewed all of the output. We recog-nized the need for categorizing the differences between the votes to report risk using a color key for risk profiles (see Exhibit 3.1). In reviewing the voting scores,

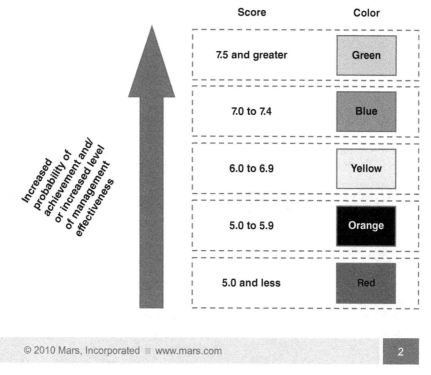

Exhibit 3.1 Color Key for the Risk Profile Score

it appeared that five groupings existed. We had some actuaries review the data as well, and they came up with the same results.

Companies frequently like to use three colors in their corporate dashboards; however, most experts seem to agree that risk is not so cut-and-dried, and recommend four or five risk categorizations. As a workshop facilitator, one can generally detect why a score was blue and not green. In discussions challenging such a vote, facilitators frequently heard general managers or other participants speak very clearly as to why an initiative is blue and not green.

Following the addition of risk categories, the ERM team developed a summary report, in priority order, consisting of each initiative, its definition, and each initiative's risk profile (see Exhibit 3.2). These were compiled by region and submitted to the Mars management team and the regional management teams, along with the complete workshop reports.

Although senior managers reviewed these reports, it was too early in the process for them to understand fully the potential of ERM. This was highlighted in January 2007 during my annual review with Oscar. David, Mars' president, entered the "fishbowl" room quite perturbed at one of the largest units. The unit had advised of a significant surprise at year-end, which had an impact on the overall business's year-end results. David looked at me and asked whether this issue had arisen during my new process. I advised him that the unit had raised this as a potential issue, which could adversely impact them entering the new year. They

Business units are responsible for submitting a summary report to corporate.

Illustrative

Initiative	Risk Profile
Grow the X Market with Relevant Brands Grow the X market through product improvement and increased accessibility to achieve sales growth of 8% and margin improvement of 7%.	Yellow
Direct-to-Customer (DTC) Increase DTC shipments by 12%.	Green
Workforce Engagement Increase workforce engagement score by 10%.	Blue
Bring New Plant Online Make the new plant fully operational by the end of Q3.	Red
Launch of New Brand Successfully launch New Brand into the market and achieve 65% distribution.	Blue

© 2010 Mars, Incorporated ■ www.mars.com   3

Exhibit 3.2   Summary Report

asked me to get them a copy of the complete report, and I took this to mean they had read but not kept the original.

The unit's ERM workshop output had the issue as a "red" in their submission. While both David and Oscar agreed that they expected some units to have initiatives with a red risk profile, they would not accept a unit to have a red issue and not address it or communicate the potential impact as appropriate. This became a basic tenet of the ERM process. This incident also proved a major win for ERM, as David became extremely interested in the quarterly updates, which began shortly thereafter.

To ensure that units used ERM throughout the year and communicated their views on risk to senior management, we developed an ERM dashboard template. This included the initiatives in priority order, the risk profile of each initiative for each quarter (beginning with the workshop in Q3), the risk profile trend—stable, improving, or declining—and a comment column for providing a view for year-end (see Exhibit 3.3). This became an excellent tool for communicating for several reasons. First, units that did not do so already had to review their risks and risk treatments quarterly. This helped them to have a risk mentality mind-set, which David had given us as a goal at the beginning. Second, senior managers could quickly identify units that were struggling with issues. For the first couple of years of the program, David would meet with the corporate controller, to review the

Business units are required to review and update a dashboard on a quarterly basis, which allows tracking of performance over time.

Illustrative

Initiative	Risk Profile					Trend	Comments
	Q3 '09	Q4 '09	Q1 '10	Q2 '10	Q3 '10		
Grow the X Market with Relevant Brands Grow the X market through product improvement and increased accessibility to achieve sales growth of 8% and margin improvement of 7%.	Yellow	Green				Improving	YTD the X Market is our second biggest growth contributor growing by 10%. Margin improvements on track.
Direct-to-Customer (DTC) Increase DTC shipments by 12%.	Green	Green				Stable	DTC operation has improved; however, some areas need improvement. We will expand when we have a holistic strategy.
Workforce Engagement Increase workforce engagement score by 10%.	Blue	Green				Improving	Managers have been provided training. All managers have held meetings with their team members.
Bring New Plant Online Make the new plant fully operational by the end of Q3.	Red	Blue				Stable	On track, construction underway Plant will be ready by the end of Q3.
Launch of New Brand Successfully launch New Brand into the market and achieve 65% distribution.	Blue	Yellow				Stable	Increased risk due to current demand exceeding supply. We have rephrased the rollout for the market to ensure current supply is adequate.

© 2010 Mars, Incorporated ▦ www.mars.com

4

Exhibit 3.3 Quarterly Update

quarterly reports. Finally, it provided units with a tool to communicate to management that things were on track, although the first or second quarter sales may not have appeared that way.

An excellent example of the latter point occurred the first year we used the reporting template. In a large market where the company had a strong number three position, the unit's reported sales appeared to fall below its plan at the end of the first, second, and third quarters of 2006.

I had facilitated the unit's workshop. As their two main competitors, which had a significant share of the market, planned to front-end load their activities (e.g., advertising, consumer promotions, trade discounts, etc.) into the first and second quarter, the unit decided to focus the vast majority of its activities into the second half, especially the fourth quarter. Each quarter the unit reported its key brands as having green risk profiles. Each quarter, Oscar had me contact and challenge the unit CFO on this point. Each quarter the unit CFO responded that the unit had back-end loaded its activity set into Q3 and Q4, and I confirmed to Oscar that this had been the case in the workshop as well. In the end, the unit delivered about 105 percent of its planned sales, and the ERM Quarterly Report gained a great deal of credibility.

One thing that we noted from both the pilot year and the launch year was that participants did not always seem to vote on the same thing on an initiative. For example, an objective may read, "Maintain market leadership while achieving growth and profitability targets." A unit might have 35 percent market share, and it could hold market leadership at 25 percent. One participant may vote low because she believes market share will fall to 32 percent while another participant votes high because this will still represent market leadership. Similarly, divergent votes

Define initiatives with <u>measurable</u> objectives.

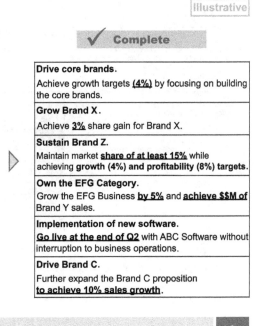

Exhibit 3.4   Targets

on achieving growth and profitability may result as different participants vote on gross sales versus net sales, and earnings versus margins.

To resolve this problem, we changed the process for the 2007 Operating Plan workshops, conducted in Q3 of 2006, and all future workshops. We required units to specify measurable targets within each objective (see Exhibit 3.4).

Units could do this for all initiatives, including intangible ones. For instance, associate engagement targets would include specific numerical scores for the units and follow-up percentage targets for management. Similarly, "Have the right people for the right jobs" would become "Have one person for each critical job in the unit's succession plan." These objectives would have measurable targets by which the unit could report progress throughout the course of the year.

2007 OPERATING PLAN WORKSHOPS

In 2006, we made two major changes. We added a strategic component to the workshop. We also pushed most of the workshop development to the units.

In terms of a strategic component, we added a column to the existing workshop template that held the activities the unit needed to undertake to successfully implement its long-term strategic objectives. The strategic component proved unsuccessful for three major reasons. First, we found that units without a completed long-term strategy did not find this worthwhile. Second, the shift from the operating plan in the morning to the strategic plan in the afternoon proved too mentally taxing. Workshop participants tend to be less effective late in the afternoon due to the mental focus required in the workshop, and the transition to the longer-term view in the afternoon seemed to make this afternoon lapse worse. Finally, we found the extra column in the strategic template unnecessary. Units preferred to use the standard workshop template for both operational and strategic issues. For all future strategic workshops, we used only the standard template.

For the 2006 Operating Plan workshops, we found it very time consuming for facilitators to build each individual workshop. To build each workshop, the two facilitators interviewed the general manager, the unit CFO, and several other unit management team members. They would then take the unit's key operating plan objectives and compile the templates by adding the risks and risk treatments based on their interpretation of the interviews. Between the interviews and the workshop compilation, it could take as much as a person-week to build a workshop. As facilitators typically had very senior positions, this did not represent an effective use of their time. This time-consuming process would greatly limit the number of workshops that we could have, unless we could find a better solution.

At this time, the company was moving to increasingly standardized planning tools. The units could use these tools to develop their own workshops, with minimal guidance and support of the workshop facilitators. This aligned well with our objective to simplify the workshop development process and aided us in pushing much of the workshop development to the unit. We developed a PowerPoint presentation that outlined the process, as summarized in Exhibit 3.5.

This new approach greatly reduced the time to build a workshop. By having initiative owners confirm the definition of the objectives, adding what they viewed as the major four or five risks and risk treatments, we not only reduced the time necessary to build a workshop, but we also improved the quality of the workshops. The latter was achieved because the facilitators no longer had to interpret what they had heard in the workshop. Instead, the actual owners populated this data, which the management team validated in the workshop. This had the additional benefit of increasing the ownership of the process within the unit.

TECHNOLOGY

When the ERM program began in 2003, the ERM team consciously did not select a technology solution. The company did not want a technology solution to drive the process. By 2007, the program had developed to the point that we needed technological support. First, we moved from using Word to Excel. This enabled us to develop a comprehensive Excel tool for workshop development and data capture. Second, we selected a software vendor whose product could most closely adapt to our process.

The Excel tool greatly streamlined the process for building workshops. It made it easier to define initiatives and for users to build individual templates in preparation for workshops. More importantly, it enabled workshop operators to revise and add information to the templates more easily during workshops. This enabled workshop participants and operators to focus better on the process.

Exhibit 3.5   Sample Planning Process

#	Activity	Timing
1	The unit CFO provides the facilitators with the key operating planning documents, standard planning documents, and so on.	—
2	The facilitators hold a teleconference with the unit's GM and CFO to identify relevant operating plan initiatives and strategic risks from last year's assessment and add new operating plan initiatives and strategic risks.	1.25 to 1.5 hours
3	The facilitators prepopulate the workshop template with initiative definitions, based on the interview, the planning documents provided, and output from the prior year.	1.5 hours
4	Facilitators send the prepopulated workshop template to the unit CFO.	—
5	The unit CFO forwards each template to the unit's Management Team and to the individual initiative owner.	—
6	Initiative owners confirm the initiative definition, including key metrics, adds four to five risks, and adds four to five risk treatments.	0.5 to 1 hour per initiative
7	The unit CFO consolidates the templates and forwards them to the facilitators and the unit GM.	1 hour
8	One facilitator has a review with the unit GM and/or CFO of the workshop template to validate the input and identify any key points.	30 minutes
9	The unit CFO distributes the final workshop template to the unit's Management Team as a preread package.	—
10	Workshop.	8 hours

The software resulted in two major improvements in the process. First, it enabled units to update their risk profiles into a system. It also provided more flexibility than previously available using Word.

Data capture and reporting represented the other major improvements provided by the software. Using the Excel tool following each workshop, we categorized each initiative and risk by function (e.g., Service and Finance, Sales, Marketing, etc.). Similarly, we categorized these using the risk definitions, which the initial working group had developed.

AGGREGATION

The company historically had very well-defined ranges of risk that it would take on in the areas of currencies, commodities, insurance, and so on. It had comprehensive reporting that aggregated such financial risks. Although these areas were well managed at the regional, segment, or corporate level, their role frequently influenced decisions at the business unit level.

While companies can easily aggregate these types of financial risks, the ERM process presented other types of information. The output of the ERM workshops produced both qualitative and quantitative data, as well as tangible and intangible risks. These included operational, supply chain, and human resources risks.

To aggregate these risks and identify emerging risks for regional, segment, and corporate management teams, the ERM team had two methodologies—human review and technology. In the early years, the ERM team would review all of the workshop output and summarize the three or four key themes for the corporate management team. In some cases, they would delegate the review of this information to the individual(s) responsible for the issue. In two cases, the ERM team led a short workshop with the corporate management team on one or two of the critical issues identified.

In many of the early workshops, the ERM team was surprised to find so many human resources issues across the world. Frequently, these rose to be near the top of the list in priority for many units. Bringing these out in workshops enabled the units to view these from the perspective of risk to the business. On a corporate, aggregated basis, this gave leadership a different perspective (i.e., risk) from which to view the issue, and over time how their initiatives worked to improve the risk at the corporate and unit levels.

Once the company moved to segments from regions, the ERM team aggregated the output from the individual units in the segment and conducted workshops with the segment management teams, to help them identify the key issues confronting their business in the coming year. These included themes and emerging risks identified across the entire business, but focused on their impact on the individual segment. This was done in conjunction with their overall planning activities, bringing risk into their evaluation process. Some segments found this quite useful in helping them to allocate resources and identify action plans to improve the likelihood of the segment's success in the upcoming year. Segments that found this helpful held these workshops annually.

In aggregating the risks in the workshops, we considered such issues as these:

- The number of business units impacted
- The number of associates impacted
- The number of business processes or functions impacted
- The impact on our consumers and customers
- The potential impact to our brands

This methodology worked very well with difficult-to-quantify risks. It also helped to identify emerging risks. The overall process identified issues that might be a nuisance in individual markets but when viewed on an aggregated basis had a potential impact on the segment or corporation as a whole.

The software solution provided another opportunity for aggregation. As workshop teams had categorized the initiatives and risks by both function and risk definition, we could run reports or aggregation by business unit; by geography (country, region, corporate); by corporate function (S&F, Sales, Compliance, Marketing); and so on. Once the system had three years of data, it could provide comparisons by year, segment, region, and business unit. This enabled the preparation of summary reports, aggregating the issues identified and changes by year, thus allowing the identification of emerging risks, such as the increasing importance of commodity pricing and availability. The reports provided a summary analysis of the data for the segments, which used this to supplement their ERM work.

Unfortunately, we lost our back-office support for these reports after the first year of developing the capability. As such we were unable to run these reports on an ongoing basis thereafter. The learning for others is to ensure that you select software that your team has the capabilities to fully utilize.

TEMPLATE EVOLUTION

Over the years our template evolved. Some changes resulted from observations made by facilitators. Others came from participants, either during workshops or from periodic global surveys.

During a workshop, facilitators attempt to limit the number of risks and risk treatments to 10 to 15 each (as many as 20 for very large units). However, having so many risks and risk treatments can lead to clarity without perspective.

The initial template simply listed risks and risk treatments in two columns, without referencing which risk treatments applied to the individual risks. The ERM team found that referencing the risk(s) that the individual risk treatments addressed provided better clarity as to the process. Furthermore, this approach helped to better identify the most critical risks and risk treatments. To leverage this opportunity, participants had to identify the three or four most critical risks, defined as those most likely to adversely impact the initiative. They did the same for the three or four most critical risk treatments (i.e., those most likely to lead to success). This led to more robust voting, as participants had a perspective on the impact and likelihood that the most critical risk would occur, as well as the effectiveness of the most critical risk treatments in aiding the team to achieve its objectives.

Initially, when units identified key actions that they believed would increase the likelihood of success, they were included in the summary reports. However, the ERM team discovered that the failure to assign accountability for the activity frequently led to it not getting done. (I have heard this same issue arise in other companies' programs.) Consequently, an "Action Plan" section was added to the bottom of the template. This improved the results; however, in one workshop the unit asked if they could assign each risk treatment to an individual. This worked very well.

Through experimentation it was found that adding both a responsible party and a completion date added to the robustness of the process. Typically, units would assign the tasks to either management team members or their direct reports. This helped identify situations where one associate or group had too many activities to address properly those things needed to achieve an initiative's objectives. More important, as the workshop progressed through the day, it frequently became clear that a unit might not have the bandwidth to complete all of their tasks in the time frame allotted. This led to changing deadlines and moving resources around the business in order to improve the likelihood of successfully achieving both individual initiatives as well as overall operating plan objectives. Exhibit 3.6 shows how a completed template from a workshop would appear.

Template for input in Workshops

#	Risks	Risk Ref #	Risk Treatment	Risk Treatment Owner	Due Date
	Initiative			Greener Green	
1	Risk 1	1,3,6,8,9,10	Risk Treatment 1	G. Smith	End Q4 2011
2	Risk 2	3,4,8	Risk Treatment 2	B. Spinard	May 2012
3	Risk 3	All	Risk Treatment 3	L. Warner	June 2012
4	Risk 4	1,2,3,4,5,8	Risk Treatment 4	B. Spinard	Q1 2012
5	Risk 5	3,6,7,8	Risk Treatment 5	B. Spinard	Q3 2012
6	Risk 6	2,7,8	Risk Treatment 6	L. Warner	Ongoing
7	Risk 7	5,8	Risk Treatment 7	G. Smith	End Q4 2011
8	Risk 8	9,10	Risk Treatment 8	L. Warner	Q4 2012
9	Risk 9				
10	Risk 10				
	Action Plan				

© 2010 Mars, Incorporated ■ www.mars.com 1

Exhibit 3.6 Mars ERM Template

SPECIAL SITUATIONS

The ERM team found that engaging key early supporters on an ongoing basis had mutually beneficial results for both. Most of the evolutionary improvements and best practices occurred as a result of these activities.

One major European unit sought to improve their growth rate. In 2006 Pete became the CFO, and in early 2007, Susan became general manager of this unit. Pete had participated in the initial South African workshop as well as his new unit's 2007 Operating Plan workshop. Susan had played the key role in having the ERM team involved in the 2004 European project.

To turn the business around, Susan and Pete wanted ERM to play a key role in the unit's growth program. They wanted to hold a series of ERM workshops to support the development of their program. The output would be built into and be monitored on an ongoing basis by their project management office (PMO). Over a period of 18 months, the unit held both the normal operating plan workshops as well as strategic ones. In order to increase the buy-in to the strategy by the entire business, they held a two-day workshop involving both the management team and their direct reports. This totaled approximately 30 associates. These associates were divided into several groups to conduct risk assessments of the proposed new strategies and to identify new activities and risk treatements that would improve the likelihood of achieving success. The output included changes to brands that the unit could best leverage. The process also developed support from multiple levels of the business, as they had an active voice in the process. This program of workshops contributed to the unit's successful achievement of its performance objectives.

In 2007 the company acquired a U.S.-based entity. About a year later Pete became the new CFO and Maria became the general manager. Maria had been general manager of Australia during the first ERM session in 2004, and has been a strong supporter of ERM ever since. They decided to use a similar approach to the one Pete had helped create in Europe, adding additional objectives. In addition to using ERM to assist in the development and stress testing of a comprehensive business strategy, they wanted to use ERM to assist in evaluating talent, embedding a new culture, and obtaining support from multiple layers of the business from their leadership team, the top 30 or so associates within the business. Over two and a half years, the unit held numerous workshops, both operational and strategic, to help them formulate their strategy and achieve their overall objectives.

Don had been the CFO for the first Australian Food workshop in 2005. In 2007, he became CFO of Japan. He used ERM to evaluate the unit's strategy. In this case, the unit had the brand manager for each brand come into the room, present the brand's strategy, and act as an equal member with the management team members in evaluating the likelihood of the brand successfully achieving its objectives. Here again, multilevel participation enhanced the buy-in within the business.

In 2010, Don became CFO of Petcare Asia/Pacific. Like Don, Richard, the GM of the business, had been a long-term supporter of ERM. They decided to use ERM with the regional management team to increase the probability of achieving their objectives. Over a two-year period, we held a series of ERM workshops to help support their development and evolution of their strategy. This included their brand portfolio, asset investment program, individual market investment, associate development, and so on. In addition to the standard workshop, we helped them with scenario planning to identify risk treatments for competitor activity, regulatory issues, and the like. In their meetings where no workshop was held, Don led the review of the risk profile, and the team voted on the risk profile of each strategic objective.

This team also took the standard template a step further. They categorized the risks and risk treatments by categories within each template. They added a fifth column that specified the actual activity. These were given to either the functional head of the region or the functional team underneath them responsible for the activity set—for example, Sales, Marketing, or Supply (i.e., manufacturing and distribution). The respective teams then provided periodic updates as part of the regional management team's risk profile update process.

The team found this approach beneficial for the team. As their objectives became "Green" and had been achieved, they developed new templates to reflect their updated strategies.

MAJOR ACQUISITION

When Mars made a major acquisition of a global confectionery company, the early supporters of ERM at Mars played a key role in the adoption of ERM at the acquired company. Jim, one of our original facilitators, took on a high-level role within the acquired business' U.S. operations. At his urging, the U.S. GM agreed to have an ERM workshop for the 2009 Operating Plan in early 2009. This workshop was well received within the acquired business.

The GM of European Sugar, during our current state assessment workshop in 2003, had been a key supporter of ERM in various senior roles within Mars. When he became a senior manager within the acquired company's European operations, he introduced ERM in this region. Here again the process was well received.

Lee, the S&F Staff Officer for Mars in Asia, who had observed the first workshop in China and overseen the process in the region thereafter, discussed ERM with Michael, the acquired company's CFO of Asia. Michael was so intrigued by the process that he had us conduct a 2010 Operating Plan workshop for his largest unit in the region. Following our first workshop, Michael advised us that he had found the process robust, and complementary to their other activities. As such he asked us to conduct additional workshops for the other major markets in his region.

Within two years, we were conducting annual operating plan workshops at business units representing the same high percentage of the acquired company's global sales that we achieved at Mars.

CONCLUSION

In 2010, Mars received the Corporate Executive Board's "Force of Ideas Award" for ERM. It was the first recipient in this category. The award was based on the view that Mars had successfully embedded ERM into its business model and that other companies had adopted its process.

The key factors in the success of ERM at Mars include:

- We ensured we aligned the program with the approved principles.
- We focused on achieving our operational and strategic objectives. We did not address compliance. We left that to the associates responsible for compliance, and assisted them in using our tools as appropriate.
- We focused on evolution and not revolution. As a result, the program had a continuous improvement process.
- Flexibility and not rigidity contributed to the program's results. By assisting units in developing the workshops and updating processes that best met their needs, the program had a demand for services as opposed to a push. Furthermore, many of the evolutions of the program directly resulted from unit requests.
- The process proved to be a good identifier of talent and an opportunity for associate development for the business.
- The ERM team never overpromised what it could deliver. Instead, we set realistic objectives on our rollout and obtained senior management support throughout.
- The ERM team engaged and conducted periodic surveys of the business units, the Mars management team, and the Mars board's advisers.

QUESTIONS

1. What represents the key success factors of the program?
2. What improvements would you make?
3. Does this represent an effective risk management program? If not, what is missing?
4. Would this program work for a publicly traded corporation of similar size?
5. How important do you view alignment and accountability among a management team?

NOTE

1. For information on Mars' history, see www.mars.com/global/about-mars/history.aspx.

ABOUT THE CONTRIBUTOR

Larry Warner is President of Warner Risk Group, which provides ERM and risk management consulting services. He has almost 30 years of experience in designing and building risk management programs in asset conservation, safety, insurance, and enterprise risk.

Prior to establishing Warner Risk Group in 2012, Larry served as Staff Officer of Risk Management for Mars, Incorporated (including Wrigley), based in McLean, Virginia. At Mars, Larry had global responsibility for developing and coordinating Mars' enterprise risk management activities, directing Mars' global asset conservation program, managing Mars' global property and casualty insurance programs and claims, coordinating the auditing of Mars' safety programs, and overseeing the placement of its global benefit insurance programs. The Corporate Executive Board awarded Mars its 2010 Force of Ideas Award for Risk Management for its embedding ERM into performance management.

Before joining Mars in 1989, Larry was Assistant Risk Manager at Texas Instruments. He has a BS in geography and an MBA in risk management and corporate finance, both from the University of Georgia. He is a frequent speaker at national risk conferences and contributor for such organizations as the American Strategic Management Institute, the Conference Board, the Corporate Executive Board, and the Risk and Insurance Management Society.

CHAPTER 4

Value and Risk

Enterprise Risk Management at Statoil

ALF ALVINIUSSEN
Independent Consultant, Norway

HÅKAN JANKENSGÅRD
Researcher, Department of Business Administration and Knut Wicksell Centre for
Financial Studies, Lund University, Sweden

The enterprise risk management (ERM) approach to managing a company's risks promises many benefits. A reading of the literature on the subject will tell you that ERM, among other things, will reduce the frequency of surprises, lead to better allocation of resources, improve risk response decisions, and reduce costly duplication of risk management activities (e.g., COSO 2004).

Many companies are finding out that these benefits don't always materialize easily. It turns out that implementing a holistic, enterprise-wide approach to risk management often challenges the organizational status quo. Powerful individuals and business units face a potential loss of autonomy and are asked to comply with new reporting requirements. "The way we've always done things around here" is no longer good enough, it may seem.

In companies where change is resisted, ERM is at risk of becoming an island, an isolated process whose outputs and opinions are largely ignored by decision makers. These so-called ghost ERM programs contribute little or nothing at all to enterprise value. In this chapter we use the experience of Statoil, a Norwegian oil and gas producer, for lessons about how to overcome these organizational challenges and make the potential benefits of ERM become reality.

At Statoil, understanding and managing risk are today considered core values. This principle has been duly integrated into the organization, and is inscribed in steering documents as well as in a booklet handed out to all employees, describing core values, corporate governance, the operating model, and corporate policies. The company has developed a sophisticated approach to ERM that centers on the principle of value creation. ERM is thoroughly embedded in the business units' way of doing things, and it appears to enjoy the wholehearted support of Statoil's executive officers and board of directors.

Statoil has, in other words, managed to make ERM into something that makes a real difference. To gain insights about the success factors behind this outcome, we will investigate how Statoil has dealt with the four main general tasks that fall on executives responsible for ERM: (1) make sure that there is an adequate process for identifying, managing, and reporting risks throughout the company; (2) act as a support function to business units in this work; (3) detect and counteract risk management decisions that are suboptimal for the company as a whole; and (4) analytically aggregate risks to support decision making concerning the company's total risk profile. The first two sections outline the history of ERM in Statoil, and the guiding principles that underpin it.

ERM AT STATOIL: A BRIEF HISTORY

Headquartered in Stavanger, Norway, Statoil is one of the world's top 10 oil and gas producers. In 2012, the company had revenues of 706 billion Norwegian krone, NOK (approximately 120 billion U.S. dollars, USD). In the same year, it had over 23,000 employees worldwide and produced 2,004 million barrels of oil equivalents per day. Known for its operational excellence, Statoil is the global leader in offshore oil production below water depths of 100 meters.

The company has a 40-year history as part of the Norwegian oil bonanza. Originally Statoil was the state-controlled company in the Norwegian model of retaining both publicly and privately owned exploration companies. The privately held company Saga Petroleum was acquired by the partly state-owned conglomerate Norsk Hydro in 2000. Norsk Hydro in turn merged its oil and gas division into Statoil in 2007. Statoil is now by far the largest producer on the Norwegian continental shelf.

In 2001, Statoil's shares were listed on the Oslo and New York stock exchanges. In early 2013, its market capitalization exceeded 80 billion USD. While the Norwegian state still owns 67 percent of the company, it operates independently of the state on strictly commercial principles.

After having sold its downstream and petrochemical businesses over the past few years, Statoil is today heavily focused on upstream activities (i.e., exploration and development of oil and gas reserves). Its three business areas focusing on development are divided according to geographical regions (Norway, International, and the United States, with the latter being much smaller). In addition, it has four more business areas focusing on marketing, technology, exploration, and strategy.

ERM in Statoil got under way in 1996. Petter Kapstad, who has a background in banking, had been asked to systematize the management of risk in the finance department, which previously had been carried out in a fragmented and uncoordinated way. The result of Petter's work was that the risks managed by the finance department were measured and managed as a portfolio of risks with central oversight. The then CEO of Statoil, Harald Norvik, realized that the same principles could be applied to the whole company, and that there would be benefits to Statoil from managing its risks in an integrated way. Again, Petter was trusted with the task of leading the company in this direction.

While Statoil's executive officers were generally positive to the idea behind ERM, they still demanded to know "What is in it for us?" An important part of the answer to this question came from a project group that investigated the costs and benefits to Statoil from various financial transactions, mostly hedging and foreign exchange (FX) transactions going on in the company. Petter and his group were able to show that the number of transactions was staggeringly high, and that they were mostly based on a silo thinking that made no sense at all as seen from the corporate perspective. And, crucially, these transactions were not harmless or mere annoyances. They came at a substantial cost and seriously complicated the company's accounting as well as the management of exposures. This struck the senior executives as unacceptable. ERM had demonstrated the economic justification it needed. A clear mandate was given.

Early on in the project, Petter met and started working with Eyvind Aven, who shared the same vision of an enterprise-wide approach to risk management. Importantly, Eyvind had a background in economic analysis, which complemented Petter's experience from trading units. This fact made them bilingual in the sense that they knew the specific terminology and ways of doing things that were prevalent both in the company's high-profile trading units, as well as in its headquarters. Their ability to speak complementary languages and not being viewed as outsiders was to prove very useful, as many tough decisions lay ahead with people who had an interest in preserving the status quo.

An important early milestone in the implementation of ERM came in 1999, when the Risk Committee, a cross-disciplinary advisory body on risk, was formed. The idea behind creating this committee was to obtain a forum to which people could put proposals and general risk issues for analysis and recommendations. From the very beginning, the committee has been chaired by the chief financial officer (CFO). Its main task is to advise the executive managers and the CFO on risk issues, and is not part of the formal decision process. It consists of a broad range of professionals with different backgrounds, such as the head of strategy, the heads of the main trading units, the chief controllers of different business units, and the head of internal control, in addition to the head of the risk department who is responsible for the agenda and calling for meetings.

In 2000, the risk department was formally set up (headed by Petter Kapstad), and started work on developing a common methodology on risk, as well as continuing the work on developing the company's consolidated risk model that had been initiated two years earlier. The risk department, furthermore, has the overall responsibility for insurance and the captive insurance company. In 2005, the first enterprise-wide risk mapping process was rolled out.

ERM FOUNDATIONS

In the early stages of the project, it was decided that Statoil would not simply implement one of the existing blueprints for ERM. Nor did Petter and Eyvind want it to be, or it would be seen as another control function.[1] They had something else in mind. They wanted a framework that made sense to Statoil, and that centered on the two basic goals of the company: to create value and to avoid accidents. Keeping people and the environment safe are the first priority and supersede any other objective.[2] Beyond those basic objectives, however, risks are to be managed in a way that maximizes the value of the company. This insight has a number of implications, which are explored in this section.

To begin with, the focus on value affects the very way risk is defined in Statoil. According to Statoil's philosophy, which is widely communicated internally, risk encompasses not only downside risk but also upside potential. This philosophy has even found its way into the corporate directives of the company, which state that "risks shall be identified and analyzed, including both upside and downside impact." On this dimension, existing off-the-shelf ERM frameworks were considered too oriented toward regulatory compliance and risk avoidance. The Statoil philosophy instead recognizes that risk taking is unavoidable, even necessary, to create value for shareholders.[3] What matters is that the risks are well enough understood and found acceptable, given their downside risk and upside potential. Reflecting this thinking, the risk maps in Statoil have been developed to show probability and impact not only for the downside, which is the most common way of constructing these maps, but for the upside as well (see Exhibit 4.1).

Statoil's risk map captures both upside potential and downside risk for any given risk factor. On the x-axis is the probability of occurrence. On the y-axis is the impact figure, measured as the pretax impact on earnings (USD millions). Note that the impact is measured relative to the forecasted value of earnings. All reported risks will be considered twice in the map. The first is its potential contribution to upside potential (to be entered above the line), and the second is its contribution to downside risk (to be entered below the line). These two points are a summary, or synthesis, of the entire range of potential outcomes for the risk factor in question. For example, the risk factor denoted Risk A in the exhibit has a 5 percent probability that the outcome will be somewhat better than expected. However,

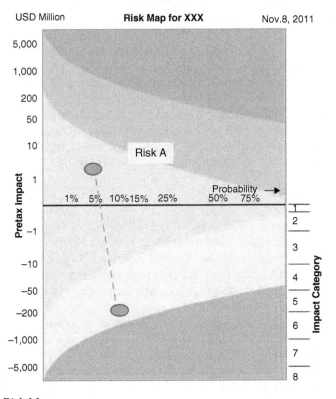

Exhibit 4.1   Risk Map

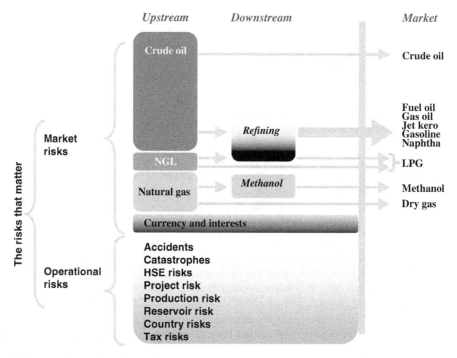

Exhibit 4.2 Statoil's Value Chain

there is a 10 percent probability of a fairly significant loss relative to the forecast (USD 200 million). For this particular risk, the downside risk is larger than the upside potential.

As already mentioned, value creation is the basic guiding principle for ERM in Statoil. That is demonstrated by the emphasis the company puts on viewing risks in a value chain perspective. In the corporate directives it is written that the company's approach is to "identify, evaluate, and *manage risk related to the value chain* to support achievement of our corporate objectives" (original emphasis). Statoil's value chain is outlined in Exhibit 4.2, showing how its main activities progress from upstream (oil exploration and development) to downstream (petroleum refinement) to market (selling its products into various global markets).

Statoil's value chain consists of three main stages: the exploration and development of oil and gas reserves (upstream); the refinement of hydrocarbons into various petroleum products (downstream); and the selling of crude oil, gas, and refined products into different markets. The most important risks ("the risks that matter") have been divided into two categories: market risks and operational risks.

What difference does the value chain perspective make? First, it serves as a clear signal to everybody involved (i.e., Statoil's employees and other stakeholders) that value creation is the metric being pursued through ERM, and it is the impact on Statoil's performance that ultimately counts. Statoil's thinking on this issue is that if ERM is limited to managing risks related to goal achievement in various business units, the result will be "satisficing" rather than value maximizing.[4]

Another important benefit of the value chain perspective relates to the fact that the large number of risks identified in the risk map can make it challenging to understand what is really going on. By sorting the risks into a value chain, one can more easily see the bigger picture and, through the lens of the company's business model, see how the different risk categories hang together. In other words, the value chain perspective allows Statoil to rework the knowledge about risk contained in the risk maps into something that is more analytically and logically coherent.

The concept of core risks further underlines the central role of value creation as a guiding principle for ERM in Statoil. To understand this concept, we need to go back to 2001, when the company's shares were listed.[5] During the listing process, there were investors looking for arguments as to why they should invest in Statoil. Recognizing that investors were entitled to information about what exposures they were getting when they invested in Statoil shares, the company formulated the idea of core risks, understood as the risk exposures that an investor would expect, and even desire, to have from buying Statoil shares (the most important of which was the exposure to oil and gas prices). The core risks are owned by the CEO of the company and are coordinated centrally in the organization. One of the practical consequences of this is that trading mandates throughout the company have been substantially restricted and placed under central scrutiny. At the end of the day, this should increase the transparency and predictability of the risk exposures obtained by investing in Statoil shares, which lowers the risk premium investors attach to the company and hence also its cost of capital (Jankensgård, Hoffman, and Rahmat 2013).

ERM PROCESSES IN STATOIL TODAY

So far we have discussed the history of ERM in Statoil and the guiding principles underpinning it. We now turn to the more practical issues of what tasks executives need to address for ERM to work in practice and for its potential benefits to be realized. The first two tasks, covered in this section, are making sure there are adequate processes in place for managing risks throughout the organization, and acting as a support function to the business units as they go about this.

Let us dispel a potential misunderstanding. ERM does not imply that all risks should be managed, or owned, centrally in a company. While some risks certainly are managed centrally in Statoil (its core risks, as discussed in the previous section), the business areas are responsible for managing the large majority of the risks that arise in their lines of business.

Just because a business area has been designated the owner of a particular risk, however, doesn't mean that sound management of this risk automatically follows. Corporate management needs to ensure that risk management in the business units is of sufficient quality. Corporate management also has a legitimate right to be informed about the main risks in each business unit and what is done about them. These considerations lead us to what for many is the bread and butter of ERM, namely the process of identifying, mitigating, and reporting risks. For brevity, we will refer to this as the "risk mapping process."

In Statoil, the risk mapping process follows a quarterly rhythm, which is the frequency at which the business units are required to update their risk maps. This is not just a numbers exercise. The units are expected to provide discussions and justifications for their assumptions, and explain what their policy on each main risk is. As part of the company's quarterly review meetings,[6] they also meet with top management to discuss the status with regard to major risks. These two facts—providing written justifications and actually meeting with representatives of top management and the risk department—go a long way toward ensuring the quality of the outputs of this process (the probability-impact estimates). Since the business units know this lies ahead, they have every reason to do a good job preparing and thinking through their estimates of risks (and their mitigation actions). It also counteracts any tendency to think along the lines that "this risk certainly exists, but it surely will not happen during my time in office, so I will just do nothing."

The risk department, in turn, writes a brief in response to the business units' risk maps, which is sent to executive management. Statoil's board of directors is also briefed on the risk profile on a quarterly basis, and they receive a condensed version of the risk map prepared by the risk department.

The risk department is not only a supervisor of the risk mapping process. It also provides support to business areas and helps spread best practices. It has the expertise and resources to assist business units in multiple ways from advice on how to manage a particular credit risk to suggesting a methodology for quantifying a certain market risk.

A useful example of the role of the risk department as a resource available to support business areas in their commercial activities comes from country risk. Statoil's risk department has, in collaboration with consultancy firm IHS Global Insight, developed a deep expertise in this area, which is of particular importance to a company active in many of the world's most risky countries. This effort has resulted in a large internal knowledge base on country risk, as well as a standardized methodology for evaluating country risk as part of new investment proposals. The business areas are able to draw on these resources, and work with the risk department to reach the appropriate policies for each country and new investment.

In the risk mapping process, rigorous quantification of probability and impact has been considered essential to make the risk maps useful to support decision making. Quantification brings a focus on the financial bottom line of the company, and makes it possible to compare different risks in a meaningful way. What one person would label a large risk may well be a small one to someone else, depending on references.

OPTIMIZING TOTAL RISK

The two tasks related to ERM discussed so far, the risk mapping process and the role of adviser to the business areas, are conceptually straightforward. The third, avoiding risk management decisions that are suboptimal for the company as a whole, is less so. To increase the understanding of the issue, we will discuss several practical examples in this section.

In Statoil, avoiding suboptimal decisions is also known as "optimizing total risk." Optimization of total risk has been unyieldingly pursued by the ERM team, with several tangible benefits for the company. The value metric that underpins ERM in Statoil implies that it is the perspective of the company as a whole that should rule in practical situations where different individuals and business units may have differing views on how to proceed.

A straightforward example of possible suboptimal behavior concerns foreign exchange (FX) risk management. Consider a situation where one business unit is selling into a market where the product is quoted in U.S. dollars, and another unit is sourcing material priced in the same currency. Whereas each unit may have an incentive to manage its own exposure, what counts for the company as a whole is the net of these exposures. Lacking a central policy, risk could be overmanaged to the extent that managers of business units use FX derivatives to cover exposures that would cancel out from the perspective of the company. Apart from the burdensome accounting that derivatives cause, there are also significant direct costs from such overmanagement of risk. Statoil calculates that if two business areas simultaneously cover a USD 10 million exposure (by no means a large hedge by Statoil's standards), it would incur transaction costs of around NOK 180,000 (assuming a USD/NOK exchange rate of 6 and a bid-ask spread of 30 basis points). Since ERM was implemented, Statoil has withdrawn the ability of business units to set their own policy with regard to FX derivative usage. Besides avoiding the transaction costs just mentioned, a centralized FX derivative policy entails a number of other advantages, such as business units focusing on their core activities and an increased ability to coordinate the derivative policy with other corporate policies; see Jankensgård (2013) for a detailed discussion.

Our second example of potential suboptimization concerns the hedging of oil and gas exposures. Prior to ERM, business units used to have fairly generous mandates to hedge their exposures to these market prices. This created a potential problem from the perspective of the company as a whole. Besides complicating the assessment of net exposures on the corporate level, the business units were basing their hedging decisions on criteria that were disconnected from the goal of maximizing value. What drove a unit's decision to hedge was instead a desire to lock in prices when they were above the price that was assumed when targets were set for the year, but to leave them unhedged otherwise. If the business plan had assumed an oil price of $100 and it later climbed to $115, the unit could use a derivative contract to lock in this level, which ensured it would beat the target and could collect a bonus for the year. As mentioned earlier, these mandates have been gradually reined in and subjected to strict limits set centrally in the organization.

A third example of a business unit optimizing its own risk/return with the result being suboptimal decisions for the company overall comes from Statoil's captive insurance unit. Previously this unit sought to justify its existence as a standalone unit by showing robust profits. In so doing, it benefited greatly from the implicit guarantee provided by Statoil's credit rating and strong balance sheet. From the perspective of ERM, this is incorrect. Rather, the captive should be a tool for Statoil in optimizing total risk. Today the captive does this. The insurance policy of Statoil now targets the things that matter: the really big risks related to business continuation. That is, the insurance program focuses on the risks that really could throw Statoil off course, and ignores (i.e., self-insures) the lesser risks that ultimately have no significance for Statoil's ability to meet its overall objectives.

TOTAL RISK OPTIMIZATION: LESSONS LEARNED

Optimizing total risk may sound simple in principle. Indeed, it is one of the supposed core principles of ERM. ERM texts routinely contain phrases like "avoid duplicating costly risk management activities" and emphasize this as one of the main benefits of ERM (as opposed to a silo or decentralized approach to risk management).

In reality, optimizing total risk is not so easily achieved. A key reason for this is that it threatens the established way of doing things. Powerful units and individuals may have little interest in conforming to ERM because it reduces their autonomy and requires a change in how they work. Some deeply rooted habits may need to change. As a result, many will resist, which may prevent an ERM program from lifting off the ground.

Consider also the way the ability to manage risk hangs together with the system for performance measurement used by the company. Let's say a business unit is evaluated on its earnings before interest and taxes (EBIT). Since the unit is responsible for its own result, it seems only reasonable that it should have the freedom to manage the risk exposures related to it. However, this conflicts with the legitimate goal of headquarters to centralize management of FX risk or other core risks (e.g., oil prices) given the substantial benefits of a centralized approach (as discussed earlier). Hence, we have a conflict between the desire to centralize risk management and the way the company measures the performance of its business units.

So how do you succeed in making the ERM mind-set take root despite these potential problems? A few factors stand out in Statoil. For example, the company has ensured that key performance indicators (KPIs) and balanced scorecards that the company uses to evaluate its business units are, to the extent possible, unaffected by the centrally managed core risks we introduced earlier. This is a very important principle, because it resolves many of the potential conflicts of interest that could arise from centralizing risk management. As mentioned, energy prices and exchange rates could greatly impact the company (e.g., its EBIT), which could create incentives for the business units to manage these risks. In Statoil, however, the performance measures used have been designed to exclude the impact of these external factors. This means that the company achieves central management of these risks but largely avoids the discontent that could result from business units having to live with large risk exposures.

Beyond established KPIs and scorecards, work has also been done to make taking the best decision for Statoil the normal and expected thing for an employee. Obvious though the foregoing may sound, many units are, for often quite understandable reasons, very focused on meeting their own targets and consequently do not see beyond the border of their unit. The ERM team has, however, sought to make it part of anyone's job description to think in terms of Statoil's net benefit. People have been made aware that this is expected of them.

Another success factor in this regard has been to spend significant amounts of time *beforehand* thinking about what the ERM should ultimately look like, and why. Petter and Eyvind call this "doing one's homework." Having a coherent set of arguments ready to defend a particular measure meant to optimize Statoil's total risk has made it much easier to stand firm when people resisted change.

The Statoil experience also illustrates the importance of getting the Risk Committee right. If not done the right way, such a committee will continue in old tracks and look at risks in a silo fashion. Attendance will be low and the committee's utterances will carry little weight. If done right, however, it will develop into an effective

ERM champion whose recommendations are widely respected and translated into action.

The Statoil Risk Committee today is indeed a guardian of Statoil's best interests in matters related to risk. It effectively functions as an ERM filter in which difficult questions are voiced and resolved. Policies that were earlier set in isolation in a particular department now have to pass through the Risk Committee. For example, Statoil's FX policy is prepared by the finance department, but needs to be thoroughly discussed and supported in the Risk Committee.

A useful example of the committee's role in resolving issues related to total risk optimization comes from the process of setting performance KPIs and scorecards for business units (as discussed earlier). Wrongly formulated targets are seen as a threat to total risk optimization, because they may encourage a behavior that runs counter to this goal. The Risk Committee counteracts such tendencies by checking if a particular target makes sense and is compatible with Statoil's overall best interests, a loop that in Statoil is referred to as "pressure testing" the targets.

What accounts for Statoil's success in turning the Risk Committee into an ERM champion? The importance of having the unwavering support of key individuals in the executive team cannot be overstated here. Moreover, setting up an interesting agenda with a certain content of education (especially in the early days of the program) seems to have been a key success factor for the Statoil Risk Committee. The Statoil experience also shows that the committee should remain a specialist forum, and that one should stay away from attempts to integrate it with top management. Ultimately the Risk Committee needs to remain an advisory body, not an executive one, though it needs to carry enough status to be seen as the real arbiter on risk-related issues in the company.

RISK AGGREGATION

Developing risk maps and assembling the risk register produces a lot of information about risks, in qualitative as well as in quantitative terms. The simple fact that these processes are in place provides some reassurance that the risks are recognized and given proper attention. This is a goal in and of itself.

While in many ways essential to an ERM program, risk maps are largely static devices that don't allow codependencies between risks to be taken into account in any meaningful way. As a straightforward example, consider the relationship between the oil price and the USD/NOK exchange rate. Given the oil dependency of the Norwegian economy, this exchange rate tends to be sensitive to the price of oil, which is quoted in USD. Over the decades, this has provided Norwegian oil companies with a natural hedge: A lower oil price tends to weaken the Norwegian krone, as less oil revenue needs to be converted into NOK. Such dynamic relationships are hard to capture in a risk map, yet they are highly relevant to the risk management strategies of these companies.

Nor do the risk maps easily translate into an overall estimate of the uncertainty in the firm's future performance, as expressed through financial bottom lines such as earnings, liquidity, or balance sheet ratios. These shortcomings of the risk maps bring us to the fourth task facing the executives responsible for an ERM program: aggregating the firm's portfolio of risks into some indicator, or metric, that can guide the company's executive team (and board of directors) in matters related to the firm's overall risk profile.

Alviniussen and Jankensgård (2009) argue that most ERM programs today are detached from the analytical work of predicting and managing the firm's financial position. Not taking into account the firm's financial situation means that, despite the ERM effort to identify and quantify risks, an estimate of aggregate risk continues to elude companies implementing ERM. In the enterprise risk budgeting (ERB) approach proposed by these authors, the risk register is integrated with the firm's financial planning process to generate risk-adjusted forecasts of important enterprise-level indicators of performance and financial health.

To address the concerns voiced in the previous paragraph, companies need to take a more analytical and quantitative approach to risk management. In practical terms this implies building a model that combines the company's many different risks into a probability distribution for some bottom line considered important, such as earnings or its debt-to-assets ratio. From such a probability distribution, summary risk statistics can be obtained—for example, the loss in earnings associated with a certain probability (this measure is known as earnings at risk). Generally, this approach requires some form of simulation methodology (e.g., Monte Carlo simulation).

Statoil's corporate risk model, briefly introduced earlier in this chapter, is based on these principles. It contains a sophisticated methodology for estimating the amount of variability in the firm's main risk exposures, based on historical time series, as well as estimates of the tendency of these risks to co-vary. It lets the user select an output from a list and, within a few minutes' time, obtain a probability distribution for this variable. Moreover, the user can learn what the probability distribution would look like under an alternative course of action. For example, the model allows the user to overlay the probability distribution for net income with a second distribution that takes into account a certain risk management strategy (e.g., buying put options covering a certain fraction of the company's net exposure to the oil price). Such an overlay is illustrated in Exhibit 4.3.

Statoil's risk model allows the company to produce a probability distribution for various financial parameters considered important, such as earnings or return on assets employed. The obtained probability distribution can be used to derive summary risk statistics of the company's overall risk. In this graph, the base case outcome distribution (the darker line) for net income is compared with what it would look like if the company implemented a large-scale hedge of the oil price (the lighter line). The values of net income on the x-axis have been deliberately hidden. The vertical dashed line represents the value of net income associated with the 5th percentile of the probability distribution, a measure commonly referred to as net income at risk (or earnings at risk).

THE FRONTIERS

Part of the philosophy of ERM in Statoil is never to lean back and consider the job done. While the progress in achieving the necessary buy-in for new approaches is gradual and sometimes slow, the frontiers are pushed ever forward. Decision makers around the company need to have their worldviews challenged, as the thinking goes, and to be provoked into new ways of looking at things.

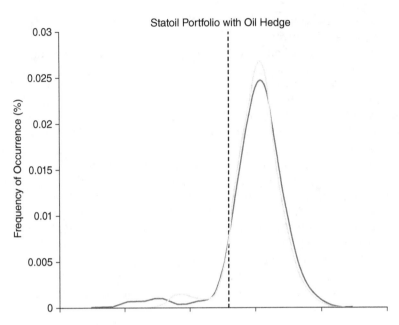

Exhibit 4.3   Comparing Different Risk Profiles

One area where work is currently being done is giving the concept of risk appetite a content that is meaningful to Statoil. Risk appetite is commonly construed as the amount of risk exposure a company is willing to retain in order to pursue the upside potential it considers appropriate and desirable. True to its tradition of quantifying risk, Statoil frames risk appetite in terms of several quantitative risk measures. The variable, return on capital employed (ROCE), is one of the performance indicators that Statoil considers useful in this regard since it sums up the net effect of a large number of risk exposures. Risk appetite in Statoil is about formulating, for a given upside, how large of a potential shortfall, or tail risk, Statoil is willing to accept in terms of a particular performance indicator; see Jankensgård (2010) for a discussion about constructing shortfall risk measures in an ERM context.

Another area where Statoil is pushing the frontiers concerns the relationship between ERM and strategy. As part of this project, the ERM team has developed estimates of how different strategic paths would contribute to different risk categories, such as reservoir risk, implementation risk, market risk, or risks related to health, safety, and environment. Depending on which strategic path is considered, the composition of the company's overall portfolio of risk would gradually shift in a particular direction (see Exhibit 4.4). This initiative is about clarifying the nature of this impact and making senior decision makers aware of the consequences of their strategic decisions.

This graph illustrates how different strategic paths would, if implemented by management and the board of directors, impact the overall composition of Statoil's portfolio of risks. Each bar represents a strategic path, and the shadings indicate the relative importance of different types of risk (country risk, market risk, implementation risk, and so on). The y-axis shows the expected risk (probability/impact)

Risk Specifications—Segments

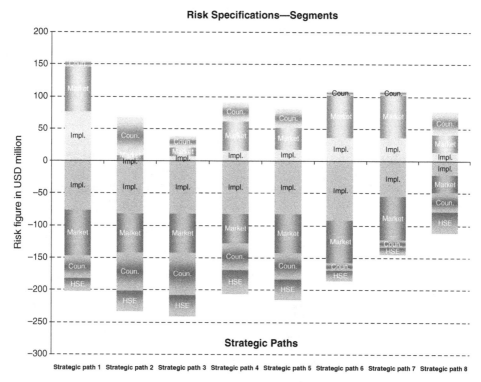

Exhibit 4.4 ERM and Strategic Risk

associated with each strategic path on both the upside and the downside. Note that certain risk categories appear on both the upside and the downside, and that these impacts need not be equally large. This asymmetry is at hand also for market risk, due to differences in marginal taxation across different income levels for oil companies. In the final decision making, the risk profile of each strategy path would have to be compared with the estimated investment outlays and the expected return on investment (not shown in the graph).

CONCLUSION

In Statoil, understanding and managing risk is today considered a core value of the company that is written into the corporate directives and widely communicated to employees. ERM is thoroughly embedded in the organization's work processes, and its Risk Committee has managed the transition from a silo mentality to promoting Statoil's best interests in areas where risk needs to be considered. The company has introduced the concept of core risks, which are the risk exposures that the company needs to manage consistently vis-à-vis its investors and which therefore require central management. In several areas where risk management used to be pursued in a silo fashion, based on incentives existing locally in the organization, risk is now optimized from the perspective of the company as a whole. ERM in

Statoil is not a control function aimed at minimizing risk, but dedicated to the goal of maximizing enterprise value given both downside risk and upside potential.

Achieving these outcomes is by no means trivial, because it challenges the organizational status quo and forces people to think and act differently with regard to risk. Statoil's success in achieving these outcomes is largely explained by the diligent work of a few key individuals, who consistently over many years have pursued a risk management program that maximizes the value of the company as a whole, as well as the strong support of the executive officers and directors. The ERM program has involved changing people's attitudes toward risk, and making Statoil's enterprise value the metric that people are ultimately expected to pursue. It has also involved thoughtfully changing the performance evaluation systems in ways that address the potential conflicts of interest that result from centralizing risk management.

QUESTIONS

1. Why might it be in a firm's best interest to centralize the management of some risks but not others?
2. Describe why the organizational status quo might lead to resistance to ERM implementation. How can this potential resistance be overcome?
3. How do you succeed in making sure that the risk committee really turns into an ERM champion, as opposed to continuing in a silo mentality?
4. What are the costs and benefits of integrating the ERM risk register in the firm's financial model to obtain "risk-adjusted" financial forecasts?
5. What are the key financial risk factors that a company could encounter?
6. What should limit Statoil's capacity to invest in profitable new oil projects, that is, take on new risks?
7. For which risk factors would it be advisable to use Monte Carlo simulation to quantify the distribution of outcome?
8. In what cases would it be relevant for an oil company to consider effects of correlation between risk factors in quantifying risk?

NOTES

1. This is not to suggest that internal audit has been excluded from the ERM process. On the contrary, internal audit has been strongly supportive of ERM and has contributed valuable resources to it.
2. This is underscored by the fact that the risks related to health, safety, and environment are the responsibility of a separate corporate function (Corporate Safety).
3. Statoil's internal communication puts it this way: "We live by taking risks."
4. The term *satisfice* was introduced by the American researcher and Nobel laureate Herbert Simon in 1956. It refers to a decision-making strategy that seeks to achieve an acceptable outcome, as opposed to the optimal outcome, which requires expending more time and effort.
5. Statoil's shares were simultaneously listed on the New York Stock Exchange.
6. The quarterly review meetings are occasions in which top management meets with business areas to discuss the unit's performance vis-à-vis previously agreed targets. This refers to the unit's overall financial performance as well as specific key performance

indicators. Risk is therefore only one of several issues on the agenda for these quarterly reviews.

REFERENCES

Alviniussen, A., and H. Jankensgård. 2009. "Enterprise Risk Budgeting: Bringing Risk Management into the Financial Planning Process." *Journal of Applied Finance* 19, 178–192.

COSO. 2004. *Enterprise Risk Management—Integrated Framework*. New York: Committee of Sponsoring Organizations of the Treadway Commission.

Jankensgård, H. 2010. "Measuring Corporate Liquidity Risk." *Journal of Applied Corporate Finance* 22, 103–109.

Jankensgård, H. 2013. "Does Centralization of FX Derivative Usage Impact Firm Value?" *European Financial Management*, forthcoming.

Jankensgård, H., K. Hoffman, and D. Rahmat. 2013. "Derivative Usage, Risk Disclosure, and Firm Value." Financial Management Association Europe Conference Paper.

ABOUT THE CONTRIBUTORS

Alf Alviniussen is former Group Treasurer and Senior Vice President of Norsk Hydro ASA, Oslo, Norway. After 42 years in the company holding leading positions within the group treasury and corporate finance, including responsibility for risk management and financial planning, he is now acting as an independent consultant.

Håkan Jankensgård holds a PhD in risk management from Lund University, Sweden. He is the former risk manager of Norsk Hydro and has more than 10 years' experience in advising companies on their risk management strategies. He is currently a researcher in corporate finance at the Department of Business Administration and Knut Wicksell Centre for Financial Studies, Lund University.

CHAPTER 5

ERM in Practice at the University of California Health System

GRACE CRICKETTE
Senior Vice President and Chief Risk and Compliance Officer, AAA Northern California, Nevada, and Utah; former Chief Risk Officer, University of California

T he University of California's Health System is comprised of numerous clinical operations, including five medical centers that support the clinical teaching programs of the university's medical and health sciences schools and handle more than three million patient visits each year. The medical centers provide a full range of health care services in their communities and are sites for the development and testing of new diagnostic and therapeutic techniques. Collectively, these centers comprise one of the largest health care systems in the world.

The University of California Office of the President's Office of Risk Services is responsible for developing and implementing enterprise risk management (ERM) systemwide, identifying and developing strategies to minimize the impact of risk, developing a center of excellence for managing risk, reducing costs, and improving safety by executing new ideas and strategic plans in a rapid manner in support of the university's mission of teaching, research, public service, and patient care.

THE ENTERPRISE RISK MANAGEMENT PROGRAM

The University of California (UC) System began an ERM initiative as a natural progression of making the decision to adopt the Committee of Sponsoring Organizations (COSO) Internal Control—Integrated Framework in 1995, and in that same year UC's vice chancellors for business and finance accepted an internal audit recommendation to adopt COSO as the Internal Control Integrated Framework for the university. In 2004, COSO's inclusion of enterprise risk management into its model led to the hiring of a chief risk officer (CRO) tasked with implanting enterprise risk management.

The chief risk officer, who had previously implemented ERM for a publicly traded company, set out to learn about the operations and culture of the university and identify what ERM activities were already in place and where there were gaps, and what would be the best approach for implementing ERM. Visits were made to all of the campuses and medical centers, and leaders from various departments and disciplines were gathered together and asked: *How do you know if you are doing well? What data do you have to let you know how you are doing?* Leadership clearly was able to articulate their objectives and the risks that could impact those objectives, but the data for measuring and monitoring were not timely and were primarily ad hoc, annual, and manual. The information gathered through these meetings was critical for understanding and developing the key performance indicators (KPIs) that would later become an important component of the ERM program. (See What Is a KPI?)

What Is a KPI?

Generally, strategic or operating plans will identify the critical success factors and key goals of an organization. Critical success factors are the areas that the organization must focus on and do well in to satisfy customer/client needs. An example may be "meeting client expectations." KPIs are derived from critical success factors and define these critical success factors into more meaningful criteria. For example, the critical success factor of "improve productivity" might have KPIs such as cost, service quality, cycle time, streamlining of processes, and reduced duplication and/or rework.

How often can KPIs be updated?

KPIs can be updated as frequently as the data they are drawn from is updated. Some examples:
Claims information, daily
Payroll information, monthly
Construction scheduling, quarterly

How is improvement measured with KPIs?

Improvement is measured by looking at ratios between time periods relative to risk. For example, in the area of workers' compensation:

Recordable rate = Number of injuries relative to the hours worked

Next, an ERM panel was formed to develop an ERM strategy. The ERM panel included management representatives from the Office of the President, the campuses, and the health system. The CRO along with the ERM panel recognized that, given the complexity of the university's operations and the general decentralization of services and information, technology would need to be leveraged to identify, manage, and monitor risks. The overall strategy was to develop a data warehouse that could manage information already being collected by various groups, existing programs, and initiatives throughout the system—an enterprise risk management information system (ERMIS). Once consolidated in a single location, the data could then be used to analyze processes, risks, and controls systemwide.

As the ERMIS was being developed, the CRO commissioned a cost of risk study to be able to measure and monitor success of the ERM program. The first Risk Summit was held with more than 100 attendees, and the charge was given to the attendees to reduce the cost of risk by 16 percent in 24 months. How? At the summit the program Be Smart about Safety (BSAS) was launched, which was the first of many initiatives focused on preventing and managing risk. The university not only met this charge, but exceeded it by meeting the target in only 18 months.

Leveraging Technology to Support ERM

UC continues to develop the ERM information system (ERMIS), a flexible and dynamic system, to give campus stakeholders at multiple levels the information they need to make business decisions in a timely and effective manner. The ERMIS essentially "democratizes" information, in that it has the ability to provide key data and reports to personnel at all levels and locations of the university. As the data integrated has become richer and its use more widespread, the value of the ERMIS has grown in creative ways.

The ERMIS started with simple risk assessment tools and expanded to include:

- Dashboard reporting on major areas of risk
- Control and accountability tracking platform
- Risk mitigation and monitoring tools
- Survey capabilities

All of these tools can be used independently or interdependently, allowing for:

- Better quantitative analysis capabilities
- Improved analytical and reporting capabilities
- Support for leading risk governance and compliance processes
- Systemwide visibility, with local flexibility
- Scalability without additional burden on UC staff

While the ERMIS dashboard system is prepopulated with some KPIs, UC continues to work with each location to develop KPIs that are helpful to supporting the location's own initiatives. ERM groups find the ERMIS to be an important tool for identifying and understanding risks. The system will also support the monitoring of internal controls and accountability, providing valuable information to the controllers and internal auditors. These capabilities lower the overall cost of risk (oftentimes associated with day-to-day operations) across the institution.

The creation of automated reports within the ERMIS increases workforce efficiency. Redundancy is reduced by the creation of automated reports made readily available to those with a need to know. Instead of having the same or similar reports being developed and maintained without the benefit of shared knowledge at different divisions, departments, schools, campuses, medical centers, and other

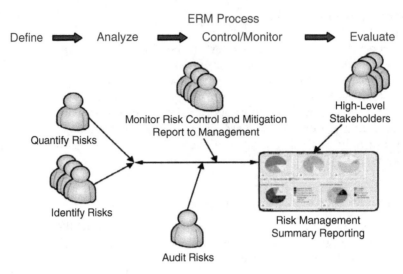

Exhibit 5.1   ERM Process

locations, the ERMIS enables sharing of analyses and information easily and efficiently across multiple different locations. (See Exhibits 5.1 and 5.2.)

Creating a Risk-Aware Culture

The foundation of the University of California's enterprise risk management program is to have people actively manage their various risks—everyone is a risk manager! One key to creating a culture where everyone is a risk manager is to give them
tools that meet their specific needs. That means developing different tools, work
groups, and initiatives, but delivering them in a cohesive and integrated manner.
Also, how can we create personal ownership for identifying, managing, and monitoring risk? A group of forward-thinking people at UC Davis came up with a solution, and the My Managed Risk portal was born!

The My Managed Risk (MMR) portal was designed as an entry point to the
services and resources provided by the Office of Risk Services. It serves as a centralized location for authorized users to access enterprise risk management–related
tools and information. The portal allows users direct access to their authorized
ERM applications, as well as the ability to view content related to the ERM Solution Set, and at the same time to stay informed of up-to-date news and articles
directly related to enterprise risk management. The streamlined design also provides an efficient way for users to search within the MMR portal in order to retrieve
contents of interest quickly. (See Exhibit 5.3.)

Health System Specialized Programs

The UC Health System participates in and benefits from all of the tools and programs that come under the umbrella of ERM, but, in keeping with delivering the
right tools to the right people, UC continues to develop programs specific to health
care.

Exhibit 5.2   ERMIS Dashboard Samples

Dashboard Name	Description
CFO Division AIM: Actionable Information for Managers	Promote positive administrative behavior at the campus level via campus-by-campus comparisons. Results are indicative of business/operational performance and are within Chancellor's realm of control.
Financial Accounting	Count of hand-postings, direct deposits, electronic W-2 and payments, CFR reports, and percentage of transaction not cleared.
Financial Services and Controls	Connexxus participation, travel spend, and savings. Purchase card expenditures, administrative efficiency, and incentives.
Procurement Services	Systemwide procurement savings, procurement spend under management, and percentage of transactions processed electronically by location.
External Finance, UC Bond Debt	Provides visibility and trending on UC bond debt by location.
Medical Quality	Extends medical quality reporting data to support risk management activities.
Travel Incidents, Calls, Claims	To correlate and report data from all travel insurance and travel agencies for UC students and staff traveling throughout the United States and world (anticipated).
UCSF PD Early Warning System Report	Provides UCSF PD leadership the ability to track and identify patterns of multiple staff complaints/investigations/incidents.
UC Travel Dashboard—Connexxus	Tracks campus adoption of the Connexxus travel system and actual savings for campuses that utilize Connexxus.
Waste Diversion	Contains results of the annual waste diversion campus survey. Allows for comparison of recycling/waste diversion between campuses.
Human Capital Dashboard	Provides human resources–related correlations by department and reason description by utilizing enrollment, FTEs, head count, hours, EPL claims, employee separation/retirement, OSHA rates, and harassment prevention training.
Safety Index Dashboard	Provides safety-related loss and exposure correlations by department and cause description by utilizing the following elements: WC claims, FTEs, hours, head count, vehicles, GL, student population, acres, property losses, and OSHA rates.
Safety Index ROI Enhancements	Illustrates the direct and indirect costs of safety risks at UC locations and enterprise-wide.
UC Ready	Provides mission (business) continuity plan completion counts for all locations at the department level.
UC Ready Department-Level Enhancements	Systemwide continuity plan completion and activity metrics at department level.
Reputational Risk (CDPH)	Provides aggregated counts and trends for medical center–related complaints and penalties as reported by California Department of Public Health.
Reputational Risk (OSHA Cube)	Allows visibility in OSHA claims against UC locations that may cause reputational risk to UC.
Office of General Counsel (OGC)	Provides visibility to legal cost by locations.
Medical Center	Provides Medical Center loss and exposure trends and correlations.
Medical Center PL Cube	Provides users the ability to create ad hoc reports utilizing selected Medical Center claims data.

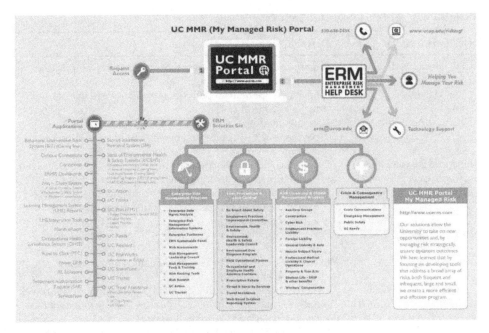

Exhibit 5.3   UC My Managed Risk Portal

Integrating Traditional Risk Management into ERM

Are traditional risk management and ERM two separate programs, concepts, and disciplines? The short answer is "No." Rather, the traditional risk management practices are critical components that make up the ERM portfolio. To get at the big enterprise picture for incidents, events, and claims arising out of the medical centers and hospitals, UC developed an approach to the evaluation of medical incidents, events, and claims. (See Exhibit 5.4.)

Trending, monitoring, and reporting of adverse clinical events and their root cause(s) are done as part of ERM:

- Each University of California Medical Center uses a web-based clinical incident reporting system that permits any staff member to report an event or near miss. The university medical centers are moving to a commercial incident reporting platform that will be consistent across all facilities and permit comparison reporting.
- Each of the UC medical centers has individuals (category managers) who are responsible for the monitoring and evaluation of certain types of events and taking action on them. The Office of Risk Services has access to this system and receives notice of significant events through the system.
- Trend reports are prepared for facility patient safety and quality committees and forwarded through the facility committee structure to the facility governing body—typically the dean of the School of Medicine.
- Adverse event incidents are monitored, and serious events that may require reporting to the state are reviewed weekly; any that are sentinel events result in a root cause analysis.

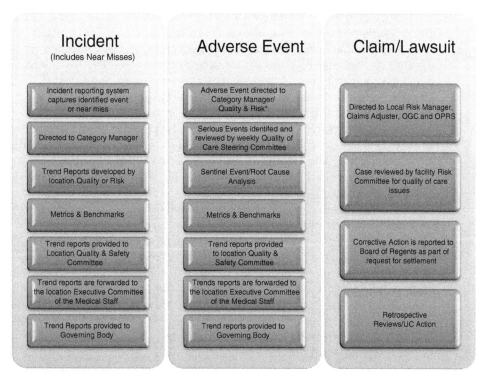

Exhibit 5.4 UC's Enterprise Risk Management Approach to the Evaluation of Incidents, Events, and Claims

*Serious events are identified and reported to location Quality of Care Steering Committee for review. This committee is multidisciplinary and includes key individuals of the Quality & Safety Committee (e.g., the chief medical officer, other physician staff members, the chief nursing officer, legal, quality, risk, and compliance).

- In addition, the medical centers measure and review data on a number of metrics from patient complaints to infection rates, patient falls, and so on.
- Hospital-level data is compared with national benchmarks, United Healthcare (UHC) data, and so on.

Individual adverse events may result in claims and lawsuits:

- Risk Services manages the Third Party Claims Administrator to ensure that the claims are promptly investigated and appropriately resolved. As part of this process, Risk Services monitors the Third Party Administrator (TPA) performance against developed performance expectations.
- Risk Services in conjunction with the Office of General Counsel (OGC) and medical center risk management staff collaborate to ensure that the cases are well managed throughout the claims and litigation process. A select panel of defense attorneys is assigned cases.
- Risk Services through Legalbill monitors law firm billing compliance with university guidelines to ensure that the university benefits from a cost-efficient and cost-effective legal defense.

- Medical Staff Risk Management Committee at each facility reviews claims and lawsuits and makes evaluations regarding the quality of care and corrective action that is needed internally; the committee monitors the action through to resolution by the responsible departments. The Risk Services director attends the committee meetings at the locations periodically.
- There are also facilities (allocation committees) that review settled claims and lawsuits and attribute responsibility to individual practitioners or to system issues. If individuals are identified as responsible, they are reported to the external state licensing boards. Risk Services and OGC are responsible to ensure that cases are appropriately reported to both the state licensing boards and the federal National Practitioner Data Bank, and work with the locations to advise them on reporting. Both the Risk Services director and an OGC representative participate with a facility medical director to review the reporting recommendations of the local facility.
- If cases result in costs to the university, inclusive of defense and indemnity, each location has to identify the risk issues involved and the corrective action taken or planned; this action is reviewed by the Risk Services professional liability (PL) program director and the CRO; for cases of certain value, the actions are also reviewed by the senior vice president for health sciences and service.
- Additionally, the General Counsel and the Board of Regents review the corrective action that is reported.
- In addition, Risk Services has developed and implemented a monitoring system to ensure that corrective actions on cases costing the university more than $50,000 are tracked through resolution through the UC Action process. UC Action is a software tool that permits the capture of events, the causes of loss, and the corrective action that was implemented across the UC System. It permits the assignment of controls to ensure that loss prevention actions are implemented and monitored to avoid recurrence of identified issues. Developed in conjunction with UC Davis, this tool supports the Risk Services and campus loss prevention efforts. All Risk Services program managers periodically review and assess the actions being taken for appropriateness.

The role and activities of UC's Risk Services in adverse event clinical audit (quality assurance) include the following:

- The Risk Services director for professional liability manages the systemwide incident report (IR) system and receives reports of certain types of events via e-mail as well as being able to evaluate trend reports.
- The Risk Services director periodically provides reports of individual events and trends to the facility chief medical directors at their systemwide meetings. In addition, each medical director typically brings events to discuss to these meetings so that locations can learn from each other.
- In addition to the IR system, the Risk Services director is often called by the facility risk managers and alerted to serious events. The Risk Services director also serves as a resource for questions from the facilities.
- The Risk Services PL director implemented a program to ensure that all of the university's claims and lawsuits are coded for loss prevention and

trended. This was accomplished through using the Controlled Risk Insurance Company (CRICO[1]) Comprehensive Risk Intelligence Tool (CRIT). This program permits the university to identify the areas of greatest frequency and cost and the underlying contributing factors in a reliable manner. The university facilities have access to the system and are able to compare their trends against the other UC system and non-UC entities.

- The Risk Services director hosts monthly conference calls with medical center risk management staff to discuss matters of interest and loss prevention opportunities.
- Risk Services funds loss prevention activities for the medical centers and student health facilities targeted at reducing university liability. Examples include the prescription rebate program, which provided grant funds for loss prevention activities; ELM Exchange,[2] which provides online risk education; EMMI Solutions information consent program, which helps ensure patient understanding of their clinical options to improve satisfaction; the Vanderbilt Patient Advocacy Reporting System (PARS) to identify and assist physicians who are outliers in terms of patient complaints; disclosure education; and operating room technology aimed at reducing retained foreign bodies.
- In addition, the senior vice president for health sciences and services collects and reviews data from multiple sources regarding hospital performance in clinical areas other than adverse clinical events.
- UC Action summary reports regarding corrective action are shared with the Regents on high-dollar-value litigated cases in the form of reports from the Office of General Counsel.

PREMIUM REBATE PROGRAM

In addition to the tools developed to assess risk and report on KPIs, the Office of the President's Office of Risk Services has developed programs to reduce the frequency and severity of loss. For the Medical and Hospital Liability Program, Risk Services developed a Premium Rebate Program in 2006–2012 that was known as the Professional Liability Prescription Program (PLPP), designed to encourage risk reduction initiatives aimed at reducing the cost of risk for the hospitals and schools of medicine. The program encouraged clinical loss prevention and patient safety and rewarded hospitals and medical groups for developing and implementing specific initiatives. PLPP is a good example of propagating the concept that *everyone is a risk manager*. It put loss control in the hands of individuals responsible for the outcomes. It gave them the financial resources and incentives to make a difference. There were several parts to the PLPP (see Exhibit 5.5).

The University of California (UC) Professional Medical and Hospital Liability Program (PL) is the second largest component of UC's cost of risk. In 2012, the Chief Risk Officer believed there was a need for more ERM focus on the university's five medical centers and began exploring ways to make this happen.

University of California Center for Health Quality and Innovation (CHQI) had established a system to encourage initiatives designed to create a culture of improvement with the support of the CHQI board, comprised of the five academic medical center CEOs, the six deans of the Schools of Medicine, and chaired by

Exhibit 5.5 Professional Liability Prescription Program (PLPP)

Grant Funds for Locally Developed Loss Prevention Initiative—Maximum Rebate 2 Percent of Premium

Requests for the 2 percent grant funds may be made at any time during the fiscal year; however, locations are encouraged to submit early.

Medical Center Risk Management offices are expected to coordinate the applications. Each project submitted for the grant funds must have both School of Medicine and a Medical Center approval if applicable. Multiple requests per site are permitted until the 2 percent is exhausted. Once the funding application is approved by Risk Services, the funds will be transferred to the campus account. The campus must transfer to the appropriate local code. The funds must be used for the approved project; failure to apply the funds to the project will result in recoupment of the funds by Risk Services. Projects will be monitored by Risk Services.

Medical Center and School Departments Allocation of Premium—Maximum Rebate 4 Percent of Premium

Allocation of premium based on loss experience and exposure is a critical underpinning of a successful loss prevention program. To qualify for this rebate, each School of Medicine and Medical Center must implement allocation to departments using the Bickmore approved methodology. Half of the premium will go to School of Medicine for its allocation to departments and half will go to Medical Centers for allocation of premium among its departments.

Criteria:

Ensuring the location organization structure for premium allocation is current and appropriate.

Reviewing and categorizing all historical and current malpractice cases to location identified Schools and Medical Centers and then to departments and divisions within each, entering the data into the Sedgwick CMS claims system on a continuous basis.

Selecting and applying an allocation model from Bickmore recommendations to the fiscal year 2011–2012 budget.

A written report, signed by the Dean and CEO of the Medical Center attesting to the methodology employed and the amounts paid by the various departments, is required.

Adoption and Implementation of EMMI—Maximum Rebate 2 Percent of Premium

Qualification for this rebate will require adoption and substantial implementation of EMMI by the individual locations during fiscal year 2011–2012. The amount of the rebate will be dependent on the degree of adoption of use as measured by EMMI data.

Use of Technology to Prevent Retained Surgical Sponges—Maximum Rebate 2 Percent of Premium

Human error in the counting process is a significant cause of retained sponges. Technical solutions such as Surgicount provide a reliable method to assure a valid sponge count. Reducing retained sponges through reliable technology contributes to improved patient safety, enhances hospital reputation, and avoids regulatory and legal expenses.

the University's Senior Vice President of Health Sciences & Services, with a small coordinating staff based at the UC Office of the President, Oakland.

ERM AND THE CENTER FOR HEALTH QUALITY AND INNOVATION

In January 2013, the chief risk officer for the University of California and the executive director for the UC Center for Health Quality and Innovation (CHQI) announced a new joint venture. The new joint venture—the Center for Health Quality and Innovation Quality Enterprise Risk Management (CHQIQERM)—will award up to $8 million in grants for projects designed to reduce the risk of clinical harm to UC surgery patients in three priority areas:

1. Development of enterprise risk management (ERM) within the Schools of Medicine and medical centers. This includes projects that are aimed at clinical improvements involving multiple departments and divisions.
2. Projects aimed at reducing medical malpractice claims. These projects should take into consideration issues creating the highest frequency and severity of malpractice claims within the university facilities. Claims data identifying these areas of exposure will be provided. Projects will be evaluated based on transferability and sustainability. Ability to demonstrate a return on investment will also be considered.
3. Projects aimed at improving patient safety, quality, and efficiency within the University of California medical centers.

The joint venture seeks to fund projects by UC Health faculty and staff that use an evidence-based, systems approach to minimize the risk of clinical harm to UC patients. UC's actuary will continue to evaluate the return on investment (ROI) of the projects and include evaluation of these loss prevention efforts in its actuarial study as it has in the past.

Funding is available to UC faculty and staff intending to engage in performance improvement activities at UC-owned and UC-operated medical centers. Individual projects are capped at $250,000 per academic medical center site. A five-campus project may be awarded up to $1.25 million.

"We're thrilled to partner with Risk Services," said Terry Leach, executive director of the UC Center for Health Quality and Innovation. "This collaboration will help leverage the talent of UC Health's faculty and staff to improve patient safety at UC medical centers."[3]

After an initial campus review, top-scored selections will receive a second round of review by the CHQIQERM Risk Advisory Committee in conjunction with the CHQI Operations Committee, with final selection by the CHQI board. Five-campus multisite proposals will automatically advance to receive a review by CHQIQERM.

The CHQIQERM will provide selected Project performance improvements (PIs), within three months of approval, a schedule to present their projects to various multicampus groups responsible for quality improvement and/or reduction of patient harm throughout UC, including the CHQI Operations Committee, the chief medical officer (CMO) and chief nursing officer (CNO) group, the UC quality officers, infection control officers, pharmacy chairs, CEOs, and so on. Presentations are designed to provide individuals responsible for integration of performance improvement projects throughout UC the opportunity to learn more about the funded projects, and to provide consultation for design modification, as appropriate, to increase support and acceptance of the funded projects.

By January 1, 2014, if project funds remain or if Risk Services provides additional resources, CHQIQERM will disseminate a second round of requests for proposals (RFPs), and will provide review and management pursuant to the previous year's round of funding, with projects to be completed by June 30, 2015, unless a project continuation agreement has been negotiated and agreed upon by all parties, including the CHQI board.

PROTECTED HEALTH INFORMATION VALUE ESTIMATOR (PHIve)

The chief risk officer was invited to serve on an American National Standards Institute (ANSI) work group. The goal of the work group was to develop and publish a guide to bring attention to the risks associated with personal health information (PHI). When hospitals and medical centers perform risk assessments, they often fail to consider the magnitude of the disruption and reputational damage from a loss of personal health information.

Following participation in the work group, UC asked Bickmore (www.bickmore.net) to develop an electronic software tool for the Protected Health Information Value Estimator (PHIve). The methodology used in PHIve is described in greater detail with examples in the American National Standards Institute (ANSI) publication, "The Financial Impact of Breached Protected Health Information." ANSI's publication is available at the ANSI website.[4]

The PHIve applies a practical methodology for protected personal health information to calculate the potential (or actual) cost of a data breach to their organization. The purpose of this exciting new tool is to help PHI protectors understand the financial impact of a PHI breach so they can evaluate and recommend the appropriate investments necessary to mitigate the risk of a data breach. This helps reduce potential financial exposure while strengthening the organization's reputation as a protector of the PHI entrusted to its care.

The tool will not make decisions for you, but it will help you organize your thinking as you consider the enterprise risk management implications of a breach of protected health information.

The five steps in PHIve are:

1. Assess risks.

    Assess the risks, vulnerabilities, and applicable safeguards for each PHI home. A PHI home is any organizational function or space (administrative, physical, or technical) and/or any application, network, database, or system (electronic) that creates, maintains, stores, transmits, or disposes of ePHI or PHI.

2. Security readiness score.

    Determine a security readiness score for each PHI home by determining the likelihood of a data breach based on the security readiness score scale.

3. Determine relevance.

    For each PHI home that has an unacceptable security readiness score, examine the relevance (i.e., likelihood or applicability) of a particular cost category, and apply a relevance factor from a provided hierarchy.

4. Determine potential repercussions.

    Relevance and consequences combined create the potential repercussions of a breach. Consequences are calculated using multiple aspects of a potential breach based on a variety of considerations for your organization. Types of repercussions include reputational (loss of patients, current customers, new customers, strategic partners, or staff), financial (including costs for remediation, communication, changes to insurance, changing associates, and business distraction), legal and regulatory, operational, and clinical.

5. Total the impacts: Add up all adjusted costs to determine the total adjusted cost of a data breach to the organization.

Relevance and consequences combined create the potential repercussions of a breach. Consequences are calculated using multiple aspects of a potential breach based on a variety of considerations for your organization.

Reputational Repercussions

Reputational repercussions of a breach may include:

- Loss of patients
- Loss of current customers
- Loss of new customers
- Loss of strategic partners
- Loss of staff (separate from staff lost due to potential disciplinary action related to a breach)

The impact of a breach may have greater reputational repercussions if it is shared through social media or other means that raise further awareness of the breach.

The demographics of those affected by a breach also change its reputational impact. Income and age are considerations for health privacy sensitivity, among other factors.

Financial Repercussions

Financial repercussions are grouped into five segments, each of which may contain multiple types of financial costs.

1. Cost of remediation may include:
   - Investigation or forensic costs
   - Corrective action plan costs
   - Workforce sanction costs
   - Identity theft monitoring costs
2. Costs of communication may include:
   - Notifying affected individuals
   - Notifying media outlets and notifying governmental agencies
   - Public relations costs
   - Investor relations
3. Costs of changes to insurance may include:
   - Broker costs
   - Presenting and negotiating with agencies
   - Increased cost of coverage
4. Costs of changing associates may include:
   - Due diligence for new vendors
   - Transitions to new vendors
   - Increased costs of new vendors
5. Costs of business distraction may include:
   - Lost productivity
   - Opportunity costs
   - Diversion of resources

Legal and Regulatory Repercussions

Legal and regulatory repercussions of a breach can be grouped into four areas:

1. Costs associated with actions by the U.S. Department of Health and Human Services' Office for Civil Rights (OCR), including:
   - Fines and penalties
   - Costs of additional corrective action plans
2. State fines and penalties
3. Lawsuit costs, including:
   - Legal costs
   - Settlement costs
   - Additional payments to affected individuals
   - Insurance deductibles
4. Costs associated with potential loss of accreditation or reinstatement of accreditation

Operational Repercussions

- Incremental cost of new hires
- Costs of recruiting and training new hires
- Costs associated with reorganization following a breach

Clinical Repercussions

- Fraudulent claims processed
- Delayed or inaccurate diagnoses
- Bad data in search results

Total the Impacts

Add up all adjusted costs to determine the total adjusted cost of a data breach to the organization.

The pilot PHIve tool was previewed by UC's medical risk managers for the first time at the University of California's 2013 Risk Summit. Bickmore is demonstrating the tool and seeking comments from the UC medical risk managers before the tool is released. The tool was demonstrated and comments were sought from the UC medical risk managers before the tool was released.

ERM and Strategy

Risk is an inherent and essential part of any organization. When properly managed, risk drives growth and opportunity. If enterprise risk management (ERM) is the process of planning, organizing, leading, and controlling the activities of an organization in order to minimize the effects of risk on an organization's capital, earnings, and operations, then it only makes sense that ERM is seen as a strategic tool for management.

The past several years have been a financially challenging time for the university. Even in the face of those challenges, however, the university has made significant strides in reducing its risk exposure, thereby allowing the campuses to focus their limited dollars on the university's mission of teaching, research, and service. ERM is seen in the university as a continuous improvement process and has been integrated into its Working Smarter initiative.[5]

The Office of Risk Services, as part of the CFO division, has integrated the Division Strategic Goals[6] into our operations:

- Reexamine the day-to-day
- Showcase our value-add
- Engage with the customer
- Develop our staff
- Be action-oriented

The Office of Risk Services continues to reexamine the day-to-day operations, looking for innovative ways to reduce risk while improving operational efficiency. It continues to showcase the savings that are generated by implementing ERM, and continually engages its customers to learn how it can better meet their needs. It not only focuses on developing its staff, but encourages the professional development of those at the campuses and medical centers by providing the Risk Summit and monthly webinars. Finally, the tools and information provided by Risk Services allow campus and medical center leadership to be action-oriented and to be able to implement quickly programs that will result in immediate impacts. The guiding principle in all of the work that Risk Services does is to support the university mission of teaching, research, and public service, as well as patient care.

QUESTIONS

1. Your Medical Group wants to expand by starting a new venture, owning and operating a pharmacy. In order to increase the success, you have been asked to perform an enterprise risk assessment that includes reputational risk. Give three examples of how starting a new venture might have risk events that could lead to repercussions that would negatively impact the organizations reputation and three examples where it might be enhanced, creating opportunity.
2. Explain how improvement is measured with KPIs and give one example related to Human Capital and how this KPI might help you improve your organization.
3. In the UC example, the ERM Program gives weight to both data-driven activities and to culture-changing activities. Give two examples of each and then your own opinion regarding which activities you believe to be most effective in implementing an ERM program.
4. What do you think is the difference between *traditional risk management* and *enterprise risk management*?
5. From the UC example, identify what aspects of their program were "carrots" and which ones were "sticks." From your own experience describe which one you think works best in creating lasting change.

NOTES

1. CRICO is the patient safety and medical liability company that serves the Harvard University medical community. It is a leader in evidence-based risk management.
2. Education in Legal Medicine.
3. UC Health, January 8, 2013.
4. http://webstore.ansi.org/phi.
5. http://workingsmarter.universityofcalifornia.edu/.
6. www.ucop.edu/finance-office/mission-goals/strategic-goals.html.

ABOUT THE CONTRIBUTOR

Grace Crickette joined AAA Northern California, Nevada, and Utah (NCNU) in May 2013 as the Senior Vice President and Chief Risk and Compliance Officer. She was the former Chief Risk Officer at the University of California. In her current position, she is charged with implementing enterprise risk management (ERM) with her legal, compliance, risk management, and internal audit team. The Risk Services team provides internal audit and consultation, legal consultation, quality assurance and compliance, risk financing and captive solutions, crisis and consequence management, and loss prevention and loss control services. The Risk Services team's ERM vision is to support AAA's Membership Promise: "We will keep you safe and secure—We will offer you the right product at the right time—We will provide you helpful and knowledgeable service—We will reward your loyalty—One Member, One AAA."

Prior to coming to AAA NCNU, Grace served as the University of California's Chief Risk Officer. Major initiatives for the Risk Services department included reducing the cost of risk, implementing system and local safety programs, improving claims management systems, developing risk financing strategies, and implementing enterprise risk management (ERM), and emergency management and business continuity planning throughout the university.

Grace joined the University of California in December 2004 after 13 years as a vice president and officer in audit, insurance, safety, and human resources capacities for the equipment and construction industry. She graduated with distinction from the University of Redlands with a bachelor's degree in business administration, and holds a variety of professional designations in the areas of claims, safety, audit, and human resources, including Associate in Risk Management and Senior Professional in Human Resources.

In 2008, Grace received the Risk Innovator Award for innovation and excellence in risk management in higher education. She received the Information Security Executive (ISE) of the Year West Award 2011 and National Award 2011 for Higher Education/Non Profit Sector for innovative problem solving related to a collaborative partnership with the University of California's chief information officer and other information technology (IT) professionals, insurance brokers, and underwriters for securing previously unavailable and much-needed cyber coverage and at the same time developing a program that will drive improvement and best practices into the future. She also received the ISE award of the decade for Higher Education/Non Profit Sector for her overall commitment to IT security. She was chosen in 2011 as one of *Business Insurance*'s Women to Watch, an annual feature spotlighting 25 women who are doing outstanding work in commercial insurance, reinsurance, risk management, employee benefits, and related fields, such as law and consulting. She was also selected by *Business Insurance* magazine for its 2011 Risk Management Honor Roll. Also in 2011, *Treasury & Risk* magazine named her one of the "100 Most Influential People in Finance." She has consulted with numerous public and private entities on the implementation of ERM, including Harvard University and SingHealth, Singapore's largest health care group.

CHAPTER 6

Strategic Risk Management at the LEGO Group

Integrating Strategy and Risk Management

MARK L. FRIGO
Director, Strategic Risk Management Lab, and Ledger & Quill Distinguished Professor of Strategy and Leadership, DePaul University

HANS LÆSSØE
Senior Director of Strategic Risk Management, LEGO Group

How can organizations manage strategic risks in a volatile and fast-paced business environment? Many have started focusing their enterprise risk management (ERM) programs on the critical strategic risks that can make or break a company. This effort is being driven by requests from boards and other stakeholders and by the realization that a systematic approach is needed and that it's highly valuable to include strategic risk management in ERM and to integrate risk management within the fabric of an organization.

In this case[1] we describe strategic risk management at the LEGO Group, which is based on an initiative started in late 2006 and led by Hans Læssøe, senior director of strategic risk management at LEGO System A/S. It's also part of the continuing work of the Strategic Risk Management Lab at DePaul University, which is identifying and developing leading practices in integrating risk management with strategy development and strategy execution. This descriptive case provides a great example of integrating risk management into the strategy development and strategy execution.

ABOUT THE LEGO GROUP

Headquartered in Billund, Denmark, the family owned LEGO Group has 12,500 employees worldwide and is the second-largest toy manufacturer in the world in terms of sales. Its portfolio, which focuses on LEGO bricks, includes 25 product lines sold in more than 130 countries. The name of the company is an abbreviation of the two Danish words *leg godt* that mean "play well." The LEGO Group began in 1932 in Denmark, when Ole Kirk Kristiansen founded a small factory for making wooden toys. Fifteen years later, he discovered that plastic was the ideal material for toy production and bought the first injection molding machine in Denmark.

In 1949, the brick adventure started. Over the years, the LEGO Group perfected the brick, which is still the basis of the entire game and building system. Though there have been small adjustments in shape, color, and design from time to time, today's LEGO bricks still fit bricks from 1958. The 2,400 different LEGO brick shapes are produced in plants in Denmark, the Czech Republic, Hungary, and Mexico with the greatest of precision and subjected to constant controls. There are more than 900 million different ways of combining six eight-stud bricks of the same color.

THE LEGO GROUP STRATEGY

To understand strategic risk management at the LEGO Group, you need to understand the company's strategy. This is consistent with the first step in developing strategic risk management in an organization: to understand the business strategy and the related risks as described in the strategic risk assessment process.[2]

The LEGO Group's mission is "Inspire and develop the builders of tomorrow." Its vision is "Inventing the future of play." To help accomplish them, the company uses a growth strategy and an innovation strategy.

- *Growth strategy.* The LEGO Group has chosen a strategy that's based on a number of growth drivers. One is to increase its market share in the United States. Many Americans may think they buy a lot of LEGO products, but they buy only about a third of what Germans buy, for example. Thus there are potential growth opportunities in the U.S. market.

  The LEGO Group also wants to increase market share in Eastern Europe, where the toy market is growing very rapidly. In addition, it wants to invest in emerging markets, but cautiously. The toy industry isn't the first one to move into new, emerging markets, so the LEGO Group will invest at appropriate levels and be ready for when those markets do move. It will also expand direct-to-consumer activities (sales through LEGO-owned retail stores), online sales, and online activities (such as online games for children).

- *Innovation strategy.* On the product side, the LEGO Group focuses on creating innovative new products from concepts developed under the title "Obviously LEGO, never seen before." The company plans to come up with such concepts every two to three years. One of the latest examples is LEGO Games System, which consists of family board games (a new way of playing with LEGO bricks) with a LEGO attitude of changeability (obviously LEGO). The company also intends to expand LEGO Education, its division that works with schools and kindergartens. And it will develop its digital business as the difference between the physical world and the digital world becomes more and more blurred and less and less relevant for children.

Now let's look at the development of LEGO strategic risk management.

Exhibit 6.1 Four Elements of Risk Management at the LEGO Group

LEGO STRATEGIC RISK MANAGEMENT

The LEGO Group developed risk management in four steps (numbered in the order in which the steps were initiated) as shown in Exhibit 6.1:

- *Step 1. Enterprise risk management* was traditional ERM in which financial, operational, hazard, and other risks were later supplemented by explicit handling of strategic risks.
- *Step 2. Monte Carlo simulations* were added in 2008 to understand the financial performance volatility (which proved to be significant) and the drivers behind it to integrate risk management into the budgeting and reporting processes. During the past two years the use of Monte Carlo simulations was refined, as described later in this chapter.

Those two steps were seen mostly as damage control. To get ahead of the decision process and have risk awareness impact future decisions as well, LEGO risk management added:

- *Step 3. Active risk and opportunity planning (AROP)*, where business projects go through a systematic risk and opportunity process as part of preparing the business case before final decisions about the projects are made.
- *Step 4. Preparing for uncertainty*, where management tries to ensure that long-term strategies are relevant for and resilient to future changes that may very well differ from those planned for. Scenarios help them envision a set of different yet plausible futures to test the strategy for resilience and relevance.

These last two steps were designed to move upstream—or get involved earlier in strategy development and the strategic planning and implementation process.

Strategic Risk Management Lab Commentary

This four-step approach is a good illustration of how organizations can develop their risk management capabilities and processes in incremental steps. It represents an example of how to evolve beyond traditional ERM and integrate risk management into the strategic decision making of an organization. This approach positions risk management as a value-creating element of the strategic decision-making process and the strategy-execution process.

In our research on high-performing companies, we've found that the LEGO Group, like those companies, achieves sustainable high performance and creates stakeholder value by consistently executing the strategic activities in the Return-Driven Strategy framework (for example, the focus on innovating its offerings toward changing customer needs) while co-creating value through its engagement platforms—that is, the online community, including its My LEGO Network, which engages more than 400 million people and helps its product development process; see Venkat Ramaswamy and Francis Gouillart, *The Power of Co-Creation* (Free Press 2010). Its strategic risk management processes incorporate distinct elements of co-creation by engaging its employees (internal stakeholders) throughout the strategic decision-making, planning, and execution processes, as well as engaging external stakeholders (suppliers, partners, customers). The LEGO Group's approach is a good example of how an organization can engage stakeholders in co-creating strategic risk/return management (see Mark L. Frigo and Venkat Ramaswamy, "Co-Creating Strategic Risk-Return Management," *Strategic Finance*, May 2009).[3]

ENTERPRISE RISK MANAGEMENT (STEP 1)

The evolution of ERM toward strategic risk management is represented in Exhibit 6.2. Strategic risk was missing from the ERM portfolio until 2006.

To fix this, based on his then 25 years of LEGO experience and a request from the CFO, Hans Læssøe started looking at strategic risk management. "I was a corporate strategic controller who had never heard the term until then," he says. The company had embedded risk management in its processes. *Operational risk*—minor disruptions—was handled by planning and production. *Employee health and safety* was OHSAS 18001 certified. *Hazards* were managed through explicit insurance programs in close collaboration with the company's partners (insurance companies and brokers). *Information technology (IT) security risk* was a defined functional area. *Financial risk* covered currencies and energy hedging as well as credit risks. And *legal* was actively pursuing trademark violations as well as document and contract management. But *strategic risks* weren't handled explicitly or systematically, so the CFO charged Hans with ensuring they would be from then on. This became a full-time position in 2007, and Hans added one employee in 2009 and another in 2011.

Exhibit 6.2 The LEGO ERM Umbrella: Adding Strategic Risk

Strategic Risk Management Lab Commentary

The 2006 situation is common. Even though strategic risks need to be integrated with risk management, many organizations don't explicitly assess and manage strategic risks within strategic decision-making processes and strategy execution. A recent study by the Corporate Executive Board found that strategic risks have the greatest negative impact on enterprise value: "strategic risk caused 68 percent of severe market capitalization declines."[4] But the LEGO Group's approach shows how strategic risk management can be a key to increasing the value of ERM within an organization. It also shows how executive leadership from the CFO played an important role in the evolution of ERM as a valuable management process. Finally, Hans came from the business side and had the attributes necessary to lead the initiative: broad knowledge of the business and its core strategies, strong relationships with directors and executive management, strong communication and facilitation skills, knowledge of the organization's risks, and broad acceptance and credibility across the organization. (For more, see Mark L. Frigo and Richard J. Anderson, *Embracing ERM: Practical Approaches for Getting Started*, at www.coso.org/guidance.htm, p. 4.)

Also, the risk owner concept at LEGO provides a good example of the importance of understanding who owns the risks as well as defining the role of risk management in the organization. The idea of "risk owners" was important to ensure action and accountability. Hans's charge was to develop strategic risk management and make sure the LEGO Group had processes and capabilities in place to do this. But as senior director of strategic risk management, Hans doesn't own the risk. He can't own the risk, because this essentially would mean he would own the strategy, and each line of business owns the pertinent strategic risks. Hans trains, leads, and drives line management to apply a systematic process to deal with risk. The mission of Hans's strategic risk management team is to "drive conscious choices." This is just like budgeting functions: They don't earn the money or spend the money, but they support management to deliver on the budget or compare performance against the budget.

MONTE CARLO SIMULATION (STEP 2)

In 2008, Hans introduced Monte Carlo simulation into the process. A mathematician by education (MSc in engineering), he started defining how Monte Carlo simulation could be used in risk management. Now it's being used for three areas:

1. *Budget simulation.* The business controllers were asked for their input about volatility, which is combined with analyses based on past performance of budget accuracy. Managers said this helped them understand the financial volatility, so it was part of the financial and budget reporting in 2012. In fact, the first analyses directed top management's attention to a sales volatility that was known but that proved to be much more significant than everyone intuitively believed. During the past two years, this approach has been refined as described by Hans: "We actually stopped this. It was found that

the volatility of the business is so significant that we have stopped budgeting altogether, as the process took a lot of effort—too little value as conditions changed. Today (2014) we use an estimate process where a small team of lead controllers defines a preliminary estimate for board of directors discussions. In March (each year) we do a detailed estimate on which we base KPIs, targets, bonus criteria, et cetera. Monthly, we then update the estimate, and hence our financial planning process is more dynamic … and we do not need the budget simulation anymore."

2. *Credit risk portfolio.* The LEGO Group uses a similar approach to look at its credit risk portfolio so it can have a more professional conversation with a credit risk insurance partner.

3. *Consolidation of risk exposure.* You could multiply the probability and impact of each risk and add the whole thing up. Risk management isn't about averages (if it were, no one would take out an insurance policy on anything). With a Monte Carlo simulation, the LEGO Group can calculate the 3 percent worst-case loss compared to budget and use that to define risk appetite and risk report exposure vis-à-vis this risk appetite, as shown in Exhibit 6.3.

Risk Tolerance

As a privately held company, the LEGO Group can't look at stock values, so it looks at the amount of earnings the company is likely to lose compared to budget if the worst-case combined scenarios happen. Not all risks will materialize in any one year, because some of them are mutually exclusive; but a huge number may happen in any one year, as we have seen during the global financial crisis. Hans

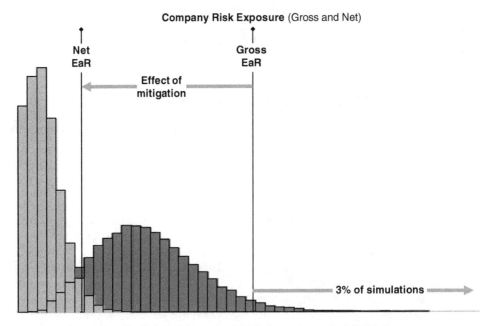

Exhibit 6.3   Monte Carlo Simulations and Risk Appetite at the LEGO Group

computes a net earnings at risk (EaR), and corporate management and later the board of directors use that net earnings at risk to define their risk tolerance. They have said that the 3 percent worst-case loss may not exceed a certain percentage of the planned earnings (the percentage is not 100). That guides management toward understanding and sizing the risk exposure. This process has helped the LEGO Group take more risks and be more aggressive than it otherwise would have dared to be, and to grow faster than it otherwise could have done.

Strategic Risk Management Lab Commentary

Risk tolerance is a difficult area for organizations to address. The approach used at the LEGO Group provides a good example of deriving risk tolerance (the term LEGO uses rather than risk appetite) in an actionable and systematic way. It also shows an approach that fosters intelligent risk taking and that avoids being too risk averse while maintaining discipline on the amount of risk undertaken. Hans has actually had cases where he recommended taking on more risks to meet elusive targets. He uses an analogy to communicate the idea of taking risks and not being too risk averse: "I used the (very normal) traffic picture … 'Guys, you are getting late for the party, yet you are still cruising at 40 mph on the highway. Why not speed up to the 70 mph you are allowed to drive—if that will more likely take you to the party in time?'"

What we've discussed so far is more or less damage control because it's about managing risks already taken by approving strategies and initiating business projects. Hans decided he wanted to move beyond damage control and be more proactive so he could create real value as a risk manager. He came up with a process he calls active risk and opportunity planning (AROP) for business projects.

AROP: ACTIVE RISK ASSESSMENT OF BUSINESS PROJECTS (STEP 3)

When the LEGO organization implements business projects of a defined minimum size or level of complexity, it's mandatory that the business case includes an explicit definition and method of handling both risks and opportunities. Hans says that the LEGO Group has created a supporting tool (a spreadsheet) with which to do this, and it differs from the former approach to project risk management in several areas. Hans has the following to say on each:

- *Identification*, "where we call upon more stakeholders, look at opportunities as well as risks, and look at risks both *to* the project and *from* the project (i.e., potential project impact on the entire business system)."
- *Assessment*, "where we define explicit scales and agree what 'high' means to avoid different people agreeing on an impact being high without having a shared understanding of the exposure."
- *Handling*, "where we systematically assign risk owners to ensure action and accountability and include the use of early warning indicators, where these are relevant."

- *Reassessment*, "where we explicitly define the net risk exposure to ensure that we have an exposure we know we can accept, the reason being that we have seen people ignore this step, and hence do too much or too little to a particular risk; here, we ask them to deliberately address whether or not they can and will accept the residual risk—and know what it is they accept. From time to time we see the individual risks being accepted, but then, when we do the Monte Carlo simulation on the project (yes, we use it here as well), we see that the likelihood of meeting the target is still too low—and more risk mitigation or opportunity pursuit is called for and included in the project."
- *Follow-up*, "where we keep the risk portfolio of the project updated for gate and milestone sessions."
- *Reporting*, "which is done automatically and fully standardized based on the data."

Common Language and Common Framework

The most important point is that the people who address and work with risks get a systematic approach so they can use the same approach from Project A for Project B. The one element that project managers really like is having the data in a database. They don't receive just a spreadsheet model. Data are entered into the spreadsheet as a database, and all the required reporting on risk management is collected from that data, so project managers don't have to develop a report—they can just cut and paste from one of the three reporting sheets that are embedded in the tool. All the reports are standardized. That's good for the project managers, but it's also good for the people on the steering committees because they now receive a standardized report on risks. They don't have a change between layouts of probability/impact risk maps or somebody comes up with severity or whatever from project to project. Everyone has the same kind of formula, the same way of doing it.

Strategic Risk Management Lab Commentary

The AROP process is a great example of integrating risk assessment in terms of upside and downside risks in the strategic decision-making process. This balanced approach to strategic risk management allows organizations to create more stakeholder value while intelligently managing risk.

PREPARING FOR UNCERTAINTY: DEFINING AND TESTING STRATEGIES (STEP 4)

To get further ahead in the decision process, the LEGO Group has added a systematic approach to defining and testing strategies. As Hans notes, "We are going one step further upstream in the decision process with what we call 'Prepare for Uncertainty.' This is a strategy process, and we're looking at the trends of the world. The industry is moving; the world is moving quite rapidly. I just saw a presentation that indicated that the changes the world will see between 2010 and 2020 will be somewhere between 10 and 80 times the changes the world saw in the twentieth century, compressed into a decade."

He offers the following story to illustrate the forces of change the company is facing: "My seven-year-old granddaughter came to me and asked, 'Granddad, why do you have a wire on your phone?' She didn't understand that. She'd never seen a wire on a phone before. We need to address that level of change and do it proactively."

Four Strategic Scenarios

A group of insightful staff people (Hans and a few from the Consumer Insight function) defined a set of four strategic scenarios based on the well-documented megatrends defined by the World Economic Forum in 2008 for the Davos meetings. Hans commented:

"We presented and discussed these with senior management in 2009, *prior* to their definition of 2015 strategies, to support that they would look at the potential world of 2015 when defining strategies and not just extrapolate present-day conditions.

"Having done that, we then prepared to revisit each key strategy vis-à-vis all four scenarios to identify issues (i.e., risks and opportunities) for that particular strategy if the world looks like this particular scenario.

"This list of issues is then addressed via a PAPA model whereby a strategic response is defined and embedded in the strategy.

"This way, we believe that we have reasonably ensured our strategies will be relevant if/when the world changes in other ways than we originally planned for."

During the past two years, LEGO refined the process and used it actively, the reason being that the original scenarios did in fact not lead to much explicit action. Today a scenario session is a five-hour workshop where participants focus on one particular strategy (e.g., market entry in China). The workshop is with the management team that owns the strategy and its implementation.

- The first hour they discuss and agree on two key drivers of uncertainty to their strategy (the axes of the 2 × 2 scenarios). Hans's team comes with a battery of potential drivers—and they (after some discussion) end up with two—leading to four quadrants of a 2 × 2 matrix.
- The next two hours the team describes the four quadrants one at a time. First, they individually use Post-it notes to write down descriptive elements or key success factors for the scenario (the Post-it session is to avoid groupthink). Then they share their descriptions and discuss their way into a reasonably consistent image of that scenario, before they move on to the next.
- The fourth hour is used to define strategic issues—again Post-it notes and sharing. Here they are diligently coached to be aware that any issue may be an opportunity (if they choose to pursue this in time). If they do not pursue this, it may become a risk, and if they still don't do anything and the risk materializes, it becomes a problem. The sharing process includes a prioritization discussion in LEGO's PAPA model (see later in this chapter).
- The last hour focuses first and foremost on actions to be taken. The team discusses and agrees on explicitly "who is doing what by when" to ensure action on the issues that the team members have themselves decided are important, likely, and fast moving.

The role of Hans's team is to coach the process, including asking provocative questions and ensuring that team members get out of their comfort zone (where the real world is). The process is mandatory for business planning and strategy definition, and in 2013 Hans's team was involved with doing 25 of these workshop sessions as the company business plans were to be updated. Subsequently it was documented that 75 percent of these business plans had taken on explicit actions on issues they had not seen prior to the session—hence the value.

Hans explains, "Once we have decided on the strategy and defined what we're going to do, we test the strategy for resilience. We very simply take that particular strategy and, together with the strategy owner, discuss: If this scenario happens, what will happen to the strategy? Some of these issues will be highly probable, and some of them will be less probable. Some of them will happen very fast; some others will happen very slowly. This is where the PAPA model comes in."

THE PAPA MODEL

When looking at the issues inspired by the scenarios, the LEGO Group uses what it calls a Park, Adapt, Prepare, Act (PAPA) model, as shown in Exhibit 6.4. Hans explains:

- *Park:* "The *slow* things that have a *low probability* of happening, we park. We do not forget about them."
- *Adapt:* "The *slow* things that we know will happen or are *highly likely* to happen, we adapt to those trends. In our case, this is a lot around demographics. We know children's play is changing, we know demographics are changing, and we know the buying power between the different realms or the different parts of the world is changing. Although we know children's play is changing, we also know it does not happen fast. So we adjust, systematically monitoring what direction it's moving in and following that trend."
- *Prepare:* "The things that have a *low probability* of happening, but, if they do, they materialize *fast*, we need to be prepared for this. In fact, this is where

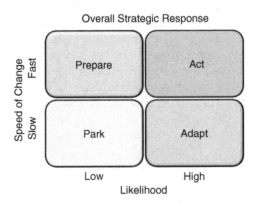

Exhibit 6.4   LEGO's PAPA Model

we identify most of the risks that we need to put into our ERM risk database, make sure that we have contingency plans for them, and apply early warnings and whatever mitigation we can put in place to make sure that we can cover these should they materialize, but they are not expected to."

- *Act:* "Finally, we have the *high-probability* and *fast-moving* things that we need to act on now in order to make sure the strategy will be relevant. In our case, anything that has to do with the concept of connectivity (i.e., mobile phones, Internet, that world)—if we can see it, we move on it. We know that it is changing so fast, and it's changing the way kids play. It's changing their concepts and their view of the world."

Hans concludes, "This way, we have a kind of model of what we do, because we shouldn't, of course, be betting on every horse in the race. That's not profitable, and it isn't even doable."

Strategic Risk Management Lab Commentary

One of the challenges of risk management is to find ways to prioritize risks that make business sense. The PAPA model provides a good example of a framework that can prioritize risks and set the stage for the appropriate actions. Our research on high-performance companies (see Mark L. Frigo, "Return Driven: Lessons from High Performance Companies," and the book *Driven: Business Strategy, Human Actions, and the Creation of Wealth* by Mark L. Frigo and Joel Litman) found that companies that demonstrate sustainable high performance exhibit a "vigilance to forces of change" that allows them to manage the threats and opportunities in the uncertainties and changes better than other companies do.[5] The approach used at LEGO is a great example of embedding this vigilance to forces of change in its strategy development and strategy execution processes. The scenario analysis approach used at LEGO provides an engagement platform for engaging stakeholders in the risk management process.[6]

STATEGIC RISK MANAGEMENT RETURN ON INVESTMENT

A great deal has happened in the LEGO Group's approach to risk management based on strong support from top management (always needed to develop processes and methodologies) and a strong focus. They have demonstrated value from the efforts they've made. They also have explicitly embedded risk management in most of the key planning processes used to run the company:

- The Strategic Scenarios used in business planning
- The LEGO Development Process—includes Monte Carlo simulation of overall project risk/opportunity exposure
- The Customer Business Planning Process—AROP in collaboration
- The Sales and Operations Planning Process—tactical scenarios
- The Performance Management Process—bonuses based on results, not efforts

"All of this has worked," Hans says. "Based on actual data, we have had a 20 percent average growth from the period between 2006 and 2010 in a market that barely grows 2 percent and 3 percent a year. It has continued so 2006 to 2012 has a cumulative annual growth rate of 20 percent, leading to a tripling of the size of the company based on official public data. Beyond that, our profitability has developed quite significantly as well. We've grown from a 17 percent return on sales in 2006 to 34 percent return on sales in 2012. And it goes beyond that. If you go back a couple more years, in 2004 we were in dire straits and had a negative return on sales of 15 percent. We changed a number of strategies.

"Risk management is not the driver of these changes," Hans continues. "I'm not even sure it's a big part. But it's one part. It's a part that has allowed us to take bigger risks and make bigger investments than we otherwise would have seen. The Monte Carlo simulation has shown us what the uncertainty is and was a key element of changing the financial planning process to a more dynamic estimation approach. The risk tolerance has shown us how much risk we are prepared to take, between the board of directors and the corporate management team. This has meant that we have been prepared to make bigger supply chain investments than we otherwise would have done and have been able to achieve bigger growth than we ever imagined we could have."

Strategic Risk Management Lab Commentary

The development of strategic risk management at the LEGO Group provides a great example of how organizations can develop their ERM programs to incorporate strategic risk and make strategic risk management a discipline and core competency within. One of the key elements was integration. During discussions with LEGO management, when Hans was asked about the ongoing development of risk management at the LEGO Group, he replied that it was "naturally integrated." It is this integration of risk management in strategy and strategy execution, and the integration of strategy in risk management, that can elevate the value of ERM in an organization.

CONCLUSION

We want to emphasize that risk management is *not* about risk aversion. If, or rather when, you want or need to take bigger chances than your competitors— and get away with it (succeed)—you need to be better prepared. The fastest race cars in the world have the best brakes and the best steering to enable them to be driven faster, not slower. Risk management should enable organizations to take the risks necessary to grow and create value. To quote racing legend Mario Andretti: "If everything's under control, you're going too slow." The approach and philosophy described in this case are reflected in the mission of the strategic risk management team at the LEGO Group to "drive conscious choices."

QUESTIONS

1. What are the advantages of integrating ERM with strategy and strategy execution as described in this case?

2. How does scenario analysis as described in this case help an organization to prepare for uncertainties?
3. What are the advantages of using the PAPA model to categorize risks?
4. How would you describe the "Strategic Risk Management Return on Investment" at LEGO?
5. The mission of the strategic risk management team is to "Drive conscious choice." How does the Active Risk and Opportunity Planning (AROP) element of strategic risk management at LEGO help to drive conscious choice?

NOTES

1. This chapter was adapted from Mark L. Frigo and Hans Læssøe, "Strategic Risk Management at the LEGO Group," *Strategic Finance* (February 2012) with the permission of *Strategic Finance* and the Institute of Management Accountants. An earlier version of this case was presented at the Risk and Insurance Management Society (RIMS) Conference, where Mark and Hans serve as members of the RIMS Strategic Risk Management Development Council.
2. M. L. Frigo and R. J. Anderson, "Strategic Risk Assessment: A First Step for Improving Governance and Risk Management," *Strategic Finance* 12 (2009), 25–35.
3. Also see Hans Læssøe, Venkat Ramaswamy, and Mark L. Frigo, "Strategic Risk Management in the Co-Creative Enterprise," Working Paper, Strategic Risk Management Lab, DePaul University, 2014.
4. See "Using ERM to Improve Strategic Decisions," CEB Risk Management Leadership Council, Corporate Executive Board, 2013.
5. Also see Mark L. Frigo, *Driven Strategy: Creating and Sustaining Superior Performance* (Palo Alto, CA: Stanford University Press, forthcoming 2015).
6. A. Mikes and D. Hamel, "The LEGO Group: Envisioning Risks in Asia," Harvard Business School Case 113-054, November 2012.

REFERENCES

Frigo, M. L. 2008. "Return Driven: Lessons from High Performance Companies." *Strategic Finance* 7, 24–30.

Frigo, Mark L. 2015. *Driven Strategy: Creating and Sustaining Superior Performance*. Palo Alto, CA: Stanford University Press, forthcoming.

Frigo, M. L., and R. J. Anderson. 2009. "Strategic Risk Assessment: A First Step for Improving Governance and Risk Management." *Strategic Finance* 12, 25–35.

Frigo, M. L., and R. J. Anderson. 2011. "Embracing ERM: Practical Approaches for Getting Started." Committee of Sponsoring Organizations of the Treadway Commission (COSO). www.coso.org/guidance.htm.

Frigo, Mark L., and Mark Beasley. 2010. "ERM and Its Role in Strategic Planning and Strategy Execution." In John Fraser and Betty J. Simkins, eds. *Enterprise Risk Management*. Hoboken, NJ: John Wiley & Sons.

Frigo, Mark L., and Hans Læssøe. 2012. "Strategic Risk Management at the LEGO Group." *Strategic Finance* 2, 27–35.

Frigo, Mark L., and Joel Litman. 2007. *Driven: Business Strategy, Human Actions, and the Creation of Wealth*. Chicago: Strategy & Execution, LLC.

Frigo, M. L., and V. Ramaswamy. 2009. "Co-Creating Strategic Risk-Return Management." *Strategic Finance* 5, 25–33.

Læssøe, Hans, Venkat Ramaswamy, and Mark L. Frigo. 2014. "Strategic Risk Management in the Co-Creative Enterprise." Working Paper, Strategic Risk Management Lab, DePaul University.

Mikes, A., and D. Hamel. 2012. "The LEGO Group: Envisioning Risks in Asia." Harvard Business School Case 113-054, November.

Ramaswamy, V., and F. Gouillart. 2010. *The Power of Co-Creation*. New York: Free Press.

Ramaswamy, V., and K. Ozcan. 2014. *The Co-Creation Paradigm*. Palo Alto, CA: Stanford University Press, forthcoming.

ABOUT THE CONTRIBUTORS

Mark L. Frigo, PhD, CMA, CPA, is director of the Center for Strategy, Execution and Valuation and the Strategic Risk Management Lab in the Kellstadt Graduate School of Business at DePaul University in Chicago. He is Ledger & Quill Alumni Foundation Distinguished Professor of Strategy and Leadership in the Driehaus College of Business at DePaul. The author of seven books and more than 100 articles, his work is published in leading journals, including the *Harvard Business Review*. Dr. Frigo is coauthor (with Joel Litman) of the book *Driven: Business Strategy, Human Actions, and the Creation of Wealth*, coauthor (with Richard J. Anderson) of the book *Strategic Risk Management: A Primer for Directors and Management Teams*, and author of a forthcoming book, *Driven Strategy*, from Stanford University Press. His research and thought leadership on strategic risk management and ERM have been published by Harvard Business Press, the Conference Board, Committee of Sponsoring Organizations of the Treadway Commission (COSO), American Accounting Association, Financial Executives International, American Institute of Certified Public Accountants, Institute of Interal Auditors, Institute of Chartered Accountants in England and Wales, Chartered Institute of Management Accountants, Institute of Management Accountants, Risk and Insurance Management Society, and other leading organizations, and he has presented keynote presentations and executive workshops on strategic risk management throughout North America, Europe, and the Asia-Pacific region. He is a member of the RIMS Strategic Risk Management Development Council. Dr. Frigo is an adviser to executive teams and boards of directors in the area of strategic risk management.

Hans Læssøe, MSc, is the LEGO Group head of and senior director on strategic risk management, a function he established in 2006 and 2007. He has more than 30 years of LEGO Group experience from a number of areas, which provides him with strong business insight and a network to drive the task of proactive strategic risk management. He is a founding member of a Danish ERM network, an executive member of the European Council of Risk Management, and a specialist member of the Institute of Risk Management (IRM). He is a member of the RIMS Strategic Risk Management Development Council. The LEGO Group and Læssøe have won multiple European awards for their unique risk management approach. Læssøe is the author or coauthor of articles in international magazines, and speaks at international risk management conferences.

CHAPTER 7

Turning the Organizational Pyramid Upside Down

Ten Years of Evolution in Enterprise Risk Management at United Grain Growers

JOHN BUGALLA
Managing Principal, ermINSIGHTS

> Strategy without tactics is the path to uncertain success; tactics without strategy is the noise before defeat.
>
> —Sun Tzu (c. 544–496 B.C.)

Few companies stand out as successful pioneers in enterprise risk management (ERM), especially one that undertook the initiative almost 15 years ago. One such ERM pioneer was United Grain Growers (UGG), a conservative 100-year-old Winnipeg, Canada–based grain handler and distributor of farm supplies. When UGG announced that it had implemented a new integrated risk-financing program in 1999, it received a great deal of attention in the financial press. *CFO* magazine hailed the UGG program as "the deal of the decade."[1] *The Economist* characterized it as a "revolutionary advance in corporate finance."[2] Harvard created a UGG case study.[3] While most outside attention focused on the direct financial benefits of implementing the program (protection of cash flow, the reduced risk capital required, and a 20 percent increase in stock price)[4], scant attention was given to the less tangible and therefore less measurable issues of governance, leadership, and corporate culture—the *conditions* that enabled such innovation. It was a combination of a collaborative leadership open to new ideas, a culture of controlled risk taking, and active risk oversight by the board that produced a strategic approach to UGG's risk management process. A combination of the same cultural factors had already contributed to the 1993 transformation of UGG from a cooperative structure to a publicly traded company with access to the capital markets. UGG's chief executive officer (CEO) had two key strategic objectives: (1) from day one of his tenure, a razor-sharp focus on improving the financial performance of the company to better serve customers and shareholders, and (2) as financial performance improved, to change the risk profile of the company to attract long-term shareholders versus short-term stock speculators.

Implementing the integrated risk program that reduced earnings volatility helped to change the risk profile of the company. However, the strategic goals of UGG went deeper than an integrated risk program. Over the next several years, financial performance continued to improve. New value was created by implementing a unique credit financing business (UGG Financial), in partnership with the Bank of Nova Scotia (ScotiaBank). This was followed by merging/acquiring the business of rival Agricore Cooperative in 2001, creating Agricore United (AU). The final act of value creation was extracting a high premium for AU's stock in 2007 from several bidders that wanted to acquire the company.

BACKGROUND—OPERATING ENVIRONMENT

The grain business is capital intensive and inherently risky in terms of supply, commodity prices, currency exchange rates, Canadian government regulation of the industry, and, from time to time, the current political climate existing with key customers. Weather is obviously a major risk, and it determines local and overall supply. Grain production in the Canadian prairies covers tens of thousands of square miles of Manitoba, Saskatchewan, and Alberta, and stretches into the Peace River district of British Columbia. The success or failure for the entire crop year, for the farmer-growers, grain handlers like UGG, and road and rail transporters, is determined by the amount of rainfall in April and May. Not enough rain in those key months translates into a drought-reduced harvest. Added complexity was demonstrated by an analysis of a century of rainfall data that revealed that weather events thought to occur every 100 years actually occur every nine to 11 years. However, UGG was a grain handler, not a crop grower. The threat to UGG was related to the volume of grain that it would process, much of it at a fixed price established by the Canadian Wheat Board (CWB).[5] UGG had an established average market share of 15 percent. UGG (and its competitors) would be allocated rail cars by the Canadian Wheat Board that were almost entirely determined by its market share in the preceding year, no matter how large or small the crop. There was, therefore, little opportunity to gain (or lose) grain handling market share. Consequently, it was overall grain production volume risk that drove revenues and profits.[6]

Grain is a commodity traded on global exchanges. The price of grain, such as wheat, like any other commodity, is driven by supply and demand. While local weather conditions impact Canada's grain-producing provinces, supply and demand are also impacted by global[7] weather conditions. Political risk is another factor in the supply-and-demand chain, as Canada is a major grain exporter. A grain embargo placed on a major customer nation is a critical threat. It has been said that wheat is 15 percent protein and 85 percent politics.

Canadian grain (wheat, barley, oilseeds, and pulse crops)[8] is harvested in the fall. The average Canadian harvest is over 60 million tons. The farmers harvest the grain and then transport it to the storage elevators operated by UGG and its competitors. The primary grain elevators are located on railroad sidings in farming communities that enable the railroad to collect the grain in special hopper cars and transport it to the two main grain terminal ports at Thunder Bay on Lake Superior for shipments going east, and Vancouver for shipments going west. As a result of almost 100 years of railroad regulation and transportation subsidies,

Western Canada was dotted with smaller wooden grain elevators, most of which could accommodate only short trains. The business was inefficient. By the 1990s the grain business was in transition. Deregulation of the railroads and the removal of transportation subsidies provided the railroad companies with the incentive to eliminate uneconomic branch lines. This, in turn, required that the smaller wooden elevators that dotted Western Canada would have to be replaced by giant modern elevators able to accommodate 100 or more grain railcars. The railroads were driving cost inefficiencies out of the system. This imposed a massive increase in capital requirements on UGG (and its competitors) as it embarked on an infrastructure rebuilding program—replacing its multitude of old wooden elevators with large, high-throughput, concrete ones capable of loading the multiple carloads demanded by railroad rationalization—reducing grain handling costs per metric ton, but adding new fixed costs.

Adding to the financial pressure of investing in grain handling infrastructure replacement, working capital requirements were also increasing rapidly. During the 1990s, the western Canadian grain handling companies responded to the increasing demand for crop inputs (seed, fertilizer, herbicides, and pesticides) by aggressively investing in the farm retail business. Farm retail sales showed dramatic growth as biotechnology delivered new products and genetics that promised to increase and protect crop yields. This substantially increased the amount of retail credit extended to farm customers.

GOVERNANCE

The financial scandals of the mid-1990s, such as Barings Bank and Orange County, were just as troubling then as the recent decade's risk management mistakes, misdeeds, and failures are to today's regulators and investors. The financial culprit then was the emerging issue of financial derivatives rather than the residential mortgage-backed securities that wreaked havoc on the global financial markets in 2008–2009. The scandals of the 1990s had the effect of sensitizing legislators, regulators, and investor advocates to start asking organizations questions about how publicly traded companies manage the inherent risks of their business. From these concerns were born a number of guidelines and standards in many parts of the world that, in general, allocated accountability to directors, officers, and organizational management to effectively manage their risks. One example, corporate governance guidelines produced by the Toronto Stock Exchange (TSX), set out five general responsibilities of directors in Canada. In addition to strategic planning, succession planning, communication policy, and internal control/management systems, directors were given responsibility for "the identification of the principal risks of the corporation's business and ensuring the implementation of appropriate systems to manage those risks."[9]

For a company historically sensitized to managing substantial business risks, particularly grain price volatility,[10] the TSX guidelines immediately struck a chord. The board of directors of UGG therefore mandated the chief executive officer to form a Risk Management Committee, establish a formal risk management policy, develop corporate-wide risk management processes, and report to the Audit Committee of the board of directors on a quarterly basis. The board of UGG created a platform for the adoption of ERM and a strategic approach to risk management.

UGG already had a solid platform on which to build its approach to ERM. Risk management was a process that was well ingrained at UGG, and had been since the 1970s. The organization had a risk management policy, applied risk management processes via inspections (identification and evaluation) as required under its corporate insurance programs, and had developed internal loss prevention programs (environment, safety, and loss control); but, unlike many other organizations at the time, UGG also applied a risk measurement metric to its risk management initiatives by tracking its "cost of risk" (net risk retention costs + risk transfer costs + risk-related administrative overhead = cost of risk).

Concurrently, UGG's leadership team was wringing out as much cost from the system as possible. Between the capital requirements for the new elevators, a lengthy depressed operating environment, and reduced crop volumes, reducing cost throughout UGG was a critical objective. Risk management expenses were no exception.

Leadership

Tracing its roots back to 1906 as a farmer-owned cooperative,[11] UGG was a mature organization entrenched in its own bureaucratic business model. There were numerous business units operating under the UGG umbrella but all reporting in a hierarchical command and control structure straight to headquarters. By the early 1990s, the company had become financially distressed—UGG was in breach of its bank covenants and losing cash. Under consideration in 1990 was the idea of exiting or selling certain noncore business units. An internal study of one business (farm supplies) produced a stark picture of not only that single business, but an entire organization, including operations, and its unresponsiveness to customer needs. The report was a candid assessment of the organization that equated the firm to a geriatric patient 85 years old in need of major care if it expected to survive. Written by the future CEO, the report projected that without dramatic change the fluid and dynamic forces taking place in the entire agribusiness sector, coupled with UGG's weak balance sheet, would simply overwhelm the cooperative in a matter of a few years.

The financial imperatives critical to survival were fixing the weak balance sheet, recapitalization, and addressing bank covenants that had been breached. Access to cash and the capital markets was of paramount concern. One way to access the capital markets efficiently was to demutualize and become a publicly traded company. While it literally took an act of Parliament to demutualize, UGG went public in 1993.[12]

The UGG Annual Report in 1994 indicated the transformational shift in thinking by the new CEO that would set in motion a series of events that propelled the company to greatly improved operating and financial performance:

> We have also taken definitive steps to organize our business so that the decisions which most affect customer service are made by the people who deal directly with customers. In the last year, we turned our organizational pyramid upside down. We can't be prompt and effective in the era of market-driven agriculture if all the decisions that impact on customers are made by senior managers, sitting in Head Office, at the top of the organizational pyramid. In the country—in our core grain

and inputs businesses—we've tipped the pyramid over. Our management team now provides support and planning services to the people who deal with customers, therefore enhancing services. This change was perhaps the most profound rethinking of our business approach in many years.[13]

Improved operational and financial performance would not have been possible without building an executive team of trusted partners who also embraced the need for change. Turning the pyramid upside down and allowing UGG staff interfacing with customers to respond quickly to their needs required a cultural shift—from the previously hierarchal management structure to one that delegated decision making and fostered personnel development. A new chief financial officer, with working experience in publicly traded companies, was appointed to help develop and implement the financial disciplines and tactics necessary to achieve the company's business strategy.

Turning the pyramid over to improve customer service also required a completely new approach to management information technology (IT) systems.

Like the oil in an engine, lubricating support processes are needed for any business to operate smoothly.... UGG also eliminated its need for mainframe computing over the past year. While the Company incurred the double cost of carrying both our new "client-server" and mainframe for a good part of fiscal 1995, from fiscal 1996 forward we will realize material benefits from this shift. UGG won international recognition from the Smithsonian Institution for innovation in applying computing technology during 1995 for the successful completion of this project.[14]

Over the decade and a half following the decision to demutualize UGG, the transformation in management philosophy and the executive team's implementation of strategic decisions proved successful in realizing the company's objectives: The confidence of the board of directors was gained progressively and cumulatively and developed into an effective partnership with management; it was decision-making capital built up over time that created a culture of welcoming and listening to new and innovative ideas—ideas that could better serve UGG's customers and other stakeholders.

Of course, no company has a straight line to success, and UGG was no exception. The ERM program was one example. Before risks can be managed and opportunities considered, they have to be identified. It is commonplace today, but, mindful of expenses and time constraints, the mandated (Toronto Stock Exchange, UGG Board, and CEO) risk identification process and subsequent risk rankings at UGG were accomplished in a single daylong meeting. The composition of this meeting exemplified the company's departure from hierarchy: Participants were selected not by the seniority of their rank in the organization but rather for their knowledge and experience of the business; they ranged from frontline representatives to vice presidents, all given an equal opportunity and showing an equal propensity to contribute to the process. However, the road to ERM would take more than two years, which, once the company's major risks were identified, included intense analysis, evaluation, and quantification of the company's principal risks. There were headwinds along the way. The process was temporarily delayed by (1) a major flood in UGG's home province and (2) a hostile takeover attempt by a combination of two competitors (which, after their failure to acquire UGG, merged to form Agricore Cooperative).

UGG did not embrace ERM as a risk management destination, but as (an important) part of a process that would support executive management's risk-adjusted decision making. It evolved as a logical progression that had begun eight years earlier with the company's strategic vision for its future and the development of a more inclusive management style.[15]

ERM/Integrated Risk Outcomes

The concept of developing an ERM process was new in the late 1990s. UGG started by identifying and assessing its principal risks. As indicated earlier, since the 1970s a substantial amount was already being done to control and measure the cost of property, casualty, liability, environment, safety, and loss control risks, in addition to potential (if unhedged) grain price exposure; the additional dimension was to apply the same systematic procedures to *all* the company's major business risks.

The major risks were identified through the ERM exercise. Quantitative risk analysis confirmed (not unexpectedly) that weather had the greatest impact on UGG's earnings, cash flow, and debt stability. Almost 100 years of data was available on the Canadian prairies' crop production levels; this revealed that major droughts, such as occurred during the late 1920s and early 1930s, could reduce grain production and, consequently, UGG's grain handling volume in the subsequent year by as much as 50 percent. Since this could pose a significant threat to UGG's profitability, cash flow, and ability to control its debt level (and, therefore, investment plans), UGG's senior finance, risk management, and treasury personnel began searching for a means to control this risk at reasonable cost.

Two different approaches to the problem were explored: Aware that financial derivatives *might* offer a solution, discussions were initiated with financial institutions; but none could be identified that were able to hedge the risk. UGG then began collaborating with its insurance broker, who conceived an insurance solution—a structure that incorporated the grain volume risk with *all* UGG's traditionally insured risks (property, casualty, freight, liability, etc.) into an "integrated risk-financing program." UGG was intrigued by this concept, particularly since a quantitative analysis suggested that such a program would cost no more than the discrete insurance policies that UGG was currently buying—without grain volume insurance. UGG's executive management worked closely with the broker and market to address this never previously insured exposure. Swiss Re, largely because of its expertise, capacity, and triple A financial rating, provided UGG with a ground-breaking integrated risk-financing program that applied to the various event risks that had previously been addressed by monoline traditional insurance policies, and a parametric risk solution tied to the expected volume of grain passing through UGG's grain handling pipeline.

The effect of this on UGG's potential financial stability was dramatic; while it "protected" (put a floor under) grain handling earnings that represented approximately 50 percent of UGG's total gross profits, it had an even greater proportionate effect on the company's net profits and cash flow—providing, by stabilizing its debt structure, greater assurance of its ability to deliver on its strategic plan. *The*

Economist pointed out that "for a large chunk of its own equity, it [UGG] substituted the imposing capital of the world's largest reinsurer."[16]

It is worth noting that while the financial media sometimes referred to UGG's risk-financing program as ERM, this was a misnomer; it was in fact an integrated risk-financing program (combining multiple property and casualty risks with the grain volume coverage). It was UGG's different approach to thinking about risk—considering both the upside as well as the downside from an enterprise perspective—that was the ERM in the company's process.

ERM CREDIT FINANCING OUTCOMES

Given the high capital demands of grain handling infrastructure renewal, UGG was also concerned about its ability to finance the rapid growth in crop inputs retailing—specifically the burgeoning demand from farmer customers for extended credit. Within UGG, a division called Crop Production Services managed the retail sales and logistics of these products, which included the extension of UGG retail credit to farm customers. As the levels of working capital and associated risk in the credit program increased, UGG sought to bring it under more rigorous control by placing credit at arm's length from the retail operation, and under the oversight of the corporate treasury.

A cultural shift gradually took place that ensured compliance with improved practices in credit extension, but growth continued to strain working capital. This was alleviated to some extent by renegotiating bank lines, and later by undertaking the first off-balance-sheet securitization of Canadian farm receivables, but then competition was driving retailers to use financing as a tool to promote sales—there was a competitive advantage in being able to provide credit terms that extended repayment until after harvest. Ideally, the solution was to retain some control over the credit product, and to have as much credit capacity as needed, at attractive terms, without putting a strain on the balance sheet.[17]

After lengthy exploration, this was finally accomplished by forming UGG Financial through a strategic alliance between UGG and Scotiabank. Essentially, UGG provided the customers, administration, and reporting while Scotiabank provided the capital. UGG shared an equal level of risk with the bank with a hard cap[18] on the maximum limit. UGG received significant fees from Scotiabank based on the performance of the portfolio. The results were dramatic, effectively freeing up to $200 million in capital, extending customer credit terms up to 12 full months, streamlining application processes and providing greater levels of customer service, and expanding product lines to livestock producers. It was also instrumental in enabling acquisitions of independent retailers' accounts and the merger of UGG with Agricore Cooperative to form AU in 2001. This arrangement forced competitors to engage in similar outsourcing credit arrangements, and it became the standard of the industry. When Saskatchewan Wheat Pool eventually acquired AU, the operation was extending $1.5 billion in credit to 20,000 customers and generating over $10 million in net profits annually.[19]

A third leg of UGG/AU's activities was its Livestock Services division. Accounting for between 10 percent and 15 percent of the company's business, its primary activity was the manufacture and sale of animal feedstuff, the largest segment being to hog farmers. Traditionally highly leveraged, hog farmers were vulnerable to cyclical fluctuations in hog prices. Learning from the statistical techniques employed in assessing UGG/AU's other risks during the ERM process, collaboration between corporate and divisional management identified an opportunity to use these methods to acquire a competitive advantage in supporting feed sales to hog producers.

By analyzing the hog price cycle, it became evident that there was an opportunity for UGG/AU to provide hog *price* risk management to customers who contracted to purchase their feed from the company. Provided that the customers met strict performance criteria (such as weight gain, morbidity, etc.), the company would agree to support shortfalls in realized prices from a preestablished minimum until prices recovered sufficiently to recover the subventions, thus protecting the producers' cash flow. Clearly there was always a risk that the historical pattern of the hog price cycle could prove an insufficient predictor of the severity or length of future price downturns; however, using statistical modeling techniques, it was possible to stress test the company's exposure to credit risk to ensure that the capital at risk did not exceed preestablished levels based on UGG/AU's required return targets (on the associated feed sales). In this way, the company was able to promote its feed sales to high-performing producers with the quantitative intelligence to provide a high degree of assurance that it would achieve its return targets without excessive risk, secure in the knowledge that if competitors provided more attractive terms under any similar program they risked eroding their financial (and, therefore, long-term competitive) positions.[20]

Apart from the obvious risk mitigation provided by the integrated risk-financing program, it could be argued that the broader ERM project further increased UGG's ability to take on more risk; as it gained a more precise quantification of the risks it faced, not only as individual risks but in aggregate, this improved understanding of its overall risk profile reduced the need for "precautionary capital."[21]

While by no means all of the risks that UGG/AU confronted could be quantified (and could only be managed procedurally or avoided altogether), the quantification of its major risks substantially enhanced the company's ability to model its anticipated financial performance. While weather could have a dramatic impact on the volume of grain produced, it could also have a significant influence on the volume, timing, and variety of seed, fertilizer, herbicide, and pesticide sales by the Crop Production Services division (e.g., an unusually wet spring that delayed planting could shift sales from one quarter to another, change farmers' planting intentions, and alter their fertilizer, herbicide, and pesticide requirements for the entire crop year).

Such variability could substantially affect UGG/AU's quarterly and annual earnings, even if the impact was not as dramatic as a full-blown drought. UGG had developed a comprehensive financial model of its expected earnings, debt levels, and cash flow. Prior to developing the intelligence derived from the quantification of its major risks during the ERM process, the model had, however, been one that produced average (or normal weather condition) projections—good for long-term planning but of limited use in the short term, as it did not anticipate the consequences of seasonal and year-to-year variability. Given the quantitatively enhanced understanding of the potential range of earnings and cash flow derived from ERM, the company was able to model the complete range of its possible financial outcomes. While this did not significantly enhance its understanding of its expected long-term average results, it did provide a powerful analytical tool: It identified its requirements for contingent capital with more precision; it provided a much better tool for judging its performance against its plans in a set of potentially variable conditions—an infinitely flexible budget; and it improved its capacity to respond appropriately to changing conditions that had, or might have, adverse financial implications.

ERM was also able to bring a more consistent and disciplined treatment of risk exposures across the organization. UGG became better positioned to allocate appropriate resources to ensure that the risks within the different divisions and activities of the company were not over- or undermanaged relative to the corporation's level of risk tolerance.[22]

AGRICORE UNITED

As the solutions to UGG's top risks started to pay financial dividends and improve its balance sheet, the management team began to apply enterprise-wide thinking to other areas that had been identified and to factor this competitive strength into its growth strategies. One of these was a merger with Agricore Cooperative, a rival grain processor whose predecessor companies had, three years previously, attempted a hostile takeover of UGG.[23]

UGG's integrated risk-financing program proved a valuable tool during the merger negotiations: The potential to expand the program to the enlarged company was perceived by Agricore Cooperative's board of directors and members as a means of providing greater stability and security to the organization.

In practical terms, though, UGG Financial was a more powerfully persuasive factor in the merger: Lacking UGG's access to the capital markets, Agricore Cooperative had become substantially overleveraged in the race to build high-throughput elevators and expand its crop inputs business in line with its competitors; consequently, the prospect of being able to roll up Agricore Cooperative's receivables into UGG Financial was a very significant advantage for a combined company—removing, as it did, the need for some $300 million in financing from the combined company's balance sheet (compared to the amount previously financed directly by Agricore Cooperative).[24]

HARVESTING VALUE

Every publicly traded company is for sale, and the price is visible to everyone in the form of the stock price. While AU would have preferred to stay independent, the company received a buyout offer from the Saskatchewan Wheat Pool (SWP) that, under Canadian law, could not be ignored even though the initial offer was considered by management to be woefully inadequate. The AU CEO and the board of directors, given their governance responsibilities, thought the offer could be substantially improved or even countered by another suitor—one prepared to put a more realistic value on AU. The CEO believed there were three possible options that could create additional stakeholder value:

1. AU could make its own offer to buy out SWP.
2. AU could seek a white knight to counter the SWP offer, effectively creating an auction that would produce the highest bid (i.e., provide the greatest possible increase in shareholder value).
3. Archer Daniels Midland (ADM) was a strategic partner and significant stakeholder in AU that had aided UGG in its defense of the hostile takeover attempt by Agricore Cooperative's predecessor companies. ADM could be offered a proposal to increase its ownership position.

The CEO and the board of directors decided upon a strategy to pursue the first two options, which also offered the greatest flexibility to ADM.

As is usual in hostile takeovers, a team of advisers and investment bankers was hired by AU to analyze the company's financial position and prospects and determine a fair value. At the same time, AU made a buyout offer to SWP that was rejected. After the evaluation was completed, it confirmed that AU was worth considerably more than the share-swap deal offered by SWP. The AU board of directors, which included representatives from ADM, rejected the buyout offer. One of the AU board members then made an overture to Richardson International, Canada's next largest agribusiness, to determine its interest in acquiring AU. Richardson International offered a friendly all-cash offer higher than the offer from SWP. Not to be thwarted in its takeover attempt, SWP countered with a higher all-cash offer. This had the effect of creating an auction process where the price for the AU stock reached a level prompting ADM to make a strategic decision. ADM could increase its holdings in AU and assume control or could sell them at a substantial profit to shareholders, knowing that AU was going to be sold to either SWP or Richardson International. Finally, the highest bid was an all-cash offer from SWP.[25]

After the buyout was complete in 2007, SWP changed the name of the combined company to Viterra, Inc., and continued to operate until being acquired by Glencore International on January 1, 2013.[26]

CONCLUSION

Thomas Edison once quipped: "Vision without execution is hallucination." Turning the organizational pyramid upside down initiated a transformation in the company—a process starting with the formulation of a strategic plan, then transforming the culture of the organization, and finally demanding execution of that plan. Without execution, innovative ideas tend to die on the vine. While one aspect of the organizational vision was intended to be operational—improving customer service—another (more subtle) effect was to transform the entire culture of the company. The cultural shift to a leadership that was aligned in their goals made for quicker and better-informed decision making. UGG and its successor company AU did not just become more responsive to the needs of customers; the new culture developed greater collaboration between senior and middle management teams, and delegated responsibility to them for their decisions. This collaborative but accountable environment allowed a number of innovative solutions to the company's business challenges to be created: developing new (client-server) computing, early adoption of the ERM process, the subsequent groundbreaking risk-financing program, and the creation of UGG/AU Financial—not just industry firsts that spawned imitators but also initiatives that significantly added value to the corporation.

QUESTIONS

1. Why does a more participative management style ("tipping the pyramid over") lead to greater responsiveness to customers' needs, increased accountability, and more innovative solutions to challenges than a hierarchical "command and control" structure?
2. Under what circumstances might the hierarchical "command and control" structure produce superior results?
3. What particular factors do you believe led UGG/AU to be pioneers in ERM? Was it industry/company/history/circumstances? Was it a changed organizational "culture"? Was it good management?

ACKNOWLEDGMENTS

This chapter could not have been written without the extensive cooperation of the following:

Peter G.M. Cox, Former Chief Financial Officer, Agricore United
Brian Hayward, Former Chief Executive Officer, Agricore United
Michael McAndless, Former Chief Risk Officer, Agricore United
George Prosk, Former Treasurer, Agricore United

NOTES

1. "Whatever the Weather," *CFO*, June 2000.
2. "Outsourcing Capital," *The Economist*, November 1999.
3. "United Grain Growers Ltd. (A)," Harvard Business Publishing, August 2003.
4. United Grain Growers Ltd as of December 2, 1999, Yahoo! Finance stock chart.
5. The CWB was created in 1935—with antecedents going back to before World War I—as a mandatory producer marketing system for wheat and barley grown in Western Canada. It was illegal for farmers under CWB jurisdiction (anywhere in Western Canada) to sell their wheat and barley through any channel other than the CWB. The CWB became a voluntary marketing organization only in 2012.
6. Interview with Peter Cox.
7. Agricultural Futures Markets.
8. Pulse crops are peas, beans, and lentils.
9. In 1994 a committee sponsored by the TSX published a report (the Dey Report) containing corporate governance recommendations to TSX-listed companies. In 1995 the TSX adopted them as "best practice guidelines." Although the guidelines were not mandatory, the TSX did require listed companies to disclose annually their approach to corporate governance and provide an explanation of any differences from the guidelines.

10. Virtually all grain purchases not matched by sales contracts, as well as sales contracts for which the company did not have purchased grain, were hedged using derivatives on long-established international grain exchanges, while very limited, unhedged positions had been closely managed and supervised for many years.

11. UGG was formed in 1917 by the merger of the Grain Growers' Grain Company, founded in 1906, and the Alberta Farmers' Co-operative Elevator Company of 1913.

12. The United Grain Growers Act was approved by the Canadian Parliament in 1992, allowing UGG to become a public company with both members (the former cooperative's members) and public shareholders.

13. 1994 UGG Annual Report, Chief Executive's Report, and interview with Brian Hayward.

14. 1995 UGG Annual Report, Chief Executive's Report, and interview with Brian Hayward and Peter Cox.

15. Interview with Michael McAndless.

16. "Outsourcing Capital."

17. Interviews with Peter Cox and George Prosk.

18. A "hard cap" means that there is a fixed upper limit on the amount of risk that UGG would absorb.

19. Interviews with George Prosk and Peter Cox.

20. Interview with Peter Cox.

21. Interviews with Peter Cox, Brian Hayward, and Michael McAndless.

22. Interviews with Peter Cox, Michael McAndless, and George Prosk.

23. Interview with Brian Hayward.

24. Interview with Peter Cox.

25. Interview with Brian Hayward.

26. Various announcements in financial media.

ABOUT THE CONTRIBUTOR

John Bugalla is Principal of ermINSIGHTS, an advisory and training firm specializing in enterprise risk management and strategic risk management. His experience includes 30 years in the risk management profession serving as Managing Director of Marsh & McLennan, Inc., Willis Group, Plc., and Aon Corporation before founding ermINSIGHTS. He led the Willis team that negotiated the integrated risk program on behalf of UGG. He is the author or coauthor of numerous articles in diverse publications such as *The Corporate Board* magazine, *CFO* magazine, the *National Law Review*, *Credit Union Management* magazine, *Risk Management* magazine, the *Journal of Risk Management in Financial Institutions*, and the *Journal of Risk Education*.

CHAPTER 8

Housing Association Case Study of ERM in a Changing Marketplace

JOHN HARGREAVES
Managing Director of Hargreaves Risk and Strategy

This case has two main aims. The first is to help develop an understanding of the importance of enterprise risk management (ERM) in a charitable context, and show that modern charities are often very active organizations that face significant risks. Second, the case aims to illustrate the need for a close relationship between risk assessment and strategy development, particularly in sectors where objectives are defined in social as well as in economic terms. This case features four real-life charitable housing associations in England and Wales, each with a different strategy and risk environment. Simple yet practical tools to assist in risk identification and prioritization are also presented.

BACKGROUND

The UK housing market is going through a difficult period. The number of households is expanding by 250,000 per year, but the rate of house building is only half of what it needs to be. There is a tradition of home ownership, but the banking sector has recently not been able (or willing?) to fund further growth, and home ownership has fallen to its lowest level for two decades. Young working people who would previously have taken out a mortgage and bought their houses are now turning to renting. There is an urgent need to provide ordinary working people with good quality homes; the private rental market provides homes of mainly low quality, and market rents are increasing to unaffordable levels.

About one-fifth of the United Kingdom's housing is owned by housing associations, independent charities that until recently have specialized in so-called social housing (i.e., rental accommodation for the United Kingdom's poorest people). The quality of this housing has been significantly improved over the past few years to meet the United Kingdom's Decent Homes Standard.[1] There are about 2,000 associations, of which 250 own more than 1,000 homes each. Currently, their tenants are mainly nominated by local authorities using prioritized waiting lists. Their rents are set at about 40 percent of market rent, and quite a high proportion of these rents are paid from welfare payments. However, £10 billion worth of welfare cuts are now being implemented, with a further £10 billion still in the pipeline. This, together with a stagnant economy, means that housing associations' tenant communities are now under significant financial stress. In the past year the associations have built a total of about 40,000 houses, mostly for rental, largely using finance from the bond market, to the tune of over £3 billion.

The building of new social housing stock has historically been subsidized by government capital grants, but these have now been reduced both in number and in value, and a typical grant (with strings attached) now covers only about 15 percent of the building cost. Now only about 40 percent of the housing associations' house building is utilizing the small grant subsidies available under the government's Affordable Homes program, to be let at rents between 60 percent and 80 percent of market rent.

In recent years, housing associations have been expanding into new product areas, including:

- Building houses for sale
- Low-cost home ownership (the association owns part of a house, on which the tenant/owner pays a low rent, and the tenant/owner owns the rest, which is financed by a mortgage; the tenant/owner progressively buys his or her share from the association, and repays the mortgage, usually over a period of 25 years)
- Market renting
- Intermediate market renting, where rent levels are set somewhere between social and market rents, for key worker tenants such as nurses, teachers, and police officers
- Services for elderly people, such as old persons' homes and visiting support services
- Nursing homes and student accommodations
- Providing services, such as building maintenance and servicing tenant repair requests, on a contract basis for other associations

SECTOR ISSUES

Each association has its own board, with a large degree of independence. The board members of most large associations are paid for their services, but in smaller associations their participation is voluntary. The sector is regulated by the Homes and Communities Agency (HCA), but only in respect of governance and viability, not the quality of service provided. Most associations cover small local areas, but increasingly associations are amalgamating to give them a regional, rather than local, coverage. The boards of housing associations now have to make difficult strategic decisions, and different associations are adopting contrasting strategies according to their individual circumstances and risk appetites. Their environment is now much riskier than previously, and all of the available strategies are riskier than the typical association is used to. The choice is broadly between four generic strategies:

1. To concentrate on continuing to provide good quality housing services to existing social housing tenants and their replacements, in a situation where

local authority financing is being cut by up to 28 percent and support services are therefore likely to be cut. This policy helps those in need, reduces leverage, and conserves resources that could be used to support a more expansive policy in a better socioeconomic climate.

2. To invest in various social services on the borderline between the private and public sectors with the aim of increasing human or environmental well-being, and in particular regarding employment generation and support.

3. To expand in the affordable rent market, by using a mix of external capital and grants, and by cross-subsidy through progressively transferring existing social-rent housing onto a higher rent level.

4. In areas of high housing demand such as London, to develop high-volume housing for sale or at full market rent, and also to build houses where the tenants pay a rent sufficient to allow them to accumulate a financial interest in the property. An association, in employing this strategy, would typically have a culture similar to that of a commercial developer.

There are a number of issues currently causing concern in the sector; in particular:

- The government currently pays housing welfare benefits to landlords where the tenant qualifies to receive the benefit. This means that the risk of tenant rent arrears is much reduced. In the future, to encourage a culture of self-sufficiency, the government will pay benefits directly to tenants, and expect them to pay their own rents. Only if rent arrears reach a level of two months will the government resort to the payment of a tenant's rent to the landlord.

- Benefit levels are being reduced, and more pressure is being put on recipients to find work.

There is an acute housing shortage in London and the South East of England, which the sector is struggling to meet. In the north of the country the housing market is weak, with some economists being of the opinion that many houses are overvalued. In the event that there is another depression or a reversion within the present one, or a sudden increase in interest rates, then there is a danger of a downward correction in house prices.

Some associations were set up several years ago to take over local authority houses, then in poor condition, and bring them up to the Decent Homes Standard using long-term bank financing specifically tied to this (low-risk) purpose. The Decent Homes Program was successful, with the required standard generally being attained by 2012. However, often the bank financing has covenants that prevent the association from borrowing more money to branch out into riskier activities without the need for refinancing their existing lending at higher interest rates, typically 1.5 percent greater than their existing finance. For these associations, known as large-scale voluntary transfers (LSVTs), a decision is needed as to whether they should stick with their knitting and limit their investment in new houses to what they can generate internally, or bite the bullet and pay the extra margin for new loans to fund an expansion.

In some respects the position of the sector is relatively stable, since the demand for its core product would be expected to increase in adverse economic times. However, the sector's finances are finely balanced, with its borrowing subject to profitability and leverage covenants, so it may be vulnerable to sudden changes in economic conditions, and in particular:

- To an economic downturn if this were to be accompanied by a sudden fall in house prices, since there could then be losses on houses being built for market sale.
- To a sudden hike in interest rates, if this were not accompanied by an equivalent increase in inflation. About two-thirds of the sector's borrowing is at fixed interest rates, thus reducing this risk. Also, the social housing rent levels of a typical association are tied to the United Kingdom's consumer price index (CPI), so if the interest rate rise were accompanied by an increase in inflation, as has commonly been the case in the past, the risk would also be covered. However, there remains a chance that a sudden change in monetary policy could result in interest rate increases without an accompanying increase in inflation rates, possibly accompanied by a sudden fall in house prices.

CHARITABLE STATUS

Housing associations are registered as charitable organizations under the UK Charities Act of 2006, being set up to provide public benefit by relieving poverty, developing communities, and supporting people who are in need by reason of their age, ill health, financial hardship, or other disadvantage. Most of them make substantial surpluses, which they retain and use for their charitable purposes. As charities, they are exempt from paying UK corporation tax. Housing associations often also engage in noncharitable activities such as market renting or building houses for sale by setting up noncharitable subsidiaries, which then will gift any profits made to the parent charity, which then exempts the subsidiary from having to pay corporation tax. Public donations do not comprise a significant part of the sector's cash flow.

Sector Risks

The housing association sector is regulated by the Homes and Communities Agency (HCA). The HCA has extensive powers to intervene if it believes an association is being poorly governed or its viability is threatened. Most associations are highly leveraged, and the presence of an efficient regulatory activity is viewed by the financial sector as extremely important in supporting its lending. To date, the regulatory system has been unbelievably successful—while a number of associations have gotten into difficulties over the past 25 years, in no case has a financial institution made lending losses, and there has been only one case of serious default. The regulator adopts a co-regulatory approach, which "gives providers full responsibility for managing their own businesses, including their own risks. The role of the regulator is to seek assurance on how those risks are being managed."[2]

The regulator's view of the financial risks facing the sector is that:

The model of social housing that has existed for approximately 25 years is chang-ing. Boards of providers more than ever need to be aware of the risks and choices they face in order to meet their objectives. They also need to understand the interac-tion between the various risks and their overall "portfolio" impact. An approach to risk that considers issues in isolation is unlikely to be effective in the current operating environment.... The risks can be summarized as:

- Asset-related risks, including risks associated with:
  - Development
  - Diversification into other activities
  - Exposure to the housing market
  - Maintaining existing stock
- Liability-related risks, including risks associated with:
  - Existing debt (gearing, loan covenant, and repricing issues)
  - Mark-to-market exposure
  - IFRS
  - New forms of debt
- Income-related risks, including risks associated with:
  - Affordable rent
  - Welfare reform
  - Supporting people
- Cost-related risks, including risks associated with:
  - Pension issues
  - Differential inflation rates

The relative importance of each of these risks and their interaction with each other will depend on the precise business models and stock holding patterns of individ-ual providers.

SOME USEFUL METHODOLOGY

The following are some notes on two risk techniques that have been found to be useful in the sector.

Risk Appetite Determination

The sector has had a number of cases where associations have taken on rather more risk than their risk capacity allowed. As part of the process of establishing the con-text for risk management in the sector, answering the following questions has been found to be helpful:

Q1: How much risk do we think we are taking (risk perception)?
Q2: How much risk are we actually taking (risk exposure)?
   What evidence have we got that the assessment is correct? If there are gaps, biases, or incorrect assessments in the risk map, our perception will be incorrect.
Q3: How much risk do we usually like to take (risk propensity/culture)?
   If this is less than Q1, then we will feel uncomfortable.

Exhibit 8.1   Sample Probability Scale

Probability Score	Description	Range
5	Very high	More than 90%
4	High	31% to 90%
3	Medium	11% to 30%
2	Low	3% to 10%
1	Very low	Less than 3%

Q4: How much risk could we safely take (risk capacity)?
This should be bigger than Q1, Q2, and Q3. It mainly depends on financial strength and covenants, but also a view of response speeds should things start to go wrong.

Q5: How much risk do we think we should be taking (risk attitude)?
We may feel we should be doing things but we don't currently have the capacity to do them.

Q6: How much risk do we actually want to take (risk appetite)?
This is perhaps a compromise!

Q7: How do we set controls and limits across products and parts of the business, so that we can be confident that our total risk appetite is not exceeded (risk limits)?

Risk Assessment Methodology

There are technical difficulties in assessing the risks in housing associations, largely concerned with their mix of financial and social objectives. A successful approach to risk assessment for the sector has been developed, as described in Chapter 13 of Fraser and Simkins (2010) and summarized in Exhibits 8.1 and 8.2.

It is difficult to assess a risk that has several types of impact, but the task is considerably simplified if you use a clear set of criteria[3] such as those given in Exhibit 8.2.

When using the scale in Exhibit 8.2 to assess a risk, one should decide which is the highest type of impact and make the assessment based on the assessed level of this type of impact. Thus if a risk has mainly staff impact, and many staff are significantly affected, then the risk would be recorded as impact score 4. Similarly, if another risk would result in major reputational damage, the score would be 4. However, if a risk has two or more types of impact at the same level, then the score would be one degree higher (i.e., a score of 5 in the example).

FOUR ASSOCIATIONS

The case considers the strategy choice, risk analysis, and risk appetite of four associations:

1. Large London association (London & Quadrant, 70,000 housing units)
This is one of the largest associations with a very strong financial position. It is following an aggressive development policy with a mix of

Exhibit 8.2 Sample Impact Scale

Impact Score	Description	Strategic	Financial % of Turnover	Customers and Staff	Reputational	Legal/Regulatory
5	Very high	Major impact on direction of business	Above 10%			Compulsory transfer of assets
4	High	Major impact on important business objective	3.1% to 10%	Significant impact on many customers or staff Significant resource to rectify	Major adverse publicity and external interest with damage to reputation and/or long-term impact	Prosecution/regulatory supervision
3	Medium	Noticeable impact but business still on course	1.1% to 3%	Noticeable impact	Longer-term adverse publicity, locally contained	Loss of regulatory approval
2	Low	Minor importance	0.3% to 1%	Minor or short-term problems	Short-term local adverse publicity	More serious breach but no long-term implications
1	Very low		Less than 0.3%	Impact both minor and short-term	No adverse publicity	Minor breach of legal/regulatory requirements

intermediate rent, market rent, and houses for sale in order to meet the expanding housing needs of London and the prosperous South East. It has invented a number of innovative financial instruments and renting regimes to make this high rate of expansion possible.

2. Medium-sized South Wales association (RCT Homes Limited, 10,000 housing units)

Based in the Welsh valleys to the north of Cardiff, an area of acute depression, this association has set up a number of social enterprise subsidiaries to help provide employment in the area. The association is also participating in a risky joint venture hoping to build 1,000 units mainly in the northern hinterland of Cardiff, the prosperous Welsh capital.

3. Specialist association (Ability Housing Association, 550 housing units)

This association provides housing and support services to disabled people living in the South of England. It works in partnership with other agencies to help deliver flexible and tailored housing and support for people who want to live more independently. Its housing stock comprises mostly either wheelchair-standard housing or supported housing for people who need additional care or support.

4. Medium-sized association in the prosperous corridor to the west of London (GreenSquare Group, 11,000 housing units)

The GreenSquare Group was originally formed in 2008 from two associations (Westlea Housing Association and Oxford Citizens Housing Association). Another Oxford-based association, Oxbode, joined the Group in November 2012. The Group has achieved an improvement in administrative efficiency and the development of product expertise, with a mixed portfolio of housing product lines and support activities.

ASSOCIATION A: LONDON & QUADRANT

Quadrant Housing Association was set up in 1963 by a group of young professionals who found out about the plight of the homeless in London, bought a house, and converted it into three flats. Initially the association operated from a church crypt, but by 1972 it had its own office and a portfolio of 1,300 homes. In 1973 it merged with the London Housing Trust, which had been set up in 1967, and by 1979 London & Quadrant (L&Q) had 6,000 homes. Quadrant Housing Finance was set up as a subsidiary of L&Q in 1997 to raise funds in the capital markets, and the expansion continued. L&Q now owns and manages about 70,000 homes in London and the South East and employs 1,200 staff.

Mission Statement

Our mission is: *Creating places where people want to live.*
For us that means two things:

1. Maximising resident satisfaction with our homes, services, and neighbourhoods.
2. Responsible growth through new, sustainable investment models and new housing options that increase choice and mobility.

Both of these are vital to our continued success as the leading provider of affordable homes and services in London and the South East.[4]

Perceived Risks

The Board considers the following risks the most likely to affect future performance and our ability to achieve our five-year plan:

- Welfare reform: L&Q has allocated time and resources to understand the longer-term risk of welfare reform. We are working with local authorities to identify residents who will be affected and contacting them to ensure they are aware and prepared. Our focus has now turned to managing the transition. This includes targeting higher risk accounts, the recruitment of additional staff to deal with increased debt, and the creation of a financial inclusion team to support residents.
- Land cost inflation: We have embarked on a progressive development strategy to give us the flexibility to adapt in a fluid marketplace. Returns from private sale and rent portfolios reduce the impact of increased land costs on our affordable housing pipeline. L&Q has adopted a shared risk approach, where appropriate, through joint ventures to counter the impact of land cost inflation.
- Sales/mortgage availability: We adopt a bespoke marketing and sales strategy for each new development and undertake scenario modelling based on revenue and cost fluctuation. We work with mortgage lenders to ensure potential customers have access to advice on how much they can borrow and the range of products available. We also undertake market research to ensure the products offered meet market requirements.
- Withdrawal of capital grant funding beyond 2015: We have developed a sustainable cross-subsidy model for new homes, supported by our annual surplus. Our development strategy assumes no additional capital grant.
- Health and safety: A dedicated health and safety team supports all of L&Q activities. . . . The Group Board receives an annual report on progress against our health and safety strategy.
- Business continuity: We have effective IT and logistical back-up arrangements in place to ensure business continuity following a major event such as a fire. In particular L&Q has a disaster recovery data centre. This provides real time data replication along with capabilities for hosting our telephony and email in the event of a major incident.
- Protection of charitable assets: Our financial strategy includes sensitivity analysis and performance indicators. These demonstrate that non-charitable activities do not place our charitable assets at risk. All non-charitable projects require Board approval and include exit plans. L&Q will respond to regulatory thinking and requirements as they develop.
- Rent control: L&Q is working with Shelter on its Stable Rental Contract. This involves market rent increases pegged at a percentage over CPI or RPI (Retail Price Index) combined with longer-term (probably five year) tenancies. In the worst scenario, current exposure to market rent is limited as a proportion of total housing stock. A greater risk relates to further rent control for existing social rented homes. Any adverse change would be met with a reduction in our development appetite.
- Property prices: Savills predicts zero percentage growth in London during 2013 but over 25 percent growth over the next four years. L&Q's financial

strategy tests a worst case scenario twice yearly and concludes that a 25 percent reduction in house prices will not have a material effect on our covenants. Whilst property prices have fallen by more than 25 percent once over the last 30 years, and taken nearly a decade to recover, L&Q is a long-term property investor and able to withstand such events. We are able to delay construction and move completed homes into alternative tenures rather than sell at a loss. Finally we may also see a fall in land prices as an opportunity to invest for the future.

- Impact of austerity/welfare reform on resident satisfaction: Welfare reform combined with continued austerity measures could have an adverse impact on the outlook of residents and their general satisfaction. Resident satisfaction is a top priority for L&Q. We have put in place a service improvement plan that will deliver sustainable improvements through investment in our social mission, our culture, systems and process change.

The summarized financial statements of London & Quadrant for the previous five years are presented in Exhibit 8.3.

Choices Made in 2012/2013

To help relieve London's housing shortage, the size of the L&Q development program has been increased in the past year from £1.25 billion to £2 billion, and there are now 12,000 homes in the program, of which £250 million is for 1,000 homes for rent at market rates. This represents a quickly accelerating growth rate—in 2012/2013 L&Q completed 1,444 new homes, 952 of which were for social rent, 25 were for affordable rent, 222 were low-cost home ownership homes, 201 were for market sale, 10 were for private rent, and 34 were for intermediate rent. L&Q's in-house contractor, Quadrant Construction Services, handled over 231 of these homes, with a further 465 in progress at year-end.

In 2011 L&Q committed £100 million to the newly launched L&Q Foundation to tackle the disadvantaged by supporting projects that help people access training and employment, give opportunities to young people, provide guidance and support with managing finances, and build stronger communities.

In 2012/2013, over 4,000 people benefited from activities supported by the Foundation; £10 million was spent as follows:

- £5.6 million on community activities
- £1.9 million on giving residents financial advice and supporting Citizens Advice Bureau and Credit Unions
- £1.4 million on schemes to increase resident employability
- £1.1 million on youth schemes

ASSOCIATION B: RCT HOMES

RCT Homes Limited is the largest social landlord on Wales and winner of Business in the Community's Welsh Company of the Year 2012 Award. RCT is based in Pontypridd, in the Welsh county borough of Rhondda Cynon Taf, situated at the confluence of the Rhondda and Cynon Taff valleys. The town is famous for its old bridge, which, when it was constructed in 1756, had the longest single-span

Exhibit 8.3   Financial Performance of London & Quadrant

Panel A: Income and Expenditure Account

Income and expenditure account (£ million)	2013	2012	2011	2010	2009
Turnover	457	368	327	330	306
Operating costs and cost of sales	(238)	(243)	(240)	(276)	(224)
Operating surplus	181	144	89	87	66
Net interest charge	(70)	(65)	(62)	(43)	(41)
Surplus on disposal of assets	11	16	17	17	12
Taxation	(4)	—	—	—	—
Surplus for the year after tax	118	95	44	61	37

Panel B: Balance Sheet

Balance sheet (£ million)	2013	2012	2011	2010	2009
Housing properties at cost less depreciation	4,787	4,618	4,411	4,247	4,023
Social housing and other grants	(2,625)	(2,564)	(2,515)	(2,336)	(2,215)
Subtotals	2,162	2,054	1,896	1,911	1,808
Other tangible fixed assets and investments	144	51	55	53	28
Net current assets	395	340	457	355	196
	2,701	2,445	2,408	2,319	2,032
Loans due after one year	1,877	1,749	1,779	1,880	1,667
Other long-term liabilities	249	216	186	28	12
Cash flow hedge reserve	(93)	(77)	(24)	(28)	(42)
Revenue reserve	668	557	467	439	395
	2,701	2,445	2,408	2,319	2,032

Panel C: Cash Flow Statement

Cash flow statement (£ million)	2013	2012
Net cash inflow from operating activities	141.3	123.3
Interest paid/received	(93.1)	(83.1)
Capital expenditure		
House construction and purchase	(146.5)	(177.2)
Capital reinvestment in existing stock	(49.9)	(70.2)
Capital grants received	57.4	65.2
Purchase of other assets	(95.8)	(1.3)
Sale of fixed assets	26.5	36.1
Subtotal	(208.3)	(147.4)
Cash outflow before financing	(160.1)	(107.2)
Cash withdrawn from term deposits	56.9	26.2
Financing		
Loans received	250.0	—
Loans repaid	(135.5)	(3.4)
Increase/(decrease) in cash and cash equivalents	11.3	(84.4)

(continued)

Exhibit 8.3 (*Continued*)

Panel D: Financial Ratios and Statistics

Financial ratios and statistics	2013	2012	2011	2010	2009
Operating margin on social housing lettings	46%	46%	34%	37%	31%
Operating margin—all activities	40%	39%	27%	26%	22%
Interest cover—excl asset sales & disposals	212%	211%	142%	202%	161%
Interest cover—incl asset sales & disposals	277%	244%	170%	242%	190%
Net gearing	56%	53%	51%	53%	56%
Operating cost per unit managed £	2,900	2,700	3,200	3,100	3,300
Net debt per unit managed £	25,400	23,700	22,600	23,400	22,700
Homes managed (000's)	70.1	68.6	67.1	62.1	60.6
Estimated open market value of homes £ bn	12.0	10.8	10.3	9.4	8.5

Panel E: Product Profitability

Product profitability	2013 Turnover £m	2013 Operating Surplus £m
Social housing		
General needs	274.7	131.9
Supported housing	22.5	5.9
Intermediate market rent	16.2	8.0
Low-cost home ownership	49.7	19.6
Affordable rent	4.4	(0.3)
Other social housing activities	7.1	(4.8)
Community investment	0.2	(9.8)
	374.8	150.5
Other		
Outright sales	76.4	27.2
Market rent	2.6	1.4
Student accommodation	2.5	1.0
Commercial	0.5	0.5
Total	456.8	180.6
Disposal of fixed assets		11.5
Interest payable/receivable		(69.3)
Other		(0.3)
Tax		(4.4)
Surplus for year after tax		118.1

stone arch in the world. The coal mines that formerly were the basis of the area's economy were closed in the 1980s, and it has been difficult to attract new industry. In Rhondda Cynon Taf, the unemployment rate and the proportion of people of working age claiming benefits remain about 50 percent greater than in other parts of the United Kingdom.

RCT Homes was set up in 2007 to take over the ownership and management of more than 10,000 homes in the borough, which had been allowed to get into bad condition. In particular, over 30 percent of them did not meet the Welsh Housing Quality Standard, which the Welsh government said should be satisfied by the end of 2012. The performance of some services that tenants had been receiving was also well below the standard they had a right to expect.

RCT is a community mutual organization with nearly 5,000 members and a board comprising 15 people: five tenants, five members nominated by the Rhondda Cynon Taff Council, and five independent members. Board members are not paid. RCT now employs more than 500 staff and has four unregistered subsidiary companies—Meadow Prospect, Grow Enterprise Wales (GrEW), Homeforce, and Porthcwlis.

At transfer, funding was agreed from the government and from Lloyds Bank to pay for the required works, and 86 performance promises were made to tenants. Eighty promises, including achievement of the Welsh Housing Quality Standard, were signed off as delivered by the RCT Homes Members' Forum and the local authority ahead of schedule in December 2012, and RCT has written to every household to inform tenants and invite challenge.

The RCT Subsidiaries[5]

RCT has a strong wider social agenda—encompassing financial, social, and digital inclusion and employment and addressing health inequalities—aimed at building individual and community capacity to improve tenancy and neighborhood sustainability. Some of these aims are planned to be realized through the four RCT subsidiaries.

RCT Homes has major pipeline proposals for development of new homes via its new development subsidiary, Porthcwlis, working with the Cardiff developer, Bellerophon. The proposals are at an early stage of development, and no homes have yet been completed. A new financing and delivery vehicle has been produced, which has secured £1 billion of private sector finance and which, it is hoped, will enable the public sector, housing associations, and private developers to come together to build many affordable homes without the need for capital grant funding from the Welsh government. An initial development of four homes, the first of a pilot for 30 homes at Cwmbach in the Cynon Valley, is now in progress.

Meadow Prospect, RCT's regeneration charity, delivers community-enhancing regeneration projects by working with partner organizations. These support three core objectives:

1. Community capacity building projects, including youth work and supported employment programs
2. Community-based renewable energy projects
3. Social enterprise development

Grow Enterprise Wales (GrEW) is an award-winning social enterprise sub-sidiary of Meadow Prospect that aims to move local people closer to the workplace by offering work experience and basic life skills training.

Homeforce was set up in 2010 as a subsidiary to carry out annual gas safety checks, which are mandatory under current safety legislation, and gas-based responsive repairs. RCT Homes Group Board agreed in 2012 that Homeforce would expand to become the sole contractor for boiler and heating installations and would undertake half of the electrical improvement works program. Home-force also became the appointed contractor for the completion of the power flush-ing program, which forms part of the long-term maintenance program of the cur-rent stock in RCT Homes' properties.

The Sheltered Housing Remodelling Programme, being achieved within the parent company is a major program for the remodeling of RCT's sheltered housing accommodation for the elderly. This continued in 2012/2013 with the commence-ment of works in seven schemes. In 2012/2013, £9.2 million was spent, with a total of £12.4 million having been spent since transfer on improving sheltered accom-modation. A further two schemes are planned to commence in 2013/2014.

Perceived Risks

The quotations that follow are from the RCT Homes 2012/2013 Group financial statements:

> During 2012 the group risk map was developed to ensure it has a greater strategic focus. It identifies the following risks and challenges to the Group:
>
> - Welfare Reform—As previously stated the changes proposed to welfare benefits will significantly change the UK housing sector and will place increased financial pressure on tenants and subsequently us. Direct pay-ments to tenants increase the risk of our bad debt provision increasing and we will need to find innovative ways to keep cash collection rates at an acceptable level.
> - Rent Restructure—The consultation document issued by Welsh Govern-ment in 2011 indicated that our rent envelope is lower than the current aver-age rents charged across the borough, resulting in lower rent increases than those currently included in the business plan. The implementation of the new regime has been delayed until April 2014. This risk coupled with Wel-fare Reform has the potential to have a major impact on the rental income of the Group.
> - Sheltered Remodelling Programme—As the project continues we need to ensure specifications are clear and build costs remain within budget. We need to ensure the preferred models are future proofed and fit for purpose whilst at the same time ensuring value for money. Active financial manage-ment, planning, and tenant input will be key to the success of this project.
> - Impact on New Build to the Group—We currently have permission to pilot 200 properties through the framework operated by Porthcwlis. Any further increase in volumes will need consent from our funders.
> - Expansion of Homeforce—As Homeforce expands into new work streams and begins to operate outside of the Group, we need to ensure growth is manageable in terms of resources and working capital. Asset investment

will need to be closely managed to ensure cash does not become over committed and profitability on contracts is maintained.
- Long-Term Financial Viability of GrEW—Work is in progress to reduce costs within GrEW and expand its customer base to make the business more financially secure. During this time Meadow Prospect will continue to support its subsidiary.

The summarized financial statements of RCT Homes for the previous five years are presented in Exhibit 8.4.

RCT Homes entered into a value-added tax (VAT)[6] shelter coincident with the date of transfer of the housing stock, to carry out an agreed schedule of refurbishment works to the properties. The value of these works was £359 million. The cost to the borough council of contracting for these works to be undertaken was offset

Exhibit 8.4 Financial Performance of RCT Homes

Panel A: Income and Expenditure Account					
Income and expenditure account (£ million)	2013	2012	2011	2010	2009
Turnover	45.9	44.6	43.6	40.0	36.6
Operating costs	(33.0)	(38.5)	(29.6)	(28.0)	(27.1)
Operating surplus	12.9	6.1	14.0	12.0	9.5
Net interest charge	(1.4)	(0.5)	(0.0)	(0.5)	0.3
Surplus on disposal of assets	0.5	0.4	0.5	0.5	1.8
Actuarial (loss) on pension scheme	(0.1)	(3.8)	(4.0)	(1.3)	(6.2)
Surplus for the year after tax	11.9	2.2	10.4	10.7	5.4

Panel B: Balance Sheet					
Balance sheet (£ million)	2013	2012	2011	2010	2009
Housing properties at cost less depreciation and grant	96.6	75.1	46.4	27.7	11.8
Other tangible fixed assets and investments	1.3	1.6	1.9	2.3	2.5
Net current assets/(liabilities)	(0.8)	(1.8)	1.6	(10.6)	(7.6)
	97.1	74.9	49.9	19.4	6.7
Loans due after one year	(47.0)	(37.0)	(18.0)	(5.0)	(3.0)
Other long-term liabilities (pensions)	(7.2)	(6.8)	(3.1)	0.0	0.0
Net assets	42.9	31.1	28.8	14.4	3.7

Panel C: Cash Flow Statement		
Cash flow statement (£ million)	2013	2012
Net cash inflow from operating activities	16.3	9.9
Interest paid/received	(1.5)	(1.0)
Capital expenditure		
Improvement works on properties	(27.0)	(33.1)
Social housing and other grants	1.6	3.7
Purchase of other assets	(0.3)	(0.3)
Sale of fixed assets	0.5	0.5
Subtotal	(25.2)	(29.2)
Cash outflow before financing	(10.4)	(20.2)
Loans advances received	10.0	19.0
(Decrease) in cash and cash equivalents	(0.4)	(1.2)

against an equal increase in the purchase price of the stock paid to the borough council by RCT Homes. This transaction is not reflected in the financial statements in accordance with Financial Reporting Council (FRS) 5,[7] reporting the substance of transactions over the legal form. The works contracted are to be carried out over an envisaged 15-year period and are being recognized as they are undertaken, in accordance with the accounting policy for major, cyclical, and responsive repairs. In the event RCT Homes does not complete the work specified, the development agreement may be terminated at no financial loss to RCT Homes.

At April 2013, it was envisaged that there will be a further £136 million of expenditure under the remaining nine years of the VAT shelter.

ASSOCIATION C: ABILITY HOUSING ASSOCIATION

Ability Housing Association is a specialist association that provides housing and support services to disabled people living in the South of England. It works in partnership with local authority housing, social services, and Supporting People teams, the Homes and Communities Agency, and mainstream housing associations to help deliver flexible and tailored housing and support for people who want to live more independently. The Ability Housing Association operates in London, Essex, Oxfordshire, Berkshire, Hampshire, Surrey, Dorset, and West Sussex. Its housing stock comprises mostly either wheelchair-standard housing or supported housing for people who need additional care or support.

The association was set up in 1999 when the Cheshire Foundation Housing Association changed its name and relaunched as Ability. At this point it had 285 homes under management, employed 47 staff, and had a turnover of £1.86 million. In 2003 the national Supporting People program began, and Ability entered into Supporting People contracts with 18 local authorities. In 2004 Ability set up its first mental health support services, in the London borough of Merton, and in 2004 Ability was rated as the second most efficient registered social landlord (RSL) in England. In 2007 it was selected to provide mental health support services in Surrey and new supported housing in Swindon. Over the next 10 years it grew steadily, and in 2009 the REAP resettlement agency transferred its activities to Ability. By 2012 Ability had over 550 homes under management, and had a turnover of £8.8 million. In 2012, for the second year running, Ability was recognized as one of the *Sunday Times'* 100 Best Not-for-Profit Organisations to Work For.

In its corporate plan Ability states its values as follows:

Our pursuit of our visions is underpinned by the following values which permeate the whole organisation:

We focus on ability not disability

– We focus on what each person *can* do—on their ability—rather than what they can't do. We work together with our customers to help them overcome barriers to their own personal independent living goals.

We engage actively for feedback

– We engage actively with our customers, colleagues, and partners to seek feedback that helps us to understand how we can improve what we do and how we do it.

We value difference

– We respect and value the individuality of each person; we believe that differences are strengths and that diversity enriches our lives and communities.

We demonstrate integrity

– We encourage a culture of openness, honesty, and personal accountability; we respond to a challenge by asking ourselves what **we** *can do* to help and always deliver on our promises.

Ability provides the following services:

Housing with Support, to promote independent living, for example:

- Assistance with learning independent living skills
- Advice and assistance with claiming welfare benefits and housing benefit
- Advice and assistance with budgeting and managing bills
- Advice on aids and adaptations
- Assistance with reporting repairs and managing tenancies
- General counseling and support with day-to-day living
- Assistance with arranging personal care and contacting other agencies involved in care and welfare

Most of the Housing with Support is provided in self-contained flats or bungalows, although some of it is in shared housing or studio apartments with some shared facilities.

Floating Support, similar support to that just described but provided without housing. This service helps people with physical disabilities, learning disabilities, or mental health–related support needs to manage their homes.

The **Accessahome database**, to enable disabled people, housing associations, and local authorities to make better decisions about housing. Accessahome records details about accessible features of properties—for example, if a property has been purpose-built to a wheelchair standard, lifetime homes standard, or mobility standard, or it has been specially adapted for a disabled person, for example, with a stair lift, level-access shower, or adapted kitchen. The database offers a matching service for both landlords and applicants and support information for disabled people, so that a landlord with an accessible or adapted property that is available for letting can search the database for applicants whose needs match the features of the property.

Perceived Risks

Extracts from 2012 Annual Report:

The removal of the Supporting People "ring-fence,"[8] coupled with extreme funding cuts faced by local authorities, has cast doubt on the future of many supported housing and social care services. At Ability we place faith in maintaining the quality and value for money of services and being able to demonstrate positive outcomes for customers and commissioners.

Exhibit 8.5   Financial Performance of Ability Housing Association

Panel A: Income and Expenditure Account					
Income and expenditure account (£ million)	2012	2011	2010	2009	2008
Turnover	8.8	8.6	8.6	7.4	5.6
Operating costs and cost of sales	(7.6)	(7.4)	(7.3)	(6.5)	(4.9)
Operating surplus	1.2	1.2	1.3	0.9	0.7
Net interest charge	(0.4)	(0.2)	(0.1)	(0.1)	(0.1)
Surplus on disposal of assets	0.1	0.4	—	—	0.1
Taxation	—	—	—	—	—
Surplus for the year after tax	0.9	1.4	1.2	0.8	0.7
Panel B: Balance Sheet					
Balance sheet (£ million)	2012	2011	2010	2009	2008
Housing properties at cost less depreciation & grant	18.9	16.7	13.0	8.8	7.2
Other tangible fixed assets and investments	1.1	1.1	1.1	0.5	0.5
Net current assets	0.8	0.2	0.8	0.4	0.3
	20.7	20.0	14.9	9.7	8.0
Creditors due after more than one year	(9.9)	(8.1)	(6.6)	(2.5)	(1.6)
Other long-term liabilities	—	—	—	—	—
	10.8	9.9	8.3	7.2	6.4

We are pleased therefore to have been able to agree with local authorities in London Borough of Hillingdon and West Sussex extensions to some of our most valuable services. Sadly this has not always been the way and, following a competitive tendering exercise, some of our floating support services in Slough have been transferred to another provider. . . .

Again this year we have seen the loss of some of our supporting people contracts with others reducing in value. We expect further reductions in the years ahead. By winning new business through competitive tender processes we have been able to replace a part of the lost income.

The summarized financial statements of Ability Housing Association for the previous five years are presented in Exhibit 8.5.

ASSOCIATION D: GREENSQUARE

Recently, locally based housing associations have been amalgamating together to form regional groups. Once the amalgamation has been accomplished, the groups often organize themselves on a product and activity basis, invest in innovative new products, develop vigorously, and continue to absorb further local associations.

GreenSquare Group Limited is typical of such a group, operating across Wiltshire, Oxfordshire, Gloucestershire, Swindon, and the surrounding areas. GreenSquare was originally formed in 2008 from two associations (Westlea

Housing Association and Oxford Citizens Housing Association). Another Oxford-based association, Oxbode, joined the GreenSquare Group in November 2012. GreenSquare now manages over 11,000 properties.

The strategy just described allows the reduction of administration costs and the development of product expertise. GreenSquare has the following:

- Development construction services provided by its in-house subsidiary Tidestone
- Property investment and maintenance of public open spaces undertaken by its commercial subsidiary Oakus
- Gas servicing and renewable energy business undertaken by a new acquisition, GW Sparrow & Company Ltd., based in Swindon

GreenSquare Group now has the following key business streams:

- General needs housing for rent, primarily by families who are unable to rent or buy at open market rates
- Supported housing and housing for older people who need additional housing-related support or additional care
- Low-cost home ownership, primarily shared ownership whereby residents purchase a share in the equity of their homes and pay rent to the association on the remainder
- Building large volumes of new affordable housing and a lead development partner under the Homes and Communities Agency (HCA)'s National Affordable Housing Programme (NAHP)
- A newly registered housing association, GreenSquare Community Housing Association, was set up in 2012. This will build houses financed by a £32 million sale-and-leaseback financing from Aviva, which will enable the Group to respond to new development opportunities as well as continuing to deliver its existing HCA program.
- The GreenSquare Academy has recently been set up to offer training and life skills development to residents, as many associations are becoming increasingly involved in education and vocational training.

Amalgamated organization structures carry a danger of reduced resident involvement; GreenSquare therefore set up three communities boards in 2012/2013 to ensure that its services and how the neighborhoods are run are kept under close review. Last year £0.9 million was allocated to support community projects. GreenSquare also has a Resident Scrutiny Panel to carry out inspections and engage directly with residents.

Objectives and Strategy

GreenSquare's mission is seen as "housing people, building communities." The achievement of this is underpinned by four key vision statements:

1. Develop good quality housing to meet a wide and growing range of needs.
2. Create places where people want to live, and support a good quality of life.

3. Provide the range and quality of services our customers want.
4. Grow our activities and improve our financial strength and sustainability.

The following list of key risks is drawn from the 2012/2013 GreenSquare Group Limited annual report:

Key Risks	Comment
Current economic climate and impact on public sector funds and the housing market	The continued restraints on government spending, changes to the housing benefit rules, along with the wider economic downturn, have been identified as key risks to the group. Such changes are likely to impact on the group's ability to deliver its planned development program and may also affect core activities.
Delivery of development program	Successful delivery of the program depends on continued support from the HCA for the Group, as well as the ability and willingness of development contractors to continue to build the Group's schemes in a challenging economic environment.
Availability of finance	Availability of loan finance is key to a thriving housing market, with potential impact on the Group's ability to deliver its development program as well as difficulty for potential shared ownership purchasers to raise finance.
Low demand for housing properties developed for sale	The Group's development program includes low-cost home ownership. Success depends on demand for the properties. Low demand in the housing market generally has an impact on low-cost home ownership schemes.
Rise in final salary pension scheme liabilities to unaffordable level	The Group could face significant liabilities for meeting pension fund deficits. The Group's contributions to the fund may need to increase significantly in order to fund the scheme.
Change in government policy or new legislation	Such changes could have significant impact on the sector and therefore the operations of the Group (e.g., changes to the planning or tax regimes may increase costs of new developments, reducing scheme affordability).
Performance failure	Performance failures in services to our customers would affect the Group's rating with the HCA and its reputation in the sector. Failure to deliver its development program may result in a withdrawal of capital grant.
Loss of key staff	Retention of quality staff and managers is key to successful delivery of the Group's business plans.

Selected summarized financial statements of GreenSquare Group Limited from the previous five years are presented in Exhibit 8.6.[9]

Exhibit 8.6   Financial Performance of GreenSquare Group

Panel A: Income and Expenditure Account					
Income and expenditure account (£ million)	2013	2012	2011	2010	2009
Turnover	56.2	48.5	45.0	45.3	45.7
Operating costs and cost of sales	(43.1)	(37.2)	(35.0)	(35.0)	(36.8)
Operating surplus	13.1	11.3	10.0	10.3	8.9
Net interest charge	(11.0)	(9.5)	(9.2)	(8.4)	(7.7)
Surplus on disposal of assets	0.8	0.3	0.1	0.2	0.1
Other income (note 1)	10.5				
Taxation	0.1	(0.3)	(0.1)	(0.02)	(0.1)
Surplus for the year after tax	13.5	1.8	0.8	2.1	1.0

Panel B: Balance Sheet					
Balance sheet (£ million)	2013	2012	2011	2010	2009
Housing properties at current valuation	545.2	384.5	350.6	343.2	301.5
Other tangible fixed assets and investments	6.3	6.2	5.7	5.7	5.7
Net current assets	20.3	3.3	(4.1)	4.3	6.9
	571.8	394.0	352.2	353.2	314.1
Loans due after one year	(281.6)	(237.3)	(211.3)	(210.3)	(194.1)
Other long-term liabilities	(6.7)	(6.7)	(5.1)	(10.2)	(4.6)
	283.3	150.0	135.8	132.7	115.4

Panel C: Cash Flow Statement					
Cash flow statement (£ million)	2013	2012	2011	2010	2009
Net cash inflow from operating activities	20.9	20.1	20.1	20.1	20.1
Interest paid/received	(10.7)	(10.6)	(10.6)	(10.6)	(10.6)
Tax paid	(0.1)	(0.1)	(0.1)	(0.1)	(0.1)
Cash from acquisition of Oxbode	2.3	(0.9)	(0.9)	(0.9)	(0.9)
Capital expenditure					
House construction and purchase	(29.2)	(39.1)	(39.1)	(39.1)	(39.1)
Capital grants received	4.1	9.3	9.3	9.3	9.3
Purchase of other assets	(1.1)	(0.7)	(0.7)	(0.7)	(0.7)
Sale of fixed assets	1.7	1.0	1.0	1.0	1.0
Subtotal	(24.5)	(29.5)	(29.5)	(29.5)	(29.5)
Cash outflow before financing	(12.1)	(21.0)	(21.0)	(21.0)	(21.0)
Cash (invested in) term deposits	(13.7)	(2.2)	(2.2)	(2.2)	(2.2)
Financing					
Loans received	31.8	26.6	26.6	26.6	26.6
Loans repaid	(1.0)	(0.8)	(0.8)	(0.8)	(0.8)
Increase in cash and cash equivalents	5.0	2.6	2.6	2.6	2.6

Note 1: Gift on acquisition when Oxbode joined the Group in November 2012.

QUESTIONS

You are asked to look at the four housing associations and choose one of them whose location most resembles your own home area, together with another association in a contrasting area. You are asked to address four questions for each of the two associations that you have chosen:

1. Given the fact that the association is a charity, with risks related both to its financial and charitable aims and any profits made being reinvested to support its charitable aims,

what do you assess as the biggest risks facing the association and what is your assessment of these risks? Note that "for-profit" activities such as building houses for sale can also contribute to an association's aims (e.g., to provide affordable housing within its chosen area of operation).

2. Considering the list of products in the "Background" section, how do you rate their potential risks and returns for the association, again in relation to its charitable aims and viability constraints and in the context of the association's operating environment?

3. In the light of the association's financial position and its charitable aims, how high should be the risk appetite of the association? Is one of the generic strategies listed in the "Sector Issues" section appropriate for the association, and if not then what should the association's strategy be?

4. Can you suggest product growth targets and appropriate risk limits that will enable the association to develop safely and dynamically in the short/medium term?
    The association data was drawn in 2013 from current real cases, and it may help you to investigate the "actual" cases and their contexts.

NOTES

1. The Decent Homes Standard is a technical standard for public housing introduced by the United Kingdom government in April 2002. It underpinned the Decent Homes Programme brought in by the Labour party, which aimed to provide a minimum standard of housing conditions for all those who are housed in the public sector (i.e., council housing and housing associations). The content of the standard is described in the House of Commons Library Research Paper 03/65 "Delivering the Decent Homes Standard: Social Landlords' Opinions and Progress."

2. For more detail, see www.homesandcommunities.co.uk/sites/default/files/our-work/sector-risk-profile-120611.pdf.

3. See section 5.3.5, "Defining Risk Criteria," in ISO 31000:2009.

4. The quotes are from the L&Q 2013 financial statements; see www.lqgroup.org.uk/_assets/files/LQ0363_Financial-Statements-2013_LR.pdf. For more information about L&Q see www.lqgroup.org.uk.

5. For more information on the RCT subsidiaries, please refer to: www.rcthomes.co.uk, www.rcthomes.co.uk/main.cfm?type=PORTHCWLIS&object_id=2745, www.bplltd.co.uk/index.php, www.meadowprospect.co.uk/default.htm, and www.meadowprospect.co.uk/growenterprisewales/default.htm.

6. A value-added tax (VAT) is a form of consumption tax. From the perspective of the buyer, it is a tax on the purchase price. From that of the seller, it is a tax only on the value added to a product, material, or service, from an accounting point of view, by this stage of its manufacture or distribution. The manufacturer remits to the government the difference between these two amounts, and retains the rest for itself to offset the taxes it had previously paid on the inputs, see HM Revenue & Customs: Introduction to VAT, www.hmrc.gov.uk/vat/start/introduction.htm.

7. FRS 5 addresses the problem of what is commonly referred to as off-balance-sheet financing. One of the main aims of such arrangements is to finance a company's assets and operations in such a way that the finance is not shown as a liability in the company's balance sheet. A further effect is that the assets being financed are excluded from the accounts, with the result that both the resources of the entity and its financing are understated. *Source:* Financial Reporting Council.

8. Ring-fencing occurs when a portion of a company's assets or profits are financially separated without necessarily being operated as a separate entity. This might be for regulatory reasons, creating asset protection schemes with respect to financing arrangements, or segregating into separate income streams for taxation purposes. Ring-fencing guarantees

that funds allocated for a particular purpose will not be used for anything else. *Source:* www.oxforddictionaries.com/definition/english/ring-fence. *Note:* The removal of the Supporting People ring-fence allows local authorities to divert to other activities the money allocated to them for this program. The result has been severe cuts in the total Supporting People funding.

9. For GreenSquare's financial statements, see: www.greensquaregroup.com/upload/5236 bbc772028GS.pdf and www.greensquaregroup.com/upload/50619fd12a9aaGS_report11 12.pdf.

REFERENCES

Fraser, John, and Betty J. Simkins, eds. 2010. *Enterprise Risk Management: Today's Leading Research and Best Practices for Tomorrow's Executives*. Hoboken, NJ: John Wiley & Sons.

Sector Risk Profile. 2012. Homes and Communities Agency, London, England. www.homesandcommunities.co.uk/sites/default/files/our-work/sector-risk-profile-120611.pdf.

ABOUT THE CONTRIBUTOR

Following a mathematics degree at Cambridge University and six years' KPMG strategy consultancy experience, John Hargreaves took up a series of financial positions, including periods as the Financial Controller of National Freight, a stint running Shell's central financial and management accounting and planning systems, and three years as the Finance Director of London Underground. Since 1991 John has specialized in risk management, initially as Corporate Finance Director of Barclays Bank, where he was responsible for introducing risk management systems following the previous United Kingdom depression.

In 1996 he became Managing Director of Hargreaves Risk and Strategy, which has clients in the housing, banking, oil, and transport sectors. The consultancy has implemented risk management systems in about 60 organizations. John is a leading expert on the quantification of risks. He has conducted research over a number of years on the risk profile of the UK social housing sector, initially through study of client risk maps but also through analysis of the risks that occurred in a sample of 41 companies. This knowledge was used in 2005 in the design of the sector's highly successful risk-related regulatory system.

John is also an authority on the relationship between risk management and strategy, and for 15 years has run a course on strategic management for an MSc program at the London School of Economics.

CHAPTER 9

Lessons from the Academy

ERM Implementation in the University Setting

ANNE E. LUNDQUIST
Western Michigan University

The tragedy at Virginia Tech, infrastructure devastation at colleges and universities in the New Orleans area in the aftermath of Hurricane Katrina, the sexual abuse scandal at Penn State, the governance crisis at the University of Virginia, American University expense-account abuse, and other high-profile university situations have created heightened awareness of the potentially destructive influence of risk and crisis for higher education administrators.[1] The recent *Risk Analysis Standard for Natural and Man-Made Hazards to Higher Education Institutions* (American Society of Mechanical Engineers–Innovative Technologies Institute 2010) notes that "resilience of our country's higher education institutions has become a pressing national priority" (p. vi). Colleges and universities are facing increased scrutiny from stakeholders regarding issues such as investments and spending, privacy, conflicts of interest, information technology (IT) availability and security, fraud, research compliance, and transparency (Willson, Negoi, and Bhatnagar 2010). A statement from the review committee assembled to examine athletics controversies at Rutgers University is not unique to that situation; the committee found that "the University operated with inadequate internal controls, insufficient inter-departmental and hierarchical communications, an uninformed board on some specific important issues, and limited presidential leadership" (Grasgreen 2013).

The situation at Penn State may be one of the clearest signals that risk management (or lack thereof) has entered the university environment and is here to stay. In a statement regarding the report, Louis Freeh, chair of the independent investigation by his law firm, Freeh Sporkin & Sullivan, LLP, into the facts and circumstances of the actions of Pennsylvania State University, said the following:

> In our investigation, we sought to clarify what occurred … and to examine the University's policies, procedures, compliance and internal controls relating to identifying and reporting sexual abuse of children. Specifically, we worked to identify any failures or gaps in the University's control environment, compliance programs and culture which may have enabled these crimes against children to occur on the Penn State campus, and go undetected and unreported for at least these past 14 years.

The chair of Penn State's board of trustees summed it up succinctly after the release of the Freeh Report (Freeh and Sullivan 2012) regarding the university's handling of the sexual abuse scandal: "We should have been risk managers in a more active way" (Stripling 2012).

The variety, type, and volume of risks affecting higher education are numerous, and the public is taking notice of how those risks are managed. Accreditation agencies are increasingly requiring that institutions of higher education (IHEs) demonstrate effective integrated planning and decision making, including using information gained from comprehensive risk management as a part of the governance and management process.[2] Credit rating agencies now demand evidence of comprehensive and integrated risk management plans to ensure a positive credit rating, including demonstration that the board of trustees is aware of, and involved in, risk management as a part of its decision making.[3] Through its Colleges and Universities Compliance Project, the Internal Revenue Service (IRS) is considering how to hold IHEs responsible for board oversight of risk, investment decisions, and other risk management matters.[4] The news media has a heightened focus on financial, governance, and ethical matters at IHEs, holding them accountable for poor decisions and thus negatively affecting IHE reputations. In response to this, many IHEs have implemented some form of enterprise risk management (ERM) program to help them identify and respond to risk.

THE HIGHER EDUCATION ENVIRONMENT

Colleges and universities have often perceived themselves as substantially different and separate from other for-profit and not-for-profit entities, and the outside world has historically viewed and treated them as such. Colleges and universities have been viewed as ivory towers, secluded and separated from the corporate (and thus the federal regulatory and, often, legal) world. Higher education was largely a self-created, self-perpetuating, insular, isolated, and self-regulating environment. In this culture, higher education institutions were generally governed under the traditional, independent "silos of power and silence" management model, with the right hand in one administrative area or unit often unaware of the left hand's mission, objectives, programs, practices, and contributions in another area.

John Nelson (2012), managing director for the Public Finance Group (Healthcare, Higher Education, Not-for-Profits) for Moody's Investors Service, observed that higher education culture is somewhat of a contradiction in that colleges and universities are often perceived as "liberal," whereas organizationally they tend to be "conservative and inward-looking."[5] Citing recent examples at Penn State and Harvard, he noted that colleges and universities can be "victims of their own success"; a past positive reputation can prevent boards from asking critical questions, and senior leadership from sharing troubling information with boards, and this can perpetuate a culture that isn't self-reflective, thus increasing the likelihood for a systemic risk management or compliance failure. The Freeh Report (2012) is instructive regarding not only the Penn State situation, but the hands-off and rubber-stamp culture of university boards and senior leaders more broadly. The Freeh Report found that the Penn State board failed in its duty to make reasonable inquiry and to demand action from the president, and that the president, a senior vice president, and the general counsel did not perform their duties.

The report calls these inactions a "failure of governance," noting that the "board did not have regular reporting procedures or committee structure to ensure disclosure of major risks to the University" and that "Penn State's 'Tone at the Top' for transparency, compliance, police reporting, and child protection was completely wrong, as shown by the inaction and concealment on the part of its most senior leaders, and followed by those at the bottom of the University's pyramid of power."

In his text regarding organizational structures in higher education, *How Colleges Work*, Birnbaum (1988) notes that, organizationally and culturally, colleges and universities differ in many ways from other organizations. He attributes this difference to several factors: the "dualistic" decision-making structure (comprised of faculty "shared governance" and administrative hierarchy); the lack of metrics to measure progress and assess accountability; and the lack of clarity and agreement within the academic organization on institutional goals (based, in part, on the often competing threefold mission of most academic organizations of teaching, research, and service). Because of these organizational differences, Birnbaum notes that the "processes, structures, and systems for accountability commonly used in business firms are not always sensible for [colleges and universities]" (p. 27).

While noting that colleges and universities are unique organizations, Birnbaum also observes that they have begun to adopt more general business practices, concluding that "institutions have become more administratively centralized because of requirements to rationalize budget formats, implement procedures that will pass judicial tests of equitable treatment, and speak with a single voice to powerful external agencies" (p. 17).

This evolution to a more businesslike culture for IHEs has been evolving since the 1960s and has brought significant societal changes while seeing the federal government, as well as state governments, begin to enact specific legislation affecting colleges and universities.[6] The proliferation of various laws and regulations, coupled with the rise of aggressive consumerism toward the end of the 1990s, has led to an increased risk of private legal claims against institutions of higher education—and their administrators—as well as a proliferation of regulatory and compliance requirements. Higher education is now generally treated like other business enterprises by judges, juries, and creative plaintiffs' attorneys, as well as by administrative and law enforcement agencies, federal regulators—and the public.

Mitroff, Diamond, and Alpaslan (2006) point out that despite their core educational mission, colleges and universities are really more like cities in terms of the number and variety of services they provide and the "businesses" they are in. They cite the University of Southern California (USC) as an example, noting that USC operates close to 20 different businesses, including food preparation, health care, and sporting events, and that each of these activities presents the university with different risks. Jean Chang (2012), former ERM director at Yale University, observed that IHEs are complicated businesses with millions of dollars at stake, but they don't like to think of themselves as "enterprises."

Organizational Type Impacts Institutional Culture

While Birnbaum (1988) notes that IHEs differ in important ways from other organizational types, especially for-profit businesses, he also concludes that colleges and universities differ from each other in important ways. Birnbaum outlines five models of organizational functioning in higher education: collegial, bureaucratic, political, anarchical, and cybernetic. In Bush's (2011) text on educational leadership, he groups educational leadership theories into six categories: formal, collegial, political, subjective, ambiguity, and cultural. In their discussion of organizational structure, Bolman and Deal (2008) provide yet another method for analysis of organizational culture, identifying four distinctive "frames" from which people view their world and that provide a lens for understanding organizational culture: structural, human resources, political, and symbolic.

Each of these models can provide a conceptual framework by which to understand and evaluate the culture of a college or university. Understanding the organizational type of a particular institution is imperative when considering issues such as the process by which goals are determined, the nature of the decision-making process, and the appropriate style of leadership to accomplish goals and implement initiatives. What works in one university organizational type may not be effective in another. The leadership style of senior administration may be operating from one frame or model while the culture of the faculty may be operating from another, thus affecting policy and practice in positive or negative ways.

While not true across the board, for-profit organizations tend to operate from what Bush as well as Bolman and Deal refer to as the *formal* or *structural* models and Birnbaum terms *bureaucratic*. The structural frame represents a belief in rationality. Some assumptions of the structural frame are that "suitable forms of coordination and control ensure that diverse efforts of individuals and units mesh" and that "organizations work best when rationality prevails over personal agendas" (Bolman and Deal 2008, p. 47). Understanding this cultural and framing difference is important when considering the adoption and implementation of ERM in the university environment, and can help to explain why many university administrators and faculty are skeptical of the more corporate approach often taken in ERM implementation outside of higher education.

Bush observes that the *collegial* model has been adopted by most universities and is evidenced, in part, by the extensive committee system. Collegial institutions have an "emphasis on consensus, shared power, common commitments and aspirations, and leadership that emphasizes consultation and collective responsibilities" (Birnbaum, p. 86). Collegial models assume that professionals also have a right to share in the wider decision-making process (Bush 2011, p. 73). Bush points out that collegial models assume that members of an organization agree on organizational goals, but that often various members within the institution have different ideas about the central purposes of the institution because most colleges and universities have vague, ambiguous goals. Birnbaum describes the *collegium* (or university environment) as having the following characteristics:

> The right to participate in institutional affairs, membership in a congenial and sympathetic company of scholars in which friendships, good conversation, and mutual aid flourish, and the equal worth of knowledge in various fields that precludes preferential treatment of faculty in different disciplines. (p. 87)

ERM (or risk management and compliance initiatives in general) tend to be viewed as more corporate functions and to align with formal, structural, and bureaucratic aims, goal setting, planning, and decision making. The chart in Exhibit 9.1 outlines management practices and how they are viewed from the

Exhibit 9.1   Distinctions between Structural and Collegial Elements of Management*

Elements of Management	Formal/Structural			Collegial/Human Resources		
	Bolman and Deal Institutional	Bush Institutional	Birnbaum Institutional	Bolman and Deal	Bush	Birnbaum
Level at which goals are determined	Institutional	Institutional	Institutional	Institutional through agreement and consensus		
Process by which goals are determined	Vertical and lateral processes	Set by leaders	Based on organizational structure and roles	Agreement	Agreement	Consensus
Relationship between goals and decisions	Organizations exist to achieve established goals	Decisions based on goals	Conscious attempt to link means to ends and resources to objectives	Shared sense of direction and commitment	Decisions based on goals	Strong and coherent culture and value consensus informs decisions
Nature of the decision process	Rational; rules, policies, and standard operating procedures	Rational	Rational; compliance with rules and regulations	Egalitarianism; teams	Collegial	Deliberative consensus
Nature of structure	Organizations increase efficiency and enhance performance through specialization and division of labor	Objective reality; hierarchical	Designed to accomplish large-scale tasks by systematically coordinating the work of many individuals	Organizations exist to serve human needs; must be a good fit between organization and people	Lateral	Collegium
Style of leadership	Established authority	Leader establishes goals and initiates policy	Leader is concerned with planning, directing, organization, staffing, and evaluating	Doesn't control or overly structure; sensitive to both task and process; use of teams	Leader seeks to promote consensus	Leader is "first among equals," consultation and collective responsibilities

*Adapted from Bush (2011), 199 (Figure 9.1).

formal/structural and collegial/human resources models. As will become clear in the University of Washington ERM implementation case described in this chapter, the culture of higher education in general, and the institution-specific culture of the particular organization, cannot be ignored when adopting or implementing an ERM program, and may be the most important element when making ERM program, framework, and philosophy decisions.

Risks Affecting Higher Education

One way in which colleges and universities are becoming more like other organizations is the type and variety of risks affecting them. Risk and crisis in higher education may arise from a variety of sources: a failure of governance or leadership; a business or consortium relationship; an act of nature; a crisis related to student safety or welfare or that of other members of the community; a violation of federal, state, or local law; or a myriad of other factors. The University Risk Management and Insurance Association (URMIA 2007) cites several drivers that put increased pressure and risk on colleges and universities, including competition for faculty, students, and staff; increased accountability; external scrutiny from the government, the public, and governing boards; IT changes; competition in the marketplace; and increased levels of litigation. A comprehensive, yet not exhaustive, list of risks affecting higher education is outlined in Exhibit 9.2. Risks unmitigated at the unit, department, or college level can quickly lead to high-profile institutional risk when attorneys, the media, and the public get involved. Helsloot and Jong (2006) observe that higher education has a unique risk as it relates to the generation and sharing of its core task: "to gather, develop, and disseminate knowledge" (p. 154), noting that the "balance between the unfettered transfer of knowledge, on the one hand, and security, on the other, is a precarious one" (p. 155).

EMERGENCE OF ERM IN HIGHER EDUCATION

In the corporate sector, interest in the integrated and more strategic concept of enterprise risk management (ERM) has grown significantly in the past 15 years (Arena, Arnaboldi, and Azzone 2010). Certain external factors affected the adoption and implementation of ERM practices in corporations, including significant business failures in the late 1980s that occurred as a result of high-risk financing strategies (URMIA 2007). Governments in several European countries took actions and imposed regulatory requirements regarding risk management earlier than was done in the United States, issuing new codes of practice and regulations such as the Cadbury Code (1992), the Hampel Report (1998), and the Turnbull Report (1999). In 2002, the Public Company Accounting Reform and Investor Protection Act (otherwise known as Sarbanes-Oxley, or SOX) was enacted in the United States. In 2007, the Securities and Exchange Commission (SEC) issued guidance placing greater emphasis on risk assessment and began to develop requirements for enterprise-wide evaluation of risk. In February 2010, the SEC imposed regulations requiring for-profit corporations to report in depth on how their organizations identify risk, set risk tolerances, and manage risk/reward trade-offs throughout the enterprise.

While widespread in the corporate sector, in large part due to regulatory compliance, ERM is fairly new in higher education. Gurevitz (2009) observes that

Exhibit 9.2   Risks Affecting Higher Education

Institutional Area	Types of Risk
Boards of Trustees and Regents, President, Senior Administrators	Accreditation
	Board performance assessment
	CEO assessment and compensation
	Conflict of interest
	Executive succession plan
	Fiduciary responsibilities
	IRS and state law requirements
	Risk management role and responsibility
Business and Financial Affairs	Articulation agreements
	Bonds
	Budgets
	Business ventures
	Cash management
	Capital campaign
	Contracting and purchasing
	Credit rating
	Debt load/ratio
	Endowment
	Federal financial aid
	Fraud
	Gift/naming policies
	Insurance
	Investments
	Loans
	Outsourcing
	Transportation and travel
	Recruitment and admissions model
Compliance with Federal, State, and Local Laws, Statutes, Regulations, and Ordinances	Americans with Disabilities Act (ADA)/Section 504
	Copyright and fair use
	Drug-Free Schools and Communities Act
	Family Educational Rights and Privacy Act (FERPA)
	Health Insurance Portability and Accountability Act of 1996 (HIPAA)
	Higher Education Opportunity Act IRS regulations
	Integrated Postsecondary Education Data System (IPEDS)
	Jeanne Clery Disclosure of Campus Security Policy and Campus Crime Statistics Act (Clery Act)
	National Collegiate Athletic Association (NCAA)/National Association of Intercollegiate Athletics (NAIA) regulations
	Record retention and disposal
	Tax codes
	Whistle-blower policies
Campus Safety and Security	Emergency alert systems for natural disaster or other threat
	Emergency planning and procedures
	Incident response

(continued)

Exhibit 9.2 (*Continued*)

Institutional Area	Types of Risk
Campus Safety and Security (*continued*)	Infectious diseases
	Interaction with local, state, and federal authorities
	Minors on campus
	Terrorism
	Theft
	Violence on campus
	Weapons on campus
	Weather
Information Technology	Business continuity
	Cyber liability
	Electronic records
	Information security
	Network integrity
	New technologies
	Privacy
	System capacity
	Web page accuracy
Academic Affairs	Academic freedom
	Competition for faculty
	Faculty governance issues
	Grade tampering
	Grants
	Human subject, animal, and clinical research
	Intellectual property
	Internship programs
	Joint programs/partnerships
	Laboratory safety
	Online learning
	Plagiarism
	Quality of academic programs
	Student records
	Study abroad
	Tenure
Student Affairs	Admission/retention
	Alcohol and drug use
	Clubs and organizations
	Conduct and disciplinary system
	Dismissal procedures
	Diversity issues
	Fraternities and sororities
	Hate crimes
	Hazing
	International student issues
	Psychological disabilities issues
	Sexual assault
	Student death
	Student protest
	Suicide

Exhibit 9.2 *(Continued)*

Institutional Area	Types of Risk
Employment/Human Resources	Affirmative action
	Background checks
	Discrimination lawsuits
	Employment contracts
	Grievances
	Labor laws
	Performance evaluation
	Personnel matters
	Sexual harassment
	Termination procedures
	Unions
	Workplace safety
Physical Plant	Building and renovation
	Fire
	Infrastructure damage
	Off-site programs
	Public-private partnerships
	Residence hall and apartment safety
	Theft
Other	Alumni
	Athletics
	External relations
	Increased competition for students, faculty, and staff
	Increased external scrutiny from the public, government, and media
	Medical schools, law schools
	Vendors

educational institutions "have been slower to look at ERM as an integrated business tool, as a way to help all the stakeholders—trustees, presidents, provosts, CFOs, department heads, and frontline supervisors—identify early warning signs of something that could jeopardize a school's operations or reputation." In 2000, the Higher Education Funding Council of England enacted legislation requiring all universities in England to implement risk management as a governance tool (Huber 2009). In Australia, the Tertiary Education Quality Standards Agency (TEQSA 2013) evaluates the performance of higher education providers against a set of threshold standards and makes decisions in relation to their performance in line with three regulatory principles, including understanding an institution's level of risk.

In the United States, engaging in risk management efforts and programs for IHEs is not specifically required by accrediting agencies or the federal government. Perhaps because it is not required, ERM has not been a top focus for boards and senior administrators at IHEs. Tufano (2011) points out that risk management in the nonprofit realm, including higher education, is significantly less developed than in much of the corporate world and often still has a focus on avoidance of loss rather than setting strategic direction. Mitroff, Diamond, and Alpaslan's (2006) survey assessing the state of crisis management in higher education revealed that colleges and universities were generally well prepared for certain crises, particularly fires, lawsuits, and crimes, in part because certain regulations impose requirements. They were also well prepared for infrequently experienced but high-profile situations such as athletics scandals, perhaps based on their recent prominence in the media. However, they were least prepared for certain types of crises that were frequently experienced such as reputation and ethics issues, as well as other non-physical crises such as data loss and sabotage.[7] A survey conducted by the Association of Governing Boards of Universities and Colleges and United Educators (2009) found that, of 600 institutions completing the survey, less than half of the respondents "mostly agreed" that risk management was a priority at their institution. Sixty percent stated that their institutions did not use a comprehensive, strategic risk assessment to identify major risks to mission success. Recent high-profile examples may be beginning to change that. The Freeh Report regarding Penn State determined that "the university's lack of a robust risk-management system contributed to systemic failures in identifying threats to individuals and the university and created an environment where key administrators could 'actively conceal' troubling allegations from the board" (Stripling 2012).

ADOPTING AND IMPLEMENTING ERM IN COLLEGES AND UNIVERSITIES

In 2001, PricewaterhouseCoopers and the National Association of College and University Business Officers (NACUBO) sponsored a think tank of higher education leaders to discuss the topic of ERM in higher education, likely in response to widespread discussion in the for-profit sector and in anticipation of potential regulatory implications for higher education. The group included Janice Abraham, then president and chief executive officer of United Educators Insurance, as well as senior administrators from seven universities.[8] The focus of their discussion was on the definition of risk; the risk drivers in higher education; implementation of risk management programs to effectively assess, manage, and monitor risk; and how to proactively engage the campus community in a more informed dialogue regarding ERM. Their conversation produced a white paper, "Developing a Strategy to Manage Enterprisewide Risk in Higher Education" (Cassidy et al. 2001). In 2007, NACUBO and the Association of Governing Boards of Universities and Colleges (AGB) published additional guidance in their white paper, "Meeting the Challenges of Enterprise Risk Management in Higher Education." The University Risk Management and Insurance Association (URMIA) also weighed in with its white paper, "ERM in Higher Education" (2007). In 2013, Janice Abraham wrote a text published by AGB and United Educators, entitled *Risk Management: An Accountability Guide for University and College Boards*. These documents provide guidance and information to institutions considering the implementation of an ERM program and discuss the unique aspects of the higher education environment when considering ERM implementation.

Several authors have discussed the transferability of the ERM model to higher education, even with the cultural and organizational differences that abound between the for-profit environment and higher education. URMIA (2007) concluded that "the ERM process is directly applicable to institutions of higher education, just as it is to any other 'enterprise'; there is nothing so unique to the college or university setting as to make ERM irrelevant or impossible to implement" (p. 17). Whitfield (2003) assessed the "feasibility and transferability of a general framework to guide the holistic consideration of risk as a critical component of college and university strategic planning initiatives" (p. 78) and concluded that "the for-profit corporate sector's enterprise-wide risk management framework is transferable to higher education institutions" (p. 79).

National conferences for higher education associations such as NACUBO, AGB, URMIA, and others had presentations on ERM. Insurers of higher education, such as United Educators and Aon, as well as consultants such as Accenture and Deloitte, among others, provided workshops to institutions and published white papers of their own, such as the Gallagher Group's "Road to Implementation: Enterprise Risk Management for Colleges and Universities" (2009). In the early 2000s, many IHEs rushed to form committees to examine ERM and hired risk officers in senior-level positions, following the for-profit model.[9] However, when specific regulations such as those imposed by the SEC for for-profit entities did not emerge in the higher education sector, interest in highly developed ERM models at colleges and universities began to wane. Gurevitz (2009) points out that the early ERM frameworks weren't written with higher education in mind and were often presented "in such a complicated format that it made it difficult to translate the concepts for many universities."

Institutions with ERM programs have taken various paths in their selection of models and methods and have been innovative and individualized in their approaches. There is no comprehensive list of higher education institutions with ERM programs, and not all IHEs with integrated models use the term *ERM*. Exhibit 9.3 shows a snapshot of IHEs that have adopted ERM; a review of their websites demonstrates the various risk management approaches adopted by IHEs and the wide variability in terminology, reporting lines, structure, and focus. In many instances, those IHEs with highly developed programs today had some form of "sentinel event" (regulatory, compliance, student safety, financial, or other) that triggered the need for widespread investigation and, therefore, the development of more coordinated methods for compliance, information sharing, and decision making. In other situations, governing board members brought their business experience with ERM to higher education, recognizing the "applicability and relevance of using a holistic approach to risk management in academic institutions" (Abraham 2013, p. 6).

Regardless of the impetus, the current focus appears to be on effectively linking risk management to strategic planning. Abraham points out that many higher education institutions are recognizing that an effective ERM program, with the full support of the governing board, "will increase a college, university or system's likelihood of achieving its plans, increase transparency, and allow better allocation of scarce resources. Good risk management is good governance" (p. 5). Ken Barnds (2011), vice president at Augustana College, points out that "many strategic planning processes, particularly in higher education, spent an insufficient amount of time thinking about threats and weaknesses." Barnds believes that "an honest and thoughtful assessment of the college's risks … would lead [Augustana] in a positive, engaged, and proactive direction." A recent Grant Thornton (2011) thought paper urges university leaders to think about more strategic issues as part of their risk management, including board governance, IRS scrutiny of board oversight

Exhibit 9.3 Sample of Colleges and Universities with ERM Programs

Institution	Title of Person with ERM Responsibility	Website
Duke University	Executive Director of Internal Audit	http://internalaudits.duke.edu/risk-assessment/index.php
Emory University	Chief Audit Officer	www.emory.edu/EMORY_REPORT/stories/2010/04/19/risk_management.html
Georgia State University	Director, Enterprise Risk Management	www.gsu.edu/accounting/63370.html
Iowa State University	Associate Vice President for Budget and Planning	www.provost.iastate.edu/what-we-do/erm
Johnson & Wales	Director of Compliance, Internal Audit, and Risk Management	www.jwu.edu/content.aspx?id=57825
Maricopa County Community College District (MCCCD)	Director of Enterprise Risk Management	www.maricopa.edu/publicstewardship/governance/adminregs/auxiliary/4_16.php
Ohio University	Associate Vice President for Risk Management and Safety	www.ohio.edu/riskandsafety/urmi.htm
Texas A&M University System	Office of Risk Management and Benefits Administration	www.tamus.edu/offices/risk/riskmanage/guide/enterprise-risk-management/
University of Alaska System	Chief Risk Officer	www.alaska.edu/risksafety/
University of California	Risk Services, Office of the President	www.ucop.edu/enterprise-risk-management/
University of Denver	Director of Enterprise Risk Management	www.du.edu/internal-audit/internal_audit/faq.html
University of Iowa	Senior Vice President of Finance and Operations and Treasurer	www.uiowa.edu/~fusrm/EnterpriseRiskManagement/index.html
University of Maryland	Vice President for Planning and Accountability	www.umaryland.edu/accountability-old/risk-management/
University of Notre Dame	Director of Risk Management and Safety	http://riskmanagement.nd.edu/about/
University of Vermont	Senior Strategist for Enterprise Risk and Planning, Office of the Vice President for Finance & Administration	www.uvm.edu/~erm/
University of Maryland	Vice President for Planning and Accountability	www.umaryland.edu/accountability-old/risk-management/
University of Washington	Risk Analyst	http://f2.washington.edu/fm/erm
Yale University	Director of ERM	http://ogc.yale.edu/riskmanagement

practices, investment performance in university endowments, indirect cost rates in research, changes in employment practices, and outsourcing arrangements.

Regardless of terminology, there is an increased priority on taking a more enterprise-wide approach to risk management and moving from a compliance-driven approach to a comprehensive, strategic approach across and throughout the organization that is used to positively affect decision making and impact mission success and the achievement of strategic goals. Tufano (2011) points out that even in the corporate environment, top leaders are not inclined to work through a detailed step-by-step risk management process, but rather take a top-level approach. In the university environment, this means asking three fundamental questions: What is our mission? What is our strategy to achieve it? What risks might derail us from achieving our mission? Richard F. Wilson, president of Illinois Wesleyan University, may best summarize the current perspective of senior-level higher education administrators:

> When I first started seeing the phrase "enterprise risk management" pop up in higher education literature, my reaction was one of skepticism. It seemed to me yet another idea of limited value that someone had created a label for, to make it seem more important than it really was. Although some of that skepticism remains, I find myself increasingly in sympathy with some of its basic tenets … [especially] the analysis that goes into decisions about the future. Most institutions are currently engaged in some kind of strategic planning effort driven, in part, by the need to protect their financial viability and vitality for the foreseeable future. … Bad plans and bad execution of good ideas can put an institution at risk fairly quickly in the current environment. Besides examining what we hope will happen if a particular plan is adopted, we should also devote time to the consequences if the plan does not work. I still cannot quite get comfortable incorporating enterprise risk management into my daily vocabulary, but I have embraced the underlying principles. (Wilson 2013)

THE UNIVERSITY OF WASHINGTON: A JOURNEY OF DISCOVERY

The University of Washington (UW) has a robust enterprise risk management (ERM) program that is moving into its seventh year. The program began with what administrators[10] at UW call a "sentinel event," settling a Medicare and Medicaid overbilling investigation by paying the largest fine by a university for a compliance failure—$35 million. This led the new president, Mark Emmert, to formally charge senior administrators in 2005 with the task of identifying best practices for "managing regulatory affairs at the institutional level by using efficient and effective management techniques" (UW ERM Annual Report 2008, p. 4). At the outset in 2006, the objective for UW was to "create an excellent compliance model built on best practices, while protecting its decentralized, collaborative, and entrepreneurial culture" (Collaborative ERM Report 2006, p. vi). The ERM process at UW has been what Ann Anderson, associate vice president and controller, terms "a journey of discovery." ERM has developed and evolved at UW, moving from what UW administrators describe as an early compliance phase, through a governance phase to a mega-risk phase. Currently, the University of Washington is focused on two objectives: (1) strengthening oversight of top risks, and (2) enhancing coordination and integration of ERM activities with decision-making processes at the university. This case study will describe the decision-making and implementation process at UW, as well as outline various tools and frameworks that UW adopted and adapted for use not only in the higher education setting in general, but to fit specifically within the university's decentralized culture.

Institutional Profile

Founded in 1861, the University of Washington is a public university enrolling some 48,000 students and awarding approximately 10,000 degrees annually (see Exhibit 9.4). The institution also serves approximately 47,000 extension students. There are nearly 650 student athletes in UW's 21 Division I men's and women's teams. There is a faculty/staff of over 40,000, making UW the third-largest employer in the state of Washington. The university is comprised of three campuses with 17 major schools and colleges and 13 registered operations abroad. It has a $5.3 billion annual budget, with $1.3 billion in externally funded research and $2.6 billion in clinical medical enterprise. UW has been the top public university in federal research funding every year since 1974 and has been among the top five universities, public and private, in federal funding since 1969. The university has an annual $9.0 billion economic impact on the state of Washington.

Culture at UW

When appointed to serve on the President's Advisory Committee on ERM (PACERM) in 2007, Professor Daniel Luchtel commented, in the context of talking about risk assessments, that "the number of issues and their complexity is stunning. The analogy that comes to mind is trying to get a drink of water from a fire hose" (2007 ERM Annual Report, p. 4). As with most higher education institutions, especially research universities, along with the core business of the teaching and learning of undergraduate and graduate students, the faculty are focused on the creation of new knowledge. "The University of Washington is a decentralized yet collaborative entity with an energetic, entrepreneurial culture. The community members are committed to rigor, integrity, innovation, collegiality, inclusiveness, and connectedness" (Collaborative Enterprise Risk Management Final Report 2006, p. v).

Faculty innovation and the idea of compliance don't always go hand in hand in higher education, and UW is no exception. Research associate professor David Lovell, vice-chair of the Faculty Senate in 2007–2008, expresses it well:

> "Compliance" [is] not necessarily a good word for faculty members. . . . What lies behind [that] is the high value faculty accord to personal autonomy. . . . The notion of a culture of compliance sounds like yet another extension of impersonal, corporate control, shrinking the arena of self-expression in favor of discipline and conformity. . . . Over the last ten months, I've come to understand that you're not here to get in our way, but to make it possible for us faculty legally to conduct the work we came here to do. . . . I hope that working together, we can try to spread such understanding further, so that we can make compliance—or whatever term you choose—less threatening to faculty and frustrating to staff. (Annual ERM Report 2008, pp. 6–7)

STUDENTS

48,022 students were enrolled at the UW in the fall of 2009

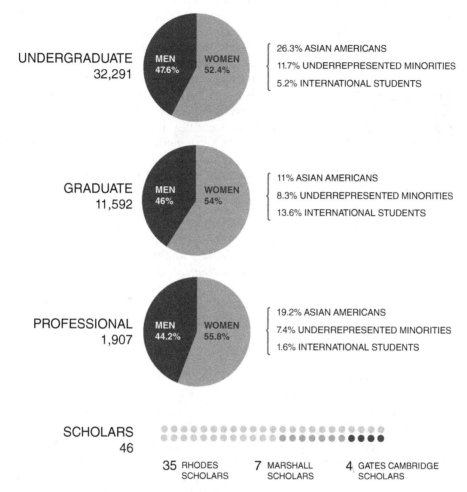

UNDERGRADUATE
32,291

MEN
47.6%

WOMEN
52.4%

26.3% ASIAN AMERICANS

11.7% UNDERREPRESENTED MINORITIES

5.2% INTERNATIONAL STUDENTS

GRADUATE
11,592

MEN
46%

WOMEN
54%

11% ASIAN AMERICANS

8.3% UNDERREPRESENTED MINORITIES

13.6% INTERNATIONAL STUDENTS

PROFESSIONAL
1,907

MEN
44.2%

WOMEN
55.8%

19.2% ASIAN AMERICANS

7.4% UNDERREPRESENTED MINORITIES

1.6% INTERNATIONAL STUDENTS

SCHOLARS
46

35 RHODES
SCHOLARS

7 MARSHALL
SCHOLARS

4 GATES CAMBRIDGE
SCHOLARS

Exhibit 9.4 University of Washington Student Profile
From University of Washington Fact Book: http://opb.washington.edu/content/factbook.

Organizationally, the institution is divided into silos, which has historically focused risk mitigation within those silos.

Implementation History at UW

On April 22, 2005, President Mark Emmert sent an e-mail to the deans and cabinet members in which he said: "With the most recent example of compliance issues, we have again been reminded that we have not yet created the culture of compliance that we have discussed on many occasions." He went on to say that "the creation of a culture of compliance needs to be driven by our core values and commitment to doing things the right way, to being the best at all we do.... We need to know that the manner in which we manage regulatory affairs is consistent with the best practices in existence."

The Sentinel Event: Largest Fine at a Medical School

The Collaborative Enterprise Risk Management Report for the University of Washington (2006) began with the following: "Over the past few years, the UW has been confronted by a series of problems with institution-wide implications, including research compliance, financial stewardship, privacy matters, and protection of vulnerable populations" (p. v). The situation with the highest impact on the university began when Mark Erickson, a UW compliance officer, filed a complaint alleging fraud in the UW's Medicare and Medicaid billing practices. The 1999 complaint prompted a criminal investigation, guilty pleas from two doctors, and a civil lawsuit resulting in the $35 million settlement, the largest settlement made by an academic medical center in the nation. The federal prosecutor claimed that "many people within the medical centers were aware of the billing problems" and that "despite this knowledge, the centers did not take adequate steps to correct them" (Chan 2004). UW's 2006 ERM Annual Report acknowledges that, in addition to the direct cost of the fines, there were also indirect costs in terms of additional resources for reviews of university procedures, increased rigor and frequency of audits, and an incalculable damage to the university's reputation. The federal prosecutor acknowledged that UW's efforts to reform its compliance program have been "outstanding" (Chan 2004). He further noted that since the lawsuit was filed, the university "has radically restructured their compliance office. The government is very pleased with the efforts the UW is taking to take care of these errors."

Leadership from the Top: President Outlines the Charge

At the time of the medical billing scandal, Lee L. Huntsman was president of UW. Huntsman had formerly been the acting provost, associate dean for scientific affairs at the school of medicine, and a professor of bioengineering. The UW Board of Regents had appointed Huntsman in a special session when Richard McCormick, the incumbent, accepted the presidency at Rutgers. Huntsman served for 18 months as president and continued as Special Assistant to the President and Provost for Administrative Transition until 2005 and as a senior adviser to the university for several more years. Mark A. Emmert, former chancellor of Louisiana State University and a UW alumnus, was appointed as the 30th president of UW and professor with tenure at the Evans School on June 14, 2004.

In April 2005, President Emmert charged V'Ella Warren, Vice President for Financial Management, and David Hodge, Dean of the College of Arts and Sciences, with conducting a preliminary review of best practices in compliance and enterprise risk management in corporate and higher education institutions. Warren engaged the Executive Director of Risk Management, Elizabeth Cherry, and the Executive Director of Internal Audit, Maureen Rhea, to conduct a literature search on enterprise risk management, particularly in higher education. Cherry and Rhea engaged Andrew Faris, risk management analyst, to assist, and the three spent nearly two years (from 2004 to 2006) conducting the literature search and finding out how risk management was functioning on other campuses. As they conducted their research, they continued to report their findings to Vice President Warren. They also piloted the risk assessment process with various departments at UW.

Based on their findings and discussions with Vice President Warren, a draft report was compiled to provide initial guidance of the development of a UW-specific framework. The report provided an overview of various approaches to compliance, described best practices at four peer universities (University of Texas system, University of Minnesota, University of Pennsylvania, and Stanford University), identified the common problems encountered in several recent compliance problems at UW, and offered suggestions for actions that UW might take in the effective management of compliance and risk. President Emmert then charged Warren and Hodge to cochair the recommended Strategic Risk Initiative Review Committee (SRIRC). The role of the SRIRC was to continue to investigate best practices in university risk management and make recommendations about a structure and framework for compliance that would fit the UW culture. In a memo to the SRIRC regarding that review, Warren and Hodge noted that they had "developed a framework for university-wide risk and compliance management which builds on [UW]'s decentralized and collaborative character." President Emmert also made it clear that the proposed model should be driven by UW's core values as well as promote "effective use of people's time and energy." In a memo to the deans and cabinet members in 2005, President Emmert declared that UW did not "want or need another layer of bureaucracy."

The SRIRC was comprised of broad university representation, including the Executive Vice President, the Associate Vice President for Medical Affairs, the Senior Assistant Attorney General, the Vice Provost-elect for Research, the Vice Provost for Planning and Budgeting, the Chancellor of the University of Washington–Tacoma, the Athletic Director, the Dean of the School of Public Health and Community Medicine, the Provost and Vice President for Academic Affairs, the Dean of the School of Nursing, the Special Assistant to the President for External Affairs, the Vice President of Student Affairs, two faculty members, and two students. Meeting throughout the fall semester, the SRIRC reviewed the preliminary research material provided by Hodge and Warren and their team and discussed a variety of issues, including the structure for risk management, how risk assessment has been and could be conducted, communication issues, methods for reporting risks, ways to report progress, and others. For each initiative, they asked the following three questions: *Does this proposal add value? What obstacles are apparent and how can they be addressed? How could this proposal be improved?*

In addition to formal meetings, Cherry, Rhea, and Faris conducted one-on-one meetings with the SRIRC members to gather more information about how they viewed implementation at the university. Because one of the recommendations was the creation of a Compliance Council, meetings were also conducted throughout the campus with director-level personnel to survey their interests and suggestions regarding that aspect of the proposed model. Prior to the formal implementation of the ERM program, resources were also dedicated to create an infrastructure to sustain the recommended model. Faris's role as risk manager was formally revised to create a full-time ERM analyst position within the Office of Financial Management in the Finance and Facilities division and a half-time ERM project manager position was created, filled by Kerry Kahl.

Advisory Committee Recommendations: Create a Culture-Specific ERM Program

In February 2006, Hodge and Warren put forth to President Emmert a Collaborative Enterprise Risk Management Proposal developed by the SRIRC. The proposal recommended that "the UW adopt an integrated approach to managing risk and compliance, commonly called enterprise risk management (ERM)." They acknowledged that the proposed changes were not intended to "replace what already works across the university," but rather to "augment the existing organization with thoughtful direction, collaboration, and communication on strategic risks" (Collaborative ERM Final Report, February 13, 2006). At the outset, the SRIRC acknowledged that the structure and priorities of the ERM program would likely evolve and develop over time, but the members of the committee were confident that they had created a "strong, yet flexible framework within which to balance risk and opportunity" (February 14, 2006, memo to President Emmert).

While the report acknowledged the impetus for the creation of the ERM program (the $35 million compliance failure fine), it focused on the positive impact an ERM program could have for UW, beyond addressing compliance concerns. The report defined key terms and made recommendations based on three basic parameters: scope of the framework, organizational structure for the framework, and philosophy of the program. Each aspect was framed in the context of the literature review and campus comparisons; UW-specific recommendations were put forth based on SRIRC discussion and analysis.

Scope of the Risk Framework

The report reviewed and discussed the various approaches taken by organizations in practicing risk management, from a basic practice of risk transfer through insurance to a more integrated institution-wide approach. It acknowledged that, prior to implementation, some key decisions would need to be made: Would the scope of the program be institution-wide or targeted at the school, college, or unit level? Would it include all risks (compliance, finances, operations, and strategy) or be focused on certain categories of risk? ERM was cited as "the most advanced point on the continuum," a model that integrates risk into the organization's strategic discussions. The report also summarized a Centralized Compliance Management approach. This model, rather than encompassing all risks, would focus primarily on legal and regulatory compliance. It was noted that "while both are university-wide approaches, they vary in a number of important aspects, including scope, objective, and benefits" (p. 6).

The report also summarized the ERM models at four IHEs, based on interviews with compliance and audit managers at those institutions. Noting that all four were institution-wide approaches, Pennsylvania and Texas were identified as having adopted a more corporate philosophy; Minnesota, a compliance approach with a centralized style; and Stanford, a collaborative ERM approach (see Exhibit 9.5). The report recommended developing a "collaborative, institution-wide risk management model" for UW, one that "ensures that UW creates an excellent compliance model based on best practices, while protecting its decentralized, collaborative, and entrepreneurial culture" (p. 28).

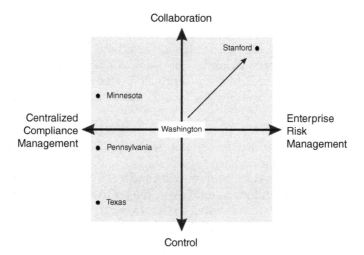

Exhibit 9.5 UW's Approach to Risk Management Compared to Other Institutions
From University of Washington Collaborative Enterprise Risk Management Final Report, February 13, 2006.

Organizational Structure

Based on a review of the literature and discussions with risk and audit managers at other universities, the report also summarized various models and structures for organizing the risk management activities. One method was to appoint a central risk officer with institution-wide oversight and responsibility. With this model, key decisions would need to be made regarding reporting lines and the placement of that position within the organization. The report also outlined UW's current approach to risk management, noting that it had moved beyond the insurance approach, "which is usually reactive and ad hoc," but also observing that responsibility for specific risks was currently distributed among the institution's organizational silos (p. 15). It further noted that "the UW does not formally integrate risk and compliance into its strategic conversations at the university-wide level" (p. 15). While acknowledging the good progress being made in several areas (including UW Medicine, the newly restructured Department of Audits, and the Office of Risk Management), the report highlighted the weaknesses of the current approach, including the fact that "due to the size, decentralization, and complexity of the institution, a proliferation of compliance, audit, and risk management activities has grown up around separate and distinct risk areas, each largely operating in a self-defined stovepipe" (p. 18).

Philosophy of the Program

The report also discussed the philosophy of a proposed risk management program, asking whether the preferred approach should focus on enforcing law and regulation—a compliance or control approach—or be one that "encouraged cooperation between faculty and staff to develop flexible compliance approaches—a collaborative approach" (p. 2). After sharing the findings from the literature review and the institutional profiles of the peer institutions, the report outlined three guiding principles to shape the evolution of compliance and risk management at UW: (1) foster an institution-wide perspective, (2) ensure that regulatory management is consistent with best practices, and (3) protect UW's decentralized, collaborative, entrepreneurial culture. In light of these principles, the report made the following eight recommendations, detailing the key elements and implementation suggestions for each:

1. Integrate key risks into the decision-making deliberations of senior leaders and Regents.
2. Create an integrated, institution-wide approach to compliance.
3. Ensure that good information is available for the campus community.
4. Create a safe way for interested parties to report problems.
5. Minimize surprises by identifying emerging compliance and risk issues.
6. Recommend solutions to appropriate decision makers.
7. Check progress on compliance and risk initiatives.
8. Maintain a strong audit team.

EVOLUTION OF ERM AT UW

The SRIRC report acknowledged that the ERM concept was not new, but that it has not been fully implemented at many organizations, especially in higher education. The development of risk management within an organization was discussed, noting that the management of risk develops along a continuum, with early models focused on hazard risks only and mitigation being accomplished primarily through the purchase of insurance. As risk models evolve at an organization, other risk types are added to the model and more cross-functional participation by other units begins to occur. Ultimately, strategic risks are added to the conversation and there is an integration of information from all units across the university. It is at this point that risk can be viewed as both an opportunity and a threat and where mitigation priorities can be more clearly linked to the strategic objectives of the organization.

In 2006, when the ERM program and model were proposed, UW viewed itself as being in the middle of the continuum (see Exhibit 9.6). The report noted:

> Although many operational units, committees, and administrative bodies handled the risks faced in their own environments well, there is little cross-functional sharing of information. The opportunity aspect of risk is therefore not fully utilized by the University and risk mitigation priorities are not consistently driven by the institution's strategic objectives. (p. 4)

The 2012 ERM Annual Report observes that "the ERM program has continued to evolve, developing structural mechanisms to support the 8 initial recommendations" (p. 2).

Faris and Kahl commented that the first few years of implementation of ERM at UW were focused on risk assessments. They spent most of their time (both working with the ERM committees and in their roles as ERM staff) performing risk

UW Evolution of ERM

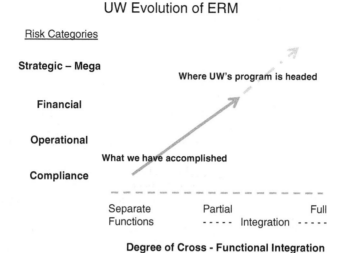

Exhibit 9.6 Evolution of ERM at the University of Washington
From University of Washington 2009 ERM Annual Report, p. 4.

assessments using the risk mapping process (e.g., writing a risk statement, ranking the risks for likelihood and impact, plotting the risks on a 5 × 5 map). In the first four or five years, they conducted nearly 35 risk assessments across the university. Based on broad cross-functional topics identified by the President's Advisory Committee on ERM (PACERM), the risk assessments were facilitated by Faris and Kahl with temporary teams put together to meet three to five times over the course of the year to write risk statements, rank them, and put together suggestions for mitigation.

The first five years of ERM at UW were "formative" and focused on the following key activities:

- Developing a common language around risk
- Conducting individual risk assessments
- Focusing discussion and mitigation on financial and enrollment challenges
- Comparing financial strength (as gauged by Moody's Investors Service) against peers
- Drafting an initial compendium of enterprise-wide success metrics

Well-written, clear annual reports to the president, the Board of Regents, and the UW community helped to connect the dots and keep the strategic overarching goals front and center, even as employees at the unit level were continuously engaged in the more operational aspects of ERM. Exhibit 9.7 summarizes the implementation time line from the formalized inception of ERM at UW to the present. A review of the chart shows how the UW has continued to focus on moving from an initial focus on hazard risk to a more integrated, strategic approach to enterprise risk management.

Exhibit 9.7   University of Washington ERM Implementation Time Line

Academic Year	Initiatives*
2005–2006	President Emmert charged administrators with review of best practices and development of broad institutional compliance/risk framework for UW. Warren and Hodge drafted report with overview of institution-wide approaches, best practices at four peer universities, common compliance problems faced by UW, and suggestions for next steps.
2006–2007	Developed a central focus and common language for evaluating risk across the university. ERM structure formed (including PACERM, Compliance Council). First UW-wide risk map was compiled. Office of Risk Management dedicated one FTE to ERM initiative. Dedicated $4.8 million in funds for integrity/compliance/stewardship initiatives, including animal care, student life counseling, human subjects, global activities, and IT security. Information about ERM program included in reinsurance renewal discussions with international underwriters. First Annual Report to the Board of Regents.
2007–2008	Identified key strategic and mega risks for the institution. Expanded Compliance Council to form COFi. Rolled out Enterprise Risk Management Toolkit for units to do self-assessments. UW Medicine and Department of Athletics presented annual reports on their compliance programs and ongoing efforts to minimize risks and address current issues. Continued development of the Institutional Risk Register. Internal Audit department expanded from nine to 15 staff.
2008–2009	Focused on financial crisis and demographics. PACERM formed two mega-risk subgroups to apply ERM processes at a strategic level: extended financial crisis and faculty recruitment and retention. HR advance planning for economic downturn and major reduction in state funding. Office of Risk Management conducted first Employment Practices Liability Seminar. ERM web pages were enhanced. Hired a new Executive Director for Audits. Second ERM Report to the Board of Regents.
2009–2010	Development of the UW Integrated Framework based on COSO model. PACERM focused discussion on how to remain competitive. Initial exploration of enterprise-wide dashboard of success metrics. Use of risk assessments in business case alternatives and research proposals.
2010–2011	PACERM evaluated the university's academic personnel profile and oversaw major information technology projects. Assessed institutional financial strength in comparison to peers (Moody's). More than 200 ERM Toolkits provided to universities and companies.
2011–2012	Development of enterprise-wide dashboard of success metrics. UW's work recognized as a "Best Practice" by the Association of Governing Boards for Universities and Colleges (AGB).

*All initiatives, including others not detailed in this chart, are outlined in more detail in the UW ERM Annual Reports, available at the website: http://f2.washington.edu/fm/erm.

ERM STRUCTURE AT UW

The organizational structure for ERM at UW arose out of the initial recommendations of the SRIRC. In its aggregate, the UW ERM program is comprised of the following areas, working together to create an effective structure: UW units; ERM staff; Compliance, Operations, and Finance Council (COFi Council); President's Advisory Committee on ERM (PACERM); Internal Audit; and the UW President and Provost (see Exhibit 9.8).

UW Units

At the unit level, staff and faculty take ownership of the activities that give rise to risk. They conduct risk and opportunities identification and self-assessments. They develop strategies and take action to mitigate and monitor risk. They are encouraged to share a summary of their risk assessments with the Office of Risk Management.

ERM Program Staff

There are 1.5 full-time equivalent (FTE) ERM program staff located in the office of the associate vice president/controller for UW. This staff supports the work of the various committees and units, in part by establishing the ERM framework, standards, and templates. They monitor and participate in risk assessments for the purpose of providing the enterprise view. They provide administrative support and

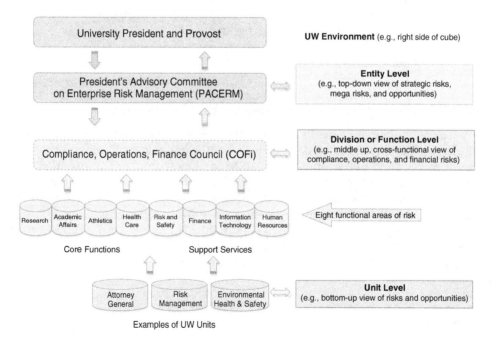

Exhibit 9.8 University of Washington ERM Structure
From University of Washington 2010 ERM Annual Report, p. 10.

summary information and analyses to the ERM committees. They also provide professional development in a train-the-trainer format.

Compliance, Operations, and Finance Council (COFi)

The COFi Council, led by the Executive Director of Audits, takes a middle-up, cross-functional view of risks and opportunities, particularly items that have university-wide potential impact or where supervisory authority for various aspects of the risk reside in different departments or divisions across the university. The COFi Council has oversight of risk assessments at the division or functional level. It provides approval of methods to monitor risks and identifies topics for outreach, particularly items that have university-wide potential impact or that involve cross-departmental or divisional silos. The six primary goals of the COFi Council are to:

1. Engage in a continual, cross-functional process that results in effective prioritization of institutional responses to compliance, financial, and operational risks, and consider the impact to strategic and reputational risks.
2. Ensure that the institutional perspective is always present in risk and compliance management discussions.
3. Identify strategies to address emerging risks and compliance management issues.
4. Support risk and compliance management training and outreach efforts throughout the university.
5. Provide external auditors and regulators with information about the university's risk and compliance programs.
6. Avoid the creation of additional bureaucracy by minimizing redundancy and maximizing resources.

President's Advisory Committee on ERM (PACERM)

PACERM, cochaired by the Provost and the Senior Vice President for Finance and Facilities, has oversight of risk assessments at the entity level. Taking a top-down view of risks and opportunities, PACERM advises the university president and other senior leaders on the management of risks and opportunities that may significantly impact strategic goals and/or priorities. They review the ERM dashboard (e.g., key risk indicators and key performance indicators). According to V'Ella Warren and Ana Mari Cauce, cochairs of PACERM in 2008–2009, PACERM "is the one place where participants set aside their individual organizational perspectives, and really think about the major risks and opportunities from an institution-wide view" (2009 ERM Annual Report, p. 6).

Internal Audit

Internal Audit provides independent verification and testing of internal controls. The department also provides administrative support and summary information to the COFi Council.

UW President and Provost

The President and Provost play a key role in acknowledging, validating, and supporting the ERM program. They verbally refer to key documents such as the ERM framework, PACERM and COFi Council charters and assessments, and the ERM dashboard. They provide entity-level reporting to the Regents.

UW'S ERM MODEL

After a careful review of models in the corporate sector and within higher education, UW settled on the following regarding its ERM model:

- Assess risks in the context of strategic objectives, and identify interrelation of risk factors across the institution, not only by function.
- Cover all types of risk: compliance, financial, operational, and strategic.
- Foster a common awareness that allows individuals to focus attention on risks with strategic impacts.
- Enhance and strengthen UW's culture of compliance while protecting the decentralized, collaborative, entrepreneurial nature of the institution.

Adopting and Adapting the COSO Model

UW has defined ERM according to its interpretation of the Committee of Sponsoring Organizations (COSO) model, adapting the framework to fit the university environment and the UW in particular (see Exhibit 9.9). COSO describes ERM

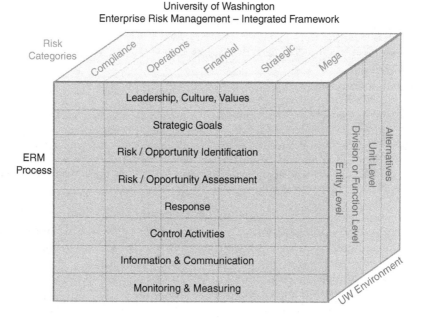

Exhibit 9.9 University of Washington's ERM Integrated Framework
From University of Washington Enterprise Risk Management Toolkit, p. 7. Copyright 2007, University of Washington.

as "a process, effected by an entity's board of directors, management, and other personnel, applied in strategy setting and across the enterprise, designed to identify potential events that may affect the entity, and manage risk to be within its risk appetite, to provide reasonable assurance regarding the achievement of entity objectives" (COSO 2004). Adopted in 2009–2010, the 2010 ERM Annual Report notes:

> The UW ERM Integrated Framework offers a schema to integrate the views of risk that have historically been addressed in silos or through a fragmented approach. The ERM framework bridges the gap between lower-level issues and upper-level issues, and it allows us to be explicit about the multiple levels on which the ERM process is deployed as a risk and/or opportunity management mechanism. (p. 4)

Risk Categories

The top of the cube identifies risk types, including compliance, operations, and financial risks. Strategic risks can impact the mission. Mega risks are major external events over which the institution has no control, but for which the institution can prepare.

UW Environment

The right side of the cube views the organizational structure at three levels: entity, which entails all operations and programs; division or function, looking at a major risk in depth; and unit, where individual departments can use the tools to assess their risks. A fourth level of ERM used in the UW environment is to evaluate alternatives.

ERM Process

The front of the cube outlines the traditional eight steps from the COSO model, including setting the tone and context for ERM at the top, identifying risks in conjunction with strategic goals, and through the complete cycle with implementation and follow-up.

The report notes:

> UW's "cube" integrates the several ERM facets into a whole, and enables ERM to be applied in a very **intentional** manner: Starting any new risk assessment requires identifying the appropriate level of the organization or environment at which the assessment will be made; focusing on which set of **risks** (compliance—strategic—mega risks) to cover; and applying all the steps in the ERM **cycle** to ensure a complete assessment and follow through.

The UW views ERM as integrating risk discussions into strategic deliberations and identifying the interrelation of risk factors across activities. Using the COSO model, its eight-step process involves the following (see Exhibit 9.10):

1. *Leadership, culture, and values.* Setting the tone at the top.
2. *Strategic goals.* At the entity or institutional level (top down), the division or function level (risk topic across shared goals of VPs and deans—"middle up"), the unit level (such as a department, school, or college—bottom up), or the alternatives level (investment alternatives or business options).

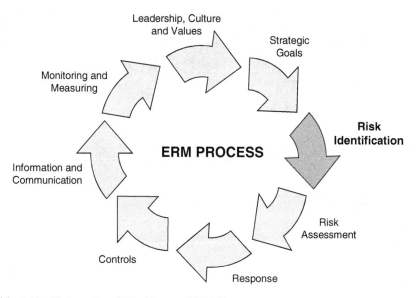

Exhibit 9.10 University of Washington ERM Process
From University of Washington Enterprise Risk Management Toolkit, p. 8. Copyright 2007, the University of Washington.

3. *Risk identification.* In the appropriate context, name the harm, loss, or compliance violation to avoid, as well as the opportunities to be identified. This typically begins with listing broad risk activities or subject areas. Risks can be identified at the entity, division, functional, unit, or alternatives level. This process includes the use of risk statements and opportunity identification.

4. *Risk assessment.* In the appropriate context, analyze the risk or opportunity in terms of likelihood and impact (see Exhibit 9.11). Create a risk map, ranking or prioritizing risks to inform decisions regarding response. For opportunities, rate the likelihood of occurrence on a scale of 1 to 5 (1 = rare, not expected to occur in the next five years; 5 = almost certain, expected to occur more than once per year). Also rank the positive impact, considering what impact the opportunity would have on the institution's ability to achieve goals or objectives (1 = insignificant, with little or no impact on objectives and no impact to reputation and image; 5 = outstanding, could significantly enhance the capability to meet objectives and could significantly enhance reputation and image).

5. *Response.* Selecting the appropriate response involves comparing the cost of implementing the option against benefits derived from it. Responses include avoid, mitigate, transfer, or accept the risk. For opportunities, the response can be exploit, enhance, share, or ignore.

6. *Controls.* Document internal controls for top risks, and rank for effectiveness. For UW, internal controls are narrowly defined to describe the methods used by staff or faculty that help ensure the achievement of goals and objectives, such as policies, procedures, training, and operational and physical barriers.

IMPACT	Catastrophic - 5 -	5	10	15	20	25
	Disastrous - 4 -	4	8	12	16	20
	Serious - 3 -	3	6	9	12	15
	Minor - 2 -	2	4	6	8	10
	Insignificant - 1 -	1	2	3	4	5
		Rare - 1 -	Unlikely - 2 -	Possible - 3 -	Likely - 4 -	Almost Certain - 5 -
				LIKELIHOOD		

Risk Level	Score Range
Extreme	19.5 – 25
High	12.5 – 19.4
Substantial	9.5 – 12.4
Medium	4.5 – 9.4
Low	1 – 4.4

Exhibit 9.11 University of Washington Risk Assessment: Likelihood and Impact
From University of Washington Enterprise Risk Management Toolkit, p. 17. Copyright 2007, the University of Washington.

7. *Information and communication.* Communicate with stakeholders and take action (the transition from analysis to action). Designate a risk owner for each of the top risks.
8. *Monitoring and measuring.* Monitor performance to confirm achievement of goals and objectives, and monitor risk to track activities that prevent achievement of goals and objectives.

Tools and Techniques

As its ERM program has developed and evolved, UW has learned from its experience and is positioned to share information not only internally, but with others in higher education as well. The university has developed a comprehensive Enterprise Risk Management Toolkit, copyrighted in 2007, with the second edition released in 2010. The second edition includes an expanded section on the ERM process and has new material on evaluating opportunities. It is comprised of a manual and a set of spreadsheets that provides a framework for assessing and understanding institutional risks. The UW allows access to the Toolkit for UW staff, faculty, and students, federal agencies, Washington State agencies, and other institutions of higher education at no charge through the UW Center for Commercialization Express Licensing Program.

As is typical with most universities, the tools utilized by UW for conducting the risk assessment process are Microsoft Office products. Excel is used to catalog risk assessment inventories and Word for report writing. While the administrators have explored many options for software to aid in the process (and to potentially provide outcomes such as dashboards), they find that, having been developed in the corporate for-profit environment, none of those options are particularly suited to capturing the needs of the higher education environment. They note, however, that at the unit level, many departments are investing in unit-specific software to aid in their data management. For example, the Finance and Budgeting Office is investigating software to run stress tests and financial simulations, and the Human Resources Office is examining payroll software. This allows the units to be able to more quickly evaluate risk specific to their areas, but UW finds that its ability to aggregate risks for examination at the entity level can be accomplished effectively with its low-tech process.

OUTCOMES AND LESSONS LEARNED

UW administrators can chart the evolution of their ERM program and the effectiveness it has on the university. They note that the early wins were at the unit level, when specific departments, such as Information Security and Environmental Health and Safety, integrated the ERM process with their well-established strategic planning processes. Those units used the risk assessment tools to identify and rank risks that could hinder or prevent the achievement of their strategic goals. Integration of ERM at the entity level is happening more slowly, but issues that impact everyone at the UW, such as faculty recruitment and retention or responding to the external financial crisis, now can happen in a more integrated fashion as the understanding of ERM evolves. For several years, due to severe budget reductions, the Office of Planning and Budgeting consciously added some questions about risk assessment into the budget request process. Vice presidents and deans were asked to address the impact of budget reductions in terms of risk. This happened, in part, because two key members of the Budget and Planning Office, as well as the Provost, have been involved with the PACERM.

UW administrators have a few other observations about their process and how and why it has worked. First, they note that they were aware from the outset that the environment at UW is highly decentralized and that appointing an "ERM czar" or chief risk officer (CRO) wouldn't fit with the culture. They made a deliberate choice not to formalize ERM through a senior-level position, but rather to engage in implementation through a committee structure. Second, they involved faculty members from the beginning. This helped with a sense of shared purpose. Faculty members came to see the business side of academia, and staff and administrators better understood the point of view of scholars engaged in teaching and learning. Third, the senior leadership has stayed dedicated to the ERM process, even with transitions in the president and other senior administrators. The 2011 ERM Annual Report points out the benefits to the UW of the ERM approach:

> The value of ERM is both qualitative (e.g., risk and opportunity maps) and quantitative (e.g., dashboards to contextualize and display metrics). Qualitative benefits accumulate because the risk mapping process allows groups throughout the University to collectively prioritize issues, and ensure that the effort and resources involved in root cause analysis, measurement, and monitoring are applied only

to the most significant concerns. Each iteration of the ERM process results in new capabilities, and insight gained into maintaining the University's competitive advantage—particularly from managing our financial risks and strategic opportunities better than our peers. (p. 5)

UW has been strategic, deliberate, and inclusive as it continues on its journey to develop and enhance its ERM program, learning lessons from what works and adapting new strategies in order to improve or modify its program. ERM began at UW in 2006 "by establishing a collaborative approach and structure to consider broad perspectives in identifying and assessing risk" (2012 Annual Report, p. 3). This strategy has helped UW overcome some of the traditional challenges facing universities when implementing ERM, including addressing concerns about the real effectiveness of risk assessment, getting agreement on definitions of risk assessment impact, identifying risk owners, and moving beyond the "risk discussion" to focus on mitigation (2012 Annual Report, p. 3). In her November 2012 presentation on UW's ERM program to the Pacific Northwest Enterprise Risk Forum, Ann Anderson, Associate VP and Controller, outlined the following seven key lessons that UW has learned by engaging in ERM for almost eight years:

1. Clarify the roles of the various risk committees.
2. Develop a "work plan" for the committees.
3. Develop engaging agendas, focused at the appropriate level.
4. Don't overemphasize "lowest common denominator" risks.
5. Gather data/information to develop expertise on specific risks.
6. Avoid discussing low-level, narrow risks—too time-consuming!
7. Don't get into the weeds with implementation and process. Delegate actions to responsible parties.

WHAT NEXT?: CURRENT PRIORITIES AND FUTURE DIRECTION

As the 2010 ERM Annual Report points out, the process of involving people in risk assessments, even with the most well-developed risk assessment tools, is only part of the process. "Successfully maintaining a large-scale organizational initiative such as ERM requires a comprehensive, broad based approach that is widely understood and used regularly to clearly articulate where risks and opportunities exist throughout the University" (p. 4). As ERM moves forward at UW, the focus is on a "greater refinement of institutional success metrics, increased assessments of risks identified, and continued expansion across the university to incorporate risk assessment into decision-making and strategic planning" (2012 Annual Report, p. 2). The objectives for 2013–2014 are: (1) strengthen oversight of the top risks and (2) enhance coordination and integration of ERM activities with decision-making processes. Several initiatives will help UW achieve these objectives, including seeking input and approval from the PACERM in order to elevate the monitoring of the top risks; a comparison of the institutional-level risks with unit-level risks; the development of quantitative visual representations of the risks, metrics, and targets; engaging the community more broadly in risk management; integrating risk management with the budget and planning cycle for the university; a retrospective analysis of risks and mitigation investments; and a forward-looking analysis to highlight gaps and areas of concern. They are also in the process of developing specific deliverables and measures as indicators of success, such as executive-level risk registers, dashboards of key risks, and a foundation and structure to integrate risk maps and dashboards with the planning and budgeting cycle.

CONCLUSION

UW's ERM implementation process and lessons learned are consistent with the guidance offered by the National Association of College and University Attorneys (NACUA). In a 2010 conference presentation, NACUA identified the following eight critical success factors:

1. Establish the right vision and realistic plan.
2. Obtain senior leadership buy-in and direction.
3. Align with mission and strategic objectives.
4. Attack silos at the outset.
5. Set objectives and performance indicators.
6. Stay focused on results.
7. Communicate vision and key outcomes.
8. Develop a sustainable process versus a one-time project.

While complex and time-consuming, effective development of a culture-specific ERM program can have positive outcomes for colleges and universities. Institutions such as UW that view ERM as a long-term investment in institutional health, rather than a fad or simply a set of tools (such as spreadsheets and heat maps), position themselves well not only to respond to the external demands from credit ratings agencies, accreditors, and federal regulators, but to situate themselves to make key strategic decisions, informed by both quantitative and qualitative data, to enhance their organization, leading to increased enrollment and graduation and strategic disbursement of resources for teaching and research, as well as increasing the likelihood that, due to their integrated, proactive approach, they will avoid future compliance scandals. Perhaps the two most important deliverables on UW's 2013–2014 agenda are those that demonstrate its awareness of the importance of the human resources component in its collegial environment: outreach to faculty and other administrators to obtain broader validation of risks and to identify additional mitigation activities, and an iterative process to involve senior leaders, the Provost, the President, and the Regents in monitoring the top risks. Through this process, UW is building a culture not only of compliance, but of shared responsibility for the future health of the university.

QUESTIONS

1. How does ERM adoption and implementation in the higher education environment differ from the for-profit environment?
2. What type of culture is at the University of Washington? Why is culture important to consider when implementing ERM?

3. What were some of the key factors in the early stages of UW's ERM adoption and implementation that led to its current success within the organization?
4. Why did UW decide to adopt a committee structure to administer its ERM program rather than designate a senior level Chief Risk Officer?
5. Who are some of the key players involved in the decision-making about the ERM model and its current administration?

NOTES

1. Many colleges and universities were affected by Hurricane Katrina in the New Orleans area (see the American Association of University Professors [AAUP] Special Committee Report on Hurricane Katrina and New Orleans Universities at https://portfolio .du.edu/downloadItem/92556). The independent report by Louis Freeh and his law firm, Freeh Sporkin & Sullivan, LLP, documents the facts and circumstances of the actions of Pennsylvania State University surrounding the child abuse committed by a former employee, Gerald A. Sandusky (available at http://progress.psu.edu/the-freeh-report). The AAUP's Committee on College and University Governance reported on breakdowns in governance at the University of Virginia as the board attempted to remove president Sullivan (www.aaup.org/report/college-and-university-governance-university-virginia-governing-board). American University trustees removed then president Ladner in 2005 after investigation of expense abuses of university funds (http://usatoday30.usatoday.com/news/education/2005-10-11-au-president_x.htm). The most tragic of these situations was, of course, the shootings at Virginia Tech on April 16, 2007. On December 9, 2010, the U.S. Department of Education issued a final ruling that Virginia Tech had violated the Clery Act by failing to issue a "timely warning" to students and other members of the campus community following the initial shootings early on the morning of April 16, 2007. In commenting on the verdict, Stetson Professor of Law Peter Lake stated, "Higher education is under the microscope now. The accountability level has definitely changed" (S. Lipka, "Jury Holds Virginia Tech Accountable for Students' Deaths, Raising Expectations at Colleges," *Chronicle of Higher Education*, March 14, 2010).
2. In order to disperse federal financial aid and grant degrees, institutions in the United States are accredited by one of several accrediting bodies. One example of the way in which accreditors are emphasizing risk management in their review is the Southern Association of Colleges and Schools Commission on Colleges (SACS COC) (www.sacscoc.org/) Standard 3.10.4: The institution demonstrates control over all of its physical and financial resources. The University of Virginia demonstrates evidence of this standard on its website by articulating the organizational structure and integrated policies and procedures related to internal and external audit, internal controls, fixed assets, procurement, facilities management, and risk management, among others (www.virginia.edu/sacs/standards/3-10-4.html).
3. The recent Special Comment by Moody's, "Governance and Management: The Underpinnings of University Credit Ratings," declares that "governance and management assessments often account for a notch or more in the final rating outcome compared with the rating that would be indicated by purely quantitative ratio analysis" (Kedem 2010, p. 1). In Moody's consideration of five broad factors that contribute to its evaluation of governance and management, the report cites "oversight and disclosure processes that reduce risk and enhance operational effectiveness" (p. 2). The report further notes: "Effective internal controls and timely external disclosure about student outcomes, research productivity, financial performance, and organizational efficiency will become the hallmark of effective university leadership and will become

increasingly critical in mitigating new risks to individual universities and the sector overall" (p. 3).

4. One significant area of change has been the Internal Revenue Service's increased oversight of compliance issues affecting tax-exempt entities, including colleges and universities. In 2008, under prompting by members of the U.S. Senate Finance Committee, the IRS developed a 33-page compliance questionnaire (IRS Form 14018) and sent it to a cross section of 400 institutions of higher education. The form focused on a number of potentially sensitive subjects, including the types and amounts of executive compensation, the investment and use of endowment funds, and the relationship between an institution's exempt activities and other taxable business activities. The IRS also revised its Form 990, "Return of Organization Exempt from Income Tax," beginning with the 2008 tax year. The purpose of the changes is to increase the transparency and accountability of tax-exempt organizations and to ensure compliance with the Internal Revenue Code by requiring more detailed information in several categories. The changes focus not only on revenue, investment, and spending issues, but also on governance, conflicts of interest, and whistle-blower policies and procedures.

5. Based on a March 13, 2012, phone interview.

6. The Higher Education Act, up for renewal again in 2014, is a law almost 50 years old that governs the nation's student-aid programs and federal aid to colleges. It was signed into law in 1965 as part of President Johnson's Great Society agenda of domestic programs, and it has been reauthorized nine times since then, most recently in 2008. Additional examples at the federal level include Section 504 of the Rehabilitation Act of 1973, the Americans with Disabilities Act (ADA) (1990), Family Educational Rights and Privacy Act (FERPA) (1974, 1998, 2009), Health Insurance Portability and Accountability Act (HIPAA) (1996), Clery Act (1990), and Campus Sex Crimes Prevention Act (2000), among others. Lawsuits brought against institutions of higher education in which they and/or certain administrators at those institutions are accused of violating a particular federal law or a related legal right can lead to case decisions that impact that institution and perhaps others. Lawsuits can also have a significant impact even if they result in a settlement rather than a court decision. In May 2006, a group of 12 current and former deaf students at Utah State University sued the institution in U.S. District Court alleging that it had violated the Rehabilitation Act and the ADA by failing to provide enough fully qualified interpreters. The lawsuit also named the Utah State Board of Regents as defendants. After negotiations, the lawsuit was settled in April 2007 with the university agreeing to hire qualified, full-time interpreters at a ratio of one translator for every two deaf students. The lawsuit, the issues it raised, and its ultimate resolution received significant media attention, as well as attention from various organizations around the country promoting the interests of students who are deaf or have hearing deficiencies.

7. Mitroff, Diamond, and Alpaslan (2006) note that "colleges and universities are in the very early stages of establishing their crisis management programs, and much remains to be done. The recent experience in New Orleans and elsewhere suggests that developing and maintaining a well-functioning crisis management program is an operational imperative for college and university leaders" (p. 67).

8. One of those administrators was Elizabeth Cherry, Director of Risk Management, from the University of Washington (UW). As will be discussed in the case study, the UW was embroiled in several high-profile risk situations at the time and was undergoing the first of several presidential transitions.

9. See A. P. Liebenberg and R. E. Hoyt, "The Determinants of Enterprise Risk Management: Evidence from the Appointment of Chief Risk Officers," *Risk Management and Insurance Review* 6:1 (2003): 37–52. Their study uses a logistic model to examine the characteristics of firms that adopt ERM programs, most of which signal the fact that they have an ERM program through the hiring of a CRO.

10. Many thanks to Andrew Faris, Enterprise Risk Management Analyst at the University of Washington, and Kerry Kahl, ERM Project Manager at UW. They provided information via an interview in April 2012 that is incorporated throughout this case study. Additional information for the case study comes from Annual Reports, memos, and other documents found on the University of Washington ERM website: http://f2.washington.edu/fm/erm.

REFERENCES

Abraham, Janice. 2013. *Risk Management: An Accountability Guide for University and College Boards*. Washington, DC: Association of Governing Boards of Universities and Colleges and United Educators.

American Society of Mechanical Engineers–Innovative Technologies Institute, LLC. 2010. *A Risk Analysis Standard for Natural and Man-Made Hazards to Higher Education Institutions*. Washington, DC: American National Standards Institute.

Arena, M., M. Arnaboldi, and G. Azzone. 2010. "The Organizational Dynamics of Enterprise Risk Management." *Accounting, Organizations and Society* 35:7, 659–675.

Association of Governing Boards of Universities and Colleges and United Educators. 2009. *The State of Enterprise Risk Management at Colleges and Universities Today*. Available at www.agb.org.

Barnds, W. Kent. 2011. "The Risky Business of the Strategic Planning Process." *University Business*. Available at www.universitybusiness.com/article/risky-business-strategic-planning-process.

Birnbaum, Robert. 1988. *How Colleges Work: The Cybernetics of Academic Organization and Leadership*. San Francisco: Jossey-Bass.

Bolman, Lee G., and Terrence E. Deal. 2008. *Reframing Organizations: Artistry, Choice and Leadership*. San Francisco: Jossey-Bass.

Bush, Tony. 2011. *Theories of Educational Leadership and Management* (4th ed.). London: Sage Publications.

Cassidy, D. L., L. L. Goldstein, S. L. Johnson, J. A. Mattie, and J. E. Morley Jr. 2001. "Developing a Strategy to Manage Enterprisewide Risk in Higher Education." National Association of College and University Business Officers and PricewaterhouseCoopers. Available at www.nacubo.org/documents/business_topics/PWC_Enterprisewide_Risk_in_Higher_Educ_2003.pdf.

Chan, Sharon Pian. 2004. "UW Failed to Address Overbilling, Probe Finds." *Seattle Times*, May 1, 2004. Available at http://seattletimes.com/html/localnews/2001917467_uwmed01m.html.

Chang, Jean. 2012. Skype interview, March 2.

Committee of Sponsoring Organizations of the Treadway Commission. 2004. *Enterprise Risk Management—Integrated Framework*. Available at www.idkk.gov.tr/html/themes/bumko/dosyalar/yayin-dokuman/COSOERM.pdf.

Committee of Sponsoring Organizations of the Treadway Commission. 2011. *Internal Control—Integrated Framework*. Available at www.coso.org/documents/coso_framework_body_v6.pdf.

Freeh, Sporkin & Sullivan, LLP. 2012. "Report of the Special Investigative Counsel Regarding the Actions of the Pennsylvania State University to Related the Child Sexual Abuse Committed by Gerald A. Sandusky," July 12. Available at http://progress.psu.edu/the-freeh-report.

Gallagher Higher Education Practice. 2009. "Road to Implementation: Enterprise Risk Management for Colleges and Universities." Arthur Gallagher & Co. Available at www.nacua.org/documents/ERM_Report_GallagherSep09.pdf.

Grant Thornton LLP. 2011. "Best-Practice Tips for Boards, Presidents and Chancellors Regarding Enterprise Risk Management." *OnCourse*, January. Retrieved from www.grantthornton.com/staticfiles/GTCom/Not-for-profit%20organizations/On%20Course/On%20Course%20-%20Jan%2011%20-%20FINAL.pdf.

Grasgreen, Allie. 2013. "Report Shows How Rutgers Botched Handling of Former Coach, Reiterates 5-year-old Recommendations to Improve Athletics." *Inside Higher Education*. Available at www.insidehighered.com/news/2013/07/23/report-shows-how-rutgers-botched-handling-former-coach-reiterates-5-year-old.

Gurevitz, Susan. 2009. "Manageable Risk." *University Business*. Available at www.universitybusiness.com/article/manageable-risk.

Helsloot, I., and W. Jong. 2006. "Risk Management in Higher Education and Research in the Netherlands." *Journal of Contingencies and Crisis Management* 14:3.

Huber, C. 2009. "Risks and Risk-Based Regulation in Higher Education Institutions." *Tertiary Education and Management* 15:2.

Kedem, K. 2010. "Special Comment: Governance and Management: The Underpinnings of University Credit Ratings." Moody's Investors Service, Report 128850.

Mitroff, I. I., M. A. Diamond, and M. C. Alpaslan. 2006. "How Prepared Are America's Colleges and Universities for Major Crises?: Assessing the State of Crisis Management." *Change* 38:1, 61–67.

National Association of College and University Business Officers and the Association of Governing Boards of Universities and Colleges. 2007. "Meeting the Challenges of Enterprise Risk Management in Higher Education." Available at www.ucop.edu/riskmgt/erm/documents/agb_nacubo_hied.pdf.

Nelson, John. 2012. Phone interview, March 13.

Stripling, Jack. 2012. "Penn State Trustees Were Blind to Risk, Just Like Many Boards." *Chronicle of Higher Education*, July 12. Available at http://chronicle.com/article/Penn-State-Trustees-Were-Blind/132943/.

Tertiary Education Quality Standards Agency. 2013. Available at www.teqsa.gov.au/

Tufano, Peter. 2011. "Managing Risk in Higher Education." *Forum Futures*. Available at http://net.educause.edu/ir/library/pdf/ff1109s.pdf.

University Risk Management and Insurance Association. 2007. "ERM in Higher Education." Available at www.urmia.org/library/docs/reports/URMIA_ERM_White_Paper.pdf.

Whitfield, R. N. 2003. "Managing Institutional Risks: A Framework." Doctoral dissertation. Retrieved from ProQuest Dissertation and Theses database, AAT 3089860.

Willson, C., R. Negoi, and A. Bhatnagar. 2010. "University Risk Management." *Internal Auditor* 67:4, 65–68.

Wilson, Richard. 2013. "Managing Risk." *Inside Higher Education*, May 20. Available at www.insidehighered.com/blogs/alma-mater/managing-risk.

ABOUT THE CONTRIBUTOR

Anne E. Lundquist has had 20 years of increasing administrative responsibilities in higher education, having served as the dean of students at four liberal arts colleges. She received a BA in religious studies from Albion College and an MFA in creative writing from Western Michigan University. Currently, she is a PhD candidate in the Educational Leadership program at Western Michigan University with a concentration in higher education administration, where she works with the vice president of student affairs on student affairs assessment and strategic planning and with the internal auditor and University Strategic Planning Committee on ERM implementation. Her dissertation research study is titled "Enterprise Risk Management (ERM) in Colleges and Universities: Administration Processes Regarding the Adoption, Implementation and Integration of ERM." Using her expertise in several areas, she has presented and been the author of articles on risk management, institutional liability, students with psychiatric disabilities, assessment and strategic planning, intercultural competence, and the development and implementation of integrated community standards/restorative justice judicial models. She is the coauthor of *The Student Affairs Handbook: Translating Legal Principles into Effective Policies* (LRP Publications, 2007). She has had three recent risk management publications in peer-reviewed journals: *URMIA Journal* (2011, 2012) and *New Directions for Higher Education, Special Issue, Disability and Higher Education* (with Allan Shackelford, July 2011).

Special thanks to Andrew Faris, Enterprise Risk Management Analyst at the University of Washington, for sharing information about the university's ERM process, answering questions, and providing material for the case study.

CHAPTER 10

Developing Accountability in Risk Management

The British Columbia Lottery Corporation Case Study

JACQUETTA C. M. GOY

Director of Risk Management Services, Thompson Rivers University, Canada and Former Senior Manager, Risk Advisory Services, British Columbia Lottery Corporation

This case study describes how enterprise risk management (ERM) has developed over the past 10 years at British Columbia Lottery Corporation (BCLC), a Canadian crown corporation offering lottery, casino, and online gambling. BCLC's enterprise risk management program has been developed over time through a combination of internal experiential learning and the application of specialist advice. The program's success has been due to the dedication of a number of key individuals, the support of senior leadership, and the participation of BCLC employees.

The approach to ERM has evolved from informal conversations supported by an external assessment, through a period of high-level corporate focus supported by a dedicated group of champions using voting technology, to an embedded approach, where risk assessment is incorporated into both operational practice and planning for the future using a variety of approaches depending on the context.

BACKGROUND

BCLC is a crown corporation operating in British Columbia (BC), Canada. The corporation was established by act of the British Columbia legislature in 1985. As a commercial crown corporation, BCLC is wholly owned by the province but operates at arm's length from government, enjoying operational autonomy while reporting to the minister responsible for gaming, currently the Finance Minister. All profits generated by BCLC go directly to the provincial government. The initial remit of the corporation was to operate the lottery schemes previously administered for British Columbia by the Western Canada Lottery Corporation. In 1997, BCLC was given responsibility to conduct and manage slot machines, and in 1998 the corporation's remit broadened again with additional responsibilities for table games in casinos. In 2004 an online service, PlayNow (www.playnow.com), was launched.

BCLC has been a highly successful organization for over 28 years, delivering over $15.7 billion in net income to the province of British Columbia. Through April 2012 to March 2013 more than $1 billion in gambling proceeds helped fund health care, education, and community programs in British Columbia (BCLC Annual Service Plan Report 2012/2013). BCLC operates the provincial lottery and instant games and provides national lottery games through the Interprovincial Lottery Corporation. Across the province, BCLC manages 17 casinos (15 casinos plus two casinos at racetracks), 19 community gaming centers, and six bingo halls through a number of private-sector service providers. PlayNow, BCLC's legal online gambling website, offers lottery, sports, bingo, slot, and table games, including online poker. BCLC employs about 850 corporate staff with more than 37,000 direct and indirect workers employed in British Columbia in gambling operations, government agencies, charities, and support services.

BCLC's mandate is to "conduct and manage gambling in a socially responsible manner for the benefit of British Columbians" with a vision that "gambling is widely embraced as exceptional entertainment through innovation in design, technology, social responsibility, and customer understanding." The organization holds the following values as key to its success:

- **Integrity:** The games we offer and the ways we conduct business are fair, honest, and trustworthy.
- **Social Responsibility:** Everything we do is done with consideration of its impact on and for the people and communities of British Columbia.
- **Respect:** We value and respect our players, service providers, and each other.

BCLC believes that playing fairly is a serious responsibility and an empowering opportunity. A commitment to social, economic, and environmental responsibility is central to everything the organization undertakes, and is reflected in the BCLC slogan, "Playing it right." BCLC strives to create outstanding gambling experiences with games evolving with the player's idea of excitement. For BCLC, playing is not all about winning; it's about entertainment.

THE BEGINNINGS OF THE RISK MANAGEMENT JOURNEY

BCLC began its enterprise risk management journey in 2003 with the initiation of an Enterprise-wide Risk & Opportunity Management (EROM) initiative. The impetus for the initiative was twofold—the 2002 inclusion of risk management in the British Columbia Treasury Board's Core Policy and Procedures Manual and BCLC's head of Audit Services championing the need for enterprise risk management (ERM).

As a first step, an external consulting firm was contracted to undertake an enterprise-wide risk assessment and to support the Internal Audit team in developing the skills and resources to manage the new ERM program. Interviews and facilitated workshops at management and executive levels were conducted, a risk dictionary was constructed, and the highest risks were identified. The assessment focused on inherent risk compared with an evaluation of management effectiveness to produce a gap analysis, and there was also a discussion around risk tolerance. A final report was produced (Deloitte and Touche 2003), and advice was also provided on potential next steps for the program.

Although the EROM initiative was well received, financial constraints put a hold on the subsequent business case. As a result, the plan to take the program forward through the appointment of a dedicated risk manager and funding for training of a number of risk champions was not implemented at that time.

LEARNING FROM THE FIRST ERM INITIATIVE

The initial assessment provided a strong starting point for the BCLC ERM program, but even though the engagement was originally intended to be the first part of a longer-term initiative, there was insufficient impetus to put the program into operation in the face of competing priorities. This is not an unusual outcome, as although using a consultant to kick-start programs can leverage experience and expertise that organizations may not otherwise have access to, using an external party contracted for a defined period of time can also lead to a project type approach, where the focus is more on getting the risk assessment completed and less on longer-term implementation. In addition, it may be easier to source short-term consultancy fees than it is to obtain longer-term resourcing commitments.

Another issue can arise where consultants bring in defined methodologies that do not easily fit with the organization's normal approach to decision making or where participants do not understand the underlying process, and so do not fully endorse and own the outcome. To overcome this issue, the consultants worked closely with the BCLC Internal Audit team with part of the stated purpose of the engagement being to build risk management expertise within BCLC.

RESTARTING THE PROGRAM–2006–2008

In early 2006, the head of Audit Services' proposal to update the 2003 risk assessment was endorsed by BCLC's executive team. Audit Services facilitated an assessment of critical strategic and operational risks facing BCLC, by developing a set of risks for analysis through consultation with the executive team, preparing an environmental scan, and concluding with a facilitated risk workshop to evaluate and prioritize each risk. The initiative was strongly informed by the successful ERM program being run at that time by another Canadian lottery organization, the Atlantic Lottery Corporation.

The intended outcome of the 2006 assessment was to inform the three-year-old audit plan, to develop new risk criteria, and to raise awareness about the importance of risk management. The success of the exercise led to the development and acceptance of a business case in August 2006 to resource a part-time risk manager, responsible for putting into operation the risk management program. This approach was endorsed by the CEO as part of an organization-wide initiative to develop and embed a high-performance culture across BCLC.

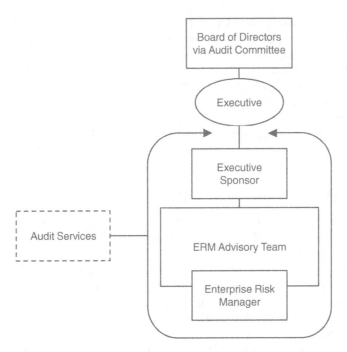

Exhibit 10.1   2006 ERM Organizational Structure

Leadership for the initiative was assigned to an executive sponsor. In the first instance, this was the chief information officer.

A cross-functional leadership team model was also approved, to be known as the ERM Advisory Team, responsible for oversight and approval of recommendations on behalf of the Executive Committee and consisting of the executive sponsor and a small number of key directors from each BCLC division. Operational support was provided by Internal Audit. The organizational structure is shown in Exhibit 10.1.

It is not entirely clear why the 2006 risk assessment exercise led to support for an ongoing ERM program while the 2003 initiative did not. The head of Internal Audit championed both initiatives, and the earlier risk assessment activity was well received. The consultants reporting in 2003 stated that "the culture in BCLC is proactive and is ideally suited to the EROM's philosophy and benefits." Executive response to both initiatives was largely positive. There does not appear to have been a so-called burning platform created in 2006; it was more a growing recognition that the time was right to adopt a more formal approach to ERM. It may be that increasing recognition of the importance of managing risk across North America with the introduction of Sarbanes-Oxley requirements[1] and publication of COSO's ERM Integrated Framework in 2004 influenced senior management. Or it could be that the simple iterative approach adopted by the head of Internal Audit when he decided to update the 2003 risk assessment—"Start slow and at the top, get learning and feedback, and then take down the ladder"—demystified the concept and increased engagement. Regardless, 2006 marked a new start for ERM, and the genesis of the current BCLC program.

KEY STEPS IN THE DEVELOPMENT OF THE ERM PROGRAM

For the second risk assessment, a streamlined process was adopted. Rather than starting with the risk statements from the dictionary, each VP was simply asked to identify their top three strategic and operational risks, with the results analyzed, combined, and allocated into the 2006 categories.

The resulting 37 risks were brought to two executive-level workshops and, as with the 2003 assessment, voting technology was used for prioritization. Nine critical risks were identified and taken forward to be integrated into the audit plan. One key difference from the 2003 assessment was the development of BCLC-specific likelihood and consequence qualitative criteria. Of interest is the correlation between the two assessments, with only two critical risks identified in 2003 not appearing in the critical zone in 2006, and no new critical risks introduced.

With the appointment of a dedicated Enterprise Risk Manager and the support of an executive sponsor, the launch of a formal ERM program became possible. The senior auditor from the Internal Audit team moved to the new position, bringing continuity with previous ERM initiatives. Between August and December 2006, the focus was on developing the core risk documentation, including terms of reference for the new steering group, an ERM policy, a project charter, and an initial plan. The initial areas of focus were to:

- Develop and continuously refine a practical ERM framework to support the identification and management of risk.
- Continuously manage risks, limiting exposure to an acceptable level while maximizing business opportunities.
- Embed a risk awareness that is a key component of instilling a high-performance culture.

A key feature of the new approach to ERM was the formation of the ERM Advisory Committee (known as ERMAC). The concept of ERMAC was to create risk champions, high-performing senior leaders from each division whose role would be to influence, communicate, and educate management and staff within their business areas about the benefits of risk management.

By January 2007, the new committee was established and the ERM policies and plan were in place, with proposals to embed risk management into project planning, business cases, and strategic planning under discussion.

In May 2007 a critical report about BCLC was issued by the British Columbia Ombudsman following an investigation into BCLC's prize payout processes (BC Ombudsman 2007). The investigation was triggered by a CBC *Fifth Estate* investigation[2] in October 2006 on issues in Ontario associated with lottery retailers winning major prizes, with the concern being that similar issues could have occurred in British Columbia. Although no incidents of wrongdoing were discovered during the investigation, the report and a subsequent audit and recommendations published by Deloitte & Touche in October 2007 marked a critical point in BCLC's transformation into a modern player-centric organization.

For risk management, the Ombudsman's review led to both a greater impetus and a broader focus for the program. BCLC had always considered integrity to be vital to the organization, but the fundamental goal of delivering revenue to government was often the dominant concern, and this was reflected in earlier risk assessments. With the advent of the Player First program,[3] significant additional resources and oversight were now dedicated to security, compliance, and reputation management, and this increased emphasis was reflected in the risk assessment conducted by the ERMAC team in April 2007.

The basis of the assessment was the risk statements completed by the Executive Committee in 2006, with new key risks facing BCLC added through consultation with key members of each of the business/support units and incorporated into an expanded risk dictionary. Once the new risk statement descriptions were agreed on, workshops were held to assess the risk ratings, and also to determine how effective were current arrangements for managing each risk. The 12 risks with the largest gaps identified between risk rating and management effectiveness were then selected for further profiling and control analysis.

Throughout 2007, the remaining enterprise risks were profiled in order to better identify the associated causes and controls. Two further enterprise risk assessments were facilitated in 2008, and a regular quarterly risk report produced from June 2008 forward provided details of both the development of the overall program and monitoring of individual risks.

Parallel to the enterprise risk assessment, a project risk assessment approach was developed and implemented, with a number of initiatives used to facilitate risk assessments, very similar to those conducted at an enterprise level. As with the enterprise risk assessments, the risk dictionary was used to support the development of potential risk statements, which were then voted on at a facilitated meeting of the core project team. Project risk assessments were piloted with four projects in 2007, and further developed with seven project risk assessments facilitated in 2008. Although the workshops were generally felt to be productive and beneficial, the volume of risks generated meant that on occasion it was not possible to assess all the risks presented.

In May 2008, the Enterprise Risk Manager was appointed director of Audit Services. Although risk assessments continued to be supported by the Internal Audit team, the further development of enterprise risk management was constrained due to the lack of dedicated resources, as the ERM manager post was not immediately filled.

REVITALIZING THE ERM PROGRAM—2009–2010

In the fall of 2008 the position of Manager, Risk Planning and Mitigation was created and an experienced risk manager was recruited to the position in late December 2008. The original intention of the appointment was to increase focus on risk treatment strategies and business-unit-level risk management activities, with the expectation that Internal Audit would continue to develop and report on the enterprise risk management framework. In late January 2009, the director of Audit Services left BCLC and the manager of Risk Planning and Mitigation assumed responsibility for managing all aspects of the ERM program.

The new risk manager brought a more operational approach, and was able to build on the excellent foundations already established to develop a new ERM strategy and supporting plan designed to move the ERM program to the next stage of maturity.

Throughout 2009, BCLC transitioned from the previous approach, where a portfolio of enterprise risk statements was assessed at a corporate level by ERMAC members, to a specific risk register with risks evaluated and agreed on at a divisional level and significant risks then escalated to the enterprise register.

One of the first changes was to move from an assessment of inherent risk with a supplementary assessment as to whether the risk was thought to be managed effectively to the use of a residual risk assessment methodology that included a more formal assessment of the effectiveness of control mechanisms in place. The next enterprise risk assessment was conducted in March 2009, and moved from the ERMAC voting approach to assessments by individual risk owners, with the committee providing more of a quality assurance function. New risk criteria were also adopted. A significant outcome was that the majority of risks were rated at a lower impact/consequence level (18 out of 29 dropping at least one rating, and three falling from critical to low risk).

Between March and July 2009, a series of risk and controls assessments workshops were held covering all divisions. The workshops brought together either functional teams or collections of specialists in thematic sessions (for example, marketing). Close to 300 managers and staff were involved. Each group attended two workshops; the first featured an educational component, brainstorming exercises, and process mapping with threats and vulnerabilities identification, while the follow-up session looked at a number of prioritized areas of risk in more detail, with a deep-dive assessment of risks and controls. The output of the workshops was the creation of divisional risk registers. Enterprise-level risks were then extracted from the divisional registers for an organization-wide view of all significant risks.

By September 2009, risk registers were established for all divisions. The new registers were more comprehensive than the previous risk documentation, with a greater focus on risk treatment and specific individuals identified as responsible for each risk treatment plan. The risk management policy was updated and new supporting guidance published.

Through 2009 and 2010, the risk management approach was further developed and embedded. In particular, the use of risk management in business case development and project management increased, while the new registers were updated on a quarterly basis. Regular quarterly reports on the risk management program were produced for discussion by the Executive Committee and at the Audit Committee.

In the summer of 2010, the risk management policy and guidelines were updated and a new risk management strategy was produced to reflect the newly published international standard on risk management, ISO 31000:2009, Risk Management—Principles and Guidelines. BCLC had previously been using the Australian risk management standard (AS/NZS 4360:2004), so the move to the new standard was a simple transition. At the same time, the government of British Columbia endorsed the new standard across all ministries, and subsequently used the approach for a number of provincially coordinated risk management activities (for example, planning for the 2010 Winter Olympics and preparing for a potential pandemic). The policy stated: "BCLC is committed to building increased awareness and a shared responsibility for risk management at all levels of the organization, and to facilitate the integration of the management and prioritization of risks into planning and operational activities."

The terms of reference for the ERMAC were also updated (see Exhibit 10.2), reflecting the change in practice from a single central risk assessment to the more devolved approach now in place.

Exhibit 10.2   Terms of Reference for the Enterprise Risk Management Advisory Committee

January 2007–March 2010	March 2010–March 2011
C. Terms of Reference	C. Terms of Reference
ERM Advisory Committee ("ERMAC")	ERM Advisory Committee ("ERMAC")
The ERMAC is an operational committee promoted and supported by the Executive to oversee the risk management process of the BCLC. The ERMAC reports to the Executive Sponsor. The ERMAC will:	The ERM Advisory Committee is tasked by the Executive to support the implementation of risk management across BCLC. The committee will:
Approve a suitable risk management mandate, terms of reference, and policy for BCLC, for endorsement by the Executive	Appraise, revise, and monitor the annual risk management program;
Approve and oversee the implementation of a flexible, adaptable Risk Management process of BCLC as a whole, on behalf of Executive	Review any changes to the Risk Management Policy prior to submission for approval by the Executive;
Recommend an appropriate risk appetite or level of exposure for BCLC to the Executive	Consider and approve procedures and guidance to support the risk management policy and process;
Identify and quantify fundamental risks affecting BCLC, and ensure that arrangements are in place to manage those risks	Review the effectiveness of risk management processes used across BCLC;
At least annually, review fundamental risks and their controls and report to Executive	Help embed a risk management culture across the organization;
Inform the Audit Committee on risks and controls that should be included in the Audit needs assessment, ensuring the integration of Audit Services into risk management	Support the development of a risk management awareness and education program; and
Ensure that critical risks are adequately dealt with	Provide support for the Divisional Risk Representatives, through encouraging sharing experience and enabling frank discussion of any risk-related issues arising.
Help embed a risk management culture into all major decisions, through risk education, high-level controls, and procedures	From time to time the committee may also focus on a particular area of risk.
Consider major decisions affecting BCLC's risk profile or exposure	

STRENGTHENING THE PROGRAM—2010–2013

In 2010, it was agreed that Internal Audit should conduct a review of the risk management program with a view to "identify any gaps and areas for improvement to ensure that the fundamental building blocks are in place to deliver on the organization's risk management needs effectively and efficiently." Interviews were conducted with Enterprise Risk Management Advisory Committee members, the executive team, CEO, and board and Audit Committee members.

The review found that the ERM process was well established and documented, with strong levels of support from all levels of the organization and an increasingly risk-conscious culture. However, risk management was not yet fully embedded within all of the organization's functions. There was some variance in perceptions of risk tolerance, and in general the program was stronger on reporting risks than it was at driving change, with significant amounts of informal risk-related discussions taking place outside of the program. Senior management also reported that too many risks were escalated to them, often at a level that was perceived to be too granular or operational.

In addition to the internal review, BCLC took part in a benchmarking exercise conducted by Ernst & Young together with seven other Canadian lottery and gaming organizations. The exercise consisted of a questionnaire completed by key risk personnel at each organization facilitated by telephone interviews conducted by the E&Y team.

The results (Ernst & Young 2010) showed that BCLC was in a similar position to many of the other gaming organizations in having a relatively young ERM program. In common with much of the gaming industry at the time, BCLC's strongest area was risk assessment, while risk tracking and the ERM structure were relatively weak (see Exhibit 10.3). The exercise included a simple self-assessment of perceived ERM maturity, where BCLC assessed itself as having risk activities in

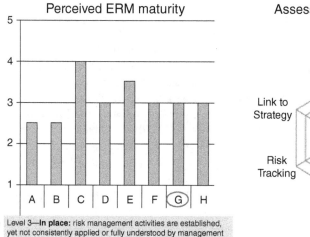

Exhibit 10.3 ERM Maturity at BCLC in 2010

Extracted from Ernst & Young ERM Benchmarking Survey, 2010.

place, but that risk management was not yet consistently applied and well understood by management and employees across the organization.

The results of the internal review and the E&Y assessment were presented to BCLC's executive team in February 2011. A number of recommendations were proposed and adopted, including strengthening senior management ownership and accountability, realigning risk criteria to better match the BCLC's tolerance for risk across organizational objectives, and broadening the focus of the program from largely operational to a more strategic level.

In April 2011, the risk management function moved to the Finance and Corporate Services division, with the CFO taking responsibility for executive leadership of the program. The risk criteria and evaluation matrix were updated and the risk review process strengthened, establishing regular review meetings for every division whereby each division's senior management team reported to their vice president (VP) on their risks every quarter. Risk oversight was also reviewed, and in addition to strengthening processes at a divisional level, dedicated time at executive meetings was scheduled to review the quarterly risk report prior to presentation to the Audit Committee. A key step in increasing accountability came from the formal assignment of each area of high risk to the appropriate VP, who would be responsible for reporting each risk in detail and providing a regular update on progress with the agreed treatment plans.

At this time, the ERM Advisory Committee was disbanded. While the committee of risk champions had played a significant role in coordinating initial assessment activities and in increasing the understanding of risk management across the organization in the early years of the risk management program, it was now felt that as all directors were expected to be fully conversant with risk management and with the movement of risk identification, evaluation, and reporting into mainstream management, the group no longer added significant value.

A new Risk Management Planning Group reporting to the CFO was established to align and coordinate a number of risk and compliance activities, in particular looking for synergies between the risk, business continuity, insurance, and antifraud programs. The intention of the group was to assist in the design of tools and approaches that deliver progress across the programs and also reduce managerial overload from potentially competing programs.

Over the next year, a series of risk reviews were undertaken with each division, with the aim to refresh the divisional registers and to make sure that each group reviewed both current and potential risks against both BCLC and divisional strategies. The format of the reviews varied across groups, dependent on divisional responsiveness and parallel activities. Several workshops were held with broader management teams, two were jointly coordinated with Internal Audit exercises, and one was externally facilitated. The review process further increased ownership and accountability by reinforcing the message that risk management and reporting are the responsibility of everyone throughout the organization.

In early 2012 BCLC invited an external consulting firm to look again at its ERM program, consider the progress made since the work in 2003, and make some recommendations as to next steps. In April 2012, the consultants delivered a presentation to the board on "Moving from a Risk Monitoring Organization to a Risk Intelligent Organization," and facilitated a discussion on risk governance and oversight. It was agreed to move risk oversight from the Audit Committee to the full board, to include more formal consideration of risk in the strategic planning process, and to continue to improve risk management processes, practices, and awareness.

In the winter of 2012 an opportunity arose to embed ERM into strategic planning when an exercise to identify and assess strategic risks was undertaken. The aim of this exercise was to identify and prioritize a set of holistic enterprise-level longer-term risks in order to inform strategic planning alongside a program of optimization. An off-site workshop was led by the CEO and the executive team with additional input from a small group of directors known as the leadership team, and supported by risk, corporate strategy, and audit services. Facilitation was provided by an external party. During the workshop, political, regulatory, economic, competitive, technology, and social business environmental factors were considered, and after a lively and informed discussion 11 key strategic risks were identified and initial sponsors assigned.

Following the workshop, a series of meetings were held with the assigned VP leads and other relevant parties, facilitated by the Senior Manager, Risk Advisory to discuss each risk in greater detail and using a bow tie approach,[4] identifying key causes, consequences, controls, and planned treatments. A formal report was developed, and a strategic risk register is now in place. Going forward, the strategic risks will be used to inform strategic planning and business optimization, while the shorter-term, more operationally focused risks continue to be reflected and addressed in business planning at an enterprise, divisional, and initiative level.

BUILDING THE RISK PROFILE

One of the first steps often taken by many organizations in developing enterprise risk management is to identify the risks that the organization faces, although ISO 31000 recommends that the risk framework is established prior to this step and that the context is established prior to risk identification. For BCLC's first risk identification exercise, the context was provided by the consultancy team in the form of a risk dictionary or universe. The idea behind the risk universe concept is that all potential risks can be identified and classified into definitive categories, which can then be used as a generic tool to identify risk within and across organizations in a consistent manner.

The universe used for the initial BCLC risk assessment contained 70 generic descriptions of risks, which were adapted after consultation to fit the BCLC environment more accurately. The resulting 2003 BCLC risk universe included 59 potential risks divided into external and internal categories with strategic, operations, technology, financial, and organizational health subcategories, and can be seen in Exhibit 10.4. Each risk was given both a two- or three-word title and a short high-level description.

Some risk practitioners consider that the development and use of a risk universe or defined classification system is essential in any enterprise risk management program (Society of Actuaries 2009, 2010). However, to be effective there must be clear rules to support consistent classification, and each set of risks must consist of like items that are relevant to management decision making.

Exhibit 10.4   The 2003 BCLC Risk Universe

External Risks

Competitor	Legal	Economic, Political &	Technological
Catastrophic Loss	Regulatory	Societal Change	Innovation
Financial Markets	Player Demands &	Industry	
	Satisfaction		

Internal Risks

Strategic

Environmental Scan	Mergers & Acquisitions	Culture
External Relations	Alignment	Governance
Business Portfolio	Organizational Structure	Strategic Alliance
Performance	Business Model	
Measurement		

Operations

Capacity	Compliance	Supply Chain
Fraud	Customer Satisfaction	Product/Service Failure
Communication	Brand Name	Knowledge
Extended Enterprise	Reputation	Management
Vendor Management	Pricing	Project Planning
Health & Safety	Product Development	Performance Gap
Change Management	Safeguarding of Assets	Gaming Integrity
Environmental	Business Interruption	

Organizational Health	**Technology**	**Financial**
Recruitment	Access, Security, & Tech.	Credit
Training & Development	Integrity	Market
Employee Satisfaction	Information Availability	Liquidity
Ethics & Values	Technology	Budget & Planning
Accountability &	Infrastructure	Valuation
Responsibility		Capital Acquisition &
Leadership		Management
Retention, Recruitment,		Financial & Management
& Succession Planning		Reporting

One common issue is that the list of risk statements may contain a mix of risk events, root causes, and outcomes, leading to imprecision and confusion, which may make assessing the level of risk or determining appropriate treatment more difficult. Another issue is that risk statements may be expressed in very generic terms that may not easily apply to the organization in question, or may make contributors feel that the risk assessment exercise is academic and not directly related to their day-to-day experiences.

The 2003 BCCL risk dictionary exhibited both of these issues, as can be shown in Exhibit 10.5.

Exhibit 10.5 Analysis of Sample Statements from the 2003 BCLC Risk Dictionary

Example	Statement Type	Issue
Catastrophic loss risk—A major disaster threatens BCLC's ability to sustain its operations and minimize financial losses.	Outcome	The outcome could arise from a variety of different circumstances, making risk response problematic.
Governance risk—BCLC does not have the appropriate governance practices in place.	Cause	It is unclear why practices might be a cause for concern, making assessing the level of risk difficult.
Health and safety risk—Failure to provide a safe working environment for its workers exposes the organization to compensation liabilities, loss of business reputation, and other costs.	Risk	This is a clear problem and outcome statement but is expressed generically, which may mean that there is a poor fit to the organization.

The intention behind the development of the risk dictionary was to provide common categorizations for specific risks identified across BCLC, and it was used effectively at a business unit level both to stimulate conversation and to identify specific risks, which were then translated to draft risk registers. At the enterprise level, the high-level statements were used for evaluation, and specific risk statements were not created.

The BCLC risk dictionary was reviewed, updated, and expanded in 2007 following the risk assessment exercise conducted by the Enterprise Risk Manager and the ERMAC team. One hundred and nine risk statements were captured in the categories of external, process, strategic, information, human capital, integrity, technical, and financial.

Through 2007 and 2008, the risk dictionary was used as the basis for assessments at an enterprise level, and the prioritized enterprise risks were then used to structure project risk assessments and also increasingly to support risk assessments in business cases.

In late 2008, as part of the ongoing development of corporate performance management, BCLC completed an exercise to implement the balanced scorecard methodology. This approach greatly assisted the risk management program in taking a fresh look into the corporate risk profile, and all of the risks were aligned to the new balanced goals. As a result, the risk dictionary was retired, with new guidance issued in 2009 recommending that all risk assessments start not from a predetermined list, but instead by looking at the objectives of the enterprise and, where relevant, the specific initiative.

The BCLC risk register generally includes around 100 risks across the nine divisions. As spreadsheets are currently used to manage the risk information, a decision was made to remove green (low) risks where it is determined that the risk level is stable and provided that there are sufficient monitoring processes embedded

into mainstream management. Each quarter, a small number of new risks are identified and an equally small number are retired as circumstances change, awareness
increases, and treatment plans come to fruition.

BCLC pays particular emphasis to the construction of clear descriptions for
each risk, with the following guidance provided to all employees:

> It is of particular importance that all risks are clearly expressed. BCLC has adopted
> a "CCC" approach where all risk statements should include not only the poten-
> tial change but also the most significant consequence and cause. Risk statements
> should start with wording equivalent to "The risk of/that" or "The opportunity to"
> and be expressed as a possibility (using "may" or "might"). Descriptions should
> be limited in length and specialized jargon or acronyms should be avoided where
> possible, so that anyone reading the risk statement can easily understand the risk.
> Care should be taken in order to avoid alarmist language. When recording partic-
> ularly sensitive risks, advice should be sought from either Risk Advisory Services
> or the Legal Services team.
> —BCLC Risk Management Guidelines, 2013

On a regular basis, the Enterprise Risk Manager assesses the full set of risks
and develops thematic risk maps, cascading from organizational goals and relating to key corporate strategies (the template schematic is shown in Exhibit 10.6).
These maps have been used as a key input to risk review workshops and are
incorporated into quarterly reporting processes. The advantage to this fluid
approach is that the maps are easily modified as organizational focus has evolved;
however, at present production is reliant on the insight and capacity of the
Enterprise Risk Manager. BCLC is currently exploring purchasing a specialist ERM

Exhibit 10.6   Thematic Risk Map Schematic

software support solution to more efficiently manage the program. Automated risk interdependency mapping is a function that the administrators hope to be able to purchase.

THE ROLE OF RISK MANAGERS, CHAMPIONS, AND COMMITTEES

BCLC's risk management program would not have been possible without the two risk managers, the ERMAC group and its champions, and the initial drive from the head of Internal Audit to implement ERM. Although most risk managers will state that the most important prerequisite for a successful risk management program is active endorsement by senior management, the provision of operational managerial resources is also essential. At BCLC, as with most organizations, the greatest progress has been made when there has been a designated risk manager assigned to the ERM program.

The role of the central risk function at BCLC, Risk Advisory Services, has not been to manage any specific risks, but rather to provide expert facilitation, coordination, and advice to management. The accountability for individual risks remains with the manager responsible for the program where the risk originates.

The two managers who have supported the ERM program came from very different backgrounds and brought different approaches to the program. Initially the program was initiated within Internal Audit and the first risk manager brought both extensive internal audit experience and, as an internal appointment, an understanding of BCLC's culture and approach. The second risk manager came with a more operationally focused risk management background and from a very different sector. Enterprise risk management is a developing discipline, and practitioners come from a wide variety of backgrounds (including finance, audit, health and safety, quality assurance, engineering, insurance, etc.), each with their own slightly different approach. Where risk management programs are supported by a single individual, change in personnel can be an opportunity to revitalize programs but also has the potential for discontinuity.

During the initial establishment of the program in 2007–2008, the active engagement of the ERMAC group of risk champions supported adoption of risk management across BCLC, bringing their knowledge and enthusiasm to both the enterprise risk assessments and the development of the program as a whole.

Risk champions are frequently advocated as a way to embed risk management into functional areas through their existing personal and professional relationships, and also as a group with diverse backgrounds and operational experience to assist with articulating a more holistic enterprise-level view of risk. However, there are some issues with the concept:

- Those selected may be the usual suspects—individuals who are chosen for every initiative either because they are felt to be particularly capable, in which case they may be overly stretched, or conversely because they are underutilized at present, leading to the possibility that they may not have the required influence to be effective.

- There may be a perception that the champion is responsible for risks in his or her division or functional area, even though other individuals hold the appropriate managerial or oversight role. This issue may lead to risks being identified but not effectively managed with formal treatment plans, and potentially to difficulties with monitoring and follow-up. Over time, champions may feel that they are put in a difficult position, or may become frustrated that their concerns are not taken forward and acted upon.

During the establishment of the ERM program, the role of the champions on the ERM Advisory Committee was clear, but as the program progressed, and in particular following the changes in 2009, the mandate became less clear and members began to feel a degree of frustration. The 2010 Internal Audit ERM review picked up on these concerns, and a new model was proposed that led to the disbanding of the committee in 2011.

The new model recognized the high level of engagement of senior management across BCLC and the more dynamic role of the Executive and the board, and also picked up on the developing concept of linking governance, risk, and compliance (GRC) matters into an integrated approach. The previous mandates of both ERMAC and a compliance committee that BCLC had established in early 2010 were brought together into the new Risk Management Planning Group (see Exhibit 10.7). This group consists of the leads from key BCLC programs, such as business planning, portfolio management, business continuity, enterprise architecture, internal audit, and policy management, with the primary role to share knowledge and improve coordination across the functions.

Early accomplishments for the group included the development and adoption of a shared lexicon of key risk management terms, and a jointly developed compliance management proposal and business case. Currently, the group is focused on developing a broad-based GRC-type dashboard, which will bring together information about the status of risks, audits, policies, regulations, performance indicators, incidents, and issues at a divisional level.

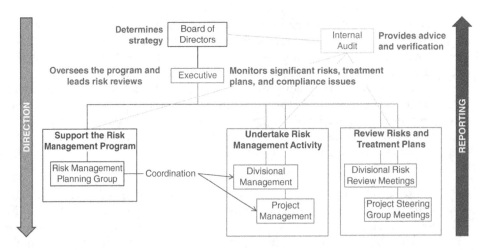

Exhibit 10.7   ERM Governance Structure, 2012–2013

DEVELOPING A MORE SOPHISTICATED APPROACH TO RISK ANALYSIS AND EVALUATION

According to ISO 31000, an essential part of developing any risk management framework is defining the criteria for evaluating risk. Risk criteria are used to reduce subjectivity and to communicate risk tolerance, and should lead to consistency across different assessments. In common with many nonfinancial organizations, BCLC uses risk tables with qualitative descriptions of a variety of potential impacts.

Over the past 10 years, a variety of risk tables and evaluation approaches have been adopted.

When BCLC conducted its initial enterprise risk management exercise in 2003, generic consequence and likelihood and management effectiveness scales with a 1 to 5 range were provided to BCLC by the consultants. The impact ratings focused on monetary and service provision consequences, while the likelihood ratings considered the chance of occurrence over the next three years.

For this initiative, risk workshops were used for the majority of risk analysis, with risk statements either predetermined or defined in advance using interviews with key internal stakeholders and then voted on by the Executive Committee, the ERMAC team, or a specific project team depending on the context. Voting technology was used at each workshop, with each participant independently rating each risk. After each vote, the software calculated the average score and derived an overall risk rating for each risk. Using voting has a number of benefits, principally allowing a large number of risks to be assessed in a relatively short period of time. Advocates also claim that voting reduces group bias, as results can be presented anonymously and any variations can be discussed.

Voters at each facilitated workshop were asked to rate the likelihood that a particular event would occur in the absence of any controls in place to mitigate the risk (known as the inherent likelihood). Each risk was then mapped to one of four categories (see Exhibit 10.8). An additional exercise considered the effectiveness of current control levels for each risk and also the desired level of control in order to identify any risks where it was considered that additional levels of control were required.

The Internal Audit–led exercise in 2006 initially used a very simple scale (high, moderate, low, and very low) when asking participants to identify/report their top three risks, and then introduced a new BCLC-specific impact and likelihood table to assess inherent impact and likelihood, using the same voting and averaging methodology as used in 2003. The new risk criteria considered a range of potential consequences, from threats to product integrity, to media reports, sales, stakeholder relations, regulatory noncompliance, and budgetary impact. The new likelihood ratings included both an assessment of the probability of occurrence and reference to historical incidence and common root causes and control effectiveness. The risks were again grouped into four categories, as can be seen in Exhibit 10.9.

The 2007 enterprise assessment developed the risk assessment framework further, reflecting the additional resources now available to the ERM program with the appointment of a dedicated manager and the engagement of the new ERMAC team. The criteria were revised once more, with metrics developed for each

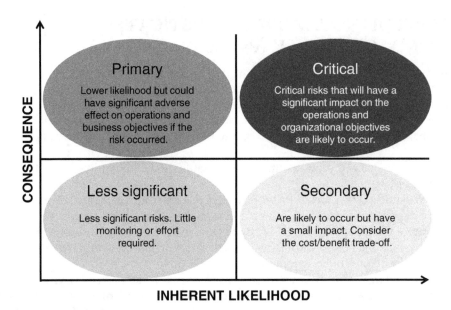

Exhibit 10.8   2003 Risk Mapping Approach

category of consequence, a cleaner likelihood table with measures of both probability and frequency, and a new management effectiveness rating table.

Assessment participants were asked to vote on the impact if the risk event were to occur and the inherent likelihood of that event occurring. As with the previous assessments, the overall rating assigned to each risk was taken as the average, giving a score from 1 to 5 for each risk. A further vote was then conducted

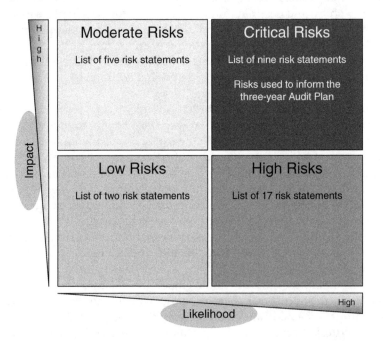

Exhibit 10.9   2006 Internal Audit Risk Matrix

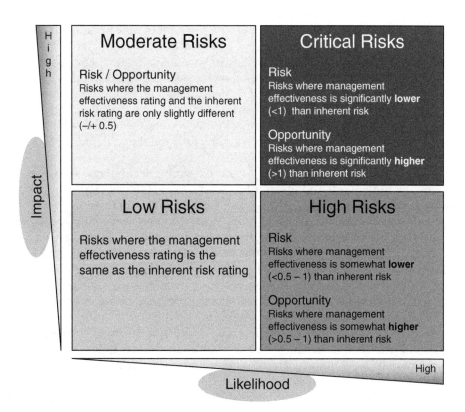

Exhibit 10.10   2008 ERM Residual Risk Rating Matrix

on how effective the ERMAC team considered current controls to be for each risk (the "current management effectiveness"). The two scores were then compared and any risks with a high-risk rating and lower management effectiveness rating were identified as requiring management attention.

The two enterprise risk assessments in 2008 in February and November used a very similar approach to the 2007 assessment, except that, instead of reporting on the inherent risk ratings and highlighting any significant gaps between the inherent risk rating and the management effectiveness rating, the management effectiveness metric was used to place each risk in a residual risk matrix, according to the size of the gap. Where the gap showed that controls were insufficient, this was termed a risk (better described as intolerable residual risk), and where the gap showed that controls were excessive, this was classified as an opportunity (to reduce control levels). The final outcome of the exercise is shown in Exhibit 10.10.

This approach was adopted partly in recognition that BCLC had not always put in place sufficient controls for the level of risk, but also because there was a perception that in some areas excessive controls had been implemented, partly in response to the Ombudsman report and subsequent recommendations and partly because some areas of the organization were considered to be risk averse.

From 2009, there was a change in emphasis from primarily inherent to residual risk assessments. This was partly due to the different approach of the new manager, partly due to difficulties with accurately assessing inherent risk, and partly because of a new opportunity with the development of new organizational goals. BCLC had been exploring the concept of balanced scorecards[5] as part of developing a more mature approach to performance management, and in early 2009 new risk criteria were introduced based on the new goals. This reinforced the link between risk and wider business and strategic planning, and enabled the development of a smaller set of risk impact categories that resonated with both management and senior leadership. The impact criteria were developed with key managers and validated with the executives, with an annual update incorporated into the risk management planning timetable.

At this time also BCLC ceased to use the voting technology for a variety of reasons, including cost and geographical limitations, and moved to an approach where group workshops prioritized risk but did not undertake formal analysis or evaluation. A variety of visual mapping techniques were introduced with a more hands-on style adopted, requiring workshop participants to engage more directly through the use of techniques such as using Post-its, voting cards, target placement, assigning spots, and drawing process maps. Formal analysis moved to the appropriate subject matter expert with quality assurance provided by the risk manager and then confirmation of risk scoring provided by the relevant member of the executive or project steering group.

In 2011, as an outcome of the Internal Audit ERM review, it was agreed that the criteria were not sufficiently aligned with leadership attitudes to risk, and that too many risks were being reported with a high rating and thus being escalated in the quarterly report. An exercise was conducted with executives to better align the existing risk criteria to organizational tolerance, and to discuss the perception that the organization, or at least some parts of it, was overly risk averse. Perspective was provided through discussion of the balance between risk aversion and excessive risk appetite and the use of the "as low as reasonably practical" principle (sometimes referred to as ALARP or ALARA [as low as reasonably achievable], and described in ISO 31010).

Two activities were undertaken, each designed to look at the four dimensions of impact in the ERM framework to ascertain whether current levels were an accurate representation of the attitude of BCLC leadership toward risk, and to initiate discussion where that attitude varied among the executives.

The first exercise (see Exhibit 10.11) used a poster showing the existing impact criteria, and each executive was asked to mark where he or she believed the current catastrophic or level 5 impact should truly fall on the scale. This clearly shows that the scales in use at the time were generally felt to be misaligned with organizational risk tolerance, in particular for financial/operations and people impacts.

The second exercise took a small number of existing and well-understood risks, all currently assessed at a similar risk rating but with impacts across the different dimensions. Each executive was asked to place the risk where he or she believed it lay on the current impact table, again displayed as a large poster. Exhibit 10.12 depicts the mapping for two of the risks, showing both the spread of opinion, and the disparity between the rating at the time and the risk attitude of the executives both as individuals and collectively.

The exercises were successful in generating discussion about relative risk tolerances and showed both that the overall evaluation tools were escalating risk at too low a level and also that the risk criteria across the different impact

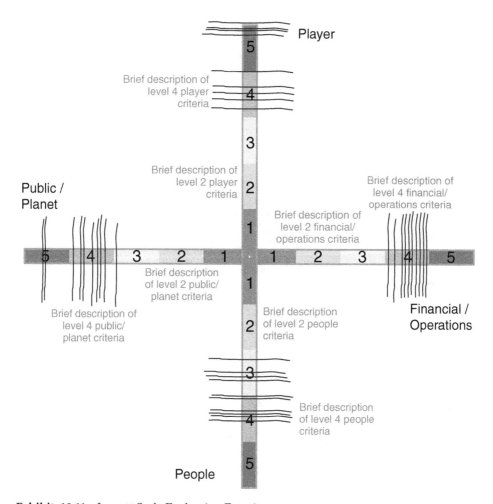

Exhibit 10.11 Impact Scale Evaluation Exercise

dimensions were not completely aligned to the collective executive risk perception and attitudes.

The impact criteria and the risk evaluation table were adjusted after the executive meeting, and the new approach adopted for the next risk review in March 2011. As a result of changing the criteria, the number of risks escalated to the executive declined from 33 to 10, allowing a much greater focus on the most significant risks, while risks now rated as having a moderate risk level continued to receive focus at the divisional risk review meetings.

In early 2012, a new risk framework was put in place describing BCLC's now maturing approach to enterprise risk management. The framework contained a section on determining appropriate risk responses, including a formal statement that BCLC had adopted the ALARP approach to determine the appropriate response to risk. This approach divides risks into three regions or zones:

1. An acceptable region, where further treatment may be undertaken but is not required

		Likelihood				
		Rare	Unlikely	Possible	Likely	Almost Certain
Impact	Insignificant	1	2 [Risk16]	3	4	5
	Minor	2	4 [Risk5] [Risk9/Risk8]	6 [Risk8] [Risk16]	8 [Risk8]	10
	Moderate	3	6 [Risk16] [Risk9] [Risk16]	9 [Risk8] [Risk16] [Risk5]	12 [Risk5] [Risk8]	15 [Risk8]
	Major	4	[Risk16]	[Risk2] [Risk9] [Risk5]	16 [Risk16] [Risk2] [Risk2]	20
	Catastrophic	5	10	15 [Risk2]	20	25

[Risk8] Original rating   [Risk3] Rating by each VP   [Risk16] Consensus

Exhibit 10.12   Specific Risk Impact/Likelihood Evaluation Exercise

2. A tolerable region where treatment should be undertaken dependent on cost/benefit analysis
3. An unacceptable region where treatment to lower the risk is mandated

Taking an ALARP approach to risk response allows for flexibility when determining the best approach to managing risk, and reflects that organizations may on occasion choose to adopt higher-risk strategies where the potential reward is deemed to be sufficient, or may elect to carry significant risk where the cost of treatment is felt to be prohibitive.

The relationships between criteria, severity, escalation, and tolerance are set out in Exhibit 10.13.

The next significant risk assessment and evaluation development was the expansion of the risk consequence criteria in August 2012 to include positive outcomes. Consideration of positive outcomes from uncertainty was introduced in ISO 31000, but has long been recommended by project management, for example in the Project Management Institute (PMI)'s Practice Standard for Project Risk Management. The concept was introduced for two reasons: to better engage those parts of the organization that were aiming to become highly innovative, and to better assess the risks associated with new initiatives. The new approach enables the comparison of risk with potential reward, and establishes the idea that both threats and opportunities are associated with uncertainty.

The new consequence table was based as previously on the key BCLC goals but for the first time included consideration of both positive and negative impacts, with benefits considered as opportunity and loss/harm as threat. The table has

The relationship between risk criteria, severity assessment, escalation, and tolerance

		Likelihood							
		Rare	Unlikely	Possible	Likely	Almost Certain			
Impact	Insignificant	1	2	3	4	5	GREEN LOW	TEAM LEADERS	
	Minor	2	4	6	8	10	YELLOW MEDIUM	DIRECTORS	
	Moderate	3	6	9	12	15	AMBER HIGH	VPs	
	Major	4	8	12	16	20	RED CRITICAL	CEO	
	Catastrophic	5	10	15	20	25			

Acceptable region
Necessary to maintain assurance that risk remains at this level

Tolerable region
Tolerable if cost of reduction would exceed the improvement gained

Tolerable only if risk reduction is impracticable or if its cost is grossly disproportionate to the improvement gained

Unacceptable region
Risk cannot be justified save in extraordinary circumstances

Exhibit 10.13 Implementing the ALARP Approach to Risk Response

four levels of positive outcomes and four levels of negative outcomes (with a neutral zone bridging the two). BCLC has opted for a symmetrical approach so that a given level of negative outcome in any of the dimensions is balanced by the equivalent level of positive outcome. For example, one of the existing financial criteria references the possibility of making a loss of up to $5 million. Therefore, the parallel positive consequence is a potential gain of up to $5 million. Likewise, in the overall severity matrix, the appetites and tolerances for positive risk follow the same principles already in use for negative risk.

The new table was incorporated into the business case template, with simple graphical maps produced as an outcome of a detailed assessment showing the overall risk profile of any proposed initiative. These maps are used as one of the factors determining both the selection of initiatives and the level of risk management support and monitoring subsequent to approval. The approach has proved very helpful for both risk mitigating proposals to be able to demonstrate value more clearly and for those initiatives that have a more balanced profile to incorporate risk treatment plans from a much earlier stage, allowing for better risk planning and resourcing.

Exhibit 10.14 shows an example of the summary charts produced as an outcome of a business case risk assessment exercise. The business case is for an initiative that is primarily designed to reduce existing risks across a number of organizational objectives. The bars show the current threat and opportunity assessment, while the lines show the anticipated effect of the initiative on the organizational risk profile. The matrix looks at the overall balance between threat and opportunity, with the pre- and post-treatment statuses showing very positive changes. This initiative was approved and is proceeding. Because of the high levels of uncertainty, monitoring of threat mitigation and benefit realization will be important.

Exhibit 10.15 shows another example, this time for an initiative with very low levels of uncertainty. The overall effect of the initiative on the organization's risk profile is broadly neutral. This initiative was also approved and is proceeding. As levels of uncertainty are low, monitoring will be minimal.

Although there was a significant learning curve both for the teams participating in the risk assessments and for senior management in interpreting the results,

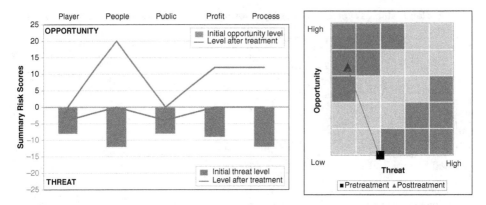

Exhibit 10.14 Business Case Risk Assessment Output Example 1

the new approach was endorsed by management and was used again in 2013 with some minor improvements to increase consistency.

Linking discussion of potential rewards with potential problems has supported the development of a more nuanced view of risk across BCLC and proved more culturally acceptable to individuals and groups tasked with developing innovative practices, as there is less of a focus on asking "What could go wrong?" and more emphasis on "What is not certain?" This has helped the ERM program to counter the viewpoint held by some groups that managing risk is a necessary but uninspiring and possibly bureaucratic exercise required by a risk-averse corporation, and has led to a better understanding that becoming risk-aware helps in embracing change and achieving objectives.

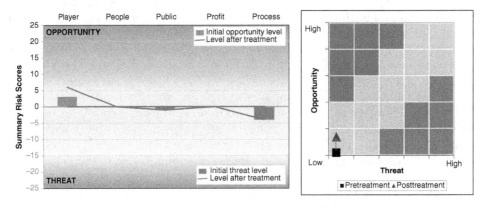

Exhibit 10.15 Business Case Risk Assessment Output Example 2

CONCLUSION

This case study has described how enterprise risk management has developed over the past 10 years at BCLC, a Canadian crown corporation offering lottery, casino, and online gambling. BCLC's enterprise risk management program has been developed over time through a combination of internal experiential learning and the application of specialist advice. The program's success has been due to the dedication of a number of key individuals, the support of senior leadership, and the participation of BCLC employees.

The approach to ERM has evolved from informal conversations supported by an external assessment, through a period of high-level corporate focus supported by a dedicated group of champions using voting technology, to an embedded approach, where risk assessments are incorporated into both operational practice and planning for the future using a variety of approaches, depending on the context. The increasing maturity of the program has been mapped to a simple scale adapted from a model developed by Deloitte (Exhibit 10.16).

BCLC's current approach to managing risk is one that recognizes that, in order to innovate and develop, it needs to embrace change with all the associated uncertainty that brings. At the same time it needs to protect its reputation and preserve the integrity of its systems and processes. Risk awareness and appropriate response are thus essential in both day-to-day and longer-term strategic planning.

BCLC is moving into a more challenging future and working to transform into an increasingly dynamic and innovative organization, where effective risk management will increasingly become a core competency for success. As its leaders reflect on 10 years of enterprise risk management, there are still plenty of challenges ahead in order to continue to sustain and develop its program. In particular they are looking to automate monitoring and reporting.

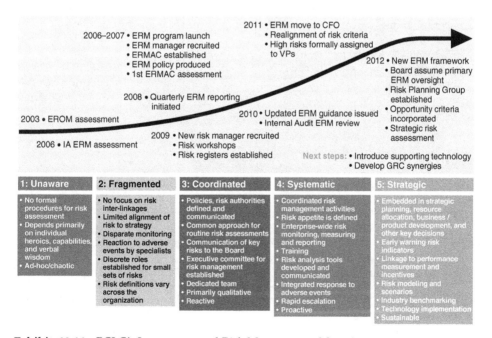

Exhibit 10.16   BCLC's Journey toward Risk Management Maturity

QUESTIONS

1. Sometimes risk workshops generate so many risks that it is not possible to assess all of them, while on other occasions only a small number of risks are identified and in-depth assessment is possible. What are the advantages and disadvantages of these two scenarios?
2. How do outcomes, causes, and risks differ, and what are the implications of confusing these?
3. Is the term *inherent risk* helpful? How could it help and/or hinder the assessment of risk?
4. What are the implications of moving from assessments of predefined sets of risks to using top-down objectives based on the balanced score card approach?
5. Contrast the advantages and disadvantages of using voting technology compared with other approaches such as those described in this case study.

NOTES

1. The Sarbanes-Oxley Act of 2002 was enacted in the United States as a response to a number of corporate governance scandals and introduced a number of financial governance regulations, including the requirement to produce a report on internal control.
2. The CBC investigative series *Fifth Estate* aired an episode entitled "Luck of the Draw" on March 14, 2007, about insider wins, featuring the story of Bob Edmonds, who was defrauded out of his lottery winnings by a retail clerk.
3. The Player First program was BCLC's response to the Ombudsman report and Deloitte recommendations, a collection of significant change initiatives under way from 2007 to 2011 designed to put the player at the forefront of BCLC activities.
4. Bow-tie analysis is a simple diagrammatic way of describing and analyzing the pathways of a risk from causes to consequences. The approach is outlined in ISO 31010 risk assessment techniques. Also see pages 291–293 of *Enterprise Risk Management: Today's Leading Research and Best Practices for Tomorrow's Executives*, ed. John Fraser and Betty J. Simkins (Hoboken, NJ: John Wiley & Sons, 2010).
5. The balanced scorecard originated by Drs. Robert Kaplan and David Norton as a performance measurement framework that added strategic nonfinancial performance measures to traditional financial metrics to give managers and executives a more balanced view of organizational performance.

REFERENCES

AS/NZS 4360:2004 Risk Management.

BCLC Annual Service Plan Report 2012/2013.

BC Ombudsman. 2007. "Winning Fair and Square: A Report on the British Columbia Lottery Corporation's Prize Payout Process."

British Columbia Treasury Board. *Core Policy and Procedures Manual (CPPM)*. "Risk Management," Chapter 14.

Committee of Sponsoring Organizations of the Treadway Commission (COSO). 2004. "Enterprise Risk Management—Integrated Framework."

Deloitte & Touche. 2003. "Enterprise-Wide Risk & Opportunity Management (EROM)— Phase 1 Final Report."

Deloitte & Touche. 2007. "Report on the Independent Review and Assessment of the Retail Lottery System in British Columbia." October.

Ernst & Young. 2010. "Results of the Enterprise Risk Management Benchmarking Study Involving 11 Participating Organizations."
ISO 31000:2009 Risk Management—Principles and Guidelines.
Society of Actuaries. 2009, 2010. "A New Approach for Managing Operational Risk."

ABOUT THE CONTRIBUTOR

Jacquetta Goy is the Director of Risk Management Services, Thompson Rivers University and former Senior Manager, Risk Advisory Services at British Columbia Lottery Corporation, responsible for establishing and developing the enterprise-wide risk management program. Prior to that she spent 14 years in the English health service, where she was responsible for setting up and developing the risk, quality, and governance programs for an inner-city health care organization. This involved preparing for a variety of accreditation reviews and inspections, managing quality assurance, audit, complaints, clinical risk, investigations, and root cause analysis. Jacquetta has both participated in and organized a number of conferences on both risk and quality management. She studied international politics at Aberystwyth University, Wales, and has a master's in public health from St. George's University of London. Currently, she is a member of the Canadian Committee for Risk Management and Related Activities, Canadian Standards Association, and one of the Canadian delegates on the international technical committee for risk management (TC262). She can often be found on various LinkedIn risk groups advocating ISO 31000.

CHAPTER 11

Starting from Scratch

The Evolution of ERM at the Workers' Compensation Fund

DAN M. HAIR
Senior Vice President, Chief Risk Officer, Workers Compensation Fund

odern workers' compensation systems are children of the industrial revolution. The concept of a social insurance program protecting workers from job-related injuries and illnesses had its modern origins in the
development of European factory, child labor, and mining regulations throughout
the eighteenth and nineteenth centuries. In the United States there was a long ges-
tation period leading to the adoption of similar schemes. In the nineteenth century
accidents in the mining and railroad industries led to early regulatory structures in
those areas. The Russell Sage Foundation's Pittsburgh Survey of 1907 along with
the Triangle Shirtwaist Factory fire in 1911 were major factors in the adoption of
the first state workmen's compensation laws from 1911 to 1915.

In 1917, the Utah legislature passed the Workers' Compensation Act, requiring
all employers to obtain workers' compensation insurance coverage. The Workers
Compensation Fund (WCF), then called the State Insurance Fund, was created to
provide competitively priced insurance to Utah employers. In the same year, the
legislature appropriated $40,000 from the state treasury for WCF to begin writing
insurance. This loan was repaid by WCF in four years, and from that time forward
WCF has operated financially independent of the state and has functioned largely
as a state agency.

A formal organizational study of WCF was completed in 1987. It recommended autonomy from state administration by establishing WCF as a quasi-
public corporation with a board of directors comprised of policyholders and individuals with expertise. In 1988 the Utah legislature again modified its statutes to
protect the state from any WCF expenses or debts and to prohibit the state from
accessing the Injury Fund. In 2005 the Utah Supreme Court ruled that WCF and all
of its assets were solely owned by its policyholders.

Today, WCF operates as a mutual insurance company owned by its policyholders and governed by a seven-member board of directors appointed by the
governor. WCF performs a public purpose relating to the state and its citizens.
Specifically, WCF serves as Utah's carrier of last resort for workers' compensation

insurance coverage. As such, any Utah employer, no matter its size, the riskiness of its business, or its prior loss history, can obtain workers' compensation insurance coverage from WCF.

WCF is under state regulatory oversight provided by the Utah Department of Insurance and Utah Labor Commission. WCF also receives annual rating agency financial oversight through the A.M. Best Company, which examines, among other things, solvency, operating performance, risk-based capital requirements, and enterprise risk management (ERM) capabilities. Currently, WCF is rated A or excellent. WCF has its headquarters in Sandy, Utah, and additional branch offices in central, northern, and southern Utah. It also owns affiliated companies that are licensed to write workers' compensation insurance and perform claims management services in other states as well.

TOWARD ERM PROGRAM INITIATION

The early 1990s were a time of transformative change at WCF. In 1992 the board hired a new president and CEO, Layne Summerhays, who soon added additional executives. The resulting executive group was an amalgam of new leaders who had spent their careers in the private sector and retained leaders with critical institutional memory and experience with the workers' compensation system in Utah. The new executive team established a focus on customer service, internal accountability, operating efficiency, and private carrier best practices.

In the ensuing years WCF obtained its initial (A–) A.M. Best rating, significantly improved operating results and customer satisfaction, grew its surplus from $67 million to more than $600 million, and returned 40 percent of net income to policyholders in dividends. These impressive results came despite the vagaries of market cycles and some very difficult strategic challenges.

Utah has been a very competitive insurance market for many years. Competitors have included large, national multiline carriers, national workers' compensation specialty carriers, and locally domiciled insurers. Their ability to quote multiple lines of insurance in and out of Utah put WCF at a distinct competitive disadvantage. Additionally, as WCF's fortunes changed, various parties initiated discussions within the legislature regarding WCF's structure, its future status as a tax-exempt market of last resort, and the ultimate ownership of company assets.

These two significant risks were tackled by the management team in close collaboration with the board. Working toward solutions involved risk assessment, evaluation of options, and envisioning potential outcome scenarios, both positive and negative. Ultimately the multistate issue was creatively resolved by working with the legislature to get limited statutory changes in an amicable fashion and the formation of an affiliated company. Resolving ownership of company assets was a more contentious issue between WCF and the executive branch of state government. This was only resolved after the board and management determined it would be necessary to take legal action by suing the State of Utah. The resulting litigation was decided in favor of WCF by the landmark 2005 Utah Supreme Court decision.

This episode in the history of the company, which involved robust discussion of risk, potential scenario development, and close collaboration with the board, was the foundation for what has followed. In addition, at the company's annual retreat and planning session for board members, senior vice presidents, and vice presidents in 2006, time was set aside for consideration of the range of potential risks to the company. Returning from this board retreat, the executive team began an ongoing discussion of key strategic risks and opportunities that continues to this day.

Although the financial trials of the Great Recession of 2007–2011 did not seriously impact the solvency of WCF or the property-casualty insurance industry, it certainly stimulated boards to think about risk, fat tails, black swans, and low-frequency, high-severity events. This watershed event also resulted in financial rating organizations such as Standard & Poor's and A.M. Best moving toward the development of much more robust questioning of rated firms' capital management, risk assessment practices, and enterprise risk management capabilities.

At this time WCF's President and CEO, Ray Pickup, along with Board Chair Dallas Bradford and other directors, began serious discussions of the need for more formality and structure in the company's risk management efforts. As the former CFO, Ray Pickup not only had a deep understanding of risk but a passion for transparency and openness, as well as a self-effacing management style that valued input from all areas of the company. As a retired partner in a public accounting firm, Chairman Bradford had long dealt with issues of risk and was a self-described "glass is half empty guy" who "imagined the worst scenario." He noted that when a company's risk management efforts fail, "a great many people would be financially damaged and the company's public image would perhaps be irreparably damaged." He also expressed that "The company had done some significant work in this arena, but little of it had been documented and there was no clear response mechanism in place. Also, there was no organized process in place to evaluate the various risks. It was an easy step for me to encourage the company to undertake a much more rigorous program to identify and manage potential risks that could severely damage our company and the important public interests we serve."[1]

INITIAL ACTIONS

In late 2010 Ray Pickup, with the approval of the board, created the chief risk officer (CRO) position, designating Dan Hair, who had been and would continue to serve as the Chief Underwriting and Safety Officer, as the first CRO. An additional committee of the board, the Risk Oversight Committee, was also created. The job description for the new CRO position contained several key elements (see WCF Chief Risk Officer Job Description). First, the CRO was to report to the president and CEO but with additional reporting responsibilities to the board and the newly formed Board Risk Oversight Committee. This was reinforced by the CEO, who encouraged direct access to the board by the CRO, including the airing of any differences of opinion. Second, the CRO was to have access to all areas of the company and its affiliates. This was fundamentally important if the CRO was to have an enterprise-wide understanding of all the risks facing WCF. Third, implicit in the job description and explicit in the WCF Risk Policy (see WCF Risk Policy) is the idea of excellence in the development of a program that is suitable and appropriate for WCF.

January 25, 2011: Initially the CRO, working with Chief Financial Officer Scott Westra, developed a preliminary risk assessment matrix to be used by the senior officers in a Delphi qualitative assessment of all risks facing the company. Each executive was asked to look at a list of risks provided by the CRO, add to it any risks they felt should be considered, and score the severity and probability of those risks. Several meetings followed with the entire senior team to come to a consensus on the matrix, scores, and risk list. Initial results were then presented to the entire Board, which resulted in further refinement of the matrix and heat maps (Exhibits 11.1 and 11.2). The Board and management were in agreement that risk appetite should primarily be evaluated by impact on WCF surplus. This was later refined to include statutory combined ratio and operating income. Senior management was explicitly tasked with developing mitigation plans for any risks scoring in the red area of the heat map.

WCF Chief Risk Officer Job Description

Position Purpose

The purpose of this position is to develop and monitor the Risk Management strategy, policies, and processes under the direction of the CEO, Board of Directors, and Board Risk Oversight Committee. Ensure that appropriate risk assessment and mitigation strategies are developed for all core functions of WCF.

Nature and Scope

The Chief Risk Officer (CRO) is a Senior Executive with 10–15 years of experience who has a broad understanding of all key areas of the business. The CRO possesses management experience in key business areas with proven ability to provide strategic direction and leadership. He/she has superior analytical, presentation, communication, and facilitation skills. The incumbent usually possesses advanced degrees and/or technical certifications in accounting, actuarial, risk management, operations, or finance.

Performance is measured on overall achievement of company financial objectives and the effectiveness of the ERM program in developing and implementing the best approaches for protecting WCF, its employees, and assets.

Principal Duties

Essential Functions

1. Develops and communicates an appropriate Enterprise Risk Management (ERM) infrastructure within WCF by working cooperatively with the Senior Officers as a group and with each department in a collaborative manner.
2. Under the direction of the CEO, works with other company executives and the Board Risk Oversight Committee to develop an ERM strategy for WCF that identifies, quantifies, and mitigates risks facing the company. Provides appropriate risk reporting.
3. Consults with and provides assistance as requested to WCF affiliates and subsidiaries. Works with them to ensure that appropriate ERM planning is in place.
4. Facilitates enterprise-wide risk assessments and monitors the capabilities around managing priority risks across the organization.

WCF Risk Policy

Failure to manage risk, whether it is financial, operational, or reputational, may subject the Company to negative outcomes. These outcomes could impact our customers, colleagues, partners, and the viability of our business. Managing risk reinforces our corporate values of compassion, accountability, and expertise.

Consequently, every employee, WCF department, and affiliate will continually assess and monitor risks of all types. Under the direction of Senior Management and the Board of Directors we will take appropriate mitigation actions consistent with our mission of excellence.

In subsequent months the CRO met with the leadership of each WCF department and affiliate to explain the importance of the ERM program, why it was being launched, and their role in the program. Basic risk management training was given to them along with a modified departmental risk matrix. Their views on risks within the company and their departments were solicited and they were guided to the development of their own heat maps. At the same time the initial meeting of the Board Risk Oversight Committee was held and the duties of the Internal Risk Committee (IRC), chaired by the CRO, were established (see WCF Internal Risk Committee Duties). This effectively created an ongoing three-level review of risk consisting of the board, senior management, and key company leaders.

Exhibit 11.1   WCF ERM Risk Management Matrix Values

Incident or exposure *probability* descriptions (Risk = $P \times S$)

Very low (1):   Improbable, no prediction confidence (P = .01/range = <.02)

Low (2):   Remote, may occur once every 10 to 50+ years (P = .02)

Moderate (3):   Occasional, may occur once every 3 to 10 years (P = .16/range = .10 to .33)

High (4):   Probable, may occur once every 2 to 5 years (P = .25/range = .20 to .50)

Very high (5):   Frequent, could occur annually (P = .50/range = .50 to 1.0)

Incident or exposure *severity* descriptions

Slight loss (1):   Inconsequential with respect to financial, personnel, or brand damage: less than 1% of surplus, or $10M loss or a 1- to 5-point impact on combined ratio.

Medium loss (2):   Important financial, personnel, or brand damage; threshold of financial materiality, 5% or more of surplus, or $11M to 25M loss or a 6- to 10-point impact on combined ratio.

Material loss (3): Material damage to financial strength, personnel, or brand; $26M–$50M loss or an 11- to 15-point impact on combined ratio.

Large loss (4):   Significant damage to financial strength, personnel, or brand; 10% or more of surplus, or a $51M to $75M loss, could damage stakeholder confidence or a 16- to 20-point impact on combined ratio.

Very high loss (5): Catastrophic impact on solvency, brand, or personnel; 50% or more of surplus; greater than a $75M loss, would damage stakeholder confidence or a combined ratio impact of >20 points.

WCF Internal Risk Committee Duties

Description

- Meets quarterly under the direction of the Chief Risk Officer.
- Attended by representatives/risk champions from each department or business unit.
- Reviews reports on department risk identification and mitigation efforts.
- Reviews risks and risk mitigation efforts company-wide.
- Receives training in risk recognition and mitigation techniques from CRO and others.
- Helps develop WCF risk policies and resources.
- Assesses risk integration and response issues.

Members

- Preferably business unit managers or leaders with interest in risk management.
- Ability to train and coach others.
- Thorough understanding of all aspects of the department/business unit.

Standing Agenda

- Review/update WCF key risks and mitigation efforts.
- Review/update department or business unit key risks and mitigation efforts.
- Training in ERM, risk identification, and control techniques (CRO or guest speakers).
- Committee member new business.
- Improving/strengthening the risk culture at WCF and affiliates.

In its initial meetings, the Board Risk Oversight Committee, which meets two or three times per year, approved the IRC Charter and gave direction and feedback regarding initial efforts. One valuable suggestion was to do a risk survey of the entire company. Although approximately one-third of WCF employees had already been involved in ERM activities to date, this was a very helpful idea. Over 50 percent of all employees responded (see 2012 All-Employee

Incident or exposure severity descriptions	Incident or exposure probability descriptions				
	Very low (1)	Low (2)	Moderate (3)	High (4)	Very high (5)
Very high loss (5)	5	(9) Large Earthquake	15	20	25
Large loss (4)	4	(8) AWCIC Failure	(12) Loss of Tax Exemption; (12) Multi-line competition, leveraging	16	20
Material loss (3)	3	(5.2) Detrimental State Regulatory Action; (4.64) Catastrophic Multi-Claim Incident; (4.5) Loss of Tax Exemption Retroactively; (5.76) Other Detrimental Federal Regulatory Action; (6.46) Terrorist Act; (5.8) Adverse Loss Reserve Development; (6) Inflation Risk; (7.02) Multi-Year High Combined Ratio	(9) Prolonged Economic Downturn Beyond 2011; (9) Prolonged Soft Market Beyond 2011	12	15
Medium loss (2)	2	(4) Violent Security Breach; (3.84) Pinnacle or AWCIC Failure; (5.04) Data Breach With Loss of Data	(6) Bond Credit Risk; (6.24) Malevolence Against Company; (5.52) Significant Number of Large Losses in Single Year; (6.9) Interest Rate Risk	8	(10) Equities or Securities Impairment
Slight loss (1)	1	(2) Other Credit Risks - Receivables	3	(4) Employee Malfeasance	5

Exhibit 11.2 WCF Risk Assessment Matrix; the increased darkness corresponds to the risk, i.e. low = least dark, medium = middle shade, and high = darkest.

Risk Score

Under 4: Category 1: Risk reduction actions discretionary, risk acceptable

4 to 8: Category 2: Ongoing risk assessment appropriate with informal mitigation but may be within risk tolerances; to be discussed with Internal Risk Committee

9 or greater: Category 3: Unacceptable risk, triggers scenario planning and development of mitigation plan to be presented to Board Committee

ERM Survey). The survey was done electronically with optional anonymity for all participants.

2012 All-Employee ERM Survey

- What are the most important challenges facing WCF today?
- What are the greatest threats to our reputation/brand?
- What local or national events or trends should cause us the most concern?
- What other issues should the Chief Risk Officer be concerned about?
- Name (optional)

Initial IRC discussions were robust and enthusiastic. The mix of company officers, managers, and risk champions worked effectively together. Many of the risks that were contained in the consolidated risk list they developed were also identified by the senior group and the company-wide survey. Having wide unanimity on which risks were most important was very helpful and allowed effective focus. Early on it was decided to split the list of risks thus developed into two sections. The first section contained the risks that, as department leaders, the IRC could impact and manage. The second-tier risks were those that were of a strategic nature or just simply could only be managed by senior management.

The initial duties of the Internal Risk Committee were to review all the department risks, consolidate them where possible, and come up with a consensus scoring using the risk matrix. The committee was split into a gold team and a blue team to accomplish this and report back to the IRC, whereupon a consensus was reached. Mitigation plans were discussed and developed where appropriate. In some cases this involved tailored mitigation steps. In many others it was determined that existing WCF and department management protocols and procedures were adequate. It is the ongoing duty of the IRC to meet quarterly to discuss the adequacy of existing mitigation efforts and to consider new risks. In each meeting of the IRC, members are asked to again consider the question "Have we adequately protected the company against these risks?" Many of the early discussions of the IRC were taken up with data security concerns, particularly relating to the Health Insurance Portability and Accountability Act of 1996. The committee also focused on cyber risk, other operational risks, affiliate risks, and compliance risks.

As a final note to this section, developing and maintaining positive and helpful relationships with other executives is very important. Two roles that are especially important at WCF are the CFO and the company's head of Internal Audit. At WCF they work closely and effectively by fully sharing information, both internal and external. Both the CFO and Internal Audit leader participate in the IRC. The CRO has no direct authority over other executives, so he or she must work in a collaborative manner, building consensus as to needed measures and ERM development. Should problems arise, the CEO has been willing to intervene in support of the ERM program, but that has rarely been needed.

MATURING: YEARS 1 AND 2

In the spring of 2011 a new tool was added to the ERM program with the introduction of the risk register (RR). Although this did not replace the risk list and heat maps, it consolidated all that information into one Excel file (see Exhibit 11.3) and added new elements necessary to properly manage risk. This is the primary document WCF uses to monitor enterprise risks.

The first cell contains each risk's assigned number and designation reflecting whether it is assigned to the IRC or to senior management. There are currently about 25 of each. A description of each risk is in the next cell, which is refined from time to time. The next cell captures risk correlation by listing the number of other risks in the document believed to be likely to occur at the same time or to be interrelated in some way. For example, a prolonged economic downturn affects other risks such as market cycle risk and pricing risk.

The next six cells in the RR deal with how the risk is scored and the potential loss to the company. The probability and severity scores are listed as currently scored. These are subject to modification to reflect changing conditions or successful mitigation. The risk score is listed and the cell is filled with light gray/medium gray/dark gray indications. The risk matrix gives ranges for both probability and severity, and selections are made for both and entered as AP (actual probability) and severity potential. These two cells are multiplied to produce a potential loss value. In a separate chart produced for the board, this cell is graphed into a tornado chart (see Exhibit 11.4) to give a representation of total potential losses at any one time. The CRO also prepares for them a separate modified heat map that shows only the most critical risks and opportunities with indications of whether we feel they are increasing or decreasing (see Exhibit 11.5).

The remaining five cells include space for probability and severity-reduction targets, mitigations recommended by the IRC or senior management, the risk owners, and who originally identified the risk. Formal mitigation steps are entered for higher-scoring risks. Usually at least a dozen or so risks have mitigation plans. A mitigation plan could be a set of active steps designed to reduce or control a risk or simply those steps that have been taken and are deemed adequate. Where this field is blank it represents a consensus that the risk is appropriately mitigated by current WCF guidelines and protocols. The risk owners are primarily responsible for actively monitoring the risk and suggesting changes or actions. The origination column just gives a record of where the concern started. Multiple people or WCF departments can appear in both cells.

In late 2011 the CRO suggested to the CEO and board that at some time a third-party review of the program might by helpful in reviewing progress to date, as well as providing some benchmarks for future improvements through the following two to three years. The board agreed, and allocations were made in the 2012 budget to engage a recognized thought leader with experience in the field to review WCF's ERM program. This was completed in the first quarter of 2012 and proved to be very helpful. The ERM expert thus engaged was Sim Segal, a Fellow of the Society of Actuaries (FSA), a Chartered Enterprise Risk Analyst (CERA), and president of Simergy Inc.

The engagement included a review of all documents relating to ERM at WCF to date, including matrices and heat maps in all their iterations. The risk register was

WCF ERM Risk Register_Version3-18-13 - Microsoft Excel

WCF - ERM - Risk Register

This version updated as of:

Items appeared at this version are red text/shading.

3/18/2013

Active Risks

	Risk	Correlated With	Current Probability Score	Current Severity Score	Risk Score	AP	Severity Potential	$ Potential	Probability Target	Severity Target	Mitigations Recommended by IRC	Risk Owner (Department)	Originated With
	Subsidiary risk (TWOIC, Pinnacle): Failure to put appropriate checks in place, conflict of interest, failure to maintain business operations in accordance with WCF standards. IF, for example, inconsistent or inappropriate HR procedures in hiring, disciplining, compensating, and terminating employees; data security breaches										•CHRO has met with AVP, DC CEO and an official ERM process has been launched. •CEO discussion with Pinnacle has resulted in progress on contract, data security, and HR issues.		
PC1	Loss of sensitive data (claims logs, medical records, claimant personal info, etc), HIPAA compliance		3		1	0.25	$15,000,000	$3,750,000				HR, IT, Legal, Finance	Investments, Legal, HR
PC2	Loss of sensitive data (claims logs, medical records, claimant personal info, etc), HIPAA compliance		3		2	6.00	0.10	$15,000,000	$1,500,000			IT	IT, Legal, Safety, UW
PC3	Transportation related catastrophic event (multi-passenger). Either aircraft exposure (multiple policyholder employees or WCF officers) or group transportation (multiple policyholder employees or someone else)		2			4.00	0.15	$25,000,000	$3,750,000			HR	Safety
PC5	Bad Faith lawsuit (failure to provide coverage, dissimilar treatment of insureds, failing to provide something marketing/someone else promised), class action lawsuit		2		3	6.00	0.10	$26,000,000	$2,600,000			Legal	Claims, Legal
PC6	Inequity in benefits administration (inconsistent approval/denials of medical treatment, etc), regulatory fines, lawsuits					1.00	0.10	$10,000,000	$1,000,000			Claims	Claims, Legal
PC7	Loss of critical vendor (Software AG, IBM/Filenet and others)		3			3.00	0.15	$10,000,000	$1,500,000			All Departments (Dan Hair will	IT
PC8	Medical advances at high cost		2		2	2.00	0.10	$11,000,000	$1,100,000			Claims	Actuarial
PC9	Premium fraud schemes		3		2	6.00	0.15	$11,000,000	$1,650,000			Premium Audit	Premium Audit
PC10	Internal employee risk exposure — inside and around building, violence in the workplace (employee, applicant, or claimant going postal)		2			4.00	0.10	$11,000,000	$1,100,000			IT & Security	Claims, Facilities, Safety, HR, IT
PC11	Negative Social Media/PR event, loss of reputation (large visibility lawsuit, loss of large agency)		3		3	3.00	0.15	$10,000,000	$1,500,000			Marketing	Marketing, Safety
PC12	Catastrophic event such as pandemic causing multiple large claims		2		3	6.00	0.10	$50,000,000	$5,000,000			Med Management	Claims, IT, Marketing, UW
PC13	Risk of widespread misclassification resulting in inadequate rates		3			3.00	0.25	$10,000,000	$2,500,000			Underwriting	UW
PC14	Loss of key employees including senior management		3		1	3.00	0.15	$10,000,000	$1,500,000			HR	HR, IT, Legal, Marketing, UW
PC15	Legal environment — case law, benefits, retroactive or prospective legislative changes that expand scope of benefits, limit subrogation, DOI lack of enforcement, potential compensation coverage changes to include occupational illness retroactive & prospective		2		2	4.00	0.10	$25,000,000	$2,500,000			Legal	Actuarial, Legal, Actuarial
PC16	Risk of delays/failures with the TOPICS rewrite project (scope creep, technology changes, systems capacity, etc)		3		2	6.00	0.15	$25,000,000	$3,750,000			IT	IT
PC17	External employee risk exposure — traveling, external appointments, working from home		1		2	4.00	0.15	$11,000,000	$1,650,000			HR	Claims, Facilities, Marketing
PC18	Approval/payment of treatments resulting in death (Rx meds, opioids, etc)		1		2	2.00	0.10	$11,000,000	$1,100,000			Claims	Med Management
PC19	Zions bank processing error/failure		1		2	2.00	0.10	$11,000,000	$1,100,000			Finance	Finance, Investments
PC20	Inadequate resources to meet business needs (employees, equipment, etc)		1		2	2.00	0.10	$11,000,000	$1,100,000			HR	HR, IT, UW
PC21	Loss of WCF computer systems/programs		2		2	4.00	0.10	$11,000,000	$1,100,000			IT	Claims, UW, IT
PC22	Compliance risk, NCCI, IRS, CMS		3			3.00	0.10	$10,000,000	$1,000,000			All Departments (Dan Hair will	Actuarial, Finance
PC23	Employee Malfeasance, System misuse		3			3.00	0.10	$10,000,000	$1,000,000			HR, IT	Claims, UW
PC24	Medicare Set Aside (MSA) reporting (fines associated with not reporting)		2		2	4.00	0.10	$11,000,000	$1,100,000			Claims	Claims
PC25	Other credit risk, receivables		1			1.00	0.10	$5,000,000	$500,000			Finance	Finance

Exhibit 11.3 WCF Risk Register

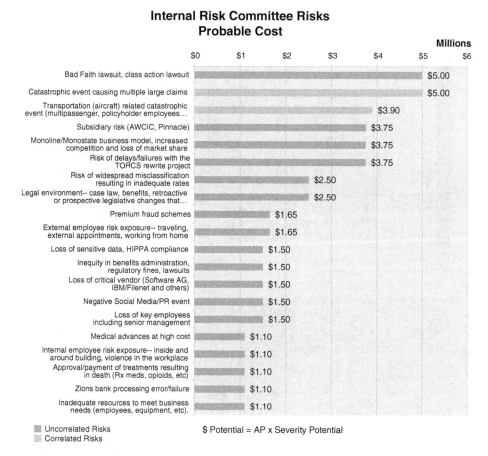

Internal Risk Committee Risks
Probable Cost

Millions

Risk	Probable Cost
Bad Faith lawsuit, class action lawsuit	$5.00
Catastrophic event causing multiple large claims	$5.00
Transportation (aircraft) related catastrophic event (multipassenger, policyholder employees…	$3.90
Subsidiary risk (AWCIC, Pinnacle)	$3.75
Monoline/Monostate business model, increased competition and loss of market share	$3.75
Risk of delays/failures with the TORCS rewrite project	$3.75
Risk of widespread misclassification resulting in inadequate rates	$2.50
Legal environment-- case law, benefits, retroactive or prospective legislative changes that…	$2.50
Premium fraud schemes	$1.65
External employee risk exposure-- traveling, external appointments, working from home	$1.65
Loss of sensitive data, HIPPA compliance	$1.50
Inequity in benefits administration, regulatory fines, lawsuits	$1.50
Loss of critical vendor (Software AG, IBM/Filenet and others)	$1.50
Negative Social Media/PR event	$1.50
Loss of key employees including senior management	$1.50
Medical advances at high cost	$1.10
Internal employee risk exposure-- inside and around building, violence in the workplace	$1.10
Approval/payment of treatments resulting in death (Rx meds, opioids, etc)	$1.10
Zions bank processing error/failure	$1.10
Inadequate resources to meet business needs (employees, equipment, etc).	$1.10

Uncorrelated Risks
Correlated Risks

$ Potential = AP x Severity Potential

Exhibit 11.4 Internal Risk Committee Risks: Probable Cost

reviewed along with minutes of all the IRC and Board Risk Oversight Committee meetings. This document review was followed by a lengthy discussion with the CRO responding to questions about the process, personalities, and content. A full day was spent by Sim Segal in one-on-one discussion with WCF's president and CEO, the board chairman, other WCF executives, and members of the IRC.

The final report with recommendations was given to and reviewed with all parties and discussed at the 2012 annual board retreat. The report was helpful in verifying WCF's initial steps and pointing it toward several key future steps with some action items. These included more rigorous risk analysis of key risks using sophisticated process safety tools, engaging more closely with the affiliates and moving toward a more formalized approach to risk/opportunity issues.

The action items have been a primary focus throughout 2012 and 2013, and two are worth specifically addressing. The most consistent failure mode for property-casualty insurance carriers is reserve failures. Workers' compensation claims have a very long tail in that costs are not finalized for many years. In fact, WCF is still paying on claims dating back to the 1950s. Case reserving involves an adjuster's considered estimate of all costs to the end of the claim and an actuary's judgment of the cumulative expected development on those claims. Some will close for less

Senior Management Risks
Threat/Opportunity Matrix (Top 10 by Risk Score)

Risk	Risk title	Risk Owner	Risk Score
3	Equities/Securities Impairments	Scott Westra	16
1	Loss of Tax Exemption	Ray Pickup, Dennis Lloyd	12
2	Multiline Competition	Peggy Larson, Dan Hair	12
8	Unsuccessful Pricing Strategy, High Multiyear Combined Ratio	Dan Hair & Sr. Team	12
4	Large Earthquake	Dan Hair	9
7	AWCIC Failure/Rating Downgrade	Ray, Dan, Scott	9
13	Inflation Risk	Scott Westra	9
15	Significant Number of Large Losses in a Single Year	Dan Hair	6.22
9	Interest Rate Risk	Scott Westra	6
12	Bond Credit Risk	Scott Westra	6
5	Prolonged Economic Downturn Beyond 2012	Sr. Group	6

Probability

	Slight Loss (1)	Medium Loss (2)	Material Loss (3)	Large Loss (4)	Very High Loss (5)
Very High (5)	Risk Score 5	Risk Score 10	Risk Score 15	Risk Score 20	Risk Score 25
High (4)	Risk Score 4	Risk Score 8	Risk Score 12	Risk Score 16	Risk Score 20
Mod (3)	Risk Score 3	Risk Score 6	Risk Score 9	Risk Score 12	Risk Score 15
Low (2)	Risk Score 2	Risk Score 4	Risk Score 6	Risk Score 8	Risk Score 10
Very Low (1)	Risk Score 1	Risk Score 2	Risk Score 3	Risk Score 4	Risk Score 5

Severity

Threat
Opportunity
Both

Risk movement since last review
Risk trend based on status and current action

Exhibit 11.5 Senior Management Risks: Threat/Opportunity Matrix (Top 10 by Risk Score)

than the estimate whereas many will ultimately exceed the estimates by a considerable margin. If a carrier gets this wrong, it will become insolvent. The same is true for pricing workers' compensation insurance. It is based on a volatile estimate of cost of goods sold and is subject to fluctuation and pricing error. While this does not usually result in insolvency, it can dramatically impact profitability. Therefore, claim reserving error and pricing error seem to be the best candidates for a more rigorous risk analysis.

To make this analysis, a simple fault tree methodology was selected (see Exhibits 11.6 and 11.7).

The fault trees were developed through consultation with subject experts. They consist of an end point failure that WCF is seeking to avoid and levels of precipitating errors built upon each other that would lead to that top-level outcome. The final bottom end points would be factors for which WCF needs to build mitigation plans. In both cases significant variables are system malfunctions, human errors, and oversight failures. The finalized analyses are then reviewed with both risk committees.

Finally, the other major focus in 2013 is on developing both a robust risk/opportunity assessment tool and determining the parameters for its use. For WCF an acceptable tool has been difficult to agree on. An initial form was developed and experimented with on a voluntary basis (see Exhibit 11.8). The form contained a restatement of WCF's risk appetite/tolerance statement guiding the users in regard to when it should be used. A description of the proposed action was required along with cost and expected value explanations.

Identified risks to successful implementation were listed and scored using a matrix embedded in the tool. Mitigation strategies for risk scoring at a certain level were completed.

Information regarding the risk owner and approvals completed the form. The usefulness of the process seemed to lie in three areas:

1. The process could help users to cover all the bases in considering their plans.
2. It could also be helpful in creating a management review and oversight circuit breaker that many companies that fared poorly in 2007–2010 might today wish they had.
3. Finally, it provides a record of risk taking. We often look back on failures and ask: How did that happen? A good risk record might show us whether the issue was an unidentified, unforeseen risk, an execution failure, or just a failure in judgment.

The question seems to come down to whether present systems are adequate or is additional formalization worth the effort and extra work? After further consultation with the Board Risk Oversight Committee in late 2013, management decided to adopt a "principle-based guideline that could be used on a voluntary basis or required by management as desired." (See pp. 223–224.) This approach gives maximum flexibility along with simplicity. Simple but fundamental questions are used to elicit understanding of a proposed action. Examples of ventures that might be suitable for an analysis are given and a simple follow-up process is described. So far, this approach has been successfully used several times and seems to meet the needs of the organization at this time.

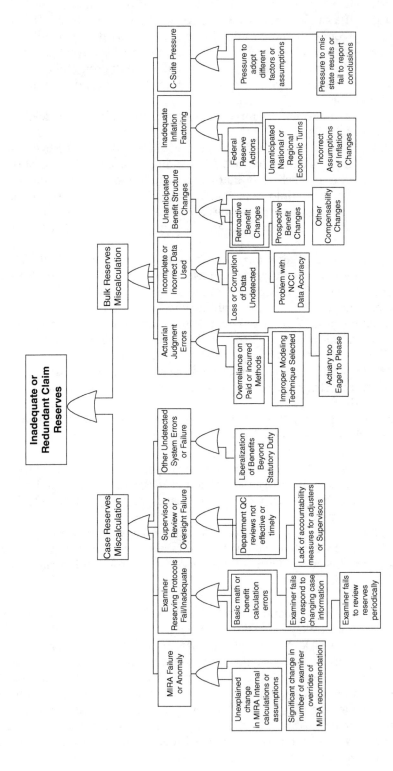

Exhibit 11.6 Claim Reserving Error Fault Tree

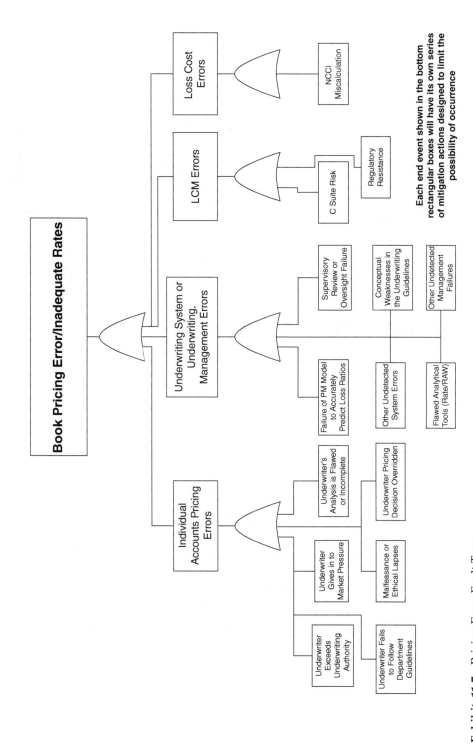

Book Pricing Error/Inadequate Rates

Loss Cost Errors
- NCCI Miscalculation

LCM Errors
- C Suite Risk
- Regulatory Resistance

Each end event shown in the bottom rectangular boxes will have its own series of mitigation actions designed to limit the possibility of occurrence

Underwriting System or Underwriting, Management Errors
- Supervisory Review or Oversight Failure
- Conceptual Weaknesses in the Underwriting Guidelines
- Other Undetected Management Failures
- Failure of PM Model to Accurately Predict Loss Ratios
- Other Undetected System Errors
- Flawed Analytical Tools (Rate/RAW)

Individual Accounts Pricing Errors
- Underwriter's Analysis is Flawed or Incomplete
- Underwriter Pricing Decision Overridden
- Underwriter Gives in to Market Pressure
- Malfeasance or Ethical Lapses
- Underwriter Exceeds Underwriting Authority
- Underwriter Fails to Follow Department Guidelines

Exhibit 11.7 Pricing Error Fault Tree

221

Risk Analysis Worksheet

It is the policy of WCF senior management to identify risk exposures that represent a potential "material" loss to the Company with an occurrence probability of "moderate" or higher. Material loss is defined as >5% of specific company surplus, or Departmental budget. In addition, management will identify correlated risks that, occuring simultaneously, would trigger either of these or an income statement loss greater than 10% of annul premium.

Company, Department, or Subsidiary: _____ Date: _____

Proposed Action, Product, or Operational Change:

Potential Risks	Prob. Score	Sev. Score	Total Score
1)			
2)			
3)			
4)			
5)			
6)			
7)			
8)			
9)			
10)			

Incident or expsoure *probability* descriptions

Very Low (1): Improbable, no prediction confidence
Low (2): Remote, may occur once every 10-50+ years
Moderate (3): Occasional, may occur once every 3-10 years
High (4): Probable, may occur once every 2-5 years
Very High (5): Frequent, could occur annually

Incident or exposure *severity* descriptions

Slight Loss (1): Inconsequential with respect to financial, personnel, or brand damage. Less than 1% of surplus or $10M loss or less
Medium Loss (2): Important financial, personnel, or brand damage; 5% or more of surplus or $11M-$25M loss.
Material Loss (3): Material damage to financial strength, personnel, or brand; 10% or more of surplus or a $26M-$50M loss.
Large Loss (4): Significant damage to financial strength, personnel, or brand; 10% more of surplus or a $51M-$75M loss, could damage stakeholder confidence.
Very High Loss (5): Catastrophic impact on solvency, brand or personnel; 50% or more of surplus, greater than a $75M loss, would damage stakeholder confidence.

*Potential risks scoring 6 or greater must have completed mitigation plans.

Spaces requiring input are shaded.

Mitigation Plans and Risk Owners (Attach additional documentation as needed)

Expected Value of Action

Implementation Costs

Completed by: _____   Dept. SVP: _____

Dept. Manager or VP: _____   CEO: _____

Chief Risk Officer: _____

Exhibit 11.8   Risk Analysis Worksheet

WCF Group—Risk Assessment Framework
February 2014

In order to protect our assets, our employees and our customers, WCF is committed to excellence and consistency in risk assessment and risk management. We are creating a risk assessment process that is transparent, scalable and productive. An effective process is one that promotes a thorough analysis and provides a framework for successful execution of the initiative.

Principle Based Format

The following questions should be addressed in a single document for new ventures or initiatives meeting the risk assessment "trigger":

1. Why do we need to take this step at this time and what are the expected costs and benefits?
2. What are the key risks (financial, operational, market, strategic, etc.) involved in the initiative?
3. How will each risk be mitigated? (Identify the specific controls to be applied.)
4. What are the most likely outcomes of the venture, as well as, the worst and best case scenarios?

Examples of initiatives triggering a risk assessment

1. Significant pricing changes, e.g. refiling Loss Cost Modifiers.
2. Legislative initiatives proposed by WCF.
3. Changes in commission structure.
4. IT software or hardware purchases in excess of $500,000.
5. Changes in claim reserving methodology or claims settlement policy.
6. Investment initiatives requiring a change in investment policy and/or including a commitment of assets of $20,000,000 or more.
7. Other non-investment initiatives requiring a financial commitment greater than $500,000.
8. Significant changes to our reinsurance structure or policy.

Approval and follow up

1. The risk assessment should be completed prior to the initiative's presentation to senior management or the Board for approval with a copy provided to the Chief Risk Officer.
2. At reasonable milestones, and at the conclusion of the project, the CRO will follow up with the project leaders to assess:
   (A) Are the original goals of the initiative being met?
   (B) Are actual costs in line with expected costs?

(C) Are the risk mitigation strategies being executed successfully?
(D) Would we make the same decision if we had it to do over again?

THE FUTURE

At the time of the preparation of this chapter, WCF is analyzing the results of its second employee survey (see 2013 All-Employee ERM Survey). The questions in the survey were reviewed with both the IRC and the Board Risk Oversight Committee prior to the survey, and again, about half of the company's 300+ employees have responded. WCF is trying to ascertain whether it is truly developing a risk-sensitive culture and whether it has any barriers to the free expression of concerns and ideas. This desire for transparency and openness has been clearly and publicly articulated by both the president and the chairman. Analysis of the survey results, when completed, will be presented to the board.

2013 All-Employee ERM Survey

- Are there any risks the company faces that you don't feel are being adequately addressed?
- Do you feel comfortable raising concerns about risk at WCF and do you feel they will be taken seriously?
- What should be done to help employees carefully consider risks, communicate concerns, and take appropriate actions to mitigate risks?
- Are there areas of WCF's Enterprise Risk Management Program that you would like to know more about?
- Name (optional)

The question of how much is enough is one WCF continues to grapple with. For better or worse, it is one in which both its regulator and its rating agency are giving specific direction as well. In the past couple of years A.M. Best has become increasingly clear regarding its expectations of the companies it is rating. Speaking at an industry conference in the spring of 2012, Group Vice President Ed Easop outlined an approach of generally matching ERM expectations to the general risk profile of the company. Where a carrier's ERM risk capabilities did not measure up to its risk profile, its rating might be notched down or capital requirements might be raised. If a carrier's capabilities matched or exceeded its risk profile, more favorable ratings treatment and lower capital requirements would be likely.

More recently A.M. Best addressed this in greater detail at its annual conference in March 2013. A.M. Best indicated that although the property-casualty industry is making progress in developing ERM programs, information gleaned from its supplemental risk questionnaires leaves little doubt that the industry has a long way to go. The rating agency also spelled out in great detail the underlying characteristics of its ERM rating levels of superior, strong, good, and weak in 17 key risk management areas. WCF will have its annual rating discussion meeting with A.M. Best in late fall 2013. It will be interesting to receive feedback in those meetings regarding the rating agency's perception of the WCF risk profile and the adequacy of WCF's efforts to date.

Since 2013, the state regulator, the Utah Department of Insurance, has not engaged WCF on this subject, but that is expected to change. As a member of the National Association of Insurance Commissioners (NAIC), it is aware of that organization's adoption in September 2012 of the Risk Management and Own Risk and Solvency Assessment (ORSA) model legislation. This model law is effective for adoption by state legislatures in 2015. Among other things, the Act requires that "An insurer shall maintain a risk management framework to assist the insurer with identifying, assessing, monitoring, managing, and reporting on its material and relevant risks. This requirement may be satisfied if the insurance group of which the insurer is a member maintains a risk management framework applicable to the operations of the insurer."[2] At this time, WCF meets the exemption requirement due to premium volume written, but the Act clearly sets out standards of best practice that should be considered.

Management has committed to, and the board expects, continued development of the ERM program and culture. This must be done to a level that matches WCF's risks and ensures it will always be able to discharge the long-term responsibilities it has to policyholders and injured workers. The depth and complexity of the ERM program will be determined through discussion and consultation between management and the board. WCF's mission is excellence.

QUESTIONS

1. What skill set or industry experience would be most valuable for a CRO to acquire?
2. If a Board has an audit, investment, and risk committee how should they work together and what would be an appropriate division of duties?
3. Should the CRO's role be a directing or a counseling one? How would this vary in small, medium, or large companies?
4. What would the ideal working relationship be between the CRO and CFO?
5. How should the Board and CEO evaluate a CRO's performance and contribution to the Company?

NOTES

1. Bradford, Dallas. June 2013. Written comments from WCF Board Chair Dallas Bradford to author.
2. National Association of Insurance Commissioners. 2012. "Risk Management and Own Risk and Solvency Assessment Model Act."

ABOUT THE CONTRIBUTOR

Dan Hair is the Chief Risk Officer (CRO) at Workers Compensation Fund, located in Utah. He joined WCF in 2005 after a 25-year career with Zenith Insurance

Company. As CRO, Dan is responsible for the enterprise risk management efforts of WCF and reports to the president and CEO. He works directly with the board of directors and the Board Risk Oversight Committee. Dan was educated at UCLA and USC, has an insurance operations and safety engineering background, and has taught and published in the areas of risk and risk management for years.

CHAPTER 12

Measuring Performance at Intuit

A Value-Added Component in ERM Programs

JANET NASBURG
Chief Risk Officer, Intuit Inc.

Intuit started small in 1983 with Quicken personal finance software, simplifying a common household dilemma: balancing the family checkbook. Today, we've improved the lives of more than 50 million people, and our annual revenue exceeds $4 billion. We are publicly traded with the symbol INTU on the NASDAQ Stock Market, and are regularly recognized as one of the best places to work in locations around the world.

Our flagship products—QuickBooks, TurboTax, Quicken, and Mint—define our commitment to revolutionize the way people manage their personal finances, run small businesses, and pay employees. Our lineup of tax preparation products helps individuals and small business owners easily and accurately file their own taxes. And working with accountants, we've become a staple of American small business, with a widespread and deep-rooted presence that's second to none.

But we're much more than that. Today, our expanding portfolio serves customers in North America, Europe, Singapore, and India. And our products have evolved from the desktop to the cloud, with many available both online and for mobile devices.

As the way we live and work evolves, we adapt our strategy to meet and lead these changes. No matter where you find us—and whether you use our products on your PC or mobile phone—we remain committed to creating new and easier ways for consumers and businesses to tackle life's financial chores, giving them more time to live their lives and run their businesses. As our business and product lines grow beyond accounting and into new areas, we will build on our heritage of innovation. That's not just our history. It's our future.

INTUIT'S ERM JOURNEY

Like most companies, Intuit's enterprise risk management (ERM) journey began with the practice of risk management on an ad hoc basis. Organized efforts came into play only when a significant problem occurred. Problems identified were primarily operational in nature and were defined narrowly to the specific issue. Well-intentioned and committed teams would attack the problem, stopping everything to focus on and solve the problem. These teams would produce long lists of issues and potential mitigation steps—some significant and some minor— to be addressed. Once the immediate problem was solved, it was back to business as usual. This ad hoc approach was not only extremely inefficient but was also not producing a lasting framework that would allow risks to be managed intelligently. In 2009 Intuit established the foundation of the ERM program that is in place today. This foundation included an enterprise-wide common risk framework, annual assessment cycle, and integration into the strategic planning process.

At Intuit, our ERM program has focused not simply on building a process but on building a sustainable risk management capability. Process is a necessary component, but process alone will not build the capability; it will not ensure that risk management is an integral part of how the company operates. Establishing operating mechanisms, practices, and processes that can be maintained well into the future and drive continuous focus on risk management was an important first step. Once the process was solidly in place, focus shifted to building risk management capability. Robust processes for identifying risk, assessing risk, and monitoring risk management progress helped our business leaders to develop and implement risk management activities as part of the normal operating processes of the company instead of reacting to risk on an ad hoc basis. This regular rhythm of risk management has built a strong risk management capability across the company.

Underlying Intuit's ERM program are some core principles that have brought Intuit's program to the leadership level it is at today.

- *A common risk framework enterprise-wide.*
  The establishment of a common risk framework has enabled business leaders to speak about risks with a common language despite the differences in business lines.
- *Assessing risks on an ongoing basis.*
  A constant lens on the risk landscape increases agility to adapt to changes in our business and the environment in which we operate.
- *Focusing on the most significant risks.*
  Targeting attention and resources on those risks with the greatest impact on Intuit's growth, product delivery, and operations drives progress.
- *Clearly defined ownership and accountability for risk management.*
  With appropriate oversight from the board and executive management, ownership and accountability for managing risk are the responsibility of business leaders across the company, thereby aligning ownership with leaders who are driving Intuit's growth strategy and operational priorities.
- *Performance measurement and monitoring.*
  Continuously monitoring performance drives progress in risk mitigation and continuously strengthens risk management capability.

Intuit's ERM program provides our business leaders with an understanding of current and emerging risks providing insights that inform strategic decisions. Each year the journey has continued to increase the level of risk intelligence across the company by building risk management strength and continuously measuring risk management effectiveness.

ERM MATURITY MODEL

ERM programs take time to establish and mature, and building the right foundation is critical.

> Patience is not an absence of action; rather it is "timing"; it waits on the right time to act, for the right principles and in the right way.
>
> *–Fulton J. Sheen*

Enterprise risk management programs are designed to drive identification of risks that may affect a company and management of those risks in order to enable achievement of the company's objectives. As the level of risk management capability matures, the value of ERM becomes more visible and impactful. The stages of risk management maturity can be described in many ways, all of which generally fall into the following levels (see Exhibit 12.1):

- *Ad hoc risk management.*
  Risk Management activities are designed to address a specific problem or task, and not intended to be adapted for wider application.
- *Targeted risk management.*
  Independent risk management activities are focused on a limited set of specific risk areas.
- *Integrated risk framework.*
  A common, repeatable enterprise framework is used for assessment, ownership and accountability, and reporting of risk management performance.

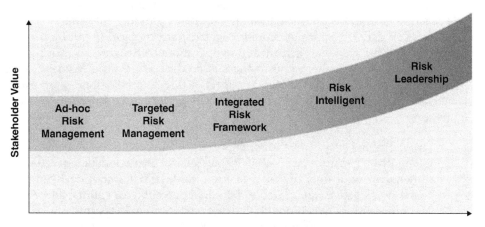

Exhibit 12.1 Enterprise Risk Management Maturity Model

- *Risk intelligent.*
  Established processes are used to continuously measure and monitor risk management effectiveness and drive optimal performance.
- *Risk leadership.*
  Risk management is seamlessly embedded in strategic decision making.

The speed at which a company moves through each level of maturity will vary, as it must be tailored to the individual needs and capacity for change of the company.

BENEFITS OF MEASURING PERFORMANCE IN ERM PROGRAMS

Performance measurement is not new. Measuring performance provides insights into where additional attention may be required or potential opportunities exist. Understanding the risk landscape enables business leaders to formulate and execute strategies informed by potential pitfalls and opportunities. The use of measurements to monitor current significant risks, highlight emerging risks, and understand the impact of both on company strategies and objectives is a key component of any ERM program.

The type of performance measures used varies based on the objective. Key risk indicators (KRIs) can be used to understand how potential emerging risks or trends may impact current risks, business opportunities, and business strategies. Key performance indicators (KPIs) can be used to measure the effectiveness of risk management activities. Both of these types of indicators are important, and using a combination of KRIs and KPIs can increase the value achieved from an ERM program.

Using Key Performance Indicators to Measure Risk Management Effectiveness

Key performance indicators are used to measure and monitor business strategies and business operations. Performance measurement provides information on the gaps between actual performance and targeted performance. It can be used to determine organizational effectiveness and operational efficiency. Measuring and monitoring risk management effectiveness is no different from measuring other performance. Measures are identified, expected targets or thresholds are established, and a starting point or baseline is set. Key performance indicators can take many forms:

- *Qualitative and quantitative indicators.*
  Qualitative measures are based on subjective characteristics or qualities rather than on a quantity or measured value. Quantitative measures are based on objective, quantifiable data, like percentages, counts, and ratios. The difference between qualitative and quantitative measures can be confusing, and there is often debate over which is better; however, both can be equally useful, and many times a combination of qualitative and quantitative measures can provide a more holistic picture of performance.

- *Leading and lagging indicators.*
  Leading indicators are predictive in nature, like early warning signals. They can highlight that an overall change in performance level is expected based on specific triggers that are monitored. Lagging indicators provide insights into the success or failure of an activity after it is complete.
- *Input, process, and output indicators.*
  These indicators are useful in evaluating an end-to-end process. Input indicators measure resources used in executing an activity. Process indicators measure efficiency or productivity. Output indicators measure the result of the process or activity.

In measuring risk management effectiveness, a combination of indicator types is often used. The biggest challenge in measuring performance is knowing what to measure. Selecting performance measures that cannot be gathered and tracked on an ongoing basis or selecting performance measures that are too complex for business leaders to understand their relevance will not provide value. To be most effective, key performance indicators need to be defined so that they are clear, meaningful, and measurable.

When defining KPIs for ERM, ensuring that the following four characteristics are incorporated can be helpful:

- *Tangible.*
  Tangible performance measures, aligned with the level of risk exposure that the company deems acceptable, provide true measures of risk management effectiveness, not just milestones in a risk management plan.
- *Flexible.*
  Flexible performance measures that can be adjusted to changes in the organization and risk landscape.
- *Standardized.*
  Common performance measures used enterprise-wide that provide a view of how each business line's performance contributes to the aggregated risk exposure at the enterprise level.
- *Outcome or objective focused.*
  Performance measures that are aligned to a specific objective or desired outcome.

Exhibit 12.2 provides some examples of key performance indicators.

Exhibit 12.2 Key Performance Indicators

Examples of Key Performance Indicators
Percentage of customer attrition
Percentage of employee turnover
Profitability of customers by demographic segments
Percentage of mission-critical business processes with tested contingency plans
Current-period write-offs or fraud losses

Analyzing Performance Data

Performance measurement alone is not enough to add value; learning from the information and applying that learning to drive changes that improve performance are important steps. Optimizing the benefits of performance measurement can be achieved by performing analysis of the data collected. Data analysis transforms the performance information making it useful input, which can help business leaders to make better risk-informed decisions. There are many types of analysis that can be used, and the choice will vary based on the objectives of the analysis.

While this list is not exhaustive, here are some examples of commonly used analyses:

- *Failure mode and effects analysis (FMEA).*
  FMEA helps to identify potential failure points based on certain conditions. The consequences of failures are further analyzed to understand their impact on other parts of a system or process. FMEA can help to design more comprehensive risk mitigation efforts.
- *Regression analysis.*
  Regression analysis provides information on the relationship between one dependent variable and one or more independent variables. This type of analysis can be helpful in understanding the correlation between different risks.
- *Pareto analysis.*
  Pareto analysis measures the frequency of issues, from most to least frequent. This type of analysis is useful in making decisions that provide the greatest results—for example, targeting resources to address issues in a specific component of a process with the greatest number of errors or control failures.
- *Root cause analysis.*
  Root cause analysis is designed to identify and correct the fundamental cause of a problem. It helps focus remediation not on merely correcting symptoms but on preventing the recurrence of problems. This type of analysis is especially useful as a method to proactively forecast probable events before they occur.
- *Scenario analysis.*
  Scenario analysis uses discrete scenarios to understand the potential outcome. Typically the worst case, best case, and most likely case are considered. Single-point estimates or a Monte Carlo simulation model using a range of values can be used. This type of analysis is useful to enhance readiness and strengthen response capabilities.
- *Benchmarking.*
  Benchmarking compares a company's current practices to best practices. This type of analysis facilitates development of strategies to improve processes and performance measures.
- *Threat analysis.*
  Threat analysis can be used to evaluate a broad spectrum of areas such as natural disasters, criminal activity, legal or regulatory factors, technology

trends, internal capabilities, and market forces. Using this type of analysis to gain insights into potential threats is useful to enhance readiness and strengthen response capabilities, as well as to enhance risk mitigation strategies.

Analyses such as these can be used to perform a deep review of a specific risk area to understand effectiveness of current risk mitigation strategies, or can be used broadly to understand potential emerging risks.

Using Key Risk Indicators to Understand Potential New Risks or Changing Risks

Most organizations use key performance indicators to monitor progress in meeting corporate objectives. Those indicators provide valuable information, including insights into risks. However, key performance indicators primarily provide insights into risks already well known by the organization. With ever-changing business environments challenging companies to take a longer-term view into potential risks, there is increased focus on understanding emerging risks. Key risk indicators are used to provide an early warning signal by not just looking at current risks but looking for leading indicators or triggers in the business environment. These triggers can be used to develop strategies that better position the company to manage new risks as they arise. Development of risk indicators can come from analysis of previous risk events to understand their root cause and triggers that can be used in the future as risk indicators. External information, such as economic indicators, industry benchmarks and trends, competitor actions, and the like, can all be utilized in developing key risk indicators. Just as with key performance indicators, key risk indicators are most effective if they are tangible, flexible, standardized, and outcome or objective focused.

Exhibit 12.3 provides some examples of key risk indicators.

Exhibit 12.3   Key Risk Indicators

Examples of Key Risk Indicators

Industry trends in customer attrition
Frequency of critical process failures
Trends in gasoline or other critical commodity prices in relevant geographies
Unexpected significant change in number of competitors or suppliers
Spreads on debt for comparably rated companies

ERM PERFORMANCE MEASUREMENT AND REPORTING AT INTUIT

Performance measurement in Intuit's ERM program has been a journey of continuous improvement. As ERM programs mature over time, increasing their complexity and value, performance measures and reporting must evolve as well. What gets measured at each level of maturity may vary greatly. The ERM performance measurement approach at Intuit has been continuously updated to keep it relevant and flexible with respect to the organization's level of risk management maturity. At each stage in the evolution of ERM maturity, objectives and expectations are adjusted. In addition, the appropriateness of current metrics is evaluated given the constantly changing business environment.

First Evolution: ERM Process Adoption

In the early stages of ERM maturity at Intuit, performance measurement was focused on adoption of the ERM process. The objective was to ensure a robust process of risk identification and prioritization facilitating focus on the most significant risks. The measures at this point were twofold: process participation and risk assessment impact and likelihood. Reporting to executive management and the board included the results of the annual assessment, participation rates and heat maps, as well as an outline of strategies to improve the company's top risks.

ERM Process Participation

Participation in the process was targeted at senior leadership at both the company and business line levels. Business line leadership provided subject matter expertise and insights into the most significant risks facing their specific businesses. Executive management provided an enterprise perspective. The desired participation rate target was 80 percent or greater. Participation rates were calculated at the individual business line level as well as at the company level. This may seem like a very simplistic measure, but you need to consider the level of risk management maturity that was in place at this point. Expecting business leaders to track complex measures when they are just beginning to build a risk management capability may be unrealistic. Measuring participation in the ERM process provided an indicator of risk awareness and risk management currently in place. This was an important benchmark. Since performance measurement provides information on the gaps between actual performance and targeted performance, this measure highlighted opportunities to help business leaders increase their risk focus and knowledge.

Risk Impact and Likelihood

Intuit's ERM program, like many other companies' programs, includes an annual risk assessment. The annual risk assessment provides an enterprise-wide understanding of key risks. Intuit conducts risk assessments at both the company level and on an individual business line level. The assessment solicits information from the company's executive management on the impact and likelihood of risks affecting the organization's strategies and objectives. Measuring impact and likelihood is clearly defined and standardized, facilitating aggregation of the information received from participants across the company. Heat maps, as illustrated in Exhibit 12.4, are used to show the results of the assessment, and attention is then focused on the risks in the upper right-hand quadrant.

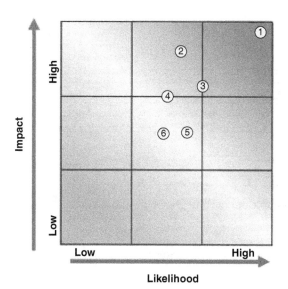

Exhibit 12.4   Risk Impact and Likelihood Diagram

This type of performance measurement and reporting provided many benefits, including:

- Helping business leaders to understand the effect of risks on performance against strategic goals and objectives
- Targeting focus to the critical few, and in doing so accelerating progress on addressing these risks
- Identifying potential events or circumstances that may impede ability to optimize performance

Second Evolution: Risk Mitigation Progress Measurement

With the rhythm of an annual ERM assessment in place and top risks at the company and business line level appropriately prioritized, the focus shifted to building risk management strength. The objective was to ensure direct alignment of risk management activities and resources to the most critical issues identified as part of the assessment process. The focus of performance measurement was one of the top risks identified at the company and business line levels. Ownership and accountability for the top risks are specifically designated to a senior leader at the company level or business line level. Performance measurement includes an indicator of the status of overall risk exposure, an indicator of current risk trending, as well as a separate measure tracking the progress on individual risk mitigation activities.

Exhibit 12.5 provides an example of the levels of status indicators.

Quarterly ERM performance reporting is integrated into Intuit's annual enterprise and business line strategic planning process and quarterly operating reviews. Exhibit 12.6 provides a sample business line top risk status report.

Color	Status of Risk Exposure	Plan Status
●	Missing or ineffective mitigation and/or significant process breakdowns. Further action required.	Plan significantly at risk.
○	Some mitigation in place, stronger additional mitigation needed. Plans developed and some risk reduction occurring.	Plan potentially at risk.
◐	Managed well with appropriate mitigation in place. Risk has been reduced to an acceptable level.	Plan on schedule.
◌	Status not available.	Plan not started.
◌	N/A	Plan complete.

Exhibit 12.5   Example of Levels of Status Indicators

This type of performance measurement and reporting provides many benefits, including:

- Demonstrating the breadth of top risk coverage with defined risk management plans
- Highlighting potential gaps in resources to execute mitigation activities
- Providing transparency to risk management activities across the organization and opportunities to leverage common risk management strategies and best practices

Risk	Status of Risk Exposure	Top Priorities	Risk Trend	Strategies to Improve and Plan Status
Risk 1	○	Xxxxx	**Stable** Xxxxx	• Plan 1 ● • Plan 2 ◐
Risk 2	◌	Xxxxx	**Increasing** Xxxxx	• Plan 1 ◌ • Plan 2 ●
Risk 3	●	Xxxxx	**Increasing** Xxxxx	• Plan 1 ● • Plan 2 ◐ • Plan 3 ◌
Risk 4	◐	Xxxxx	**Stable** Xxxxx	• Plan 1 ● • Plan 2 ◐
Risk 5	◐	Xxxxx	**Decreasing** Xxxxx	• Plan 1 ● • Plan 2 ◐

Exhibit 12.6   Sample Business Line Top Risk Status Report

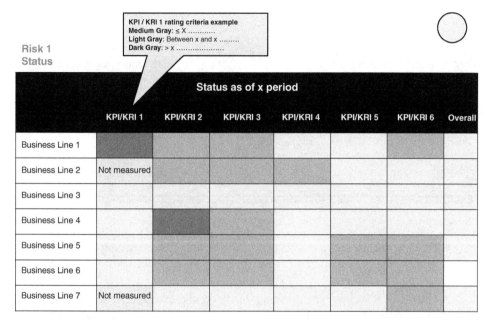

Risk 1 Status	KPI / KRI 1 rating criteria example Medium Gray: ≤ X .... Light Gray: Between x and x .... Dark Gray: > x						

	Status as of x period						
	KPI/KRI 1	KPI/KRI 2	KPI/KRI 3	KPI/KRI 4	KPI/KRI 5	KPI/KRI 6	Overall
Business Line 1							
Business Line 2	Not measured						
Business Line 3							
Business Line 4							
Business Line 5							
Business Line 6							
Business Line 7	Not measured						

Exhibit 12.7 Sample Executive Dashboard

Third Evolution: Multidimensional Risk Management Performance Measurement

As Intuit's program evolved, performance measurement and reporting focus moved from tracking progress on risk mitigation to a more holistic approach. The objective was to actively monitor the most important risks facing the company and ensure that business leaders were proactively adjusting strategies to balance managing these risks and leveraging the opportunities they provide. To this end, executive dashboards were developed, which use a combination of key performance indicators and key risk indicators. Aggregation of a number of different KPIs provides a multidimensional view of risk and an overall risk score. Standard metrics are used enterprise-wide to ensure that all business lines are aligned to the objectives. Additionally, an overall risk rating is assigned that demonstrates the collective effect of these activities on the risk exposure at the company level. Dashboards for each of the company's top risks and an overall summary are routinely reported to the board and executive management. Exhibit 12.7 provides a sample executive dashboard.

This type of performance measurement and reporting has provided many benefits, including:

- Providing visibility into business line risks to aid understanding of the cumulative impact of these risks on Intuit as a whole
- Enabling the company to drive focus and allocate resources to the highest-impact work, and to accelerate progress on specific risks by leveraging a rigorous program from the center and coordinated business line effort

From: **To:**

- Tactical activities to      - Better understanding of the
  address current gaps   risks and their effect on
                                                              company growth
- Narrow scope
                                                            - Longer term view of
- Long road maps   strategies to address risk,
                                                              with tighter timelines to
                                                              accelerate progress

                                                            - Embrace Innovation

Exhibit 12.8   From Tactical Risk Management to Strategic Risk Management

- Driving the development and adoption of enterprise standards and best practices (e.g., hosting principles, security standards, technology principles)

As Intuit's ERM program, and the approach to performance measurement and reporting, has matured, we have a higher bar for risk management—it is more strategic, and we have significantly improved execution. We have moved from tactical risk management to strategic risk management, as shown in Exhibit 12.8.

CONCLUSION

This chapter has described the value of performance measurement as a component of ERM programs.

At Intuit, risk management is the responsibility of everyone in the organization, from the board and executive management all the way down to the individual employees. To ensure that risk management is effective, it must be a core business competency, and measuring performance facilitates tracking that the appropriate level of competency is achieved.

Intuit's ERM program provides a rigorous and coordinated approach to assessing and responding to risks. It recognizes the upside opportunity and downside nature of risks. Routine performance measurement is a critical component of the program and not only ensures a focus on the most significant risks but also accelerates progress on managing current and emerging risks and assuring alignment with strategic goals.

Performance is reviewed regularly with the Audit and Risk Committee of the board, and, as a result, feedback drives continuous innovation around performance measurement and reporting. ERM is viewed as an integral part of the company's current operating model, and continuously improves enterprise-wide risk awareness, monitoring, and management.

QUESTIONS

1. How do Key Risk Indicators help companies identify emerging risks?
2. How do Key Performance Indicators help companies to manage existing risks?

3. If measuring performance is not a component of an ERM program, what is the effect on the overall quality of the program?
4. How can the Board be confident in the information reported on management's progress in responding to significant risks?

ABOUT THE CONTRIBUTOR

Janet Nasburg is Chief Risk Officer at Intuit, makers of QuickBooks, TurboTax, Quicken, and Mint. Intuit is committed to revolutionizing the way people manage their small businesses and personal finances. Ms. Nasburg is responsible for driving Intuit's enterprise risk management capability to ensure that the company appropriately balances opportunities and risks to achieve optimal business results. She reports routinely to the board of directors on the company's risk landscape, risk tolerance, and emerging risks.

Ms. Nasburg has more than 30 years of experience in finance and risk management. She is on the executive committee of the Conference Board's Strategic Risk Management Council, and is also a member of the Institute of Internal Auditors. She is a Certified Internal Auditor (CIA), Certified in Risk Management Assurance (CRMA), and Certified in Control Self Assessment (CCSA). She has a BS in agricultural economics and business management from the University of California, Davis, and an MBA in finance from the Graduate School of Business, San Francisco State University.

CHAPTER 13

TD Bank's Approach to an Enterprise Risk Management Program

PAUL CUNHA
Vice President, Enterprise Risk Management for TD Bank Group

KRISTINA NARVAEZ
President and Owner of ERM Strategies, LLC

This case study focuses on how TD Bank Group uses enterprise risk management (ERM) to grow profitably while keeping in mind the balance between taking and managing its risks. TD recognizes that having a strong risk culture and approach to risk management is fundamental to success. TD's ERM approach is comprehensive and proactive. It combines the experience and specialized knowledge of individual business segments, risk professionals, and the corporate oversight functions. It is based on enabling TD's business to understand the risks it faces and to develop the policies, processes, and controls required to manage them appropriately in alignment with the bank's strategy and risk appetite.

BACKGROUND

Headquartered in Toronto, Canada, with more than 85,000 employees in offices around the world, TD and its subsidiaries offer a full range of financial products and services to approximately 22 million customers worldwide through three key business lines:

1. Canadian retail, including TD Canada Trust, TD Auto Finance Canada, Canadian credit cards, Canadian wealth, and TD Insurance
2. Wholesale Banking, including TD Securities
3. U.S. retail, including TD Bank ("America's Most Convenient Bank"), TD Auto Finance U.S., U.S. wealth, and U.S. credit cards

As of April 30, 2014, TD had $896 billion (Canadian) in assets. TD also ranks among the world's leading online financial services firms, with approximately eight million active online and mobile customers. It is the second-largest bank in

Canada and the tenth-largest bank in the United States (by market capitalization). TD trades on the Toronto Stock Exchange and New York Stock Exchange under the symbol "TD."

ERM at TD Bank

TD's risk management approach is comprehensive with TD Bank's Enterprise Risk Framework (ERF), reinforcing TD's risk culture and ensuring that all stakeholders have a common understanding of how TD manages risk. The ERF addresses: (1) the nature of the risks to TD's business strategy and operations; (2) how TD defines the types of risk it is exposed to; (3) risk management governance; and (4) how TD manages risk through processes that identify, measure, assess, control, and monitor risk. TD's risk management resources and processes are designed to enable all of its businesses to understand the risks they face and to manage them within TD's risk appetite.

TD's Risk Appetite Statement is the primary means used to communicate how TD views risk and determines the risks it is willing to take in order to grow its business. TD takes into account its mission, vision, guiding principles, and strategy, as well as risk philosophy and capacity to bear risk, in defining its risk appetite.

TD takes risks required to build its business, but only if those risks:

- Fit its business strategy, and can be understood and managed
- Do not expose the enterprise to any significant single-loss events
- Do not risk harming the TD brand

In applying its risk appetite, TD considers both the current conditions in which it operates and the impact that emerging risks will have on TD's strategy and risk profile. Adherence to the enterprise risk appetite is managed and monitored across TD and is based on a broad collection of principles, policies, processes, and procedures, including risk appetite statements and related performance measures for major risk categories and the business segments.

At the enterprise level, metrics are tracked against key risks like capital adequacy, market risk, liquidity risk, credit risk, and operational risk. These metrics and compliance with the Risk Appetite Statement are monitored and reported by risk dashboards on an ongoing basis. To ensure that TD Bank's Risk Appetite Statement remains current and relevant, TD has established a Risk Appetite Governance Framework approved annually by the Risk Committee of the Board (RCoB). This framework describes TD's processes, structure, and responsibilities to develop, govern, and approve the Enterprise and Business Segments Risk Appetite Statements and the requirements for monitoring and escalating exceptions. Specifically, the governance process provides that:

- The Enterprise and Business Segments Risk Appetite Statements and related metrics must be reviewed at least annually.
- Updates and amendments are developed by Risk Management with input from business segments, corporate functions, the senior executive team, and the RCoB.

- The TD Enterprise Risk Appetite Statement and related metrics must be reviewed and approved by the RCoB annually.
- The Business Segment Risk Appetite Statements must be recommended by each of the Business Group heads and approved by the president and chief executive officer (CEO) and chief risk officer (CRO) annually.
- Performance against the Enterprise and Segment Risk Appetite Statements must be monitored and reported on an ongoing basis.

Understanding an Organization's Risks Helps Reinforce the Risk Culture

Each of the ERF's components reinforces the desired risk culture of TD Bank, and they are all equally necessary to ensure that TD successfully manages its risk. The ERF sets the direction of how TD manages enterprise risk. The TD Risk Inventory sets out TD's major risk categories and related subcategories to enable a consistent language and approach to measuring, reporting, and disclosing TD's risks. This inventory of risks facilitates consistent enterprise risk identification and becomes the starting point to develop the appropriate risk strategies and processes to manage TD's risk exposure. Definitions of common terms include:

> **Strategic risk** is the potential for financial loss or reputational damage arising from ineffective business strategies, improper implementation of business strategies, or a lack of responsiveness to changes in the business environment. The CEO manages strategic risk supported by the members of the senior management team. Together they define the overall strategy, in consultation with and subject to approval by the board.
>
> **Credit risk** is the risk of loss if a borrower or counterparty in a transaction fails to meet its agreed payment obligations. Credit risk is one of the most significant and pervasive risks in the banking sector. Every loan, extension of credit, or transaction that involves transfer of payments between TD and other parties or financial institutions exposes TD to some degree of credit risk. The responsibility of credit risk management is enterprise-wide. Each business segment's credit risk control unit is primarily responsible for credit decisions and must comply with established policies, exposure guidelines, and credit approval limits.
>
> **Market risk** is the risk of loss in financial instruments or the balance sheet due to adverse movements in market factors such as interest and exchange rates, prices, credit spreads, volatilities, and correlations. TD is exposed to market risk in its trading and investment portfolios, as well as through its nontrading activities. The primary responsibility for managing market risk in trading activities lies with Wholesale Banking with oversight from Market Risk Control within Risk Management.
>
> **Liquidity risk** is the risk of having insufficient cash or collateral resources to meet financial obligations without raising funds at unfavorable rates or being unable to sell assets at a reasonable price in a timely manner. Demand for cash can arise from deposit withdrawals, debt maturities, and

commitments to provide credit or liquidity support. The Asset/Liability and Capital Committee oversees the liquidity risk management program.

Operational risk is the risk of loss resulting from inadequate or failed internal processes, people, and systems or from external events. Operational risk is embedded in all of the bank's business activities, including the practices for managing other risks such as credit, market, and liquidity risk. Operational Risk Management is an independent function that designs and maintains TD's overall operational risk management framework. This framework sets out the enterprise-wide governance processes, policies, and practices to identify, assess, report, mitigate, and control operational risks.

Insurance risk is the risk of financial loss due to actual experience emerging differently from expected in insurance product pricing or reserving. This could be due to adverse fluctuations in timing, actual size, and/or frequency of claims mortality, morbidity, policyholders' behavior, or associated expenses incurred. Senior management within the insurance business units has primary responsibility for managing insurance risk with oversight by the Chief Risk Officer for Insurance, who reports into Risk Management.

Legal, regulatory, and compliance risk is the risk of negative impact to business activities, earnings or capital, regulatory relationships, or reputation as a result of failure to comply with or to adapt to current and changing regulations, laws, industry codes, rules, or regulatory expectations. Legal risk includes the potential for civil litigation or criminal or regulatory proceedings being commenced against the bank that, once decided, could materially and adversely affect its business, operations, or financial condition. Business segments and corporate areas are responsible for managing day-to-day regulatory and legal risk, while the Legal, Compliance, Global Anti-Money Laundering, and Regulatory risk groups assist them by providing advice and oversight.

Capital adequacy risk is the risk of insufficient capital available in relation to the amount of capital required to carry out the bank's strategy and to satisfy regulatory capital adequacy requirements. Capital is held to protect the viability of the bank in the event of unexpected financial losses. The board of directors has the ultimate responsibility for overseeing adequacy of capital and capital management. The board reviews the adherence to capital limits and targets, and reviews and approves the annual capital plan and the Capital Management Policy.

Reputational risk is the potential that stakeholder impressions, whether true or not, regarding an institution's business practices, actions, or inactions, will or may cause a decline in the institution's value, brand, liquidity, or customer base. TD Bank's enterprise-wide Reputational Risk Management Policy is approved by the Risk Committee of the Board. This policy sets out the framework under which each business unit is required to implement a reputational risk policy and procedures. These include designating a business-level committee to review reputational risk issues and to identify issues to be brought to the Enterprise Reputational Risk Committee.

Risk Governance Structure

TD's risk governance structure emphasizes and balances strong central oversight and control of risk with clear accountability for, and ownership of, risk within each business unit. Under TD's approach to risk governance, the business owns the risk that it generates and is responsible for assessing risk, designing and implementing controls, and monitoring and reporting its ongoing effectiveness to safeguard TD from exceeding its risk appetite.

TD's risk governance model includes a senior management committee structure to support transparent risk reporting and discussion with overall risk and control oversight provided by the board and its committees. The CEO and Senior Executive Team determine TD's long-term direction within the bank's risk appetite and apply it to the businesses. Risk Management, headed by the Group head and chief risk officer (CRO), sets enterprise risk strategy and policy and provides independent oversight to support a comprehensive and proactive risk management approach for TD.

TD employs a "three lines of defense" model that describes the roles of the business, governance, risk, and oversight groups in managing TD Bank's risk profile. The first line of defense is the business and corporate line of accountabilities and includes the following:

- Managing and identifying risks in day-to-day activities
- Ensuring that activities are within TD's risk appetite and risk management practices
- Designing, implementing, and maintaining effective internal controls
- Monitoring and reporting on the risk profile

The second line of defense deals with setting standards and challenging business assumptions to improve governance, risk, and control groups' responsibilities and accountability. These include the following:

- Establishing enterprise governance, risk, and control strategies and practices
- Providing oversight and independent challenge to the first line through review, inquiry, and discussion
- Developing and communicating governance, risk, and control policies
- Providing training, tools, and advice to support policy compliance
- Monitoring and reporting on compliance with risk appetite and policies

The third line of defense is independent assurance through the internal audit department, which allows for the following:

- Verifying independently that TD's ERF is operating effectively
- Validating the effectiveness of the first and second lines of defense in fulfilling their mandates and managing the risk profile

The RCoB oversees TD's risk direction and the implementation of an effective risk management culture and internal control framework across the enterprise. In support of this oversight, the RCoB reviews, challenges, and approves certain risk policies while also reviewing and approving TD's Risk Appetite Statement.

TD's executive committees provide oversight at the most senior level and support management by guiding, challenging, and advising executive decision makers. The following committees oversee governance, risk, and control activities relating to the bank's key risks, and review and monitor the risk strategies and associated risk activities and practices:

- The Enterprise Risk Management Committee oversees the management of major enterprise governance and risk and control activities.
- The Asset/Liability and Capital Committee (ALCO) oversees the management of TD's nontrading market risk and each of its consolidated liquidity, funding, investments, and capital positions.
- The Operational Risk Oversight Committee oversees the strategic assessment of TD's governance, control, and operational risk structure.
- The Disclosure Committee ensures that appropriate controls and procedures are in place and operating to permit timely accurate, balanced, and compliant disclosure to regulators, shareholders, and the market.
- The Reputational Risk Committee ensures that corporate or business initiatives with significant reputational risk profiles have received adequate review for reputational risk implications prior to implementation.

The Risk Management function, headed by the CRO, provides independent oversight of risk governance and control, and is responsible for establishing risk management strategy, policies, and practices. Risk Management's primary objective is to support a comprehensive and proactive approach to risk management that promotes a strong risk management culture. Risk Management works with the business segments and other corporate oversight groups to establish policies, standards, and limits that align with TD's risk appetite, and monitors and reports on existing and emerging risks and compliance with TD's risk appetite.

Each business segment has an embedded risk management function that reports directly to a senior risk executive, who in turn reports to the CRO. This structure supports an appropriate level of central oversight while emphasizing ownership and accountability for risk within the business segment. Business management is responsible for recommending the business-level risk appetite and metrics, which are reviewed and challenged as necessary by Risk Management and ultimately approved by the CEO.

TD's audit function provides independent assurance to the board of the effectiveness of risk management, control, and governance processes, employed to ensure compliance with TD's risk appetite. Internal Audit reports on its evaluation to management and the RCoB. The Compliance group establishes risk-based programs and standards to proactively manage known and emerging compliance risks across TD to provide independent oversight and delivers operational control processes to comply with the applicable legislation and regulation requirements.

The Global Anti Money Laundering (AML) group establishes a risk-based program and standards to proactively manage known and emerging money laundering compliance risks across TD. The AML group provides independent oversight and delivers operational control processes to comply with the applicable legislation and regulatory requirements. The Treasury and Balance Sheet Management (TBSM) group manages, directs, and reports on TD's capital and investment positions, interest rate risk, liquidity and funding risks, and the market risks of TD's nontrading bank activities. The Risk Management function oversees TBSM's capital and investment activities.

Risk Identification, Assessment, and Reporting

TD applies the following principles to how it manages risks:

- *Enterprise-wide in scope.* Risk management spans all areas of TD, including third-party alliances and joint venture undertakings and all boundaries, both geographic and regulatory.
- *Transparent and effective communication.* Matters relating to risk are communicated and escalated in a timely, accurate, and forthright manner.
- *Enhanced accountability.* Risks are explicitly owned, understood, and actively managed by business management and all employees, individually and collectively.
- *Independent oversight.* Risk policies, monitoring, and reporting will be established independently and objectively.
- *Integrated risk and control culture.* Risk management discipline is integrated into TD's daily routines, decision making, and strategy.
- *Strategic balance.* Risks are managed to an acceptable level of exposure, recognizing the need to protect and grow shareholder value.

Risk identification and assessment are focused on recognizing and understanding existing risks, risks that may arise from new or evolving business initiatives, and emerging risks from the changing environment. TD looks to establish and maintain integrated risk identification and assessment processes that enhance the understanding of risk interdependencies, consider how risk types interact, and support the identification of emerging risks.

Depending on the risk type, the risk identification and assessment process may be developed and/or controlled by the business segment with oversight provided by Risk Management, or it may be controlled by a function within Risk Management. For example, credit risk assessment processes developed by a business segment exist for both retail and nonretail clients. The nature of those processes may vary by and/or within a business segment depending on the specific nature of the risk. Risk Management's role in these processes is to provide oversight and challenge to ensure that the analysis and results produced by the process focus on the relevant issues.

Other risk assessment identification and assessment processes that can and/or need to be applied on a consistent basis across TD have been developed by Risk Management at the enterprise level. Examples of such processes would include the Risk and Control Self-Assessment (RCSA) report, the Emerging Risk Identification process, scenario analysis and stress testing, and the Internal Capital Adequacy Assessment Process (ICAAP).

Risk Measurement

The ability to quantify risks is also a key commitment of TD's risk management processes. These processes align with regulatory requirements for capital adequacy, leverage ratios, liquidity measures, stress testing, and maximum credit exposure guidelines. TD has a process in place to quantify risks to provide accurate and timely measurements of the risks it assumes.

In quantifying risk, TD uses various risk measurement methodologies, including value at risk (VaR) analysis, scenario analysis, stress testing, and limits. Other examples of risk measurements include credit exposures, provision for credit losses, peer comparisons, trending analysis, liquidity coverage, and capital adequacy metrics. TD also conducts structured Risk and Control Self-Assessment (RCSA) programs and monitors internal and external risk events. This allows TD to identify, escalate, and monitor significant risk issues as needed.

TD's Enterprise-Wide Stress Testing involves the development, application, and assessment of severe but plausible stress scenarios on earnings, liquidity, and capital of the bank. It enables senior management and the board and its committees to identify and articulate enterprise-wide risks and understand potential vulnerabilities for TD. It informs and supports risk appetite, capital adequacy, and liquidity requirements, providing a framework to assess emerging, concentration, and contagion risks.

Risk Control

TD's risk control processes are established and communicated through risk committees and approved policies, procedures, and control limits. Policies are used as a key risk control tool to provide consistency, predictability, and alignment with risk appetite by communicating the principles, rules, and limits to guide and determine decisions and behaviors. TD's Policy Governance Framework provides a common structure and requirements for the consistent development, implementation, approval, and management of policy at TD.

TD's approach to risk control includes risk and capital assessments to appropriately capture key risks in TD's measurement and management of capital adequacy. This involves the review, challenge, and endorsement by senior management committees of the ICAAP practices. The Internal Control Framework describes enterprise principles governing internal control and management accountability to own and manage risk across the enterprise by practicing ongoing risk and control self-assessment; designing, implementing, and monitoring the effectiveness of a comprehensive program of internal control; and responding in a timely manner to control weaknesses identified by management, governance, risk and control groups, Internal Audit, or other parties.

In recognition of the importance of technology risk control and management, TD has established the Technology Risk Management and Information Security Program, which is designed to reduce business risk with technology controls, and to protect the bank, its customers, and its employees. This enterprise-wide program is delivered through governance and policy setting, along with the Technology Risk Assessment and Control Framework that generates awareness, communications and ongoing assessments, information security architecture and strategy, and vulnerability and incident management.

Risk Monitoring and Reporting

TD monitors and reports on risk levels on a regular basis to senior management, the RCoB, and the board. Complementing regular risk monitoring and reporting, ad hoc risk reporting is provided as appropriate for new and emerging risk or any significant changes to the bank's risk profile. Risk-specific reporting is also in place as described in the relevant risk-specific frameworks.

TD's risk dashboards provide a comprehensive quantitative and qualitative assessment of key risk types across the enterprise. The risk dashboards reflect established guidelines and risk tolerance based on TD policies that encompass key aspects of risk to the businesses.

TD measures management's performance against risk appetite using the Risk Appetite Scorecard, which is a consolidated assessment of enterprise and business segment risk performance measured against risk appetite metrics. In completing the Risk Appetite Scorecard, TD Risk Management assesses various factors to determine whether the bank takes risks consistent with the Risk Appetite Statement and whether the risk level changed in the businesses as a result of management actions or external factors. This annual assessment of management's performance against TD's risk appetite is used as a key input into compensation decisions.

Extensive external reporting is produced to comply with legal and regulatory requirements. TD also discusses the ERF and related risk management practices in the Management Discussion and Analysis (MD&A) section of its annual report. All forward-looking statements to external stakeholders included in the MD&A are, by their very nature, subject to inherent risks and uncertainties, general and specific, which may cause the bank's actual results to differ materially from the expectations expressed in the forward-looking statements.

CONCLUSION

TD Bank's earnings are affected by the general business and economic conditions in Canada and the United States. These conditions include short-term and long-term interest rates, inflation, fluctuations in debt and capital markets, consumer debt levels, government spending, exchange rates, the strength of the economy, threats of terrorism, civil unrest, the effects of public health emergencies, the effects of disruptions to public infrastructure, and the level of business conducted in the regions where the bank operates.

TD Bank employs an ERM framework that emphasizes and balances central oversight and control of risk with clear accountability for and ownership of risk within each business segment. TD's approach to ERM is based on six key principles: enterprise-wide in scope, transparent and effective communication, enhanced accountability, independent oversight, integrated risk and control culture, and strategic balance.

QUESTIONS

1. How does an ERM program help an organization to better understand their risk culture?
2. How would you describe TD Bank's risk profile to a financial analyst on Wall Street?
3. What are the determining factors in deciding which risks TD can take?
4. How does TD measure the risks in their organization?

REFERENCES

TD Bank. 2012. ERM Framework, June.
TD Bank. 2012. Management and Decision Analysis Report.

ABOUT THE CONTRIBUTORS

Paul Cunha is Vice President, Enterprise Risk Management, at TD Bank. He graduated from Wilfrid Laurier University with an honors bachelor of business administration and is a CFA charterholder. During his career at TD Bank, he has spent time in risk management, internal audit, retail banking, commercial banking, and corporate and investment banking.

Kristina Narvaez is the president and owner of ERM Strategies, LLC. She graduated from the University of Utah in environmental risk management and then received her MBA with two advanced certificates in finance and information technology from Westminster College. She is a two-time Spencer Education Foundation Graduate Scholar from the Risk and Insurance Management Society, and has published more than 25 articles and papers on topics relating to enterprise risk management and board risk governance.

Note: The material contained in this chapter represents the views of the authors and not necessarily those of the TD Bank Group.

PART III

Linking ERM to Strategy and Strategic Risk Management

CHAPTER 14

A Strategic Approach to Enterprise Risk Management at Zurich Insurance Group

LINDA CONRAD
Director of Strategic Business Risk at Zurich Insurance Group

KRISTINA NARVAEZ
President and Owner of ERM Strategies, LLC

This case study describes how the Zurich Insurance Group has implemented and evolved its enterprise risk management (ERM) approach for more than 10 years across the globe. It describes how Zurich has organized its governance structures and ERM champions to help integrate ERM into the business model that focuses on promptly identifying, measuring, managing, monitoring, and reporting risks that affect the achievement of strategic, operational, and financial objectives. This includes adjusting their risk profiles to be in line with Zurich's stated risk tolerance to respond to new threats and opportunities in order to optimize returns.

ENTERPRISE RISK MANAGEMENT AT ZURICH

As a large global insurance carrier, Zurich Insurance Group has relied on its ERM program for more than 10 years as a means to help Zurich remain profitable. With over 60,000 employees around the world and serving customers in more than 170 countries and territories, Zurich is exposed to a wide range of risks from its customers to its own operations. Yet Zurich recognizes that taking the right risks at the right time is a necessary part of growing and protecting shareholder value. Naturally, Zurich aims to capitalize on appropriate market opportunities that could attract the best talent and investor capital. To achieve this, Zurich utilizes insight from its ERM program to help balance growth opportunities with the reality that it is operating in a complex world economy.

ERM not only is embedded in Zurich's business, but is also aligned with its strategic and operational planning and budgeting process. Zurich assesses risks systematically and from a strategic perspective through its proprietary tools that allow it to identify and then evaluate the probability of a risk scenario occurring, as well as the severity of the consequence should it occur. Zurich then develops, implements, and monitors appropriate improvement actions. Its ERM tools are integral to how Zurich deals with change, by helping to evaluate strategic risks as well as risks to its reputation. At the senior management level, the ERM process is annually reviewed and tied to the strategic planning process, but is also embedded in the ongoing business.

Listed here are Zurich's major ERM objectives, and a tangible proof point:

- Protect the capital base by monitoring that risks are not taken beyond Zurich's risk tolerance.
- Enhance value creation and contribute to an optimal risk/return profile by providing the basis for efficient capital deployment.
- Support Zurich's decision-making processes by providing consistent, reliable, and timely risk information.
- Protect Zurich's reputation and brand by promoting a sound culture of risk awareness and disciplined and informed risk taking.

Tangible Results

By aligning ERM with its business strategy, Zurich has been able to use certain tools to create new value to its organization in a variety of areas. Zurich's ERM program has sustained business growth throughout the recession, contributing to more than 40 consecutive quarters of growth. One way it added value through ERM was when Zurich introduced an enhanced operational risk management framework. One business unit reduced operational risk-based capital (RBC) consumption by 21.7 percent when Zurich moved from an asset-based to a risk-based approach for operational risk quantification. Tools such as Total Risk Profiling (TRP, described later in this chapter) and the business unit then identified high risk exposures, performed a deeper assessment and developed mitigation measures, The business unit experienced an additional reduction of 28.9 percent in operational risk capital consumption the following year. Operational risk capital not consumed was then available to fund profitable growth for Zurich

Optimizing the Risk and Reward Balance at Zurich

To consistently achieve the right balance between risk and reward to optimize capital, many corporate leaders around the world have adopted ERM within their organizations. Zurich has a well-established ERM program, which it sees as a critical component to its success. Zurich's comprehensive ERM and risk tolerance framework links risk taking, strategic planning, and operational planning with a comprehensive risk limit system. It enables active risk-taking within a consistent framework across the entire organization. It also allows for the flexibility to either increase or limit risk levels as appropriate for specific applications, geographies, or business units on a case-by-case basis, in accordance with Zurich's risk policy.

Global businesses like Zurich are increasingly focused on the challenge of mapping and managing their risk profiles, looking beyond a single dimension to understand the complex interactions between many different types of risks. Zurich's risk landscape outlines the number of risks, types of risks, and potential effects of those risks to the organization. This outline supports each business unit within Zurich as they strive to anticipate additional costs or disruption to its operations. Also, it describes the willingness of Zurich to take risks and how those risks will affect the operational strategy of the organization. Managing the vast scope of business exposures and growth initiatives requires taking a broader view on risks from a strategic perspective. In defining its desired risk profile, Zurich must determine which risks will optimize its returns. Its ERM mission is to promptly identify, measure, manage, report, and monitor the risks that affect the achievement of its strategic goals.

Risk Culture at Zurich

The risk culture at Zurich could be defined as the individual and group behavior within the organization that determines the way in which Zurich identifies, understands, discusses, and acts on the organization's risks and opportunities. Embedding a positive risk culture is the responsibility of the Zurich leadership team because it is critical to the effective management of the business.

The core characteristics expected from an effective risk culture include committed leadership, an effective governance structure with clear risk responsibilities and timely escalation procedures, continuous and constructive challenges, active learning from past mistakes, and incentives that reward consideration of risk management objectives and risk appetite in the organization's management of the business.

Zurich recognizes the need to constantly improve on its ERM program. Senior leadership also wishes to have an effective way of understanding and reporting on the risk culture and framework of the company, both to support internal management and oversight and to be able to report externally. In principle, the risk culture should not be seen as something separate from the overall culture of the organization, and, for risk to be truly embedded, it should be regarded as one element, albeit one that currently deserves specific attention.

ZURICH GROUP'S ENTERPRISE RISK MANAGEMENT FRAMEWORK

At the heart of Zurich's ERM framework is a governance process with clear responsibilities for taking, managing, monitoring, and reporting risks. (See Exhibit 14.1.) Zurich articulates the roles and responsibilities for risk management throughout the organization, from the board of directors and the chief executive officer (CEO) to its businesses and functional areas. In fact, each business and functional or project team will have someone designated as a risk owner to be responsible for identifying and addressing relevant risk exposures and to help embed ERM further in the business unit and build a more open, positive risk culture.

One of the key elements of Zurich's ERM framework is to foster transparency by establishing risk reporting standards throughout the organization. Zurich regularly reports on its risk profile, current risk issues, adherence to its risk policies, and improvement actions both at a local and on a senior management level. Zurich has procedures in place for the timely referral of risk issues to senior management and the board of directors. Various governance and control functions coordinate

Exhibit 14.1   Zurich Risk Management Framework

to help ensure that objectives are being achieved, risks are identified and appropriately managed, and internal controls are in place and operating effectively.

Risk Governance Approach at Zurich with Three Lines of Defense

Zurich uses a "three lines of defense" model to help ensure governance and control. (See Exhibit 14.2.) This model consists of the following:

1. The first line of defense in the business or functional areas involves the employees making day-to-day business decisions like underwriting, managing projects, developing information technology (IT) solutions, or managing human capital issues.
2. The second line of defense is Group Risk Management, which oversees the company's efforts to apply appropriate risk identification and governance processes and provides tools and frameworks to manage decisions. Group Risk Management also coordinates very closely with the Compliance and Legal departments, Business Continuity Management, IT, Procurement, and other areas, to encourage better coordination across various silos to build an enterprise lens on risk management.
3. The third line of defense is the independent internal audit function, which is responsible for verifying the functionality of the ERM and internal controls framework.

To support the governance process, Zurich relies on documented policies and guidelines. The Zurich Risk Policy is its risk governance document; it specifies Zurich's risk tolerance, risk limits and authorities, reporting requirements,

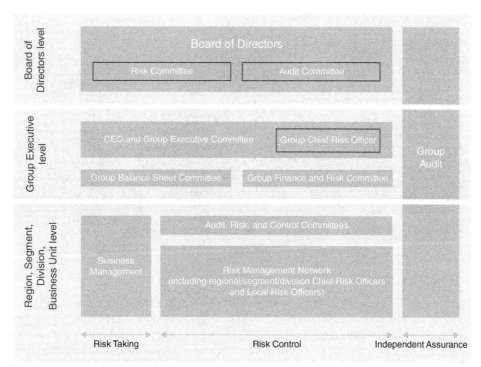

The overview above highlights only key elements of the governance framework that apply to risk management;

Exhibit 14.2 Zurich Risk Governance Overview

procedures to approve any exceptions, and procedures for referring risk issues to senior management and the board of directors. The limits are specified per risk type, reflecting the willingness and ability to take risks, considering issues such as earnings stability, economic capital adequacy, financial flexibility and liquidity, franchise value, and reputation. Zurich's strategic direction and operational plan seeks to achieve a reasonable balance between risk and return, and to be aligned with economic and financial objectives.

An important element of Zurich's ERM framework is a well-balanced and effectively managed remuneration program. This includes a groupwide remuneration philosophy and robust short- and long-term incentive plans, with strong governance and links to the business planning, performance management, and risk policies. Based on Zurich's Risk Policy, the board establishes the structure and design of the remuneration arrangements so that they do not encourage inappropriate risk taking.

As an ongoing process, adherence to requirements stated in the Zurich Risk Policy is assessed. Zurich regularly enhances its Risk Policy to reflect new insights and changes in the environment and to reflect changes to the risk tolerance. For example, the Zurich Risk Policy was recently updated and strengthened for various areas, including actuarial reserving in General Insurance, reinsurance, receivables, operational risk management, and particularly outsourcing and business continuity management. Related procedures and risk controls were also strengthened or clarified for these areas.

Group Risk Management
- Coordinate risk identification, risk assessment, and financial quantification of risk to achieve a holistic view of the organization's risks.
- Responsible for coordinating risk reporting.
- The resultant risk landscape will inform the risk-based assurance activities of the other functions.

Group Compliance
- Specialist function that contributes insights regarding compliance matters.
- Coordinates with other assurance functions in the discharge of its mandate.

Group Audit
- Facilitate alignment of assurance methodology and assurance coverage (including raising any gaps in assurance coverage). Includes assurance work of Group Audit, Group Compliance, External Audit, Technical Underwriting, and Claims QA.
- Responsible for coordinating assurance reporting.

Exhibit 14.3   Zurich's Core Assessment and Assurance Functions

Integrated Assessment and Assurance

Integrated Assessment and Assurance (IAA) is a coordinated view from the Assurance functions to provide greater confidence that risks are identified, those risks are appropriately managed, and mitigation actions are implemented and controls are operating effectively. The Assessment and Assurance functions include Group Risk Management, Group Compliance, and Group Audit. (See Exhibit 14.3.) Close coordination is also maintained with Group Legal, External Audit, and management's review functions such as underwriting or claims reviews and actuarial peer reviews.

Internal Control Framework

Swiss law prescribes the existence of an Internal Control System (OR 728a) to all "listed companies" and "companies of economic significance." Zurich Insurance Group was one of the early firms to pioneer the industry with the establishment of its internal control system in 2004. The framework is of core importance in ensuring that company objectives are adhered to and that risks are controlled. The board of directors wants to have positive assurance that an effective internal control system is embedded in the business processes.

Zurich's Internal Control Framework (ICF) provides to the board the requested global overview of the risks in each business unit and how they are controlled. The evidence of these controls and its documentation serve as proof of the ICF's existence for regulatory and auditing purposes. Zurich's three lines of defense help ensure that the Internal Control Framework is enabled.

ROLE OF THE CHIEF RISK OFFICER AND GROUP RISK MANAGEMENT AT ZURICH

Zurich's chief risk officer (CRO) consults with the other assurance, control, and governance functions to provide the chief executive officer (CEO) with a review of risk factors to consider in the annual process to determine variable compensation. The CRO leads the Group Risk Management function, which develops methods and processes for identifying, measuring, managing, monitoring, and reporting risks throughout Zurich. The CRO is responsible for the oversight of risks across Zurich and regularly reports risk matters to the CEO, senior management committee, and the Risk Committee of the board.

The Group Risk Management organization at Zurich consists of central functions at the Corporate Center and a decentralized risk management network at all the segment, regional, business unit, and functional levels. At the Group level there are two centers of expertise: risk analytics and risk and control. The Risk Analytics department quantitatively assesses insurance, financial market, asset/liability, credit, and operational risks, and is Zurich's center of excellence for risk quantification and risk modeling. The Risk and Control department includes operational risk management, internal control framework, risk reporting, risk governance, and risk operations. Group Risk Management proposes changes to the risk management framework and Zurich's risk policies; it makes recommendations on the organization's risk tolerance and assesses the risk profile.

The risk management network consists of the chief risk officers (CROs) of the Group's segments and regions, and the local risk officers (LROs) of the business units and functions and their staff. While their primary focus is on operational and business-related risks, they are also responsible for providing a holistic view of all risks for their areas. The risk officers are part of the management teams in their respective businesses and therefore are embedded in the business units. The LROs also report to the segment or regional CROs, who in turn report to the Group's chief risk officer. The CROs of the Group's segments and regions are members of the leadership team of the Group's chief risk officer.

In addition to the risk management network, Zurich has audit and/or oversight committees at the major business and regional levels. These committees are responsible for providing oversight of the risk management and control functions. This includes monitoring adherence to policies and periodic risk reporting. At the local level, these oversight activities are conducted through risk and control committees or quarterly meetings between senior executives and the local heads of governance functions.

In 2012, Zurich strengthened the process through which the assurance, control, and governance functions provide risk and compliance information about each business unit as part of the annual individual performance assessment. Through these processes, Zurich encourages a culture of disciplined risk taking across the organization. It continues to consciously take carefully selected risks for which it expects an adequate return.

Board-Level Risk Committee and Executive Risk Committee Responsibilities

The board of directors of Zurich Insurance Group has ultimate oversight responsibility for Zurich's risk management program. The board approved the guidelines for the Group's risk management framework and key principles, particularly as articulated in the Zurich Risk Policy, and decides on changes to such guidelines and key principles, as well as transactions reaching specified thresholds.

The Risk Committee of the board serves as a focal point for oversight regarding Zurich's risk management. In particular its risk tolerance, including agreed limits that the board regards as acceptable for Zurich to bear, the aggregation of these limits across the entire organization, the measurement of adherence to risk limits, and its risk tolerance in relation to anticipated capital levels. The Risk Committee further oversees the organization-wide risk governance framework, including risk management and control, risk policies and their implementation, as well as risk strategy and the monitoring of operational risks.

The Risk Committee also reviews the methodologies for risk measurement and its adherence to risk limits. The Risk Committee further reviews, with business management and Zurich's Risk Management functions, its general policies and procedures and satisfies itself that effective systems of risk management are established and maintained. It receives regular reports from Zurich's Risk Management Group and assesses whether significant issues of a risk management and control nature are being appropriately addressed by management in a timely manner. The Risk Committee assesses the independence and objectivity of Zurich's Risk Management functions; approves its terms of reference; reviews the activities, plans, organization, and quality of the function; and reviews key risk management principles and procedures. To facilitate information exchange between the Audit Committee of the board and the Risk Committee of the board, at least one board member is a member of both committees. The Risk Committee generally meets seven times per year, including once jointly with the Remuneration Committee.

Zurich's Executive Risk Committee, which consists of the CEO together with the Group Executive Committee (GEC), oversees the Group's performance with regard to risk management and control, strategic, financial, and business policy issues of organization-wide relevance. This includes monitoring adherence to and further development of the Group's risk management policies and procedures. The Group Balance Sheet Committee and the Group Finance and Risk Committee regularly review and make recommendations on the Group's risk profile and significant risk-related issues.

The chief risk officer is a member of the GEC and reports directly to the CEO and the Risk Committee of the board. The CRO is a member of each of the management committees listed below, in order to provide a common and integrated approach to risk management, to allow for appropriate quantification and, where necessary, mitigation of risks identified in these committees.

Emerging Risk Group

Zurich's Emerging Risk Group (ERG) seeks to preempt potential downsides of emerging risk and help its employees and customers understand and address them. The ERG looks to serve customers and society and build business opportunities to increase, not exclude, insurability of emerging risks. The ERG's remit is to respond to emerging risk threats and opportunities with strategies that help customers understand and protect themselves from risk and that drive profitable underwriting results.

The Zurich Emerging Risk Radar shows potential risks and opportunities that the ERG has currently identified. The online, internal version of Zurich Risk Radar is interactive, and one can roll the cursor over each threat to see a description of a risk and its potential harm—and each risk is classified by its primary scope (Science and Technology, Regulatory, Environmental, Social, or Legal), as well as the time over which the risk will potentially emerge (zero to three years, three to five years, five or more years), plus its potential impact on Group earnings. (See Exhibit 14.4 for a public version.)

WORKING WITH EXTERNAL STAKEHOLDERS

Various external stakeholders, among them regulators, rating agencies, investors, and accounting bodies, have placed emphasis on the importance of a sound risk management program in the insurance industry. Regulatory requirements, such as the Swiss Solvency Test in Switzerland and the regulatory principles of Solvency III in the European Union, have emphasized a risk-based and economic approach, based on comprehensive quantitative and qualitative assessments and reports.

Rating agencies are now interested in enterprise risk management as a factor in evaluating companies' creditworthiness. Standard & Poor's, a rating agency with a separate rating for ERM, has rated Zurich's overall ERM as "strong." Reinsurance and credit risk controls remain "excellent." Market, asset/liability management (ALM), reserving, catastrophe, and operational risk controls, as well as strategic and emerging risk management, are seen as "strong." Zurich is rated either "excellent" or "strong" in all of the Standard & Poor's dimensions for ERM.

Zurich also seeks external expertise from its International Advisory Council and Natural Catastrophe Advisory Council to better understand and assess risks, particularly regarding areas of complex change. In addition, the Investment Management Advisory Council provides feedback to Investment Management on achieving superior risk-adjusted returns versus liabilities for the Group's invested assets. Zurich also organizes various regional Risk Management Councils comprised of key customers, which engage to help identify and address issues together.

Zurich is involved in a number of international industry organizations engaged in advancing the regulatory dialogue and sound risk management practices pertaining to the insurance industry. It is also a standing member of and actively contributes to the Emerging Risk Initiative of the CRO Forum (an organization composed of the chief risk officers of major insurance companies and financial conglomerates that focuses on developing and promoting industry best practices in risk management).

Zurich actively participates in professional risk management bodies such as the Risk and Insurance Management Society (RIMS), the Institute of Risk Management (IRM), the Federation of European Risk Management Association (FERMA), and the Association of Insurance and Risk Managers in Industry and Commerce. For example, Zurich's staff serves on the RIMS ERM Committee and on the global Education Advisory Board of the IRM. It is also involved in various working groups in the Conference Board, supports the Red Cross in crisis recovery, and collaborates with other entities to help promote better risk identification, assessment, prevention, and mitigation.

Zurich is a main contributor to the Global Risk Report that is produced by the World Economic Forum in cooperation with other corporations (Swiss Re, Marsh & McLennan Companies, the Oxford Martin School [University of Oxford], the National University of Singapore, and the Wharton Risk Management and Decision Processes Center [University of Pennsylvania Center for Risk Management] [www.weforum.org/reports/global-risks-2012-seventhninth-edition]). The

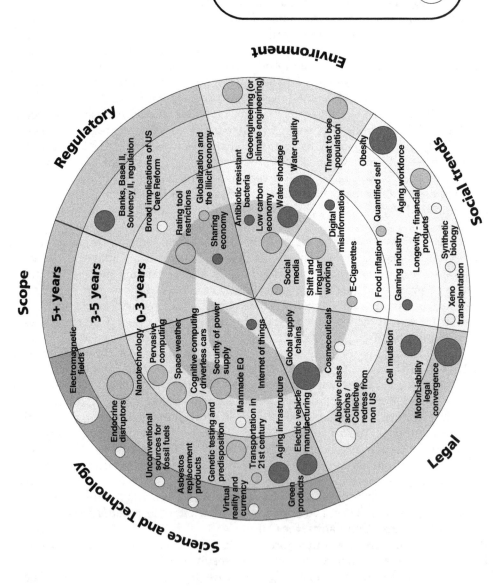

Exhibit 14.4 Zurich Risk Radar

262

report's assessment of the most pressing global risks and the interconnections among them provides valuable information for risk mitigation worldwide. Supporting the report is also part of the Group's commitment to corporate responsibility by sharing Zurich's expertise to help businesses, nations, and society.

ZURICH'S PROPRIETARY TOOLS USED IN ERM FRAMEWORK

Zurich uses a variety of methodologies and tools to manage its business risk, with the following aims. More information on Zurich's Strategic Risk Management work can be found at www.zuricherm.com.

- Understand issues in enterprise strategy, resilience, supply chain, and business continuity.
- Identify scenarios that could—or should—be built into a strategic and/or operational resilience plan.
- Develop action points and risk responsibilities to help protect profitability.

Total Risk Profiling Tool

One of Zurich's key proprietary tools is called Total Risk Profiling (TRP); it is a workshop-based approach where a facilitator-led team develops a risk profile by determining relative ratings in probability and severity (likelihood and impact) for potential risk scenarios. (See Exhibit 14.5.) TRP is a structured approach to identifying, assessing, and monitoring holistic risks and improvement

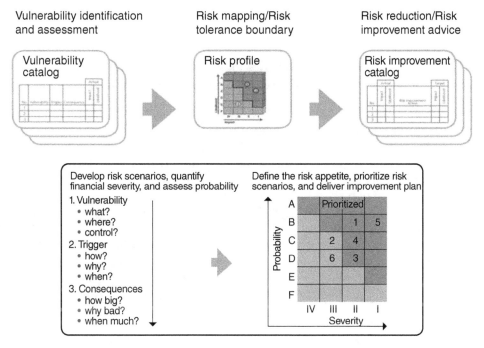

Exhibit 14.5   Zurich Total Risk Profiling Tool

actions needed. By embedding its Total Risk Profiling methodology into its risk culture, this has helped ensure its risk management culture is consistent and effective across its various business units. It uses these risk scenarios to define the underlying issues and break them into components of vulnerability, trigger, and consequences. The TRP tool can also help a business unit define and quantify its risk tolerance limit. A short video explains more about Total Risk Profiling (http://zdownload.zurich.com/zna/TotalRiskProfiling.html).

A risk tolerance limit is defined as part of the risk appetite, and action plans are developed to improve the prioritized risks and bring them within the business unit's tolerance for risk. The structure of the TRP risk identification process provides a sound basis for detailed quantification of more complex risks. TRP has helped Zurich's business units set the agenda for internal audit or enterprise risk management to monitor risks at or just below the risk tolerance boundary.

By being able to define multiple risk triggers with different potential consequences, the TRP tool has helped Zurich to identify the true drivers of risk by undertaking various stress tests or even to define new risk exposures. A facilitator-led team develops a relative rating for each risk scenario, often without a predefined scale of impact and likelihood, to improve the business unit's understanding of the risk.

Another main aim of the flexible TRP tool is to help embed a risk culture that will sustain shareholder value through better enterprise risk management practices and strategic planning processes. Zurich performs nearly 200 TRP workshops per year, ranging from assessing strategy execution, project management, human resources (HR), mergers and acquisitions (M&A), or business interruption (BI) exposures to new product development. In fact, completion of a TRP is a requisite part of the submission for a project budget or operational plan. The TRP tool helps to enable the following:

- Assessment of current and emerging risks to business resilience and profitability
- Alignment of business strategy with key performance indicators
- Communication of board discussion on risk appetite to investors and other stakeholders
- Reviewing the environmental scanning tool for corporate or competitive business strategy development
- Embedding of ERM in the strategic planning process
- Product launches, acquisitions or divestitures, and project management
- Considering the vulnerabilities in the supply chain
- Evaluation of business interruption risk scenarios
- Testing of existing strategies in the context of unrealized/underrealized risks and opportunities
- Use in the objective-setting stage of the business cycle to determine the budget

Zurich Hazard Analysis Tool

The Zurich Hazard Analysis is a powerful methodology to systematically identify, address, and manage various types of hazards or vulnerabilities and to address and manage the corresponding risks. The methodology is closely related to Total Risk Profiling, and is helpful in defining "pathways" of risks. Zurich has been successfully applying and using it within its operations and with customers for over 20 years in various industries, commercial enterprises, and, more recently, in the financial services industry, as well as public entities.

Zurich's Risk Room

Another of Zurich's proprietary tools, called the Zurich Risk Room, helps the organization and its customers to systematically explore major global risks, investigating how they are expressed on a country-by-country basis. (See Exhibit 14.6.) It shows on a 3-D screen how risks and geographies combine (sometimes unexpectedly) to be relevant to Zurich's business concerns. This tool allows one to see which countries reflect similar profiles, and which risks begin to stand out on mapping various risk correlations. By working across different types of risks, risk correlations are identified that illustrate whether relevant risk connections exist and which ones are the strongest.

The Zurich Risk Room creates a statistical, fact-based assessment of global threats as they relate to business planning and implementation. Its output can complement departmental, regional, or consultant-based research and data, providing an additional objective lens to risk evaluation and reducing the issues related to silo-based risk assessments. Using a consistent global framework, the Zurich Risk Room can help identify threats that may cross boundaries and provide key decision makers with relevant risk information that can help them make more informed business decisions, even if they are not experts in risk analysis.

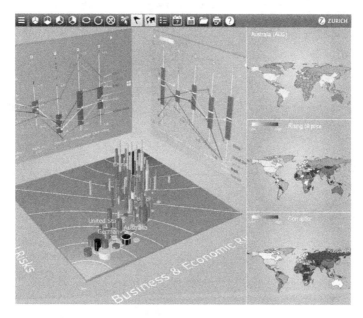

Exhibit 14.6 Zurich's Risk Room

By examining risks and interconnections in detail, Zurich is able to compare both individual issues and overall country risk characteristics of one country to those of another. This allows Zurich to see whether a country's risk profile is unique or it shares similarities with other countries. For international businesses, it is vital to form a picture of where operations and investments are vulnerable and where these vulnerabilities may reside. Zurich is then able to identify how risks are bundled, or where a threat in one area might cascade to another.

A demo version of the Zurich Risk Room software for an iPad or Android tablet can be downloaded by searching for Zurich Risk Room in iTunes or Google Play. In addition, this is a link to a short video that will give a brief overview of the Zurich Risk Room application: www.youtube.com/watch?v=_UMaYJtDu6Q.

CATEGORIZING VARIOUS RISKS AT ZURICH

In order to enable a consistent, systematic, and disciplined approach to ERM, Zurich categorizes its main risks. (See Exhibit 14.7.) This grouping assists Zurich in monitoring any aggregation of exposures that may be accumulating across the enterprise and could, therefore, have a greater impact on the company.

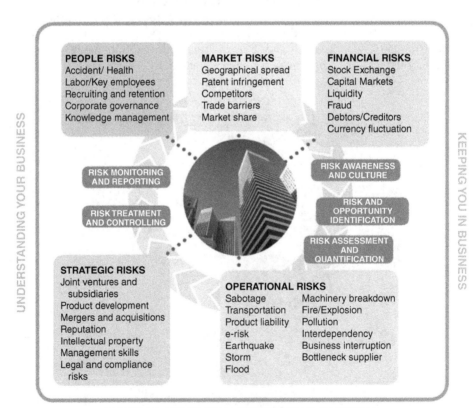

Exhibit 14.7 Categorizing Various Risks at Zurich

Strategic Risks

Strategic risks are the unintended risks that can result as a by-product of planning or executing a strategy. For example, they can arise from the following:

- Inadequate assessment of strategic plans
- Improper implementation of strategic plans
- Unexpected changes to assumptions underlying plans

Risk considerations are a key element in the strategic decision-making process. The senior leadership team assesses the implications of strategic decisions on risk-based return measures and risk-based capital in order to optimize the risk/return profile and to take advantage of economically profitable growth opportunities as they arise.

Zurich works on reducing the unintended risks of strategic business decisions through its risk assessment processes and tools. The Group Executive Committee regularly assesses key strategic risk scenarios for the Group as a whole, including scenarios for emerging risks and their strategic implications.

An example of this is when Zurich evaluates the risks of mergers and acquisitions (M&A) transactions from both a quantitative and a qualitative perspective. Zurich conducts risk assessments of M&A transactions to evaluate risk, especially related to the integration of acquired businesses, to help increase the likelihood of successfully attaining the expected benefits. They may also review country-level exposures using the Zurich Risk Room tool.

Insurance Risks

Insurance risk is the inherent uncertainty regarding the occurrence, amount, and timing of insurance liabilities. The exposure is usually transferred to Zurich through the underwriting process. Zurich assumes certain customer risks and aims to manage that transfer of risk and to minimize unintended underwriting risks through the following:

- Establishing limits for underwriting authority
- Requiring specific approvals for transactions involving new products or where established limits of size and complexity may be exceeded
- Using a variety of reserving and modeling techniques to address the various insurance risks inherent in the insurance business
- Ceding insurance risks through proportional, nonproportional, and specific risk reinsurance treaties

Market Risks

Market risks can be associated with the Group's balance sheet positions where the value or cash flow depends on financial markets. Fluctuating risk drivers resulting in market risk may include:

- Equity market prices
- Real estate market prices

- Interest rates and credit spreads
- Currency exchange rates

Zurich has policies and limits to manage market risk. Zurich aligns its strategy asset allocation to its risk-taking capacity. The Group centralizes the management of certain asset classes to help control aggregation of risk, and provides a consistent approach to constructing portfolios and selecting external asset managers. Zurich also diversifies portfolios, investments, and asset managers. It regularly measures and manages market risk exposure. Zurich has established limits on concentration in investments by single issuers and certain asset classes, as well as deviations of asset interest rate sensitivities from liability interest rate sensitivities, and also has limits on investments that are illiquid.

Credit Risks

Credit risks are associated with a loss or potential loss from counterparties failing to fulfill their financial obligations. Zurich's exposure to credit risks may be derived from the following main categories of assets:

- Cash and cash equivalents
- Debt securities
- Reinsurance assets
- Mortgage loans and mortgage loans given as collateral
- Other loans
- Receivables
- Derivatives

Zurich strives to manage individual exposures as well as credit risk concentrations. Its objective in managing credit risks is to maintain them within parameters that reflect its strategic objectives and risk tolerance. Sources of credit risks are assessed and monitored, and Zurich has policies to manage special risks within various subcategories of credit risk. To assess counterparty credit risk, Zurich uses the rating assigned by external rating agencies, qualified third parties such as asset managers, and internal rating assessments. When there is a difference among external rating agencies, Zurich assesses the reason for the inconsistencies and applies the lowest of the respective ratings unless other indicators of credit quality justify the assignment of alternative internal credit ratings. Zurich maintains counterparty credit risk databases that record external and internal sources of credit intelligence.

Liquidity Risks

Risks that Zurich may not have sufficient liquidity to meet its obligations when they fall due, or would have to incur excessive costs to do so, are categorized as liquidity risks. Zurich's policy is to maintain adequate liquidity and contingent liquidity to meet its liquidity needs under both normal and stressed conditions.

Zurich has groupwide liquidity management policies and specific guidelines as to how local businesses have to plan, manage, and report their local liquidity. These include regularly conducting stress tests for all major carriers within Zurich.

The stress tests use a standardized set of internally defined stress events and are designed to provide an overview of the potential liquidity drain that Zurich would face if it had to recapitalize local balance sheets.

Operational Risks

Operational risks can be associated with Zurich's people, processes, and systems, and external events such as outsourcing, catastrophes, legislation, or external fraud. Zurich has a comprehensive framework with a common approach to identify, assess, quantify, mitigate, monitor, and report operational risks within the scenario-based assessments, internal controls evaluations, and loss event data.

In the area of information security, Zurich continues to focus on its global improvement program with special emphasis on protecting customer information, improving security with its suppliers, and monitoring that access to information is properly controlled. This helps Zurich better protect information assets and ensure greater alignment with regulation and policies. A key consideration is maintaining and developing the capability of Zurich's business continuity with an emphasis on recovery from possible risk events such as natural catastrophe or pandemic. Zurich continues to develop its existing business continuity capability by further implementing a more globally consistent approach to business continuity and crisis management.

Focusing on the risk of claims fraud and nonclaims fraud continues to be of great importance to Zurich. Zurich continues its global antifraud initiative to further improve Zurich's ability to prevent, detect, and respond to fraud. While claims fraud is calculated as part of insurance risk and nonclaims fraud is calculated as part of operational risk for risk-based capital, both are part of the common framework for assessing and managing operational risks. Zurich considers risk controls to be key instruments for monitoring and managing operational risks. The operational effectiveness of key controls is assessed by self-assessments and independent testing of controls supporting the financial statements.

Reputation Risks

Reputation risks are risks that might arise from an act or omission by Zurich or any of its employees that could result in damage to the Group's reputation or loss of trust among its stakeholders. Every risk type could have potential consequences for Zurich's reputation, and therefore effectively managing its exposures holistically and systematically helps Zurich reduce threats to its reputation.

CAPITAL MANAGEMENT

Capital and solvency are managed through an integrated and comprehensive framework of principles and governance structures as well as methodology, monitoring, and reporting processes. The capital management process is illustrated in Exhibit 14.8. At the group executive level, the Group Balance Sheet Committee defines the capital management strategy and sets the principles, standards, and policies for the execution of the strategy. Group Treasury and Capital Management are responsible for the execution of the capital management strategy within the mandate set by the Group Balance Sheet Committee.

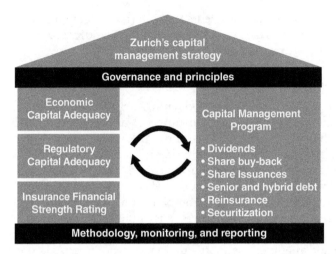

Exhibit 14.8 Zurich's Capital Management Strategy

Within these defined principles, the group manages its capital using a number of different capital models, taking into account regulatory, economic, and rating agency constraints. The capital and solvency position is monitored and reported on a regular basis. Based on the results of the capital models and the defined standards and principles, Group Treasury and Capital Management has a set of measures and tools available to manage capital within the defined constraints. This tool set is referred to as the Capital Management Program.

The Capital Management Program comprises various measures to optimize shareholders' return and to meet capital needs, while enabling Zurich to take advantage of growth opportunities as they arise. Such measures are used as and when required and could include efficient balance sheet structuring as well as cash dividends, share buy-backs, special dividends, issuances of shares or senior and subordinated debt, and purchase of reinsurance.

The group seeks to maintain the balance between higher returns for shareholders on equity raised, which may be possible with higher levels of borrowing, and the security provided by a sound capital position. The payment of dividends, share buy-backs, and issuances and redemption of debt can have an important influence on Zurich's capital levels.

Zurich Economic Capital Model

In addition to a qualitative approach to measuring risks, Zurich regularly measures and quantifies material risks to which it is exposed through both TRP and the Zurich Economic Capital Model (Z-ECM). This model provides a key input into the strategic planning process, as it allows an assessment as to whether its risk profile is in line with its risk tolerance level. In particular, Z-ECM forms the basis for optimizing Zurich's risk/return profile by providing consistent risk measurement across the Group.

Zurich uses Z-ECM to assess the economic capital consumption of its business with a balance sheet approach. Under the balance sheet approach one looks at the change in stockholders' or owners' equity to determine the amount of net income during the period between balance sheets. The Z-ECM framework is embedded in Zurich's risk culture and plays a critical role in decision making, and is used in capital allocation, business performance management, pricing, reinsurance purchasing, transaction evaluation, and risk optimization, as well as regulatory, investor, and rating agency communication. Z-ECM quantifies the capital required for insurance-related risk (including premium and reserve, natural catastrophe, business, and life insurance), market risk (market/ALM [asset/liability management]), credit risk (including reinsurance credit and investment credit), and operational risks.

At the Group level, Zurich compares Z-ECM capital required to the Z-ECM available financial resources (Z-ECM AFR) to derive an economic solvency ratio (Z-ECM ratio). Z-ECM AFR reflects financial resources available to cover policyholder liabilities in excess of their expected value. It is derived by adjusting the International Financial Reporting Standards (IFRS) shareholders' equity to reflect the full economic capital base available to absorb any unexpected volatility in Zurich's business activities. As part of Z-ECM, Zurich uses a scenario-based approach to assess, model, and quantify the capital required for operational risk for business units under extreme circumstances and a very small probability of occurrence (internal model calibrated to a confidence level of 99.95 percent over a one-year time horizon).

Analysis of Capital Adequacy

Zurich maintains interactive relationships with three global rating agencies: Standard & Poor's, Moody's, and A.M. Best. The Insurance Financial Strength Rating (IFSR) of Zurich's main operating entity is an important element of its competitive position. Moreover, Zurich's credit ratings that are derived from its financial strength rating do, in fact, affect its cost of capital, just like any other credit-rated company.

In each country in which Zurich operates, the local regulator specifies the minimum amount and type of capital that each of the regulated entities must hold in relation to its liabilities. In addition to maintaining the minimum capital required to comply with the solvency requirements, Zurich targets holding an adequate buffer of capital reserves to ensure that each of its regulated subsidiaries meets the local capital requirements. Zurich is subject to different capital requirements depending on the country in which it operates. The main areas are Switzerland and European Economic Area countries, and the United States.

Since January 1, 2011, the Swiss Solvency Test (SST) capital requirements are binding in Switzerland. The Group uses an adaptation of its internal Risk-Based Capital (RBC) model to comply with the SST requirements and runs a full SST calculation twice a year. The model is still subject to Swiss Financial Market Supervisory Authority (FINMA) approval.

ZURICH'S BUSINESS RESILIENCE TOOLS

Business resilience management helps provide Zurich with the structure for dealing with risks systematically, holistically, and successfully. Zurich's Business Resilience program is supported by an enterprise risk management framework that identifies particular events or circumstances relevant to its business objectives,

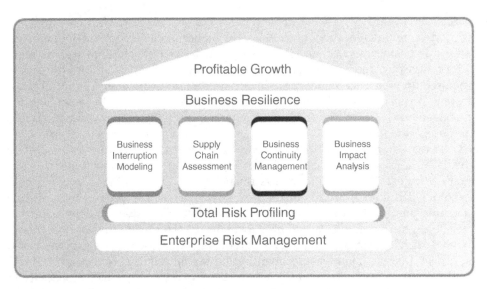

Exhibit 14.9   Zurich's Business Resilience Program

assesses them in terms of likelihood and magnitude of impact, and then determines a response strategy. (See Exhibit 14.9.) A resilient enterprise is better able to anticipate surprises, recover more quickly from disruptions, adapt to changing conditions, and leverage emerging opportunities.

The objective of Zurich's Business Resilience program is "Prepared, Informed, and Resilient." This tagline is regularly communicated to staff, especially during Business Resilience Awareness week. Some of Zurich's proprietary Business Resilience tools are listed here.

Business Interruption Modeling allows Zurich the capability to better manage its risks based on an in-depth understanding of the value chain, with a main focus on the business critical value flow, followed by identification, assessment, and quantification of business interruption exposures and optional mitigations. Like all organizations, a business interruption for Zurich could have the potential to inhibit productivity and could have multiple negative impacts on its organization. Some examples of business interruption impacts could include loss of customers, diminished customer service, legal and/or regulatory issues, lower employee morale, and even delays in projects, products, or other strategic growth. Thus, it is essential that organizations try to map and quantify how they serve customers, in order to proactively protect where they generate value.

Key stages of Business Interruption Modeling include:

- Defining scope by identifying the business-critical part(s) of the value chain
- Building an interdependency framework of business-critical value flows
- Identifying relevant business interruption vulnerabilities as loss of resources such as supplier, production, storage, and customer
- Assessing the extent based on interruption scenarios, and modeling the effects quantitatively

- Prioritizing risks based on financial impact of scenarios, with focus on unacceptable risks in order to develop a beneficial mitigation plan
- Assessing the effectiveness of current business continuity plans and identifying improvement actions

Supply Chain Risk Assessment allows Zurich to improve its reliability and minimize the effects of a supply chain disruption on its capital and earnings. Zurich's supplier risk assessment should help address vulnerabilities that could inhibit Zurich's ability to respond to a changing risk landscape. Its supply chain risk evaluation, mapping, and grading are designed to assess and quantify the broad areas of exposures and risk controls in its supply chain. This gives Zurich actionable insights to help facilitate mitigation strategies that can address the characteristics of each supplier individually, including risk transfer options.

The stages of a Supply Chain Risk Assessment include:

- Develop a supply chain/value chain map.
- Gather key supply/supplier details.
- Evaluate risk factor information.
- Define and evaluate potential risk or loss scenarios.
- Develop risk grading for each critical supplier.
- Determine risk strategies.

Business Continuity Management (BCM) includes the mitigation strategies used to minimize the impact after an incident, with the possible scope of risks coming from supply chain risks, strategic risks, operational risks, technological risks, or natural hazards. BCM is very useful in identifying gaps in risk mitigation strategies and improving risk controls to manage those exposures more effectively. As part of Zurich's business resilience process, BCM is important for managing the multitude of risk exposures and potential interruptions scenarios and thus strengthening Zurich's business resilience program.

Zurich's Six-Stage Business Continuity Management Life Cycle

1. Modeling key business processes
2. Business impact analysis
3. BCM strategy and processes
4. Business continuity planning
5. Crisis management
6. Training, exercise, maintenance, and assessment

Zurich is able to undertake a regular gap analysis of its business continuity plans against best practices and common BCM-related standards such as International Standards Organization (ISO), National Fire Protection Association (NFPA) and the British Standard. It also routinely tests its crisis response activities. For example, it has planned or completed simulation exercises such as:

- Eurostar trains caught in tunnel
- India: Bomb explosion in hotel where Zurich has employees, impacting the country where company has operations in Pune, Bangalore, and Chennai

- Fire in Home Office location injuring employees, impacting critical processes, and possibly preventing occupancy in location for up to three to four months
- Los Angeles earthquake
- Kansas tornado
- Political demonstration in New York City

Business Impact Analysis is designed to provide the method to identify the systems that, when absent, would create a danger to the survival of the organization. This analysis can also ensure that these systems receive the correct priority in any subsequent business continuity plan.

Key stages of Zurich's Business Impact Analysis include:

- Prioritize the key business services or processes.
- Identify the internal and external risks to the continuity of these business processes.
- Assess the importance of each risk in terms of both the likelihood and the financial impact of potential outcomes.
- Establish priorities for mitigating the critical risks.
- Develop a management plan of action.
- Assess the business continuity plan and management plan of action.

HOW ZURICH USES ITS ERM TOOLS TO CREATE NEW VALUE

In the area of mergers and acquisitions, Zurich may use two opportunity analysis tools to supplement traditional due diligence practices. Both the Total Risk Profiling tool and the Zurich Risk Room can be used to simulate various risk scenarios and investigate potential outcomes. (See Exhibit 14.10.) When Zurich acquired holdings in Asia and Latin America, these tools served to help identify and understand the risks associated with the strategy, so they could be managed accordingly and increase the likelihood of success on these opportunities.

While key performance indicators (KPIs) can help an organization understand how well it is performing in relation to its strategic objectives, key risk indicators (KRIs) are leading indicators of risks to business performance. (See Exhibit 14.11.)

Zurich's ERM tools can add value by helping to determine and embed KRIs within an operations to provide an early warning that potential risks are on the rise. Some examples of Zurich using KRIs to monitor risks are in the areas of natural catastrophe risks (percentage of group shareholder equity), asset-liability matching (duration mismatch), strategic asset allocation (mix of investment across categories), and credit risk (weighted average credit rating).

Zurich has the opportunity to create value through business resiliency as well, which addresses disruption to business operations. It can use a combination of modeling software, supply chain risk assessment software, and business continuity gap analysis techniques to evaluate its exposure. It has recently appointed a supply chain risk officer, who reports into Zurich's CRO organization and is tasked with finding the appropriate balance between cost and reliability. It has a business

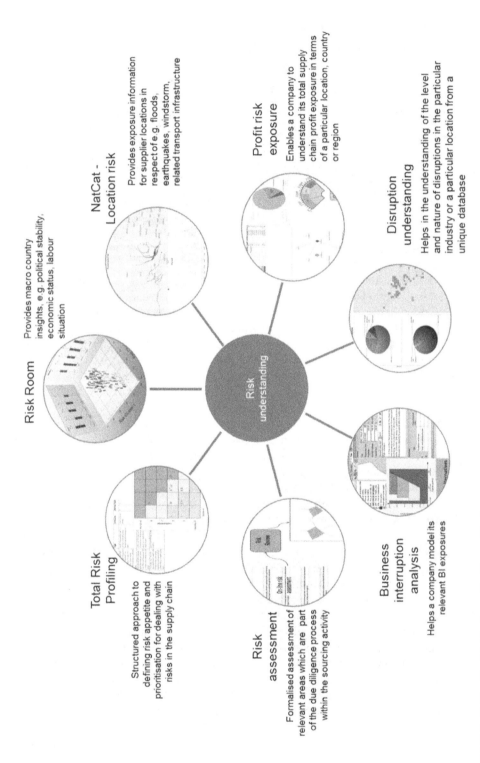

NatCat - Location risk

Provides exposure information for supplier locations in respect of e.g. floods, earthquakes, windstorm, related transport infrastructure

Profit risk exposure

Enables a company to understand its total supply chain profit exposure in terms of a particular location, country or region

Disruption understanding

Helps in the understanding of the level and nature of disruptions in the particular industry or a particular location from a unique database

Risk Room

Provides macro country insights, e.g. political stability, economic status, labour situation

Risk understanding

Total Risk Profiling

Structured approach to defining risk appetite and prioritisation for dealing with risks in the supply chain

Risk assessment

Formalised assessment of relevant areas which are part of the due diligence process within the sourcing activity

Business interruption analysis

Helps a company model its relevant BI exposures

Exhibit 14.10 Zurich Business Resilience Tools

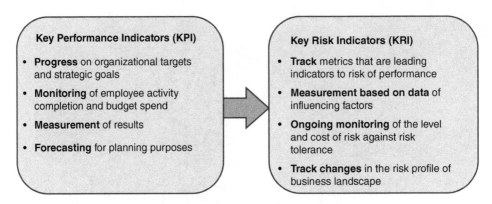

Exhibit 14.11   Zurich Key Performance Indicators and Key Risk Indicators

continuity planning team throughout its operating regions, and maintains a robust network of champions within the business, trained to return the business to operation quickly and efficiently after a disruption. The business continuity team regularly exercises a variety of plans to ensure that Zurich can be ready for many potential risk situations. Stress-testing activities take place in parallel to ensure that the network is prepared to shift workload, deploy contingencies, and remain operational, particularly when customers may have suffered from the same event.

With new projects or product development opportunities, Zurich can also use its Total Risk Profiling (TRP) tool to evaluate risk scenarios that may prevent it from delivering on time, on budget, and with the expected results. Completion of a TRP analysis is normally required as part of most requests for project approval and budget. Improvement actions are assigned to risk owners during TRP sessions, and monitored regularly to ensure risk reduction. The TRP tool can also help with quantifying the potential exposure and risk tolerance level. For example, TRP was used as an analysis tool before considering outsourcing IT services, helping to vet the solution as a viable alternative. The risk assessment team assigned risk improvement actions to individuals, and proceeded with the project. The TRP was regularly updated and benchmarked throughout the course of the project, as risks changed and new ones surfaced. The TRP assessment can even be used as a yes/no decision gate during the project phases to help determine that the expected project benefits still outweigh the risks.

The TRP methodology can also be used at the board and senior management levels to help develop strategic (top-down) scenarios that can be applied consistently during operational (bottom-up) assessments across the enterprise. This has helped to ensure uniform handling of certain systemic issues and exposures to better balance the risks and rewards of new opportunities. It is very important to Zurich to set financial parameters around managing current risk issues and guiding key business decisions going forward. The TRP process can build team commitment and focuses management expertise on dedicating resources to mitigate those risks that are outside the risk tolerance level and pose the greatest barriers to achieving corporate objectives.

Another use of the TRP methodology is its employment in a risk tolerance workshop. Establishing a corporate risk tolerance is a critical step in helping increase business controls and profitability across an enterprise. The corporate risk boundary provides a clear indication of both an acceptable risk appetite for new opportunities and an unacceptable risk threshold for downside cost on potential exposures. Risk tolerance is often defined as the level of variability that an organization is willing to accept in its aggregate earnings and capital value at risk (VaR) limits. It is essential to both define and apply corporate risk tolerance in order to prioritize the most critical areas for risk improvement. The risk appetite at Zurich is set by senior management, and then broadly articulated and followed by business and functional areas.

Zurich's ERM program also contributes to its core business through the processes and procedures to review customer risks. Zurich performs credit checks to monitor collateral and financial viability of many of its customers and suppliers. Its cross-divisional Emerging Risk Group is tasked with scanning the horizon for new exposures that may impact Zurich and its customers. Zurich reviews customers' loss control techniques and provides best practices guidance through nearly 1,000 risk engineers who specialize in safety and operational risks around the world, serving the dual purpose of supporting customers' needs as well as protecting Zurich's own portfolio. Last, accumulations within Zurich's risk portfolio are monitored via a database to identify areas of disproportionate exposure to a single company, industry, supplier, or geographic location.

CONCLUSION

Every organization's directors and officers will approach ERM differently in order to achieve their unique objectives. Zurich has taken many steps to help develop a strong and effective ERM program. This program did not emerge overnight, but today Zurich views its ERM program as a competitive advantage well worth the investment. Despite having embedded a robust program into the fabric of its business, Zurich does not rest on its laurels. The program is constantly scrutinized in search of better ways to identify, assess, manage, and monitor Zurich's key risks. The company has even developed an ERM Gap Analysis that can be done yearly to help determine risk maturity and focus on its top areas for improvement. The organization's management continuously looks for opportunities to create a closer partnership between ERM and the core business, so that its ERM team is ready to consult and assist the business in understanding risk in pursuit of profit. ERM is certainly a long journey defined by many paths, but one that can continue to yield tremendous benefits for the organization.

APPENDIX

Internally, Zurich uses its Risk-Based Capital (RBC) model, which also forms the basis of the SST model. The RBC model targets a total capital level that is calibrated to an AA-rated financial strength. Zurich defines RBC as being the capital required to protect the Group's policyholders in order to meet all of their claims with a confidence level of 99.95 percent over a one-year time horizon.

While the Group's RBC model and the SST model are broadly the same, the following is a summary of the main differences between the three approaches:

- *Model calibration.* The RBC calibration is based on a value at risk at a 99.95 percent confidence level, whereas SST calibration is based on an expected shortfall at a 99 percent confidence level. The Group thereby sets itself a higher financial strength target than the SST regulatory requirement.
- *Scope.* Operational and business risks for General Insurance are reflected in RBC, but are not required in SST.
- *Market/ALM risk.* The extreme scenario for market/ALM risk in RBC is directly attributed to that risk, whereas extreme scenarios in SST are aggregated to the combination of all risk types. This treatment of the extreme scenario in the RBC model leads to a more conservative result than in the SST model.
- *Available financial resources (AFR).* Senior debt is included in AFR for RBC purposes, but not included in AFR for the SST calculation.

Zurich uses RBC to assess the economic capital consumption of its business in a one-balance-sheet approach. The RBC framework is an integral part of how Zurich is managed. The RBC framework is embedded in Zurich's organization and decision making, and is used in capital allocation, business performance management, pricing, reinsurance purchasing, transaction evaluation, and risk optimization, as well as regulatory, investor, and rating agency communication.

Zurich compares RBC to its AFR to derive an economic solvency ratio. AFR reflects financial resources available to cover policyholder liabilities in excess of their expected value. It is derived by adjusting the IFRS shareholders' equity to reflect the full economic capital base available to absorb any unexpected volatility in the Group's business activities.

At a Group level, the management committees dealing with risks are:

- The Group Balance Sheet Committee (GBSC) acts as a cross-functional body whose main function is to control the activities that materially affect the balance sheets of the Group and its subsidiaries. The GBSC is charged with setting the annual capital and balance sheet plans for the Group based on the Group's strategy and financial plans, as well as recommending specific transactions or unplanned business changes to the Group's balance sheet. The GBSC has oversight of all main levers of the balance sheet, including capital management, reinsurance, asset/liability management, and liquidity. The GBSC reviews and recommends the Group's overall risk tolerance. It is chaired by the CEO.
- The Group Finance and Risk Committee (GFRC) acts as a cross-functional body for financial and risk management matters in the context of the strategy and the overall business activity of the Group. The GFRC oversees financial implications of business decisions and the effective management of the Group's overall risk profile, including risks related to insurance, financial markets and asset/liability, and credit and operational risks, as well as their interactions. The GFRC proposes remedial actions based on regular briefings from Group Risk Management on the risk profile of the Group. It reviews and formulates recommendations for future courses of action with respect to potential mergers and acquisitions (M&A) transactions, changes to the Zurich Risk Policy, internal insurance programs for the Group, material

changes to the Group's risk-based capital methodology, and the overall risk tolerance. The GFRC is chaired by the chief financial officer, while the chief risk officer acts as deputy.

The management committees rely on output provided by technical committees, including:

- The Asset/Liability Management and Investment Committee (ALMIC) deals with the Group's asset/liability exposure and investment strategies and is chaired by the chief investment officer.
- The General Insurance Global Underwriting Committee (GUC) acts as a focal point for underwriting policy and related risk controls for General Insurance and is chaired by the Global Chief Underwriting Officer for General Insurance.
- The Group Reinsurance Committee (GRC) defines the Group's reinsurance strategy in alignment with its risk framework and is chaired by the Global Head of Group Reinsurance.

QUESTIONS

1. How do Zurich ERM tools help them better understand their existing and emerging risks?
2. How are Zurich's risk roles and responsibilities impacting their risk culture?
3. Why is it important to include a Business Resilience program in your organization's ERM program?
4. How is Zurich's Capital Management program helping their ERM program?
5. Give some examples on how Zurich has created new value through their ERM program?

REFERENCES

Bugalla, John, Linda Conrad, and Kristina Narvaez. 2013. Presentation given at Risk and Insurance Management Society Annual Conference in Los Angeles, April 22.
Conrad, Linda. 2013. Presentation given at Risk and Insurance Management Society ERM Conference in San Francisco, November 4.
Zurich Insurance Group. 2012. Zurich Risk Report.

ABOUT THE CONTRIBUTORS

Linda Conrad is Director of Strategic Business Risk Management for Zurich. She leads a global team responsible for delivering tactical solutions to Zurich and to customers on strategic issues such as business resilience, supply chain risk, enterprise risk management (ERM), risk culture, and Total Risk Profiling. Linda also addresses enterprise resiliency issues in print and television appearances, including CNBC, Fox Business News, and the *Financial Times*, and is featured in a *Wall Street Journal* microsite at www.supplychainriskinsights.com.

Linda holds a Specialist designation in ERM, and serves on the global Education Advisory Board of the Institute of Risk Management in London. Linda is deputy member of the ERM Committee of the Risk and Insurance Management

Society (RIMS), sits on the Supply Chain Risk Leadership Council, and was chair-woman of the Asian Risk Management Conference. She taught at the University of Delaware Captive program and in the Master's on Supply Chain Management program at the University of Michigan's Ross School of Business, where she serves on the Corporate Advisory Council. Linda studied at the Graduate Institute of International Studies in Geneva, Switzerland, and Fox Business School.

Kristina Narvaez is the president and owner of ERM Strategies, LLC, which offers ERM research and training to organizations on various ERM-related topics. She graduated from the University of Utah in environmental risk management and then received her MBA from Westminster College. She is a two-time Spencer Education Foundation Graduate Scholar from the Risk and Insurance Management Society and has published more than 30 articles relating to enterprise risk management and board risk governance. She has given many presentations to various risk management associations on topics of ERM. She teaches a Business Strategy class at Brigham Young University.

CHAPTER 15

Embedding ERM into Strategic Planning at the City of Edmonton

KEN BAKER

ERM Program Manager at the City of Edmonton, Alberta, Canada

To me, the only good reason to take a risk is that there's a decent possibility of a reward that outweighs the hazard. Exploring the edge of the universe and pushing the boundaries of human knowledge and capability strike me as pretty significant rewards, so I accept the risks of being an astronaut, but with an abundance of caution: I want to understand them, manage them, and reduce them as much as possible.

—Commander Chris Hadfield[1]

The Administration of the City of Edmonton in 2012–2013 explored ways to implement enterprise risk management (ERM), with a focus on strategic risk.

Previous attempts at ERM were not fully implemented, but a new opportunity arose when Edmonton created a new strategic plan, *The Way Ahead*, in 2008. With the strategic plan and goals well established, they required risk analysis to determine what could prevent the city from achieving its goals and objectives, and how to allocate scarce resources most effectively to mitigate risks to achieving those goals and objectives.

The City Administration hired an Enterprise Risk Management Program Manager in 2012 to address the need to implement ERM at a strategic level.

After studying several models and frameworks for addressing risk, and conducting pilot workshops for two of the six directional plans that supported the strategic plan, *The Way Ahead*, the ERM Program Manager worked with the Administration to determine a course of action going forward based on these workshops.

CONTEXT—CITY OF EDMONTON

The City of Edmonton, capital of the western Canadian province of Alberta, has been a meeting place since the end of the last Ice Age. First settled by Europeans as a fur-trading post in 1795, Edmonton has grown incrementally, driven by prairie settlement in the 1880s, rail connections in 1891 and 1905, and the Klondike Gold Rush of 1897. Already an agricultural center, its reputation as "Oil Capital of Canada" was cemented in 1947 with the discovery of major oil deposits nearby. Growth since that time was largely based on resource development, and further accelerated as Edmonton served as hub for new oil sands development in northern Alberta starting in the 1970s.

Edmonton has grown significantly. In 2013, it was a city of over 800,000, anchoring an Alberta capital region of over 1.1 million. The city is experiencing nation-leading economic and population growth[2] and is expected to reach 900,000 by 2018.[3] It is home for world-leading research in several fields, including medicine, energy, nanotechnology, and winter city design. Its commercial and cultural life has earned it the nicknames "Gateway to the North," "Canada's Festival City," and "City of Champions."

City Government

Constitutionally, municipalities in Canada are the responsibility of their respective provincial governments. As such, the City of Edmonton is subject to provincial legislation, mainly the Alberta Municipal Government Act. In 2013 the elected City Council consisted of the mayor as well as a councillor for each of Edmonton's 12 geographic divisions (wards). Reporting to Council is the City Manager, and through him the City's 11,000 employees,[4] divided into five departments.

The Edmonton City Council operates the two-employee model, the second employee being the City Auditor.

ERM DEVELOPMENT IN THE PAST

In 2003 the Office of the City Auditor (OCA) and Administration jointly created an ERM framework, the Corporate Business Risk Planning (CBRP) model. Using input from several city departments as well as external subject matter experts, the CBRP model was based on the Committee of Sponsoring Organizations (COSO) risk management framework, with modifications to allow for weighting of risks at multiple levels of management. The Conference Board of Canada requested permission to use parts of the framework, in particular the Risk Management Assessment Framework tool. CBRP was presented to senior leadership in 2005 and piloted but not fully implemented; it is believed that Edmonton was not yet ready to undertake the discipline at that time.

City Auditor's Report

In a 2005 audit report,[5] the city auditor reported to the City Council's Audit Committee that:

- Known risks were being managed reasonably well.
- Risks that are strategic in nature were not clearly identified.
- ERM results were not consistently incorporated into business plans.

Administration Response to City Auditor's Report
Following the 2005 city auditor's report, several steps were undertaken to address the issues raised in the report:

- The chief financial officer was appointed sponsor for the ERM program.
- ERM governance was added to the responsibilities of the City Council's Audit Committee, which consists of the mayor, four city councillors, and two members of the public.
- In 2011 a Program Manager and an ERM Working Committee, made up of subject matter experts from throughout the Administration, were appointed to advise on a framework for strategic risk. At this point the 2005 city auditor's report was closed.[6]
- An ERM Program Manager was hired in 2012 to assist the Program Manager. In addition, oversight of the ERM framework selection process was passed to the Transforming Edmonton Committee (TEC), comprised of senior leaders responsible for the goals within the strategic plan (*The Way Ahead*), and from the ERM Working Committee, although the entire ERM Working Committee was kept abreast of developments.

CURRENT OVERALL ERM DEVELOPMENT

After the city auditor's report in 2005, Edmonton adopted a 30-year vision and six 10-year goals, forming the City of Edmonton Strategic Plan, *The Way Ahead*. From it were derived six "Ways" plans (directional goals, objectives, performance measures, and targets) in support of *The Way Ahead*:

Transform Edmonton's Urban Form	*The Way We Grow*
Shift Edmonton's Transportation Mode	*The Way We Move*
Improve Edmonton's Livability	*The Way We Live*
Preserve and Sustain Edmonton's Environment	*The Way We Green*
Ensure Edmonton's Financial Sustainability	*The Way We Finance*
Diversify Edmonton's Economy	*The Way We Prosper*

At the time of writing, all the directional plans have been approved by City Council, except for *The Way We Finance*.

A summary of *The Way Ahead* and the six "Ways" plans derived from it can be found in the Appendix at the end of this chapter.

LINKS TO STRATEGIC PLAN AND TO OTHER STRATEGIC TOOLS

When developing ERM strategy, the following five questions are asked:

1. What are our long-term vision and goals?
2. What strategy will help achieve the vision?
3. What objectives will achieve the strategy?
4. What performance measures will show whether the objectives are achieved?
5. What risks will interfere with achievement of the objectives?

Both performance measurement (PM) and ERM need to be considered when advancing the strategic objectives. Recognizing this, the Office of the Chief Financial Officer realigned its Corporate Strategy and Performance section so that the ERM Program Manager, strategy, and PM staff work together in the same section. This provides possible opportunities to combine the processes of ERM, strategy, and PM to gather information for each more efficiently.

Results-Based Budgeting

ERM assists in resource allocation decisions (as shown in Exhibit 15.1) and so was seen to possibly conflict with budgeting models, including a results-based

ERM provides risk assessments to mitigate risks to achievement of the Ways.

Performance Measurement provides Key Performance Indicators (KPIs) to determine the successful achievement of the Ways.

Results-Based Budgeting provides information to assist with determining funding of programs, initiatives, and projects to fulfill the strategic objectives of the Ways.

1. ERM receives measures of success from Performance Measurement, determines risks to achieve the objectives.

2. Performance Measurement sends list of desired outcomes to Results-Based Budgeting, and receives lists of prioritized programs and costs.

3. Results-Based Budgeting receives list of risk mitigations from ERM, creates a list of budgeted mitigation priorities.

Exhibit 15.1   Relationship between ERM, Performance Measurement, and Results-Based Budgeting

budgeting (RBB) model concurrently piloted by the Administration. The two models can be reconciled, however. For instance, one of the criteria in the RBB model for evaluating city programs was the amount and likelihood of risk relative to the amount of benefit the program was deemed to provide. Conversely, a program's quartile rating in RBB could be used as an indicator in the ERM model to determine a program's effectiveness in achieving its desired outcome. In this way, both models could inform each other.

Capital Budgeting Models

Edmonton's infrastructure branches use sophisticated risk management models for maintaining and replacing current capital assets, and are introducing risk assessment into business cases for new capital projects. The strategic ERM model needs to incorporate these projects at the strategic level.

A graphic showing the linkages between ERM, Performance Measurement, and Results-Based Budgeting is shown in Exhibit 15.1.

SELECTING AND TESTING A STRATEGIC RISK MANAGEMENT MODEL

After a review of several ERM frameworks (CBRP, ISO 31000, COSO, etc.), the Administration decided on a strategy-focused approach. The relationship of strategic ERM as part of the risk universe is shown in Exhibit 15.2.

Such a method was provided in the Risk Scorecard model devised by pm^2 Consulting (www.pm2consulting.com). The Financial Services and Utilities department (facilitated by the ERM Program Manager) conducted two pilot Risk Scorecards using the pm^2 model, for *The Way We Move* and *The Way We Live*. Following is a description of the pm^2 Risk Scorecard methodology.

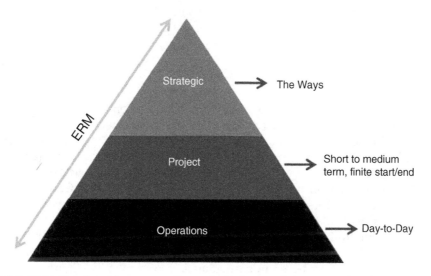

Exhibit 15.2 Relationship between Strategic, Project, and Operational Risks

Pilot pm^2 Risk Scorecard Methodology

The Risk Scorecard consisted of six steps, each dependent on the previous one:

1. Weighting of goals in the plan based on what is the highest priority in the organization to advance
2. Linking of strategic objectives to goals—determine how the strategic objectives contribute to goals, and to what degree (relationship expressed as low/medium/high)
3. Identification of risks to each strategic objective, scored 1 to 5 in likelihood and 1 to 5 in impact
4. Identification of how current programs (processes) contribute to achieving strategic objectives; currently performed—scored 1 to 5 in relationship to strategic objective and in effectiveness in meeting expectations
5. Identification of planned future initiatives—scored 1 to 5 in relationship to strategic objectives
6. Identification of possible future mitigations and risk indicators

Deliverables from this process include a risk register, a heat map, and charts showing each strategic objective's cumulative levels of risk, program contribution, and initiative contribution, to show relative effort toward areas of relative risk. In addition, a list of possible future mitigations and a list of risk indicators (measures to show as early as possible that a risk may be occurring) can be derived. The methodology is shown in Exhibit 15.3.

Ideally, risk assessment would have taken place during the creation of strategic planning documents to help determine the most risk-appropriate actions to achieve the vision and goals. However, the "Ways" documents were created before ERM was conceptualized in Edmonton. Therefore, pilots were conducted to catch up to each Ways document by conducting a Risk Scorecard workshop for each one. Because of the resource commitment of this exercise, workshops could realistically only be done one at a time. By the summer of 2013, pilot Risk Scorecards for two Ways documents had been completed or nearly completed: *The Way We Move* and *The Way We Live*.

Initial Planning

After agreeing to the plan between Administration and pm^2 Consulting, a facilitator conducted workshops. For the first pilot, three staff members from pm^2 Consulting facilitated the workshop; for the second, the ERM Program Manager was the facilitator. For both pilots, permission for the participation of lead department staff was sought and received from the general manager of the lead department: for *The Way We Move*, Transportation Services; for *The Way We Live*, Community Services. Branch managers for strategic planning for both departments were tasked to provide subject matter experts from their staff for the entire workshop; each provided three to five staff members to bring department expertise. In addition, for steps 2 and 3 (risk Identification and Scoring), senior department staff, mainly branch managers, were asked to participate in scoring the likelihood and impact of risk events, and to add to or amend the list of risk events.

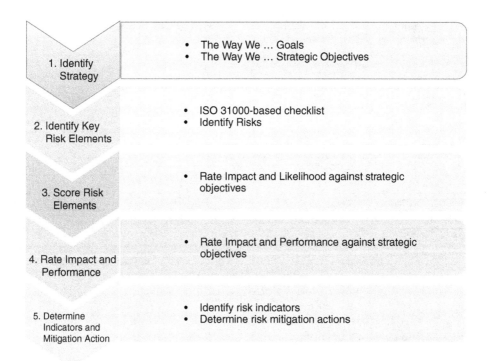

Exhibit 15.3   pm² Risk Scorecard Process Diagram
Source: pm² Consulting, 2012.

Each of the workshops took approximately 60 to 70 hours to complete. To keep time commitments, some portions of steps that were deemed to be less critical were omitted.

Step 1: Identify Strategy

The first step in the process is to identify strategic direction. Edmonton had a 30-year strategic plan, *The Way Ahead*. Using input from the public as well as subject matter experts, *The Way Ahead* was approved by the City Council and is the key planning document for the city going forward. To assist in its implementation are the six Ways plans noted previously. These documents made strategy identification straightforward. For the first pilot, *The Way We Move* (transportation plan) was selected. It was considered the best place to start because it was the most homogeneous of the plans; responsibility for its implementation was overwhelmingly with one department, Transportation Services. As well, its format made it essentially a capital plan, with easily understood objectives and goals.

At this point the ERM team had to decide at what level the strategic weightings were to occur. Options included the six 10-year goals or the 19 strategic objectives, among others. It was decided that the strategic objectives would be the appropriate level of analysis for the risk register. The goals would be at too high a level to be meaningful, and other criteria would not serve the city's purpose in addressing the risk needs of the Ways.

THE WAY WE LIVE	STRATEGIC OBJECTIVE		
	1.1	1.2	1.3
GOALS	Vibrant Communities Using Public Spaces	Create Connections Using Infrastructure	Integrate Transit with Local Hubs
	A Wgt / B		
Vibrant, Connected, Engaged, Welcoming	21 / 5	5	5
Celebrates Life	12 / 4	1	2
Caring, Inclusive, Affordable	24 / 4	3	5
Safe City	19 / 2	1	1
Attractive City	10 / 2	2	1
Sustainable City	14 / 3	4	4
100.0	C / 4	3	4

Exhibit 15.4 Relationship between Strategic Goals and Objectives
Source: Adapted from pm² Consultants Risk Score Card Model, 2012.

At this point a weighting of the goals was attempted. Subject matter experts, including the department general manager, allocated a percentage of support to each of the six goals. (It should be noted that, for political reasons, this weighting of the goals may be skipped as management may not want to prioritize these at this time.) The goals were then placed on the vertical axis of a table, with the strategic objectives across the top. An example of this table can be found in Exhibit 15.4.

For each strategic objective, the subject matter experts (in this case, four people from the Community Services department) indicated the link to each goal on a scale of 1 to 5. The larger an objective, the more goals it would relate to, and the higher weighting it would receive. When this was completed, each strategic objective had a weighting (C), expressed as a percentage, calculated as:

$$C = \Sigma\,(A \times B)/\Sigma \text{ all columns } [\Sigma\,(A \times B)] \times 100$$

where:

A = Goal weighting (expressed as a percentage)
B = Relationship to objective (1 to 5)

The sums for each column are added together to get a total weighting; the sum for each column is divided into this total to derive its relative weighting (in this example, 4 percent).

This gave each strategic objective a weighting. This weighting was then compared to that of every other strategic objective to arrive at a percentage of the total weighting. This kept the weightings constant in relative terms.

The objectives were then transposed to another table where they formed the vertical axis, then sorted by their percentage of the total objective weighting, with the highest weightings at the top. This allowed the group to select high, medium, or low weightings for each strategic objective. This categorization would be carried on to the next step, risk identification.

Step 2: Identify Key Risk Elements

Using a risk category checklist (a list of categories of potential risks covering all possible types of risk—e.g., financial, political, partner), the workshop group, with assistance from a number of subject matter experts, including branch managers, created a list of risks that could impact the achievement of the strategic objectives.

Step 3: Score Risk Elements

The risks agreed on by the group were then placed across the top of a table with the strategic objectives listed vertically along the left side. Directly below each risk was a measure of likelihood of the risk occurring (again on a 1 to 5 scale). The likelihood score was agreed on by the subject matter experts. The team then scored each risk to each strategic objective, again on a 1 to 5 scale. This provided two outputs: the scoring of risks and the risk weighting of each strategic objective. A sample of this table is shown in Exhibit 15.5.

The risk scores were calculated as:

$$\Sigma\,(D \times E \times F)$$

where:

D = Strategic objective weighting (1 for low, 3 for medium, 5 for high)
E = Risk impact on objective (1 to 5)
F = Risk likelihood (from top of column) (1 to 5)

These were summed vertically for each risk.

The risk weighting of each strategic objective was calculated using the same formula but summed horizontally for each strategic objective.

The risks were then transposed onto a data table with their likelihood and their weighted impact score (the sum of each D × E calculation for each cell in the column). This provided the basis for the risk register and the heat map.

At this point, several graphs can be created to show the relative nature of the risks and the strategic objectives. From a risk-based perspective, a heat map can be created showing the risks with the highest likelihood and weighted impact score. The more strategic objectives a risk can affect, the greater is the weighted impact score for that risk. For strategic objectives, a graph can be produced to show the strategic objectives most impacted by risk. The more risks affecting a strategic objective, and with greater impacts, the greater that objective's weighted risk score.

Step 4: Link Programs, Initiatives, and Risks

The next list required was that of the existing programs currently in place to fulfill the strategic objectives. For the ease of the workshop, it was decided to use

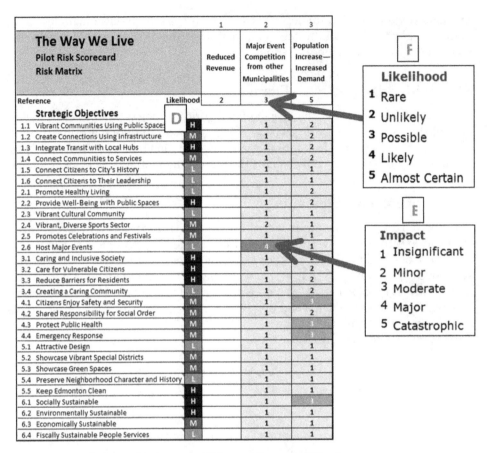

The Way We Live — Pilot Risk Scorecard — Risk Matrix			1 Reduced Revenue	2 Major Event Competition from other Municipalities	3 Population Increase—Increased Demand
Reference	Strategic Objectives	Likelihood	2	3	5
1.1	Vibrant Communities Using Public Spaces	H		1	2
1.2	Create Connections Using Infrastructure	M		1	2
1.3	Integrate Transit with Local Hubs	H		1	2
1.4	Connect Communities to Services	M		1	2
1.5	Connect Citizens to City's History	L		1	1
1.6	Connect Citizens to Their Leadership	L		1	1
2.1	Promote Healthy Living	L		1	2
2.2	Provide Well-Being with Public Spaces	H		1	2
2.3	Vibrant Cultural Community	L		1	1
2.4	Vibrant, Diverse Sports Sector	M		2	1
2.5	Promotes Celebrations and Festivals	M		1	1
2.6	Host Major Events	L		4	1
3.1	Caring and Inclusive Society	H		1	2
3.2	Care for Vulnerable Citizens	H		1	2
3.3	Reduce Barriers for Residents	H		1	2
3.4	Creating a Caring Community	L		1	2
4.1	Citizens Enjoy Safety and Security	M		1	3
4.2	Shared Responsibility for Social Order	M		1	2
4.3	Protect Public Health	M		1	3
4.4	Emergency Response	M		1	3
5.1	Attractive Design	L		1	1
5.2	Showcase Vibrant Special Districts	M		1	1
5.3	Showcase Green Spaces	M		1	1
5.4	Preserve Neighborhood Character and History	L		1	1
5.5	Keep Edmonton Clean	H		1	1
6.1	Socially Sustainable	H		1	3
6.2	Environmentally Sustainable	H		1	1
6.3	Economically Sustainable	M		1	1
6.4	Fiscally Sustainable People Services	L		1	1

F

Likelihood
1 Rare
2 Unlikely
3 Possible
4 Likely
5 Almost Certain

E

Impact
1 Insignificant
2 Minor
3 Moderate
4 Major
5 Catastrophic

Exhibit 15.5   Relationship between Risks and Strategic Objectives
Source: Adapted from pm² Consulting Risk Scorecard model, 2012.

the list of programs shown in the annual operating budget. Other program levels could have been used, such as that used in the city's results-based budgeting (RBB) initiative. This initiative divided budget-level programs into smaller components, which would be easier to change but increased the number of programs tenfold. It was for this reason the RBB-level program list was rejected; the number of programs in that initiative was exceedingly high.

Once a program level was agreed on, a new table was created, with the programs across the top and the strategic objectives down the left side. On this table, the subject matter experts scored the impact of the relationship between each program and each strategic objective (on a 1 to 5 scale). In addition, the participants estimated the effectiveness of each program (i.e., whether it fulfilled the requirements of the program), again on a 1 to 5 scale, with 5 meaning the program was performing as required and 1 meaning the program's performance was well below what was required. The difference between what was required of the program and its actual performance (i.e., 5 minus the effectiveness score) was known as the strategic gap. An excerpt from this table can be found in Exhibit 15.6.

The Way We Live Pilot Risk Scorecard Process (Program) Analysis		Fire Rescue											
		Fire Rescue Operations			Office of Emergency Management (OEM)			Public Safety			Technical Services		
Strategic Objectives	Wgt	I	P		I	P		I	P		I	P	
1.1 Vibrant Communities Using Public Spaces	H	2	5		1	5							
1.2 Create Connections Using Infrastructure	M				1	4							
1.3 Integrate Transit with Local Hubs	H												
1.4 Connect Communities to Services	M	2	4		3	3		2	4		2	5	
1.5 Connect Citizens to City's History	L												
1.6 Connect Citizens to Their Leadership	L												
2.1 Promote Healthy Living	L												
2.2 Provide Well-Being with Public Spaces	H	2	4										
2.3 Vibrant Cultural Community	L												
2.4 Vibrant, Diverse Sports Sector	M												
2.5 Promotes Celebrations and Festivals	M				1	4							
2.6 Host Major Events	L												
3.1 Caring and Inclusive Society	H	4	4		3	5		3	4		3	5	
3.2 Care for Vulnerable Citizens	H	1	4		2	4		3	4		1	5	
3.3 Reduce Barriers for Residents	H				1	5							
3.4 Creating a Caring Community	L	5	4		2	5		3	5		3	5	
4.1 Citizens Enjoy Safety and Security	M	5	4		2	5		3	5		3	5	
4.2 Shared Responsibility for Social Order	M	5	4		3	3		3	5		2	5	
4.3 Protect Public Health	M	5	4		1	4					5	5	
4.4 Emergency Response	M	5	4		5	5		1	5		5	5	
5.1 Attractive Design	L												
5.2 Showcase Vibrant Special Districts	M												
5.3 Showcase Green Spaces	M												
5.4 Preserve Neighborhood Character and History	L												
5.5 Keep Edmonton Clean	H	3	4										
6.1 Socially Sustainable	H	2	4		1	3		1	4		2	5	
6.2 Environmentally Sustainable	H	3	3								3	4	
6.3 Economically Sustainable	M	3	5										
6.4 Fiscally Sustainable People Services	L	3	4		1	3		1	3		2	5	

For each Strategic Objective, each program (e.g., Fire Rescue Operations) is assessed for its impact (I) on the strategic objective and its performance (P) relative to what is required of it. The higher the Objective weighting, the larger the impact, and the lower the performance rating, the larger the strategic gap for that program (shown in the color column next to the performance rating as medium gray (small), light gray (medium) or dark gray (large)).

Exhibit 15.6   Linkages between Strategy and Programs
Source: Adapted from pm^2 Consulting Risk Scorecard model, 2012.

At this point a new graph could be created, with a vertical bar for each strategic objective and its cumulative program requirements. Adding the cumulative effectiveness and cumulative strategic gap gave a stacked bar graph whose height was its cumulative program requirement. The bigger the objective, the more programs it had and therefore the higher cumulative program requirements (and likely a proportionally large strategic gap).

The last dimension in step 4 was to list new initiatives the City planned to implement, and rate their importance to each strategic objective. For the purposes of the workshop, it was decided to limit the list to those in the Implementation Plan for each Ways document. Within this set of possibilities, only the initiatives coded as "will do" (not "already done," "already doing," "could do," or "aspire to

The Way We Live Pilot Risk Scorecard Initiatives Analysis		1 Renew and implement the Neighbourhood Revitalization Framework	2 Renew the community indicators	3 Integrate social sustainability into the neighbourhood revitalization approach	4 Review Dogs in the Park Program
Strategic Objectives	**Wgt**				
1.1 Vibrant Communities Using Public Spaces	H	5	3	5	3
1.2 Create Connections Using Infrastructure	M	4	2	4	2
1.3 Integrate Transit with Local Hubs	H			4	
1.4 Connect Communities to Services	M	5	2	5	1
1.5 Connect Citizens to City's History	L	1	1	3	
1.6 Connect Citizens to Their Leadership	L	2	2	2	1
2.1 Promote Healthy Living	L	1	1	1	3
2.2 Provide Well-Being with Public Spaces	H	1	1	1	4
2.3 Vibrant Cultural Community	L				
2.4 Vibrant, Diverse Sports Sector	M				
2.5 Promotes Celebrations and Festivals	M				
2.6 Host Major Events	L				
3.1 Caring and Inclusive Society	H	4	1	4	3
3.2 Care for Vulnerable Citizens	H	3	3	4	
3.3 Reduce Barriers for Residents	H	1	2	1	
3.4 Creating a Caring Community	L	5		5	3
4.1 Citizens Enjoy Safety and Security	M	2	1		4
4.2 Shared Responsibility for Social Order	M	2			3
4.3 Protect Public Health	M	2		2	
4.4 Emergency Response	M				
5.1 Attractive Design	L	2		2	
5.2 Showcase Vibrant Special Districts	M	1			
5.3 Showcase Green Spaces	M	1		1	4
5.4 Preserve Neighborhood Character and History	L	1		1	
5.5 Keep Edmonton Clean	H	1	1	1	4
6.1 Socially Sustainable	H	5	4		2
6.2 Environmentally Sustainable	H	1		1	0
6.3 Economically Sustainable	M	3	3	3	
6.4 Fiscally Sustainable People Services	L	2		2	

Exhibit 15.7   Linkages between Strategy and Initiatives
Source: Adapted from pm^2 Consulting Risk Scorecard model, 2012.

do") were used for the initiatives list, to keep it to a manageable size. With this list scored by each strategic objective on a 1 to 5 scale, a graph could be produced showing the cumulative impact of future initiatives on each strategic objective. A table linking initiatives to strategy is found in Exhibit 15.7.

With the strategic gap and initiatives impact established, the two graphs for each objective could be combined on one graph to show the cumulative strategic gap and cumulative initiative impact for each strategic objective. If resources were properly allocated, one would expect to see a correlation between the height of the strategic gap bar and the height of the cumulative initiative impact point for each objective. For viewing purposes, it was necessary to use different scales for each data series, to best show the correlation. Finally, the risk weighting for each strategic objective could be added to the graph. This showed the relative risks associated with each strategic objective in relation to its required programs and initiatives.

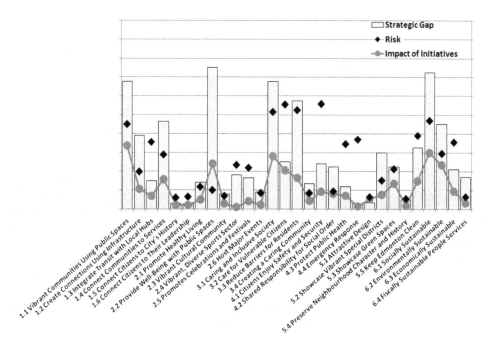

Exhibit 15.8   Strategic Objectives—Risk, Strategic Gap, and Impact of Initiatives
Source: Adapted from pm² Consulting Risk Scorecard model, 2012.

Overall, a correlation between risk, strategic gap, and initiatives may be observed. For objectives whose risks do not correlate with strategic gap and initiatives, this forms the basis of discussion for the objective; in-depth analysis shows the types of risks, whether they are caused by or independent of the programs comprising the strategic gap, and whether future initiatives address the risks, either directly or indirectly. The graph showing risk, strategic gap, and impact of initiatives on strategic objectives is found in Exhibit 15.8.

Step 5: Determine Indicators and Mitigation Actions

The final step involved completion of a risk indicator worksheet for each risk/strategic objective combination. This sheet required the user to list potential mitigation strategies, including required lead time, as well as indicators of inputs, actions, or outputs that would signal the potential onset of a risk event. The worksheet data were then summarized in a database indicating strategic objective, risk, mitigation, lead time, and whether the organization is already undertaking the mitigation. The database could then be grouped by objective, risk, or mitigation as needed.

On completion of the mitigation database, the final risk scorecard could be completed. This was a table showing strategic objectives on the left and risks across the top. For each data point, the impact of the risk on that objective was indicated, as was its performance (good, fair, or poor shown as medium gray, light gray, dark gray), and showed the risk level for each objective (the level of potential risk of the risk element impacting this strategic objective).

This provided a basis of discussion to identify key risks affecting strategic objectives.

SELECTING AN ERM FRAMEWORK

At the end of the second pilot, each department involved (Transportation Services for *The Way We Move* and Community Services for *The Way We Live*) was consulted to provide feedback on the process. As a result of the consultations it was decided to componentize the pm^2 model, as some aspects were seen to add more value than others. In addition, the model as a whole was found to provide levels of complexity that, while useful, might preclude its successful implementation. Each individual component could then be compared with other frameworks.

During this time, staff from the Edmonton Police Service (EPS) met with the Financial Services staff and presented its ERM process, based on the ISO 31000 framework. By provincial law, EPS maintains a separate command structure, reporting to the City Council through the Edmonton Police Commission. Independently, the EPS had, over a span of five years, evolved a mature ERM process based on in-depth performance measurement tools and impetus from the Police Commission to proactively identify and treat its risks. The EPS felt at this time that it could offer to share its ERM model with other city departments on an operational level. This provided an incentive for the Financial Services department to compare the pm^2 model with the ISO 31000 framework to determine a best solution going forward. A diagram of the ISO 31000 ERM process is found in Exhibit 15.9.

Comparison of pm^2 and ISO 31000 Frameworks

After two pilots of the pm^2 framework (with *The Way We Move* and *The Way We Live*), the ERM team evaluated the pilots to provide recommendations for strategic

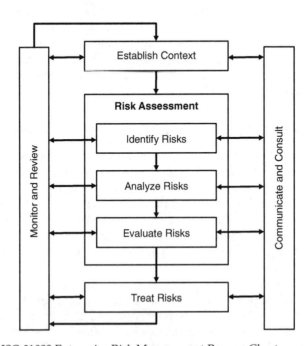

Exhibit 15.9   ISO 31000 Enterprise Risk Management Process Chart
Source: Based on CAN/CSA-ISO 31000-10, Risk Management—Principles and Guidelines, International Standards Organization/Canadian Standards Association, 2009.

PM^2 RISK SCORECARD	ISO 31000
PROS	**PROS**
Strong weighting method	Simpler to implement
Includes programs and initiatives	Robust global standard
Powerful tool	Required for Enviso
CONS	**CONS**
Part of a larger process	No programs and initiatives
Complex—hard to implement	No direct tie to other processes
Mitigation process hard to implement	

Exhibit 15.10   Comparison—pm^2 Risk Scorecard versus ISO 31000 Model

ERM going forward. Elements were taken from ISO 31000 and the pilot project. A comparison of the two frameworks is found in Exhibit 15.10.

RECOMMENDED STRATEGIC ERM MODEL

After reviewing the results from the two pm^2 pilots, the ERM team consulted with the subject matter experts from both operating departments involved in the Risk Scorecard workshops. The participants saw the logic in the model and had a good understanding of what was required in the workshop. They also provided valuable feedback on the usefulness of each section of the model.

All participants regarded step 1, the linking of goals and strategic objectives, as a strength; in fact, it was believed that this methodology would add value to other processes as well, such as results-based budgeting. Steps 2 and 3, identifying and scoring risks, would be core processes for any risk model. Step 4, linking programs, initiatives, and risks, was regarded as powerful but potentially confusing to branch managers and, as a result, might not add the expected value to the process. Moreover, linking programs and initiatives may have also been done with other processes, making this a duplication of effort. Finally, step 5, while necessary to the ERM process, was considered to be excessively complex and time-consuming. A simpler process for determining mitigations and following up was needed. From discussions with EPS and other research regarding ISO 31000, it was determined that the ISO 31000 framework held the key to a simpler risk mitigation and review process. It was also superior to the Risk Scorecard model in that it focused on mitigation at the risk level, rather than the strategic objective level, and did not require a separate worksheet for each risk/objective combination. Finally, because several city branches were certified to the ISO 14001 (Environmental Management) standard under Edmonton's Enviso program, it was noted that upcoming recertifications would require risk assessment conforming to the ISO 31000 standard.

The final recommended strategic ERM model for the City of Edmonton consisted of four steps, and is shown in Exhibit 15.11.

Step 1 (Weight Goals and Objectives), step 2 (Identify Risks), and step 3 (Assess Risks) are the same as steps 1 to 3 in the pm^2 Risk Scorecard model. Step 4, however, is based on the "Evaluate Risks" and "Treat Risks" sections of the ISO 31000 RM

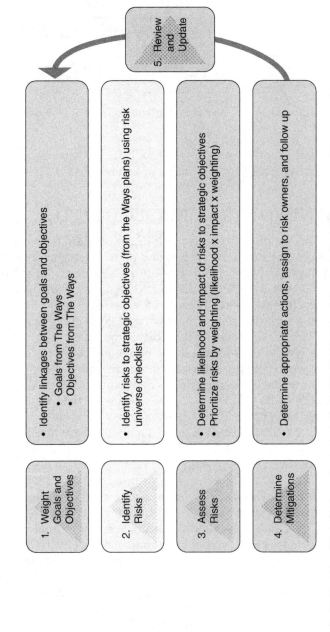

Exhibit 15.11 The City of Edmonton's Proposed ISO 31000–Based Strategic Risk Management Framework

(risk management) standard. In Step 4, the risks are transposed onto a risk register, where each row contains the necessary information for that risk: category, description, likelihood score, weighted impact score, weighted risk score, risk rating, risk acceptance, summary comments, current mitigations, future mitigations, risk owner, status update, and update interval.

An example of the proposed risk register is found in Exhibit 15.12.

LESSONS LEARNED

Several lessons were learned in terms of (1) key success factors and (2) the process of selecting and implementing a framework. The findings from these two categories are shown next.

Key Success Factors

Buy-In by Senior Management

Edmonton's Corporate Leadership Team (CLT, comprised of the city manager and the general manager of each department) has supported the concept of ERM. At a senior management level, staff must be able to perceive the value added by ERM. This makes design of an appropriate ERM process, which can show value to management, critical to its success. An example of the value proposition is found in Exhibit 15.13.

In general, the process must have two properties: it must be simple and it must show the value of doing it.

A critical balance must be struck between model power (i.e., how much information it provides) and user-friendliness. A model can provide large amounts of information but will not be helpful if it is too complex to be understood or too time-consuming to be considered worthwhile by the users. Conversely, a model that is too simple will not be helpful, as it will lack the relevance to achieve buy-in.

The pm^2 model consists of a number of simple steps performed in sequence to produce powerful results. These results include comparisons of risk, effectiveness of current programs, and the impact of future initiatives on achievement of strategic objectives. The challenge for the ERM team is to show the simplicity of the steps in the model to leaders, to ensure their understanding of the concept and buy-in to the model. Concerns have been voiced by department staff that the model, as followed in the pilot Risk Scorecard workshop, may include steps deemed too complex by branch managers. If necessary, some steps can be removed, and the model stripped to its risk analysis component if other levels of analysis are deemed not to add value to management, without losing the robustness of the model.

Whatever model is used, it must be customizable to the city's circumstances. For example, if branch managers believe a process to be too time-consuming or too difficult, it must be shortened and simplified to overcome this concern. Conversely, if the model is considered too simplistic to add value, rigor must be added to the model to show the value added and to show the time spent to be worthwhile.

Culture of Innovation (Risk-Smart)

In addition to buy-in from senior leadership, ERM also requires a culture of innovation, where new ideas are embraced and failure is tolerated. At a senior

Exhibit 15.12 Sample Proposed Risk Register

Risk Category	Risk Element	Current Risk Rating	Risk Accepted? (Y/N)	Summary Comments	Current Mitigation Actions	Future Mitigation Actions	Risk Owner	Status Update	Update Required
Economic	Economic slowdown results in increased demands on Social Supports	Medium	No	**Strategic Outcomes:** Higher demands are placed on existing programs, resulting in reduced overall service levels **Risk Not Acceptable:** Economic slowdown will require the City to prioritize programs and reallocate resources to provide social services in the most effective manner		Devise scalable plan for program prioritization	CLT	Economic conditions are monitored constantly no downturn detected to date (4 Oct. 13)	6 Months

Exhibit 15.13 The ERM Value Proposition
Source: Integrated Risk Management "Building Bridges: City of Winipeg, Audit Department", February 2009.

management level, the Transforming Edmonton Committee (TEC) is responsible for overseeing strategic planning and successful achievement of the city's strategic goals under *The Way Ahead*. Ensuring that the TEC understands the relationship between strategy, ERM, and performance measurement (PM) is key to successful ERM implementation.

Governments have traditionally been regarded as risk-averse, as political opponents would pounce on any perceived error by the government. To enable a culture of innovation, however, the organization must move from a risk-averse view to a risk-aware view, in which it openly recognizes the risks it faces. Finally, as the organization fully embraces its culture of innovation, it must move from a risk-aware view to a risk-smart view, where risks are embraced, well-managed, and mined for opportunities.

Consistency of Model across the Ways

The ERM Program Manager, as facilitator of the workshops, must ensure that consistent standards are maintained in weighting objectives, defining risks, and determining mitigations and feedback.

A strength of the pm^2 model is its robustness. This robustness stems from the model's system of weighting of strategic goals and objectives. Even if a future City Council drastically changed the prioritization of the goals, the model would automatically adjust for this change and update the risk register and other outputs accordingly. Other models would require an in-depth review of each risk in light of such a change.

This weighting system for goals and objectives can potentially be carried over to other management processes as well. For example, the results-based budgeting (RBB) model currently being tested by the City also has a weighting system for city programs to prioritize them. In addition, performance measures can be similarly prioritized to determine which ones carry the highest priority and therefore warrant the most scrutiny.

Another strength of the pm^2 model is that it does not differentiate between operating and capital items. Often a strategic objective has both a capital and an operating component (e.g., construction of a new recreation center and staffing and maintaining it afterward), which are dealt with in separate operating and capital budget cycles.

Resource Requirements on Department Subject Matter Experts

Each step in the ERM framework requires input at a senior management level in each operating department. Cumulatively these time requirements can be material for senior management already dealing with the resource constraints of their regular duties. The challenge for the ERM and other models is to minimize the time required of city staff to avoid push-back from project fatigue, which would impact the success of the ERM program.

Department Accountability for Key Risks
When key risks are identified, the department in question must take ownership of the model and assign key risks to designated risk owners. These individuals will be responsible for devising and implementing mitigation strategies and reporting results at appropriate intervals.

Findings on the Process of Selecting and Implementing a Framework

Implementing an ERM framework typically takes longer than expected. More time seems to be spent getting buy-in for the concept from the C-suite and devising an appropriate model than one could ever predict. Rarely do off-the-shelf frameworks exist that can be employed in short order; plans usually have to be tailored to fit the organization's unique circumstances. Some of Edmonton's learnings from this ERM implementation include the following.

There is no perfect system. What works for one organization may not work for another. What is necessary is flexibility. Any system must be simple enough to understand, robust enough to be usable in any area of the organization, and powerful enough to add value in decision making. In addition, it may be preferable to create a hybrid approach, taking the best parts of two or more competing systems to create one that best meets the organization's needs.

No matter how good an ERM framework is, if senior leadership does not buy in to the framework, it cannot succeed, as management will need to see the usefulness and cost justification. Three frameworks were presented to senior leadership between 2005 and 2013; all were sound and based on extensive research and knowledge of risk management principles. All were found by senior leadership to be either too complex or not a fit to Edmonton's needs.

It may be problematic to try to roll out an entire system at once. In the initial ERM planning phases there seems to be a tendency to try to hit a home run; that is, to roll out a perfect ERM system at strategic, project, and operating levels all at once. It may be the most efficient in theory, but in practice it requires a prohibitive amount of up-front resources. It ignores the learning curve managers have in learning about ERM, how it applies to them, and how to do it. This leads to the next point.

It may be preferable to introduce one phase of ERM at a time. In Edmonton's case, previous attempts at an ERM framework were unsuccessful because they went against the stated wishes of the Corporate Leadership Team (CLT). One of the CLT's main drivers for action on ERM was the 2005 city auditor's report, which identified issues mainly with strategic risk. With this in mind, the CLT wanted primarily to focus just on strategic risk, not on an overall framework. In terms of a corporate rollout, then, phase 1 was to be strategic risk; project risk and operational risk could be dealt with later, as these were lower priorities for the CLT and the city auditor.

When working with operating departments on a framework (even a pilot), it is important to define clearly what you want to accomplish with the operating departments in question. In this case, it was clearly defined that the department owned the risk register and was responsible for its content; the ERM team's role was to maintain it. Going forward, the ERM team's role was also that of facilitator, coach, and mentor to the department staff.

CONCLUSION

At time of writing, the recommended strategic ERM model was being fine-tuned for the remaining Ways documents, pending feedback from the teams involved in the two pilot Risk Scorecards.

In the longer term, the ERM Program Manager recommended further consolidation of the ERM model by ensuring links to project risk management, and by harmonizing operations' risk management practices with the ISO 31000 risk management standard, to provide consistent risk management methods to all areas, many of which are already practicing ERM, but using different formats.

Finally, the process of ERM needs to be tied to the process of performance measurement going forward. As strategic performance measures are created or amended, the risks to achieving them need to be identified at the same time, to provide the most efficient and effective means of ensuring that the measures of success can be achieved.

APPENDIX: SUMMARY OF *THE WAY AHEAD,* EDMONTON'S STRATEGIC PLAN

The City of Edmonton developed a strategic plan in 2008 called *The Way Ahead*. It contains:

- A 30-year citizen-built City vision, describing Edmonton's future
- Six 10-year strategic goals: Transform Edmonton's Urban Form; Shift Edmonton's Transportation Mode; Improve Edmonton's Livability; Preserve and Sustain Edmonton's Environment; Ensure Edmonton's Financial Sustainability; and Diversify Edmonton's Economy
- Corporate outcomes, performance measures, and targets

The Way Ahead was developed using the principles of integration, sustainability, livability, and innovation. It was built on a strong base of programs and services that already exist.

The Way Ahead has provided a foundation for prioritization and decision making. Since 2008, continual improvement has been made to the plan.

To better understand and measure how Edmonton is advancing the vision and 10-year goals, corporate outcomes for all six 10-year goals and performance measures for five of the six goals were developed in 2010. Performance measure targets for three of the six goals were approved in 2011. *The Way Ahead* was updated in 2011 to reflect this progress.

Over the past five years, the city has developed several directional plans to help achieve *The Way Ahead*.

Directional plans, referred to as the Ways plans, have been established to focus the city's work in both the achievement of the 10-year strategic goals and in delivering existing services to citizens. Accompanying Ways implementation plans were also developed to outline specific initiatives and actions that contribute significantly to the achievement of the Ways plans. The following chart shows each of the plans and when they were created.

Directional Plans	Implementation Plans
• *The Way We Grow*: Municipal Development Plan (2010) • *The Way We Move*: Transportation Master Plan (2009) • *The Way We Live*: Edmonton's People Plan (2010) • *The Way We Green*: Edmonton's Environmental Strategic Plan (2011) • *The Way We Finance*: Edmonton's Financial Sustainability Plan (under development) • *The Way We Prosper*: Economic Development Plan (2013)	• *The Way We Grow Implementation Plan* (2013 to Council) • *The Way We Move Implementation Plan* (2012) • *The Way We Live Implementation Plan* (2012) • *The Way We Green Implementation Plan* (2013 to Council) • *The Way We Prosper Implementation Plan* (under development)

In addition, the city is taking a results-based approach to aligning resources with the vision and 10-year strategic goals. Results-based budgeting is about emphasizing performance and accountability.

The following chart shows the alignment between *The Way Ahead*, Ways plans, and operational planning.

Corporate Planning Framework

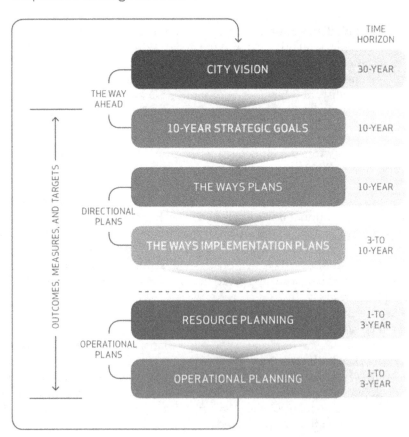

QUESTIONS

1. What other strategic processes are closely tied to ERM?
2. What three kinds of risks are identified within the City of Edmonton?
3. What two criteria must be balanced in a successful ERM model?
4. Who is responsible for dealing with and mitigating risks?
5. To what body must the City's strategic risks be reported?

NOTES

1. Chris Hadfield, *An Astronaut's Guide to Life on Earth* (Toronto: Random House Canada, 2013).
2. Conference Board of Canada, "Economic Insights into 13 Canadian Metropolitan Economies," August 20, 2013.
3. City of Edmonton, "Economic Insights, Economic Outlook 2012–2013," October 26, 2012.
4. City of Edmonton, Corporate Services, Human Resources Branch, HR Research, Statistics & Reporting Group, November 25, 2013.
5. City Auditor Report, "ERM Corporate Business Risk Planning," August 25, 2005.
6. Ibid.

ABOUT THE CONTRIBUTOR

Ken Baker is ERM Program Manager for the City of Edmonton. He is responsible for developing and implementing a strategic ERM model for the city. In addition to strategic risk, he also liaises with other areas of risk management within Edmonton to find areas of commonality, to assist with project risk management, and to investigate standardization of operational risk management among city departments. Finally, he acts as mentor and subject matter expert for areas requesting ERM expertise, as well as implementation of risk management into other business planning models such as operating budgets, operating business plans, and capital plans.

Ken is a Certified Management Accountant (Alberta) and serves on the Finance Committee of the Risk and Insurance Management Society (RIMS). Prior to his work with the City of Edmonton, he was Controller at the Alberta Urban Municipalities Association, where ERM development was included in his mandate. He also held a number of accounting positions in Canada and Sweden. Ken has a bachelor of commerce degree from the University of Alberta School of Business.

CHAPTER 16

Leveraging ERM to Practice Strategic Risk Management

JOHN BUGALLA
Managing Principal, ermINSIGHTS

JAMES KALLMAN
Assistant Professor, St. Edward's University

Enterprise risk management (ERM) emerged more than 15 years ago as an all-encompassing alternative to the then traditional fragmented approach to risk management. This previous disjointed style is sometimes referred to as managing individual risks in stand-alone silos or stovepipes. Risk management practitioners started to flesh out and test the theory. Early practical applications took the form of integrated risk programs that combined selected hazard risks and financial risks.[1]

As the ERM process was debated and matured, practitioners started to include operational risks within their portfolio. Risk registers emerged that organized the various identified risks into categories that now included hazard, financial, and operational risks. Hazard risk examples include fires, lawsuits, and strikes. Financial risk examples include commodity price volatility, inflation, and currency exchange rate fluctuations. Operational risk examples include process disruptions, compliance failures, and technology breakdowns.[2]

ERM practitioners began encountering internal organizational push-back because the process was inappropriately seen as (1) reactionary and (2) an unnecessary expansion of audit and compliance. Peter Drucker once stated, "The purpose of business is to create and keep a customer."[3] Recognizing the corporate imperative to grow the business, proponents of ERM postulated that they could indeed bring new utility to the process by aligning with, and supporting, corporate business goals, rather than just focusing on the downside of risk management. The methodology utilized to integrate ERM into alignment and support of overall business goals is to incorporate the ERM process into longer-range strategic planning and annual business plans. ERM practitioners added another new risk category to their portfolio: strategic risks. Strategic risk examples include social, technological, economic, environmental, and political situations that are much broader in scope and longer in impact. The expanded risk portfolio is far more vibrant because it inserts the ERM process into the growth side of the business. ERM moves from supporting only a defensive function to include a more balanced approach that supports growing the business.

The original vision of ERM as an all-encompassing alternative to traditional risk management expands if executive management utilizes the ERM process to support improved decision making to both protect and grow the business. Practicing strategic risk management requires risk-adjusted decision making.[4] However, leveraging ERM to practice strategic risk management depends on executing on three different, but related, variables:

1. Executive managements' willingness to reexamine the purpose of ERM—away from purely control and compliance to a strategic function
2. Positioning and leveraging ERM within the organization to support longer-range strategic planning and annual operational business goals
3. Making risk-adjusted decisions and practicing strategic risk management by utilizing new tools and techniques to measure the value created or protected by adopting the ERM process

ERM: A REEXAMINATION OF PURPOSE

Metaphorically, ERM can be compared to a tree[5] with branches growing in various directions. The enterprise risk management process has emerged from its fundamental risk management roots: preserving assets, protecting people, and complying with laws and regulations. The ERM tree developed several new branches growing in multiple directions during its initial growth period.

A standard ERM framework does not yet exist. After more than a decade of evolution, the various different national standards or artificially created frameworks and differing lexicons for marketing and commercial purposes that had existed have been reduced to two.[6] There is the framework developed by the Committee of Sponsoring Organizations (COSO) and the framework and lexicon developed by the International Organization for Standardization (ISO). These two different frameworks have different DNA. The COSO sponsoring organizations are (1) the American Accounting Association, (2) the American Institute of CPAs, (3) Financial Executives International, (4) the Association of Accountants and Financial Professionals in Business, and (5) the Institute of Internal Auditors. COSO's DNA is the financial reporting scandals of the early twenty-first century. ISO 31000:2009 is designed to be the standard principles and guidelines; it provides principles, framework, and a process for managing risk. However, actual risk management practice by a cross section of organizations indicates that hybrid frameworks are being utilized because some organizations reject strict adherence to either of the two self-proclaimed standards.[7] The hybrid idea is that the best parts of both frameworks produce a more customized model that better serves the needs of an organization, such as providing a unique competitive advantage. There also is still considerable confusion over the purpose of ERM. Some organizations view ERM as a strategic function, while others still see ERM as only a control and compliance function.

Another reason ERM has lacked a uniform standard is the way commercial firms sell ERM. The marketing of ERM by professional services firms mirrors the services and product offerings that are the core business services of those firms. For example, accounting and audit firms view ERM through the lens of audit, compliance, and control, whereas insurance brokers see ERM through the supply chain lens that leads them to a range of insurance-based products. Financial institutions, such as banks, see ERM as a methodology to comply with laws and regulations. And consulting firms focus on utilizing ERM in strategy and organizational structure. Additional branches on the ERM tree have been created by other specialties such as information technology (IT), business continuity, and crisis management.

The shape of ERM within organizations is largely dependent upon which branch of the ERM tree it emerged from. The practice of ERM will be biased toward the partisan internal forces claiming ownership of the process. For example, accounting firms may place compliance at the top of the tree. In contrast, insurers put financial outcomes and statutory regulatory requirements at the top, subjugating all other actions to creating economic value. As another example, utilities place reliability at the pinnacle of the ERM tree, knowing that is their core mission.

The lowest branch on the tree closest to the base represents the earliest forms of ERM. They were called ERM programs in the financial press, but were in actuality integrated risk programs. One such program that received a great deal of attention in the financial press in the late 1990s was the United Grain Growers (UGG) ERM program.[8] The fruit of this branch was creative financing of historically heterogeneous risk categories into new blended programs (i.e., volume risk combined with hazard risks). Creative financing came from aggregating these different kinds of risks into a blended multiyear basket, sometimes coupled with an exotic trigger.

Two additional limbs appeared in quick succession in 2001 and 2002. In the wake of 9/11, the business continuity planning branch emerged with a focus on disaster preparedness and emergency response planning. A renewed emphasis on physical security and system redundancy was accompanied by terrorism risk assessments, modeling of man-made disasters, and the passage of the Terrorism Risk and Insurance Act (TRIA).[9] IT departments and asset managers led the way in nurturing these branches. Another compliance-related branch grew out of the Enron implosion and other issues of corporate fraud. These fiduciary breaches led ultimately to the Sarbanes-Oxley Act,[10] the creation of the COSO ERM Framework,[11] and passage of the Dodd-Frank Wall Street Reform and Consumer Protection Act.[12]

Yet another branch in the compliance and audit family that emerged over the past few years is called governance, risk, and compliance (GRC). This branch focuses on blending the ERM approach to include corporate governance and risk management requirements from entities such as the New York Stock Exchange. This branch gains its support from audit firms and information technology providers.

As the United States embraces the general concept of sustainability, a new ERM branch has grown to include the green movement. One such branch includes John Elkington's concept of the triple bottom lines of profit, people, and planet.[13] From this perspective, ERM is seen as being more holistic about the risks faced by businesses in executing their strategies. In addition to managing variation in a business's economic performance, this ERM approach also includes assessing the impact on social justice performance and environmental stewardship. The social justice aspect requires an analysis of how risks impact stockholders, but also customers, vendors, governments, and employees. The environmental aspect has broadened the vocabulary of ERM. Terms like *cap and trade*, *carbon footprint*, and *sustainable development* have worked their way into the risk management lexicon. Company stakeholders have expanded far beyond employees, owners, and customers to encompass literally the entire world.

Several years ago another new branch started to grow where the idea was that the ERM process could support the addition of new measurable value to an organization. Adherents to this philosophy view ERM as encompassing both threats and opportunities. The practitioners in this camp consider leveraging risk to take advantage of the upside of opportunities, while at the same time addressing the traditional downside of risk. While some of the opportunities identified can be transactional or product-related in nature, by and large ERM should be focused on supporting business strategies. In this way ERM can be utilized to take advantage of operating conditions by aligning business growth opportunities with agreed risk appetites and tolerances to overall organizational goals: risk-adjusted decision making. Executive managements' willingness to reexamine the purpose of ERM is the first key element toward recognizing that it is a strategic function that supports reducing the impact of adverse advents and exploiting opportunities to achieve better outcomes.

REGULATORY ENVIRONMENT

The metaphoric ERM tree, like its counterpart in nature, must adapt to its environment in order to thrive. The ERM tree is growing in an environment of increased regulation by various federal agencies. Reacting to the consequences of the recent Great Recession, provoked mainly by the financial crisis of 2008–2009, the two most important new (2010) regulations (at least in the United States) affecting both the growth and practice of ERM are (1) Securities and Exchange Commission (SEC) Amended Rule 33-9089,[14] and (2) the Dodd-Frank Wall Street Reform and Consumer Protection Act.[15]

SEC 33-9089 clearly places the oversight of risk management with the board of directors at publicly traded companies. Dodd-Frank's Section 165 mandates the formation of a stand-alone board-level risk committee consisting of independent directors, practicing enterprise-wide risk management, and requiring a chief risk officer (CRO) within the financial sector.

More recently (January 5, 2012), the Board of Governors of the Federal Reserve proposed "Enhanced Prudential Standards and Early Remediation Requirements for Covered Companies."[16] Far more prescriptive and detailed mandates have been added to the original Section 165 that include:

- Board-level risk committees to be chaired by an independent director for bank holding companies over $10 billion, increasing the reach of the legislation to a greater number of institutions than the originally announced $50 billion
- A specific list of "Responsibilities of Risk Committee"
- "Appointment of CRO" who will report directly to the chief executive officer and board-level risk committee
- A specific list of responsibilities and actions by the CRO

The proposed "Enhanced Prudential Standards and Early Remediation Requirements for Covered Companies [R-1438]," provides not only the detailed responsibilities of the risk committee of the board of directors, but insights into just how deep the Federal Reserve is attempting to reach within the governance structure of publicly traded companies within the broader financial sector.

The requirement for a separate and stand-alone risk committee of the board of directors with a CRO, reporting directly to the risk committee and the CEO, indicates the high level of importance the Federal Reserve is giving to the implementation and administration of enterprise-wide risk management. Tearing down individual internal risk silos that inhibit collaboration and communication across the enterprise about identified risks and intelligence about emerging risks and opportunities should be a priority on the risk management agenda.

- "[T]he board proposes that covered company and over $10 billion bank holding company risk committee must be chaired by an independent director. The board views the active involvement of independent directors as vital to robust oversight of risk management and encourages companies generally to include additional independent directors as members of their risk committees."[17]
- "Specifically, the Board believes that best practices for covered companies require a risk committee that reports directly to the Board and not as part of or combined with another committee." Thus, "the proposed rule would require a covered company's risk committee not be housed within another committee or be part of a joint committee." In addition, "the proposed rule would require a covered company's risk committee to report directly to the covered company's board of directors."[18]
- A separate stand-alone risk committee, not a part of or combined with the existing audit committee, is a signal or reminder by the Federal Reserve that the two committees (audit and risk) have different functions and responsibilities. The risk committee's responsibilities are to document and oversee the enterprise-wide risk management policies and practices of the company.

The risk committee's agenda is:

> [to review and approve] an appropriate risk management framework that is commensurate with the company's capital structure, risk profile, complexity, size, and other appropriate risk-related factors. The proposed rule specifies that a company's risk management framework must include: risk limitations appropriate to each business line of the company; appropriate policies and procedures relating to risk management governance, risk management practices, and risk control infrastructure; processes and systems for identifying and reporting risks, including emerging risks; monitoring compliance with the company's risk limit structure and policies and procedures relating to risk management governance, practices, and risk controls; effective and timely implementation of corrective actions; specification of management's authority and independence to carry out risk management responsibilities; and integration of risk management and control objectives in management goals and the company's compensation structure.[19]

- Appointment of a chief risk officer (CRO): "... in ensuring the effective implementation of a covered company's risk management practices, the proposed rule would require a covered company's CRO to report directly to the risk management committee and the chief executive officer."[20]

As the name Dodd-Frank Wall Street Reform and Consumer Protection Act states, the law is aimed at the financial sector. However, the Act provides a model, or benchmark, of sound risk management practices that could be utilized (with some modification) in all industry sectors. The Federal Reserve model could strengthen ERM's core trunk if it does indeed become the de facto enterprise risk management standard and migrate from the financial sector to general business. The influence of the Federal Reserve cannot be understated, but adoption of its model by all publicly traded companies will take many more years without a specific push from regulators in other industries.

One example of how Dodd-Frank can extend the Federal Reserve model and reach, and has now done so, is the creation of the Financial Stability Oversight Council (FSOC). This group identifies and monitors excessive risks to the U.S. financial system arising from the distress or failure of large, interconnected bank holding companies or nonbank financial companies. In July 2013, the FSOC named the first nonbank financial companies considered systemically important financial institutions (SIFIs): American International Group and GE Capital. Prudential Financial, Inc. was added to the list in September 2013. These companies will now come under the supervisory standards, including examinations, established by the Board of Governors of the Federal Reserve for the first time.

LEVERAGING ERM TO PRACTICE STRATEGIC RISK MANAGEMENT

ERM is a business management support process. For several years, proponents of ERM have been advocating incorporating the ERM process into strategic and business planning to increase its utility. Their goal is to promote risk-adjusted decision making that can better assist management in addressing the outside forces (such as political, economic, technological, legislative, social, and environmental) that will cause the variations from performance or planned outcomes that will inevitably occur over a multiyear time line. Some outside forces will inhibit success, while others will improve the operating environment. The specific purpose is to reduce the impact of adverse events and be ready to exploit emerging opportunities. The challenge is adapting the ERM process within the existing strategic and business planning methodology.

The word *strategy* has its roots from the Greek *strategos* (a compound of *stratos*, for an encamped army spread out over ground, and *agein*, to lead,[21] which explains its initial definition of "the art of generalship"). Strategy can be defined as a careful plan or method for achieving a particular goal, usually over a long period of time, and the skill of making or carrying out plans to achieve a goal.[22] Another definition is: "A company's strategy is a series of choices, to be effective it must remain consistent with what's happening in its competitive environment."[23]

Organizations that view the ERM process as supporting business strategies should consider positioning it where the primary goals are both to grow the business and to protect value: corporate planning (longer range) and the business units (annual). Exhibit 16.1 is a model designed by the authors that can be utilized to incorporate ERM into the strategic and annual business planning process. However, before positioning can occur, the entire organization should understand the vision, mission, and purpose of ERM. This can be accomplished by creating a

Incorporating ERM into Strategic Planning Model

Internal Scan Risk Context	External View PESTLE*	Assessment Process	Articulation
Risk Perception Map** Senior Management's Perceived Levels of Risk and Current Risk Response	**Political**	**Risk Appetite(s) and Risk Tolerance Statement** What Risks Can We Take? How Much Risk Can We Take? When Do We Take the Risk? Who is Willing to Take the Risk?	**Longer Range Strategic Plan**
	Economic		
	Technological		**Annual Business Plans Risk Owners Identified**
ERM Risk Register	**Socio-Demographic**	**Scenario Planning & SWOT Analysis**	
	Environmental		
Internal Audit Perspective of Controls	**Legislative**	**Value Mapping** What Are the Measurable Benefits to Taking the Risk?	**Budget Allocation and Resources**

Execution

*From Francis J. Aguilar, *Scanning the Business Environment* (New York: Macmillan, 1967).
**From Pedro C. Ribeiro, "Predictable Project Surprises: Bridging Risk-Perception Gaps," *Ask Magazine*, August 11, 2013.

Exhibit 16.1   Incorporating ERM into the Strategic Planning Process
Used by permission of John Bugalla and James Kallman, © Copyright 2013, John Bugalla and James Kallman.

formal ERM charter. The ERM charter serves as an internal blueprint for both executive leadership and middle management to follow. The optimal time to create the charter is in the ERM planning stage, before it has been implemented. The charter will set the tone at the top for ERM in one of two directions: (1) Risk management is a strategic support function, or (2) risk management is a control function. In Exhibit 16.1 risk management is a strategic support function.

The initial step comprises three internal scan elements: (1) surveying the C-suite about leaders' current perceptions about risks and their management, (2) surveying Internal Audit about their perspectives on the current level and effectiveness of risk controls, and (3) creating an ERM risk register. The surveys will enable a comparison between the current state of risk management activities and the corresponding risk control efforts. The ERM risk register is a tool for organizing the identified risks and their internal owners.

The external view serves several purposes. It begins to incorporate the ERM process into strategic planning steps. The external view provides an opportunity to identify the outside forces that present both risks and opportunities to the organization—the two sides of the business decision coin. Coupling risks and opportunities together provides a broader and more complete view that makes for a far better assessment process and decision making. The authors have indicated some of the tools and techniques that can be utilized to complete the assessment process, including a detailed description of a new tool that is presented later in this chapter.

If the ERM and strategic planning process have been merged, the results should be seamlessly incorporated and articulated into the longer-range strategic and annual business plans. Both plans articulate how the organization will achieve its business goals. However, neither plan provides certainty that the planned performance will be achieved—analogous to von Moltke's statement "No battle plan survives contact with the enemy."[24] The goal is to reduce the impact of adverse events and exploit opportunities to achieve better outcomes around the planned performance objectives.

MANAGING AND MEASURING VALUE CREATION

At the enterprise level, a risk identification and assessment exercise at a global company can develop a list of risks sometimes numbering in the hundreds. Such an expansive list of risks requires organization. One approach to organizing the list is to create a risk register. The purpose of a risk register is to sort the risks into categories, describe their characteristics, and rank them. Bringing additional order to a cumbersome risk register is a risk map—a kind of executive summary of the risk register in a pictorial format. A risk map is a graphical snapshot of the key identified risks—usually the top 10 risks. Including all the risks identified on a risk map would render it indecipherable.

The key question practitioners should be asking about these tools is: Who benefits from the time-consuming and expensive exercise of creating a risk register that sometimes contains hundreds of risks, and the associated risk map? If the benefit is limited to a single function, that suggests a limited and narrow purpose of the organization's risk management program.

Traditional risk maps are insufficient for many reasons. One key shortfall is that traditional risk maps do not properly plot risks. The common objective definition of risk in risk management, finance, and statistics—"the variation from an expected outcome over time"[25]—includes three parameters. Traditional risk maps plot only two variables that make up the expected outcome: (1) the probability of an event and (2) the value of that loss. Rarely do they plot gains. But conspicuously missing from traditional risk maps are variation and time. All four variables must be plotted in order to provide complete information about the risks.

RISK MANAGEMENT FAULT LINE

Being in business, however, is about taking risks. Examples include expanding new product lines, investing in research and development, looking for mergers and acquisitions, and exploring geographical expansion. Organizations undertake these and other activities to grow the business. All involve taking risks. None are guaranteed successes. Managing the threats associated with taking risk is required (traditional risk management), but so should identifying and assessing the upside gain of the opportunities associated with taking those risks (speculative risk management). Measuring both the downside and the upside of risk taking in terms of a metric that is meaningful to the organization, such as earnings per share for a publicly traded company, provides a context that can be utilized to determine the type and amount of the resources needed to support the favorable outcomes as projected by the strategic planners and executive management. An additional benefit is that, by analyzing the range of possible outcomes against what was actually achieved, executive management may also gain insights into individual operational performance capabilities.

Identifying and assessing both risks and opportunities simultaneously might seem obvious, but it is atypical—at least in the first decade of the twenty-first century. One reason is that the two most widely utilized tools and techniques currently employed during the ERM risk identification and assessment process are a risk register and a risk heat map. They received their monikers for a reason. The focus of both is the perceived threats to an organization. There is no consideration of the value that could be created by taking on risks.

Academics have now spent many years researching the benefits of risk registers and risk maps.[26] While it is undeniable that risk registers and risk maps do have value, our research and analysis conclude the following:

- If the organizational goal is to respond only to known, identified risks, and the ERM process is viewed as an extension of audit and compliance, then risk registers and traditional risk maps can be useful.
- If the organizational goal is to respond to known threats (risks) and opportunities, and also to gain risk intelligence about emerging risks on the horizon, a traditional risk register and risk map fall short. This is because they fail to show both the upside of risk and the relationships between events and volatility.
- If the organizational goal is to grow the business and create value for stakeholders, a traditional risk map is useless. Again, this is because risk maps fail to enable executives to see the upside of taking risks and relationships between risks, and fail to show trends.
- A new tool is required to measure both risks and opportunities—which we call a "value map."[27]

VALUE MAPS

A value map is a graphical illustration of both threats and opportunities. Because threats and opportunities are two sides of the same coin, a value map also has two sides, as illustrated. Reference points have been added for valuation and measuring variation from the expected outcome. Threats are plotted on the left side of the map while opportunities are located on the right side. Rather than plotting a single point on a risk map, the value map illustrates the range of the magnitude of each threat and the potential gain of each opportunity. This is an important consideration because operational conditions during the year or years are not stagnant. A value map can also plot the time duration of risks. Some risky events occur and last for only a short period—perhaps a matter of days. Others have long tails and last for many years. Some long-lasting risks can have significant strategic importance. A value map can also plot correlations between risks. Some volatile situations are highly associated with others. For example, the threat of a patent lawsuit may have a strong link to a consequential decrease in revenues. A weather-related catastrophe may be highly correlated with the chance of personnel being injured, property damage, business interruption expenses, crisis management, and perhaps a

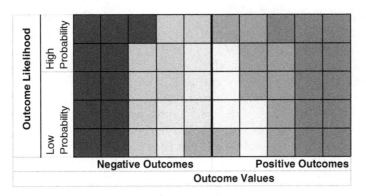

Exhibit 16.2　Value Map Outcomes

declining stock price. These associations can be shown on the value map so senior management is fully aware of the total consequences of an event.

Exhibits 16.2 through 16.4 show how a value map differs from traditional heat maps. Exhibit 16.2 shows that the outcomes from a volatile situation are not necessarily negative. In fact, organizations take on risky projects in order to create value. The value map provides cells to record both negative and positive outcomes of business situations. These events may be investments in new products, operating a factory, or providing a customer service.

Exhibit 16.3 plots two risks in their current state. That is, the ellipses show the expected outcomes (the center of the ellipses) as well as the spread of possible outcomes. On the vertical axis, the range of possible probabilities is shown; on the horizontal axis, the range of possible values is shown. This mapping differs significantly from traditional heat maps in that for the first time the *variation* (the risk) is plotted. The outcome is plotted as the Cartesian product of the event's value (on the horizontal x-axis) and its likelihood (on the vertical y-axis). This plotting of so-called expected outcomes is typical of all traditional heat maps as well. But where value maps improve on this display is in also showing the range of both inputs. These ranges are shown as ellipses. The wider (on the x-axis) the ellipse

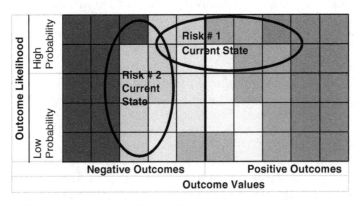

Exhibit 16.3　Value Map with Two Risks—Current State

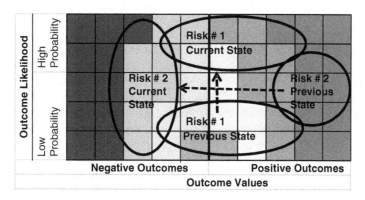

Exhibit 16.4   Value Map Showing Risk Evolution

is, the greater the range of outcome values. Risk #1 in Exhibit 16.3 shows such an outcome. The taller (on the y-axis) the ellipse is, the greater the uncertainty of the outcome. Risk #2 in Exhibit 16.3 shows an example of this uncertain outcome. In contrast, a narrow and short ellipse displays an outcome that is certain in both value and probability.

Exhibit 16.4 shows how the risks are evolving over time. There are several methods to include a risk's time dimension. In this graph, a two-period scale is used. For example, risk #1 has not changed in its possible spread of value outcomes. However, it has become much more likely in the current state. Risk #2 changed in both dimensions. Its probability range has grown, which indicates there is much less certainty in what outcome might occur. In addition, although its values have the same spread, they are all negative in the current state. Risk #2's situation has drastically degraded. The value map in Exhibit 16.5 shows risk correlations.

ADDITIONAL TOOLS AND TECHNIQUES

Making risk-adjusted decisions and practicing strategic risk management by utilizing new tools and techniques to measure the value created or protected by adopting the ERM process is not limited to value mapping. Risk managers now have multiple options that, depending on the potential impact to the organization and its executive management and the level of complexity, could be employed to improve

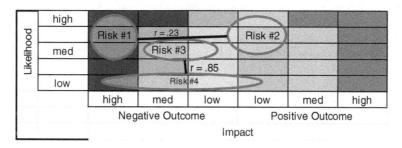

Exhibit 16.5   Value Map Showing Risk Correlations

the quality of their decisions. These tools can be quite sophisticated, and might require outside experts to facilitate a specific project, especially strategic issues that could be a destiny-determining event for the CEO. One example is game theory. Especially useful in situations involving outside suppliers, competitors, and regulators, game theory can provide insights and recommended courses of action about the various players' interests and options. If there are multiple players involved in complex negotiations, competitive strategy, crisis management, and public policy, game theory can be utilized to develop specific strategic and tactical options.

CONCLUSION

Risk management is evolving from focusing only on the downside of risks to a far broader understanding that strategic decisions have the potential of producing both downside and upside outcomes. By employing the ERM process at the strategic planning level, the organization has a far greater chance of exploiting opportunities that may arise during a typical multiyear planning cycle. Likewise, the organization has a greater chance of protecting organizational value when adversity strikes. However, to enable the organization to adopt and adapt the broader view of enterprise risk management and use the ERM process to practice strategic risk management, executive management must:

- Reexamine the purpose of ERM within the organization.
- Position and leverage ERM into strategic planning to support business goals.
- Utilize value maps to measure the value created or protected as a consequence of practicing strategic risk management.

One way to start or reignite the ERM process within an organization is to create or redraft an ERM charter. The charter should set forth a vision, mission, and purpose of ERM within the organization as a strategic function. To ensure that all levels of management are speaking a common language when it comes to risk, greater clarity will be attained by including a definition of ERM, risk, and strategic management within the charter; then utilizing modern risk registers and value maps will enable executives to better achieve their strategic goals.

QUESTIONS

1. Do you believe that ERM will continue to evolve, and if so, how?
2. Do believe that risk is a two-sided coin with both upside gains and downside losses?
3. How is value measured in your organization and do you believe the ERM process can add new value?
4. Besides risk maps and value maps, what other tools and techniques are available to manage risk and make risk-informed decisions?

NOTES

1. One of the first integrated risk programs to be labeled ERM was United Grain Growers. It combined selected hazard risks such as general liability and property with a selected economic risk (grain processing volume). (See Chapter 7 of this book.)

2. Torben Juul Andersen and Peter Winther Schroder, *Strategic Risk Management Practice* (New York: Cambridge University Press, 2010).

3. Peter F. Drucker, Goodreads.com.

4. A good discussion of strategic risk management can be reviewed at the Risk and Insurance Management Society (RIMS) website and others. For example, see www.rims.org/resources/ERM/Pages/StrategicRiskManagement.aspx.

5. John Bugalla, Barry Franklyn, and Corey Gooch, "Climbing the ERM-Enterprise Risk Management Tree," *Risk Management*, May 2010; and *National Law Review*, www.natlawreview.com/article/climbing-erm-enterprise-risk-management-tree.

6. The two major frameworks are ISO 31000, accepted in approximately 25 countries, and COSO, which is mainly utilized in the United States. Other frameworks include those created by AS/NZ 4360 and the Conference Board of Canada.

7. For a discussion of the benefits and disadvantages of ERM standards, there are many articles; for example, see www.niso.org/workrooms/ermreview, www.coso.org/documents/coso_erm_executivesummary.pdf and www.theirm.org/ISO31000guide.htm.

8. See "United Grain Growers Limited (A)," Harvard Business School Case Study 9-201-015, June 11, 2001.

9. For the full Terrorism Risk Insurance Act of 2002 Reauthorization Act of 2013, see http://beta.congress.gov/bill/113th/house-bill/508.

10. To read the full act, Public Law 107-204-July 30, 2002, see www.sec.gov/about/laws/soa2002.pdf.

11. www.coso.org/-erm.htm, accessed December 8, 2013.

12. www.sec.gov/about/laws/wallstreetreform-cpa.pdf, accessed December 2013.

13. www.johnelkington.com/activities/ideas.asp, accessed December 8, 2013.

14. To read the full rule see: www.gov.rules/final/2009/33-9089.pdf.

15. See www.sec.gov/about/laws/wallstreetreform-cpa.pdf.

16. Federal Register, January 5, 2012.

17. Ibid.

18. Ibid.

19. Ibid.

20. Ibid.

21. Lawrence Freedman, *Strategy: A History* (NY: Oxford University Press, 2013).

22. www.merriam-webster.com/dictionary/strategy.

23. John R. Wells, www.exed.hbs.edu/assets/Documents/wellsQAsa11.pdf.

24. Helmuth von Moltke, Field Marshal, German military strategist.

25. Stephan R. Leimberg, Donald J. Riggin, Albert J. Howard, James W. Kallman, and Donald L. Schmidt, *The Tools & Techniques of Risk Management & Insurance*, 2009 supplement (Cincinnati, OH: National Underwriter Co.), 8.

26. Examples of the benefits of risk registers and risk maps include www.interrisk.com.au/wp-content/uploads/2012/09/Risk_register_September2012.pdf, www.google.com/url?sa=t™rct=j™q=™esrc=s™source=web™cd=7™ved=0CFUQ FjAG™url=http%3A%2F%2Fwww.qrc.org.au%2Fconference%2F_dbase_upl%2F,Cri tical_Control_Risk_Registers.doc™ei=zCemUvrvG6Xr2QXEhoFI™usg=AFQjCNFWX ZqE8_kS9HA9aK9NZQskOEkpOQ™bvm=bv.57752919,d.b2I, and http://blog .lrenergy.org/the-benefits-of-an-effective-risk-management-process/.

27. John Bugalla and Dr. James Kallman, "How to Map Your Risks," CFO.com, February 2013.

ABOUT THE CONTRIBUTORS

John Bugalla is Principal of ermINSIGHTS, an advisory and training firm specializing in enterprise risk management and strategic risk management. His experience includes 30 years in the risk management profession serving as Managing Director of Marsh & McLennan, Inc., Willis Group, Plc., and Aon Corporation before founding ermINSIGHTS. He led the Willis team that negotiated the integrated risk program on behalf of United Grain Growers. He is the author or coauthor of numerous articles in diverse publications such as *The Corporate Board* magazine, *CFO* magazine, the *National Law Review, Credit Union Management* magazine, *Risk Management* magazine, the *Journal of Risk Management in Financial Institutions,* and the *Journal of Risk Education.*

James Kallman is Assistant Professor at St. Edward's University, Austin where he teaches courses in finance, and statistics, and risk management. Dr. Kallman holds a doctoral degree and master's of science degree in risk management and insurance from the University of Wisconsin, a bachelor of science degree from the University of Minnesota, and an Associate of Risk Management and RIMS Fellow degree. He is author or coauthor of numerous articles in diverse publications such as *The Corporate Board* magazine, *CFO* magazine, *Risk Management* magazine, *Journal of Risk Management in Financial Institutions,* and the *Journal of Risk Education.*

PART IV

Specialized Aspects of Risk Management

CHAPTER 17

Developing a Strategic Risk Plan for the Hope City Police Service

ANDREW GRAHAM
Adjunct Professor and National Editor, Case Studies, Institute of Public
Administration of Canada, Queen's University

Hope City is a midsize urbanized community, part of a larger conurbation and therefore part of larger and more complex forces. It is changing in terms of demographics and the demands on policing. While there is no central crisis in this case, there are a number of disturbing trends that represent risks to the Police Service business model now in play and to the ability of the Police Service to meet the emerging needs of its community.

The Hope City case is one that forces integrative thinking about risk management. It is a holistic set of facts and information designed to lead to the creation of a strategic risk management plan for the Police Service of Hope City. It is centered on the qualitative and impressionistic assessment of risk, rather than the quantitative. Therefore, coming to an assessment of the risks in this circumstance and rendering them relative weights will entail some form of collective, consensus-driven or centrally driven exercise. Further, aside from being a good platform for the effective assessment of risk and the assignment of weights, it is also useful when linked to the creation of a strategic or action plan for the Police Service as a whole. The case lends itself well to group work as well as written analysis.

THE CONTEXT

Like most police services, the Hope City Police Service is a busy place. There is no end of activity. Chief Karl Paulson has been in the job for 10 months now and feels that he is getting a handle on the culture and way things are done around Hope City. He came in from another service. This is his first job as chief, although he has held both operational and planning roles at the deputy level elsewhere. He finds working in a growing community of 500,000 like this one interesting. However, at the end of the day, while he fits in fine, he still does not feel in control of things. Being a good police leader and being used to rapidly changing time and resource priorities, he can certainly fit into the "What's next?" approach to management. He feels he and his organization are adept at responding and adapting to both operational challenges and changing situations. But is that what it is all about? He is also seeing some changes happening that he is not sure the Police Service is ready for.

Hope City is indeed a growing and changing place. It is situated not far from a larger metropolitan area, one that gives a lot of employment to Hope City residents. In fact, about 20 percent of the Hope City working population commutes the 50 to 75 kilometers every day by way of the multilane highway that passes just west of town, the commuter rail link into downtown Benville, or the commuter bus systems. The others work in the large service sector or the many secondary manufacturing plants on the west side of the city. There is also a community college with extensive programming that employs about 500 people. It really is a regional hub, one that Hope City residents are proud of. Right now, as this community grows and changes, there is a lot to be optimistic about for the future. On the other hand, the more the community changes, the more that future changes. Having been a small city with a homogeneous population and relatively isolated for a long time, it is now becoming part of the growing conurbation around Benville.

Taken at first blush, Hope City seems to be doing well. There is growth in residential and commercial construction as the result of an influx of new workers into the high-tech industries that are growing here. Many of these new workers are new Canadians, often well educated, some of whom come through family sponsorships. They have settled primarily in four communities in Hope City, often forming fairly close-knit communities. New services are arising to meet their needs, although schools, churches, and social organizations are at capacity.

Working with the notion that it is always best to get ahead of issues before they get ahead of you, Chief Paulson decided to pull together his top managers for a planning session and a bit of a look forward. He is allergic to flip charts, consultants, and detailed reports that do not get used. However, he wanted to not just be a good day-to-day chief, but to set the future direction of the Police Service as well. He also had an uneasy feeling that the Police Service needed to get a handle on the challenges that it was facing, develop a better understanding of the communities it was serving, and get a bit savvier on the political developments in the area. All this was also part of his desire to bring along a number of top-notch operational commanders and broaden their perspective so they could take on more senior roles. Paulson clearly wanted to move to becoming a strategic leader.

The Chief decided to get some help on an environmental scan. He was able to get the help of an old colleague (a consultant) who had retired from a senior police job (not in Hope City) and was known for her ability to talk to people. He asked her to do some interviews in preparation for the senior staff retreat. Her mandate was to gather information and impressions that would help the senior management team identify its challenges and risks. What follows is the result of those interviews.

SOME BACKGROUND ON THE HOPE CITY POLICE SERVICE

The Police Service Board is made up of seven people who meet regularly with the Chief. Board members are appointed under the provincial legislation as a mix of provincial and municipal appointees. Two Hope City Council members sit on the board. Membership tends to turn over every four years, with some continuing members serving more than one term. It is this current board that hired Chief Paulson after an executive search process. The board has a legislated responsibility to oversee the direction of the Hope City Police Service, set broad policy and strategy, and monitor the performance of the chief. It has the power to hire and fire the chief.

The Hope City Police Service deployed 790 police officers and 267 civilian members and responded to more than 85,000 calls for service during 2010. Its operating budget for 2010 was $129,600,000. The area covered is 1,382 square kilometers, serving a population of 508,000. The police also have an active volunteer program with 250 volunteers, plus 64 auxiliary officers.

Hope City is governed by a municipal council and mayor. The Police Service is part of the mandated municipal services. Hope City views the Police Service as a department of the city and budgets for it in that manner. This creates some friction, as the police chief reports formally to the Police Service Board, not the city. However, in reality, the chief must also work with the city, most notably the mayor and the Chief Administrative Officer (CAO). Formal and informal lines cross frequently, and it requires a certain measure of diplomacy, tolerance, and restraint to make the system work. Generally, it does until the budget crunch, an annual event. The police budget is a significant portion of Hope City's budget. For 2010, policing will take up 22 percent of the total municipal budget. While these costs are supported generally and there is broad City Council backing of good policing, the city chafes at how little it actually controls these costs. The budget is set by the Police Service Board, and the City Council feels there is little incentive to restrain growth. Further, if there is a disagreement, the board can appeal to the province. Generally, the police win if there is a showdown. However, the process can be messy and leaves a lot of bad feelings.

As a first step in the process of reaching a strategic plan, the work of the consultant began with interviews of key players. What follows is the result of those interviews.

WHAT THE CONSULTANT HEARD

In setting up the interviews, all those canvassed were informed of the purpose by the consultant: to help the Hope City Police Service develop a strategic plan. What follows is the report offered to the Chief at the end.

The following groups of people were interviewed:

- Chief and all direct reports
- Association president
- Chair, Police Service Board
- Chief Administrative Officer, Hope City
- Chair, Hope City Chamber of Commerce
- Citizens against Racism Community Group
- President, East End Residents Association
- Hope City Citizens for Responsible Government

Chief Administrative Officer of the City

In practical terms such as the formal budget, the Police Service is a department of the city. Therefore, the CAO has responsibility for it. This is clouded by the role of the Police Service Board, a provincially mandated oversight body. This is part of the municipal reality of the province, and the CAO is no stranger to it. However, the dynamic can sometimes create amazing tensions. His first concern about this interview was what this plan would look like in relation to Hope City's plans. However, he also realizes that working together is ultimately smarter than working apart or at odds. So, he weighed in.

The CAO noted that the demographic shift in Hope City has only just begun. In spite of the lack of some services for recent arrivals, new residents still keep coming. He sees some distinct ethnic communities as growing and developing their own infrastructures and identities. Housing starts, especially for townhouses and apartments, are growing. There has also been an increase in the number of youths in these communities. Birthrates in these ethnic communities are generally higher, and there is evidence of that already. In some of the schools in those areas, the majority is now from these recently arrived families. This is creating pressure for more schools and also adjustments in school programming. The issue of English as a second language among the older cohorts of these groups is emerging as a service issue. They hardly use the 311 civic services line.

When asked about city plans that might affect police, the CAO noted that several new major subdivisions were in the works or already approved. The Police Service will have to expand to provide adequate policing to those expansion areas. He recognizes that this will stress resources to adequately police these areas. He was not certain if the development charges[1] would adequately cover the cost of the increase needed for public services. He thought that the Police Service needed to factor this into its capital planning; for example, would a new station be needed? His concerns extended to question whether the emergency services communications infrastructure was going to be sufficient.

The high-use stress on highway infrastructure will mean construction on both of the two main north–south routes over the next two years. There will also be work on downtown main streets, including a long-term restoration of the main city square through which most of the downtown traffic now is routed. The CAO was concerned whether police were up to speed on the implications. This involves work by both the city and the province.[2]

The CAO noted that several city councilors want to develop a new strategy for the downtown core, which is plagued by many of the usual problems of lower retail presence, some gang activity, and certainly a general degradation. He feels the Police Service needs to come up with some cost-effective safe street strategies or face pressure from both the City Council and neighborhood groups along with retailers. There is certainly a desire to get more condo development downtown.

It was hard to keep the CAO off the issue of money in general. He feels that, while the Police Service takes up a major portion of the municipal budget, there is very little he can do about affecting what it will look like. The City Council does not feel there is adequate control either at the budget time or as the budget is managed over the year. Of course, the City Council theoretically has ultimate control over the budget, but it often feels it is being handed a fait accompli and that the Police

Service Board and the Chief are not really team players, willing to take their hit along with the others. Whether it is the Police Service Board or the Chief, he does not know, but he feels left out of the loop and is often surprised at budget time. He feels it would be easy to say that the budget is too high and that the police get theirs while other services suffer, but he is more annoyed at the process than opposed to good policing. One example he cited was the number of years that overtime budgets had been exceeded, forcing a return for funding to the City Council. He could see one or two years and for exceptional circumstances, but he sees a pattern of poor management here—his words. He also noted that this preceded the current chief, but he has not seen much sign of any change. Also, he believes that the policing model, as he calls it, will only drive costs up more. Why are the Police Service Board and the Chief not pushing new ways of doing things?

The CAO also noted that, while there were Provincial Adequacy Standards for police, Hope City did not appear to be following all of them. For instance, he noted that the Police Service did not have a business plan. He thought that would go a long way to making it more credible. He also had a few figures at hand, based on a comparison of most of the cities in the province:

- While the provincial clearance rate[3] on violent crime was about 74 percent, Hope City's was only 53 percent.
- While the provincial median for total crime rate was 5,900 per 100,000, in Hope City it was only 5,300.

He asked how these two facts squared. If you have a lower crime rate, surely you should expect a better clearance rate.

The CAO was concerned that the increase in cross-jurisdictional police teams would lead to problems of financial control. He observed that Hope City had been a big player in the recent regional efforts on biker gangs that the province led. He noted, however, that there seemed to be a disproportionate number of resources devoted to this and very little compensation from the regional funding that was available from the province. He worried that there was not good costing and an aggressive effort to recoup funds to pay the bills. He also wondered about tracing costs and responsibilities for such horizontal-type work. Although he noted that he was no expert on these issues, he also pointed out that quite a number of municipalities across the country are complaining about what they see as the federal downloading of costs for policing in new crime areas such as terrorism and cyber crime.

Chair of Police Service Board

The chair of the Police Service Board is appointed by the province for a three-year term. This is her second term and probably her last one.

At the outset, she expressed strong confidence in Chief Paulson and his management team. She felt there was a good working relationship, at least at the level of meetings and sharing information on current issues. She did have some reservations about the capacity of the Police Service to adapt, especially around emerging crime patterns, policing methods, and the changing population profile. She reported on what she sees happening in Hope City and the police's role in it.

Like the CAO, she sees the city changing. While she sees the rise in ethnic groups, she also sees parts of the city being nothing more than commuter subdivisions. The ones closest to the arterial roads seem to be deserted or ignored as far as active community policing goes. She also notes how there is a lack of community resources and activities to keep youths out of trouble.

She feels that the issues of rising youth crime, vandalism, and drug use are not getting the attention they deserve. She even disputes a lot of the public opinion poll results, saying that these numbers are general and not community based.

The chair is worried about succession planning for the Police Service. She sees an aging service with a lot of senior people ready to retire. More important, as far as she is concerned, she also sees that a lot of seasoned street-wise officers are leaving. She sees this as two issues, not one. In fact, she thinks the loss of street experience is more of a concern than the loss of managers. She also cites the inspector ranks with long experience in areas such as homicide who will be leaving soon. She notes that the rank below this, staff sergeant, is a small cohort populated by "a bunch of guys the same age as the bunch of guys they report to."

Generally, the Police Service Board feels that Chief Paulson tries to provide the information that is needed for the board to function well. She feels that he is overly protective of his operational role, insisting, for instance, on being the only senior officer to appear before the board. While the board members have plenty of informal interaction with line command staff, they seldom see them performing in a formal way. They miss out on seeing what their potential is. She feels that it is a lost opportunity not to use the board to profile senior staff accomplishments. The Chief argues (not aggressively) that he would rather his command group spend their time on operational priorities and he would handle external relations. The board members' view is that they are not external.

The budget is a concern of the Police Service Board. The board supports the need for the best resourcing, but feels that the lack of a long-term perspective, especially for big-ticket items like computer systems and vehicle replacement, always puts them in opposition to the City Council. The board is responsible for setting the budget, but worries about whether the Police Service knows what it will need in the longer term to be sustainable. No matter what anyone says about who is responsible for what, the board needs the chief's advice in these areas. The board is concerned about the level of good professional advice on the financial and administrative side. The board feels it is often surprised by budget requirements. Board members are also aware that this surprise and its negative consequences are something the City Council and city staff note about the Police Service.

She feels the police are responsive and professional. However, they are not as active in pursuing preventive measures generally associated with community-based problem solving as they might be. To date, she sees only token efforts; for example, even the community liaison officers, it would seem, are appointed only as a break from their car and street duty, and not with a strong mandate. She has also become aware of the move in some Canadian and American communities toward what is called intelligence-led policing, which is the application of computer analytics to both crime and police contact information to better understand trends, hot spots, and key priorities. She has seen demonstrations of this and was impressed.

She also pointed out that the growing ethnic communities have little formal or informal contact with the Police Service. In fact, the gulf appears to be widening. She pointed to the number of comments that some ethnic community leaders make to the press about police insensitivity, even though she has no evidence of it. She wonders what the Police Service actually knows about these communities and what crime potential they pose (e.g., terrorism).

The chair wonders how well some hot spot issues are being addressed. For instance, she noted that some neighboring communities had developed aggressive antigraffiti programs to increase community mobilization. She did not think that the Police Service had to do it on its own but should be open to partnerships.

The chair felt that Chief Paulson was open to the public, but that the Police Service as a whole was not as active in such matters as consultation and outreach as it could be. She worried that the ethnic changes in Hope City had left the Police Service behind. Further, she often gets complaints from business groups that they are not being heard by the police, especially around issues of graffiti, and also youth in the downtown area who are intimidating seniors who shop there.

Finally, she cited the relatively poor performance of the Hope City Police Service in comparison with other services, based on the Provincial Adequacy Standards program that uses performance data to compare services. She noted deterioration in some response time issues and the number of uncleared major crime cases. "I'm not one to proclaim we are the best. But it is not exactly satisfying proclaiming we are happily stuck in the middle."

Interviews within the Police Service

A number of trends emerged from these interviews. First and foremost was the aging workforce challenge. It appears that recruitment is not keeping pace with departures, or rather, while there was a good intake, the promotion rate was not keeping up. Further, the Police Service is losing some valuable organizational know-how without doing anything about it, in terms of either retention or knowledge transfer. The expression "too damned busy" kept cropping up. The other factor, given that Hope City was in a cluster of urban development with similar services in nearby cities, was the theft of up-and-coming officers by other services. It was felt that Hope City had a good reputation for training new officers but then lost them to other services. There have been a lot of successes, too, in terms of transfers in and promotions. It just seemed to be taking a lot more time staying on top of things. The transaction costs of this churn were considerable.

Several senior officers expressed concerns about emerging crime issues. Some were evident already. Some may or may not be on the horizon. For instance, computer pornography and child exploitation seemed to be on the rise. There was some notion that some is based in Hope City although there was no firm evidence to confirm this. Certainly, at this point the Police Service did not devote many resources in this area. Some officers had become more skilled in this area, but the Service had yet to move on creating a unit devoted to investigating child pornography. On the other hand, the concern about the potential for the development of terrorist-type activity in some of the newly opened ethnically focused private schools was an issue. Senior staff members were very worried about this in two ways. If they focused on it too much, they might be accused of profiling and lose any hope of building the intelligence and confidence links they needed with emerging ethnic communities. If they did not take some reasonable steps to inform themselves of the kind of new policing challenges the world was bringing to their doorsteps, they would be negligent in active policing.

As a summary, the following crime rate trends were recorded:

- Generally following national and regional trends but rates slightly lower than the provincial patterns
- Overall decrease in the number of crimes, especially assaults on persons
- Decrease in homicide and related crime
- Slight increase of sexual assault, in isolated areas
- Decrease in robberies
- Increase in car thefts but a shift from individual thefts to more systematic patterns, suggesting a more organized approach
- Increase in credit card fraud
- Sharp increase in complaints or inquiries about identity theft with no real pattern emerging in the statistics
- Youth-on-youth assaults up, especially in a number of both ethnic and nonethnic housing projects that have police presence but little interaction with the community
- Increase in hate/bias crimes and complaints—full range from graffiti to personal threats
- Sharp increase in illegal ATM bank entries with a strong suspicion of organized crime involvement

More and more of the budget and management time are going to the information technology (IT) infrastructure. While direct entry from patrol vehicles has been in place for a couple of years now, it is mostly used by officers to download information that is already on the system rather than for direct input from their cars and station points. Summary data on contacts that would establish patterns of interaction, most notably among gang members and between gangs, is not yet regularly input. Further, the ability of Hope City to go anywhere on a COMSTAT[4] type information management system is very low. Senior staff receive crime statistics on a weekly or monthly summary basis. The roll-ups are always questioned because of the amount of so-called dirty data they contain. This may also be why Hope City looks so bad in comparison with others. On the other hand, there was resentment of the amount of time that these administrative matters took. Reports and paperwork seem to have precedence over face time and street presence. Chief Paulson and his deputy were certainly aware of emerging technology trends, but to date there has been little internal interest in trying them out. This contrasts with one neighboring police service that has gone full tilt on geospatial intelligence analytics. This positions crime patterns onto maps to link trends to location. It also drives resource distribution.

Senior service personnel felt that they had real strengths in the area of joint task force work and collaboration with other police services. They pointed with pride to their major contribution on the recent biker initiatives, which saw several of the key biker houses or chapters closed down as well as some important arrests. They felt that they were not encumbered by a "my turf or else" mentality. They saw this as a plus for the line officers who got to work with counterparts. They also saw it as a link to public security issues at the national level, such as the protection of critical infrastructure that the bikers had targeted for copper wire and electricity diversion for grow operations.

President of the Police Association

The president had a lot of praise for Chief Paulson and his personal openness. However, she felt that this was personal and that it was not being pushed into the senior ranks. She also felt that most consultations were a joke, usually more of an announcement than a real effort to consult, which should involve, in her view, actually asking for and listening to the other party's opinion.

In general, working conditions were good for most of the officers. She noted that one recent survey of sworn officers indicated that 60 percent reported they had enough time to do their work. She was surprised at that.

The president felt that the Police Service was like all the rest—mostly white men—at a time when society was changing. However, she acknowledged that there were no ready answers and that she would speak for all her members, even the white men. However, the hiring practices should beef up recruitment of minorities, but without sacrificing standards. She has a personal focus on harassment in the workplace and had personally filed complaints about inappropriate sexual comments by senior staff.

The Police Service just seems to be keeping up to the minimum of training requirements. It is always scrambling to meet standards without thinking about staff development. As such, there is a rush for the mandatory training and very little else. She feels the Police Service should be working harder on such issues as diversity awareness, use of technology, and emerging crime issues. Often the younger staff members are way ahead of the senior people on computer crime, but their capabilities are never used.

The president doesn't feel that the Chief does enough to build up the image of frontline staff. He is too quiet with the media and seems to be responsive but not proactive on issues. He seems cautious in defending officers when something goes wrong. He should be more aggressive.

While she has been with the Police Service for 12 years, the president says she feels like an old-timer. That's because she is. She is worried about the influx of younger officers who lack experience. She is also seeing promotions much earlier in people's careers than in the past. She supports the members getting ahead, but all this change can destabilize the Police Service. She sees management as responsible for making sure that these people succeed.

Chair of Hope City Chamber of Commerce

Members of the Hope City Chamber of Commerce, too, are noticing the changing face of Hope City and are concerned that the Police Service is not intervening before things get out of hand. They know from their own surveys that many people are retiring there to get out of the big city, and young families want a safe community in which to raise their families. The problem is that some of the harbingers of big city youth issues are just beginning to surface—things like graffiti and increased vandalism—and the chamber of commerce feels that the police are not taking an aggressive enough approach to the problem.

In fact, the chamber of commerce is looking at increasing its use of private security firms and will ask the city to deduct some of these costs from the Police Service budget—the chamber members are that upset. They want a more visible presence and a more serious arrest policy, not just giving these young criminals a talking-to and a ride home.

The chamber of commerce invests a lot of energy into promoting the city as safe, and encouraging folks to come downtown for shopping and other social activities. If people begin to feel threatened, business will suffer. The chamber is seeing this in a number of instances in the downtown core.

In addition, the chamber of commerce is concerned about upcoming road construction and traffic diversion projects that will disrupt shopping patterns and the routine functions of businesses. At this point, time lines for construction, both the "when" and "for how long," have not been firmly set, or if set, not communicated to the chamber. Chamber members wonder about the challenges of policing business areas that have closed or impeded roads. In particular, they are concerned about the increased likelihood of vandalism and other crimes in these areas, and the likelihood of longer response times by police to emergency calls from businesses there. They feel that they have not been adequately consulted by the city or adequately reassured by police as to what steps will be taken to mitigate potential problems arising from the major traffic disruptions that are anticipated.

Editor of the Hope City *Telegraph*

The editor expressed the view that overall the Police Service is run well but not very much in line with more modern views of community involvement. The Chief does not often volunteer to speak with the press but waits to be asked. As a result, not too many of the key newspaper reporters and editors know him or his deputies very well. In other cities, chiefs and deputies have adopted a more proactive approach and are coming to the press with news and issues—not just the usual press release stuff designed to make them look good.

Situating his paper as a watchdog over municipal spending, the editor noted that the *Telegraph* frequently takes issue with growing municipal expenditures, of which police expenditures represent an ever-increasing portion. In particular, he noted that overtime expenditures appear to be out of control, and that the annual ritual of demanding extra money to cover these growing costs suggests that the police budget needs a major overhaul (i.e., better forecasting and more controls).

Citizens against Racism Community Group

The informal leader of this group reported that she feels that the Police Service is often too quick to pick on visible minority youths and men. She does not feel the police are in tune with modern Canadian society, and wants to see a lot more visible minority officers, as well as mandatory diversity training for officers.

She stated that some of the group's members are getting very upset with this perceived racism and are ready to make this an issue for the courts. They are talking about civil suits and lots of media interviews. She also admits that they have no real data on which to base their conclusions but they know racism when they see it—and it is clearly in the Hope City Police Service culture. She wants to see fewer arrests of young people and more diversity.

While complaining of police heavy-handedness and racism, she noted that some communities with large ethnic populations are seeing little or no police presence in spite of increased complaints from residents about growing youth problems, including vandalism, noise, and assaults. When pressed on how this increase was recorded, she indicated that this is anecdotal, as many ethnic groups are reluctant to seek formal police help through 911 or even 311. Presumably, she would like any increased police presence to occur in the person of visible minority officers.

Moreover, as an alternative to increased policing to deal with youth problems, she put forth her group's position that more of the city budget should be going to community-based groups to establish recreational and social programs for young people. She does not view the police as a potential partner in this process. In fact, she and her supporters are actively working with other community groups to make sure they get a bigger piece of the pie and the police get less. They are also actively lobbying city councillors, many of whom she feels seem to be agreeing with them. She intends to make this case to the mayor and CAO before the next budget talks occur.

East End Residents Association

The president of the influential East End Residents Association stated that its members have been campaigning for the past two years for the police to address traffic problems arising from rapid growth in their part of the city. The association identifies traffic control as the number one policing issue in the city. While the number of vehicles has increased dramatically, road construction has not kept up. What were once rural roads are now used as arterial connectors leading to Benville, or to the expressway ramps to Benville. During commuting hours these roads are often totally gridlocked. Impatient and aggressive drivers add to the problem, and because these roads do not have sidewalks or large shoulder areas, pedestrians and bicycle riders are increasingly at risk.

Further, where there is road construction—and there has been lots of it this year—there seems to have been very little planning on how best to keep traffic moving safely and fluidly, especially to allow the movement of ambulances and fire trucks. The association president maintained that when traffic completely bogs down, particularly at minor accident sites or intersections where lights are out of commission, there is rarely a police presence to sort it out.

The association president complained that he and some of the association's members have met with community police officers on these and other issues, including increased youth crime, but feel that these officers are not really committed to the exercise and/or have no real power. The president confided that his perception is that community policing officers seem to be "on sabbatical" (i.e., taking a break from real policing) rather than really working with the association's members to address community policing issues. In closing, he expressed the view that policing in Hope City appeared to be reactive rather than preventive, and committed to token consultation rather than real partnerships.

Hope City Citizens for Responsible Government

Lowell Black, a local radio talk show host and leader of this group, expressed the view that it is high time that the city and Police Service got their finances in order. He noted that the Hope City police force seems to be trying to do more with less than other like-sized communities (i.e., answer more police calls with fewer officers and less annual money). In response, for years the force has had to make emergency appeals to the city for millions of dollars to cover overtime. He says that Hope City's citizens deserve a sufficiently funded police force, one that forecasts its future expenditures accurately and that does not waste millions of dollars annually on excessive overtime.

Mr. Black maintains that his group has sought meetings with the police chief and the Police Service Board to put forth its views but has yet to get an audience. He is strongly supportive of a well-funded Police Service, but wants it managed in a more businesslike manner.

Other Input

As part of her report, the consultant summarized some recent surveys that Hope City and the Police Service had conducted. These survey results are presented in Exhibit 17.1. She was not asked to draw any conclusions from these; that is the job of the senior Police Service managers.

On the legal front, the Police Service has also faced some challenges. A recent court case found that evidence in a case had been gathered improperly, leading to a City Charter violation. The exclusion of the evidence led to a dismissal of serious criminal charges. In dismissing the case, the judge expressed concern that the Hope City police officers lacked proper knowledge and training in the area of search and preservation of evidence.

The Police Service is in the middle of a human rights complaint from one of its uniformed employees. She claims that she was not properly accommodated as the result of a medical condition that prevented her from riding in patrol vehicles. There is considerable resentment within the ranks of these special forms of accommodation.

Exhibit 17.1 Survey Results for Offense/Complaint Types

Type	Very Concerned	Somewhat Concerned	Not Concerned
Noise	10%	28%	62%
Suspicious persons	35%	5%	40%
Speeding traffic	39%	32%	28%
Breaking and entering	18%	45%	37%
Theft of property	18%	42%	36%
Car theft	15%	40%	46%
Vandalism	25%	40%	35%
Being assaulted on the street	22%	25%	52%
Being verbally abused	19%	22%	58%
Domestic disputes	5%	30%	65%

Finally, the consultant listed some developments that she was aware of in her other work in the police community:

- The Provincial Ministry of Public Safety, which supervises policing in the province, is conducting a study on the creation of regional police services, one for the four cities east of Benville and one for the three cities to the west and north. This will be completed sometime in the next year. One of the currently favored options is the creation of two mega-services.
- Police Service Board appointments are up for renewal this year. Many of the current board members have been around for a couple of terms, and change can be expected.
- Vancouver has just launched an aggressive recruitment campaign in this part of the country, and the packages offered for young officers are attractive.
- Benville has launched a job search for two new deputy chiefs. All chiefs in the adjacent areas have been approached by the headhunter, including Chief Paulson. So have a number of deputies.

COMMUNITY VIEWS ON POLICE ISSUES

A Community Police Survey of Hope City was completed four months ago. Its objective was: "To gather information from the adult residents in Hope City about their contact with the police; their attitudes regarding the quality of policing services provided by the police; their level of concern regarding neighborhood crime issues; their attitudes about personal safety; and their home security and protection measures."

The target population for the survey consisted of people over the age of 18 residing in Hope City. Results are presented in Exhibit 17.2.

Exhibit 17.2 Views on the Police Service

Performance	Good	Adequate	Poor	No Opinion
Overall	62%	22%	15%	
Responding to calls	45%	20%	25%	10%
Relating to minority groups	33%	22%	25%	20%
Present in my neighborhood	40%	21%	34%	5%
Follow-up on complaints	44%	18%	18%	20%
Treat all citizens fairly	39%	11%	39%	11%
Being approachable	60%	20%	20%	
Enforce the laws	55%	15%	25%	5%
Do good crime prevention	30%	18%	30%	22%
Provide enough police officers in my neighborhood	39%	14%	35%	12%
Catch the right criminals	45%	18%	33%	3%

QUESTIONS

You have been hired by the Chief of Police of Hope City to assist him in briefing the Police Services Board and the Mayor in understanding the most critical risks to their objective of having a best-in-class police service for their citizens. He has asked you to provide him with a report that will provide a risk profile and explain the risks to their objectives and what is being done or should be done to treat these risks. You may make any reasonable assumptions to complement the information given (e.g., priorities). Your report should not exceed five pages or 1,800 words. Figures and charts are welcome.

NOTES

1. Development charges are charges paid by developers that are used to pay for the majority of the cost of new capital projects required as a result of growth (e.g., new roads, parks, trails, community centers, fire stations, etc.). Note that this does not cover additional operational costs, which are to be recovered by taxation of the residents.
2. To date, no formal notification of next year's street construction plans have been received in the Police Service.
3. Clearance rate is calculated by dividing the number of crimes for which a charge is laid by the total number of crimes recorded. Clearance rates are used by various groups as a measure of crimes solved by the police.
4. COMSTAT is a performance indicator tracking system using fast turnaround of information for senior manager review based on integrated computer technology. It is seen as being the most advanced accountability system in modern policing.

ABOUT THE CONTRIBUTOR

Andrew Graham researches, teaches, and writes on public-sector management, financial management, integrated risk management, and governance. He teaches at Queen's University School of Policy Studies as well as a variety of international and Canadian venues. He is Series Editor of the Case Study Program of the Institute of Public Administration of Canada, Canada's leading source of public-sector case studies. Professor Graham had an extensive career in Canada's criminal justice system and has taught and worked with police services, police boards, and police commissioners in a variety of ways for the past 10 years. He continues to research public safety management issues. He is the author of Canada's leading textbook on managing public money, *Canadian Public-Sector Financial Management* (McGill-Queen's University Press, 2007), which has been adopted by a number of Canada's leading universities as a text and is used in governments for staff training. He is also the author of *Making the Case: Writing and Teaching Case Studies*, also available through McGill-Queen's University Press. He recently edited *Innovations in Public Expenditure Management*, a publication of the Commonwealth Secretariat, and *Canada's Critical Infrastructure: When Is Safe Enough Safe Enough?* for the Macdonald Laurier Institute of Canada. Professor Graham teaches in both the graduate and professional development programs at Queen's and elsewhere. He also writes a regular column on management issues, "Briefly Noted," for *Public Management*, a periodical of the Institute of Public Administration of Canada. He has taken a special interest in emerging management issues, including strategic planning, modern police governance, performance measurement, and integrated risk management. He has written extensively in this area, including an e-book, *Implementing Risk Management*, available free on his website.

CHAPTER 18

Blue Wood Chocolates

STEPHEN McPHIE, CA
Partner, RSD Solutions Inc.

RICK NASON, PHD, CFA
Partner, RSD Solutions Inc., and Associate Professor of Finance,
Dalhousie University

This case highlights many issues around enterprise risk management (ERM). It concerns a company that has turned in a satisfactory performance in the past, although this has been a result, at least in part, of luck rather than design. There is a variety of risk and governance issues that can be discussed. They include prioritization of actions and implementation of an ERM framework when considering how to deal with a diversity of personalities and opinions.

BACKGROUND

Sally Holton, the newly appointed chief financial officer (CFO) of Blue Wood Chocolates, gazed from her office window at the sunny scene outside. Her mood was far from sunny, however, as she pondered what seemed like a mountain of urgent issues facing her. It seemed that there were no easy solutions to any of them.

Blue Wood Chocolates makes chocolate products at its plants in the Midwestern United States for sale domestically and internationally. The company has delivered a mixed financial performance over the past couple of years with volatility that management has not been able to explain, and that the board of directors and owners consider unsatisfactory. There has been an ongoing debate among board members as to whether the lackluster results are due to operations or the vagaries of the commodities markets.

When the long-serving CFO recently retired, Sally Holton was brought in as an outsider to replace him. Her appointment was controversial among some finance and treasury people in the company who expected an internal appointment. Several senior, long-serving, and experienced employees were thought to be well qualified for the role. However, the CEO, John Ferguson Junior, determined that it was an appropriate time to bring in an outsider with new ideas to shake up the finance and treasury functions. Quarterly results had been variable and unpredictable. Ferguson felt that the company needed a better planning process and had to improve its ability to explain its performance to shareholders, the board, and the banks.

He considered the main problems the company faced to be due to poor reporting and presentation. Sally wondered whether the problems were more significant and fundamental. In any case, she knew that she needed to make an impression and make an impression fast.

Originally trained as an accountant and auditor working for one of the major accounting firms, Sally left accounting to work for a small mining company. That led to a job with an international mining conglomerate where she was promoted through various treasury and finance roles. Most recently, she had been responsible for managing commodity price and foreign currency risks. This was thought to position her well for dealing with Blue Wood's exposures to cocoa and sugar prices and foreign currencies. However, her new role was much broader than anything she had experienced before, and she soon realized that she had walked into a job that was going to be far more challenging than she had anticipated.

One of the first major projects Sally was tasked with was to present the latest quarterly results to the board at the end of her first month in the job. From brief conversations with some board members, she knew that they were concerned about the company's situation, and she had learned enough to know that she would have difficulty explaining the underlying reasons for the company's unsatisfactory financial position and recent performance shortfalls.

In the middle of her first week at the office, Sally received a call from Robert Klein, who was relationship manager at Blue Wood's lead bank. He introduced himself and they exchanged a few pleasantries, discovering that their kids attended the same high school, although in different grades. The conversation quickly turned to business. Robert said he was looking forward to working with Sally and seemed sympathetic about the wide-ranging tasks that he knew Sally faced. Unexpectedly, though, he jolted her by expressing his concern about Blue Wood's risk management practices and how this might be contributing to the company's unpredictable financial results. It wasn't just the weak financial results that were troubling; it was the volatility. He mentioned Blue Wood's inability to explain fluctuations adequately to the banks, and noted that the company had been very close to breaching its interest coverage covenant twice in the prior two years and looked like it would actually breach it in the current quarter. Robert was under pressure at his bank to take some form of action, including limiting or reducing exposure to Blue Wood and increasing margins and fees. He told Sally that he needed a report and plan addressing how Blue Wood was going to control and improve the volatility and unpredictability of its financial performance to present internally at his own bank, as well as to the other banks in the lending syndicate. He needed this very soon to determine what mitigating factors could be taken into account in this process.

Sally realized that her brief honeymoon in the new job was over and she needed to get to grips with the company's problems that appeared much more complex than she had been led to believe at the interview stage. She needed to formulate a comprehensive and detailed plan of action before being forced by the banks into taking certain measures that might not be in Blue Wood's best interests. She could certainly blame her predecessor for increased margins and fees on the bank financing, but she was determined to limit the extent of this by demonstrating how the company planned to improve controls, reporting, and, she hoped, financial performance.

Over the next few days, Sally spoke to as many executives in different areas of the company as possible. It became clear that there was little ongoing communication between major functions within the company. Areas like purchasing, operations, and sales did not coordinate or discuss current difficulties, future trends, and plans. They each made quarterly contributions to the business plan and got on with their business as they saw it. These contributions appeared manipulated to allow for adjustment when they were told to improve their targets. When plans were not met, which was most of the time, each area blamed the others and reporting was not adequate to identify reasons for shortcomings.

Worse still, the two cocoa purchasers did not get along and bad-mouthed each other to Sally. They were each pursuing their own purchasing strategies in isolation. The cocoa and sugar purchasing managers had discretion to use futures and options contracts as well as supply agreements to hedge quantities and prices of commodities, and they were doing this according to their views of the market and information about requirements from the production managers. The only restriction was that all contracts had to have a maximum maturity of one year.

Sally also spoke to two of the board members. Irene Dawson had been nominated to the board by one of the private equity funds that had a significant ownership stake in Blue Wood. She was not one for small talk, and appeared comfortable only when she had an Excel spreadsheet in front of her and a ruler in hand. She laid out a long list of detailed analysis and information she wanted Sally to provide to the board. Her fund wanted out of Blue Wood, but not at current values. Irene's mandate was to push Blue Wood to maximize value in the short term.

David Rennie represented a pension fund that had invested in Blue Wood. The fund saw its position as a long-term investment in a sector that promised steady growth, with Blue Wood well positioned to participate in this growth over time. The fund did see some current issues, but David considered these to be little more than a blip. In his view, management had a good grasp of the business and would soon be on top of things again. Each time Sally tried to discuss the business and the company's strategy, David was quick to steer the conversation in a different direction. He liked to be photographed with the board and attend publicity functions. He also appeared to have a weakness for chocolate, constantly feeding his not inconsiderable frame with the stuff. He bemoaned the fact that being a board member did not entitle him to a constant free supply of the company's product, although he offered the opinion that it was not nearly as good as some of the competitors' products.

Sally learned that discussions about the business plan and results at recent board meetings had degenerated into long and often heated discussions and disagreements about Blue Wood's business strategy and objectives. It seemed the arguments always circled back to the latest financial results.

In her two weeks between jobs, Sally had been reading a book about ERM frameworks and implementation guidance. The sections about the ISO 31000 framework seemed particularly interesting, but there was a variety of other risk management and financial approaches with differing levels of detail. As Sally pondered the results of her inquiries, it seemed to her that Blue Wood was sorely and urgently in need of such a framework. But which type of framework would be best for Blue Wood? And how should she go about applying this in practice? She even wondered if this would be a good time to try to implement such a system, with her being so new in her role. It would be a lot to explain to many people in a very short period of time in which she had to demonstrate competence.

She worried that if not done properly, implementing ERM would be seen as a bureaucratic exercise and resisted, or at least not applied usefully. How could it be more than a compilation of a list of risks, most of which were already known? Such a list would certainly be useful, as major risks were currently dealt with in different ways by different people and nobody had a big picture view of the company's risk profile. However, such a list would also be a static snapshot that would soon be out of date.

Upon further reflection, Sally wondered if she should set her sights lower and start by considering implementing a narrower form of financial risk management for the areas directly within her purview. She was certainly more confident of her abilities to understand what would be needed and how to do it. Perhaps a comprehensive ERM framework encompassing financial risk management would be too much to achieve and could even conflict with the financial risk management part.

THE COMPANY

Blue Wood is a midsize producer of bulk chocolate for use in other final products (e.g., candy bars, cereals, cookies, cakes, and desserts) and also has a small business supplying specialty private-label products to a variety of companies. The company has grown steadily from being a small local producer serving local retailers in its home state when it was founded 50 years ago to a midsized international company. However, growth has been unsteady, with many peaks and troughs along the way.

The company was founded by John Ferguson Senior, now in his mid-eighties. He named the company after a distinctive blue-painted barn that was on his family property and where he used to play as a child. Ferguson retains the role of chairman, but after a heart attack scare five years ago, he reluctantly passed the day-to-day running of the business to his son, John Ferguson Junior. Ferguson Senior is still a dominant and feared figure around the company. Much to the irritation of his son, he is frequently seen around the office questioning people about what they are doing and often berating them for one thing or another. At board meetings his approach is to steamroller any opposition. Woe betide the board member who has not got all his or her facts straight. He believes that the company should stick to its knitting, which brought success when he ran things, and is suspicious of what he considers "newfangled theories like ERM coming from schoolkids just out of diapers."

Customers are retail businesses, distributors, and food processors that include chocolate in their final products. Around 75 percent of sales are to the domestic U.S. market. The main international customers are located in Canada (8 percent of sales), Mexico (3 percent), the United Kingdom (4 percent), and Eurozone countries (10 percent). Almost all of these sales are denominated in local currencies.

All production is carried out at the company's two plants in Illinois and Indiana. There are local subsidiaries with sales and accounting offices in Canada, Mexico, the United Kingdom, and Ireland that each have a small sales force, deal with distribution, and collect sales revenues. These offices retain amounts sufficient to cover local expenses, and the remainder is converted to U.S. dollars with local banks and remitted to the head office monthly. Any shortfall for local expenses, including expansion of distribution networks and promotional costs, is financed by short-term borrowings from local banks. These borrowings are guaranteed by the parent company.

Blue Wood sources cocoa beans from large producers in Brazil, Ecuador, Costa Rica, and the Dominican Republic, as well as U.S.-based importers. Other main ingredients used in manufacturing the company's products are sugar and milk, which are sourced from U.S. producers. More minor ingredients include nuts, raisins, lecithin (an emulsifier processed from cellular organisms, including soybean and sunflower oils), vanilla, and other flavorings. These are all sourced domestically. Purchases are denominated in U.S. dollars.

The company's facilities are considered to be in a good state of repair, although they are not up to the standards of the best state-of-the-art facilities used by some of the largest producers. In recent years, there has been no agreement at the board level about investing in new equipment, so excess cash has been paid out in dividends, which was in keeping with the short-term focus of most of the company's investors.

The workforce is unionized and had a history of good industrial relations until two years ago when there was a strike over a change in shift patterns imposed without consultation. The strike was settled after three days by awarding increased shift allowances to affected workers. By chance, inventories were at a high level due to overproduction, resulting from errors in the budgeting and planning processes. This resulted in the strike having no significant effect on customers. However, the unions have since been adopting a noticeably tougher stance in negotiations with management.

Blue Wood is privately owned by the founder, John Ferguson Senior, and family (20 percent), other senior employees (5 percent), a pension fund (20 percent), three private equity funds (15 percent each), and certain private investors (10 percent). The outside investors were brought in as the company needed cash to expand. The pension fund made its investment around 15 years ago. The private equity funds came in seven years ago as a group with the expectation that they would be able to exit through either sale of the company or an initial public offering (IPO) and bond issue within a maximum of five years. Projections were favorable and there was a plan to prepare the company for this outcome, including a focus on improving corporate governance and risk management as well as reinvesting funds in improved sales and production. However, implementation of the plan was halfhearted at best. Funds continued to be paid out in dividends rather than reinvested internally. Little was done on the governance and risk management side, and fairly weak financial performance precluded marketability of an IPO/bond issue as well as making any possible sale price highly unattractive for the fund managers. Additionally, the rating agencies had indicated that they would not be able to give Blue Wood a favorable rating under the current circumstances.

The private equity funds would like to exit their investment but consider that they would not receive full value. They are of the view that value could be substantially improved and are pushing for a strategy to maximize profitability in the short term. This could make the company a takeover target for a larger producer. However, the private equity funds are concerned about succession. They consider Ferguson Junior to be a weak CEO who is dominated by his father and unable to make major decisions without his father's approval.

The pension fund sees its investment as a long-term growth prospect and would like to see a stabilization and steady improvement in performance. It considers the steady and significant dividends paid by Blue Wood as a stable and important flow of cash, reflective of a good investment. The pension fund favors a conservative strategy with possible retrenchment in the domestic market and withdrawal from European markets that have not been profitable in the recent past.

Ferguson Junior is in his early sixties and would like to monetize the family holdings and retire. However, given Blue Wood's recent results, he does not believe the family would obtain full value for its holdings. He would face the additional difficulty of having to dispose of the family holdings "over his father's dead body." Proud of his role in developing the company, he is frustrated that profitability has not been better and blames operating and financial staff for forays into new foreign markets and what he sees as fads like fair trade[1] and organic products.

MARKET OVERVIEW

The chocolate market has experienced steady growth in recent years. North America and Western Europe still dominate, but growth has been very strong in the BRIC countries (Brazil, Russia, India, and China). Significant growth in the latter markets has the potential to cause supply shortages of cocoa and hence increasing prices. Brand loyalty, reinforced by advertising by major producers, is strong. Consumers often stick to their favorite brands, and chocolate has proven to be relatively recession proof.

In the traditional areas, where markets are saturated, emphasis has switched to differentiating products, with new flavor combinations and bolder health claims, as well as vegetarian, organic, and premium offerings. In the developing world, market growth is expected to mirror growth in personal disposable incomes.

There is a big seasonal boost in demand at Easter, in particular, and also at Christmas. Chocolate's popularity as a gift has increased. With more premium products available, it is a relatively cheap luxury item. This helps keep demand up in times of recession when people tend to forgo more expensive luxuries. As chocolate has a relatively long shelf life, online sales have been an avenue of growth. Unlike perishable food products, delivery times for online sales of chocolate are not a problem.

Major Competitive Factors

The market is dominated by a few large producers (e.g., Kraft, Hershey, Mars, and Nestlé) with advertising being a major driver. Barriers to entry are quite high, as new operations require major capital investment. Competition is strong in the premium segment, with less domination by large producers and better opportunities to set premium prices with brand recognition. However, the large producers are increasingly entering the premium segment and are also expected to acquire many of the small producers.

Brand recognition and reputation are important at the premium end of the market where chocolate is increasingly seen as having health benefits, and many craft producers have sprung up in recent years. This portion of the market is relatively small but growing.

Conversely, nonpremium products and desserts with higher sugar content are under attack from health professionals and governments concerned about health and obesity. Quality control is important—a brand can be ruined if an inferior batch enters the supply chain and causes mass sickness. As a food producer, Blue Wood is regulated by the U.S. Food and Drug Administration (FDA).

A further factor that is increasing in importance is a greater focus on the plight of cocoa farmers who receive only a tiny fraction of the retail price, as well as on the use of child labor in developing countries. In fact, few cocoa farmers are thought to have ever actually tasted the end product of their labors. Fair trade products have sprung up in recent years to salve consumers' consciences in this regard.

Selling prices are a factor for mainstream products. Not only can people switch to other chocolate brands, but there are many other candy, dessert, and snack food products around that they can select. At the premium end of the market, price competition is less of a factor than perception of quality and luxury based on product branding.

Cocoa prices depend on demand and supply and can be heavily affected by factors such as weather and politics. U.S. sugar prices are inflated compared to world prices due to market manipulation through price support for U.S. producers, domestic market controls that limit production by individual producers, and tariff rate quotas applied to sugar imports.[2] This puts domestic chocolate manufacturers at a competitive disadvantage to foreign competitors. Prices have also been affected on occasion by speculators buying large positions of physical product or futures. Much of the world's supply comes from countries with a history of political instability, and this can cause (and has caused) supply disruptions.

Cocoa Markets Overview

Cocoa (or cacao) trees grow in a limited region approximately 20 degrees north and south of the equator. Around 70 percent of world production is grown in West Africa, with Ivory Coast and Ghana accounting for around 40 percent and 20 percent, respectively. Next is Indonesia with around 14 percent of world production. Cameroon, Nigeria, Brazil, and Ecuador are the next largest producers but with much smaller volumes.

Most cocoa is grown on small family farms. The farmers receive only a very small proportion of the international price of cocoa, and this has been falling in both absolute and real terms. Chocolate demand has been increasing steadily, helped by belief in its added health benefits. However, increasing attention is being paid in consuming countries to the poor conditions of the farmers and the use of child labor in cocoa farming. This has led to increasing sales of fair trade products.

Cocoa pods, which each contain 20 to 50 cocoa beans on average, are harvested from cocoa trees throughout the year and split open by hand (usually using a machete), and the beans are extracted along with the pulp. They are laid out for several days undergoing "sweating" when the pulp flows away. The beans are then taken to a facility where they are fermented and dried for four to seven days on trays or grates under the sun or artificial heat, after which the beans are trodden on and shuffled about (often with bare feet). Once dry, the beans can be shipped.

Beans are roasted and processed in factories to make final chocolate products. Once roasted, the beans are winnowed to remove their shells, leaving cocoa nibs.

These are alkalized before, during, or after roasting to determine the color and taste of the cocoa. The nibs are then milled to create cocoa liquor consisting of cocoa particles suspended in cocoa butter in about equal quantities. The liquor is pressed to extract the cocoa butter, leaving cocoa press cake, which is processed into cocoa powder. Cocoa butter is used to make chocolate. Cocoa powder is used in making numerous dessert and confection products.

Although cocoa beans are perishable, they can be held in storage for several years. Consequently, cocoa can be traded as a commodity for profit and change ownership many times over its life.

Cocoa production is currently around 3.5 million metric tons annually and has been steadily increasing. Demand is expected to continue to grow and reach 4.5 million metric tons by 2020. Cocoa prices have been volatile. They reached a 27-year low of $714 per ton in November 2001 mainly due to favorable weather conditions in the Ivory Coast, and a 32-year high of $3,775 per ton in March 2011. High prices from 2006 to 2011 resulted from production deficits and disruption caused by the disputed presidential election in the Ivory Coast in November 2010.

Cocoa beans, cocoa butter, and cocoa powder spot and futures contracts are traded on the NYSE Euronext Exchange in London and the Intercontinental Exchange (ICE) in New York. Cocoa futures and options on futures are traded on the NYSE Euronext Exchange (pounds sterling) and New York ICE (U.S. dollars). Cocoa futures trading volume on the ICE was 4.95 million metric tons in 2011, 750,000 metric tons more than production. Trading volumes on the NYSE Euronext market have traditionally been higher than on ICE, but the gap has been closing. ICE has been known as the market for speculative trading. It is unusual for a commodity to be traded in two major currencies.

NYSE Euronext[3] and ICE[4] contracts are standardized in 10-ton sizes. Standard contracts specify that future delivery can be made in any of the months of March, May, July, September, and December with 10 future delivery months (i.e., two years) available for trading. However, liquidity falls off sharply beyond delivery months within the first year. Contracts representing product from all country origins can be traded, some at a discount or a premium. Delivery for ICE contracts is at certain U.S. East Coast ports. Delivery for London International Financial Futures and Options Exchange (LIFFE) contracts is at certain specified northern European ports in the Netherlands, the United Kingdom, Germany, Belgium, and northern France. Options on futures are also available for months between the futures delivery months.

Prices are affected by various factors, including weather, crop disease, political instability, availability and cost of fertilizers and pesticides, or withholding of stocks by producers and speculation.

An illustration of the latter point came in August 2002 when London-based Armajaro Holdings, a hedge fund run and cofounded by Anthony Ward, bought three quarters of the 204,380 metric tons of cocoa delivered through the Euronext.liffe exchange under futures contracts. Cocoa prices soared to a 15-year high. In mid-2010, Armajaro purchased 241,000 tons of cocoa beans representing 7 percent of annual global cocoa production (enough to manufacture 5.3 billion quarter-pound chocolate bars). This was the largest single cocoa trade in 14 years and caused prices to rise to a 33-year high. Armajaro had closed its position by

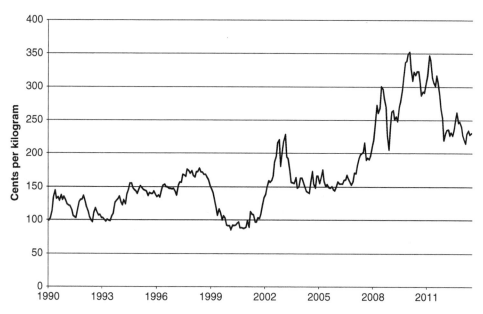

Exhibit 18.1 Cocoa Prices, 1990–2013 (Daily Average)
Source: International Cocoa Organization Secretariat; World Bank.

the end of the year. Anthony Ward is based in London and started out as a motorcycle dispatch rider before becoming a commodities trader at a series of well-known trading companies specializing in cocoa and coffee. City of London traders are rumored to have nicknamed him "Chocfinger." He has amassed a considerable personal fortune and lives in a highly expensive area of London.

Exhibit 18.1 shows world cocoa prices from January 1990 to July 2013.

Sugar Markets Overview

Global sugar production for 2013/2014 is forecast at 175 million metric tons,[5] very slightly up from the previous year, of which the United States accounts for around eight million metric tons, about 5 percent down from the previous year. Supply has grown steadily from 144 million metric tons produced in 2008/2009. The United States is both the fifth-largest producer and the fifth-largest consumer of sugar. Over the same period, demand grew from 153 million metric tons in 2008/2009 to 167 million metric tons forecast in 2013/2014 (i.e., from a supply shortfall to a surplus).

Exhibit 18.2 shows world and U.S. monthly sugar prices from January 1990 to July 2013. U.S. consumers pay substantially more than world prices for sugar, as the U.S. market is manipulated through price support, domestic market controls, and tariff rate quotas. Better growing conditions and hence cheaper costs of sugar in other producing countries would make U.S. producers struggle to survive without such support. Opposition to support, especially among beverage makers, has been increasing in recent years, and both producers and consumers have substantially increased their political contributions and lobbying efforts.

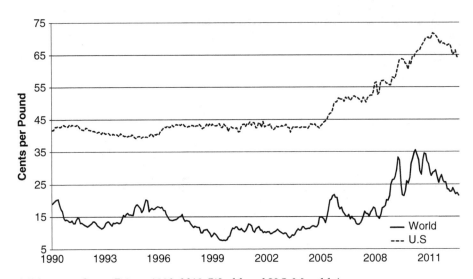

Exhibit 18.2   Sugar Prices, 1990–2013 (World and U.S. Monthly)
World source: London International Financial Futures and Options Exchange (LIFFE); *U.S. source:* Bureau of Labor Statistics.

Price Support

The U.S. Department of Agriculture (USDA) makes loans to producers who can either sell their product to the USDA at the minimum price to repay their loans or to the market if prices are higher. In attempting to avoid anticipated minimum price purchases, the USDA is often an active participant in sugar markets. It recently purchased 15.5 million metric tons of sugar from U.S. producers to bolster low market prices. In 2013, around $1.1 billion of loans were made to 17 producers representing about half of the country's producers.

Domestic Market Controls

Producers are each allotted maximum sales volumes each year. Excess production must be stored until permission is given to sell it in the future. Aggregate allotments must amount to at least 85 percent of anticipated demand.

Tariff Rate Quotas

Tariff rate quotas are used as a strict control on sugar imports. The USDA establishes quota volumes annually for sugar that can enter at low or zero duty. There is a minimum quota of around 1.1 million tons to satisfy U.S. obligations to the World Trade Organization. This can be increased if shortfalls of domestic production versus demand are expected.

Milk Markets Overview

Milk has suffered a long-term decline in consumption since its peak in World War II and has fallen by over 30 percent since 1975. Much of the decline has been offset by increased sales of yogurt, cheese, and other dairy products. The industry has endeavored to combat the decline in milk consumption with measures such as convenient packaging and healthy brands with protein additives. The decline can be attributed, partly at least, to factors such as a lower proportion of children in the population, price increases due to increasing costs of grains fed to cows, and milk no longer being seen as healthy as it once was.

The milk industry is around the size of corn production and second only to beef in the livestock industry. Milk is produced in all 50 states, mostly on family farms that are generally members of cooperatives. The cooperatives collect the milk and deliver it to processors and manufacturers. Dairy farms have been reducing in number and increasing in size, with higher output per cow more than offsetting fewer cows.

As with sugar, the U.S. milk market is heavily regulated and manipulated. There have been federal and state dairy programs since the 1930s, with subsequent programs added and discontinued over the years with changing market conditions. There are a number of reasons for the existence of such programs. These include the fact that milk is a highly perishable product that must be harvested daily, while quantities produced can vary daily according to the weather and feeding conditions. At the same time, consumption can also vary daily due to consumer shopping patterns.

The two main federal programs are the price support program and the system of milk marketing orders. Under the former, the Commodity Credit Corporation purchases manufactured products like butter and cheese, but not milk, at specified support prices and can sell at prices at least 10 percent above the purchase prices. The marketing orders are intended to establish orderly market conditions by setting the relationship between fluid and manufactured dairy products and a geographic price structure. There is also a program to provide income stabilization payments to producers.

Exhibit 18.3 shows U.S. milk prices from January 1995 to August 2013.

BLUE WOOD FINANCIAL PERFORMANCE

Sally Holton examined Blue Wood's recent results and these are summarized in Appendix I. She could not find many comparable U.S. companies with published financial results. The only ones she could find that were vaguely comparable were The Hershey Company and Rocky Mountain Chocolate Factory, Inc., although these companies were of significantly different scale and scope of operations. Their results are summarized in Appendixes II and III, respectively.

The first things Sally noted were that almost all of Blue Wood's profitability measures were significantly worse than those of Hershey and Rocky Mountain. Sales growth had been sluggish compared with the others, and Blue Wood's gross margin was substantially lower. Moreover, Blue Wood's gross margin was quite volatile. Sally determined that the largest factor causing this volatility was gains, losses, and changes in the fair value of commodity derivatives. The one favorable comparison was selling, general, and administrative (SG&A) expenses.

Discussions with the sales department convinced Sally that the main problem was on the production side, although a drop in sales in the first half of 2013

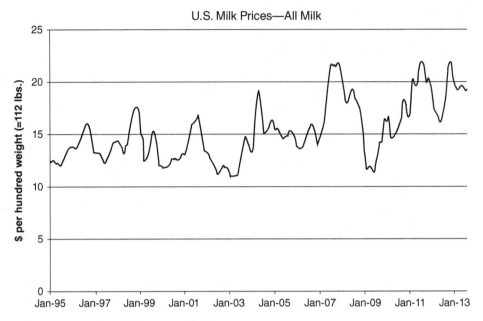

Exhibit 18.3 U.S. Milk Prices, 1995–2013
Source: U.S. Department of Agriculture.

was worrying. She had been shown correspondence from customers complaining about unreliability of delivery schedules and returns of substandard product due to poor quality control. The sales and marketing department had also provided market research showing that Blue Wood's published selling prices were broadly in line with those of competitors, although she suspected that discounts might shine a slightly less favorable light on the situation.

Blue Wood's cash position had been deteriorating over the periods Sally examined. A healthy cash balance had disappeared and the company was now borrowing under the bank revolver line. Retained earnings had also been falling. Part of this was due to the high dividend payments, particularly in 2012.

Sally noted that Blue Wood's long-term debt, both the senior notes and the bank term loan, were to mature in two years' time. Scheduled reductions of the bank loan had started in 2012. No consideration had been given as to how these may be repaid or refinanced, nor did anyone seem particularly concerned. The CEO, John Ferguson Junior, was confident that the bank would support the company. It had always done so in the past, and he and the bank's chairman were members of the same golf club. He did refer to the bank's chairman in rather colorful language that was not particularly respectful of the latter's intelligence.

On the plus side, Blue Wood had built up a significant balance of investments amounting to around $56 million at the end of June 2013. Sally was informed that this was to enable future payments of dividends in case cash flow was insufficient. These investments were not available to be used in the business. The investments consisted of stocks, bonds, exchange-traded funds, and some investments in private companies. Sally could find little information on the last of these. There was no company policy regarding management monitoring of investments. Funds were managed and invested upon the recommendation of the chairman's personal broker. His recommendations had always been followed without exception.

Sally had also learned from speaking to internal counsel that Blue Wood faced a possible $10 million lawsuit from parents of a child who had suffered from severe poisoning after eating one of the company's products. The parents claimed that the child has had difficulty concentrating and learning and has also become incontinent since eating the chocolate. Counsel considered the lawsuit frivolous and recommended resisting it or, at most, offering a small settlement to make it go away without accepting liability and while insisting upon confidentiality. He did agree with Sally that, regardless of the merits of the case, there could be significant adverse publicity if it went to a jury trial, and the result could be a bit of a lottery. When Sally mentioned the potential lawsuit to the CEO, he said he had not heard of it, but was happy to concentrate on running the business while counsel took care of such legal things.

Sally also found that certain foreign exchange futures had been transacted by the previous CFO to hedge his estimate of 50 percent of exposure to Canadian dollars (CAD), euros (EUR), and pounds sterling (GBP) over a one-year horizon. His estimates were essentially back-of-the-envelope approximations and appeared to have little relation to reality. Moreover, some of the local offices had also entered forward contracts with local banks that duplicated what the previous CFO had done. Exhibit 18.4 shows historical exchange rates for CAD, EUR, GBP, and MXN (Mexican peso) against the U.S. dollar. Note: MXN is divided by 10 for scaling to fit the graph.

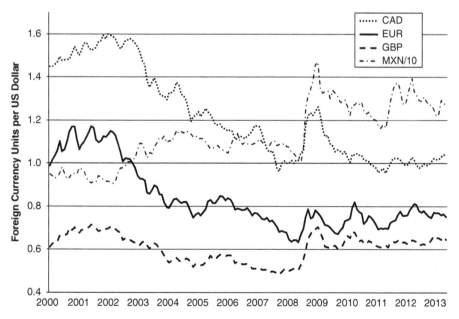

Exhibit 18.4   Exchange Rates
Source: www.oanda.com.

CONCLUSION

Sally Holton felt she had walked into a hornet's nest in her new position as CFO of Blue Wood Chocolates. The business was underperforming, and urgent action was required to respond to pressure from the banks and provide an action plan to the board of directors. There was disagreement among senior executives and board members about the strategy and overall objectives the company should pursue, and nobody had a grasp of all major risk factors. There was no oversight of the hedging practices and little effective internal communication among various functions, or even within some of the functions.

Sally needed to have an overall view of the corporate objectives before developing and implementing specific operating procedures. She needed to get a grasp on the major risks facing the company so that she could develop appropriate responses to these risks. An ERM framework seemed appropriate. However, this would need buy-in from the top, specifically the CEO, chairman, and the board. She needed to develop an overarching proposal incorporating objectives, strategy, and an ERM outline framework for presentation to the board. She would first need to get the CEO on board, not an easy task given his disinterest in what he considers bureaucratic matters that he hires people like Sally to deal with. The CEO's domination by his father, the chairman, would also likely be an obstacle.

Operational procedures, including commodity and currency hedging, would be important but would need to be developed within an overall ERM framework. It was time for Sally to get to work. She also needed to determine how financial performance could be improved. Profitability seemed lackluster, with a high expense base and no real control on major purchasing inputs. Revenues had held up fairly well but could be under competitive threat if margins continued to fall below the industry average.

Overhanging all other issues was the debt maturity profile. Both the senior notes and the bank term loan had maturity dates falling in mid-2014. No planning or discussion had taken place about how to repay and/or refinance these facilities, and the banks were already indicating dissatisfaction with Blue Wood.

APPENDIX I: BLUE WOOD CHOCOLATES

STATEMENTS OF INCOME AND RETAINED EARNINGS

($000's)	6 Mos to June 30			Year to December 31		
	2013	2012	2012	2011	2010	2009
Sales	95,188	97,760	244,387	236,669	231,755	221,925
Cost of sales	62,421	66,109	163,169	166,307	153,671	142,294
Gross profit	32,767	31,651	81,218	70,362	78,084	79,631
Selling, general, and administrative expenses	29,202	28,227	60,596	58,123	57,252	56,113

($000's)	6 Mos to June 30			Year to December 31		
	2013	2012	2012	2011	2010	2009
Income before interest and income taxes	3,565	3,424	20,622	12,239	20,832	23,518
Impairment charge	0	0	0	0	0	(6,222)
Interest & other income	1,409	1,035	1,582	1,059	3,715	933
Interest expense	(6,000)	(6,000)	(12,000)	(12,000)	(12,000)	(12,000)
Income before income taxes	(1,026)	(1,541)	10,204	1,298	12,547	6,229
Provision for income taxes	(308)	(462)	3,061	390	3,764	1,869
Net income	(718)	(1,079)	7,143	908	8,783	4,360
Retained earnings start of period	40,401	54,471	54,471	61,723	60,975	64,522
Dividends	(4,187)	(4,128)	(21,213)	(8,160)	(8,035)	(7,907)
Retained earnings end of period	35,496	49,264	40,401	54,471	61,723	60,975
Gains/(losses) on derivatives included in income statement	(370)	(211)	(259)	(3,523)	2,072	207

FINANCIAL RATIOS

	6 Mos to June 30			Year to December 31		
	2013	2012	2012	2011	2010	2009
Sales growth	−2.6%		3.3%	2.1%	4.4%	
Gross margin	34.4%	32.4%	33.2%	29.7%	33.7%	35.9%
SG&A expense growth	3.5%		4.3%	1.5%	2.0%	
SG&A/Sales	30.7%	28.9%	24.8%	24.6%	24.7%	25.3%
Operating margin	3.7%	3.5%	8.4%	5.2%	9.0%	10.6%
EBITDA/Interest coverage	1.3	1.3	2.5	1.7	2.4	2.8
Debt/Equity	2.0	1.7	1.9	1.7	1.5	1.5
Current ratio	1.8	2.0	1.8	2.4	3.3	3.3

STATEMENTS OF CASH FLOWS

($000's)	6 Mos to June 30			Year to December 31		
	2013	2012	2012	2011	2010	2009
Operating Activities						
Net Income	(718)	(1,079)	7,143	908	8,783	4,360
Adjustments for noncash items	5,212	4,977	10,474	9,195	8,508	10,141

($000's)	6 Mos to June 30			Year to December 31		
	2013	2012	2012	2011	2010	2009
Changes in operating assets and liabilities	(1,276)	736	9,547	(4,469)	2,705	1,049
Cash from operations	3,218	4,634	27,164	5,634	19,996	15,550
Investing Activities						
Additions to property, plant, and equipment	(2,649)	(2,388)	(3,949)	(7,267)	(5,695)	(9,258)
Net purchases of trading securities	(1,008)	(963)	(1,331)	(1,437)	(1,290)	(761)
Purchase of available for sale securities	(8,441)	(8,920)	(17,340)	(7,445)	(4,134)	(5,036)
Sale and maturity of available for sale securities	8,236	1,375	4,649	3,413	3,648	7,783
Net cash used in investing activities	(3,862)	(10,896)	(17,971)	(12,736)	(7,471)	(7,272)
Financing Activities						
Bank term loan repayments	(5,000)	(5,000)	(5,000)	0	0	0
Dividends paid	(2,111)	(4,123)	(23,303)	(8,181)	(8,058)	(7,922)
Net cash use in financing activities	(7,111)	(9,123)	(28,303)	(8,181)	(8,058)	(7,922)
Net increase/(decrease) in cash	(7,755)	(15,385)	(19,110)	(15,283)	4,467	356
Opening (bank revolver)/Cash	(2,278)	16,832	16,832	32,115	27,648	27,292
Closing (bank revolver)/Cash	(10,033)	1,447	(2,278)	16,832	32,115	27,648

BALANCE SHEETS

($000's)	6 Mos to June 30			Year to December 31		
	2013	2012	2012	2011	2010	2009
ASSETS						
Current Assets						
Cash and cash equivalents	0	1,447	0	16,832	32,115	27,648
Investments	11,052	5,698	8,332	4,842	3,554	3,850
Receivables	17,905	10,358	20,513	17,375	15,320	15,318
Prepaid expenses and other receivables	2,352	2,319	2,457	2,935	7,396	3,732
Inventory						
Finished goods and WIP	30,984	27,941	16,465	18,967	15,740	15,809
Raw materials	13,263	14,716	11,261	12,926	9,438	8,854
Deferred income tax	2,193	257	207	257	306	608
Prepayments and other	987	2,568	1,844	2,253	2,888	7,391
Total Current Assets	78,736	65,304	61,079	76,387	86,757	83,210

BALANCE SHEETS (*continued*)

($000's)	6 Mos to June 30			Year to December 31		
	2013	2012	2012	2011	2010	2009
Property, plant, and equipment at cost	208,144	204,680	206,101	202,265	195,988	190,043
Less accumulated depreciation	(120,368)	(112,348)	(116,639)	(107,971)	(100,214)	(91,945)
Net property, plant, and equipment	87,776	92,332	89,462	94,294	95,774	98,098
Goodwill and trademarks	80,338	80,338	80,338	80,338	80,338	80,338
Investments	45,000	41,062	45,416	32,739	28,650	25,838
Split dollar life insurance	18,400	31,357	29,737	32,982	33,085	33,174
Equity method investments	721	1,453	945	1,749	1,891	2,205
Deferred income tax	2,634	3,432	2,765	3,429	4,090	5,147
Total Assets	**313,605**	**315,278**	**309,742**	**321,918**	**330,585**	**328,010**

LIABILITIES AND STOCKHOLDERS' EQUITY
Current Liabilities

	2013	2012	2012	2011	2010	2009
Bank revolver	10,033	0	2,278	0	0	0
Payables and accruals	25,512	25,450	24,041	23,890	23,989	22,937
Dividend payable	2,121	2,095	0	2,046	2,013	1,981
Current portion of bank term loan	5,000	5,000	5,000	5,000	0	0
Postretirement health care and life insurance	247	255	247	255	0	0
Accrued income taxes	111	0	2,719	0	0	0
Total Current Liabilities	**43,024**	**32,800**	**34,285**	**31,191**	**26,002**	**24,918**
Long-term debt—senior note 8% due 2014	100,000	100,000	100,000	100,000	100,000	100,000
Bank term loan due 2014	35,000	40,000	40,000	45,000	50,000	50,000
Postretirement health care and life insurance	12,528	12,023	11,923	11,348	9,195	7,411
Liability for uncertain tax positions	3,672	3,369	3,496	3,709	4,371	8,199
Deferred income taxes	19,050	19,249	17,221	19,343	21,273	19,814
Deferred compensation and other liabilities	27,085	22,953	24,541	21,374	20,514	17,706
Total Liabilities	**240,359**	**230,394**	**231,466**	**231,965**	**231,355**	**228,048**

BALANCE SHEETS (*Continued*)

	6 Mos to June 30			Year to December 31		
($000's)	2013	2012	2012	2011	2010	2009
Stockholders' Equity						
Common stock and additional paid in capital	44,000	44,000	44,000	44,000	44,000	44,000
Retained earnings	35,496	49,264	40,401	54,471	61,723	60,975
Other comprehensive income/(loss)	(6,250)	(8,380)	(6,125)	(8,518)	(6,493)	(5,013)
Total Stockholders' Equity	**73,246**	**84,884**	**78,276**	**89,953**	**99,230**	**99,962**
Total Liabilities and Stockholders' Equity	**313,605**	**315,278**	**309,742**	**321,918**	**330,585**	**328,010**

STATEMENTS OF OTHER COMPREHENSIVE INCOME

	6 Mos to June 30			Year to December 31		
($000's)	2013	2012	2012	2011	2010	2009
Other Comprehensive Income/(Loss) Net of Tax						
Foreign currency translation	(45)	152	579	(1,109)	380	(487)
Pension and postretirement plans Gains/(losses)	0	0	474	(1,597)	(1,393)	811
Reclassification to earnings	0	0	460	223	57	328
Unrealized gains/(losses) on investments	(80)	(14)	880	458	(524)	1,207
Total other comprehensive income net of tax	(125)	138	2,393	(2,025)	(1,480)	1,859
Opening other comprehensive income	(6,125)	(8,518)	(8,518)	(6,493)	(5,013)	(6,872)
Closing other comprehensive income	(6,250)	(8,380)	(6,125)	(8,518)	(6,493)	(5,013)
Derivatives included in OCI						
Opening balance	(49)	115	115	2,334	1,028	98
Unrealized gain/(loss)	(770)	(86)	(151)	(176)	3,250	1,929
Reclassified to earnings	400	(125)	(108)	(3,347)	(1,178)	(451)
Net	(370)	(211)	(259)	(3,523)	2,072	1,478
Tax effect	134	78	95	1,304	(766)	(548)
Closing balance	(285)	(18)	(49)	115	2,334	1,028

APPENDIX II: THE HERSHEY COMPANY

CONSOLIDATED STATEMENTS OF INCOME AND RETAINED EARNINGS

($000's)	6 Months to		Year to December 31			
	June 30 2013	July 1 2012	2012	2011	2010	2009
Sales	3,335,940	3,146,508	6,644,252	6,080,788	5,671,009	5,298,668
Cost of sales	1,768,029	1,784,591	3,784,370	3,548,896	3,255,801	3,245,531
Selling, general, and administrative expenses	896,739	796,967	1,703,796	1,477,750	1,426,477	1,208,672
Business realignment and impairment charges	10,438	8,149	44,938	(886)	83,433	82,875
Total costs and expenses	2,675,206	2,589,707	5,533,104	5,025,760	4,765,711	4,537,078
Income before interest and income taxes	660,734	556,801	1,111,148	1,055,028	905,298	761,590
Interest and other income	1,413	1,350	2,940	2,597	1,270	877
Interest expense	(46,140)	(49,718)	(98,509)	(94,780)	(97,704)	(91,336)
Income before income taxes	616,007	508,433	1,015,579	962,845	808,864	671,131
Provision for income taxes	214,597	174,097	354,648	333,883	299,065	235,137
Net income	401,410	334,336	660,931	628,962	509,799	435,994
Retained earnings start of period	5,027,617	4,699,597	4,707,892	4,383,013	4,156,648	3,984,057
Dividends	(182,895)	(167,094)	(341,206)	(304,083)	(283,434)	(263,403)
Retained earnings end of period	5,246,132	4,866,839	5,027,617	4,707,892	4,383,013	4,156,648

FINANCIAL RATIOS

	6 Months to		Year to December 31			
	June 30 2013	July 1 2012	2012	2011	2010	2009
Sales growth	6%		9%	7%	7%	
Gross margin	47%	43%	43%	42%	43%	39%
SG&A expense growth	13%		15%	4%	18%	
SG&A/Sales	27%	25%	26%	24%	25%	23%
Operating margin (excluding realign. & impair.)	20%	18%	17%	17%	17%	16%
EBITDA/Interest (excluding realign. & impair./including capitalized interest)	16.9	13.7	14.7	14.6	12.4	11.6
Debt/Equity	1.7	1.8	1.8	2.1	1.9	2.0
Current ratio	1.8	1.4	1.4	1.7	1.5	1.5

Source: www.thehersheycompany.com/investors/financial-reports.aspx.

CONSOLIDATED STATEMENTS OF CASH FLOWS

($000's)	6 Months to		Year to December 31			
	June 30 2013	July 1 2012	2012	2011	2010	2009
Operating Activities						
Net Income	401,410	334,336	660,931	628,962	509,799	435,994
Adjustments for noncash items	60,127	114,940	234,364	270,762	260,926	178,671
Changes in operating assets and liabilities	(112,091)	(135,118)	199,532	(311,857)	130,698	451,084
Net cash provided from operating activities	349,446	314,158	1,094,827	587,867	901,423	1,065,749
Investing Activities						
Capital additions	(151,735)	(139,488)	(258,727)	(323,961)	(179,538)	(126,324)
Capitalized software additions	(6,854)	(8,319)	(19,239)	(23,606)	(21,949)	(19,146)
Proceeds from sale of property, plant and equipment	15,107	76	453	312	2,201	10,364
Proceeds from sale of trademark licensing rights	0	0	0	20,000	0	0
Loan to affiliate	(16,000)	(16,000)	(23,000)	(7,000)	0	0
Business acquisitions	0	(172,856)	(172,856)	(5,750)	0	(15,220)
Net Cash Used by Investing Activities	(159,482)	(336,587)	(473,369)	(340,005)	(199,286)	(150,326)
Financing Activities						
Net (decrease)/increase in short-term debt	(13,624)	95,130	77,698	10,834	1,156	(458,047)
Long-term borrowings	249,785	49	4,025	249,126	348,208	0
Repayment of long-term debt	(250,143)	(2,134)	(99,381)	(256,189)	(71,548)	(8,252)
Proceeds from lease financing agreement	0	0	0	47,601	0	0
Cash dividends paid	(182,895)	(167,094)	(341,206)	(304,083)	(283,434)	(263,403)
Exercise of stock options	114,157	185,600	261,597	184,411	92,033	28,318
Excess tax benefits from stock-based compensation	36,938	23,849	33,876	13,997	1,385	4,455
Payments from/(to) noncontrolling interests	1,470	1,470	(12,851)	0	10,199	7,322
Repurchase of common stock	(305,564)	(218,345)	(510,630)	(384,515)	(169,099)	(9,314)
Net cash used by financing activities	(349,876)	(81,475)	(586,872)	(438,818)	(71,100)	(698,921)

CONSOLIDATED STATEMENTS OF CASH FLOWS (*Continued*)

| ($000's) | 6 Months to | | | Year to December 31 | | |
	June 30 2013	July 1 2012	2012	2011	2010	2009
Increase/(Decrease) in Cash and Equivalents	(159,912)	(103,904)	34,586	(190,956)	631,037	216,502
Opening cash and equivalents	728,272	693,686	693,686	884,642	253,605	37,103
Closing Cash & Equivalents	568,360	589,782	728,272	693,686	884,642	253,605

CONSOLIDATED BALANCE SHEETS

| ($000's) | 6 Mos to | | | Year to December 31 | | |
	June 30 2013	July 1 2012	2012	2011	2010	2009
ASSETS						
Current Assets						
Cash and cash equivalents	568,360	589,782	728,272	693,686	884,642	253,605
Receivables—trade	366,288	353,337	461,383	399,499	390,061	410,390
Inventories	778,988	791,805	633,262	648,953	533,622	519,712
Deferred income taxes	102,762	121,192	122,224	136,861	50,655	34,763
Prepaid expenses	182,489	237,457	168,344	167,559	141,132	161,859
Total Current Assets	**1,998,887**	**2,093,573**	**2,113,485**	**2,046,558**	**2,000,112**	**1,380,329**
Property, plant, and equipment at cost	3,650,777	3,564,028	3,560,626	3,588,558	3,324,763	3,242,868
Less accumulated depreciation	(1,941,431)	(1,980,724)	(1,886,555)	(2,028,841)	(1,887,061)	(1,838,101)
Net property, plant, and equipment	1,709,346	1,583,304	1,674,071	1,559,717	1,437,702	1,404,767
Goodwill	578,906	589,464	588,003	516,745	524,134	571,580
Other intangibles	202,495	219,028	214,713	111,913	123,080	125,520
Deferred income taxes	30,925	28,072	12,448	33,439	21,387	4,353
Other assets	176,309	154,531	152,119	138,722	161,212	183,377
Total Assets	**4,696,868**	**4,667,972**	**4,754,839**	**4,407,094**	**4,267,627**	**3,669,926**

LIABILITIES AND STOCKHOLDERS' EQUITY

	June 30 2013	July 1 2012	2012	2011	2010	2009
Current Liabilities						
Accounts payable	413,144	388,472	441,977	420,017	410,655	287,935
Accrued liabilities	564,080	569,902	650,906	612,186	593,308	546,462
Accrued income taxes	4,585	1,930	2,329	1,899	9,402	36,918
Short-term debt	99,081	139,356	118,164	42,080	24,088	24,066
Current portion of long-term debt	3,316	347,312	257,734	97,593	261,392	15,247
Total Current Liabilities	**1,084,206**	**1,446,972**	**1,471,110**	**1,173,775**	**1,298,845**	**910,628**

LIABILITIES AND STOCKHOLDERS' EQUITY (Continued)

($000's)	6 Mos to		Year to December 31			
	June 30 2013	July 1 2012	2012	2011	2010	2009
Long-term debt	1,794,493	1,498,669	1,530,967	1,748,500	1,541,825	1,502,730
Other long-term liabilities	663,519	608,664	668,732	603,876	481,061	487,934
Deferred income taxes	32,923	27,696	35,657	0	0	0
Total Liabilities	**3,575,141**	**3,582,001**	**3,706,466**	**3,526,151**	**3,321,731**	**2,901,292**
Stockholders' Equity						
Common stock and additional paid-in capital	987,292	917,293	952,876	850,718	794,766	754,579
Retained earnings	5,246,132	4,866,839	5,027,617	4,707,892	4,383,013	4,156,648
Treasury common stock at cost	(4,740,944)	(4,324,278)	(4,558,668)	(4,258,962)	(4,052,101)	(3,979,629)
Accumulated other comprehensive loss	(380,658)	(395,527)	(385,076)	(442,331)	(215,067)	(202,844)
Noncontrolling interests in subsidiaries	9,905	21,644	11,624	23,626	35,285	39,880
Total Stockholders' Equity	**1,121,727**	**1,085,971**	**1,048,373**	**880,943**	**945,896**	**768,634**
Total Liabilities and Stockholders' Equity	**4,696,868**	**4,667,972**	**4,754,839**	**4,407,094**	**4,267,627**	**3,669,926**

Note: 2009 and 2010 as restated.

CONSOLIDATED STATEMENTS OF OTHER COMPREHENSIVE INCOME

($000's)	6 Months to		Year to December 31			
	June 30 2013	July 1 2012	2012	2011	2010	2009
Other Comprehensive Income/(Loss) Net of Tax						
Foreign currency translation	(18,981)	1,662	7,714	(21,213)	14,123	38,302
Pension and postretirement plans	13,621	12,608	(9,634)	(85,823)	5,130	38,643
Cash flow hedges						
Gains/(losses) on derivatives	4,010	(769)	(868)	(107,713)	1,001	78,257
Reclassification adjustments	5,768	33,303	60,043	(12,515)	(32,477)	1,862
Total other comprehensive income net of tax	4,418	46,804	57,255	(227,264)	(12,223)	157,064
Opening Other Comprehensive Income	(385,076)	(442,331)	(442,331)	(215,067)	(202,844)	(359,908)
Closing Other Comprehensive Income	(380,658)	(395,527)	(385,076)	(442,331)	(215,067)	(202,844)

APPENDIX III: ROCKY MOUNTAIN CHOCOLATE FACTORY, INC.

CONSOLIDATED STATEMENTS OF INCOME AND RETAINED EARNINGS

($000's)	3 Months to May 31		Year to February 28			
	2013	2012	2013	2012	2011	2010
Revenues	10,178	9,658	36,315	34,627	31,128	28,437
Cost of sales	5,027	5,022	18,955	18,309	16,228	14,911
Other costs and expenses	3,333	3,013	12,174	10,465	8,950	7,883
Loss on asset sales and restructuring charges	0	0	2,647	0	0	0
Total Costs and expenses	8,360	8,035	33,776	28,774	25,178	22,794
Income before interest and income taxes	1,818	1,623	2,539	5,853	5,950	5,643
Interest and other income	12	11	44	59	59	27
Income before income taxes	1,830	1,634	2,583	5,912	6,009	5,670
Income tax expense	584	571	1,233	2,036	2,098	2,090
Net income after income taxes	1,246	1,063	1,350	3,876	3,911	3,580
Attributable to noncontrolling interest	(67)	0	128	0	0	0
Net income attributable to RMCF	1,179	1,063	1,478	3,876	3,911	3,580
Retained earnings start of period	8,642	9,838	9,838	8,412	6,924	5,751
Dividends	(668)	(676)	(2,674)	(2,450)	(2,423)	(2,407)
Retained earnings end of period	9,153	10,225	8,642	9,838	8,412	6,924

Source: www.irdirect.net/RMCF/sec_filings/view.

FINANCIAL RATIOS

	3 Months to May 31		Year to February 28			
	2013	2012	2013	2012	2011	2010
Sales growth	*5%*		*5%*	*11%*	*9%*	
Gross margin	*51%*	*48%*	*48%*	*47%*	*48%*	*48%*
Other costs and expense growth	*11%*		*16%*	*17%*	*14%*	
Other costs and expenses/sales	*33%*	*31%*	*34%*	*30%*	*29%*	*28%*
Operating margin (excluding loss on asset sales and restructuring charges)	*18%*	*17%*	*14%*	*17%*	*19%*	*20%*

FINANCIAL RATIOS (*Continued*)

	3 Months to May 31			Year to February 28		
	2013	2012	2013	2012	2011	2010
EBITDA/Interest	n/a	n/a	n/a	n/a	n/a	n/a
Debt/Equity	n/a	n/a	n/a	n/a	n/a	n/a
Current ratio	3.2	4.7	2.6	4.0	3.7	3.7

CONSOLIDATED CASH FLOW STATEMENTS

	3 Months to May 31			Year to February 28		
($000's)	2013	2012	2013	2012	2011	2010
Operating Activities						
Net Income	1,179	1,062	1,478	3,876	3,911	3,580
Adjustments for noncash items	409	406	2,767	2,409	1,569	1,187
Changes in operating assets and liabilities	(776)	663	2,126	(138)	(1,685)	767
Net cash provided by operating activities	812	2,131	6,371	6,147	3,795	5,534
Investing Activities						
Additions to property, plant, and equipment	(58)	(253)	(743)	(3,261)	(1,298)	(499)
Proceeds from sale or distribution of assets	3	0	889	53	19	117
Franchising rights	0	0	(802)	0	0	0
Other	(59)	21	(320)	85	(518)	(260)
Net cash used in investing activities	(114)	(232)	(976)	(3,123)	(1,797)	(642)
Financing Activities						
Dividends paid	(668)	(616)	(2,623)	(2,441)	(2,418)	(2,403)
Tax benefit of stock option exercise	20	6	58	25	11	0
(Repurchase)/Issue of common stock	0	(363)	(1,633)	173	10	0
Net cash used in financing activities	(648)	(973)	(4,198)	(2,243)	(2,397)	(2,403)
Net Increase/(Decrease) in Cash and Equivalents	50	926	1,197	781	(399)	2,489
Opening Cash and Equivalents	5,322	4,125	4,125	3,344	3,743	1,254
Closing Cash and Equivalents	5,372	5,051	5,322	4,125	3,344	3,743

CONSOLIDATED BALANCE SHEETS

($000's)	May 31 2013	May 31 2012	February 28 2013	February 28 2012	February 28 2011	February 28 2010
ASSETS						
Current Assets						
Cash and cash equivalents	5,372	5,051	5,322	4,125	3,344	3,743
Receivables	3,413	3,488	4,113	4,362	5,194	4,519
Inventory	4,175	3,744	4,221	4,119	4,125	3,281
Deferred tax	644	677	629	1,212	565	461
Prepayments and other	658	741	259	281	279	220
Total current assets	**14,262**	**13,701**	**14,544**	**14,099**	**13,507**	**12,224**
Property, plant and equipment at cost	17,571	18,004	17,490	17,835	15,254	13,797
Less accumulated depreciation	(10,942)	(9,552)	(10,713)	(9,319)	(8,978)	(8,610)
Net property, plant, and equipment	6,629	8,452	6,777	8,516	6,276	5,187
Goodwill	1,047	1,047	1,047	1,047	1,047	1,047
Other intangibles	800	20	801	22	59	110
Other assets	733	457	665	479	550	352
Total Assets	**23,471**	**23,677**	**23,834**	**24,163**	**21,439**	**18,920**

LIABILITIES AND STOCKHOLDERS' EQUITY

	May 31 2013	May 31 2012	February 28 2013	February 28 2012	February 28 2011	February 28 2010
Current Liabilities						
Payables	1,246	924	1,999	1,356	1,541	878
Accruals and deferred income	2,538	1,314	2,897	1,570	1,528	1,814
Dividend payable	669	676	668	616	607	603
Total Current Liabilities	**4,453**	**2,914**	**5,564**	**3,542**	**3,676**	**3,295**
Deferred income taxes	859	1,862	882	1,885	1,109	894
Total Liabilities	**5,312**	**4,776**	**6,446**	**5,427**	**4,785**	**4,189**
Stockholders' Equity						
Common stock and additional paid in capital	7,905	8,676	7,741	8,898	8,242	7,807
Retained earnings	9,153	10,225	8,642	9,838	8,412	6,924
Noncontrolling interest	1,101	0	1,005	0	0	0
Total Stockholders' Equity	**18,159**	**18,901**	**17,388**	**18,736**	**16,654**	**14,731**
Total Liabilities and Stockholders' Equity	**23,471**	**23,677**	**23,834**	**24,163**	**21,439**	**18,920**

QUESTIONS

The following questions are intended to guide discussion about Blue Wood and how such a company can face up to and deal with issues of risk management throughout the enterprise. The questions are not necessarily exhaustive for the case and it is intended that examination and discussion can be developed further if desired.

Discussion can center on the importance of culture within an organization, how to change it, how to set priorities, how much is possible and how fast, as well as the related costs and benefits.

1. What are the prospects and consequences for Blue Wood if it carries on the way it has been?
2. Are corporate objectives and strategy important and if so, why?
3. Discuss why and how either an FRM (financial risk management) or an ERM framework might benefit a company like Blue Wood.
4. What are the main challenges in developing and implementing a risk management framework for Blue Wood? How does the ownership structure affect these challenges?
5. If the company is to develop a risk management framework, who should lead the process? Should a Chief Risk Officer (CRO) be appointed? If so, to whom should he/she report and have access to? How could smaller companies without the resources for a dedicated CRO deal with ERM? What is the role for the board in such a process?
6. Should Blue Wood hedge its exposures to commodities and foreign currencies? If so, how should it go about hedging; for example, in terms of:
   - managing, monitoring, and evaluating the hedging program
   - amounts hedged
   - time horizon of the hedges
   - instruments used
   - budget for option premiums
   - accounting and reporting the hedging program
7. Are there other areas where Blue Wood should consider a risk management program?

NOTES

1. "Fair trade" products are food products that are marketed under the auspices of a Fair Trade organization. A core objective of the organization is to promote better prices and working conditions, and secure the rights of food producers and workers in developing countries. The food is packaged with the distinctive Fair Trade logo. This branding has become popular among consumers having a social conscience.
2. See: http://sugarcane.org/global-policies/policies-in-the-united-states/sugar-in-the-united-states. See also, for example, www.nytimes.com/2013/10/31/us/american-candy-makers-pinched-by-inflated-sugar-prices-look-abroad.html?_r=0 and http://commodities.about.com/od/researchcommodities/a/The-Two-Sugar-Markets-Us-Sugar-And-World-Sugar.htm.
3. NYSE Euronext contract summary: https://globalderivatives.nyx.com/products/commodities-futures/C-DLON/contract-specification.
4. ICE contract summary: https://www.theice.com/productguide/ProductSpec.shtml?specId=7.
5. http://usda01.library.cornell.edu/usda/current/sugar/sugar-05-23-2013.pdf.

ABOUT THE CONTRIBUTORS

Stephen McPhie, CA, in his current position as partner of RSD Solutions Inc., advises businesses internationally on various aspects of financial strategy and risk mitigation. From 2000 to 2004, Stephen worked in London for Italy's largest bank. In the financial engineering group, he successfully created innovative cross-border financing structures that included private equity instruments with embedded derivatives. Previously he structured and distributed primary market debt and traded distressed and near-par debt in secondary markets. Prior to 2000, Stephen held various positions in the United States, Canada, and the United Kingdom with a "big five" Canadian bank. His experience stretches from structuring and distributing leveraged and investment grade corporate transactions to relationship management, par and distressed secondary market trading, structured credit derivative products, workouts and credit and financial mandates, structuring and negotiating transactions (including leveraged, project finance, and recapitalization of distressed situations), as well as negotiating complex legal documentation.

Stephen holds a BA in economics from Heriot-Watt University in Edinburgh, Scotland, and has qualified as a Chartered Accountant in both the United Kingdom and Canada. In this respect he worked for one of the large accounting firms carrying out assignments in the fields of audit, consultancy (including business valuations), and taxation.

Rick Nason, PhD, CFA, has an extensive background in the capital markets and derivatives industry, having worked in equity derivatives and exotics, credit derivatives, and capital markets training in a senior capacity at several different global financial institutions. Rick is a founding partner of RSD Solutions, a risk management consultancy that specializes in financial risk management consulting and training for corporations, investment funds, and banks. Dr. Nason is also an Associate Professor of Finance at Dalhousie University in Halifax, Nova Scotia, where he teaches graduate classes in corporate finance, investments, enterprise risk management, and derivatives. He has been awarded several teaching awards as well as being selected MBA Professor of the Year several times. His research interests are in financial risk management, enterprise risk management, and complexity.

Rick has an MSc in physics from the University of Pittsburgh and an MBA and a PhD in finance from the Richard Ivey Business School at the University of Western Ontario. Additionally, he is a Chartered Financial Analyst charterholder. In his spare time he enjoys practicing risk management principles as he plays with his collection of pinball machines.

CHAPTER 19

Kilgore Custom Milling

RICK NASON, PHD, CFA
Partner, RSD Solutions Inc., and Associate Professor of Finance,
Dalhousie University

STEPHEN McPHIE, CA
Partner, RSD Solutions Inc.

T his case study provides a broad spectrum of issues—both opportunities and
potential threats—that arise from creating growth opportunities. Many risks
can be explored and debated as part of various approaches to enterprise
risk management (ERM), including using strengths, weaknesses, opportunities,
and threats (SWOT) analysis and risk profiles. In particular, this case focuses on
financial risk management as taught in Chapter 14, "Market Risk Management
and Common Elements with Credit Risk Management," in *Enterprise Risk Management: Today's Leading Research and Best Practices for Tomorrow's Executives*, edited by
John Fraser and Betty J. Simkins (John Wiley & Sons, 2010). Thus, teachers of ERM
can focus at the corporate level and include all risks, or delve more specifically into
financial risks, or go even more specifically into liquidity or foreign exchange risks.

BACKGROUND

"Hope is not a risk strategy! Wishful thinking is not the best we can do, and furthermore we can't repeat the mistakes of the past if we want to move to the next
level. We need to think this through more carefully!" Cathy Williams was growing
ever more tired and frustrated. She and her four-person treasury team had been
struggling with various aspects of the new supply contract for weeks, and all that
remained was how the company would hedge the resulting currency risk. This
issue had been highlighted as part of the management team's discussions about
risk management generally, and it was still an issue as to how this aspect of currency hedging would fit into the firm's attempt at creating an enterprise risk management framework. As she sat with her boss, Steve MacLinden, and the rest of the
company's senior management team, it was clear that they were not any further
ahead than they had been when the financial hedging strategy meeting began over
two hours ago.

Kilgore Custom Milling was a small private manufacturer of power window assemblies for automobile manufacturers' plants based in southern Ontario,

Canada. Just over a year ago, as part of a strategic planning session, the company made a decision to seek out contracts to supply plants in the United States. Due to the successful efforts of the entire management team, they were in the final stages of finalizing a contract to supply a Japanese car company that was expanding its operations in Michigan. The deal included a possible extension to supply a plant in Tennessee and one in Mexico that would be coming on line in nine months. Supplying plants in the United States was a major move for the company, a move it had tried before but which had produced results that almost bankrupted the company.

The process of securing the contract had been an exhausting exercise. The Japanese manufacturer involved was very thorough in its due diligence of its supplier agreements. Additionally, in the current economic manufacturing environment, the competition was tough. The five-year contract, with an option to extend to eight years, could potentially mean the difference between a supplier such as Kilgore staying in business and it failing. The operational and technical demands of the Japanese manufacturer were high, but the main point of competition was price, as several different suppliers had the necessary track records and operational platforms to satisfy the conditions and standards necessary to win. In the 1990s, Canadian manufacturers such as Kilgore could rely on the relatively weak Canadian dollar to help them win price-based contracts. That advantage was now gone with the Canadian dollar near parity to the U.S. dollar, and thus it was manufacturing ability and geographical placement that were key determining factors—along with the bottom-line pricing, of course.

The prospect of selling to a U.S.-based manufacturer for the first time in almost 25 years was very exciting, but also scary. Kilgore had supplied a U.S.-based plant in the late 1980s for a while, but exchange rate volatility had caused Kilgore trouble and had led to significant losses. As a result, Kilgore made a decision to stick with supplying Canadian-based manufacturers. Many of its competitors in the automotive supply industry continued to focus on supplying the large U.S. manufacturing plants. Over this period of time, the focus on Canadian sales had provided Kilgore with a stable and profitable stream of business. However, with the changing manufacturing strategies of global manufacturers after the 2008 financial crisis, Kilgore needed to rethink its own strategy.

The contract was to be finalized in less than a week, with shipments to begin in six months, but exactly how Kilgore Custom Milling was going to be able to deliver profitably on the contract was still in doubt. To be sure, the operational and manufacturing details were set, but the contract was finely priced based on the competition. Any hiccups in production or in managing the exchange rate risk could turn the five-year, and possibly eight-year, contract into a guaranteed loss for Kilgore.

"Okay, I think we should all take a break for the weekend and tackle this with fresh minds on Monday," said Steve MacLinden, the CEO and cofounder of the company. "That's just great," thought Cathy. "What he really means is that I have to spend the weekend coming up with a solution for first thing Monday!" With that the meeting broke up with pleasantries exchanged for everyone to have a nice weekend—a weekend that Cathy knew she would be spending coming up with a workable plan for managing the currency risk that Kilgore would be taking on with this new phase of the company's evolution.

KILGORE CUSTOM MILLING

Kilgore Custom Milling began in late 1980. Steve MacLinden and a fellow business school graduate were wondering what sort of a career they should embark on when they came up with the idea of getting into manufacturing. Before earning his MBA, Steve had worked for five years with a major accounting firm. He went back to business school looking for a way to expand his horizons and thinking he wanted to work in marketing for a multinational company. Upon graduation, however, he thought it might be more of an adventure to be his own boss as an entrepreneur. Along with a classmate, Steve began to explore opportunities. With a government grant for young entrepreneurs, monies from an inheritance, and loans from family and friends, the two young men were able to buy a working tool and die company that had 11 employees; it made custom parts for various repair shops and had a few small contracts with various manufacturing companies. Steve was a big fan of the novelist Kurt Vonnegut, so they renamed the company Kilgore Custom Milling after a recurring character who appeared in several Kurt Vonnegut novels.

For the first few years the company struggled and relied on heavy levels of bank debt and personal loans to stay in business. Steve's business school buddy wanted out as a partner and sold his interest to Steve for a single dollar and a release from the debt obligations of the company. By then the workforce was down to four employees on a full-time basis who were supported by the occasional hiring of short-term contract workers when the work orders required them. While the company started to eke out a very modest profit, its long-term viability was far from guaranteed. It was at this point that the company caught a lucky break when a fire at a competing small auto parts manufacturer caused the latter to cease production for two months. Kilgore stepped in and secured a contract to become a short-term supplier of parts required for power windows in automobiles. That contract provided a springboard for further contracts, and soon the operations and business of the company were streamlined to focus solely on power window assemblies for direct supply to several auto manufacturers based in southern Ontario. The company grew to employ 128 workers at the company's two manufacturing facilities and a separate warehouse facility. Recent financial statements for Kilgore are provided in Exhibit 19.1.

The production of power window assemblies was a relatively simple task, and the technology was widely available and considered a commodity. The production of a power window consisted of a small electric motor (which Kilgore purchased from a variety of Canadian suppliers), a support bar on which the glass rode, a series of gears, and a variety of metal and plastic components to ensure smooth operation. See Exhibit 19.2 for an illustration of a power window assembly.

Kilgore became a relatively successful manufacturer in the original equipment manufacturer (OEM) field mainly because of its focus on low-cost manufacturing, which in large part was due to the relatively large pool of skilled manufacturing workers available in the Windsor area of southwest Ontario.

Based in southern Ontario, which was also home to the majority of Canada's OEM industry, Kilgore had ready access to labor and, based on operational efficiencies and a focus on a single product, also had a low cost of manufacturing. Indeed, since power window assemblies were low-tech and considered a

Exhibit 19.1   Kilgore Custom Milling Financial Statements

INCOME STATEMENT	(CAD MM)	12/31/12	12/31/11	12/31/10	12/31/09
Net sales		204.8	184.8	154.6	158.4
Costs of goods sold		190.1	169.4	141.0	141.3
Selling, general, and administrative expenses		8.6	8.9	7.8	8.9
Operating income		6.0	6.5	5.8	8.2
Interest expense		2.9	2.5	2.4	2.4
Net nonoperating loss (gain)		2.3	0.0	0.0	0.0
Income tax expense		0.1	1.0	1.0	1.7
Net income		0.6	3.0	2.3	4.1
Common dividend (total cash)		(0.6)	(2.3)	(2.3)	(2.9)
Opening retained earnings		19.1	18.4	18.4	17.2
Closing retained earnings		19.2	19.1	18.4	18.4

CASH FLOW STATEMENT	(CAD MM)	12/31/12	12/31/11	12/31/10	12/31/09
Operating activities					
Net income		0.6	3.0	2.3	4.1
Depreciation		5.1	4.8	4.7	4.6
(gain)/loss on fixed asset disposals		0.5	0.1	0.0	(1.9)
Cash from/used for working capital		3.7	(1.5)	0.1	(4.6)
Cash from operating activities		9.9	6.5	7.2	2.2
Investing activities					
Additions to fixed assets		(6.5)	(3.4)	(1.9)	(1.9)
Fixed asset disposal proceeds		1.4	0.0	0.6	1.9
Other LT assets		(13.7)	(3.0)	(10.8)	(4.2)
		(18.8)	(6.4)	(12.1)	(4.1)
Financing activities					
Short-term borrowings		3.0	0.0	0.0	0.0
LT borrowings		(0.8)	(0.8)	(0.8)	(0.5)
Other LT liabilities		8.6	0.1	1.6	0.7
Dividend paid		(0.6)	(2.3)	(2.3)	(2.9)
		10.2	(3.0)	(1.5)	(2.7)
Net cash change in year		1.3	(2.9)	(6.5)	(4.6)
Opening cash balance		3.0	6.0	12.5	17.1
Closing cash balance		4.3	3.0	6.0	12.5

Exhibit 19.2 Power Window Assembly
Source: www.monsterauto.com.

commodity, cost factors largely dictated the degree of success of a firm in winning orders from the major auto manufacturers.

A second competitive factor was quality. Power window assemblies were not seen by the car purchaser, and thus cosmetics, fit, and finish were not an issue. However, a faulty assembly was expensive to repair and considered a serious and annoying quality flaw by car buyers. Although not a drive-train part, the power window was still a moving part and could experience relatively heavy or abusive use. Thus a reputation for building sturdy and reliable quality parts was a key aspect of winning supply bids. With an experienced and dedicated workforce, Kilgore had built an enviable reputation as a reliable supplier of quality assemblies. However, given the simplicity of the technology, this was a difficult competitive advantage on which to differentiate the company from its competitors. The technology of window assemblies had changed little in the past 10 years and was not expected to change much going forward.

A third competitive factor for Kilgore was its philosophy of "sticking to its knitting," a favorite phrase of Steve MacLinden. Before settling on the manufacture of power windows, Kilgore had tried custom manufacturing as well as an expansion of the types of components manufactured for the OEM industry. The operational and financial results were mediocre at best. With a small management team and no special expertise in operations management, the operational and innovation demands of nonspecialization proved too challenging for Kilgore to manage successfully.

An additional argument for "sticking to its knitting" was Steve's lack of a background in engineering or operations. By staying with the production of a commodity product that was sold on the basis of cost and reliability and not innovation or changing functionality, Kilgore did not have to concern itself as much with the ongoing maintenance of a joint venture type of relationship with its customers. Participating in the major industry trade shows and Steve's natural inclination toward sales were generally enough contact with customers to keep Kilgore in the loop and competitive. In this way Kilgore was able to fly below the radar of the large consolidated OEM manufacturers and survive within its niche.

In terms of its own suppliers, Kilgore utilized Canadian specialty manufacturers and raw metal suppliers. This kept the company's own supply issues simple, and allowed it to work with lower levels of inventory, which in turn helped alleviate at least some of its cash flow problems. For heavy demand periods, many potential U.S.-based suppliers existed, but had been used only sparingly. Buying in bulk from Asian suppliers was attractive in terms of pricing, but financing such transactions was difficult and Steve preferred having strong local connections in case any issues arose. Steve was well aware of the horror stories that were common in the industry of trying to fix a problem with a foreign supplier who spoke a different language, was in a time zone that was different by 12 hours, and was at least an 18-hour plane flight away from a potential meeting. Additionally, the use of foreign suppliers complicated exchange rate transactions, which was another management hassle that historically the management team did not feel was justified or necessary. Going forward, Steve believed that Kilgore's existing suppliers would be able to fulfill the company's increased needs with the new contract.

THE MANAGEMENT TEAM

The management team at Kilgore was led by Steve MacLinden, who was now in his late fifties; his role was that of owner and chief executive officer. Although he participated in all major decisions of the company, he basically left the day-to-day operations of the company to the rest of the management team and focused on customer relationships and making sure the company kept a good profile in the industry.

Another member of the senior management team was Rory Sullivan, who was in his late sixties and was a long-term veteran of auto manufacturing. Rory had an engineering background and had worked his way up to plant manager for one of the big three auto manufacturers before joining Kilgore upon his retirement. Rory was responsible for all manufacturing and plant operations.

Casey Dobbelstyn was the youngest and also the newest member of the management team. Casey, who had a background in international heavy equipment sales, was in charge of sales and client relationships. He also managed supplier relationships.

Completing the management team was Cathy Williams, who was the treasurer and de facto chief financial officer. After graduation from university, Cathy started her career with one of the large accounting firms and quickly obtained her Chartered Accountant qualifications. However, rather than continue within the confines of a large firm, Cathy set up a small independent accounting firm with a few like-minded colleagues so she could focus on her family and maintain what she believed was a better work/life balance. When her children started in university, Cathy returned to a large accounting firm where she was involved in a number of different accounting and auditing roles. She was being considered for partnership in the accounting firm when she was approached three years ago by her B-school acquaintance Steve MacLinden to fill the vacancy of treasurer at Kilgore. Cathy was easily persuaded that life in a large firm was not for her and jumped at the chance to embark on what she considered a more challenging future and one where she could help shape strategy. Cathy had built up the treasury team from two to five persons, including herself, and had gained the respect of all team members as smart and capable. One of her major decisions as treasurer was to implement a cash management system that significantly helped to reduce, but not eliminate, the chronic cash flow problems that plagued Kilgore. She also played a major role in Kilgore's decision to implement enterprise risk management that was a slightly modified version of ISO 31000.

THE COMPANY

Kilgore is a private company 100 percent owned by Steve MacLinden. Steve's long-term plan is to exit the business when he is ready to retire in probably five to 10 years. Steve's only child is a daughter who has gone into acting and has no desire to join the company. Therefore, Steve's view is that the company must either be sold to one of the large publicly traded OEM manufacturers or be floated as a public company as a way for him to exit the company profitably. Either way, the next few years would be pivotal in ensuring that the business is on a sound footing and increasingly profitable, and hence has an enhanced exit value. It is also in his plans, if possible, to leave a portion of the company through a share distribution to the employees who stayed with him throughout the years and who helped him keep the company a going concern.

The main focus of the company had always seemed to be cash flow management. While the business had managed to be profitable on an accounting basis over the past five years, it seemed that Kilgore was always short of cash at critical times of the year. In part this was due to thin margins and generous payment terms demanded by the auto manufacturers that were Kilgore's key clients. With tight market conditions, the major auto manufacturers were able to demand and get extended payment terms. Thus management of cash flow was a key function for Cathy Williams and her treasury team to focus on. While economic conditions in the automobile industry had improved dramatically since the depths of the 2008 financial crisis, banks were still wary of extending operational lines of credit. Many industry observers felt that the overall market conditions were still shaky and the recent increase in automobile sales and profits might be a consequence of necessary replacement of aging vehicles, rather than a sustained improvement in the mind-set of consumers, as many consumers delayed new car purchases as a result of the 2008 crisis. A chart of U.S.-based auto sales is shown in Exhibit 19.3.

The new U.S. auto supply contract held the risk of dramatically increasing the concerns about cash flow management. While the addition of accounting and control systems that Cathy and her team had implemented had improved the cash flow situation significantly, the net profit margins were still quite tight. The added uncertainty of exchange rate fluctuations might throw things out of balance, and the company would be forced to scramble on a monthly basis to make payroll as it had done previously.

THE NEW CONTRACT

The new contract would dramatically increase the existing sales of Kilgore, and if all of the embedded options were exercised, the effect on Kilgore could be an additional increase in sales over the next five years of more than 100 percent. In terms of the potential for enhancing the valuation of Kilgore, and Steve's considering liquidating at least some of his sole ownership in the company in 5 to 10 years, the timing of the deal could not be better.

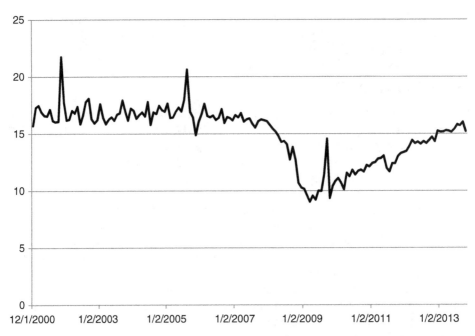

Exhibit 19.3   U.S. Monthly Auto Sales, Million of Units
Source: Bloomberg LLC.

While the technical specifications of the contract seemed highly complex and exacting, they basically laid out the design specifications for power window assemblies that Kilgore had extensive experience in producing. Some of the more complex parts of the contract dealt with unexpected, but potential, implications of significant design and production changes. In essence the contract had provisions that compensated Kilgore for any necessary modifications in the technical details of what would be produced. Thus, in terms of operational risk, it was felt that the contract was of low risk to Kilgore. While changes would have to be made to manufacturing processes and capacity, it was expected that these would proceed relatively smoothly given Rory's experience.

The more troubling aspects of the contract were financial, and more specifically the need to manage the financial risk. Under the terms of the contract, all proceeds to Kilgore were to be in U.S. dollars, even though virtually all of Kilgore's expenses were in Canadian dollars. The Japanese car manufacturer was setting up a plant to supply the U.S. market and in turn demanded that all supply contracts also be denominated in U.S. dollars. Part of the reason for doing so was to mitigate its own potential cyclical profitability due to exchange rate cycles. A second reason was the need for geographic diversity. The 2011 earthquake and tsunami in Japan had exposed a weakness of basing too much of a company's supply chain within a single region. While it wanted to diversify its supply chain across North America and utilize not only U.S. but also Mexican and Canadian suppliers, it did not want to incur currency risk.

Exhibit 19.4 USD/CAD Exchange Rate
Source: Bloomberg LLC.

Additionally, the contract had several built-in options whose exercise would benefit the Japanese manufacturer. For example, the contract could be extended by an additional three years. While there were provisions for payment of development expenses of retooling for any unforeseen model changes, the base profit margin in U.S. dollars was fixed. A second option embedded in the contract would allow the Japanese manufacturer to increase the number of units bought per year by up to 50 percent at the same fixed price. If the full range of options were exercised, this one supply contract would comprise almost 60 percent of Kilgore's total sales.

A major concern of Cathy Williams was the potential profitability of the contract, particularly when the embedded options were considered. With current U.S./Canadian dollar exchange rates, the contract was relatively profitable for Kilgore. Cathy calculated that there was approximately an 8 percent net profit margin built into the contract, which was only slightly below industry standards. The lower profit margin was considered to be a trade-off for the longer-term stability of the contract. However, a shift to a stronger Canadian dollar could quickly eliminate any profitability and potentially even lock Kilgore into a long-term loss. A chart of the history of the USD/CAD exchange rate is shown in Exhibit 19.4. Of particular concern was the potential for the Canadian dollar to creep above par as it had done periodically over the past five years.

A second concern was the potential for any inflation differentials between Canada and the United States. The contract had a built-in quarterly pricing adjustment based on the U.S. Producer Price Index (PPI). Kilgore's manufacturing costs, however, were more closely linked to the Canadian PPI, particularly as Kilgore's

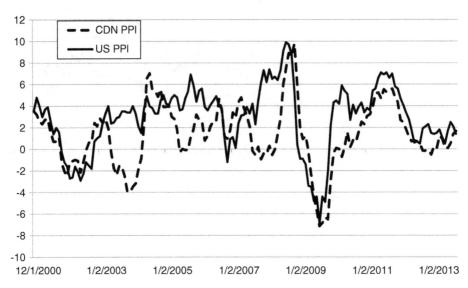

Exhibit 19.5　U.S. and Canadian Producer Price Indexes
Source: Bloomberg LLC.

union contract was linked to Canadian PPI, as were the union contracts of most of its own suppliers. While the U.S. PPI and the Canadian PPI were closely linked, the relationship was not perfect. Political events on either side of the border could potentially change the economics of the deal for Kilgore. The respective PPIs for the United States and for Canada are shown in Exhibit 19.5.

If the full range of embedded options were exercised, and if exchange rates or inflation differentials moved adversely, the contract could potentially lock Kilgore into a long-term loss and essentially scuttle any plans to take the company public or to sell it as a going concern. Conversely, if the profitability of the contract could be maintained, it had the potential to significantly alter the profitability of Kilgore and give it the scope and economy of scale necessary to seek out other opportunities and to provide Steve MacLinden with a very attractive valuation for his company.

THE FINANCIAL RISK MANAGEMENT MEETING

To deal with the financial risk arising from the new contract, Cathy and her team had been discussing the issues and ideas for managing them with Steve since the start of negotiations with the Japanese manufacturer. Everyone recognized the central importance of getting the risk management strategy right, even if the nuanced details of how to hedge created a series of quandaries. That led to Steve bringing in Rory and Casey to apply a fresh perspective to the problem. However, they proved to be of limited help, and Cathy thought they made the discussion regress with their questions about how the various hedging products worked.

Up until now, Kilgore did not have to concern itself much with currency hedging. With sales and expenses almost exclusively in Canadian dollars, there was little need for it. Likewise, the low Canadian dollar from the mid-1990s through 2004 had meant that the threat of U.S.-based suppliers entering the Canadian OEM market was minimal. That all changed of course with the new contract and with the Canadian dollar close to par with the U.S. dollar.

Cathy and her team had been discussing the various issues and how best to handle them for a couple of weeks, but in the process they were generating more questions than answers. That had precipitated the meeting with the management team that had begun two hours before. Steve was a little lost, and frankly intimidated by the choices that Cathy and her team had put forward. While conceptually Steve understood options, forwards, and swaps, the details and the implications of using the different contracts were confusing to him. Deep down he liked making things and selling things, and preferred to leave the finer financial details to others.

Casey, the sales manager, for the most part stayed out of the discussion. He felt that currency risk was something that was beyond both his control and his area of expertise. However, he did appreciate how a sound hedging strategy could give him an edge in negotiating new sales contracts with other foreign customers.

Rory, however, pounced on the opportunity to give his opinion about a hedging strategy. He liked the certainty of cost projections and believed that entering into long-term swap contracts would be best. He particularly favored doing a currency swap, which would allow Kilgore to fix the exchange rate at which it would exchange a set amount of U.S. dollars for Canadian dollars throughout the period of the contract. Cathy, however, was concerned that it could lock them in too much and potentially eliminate the opportunity for bigger upside profits. Casey at this point wondered aloud if it was possible to just hedge 50 percent of the size of the contract: "That way we will be right on at least half of the hedge." Cathy just glared at him for that comment, and thus Casey remained quiet thereafter.

There was also the issue of how to structure a swap to account for the embedded options in the manufacturing contract. If the options in the manufacturing contract were exercised by the customer, a standard swap could leave Kilgore exposed at unfavorable rates. Conversely, if Kilgore entered into swaps expecting the contract options to be exercised and they weren't, then it exposed Kilgore to being overhedged.

While he didn't fully appreciate all the nuances, Steve did recognize that they could be at a significant disadvantage on new contracts to U.S. competitors (and even Asian competitors) if the Canadian dollar appreciated in the long term and they were locked into a long-term currency swap agreement. This could dramatically affect the value of any exit strategy he might choose.

Cathy explained that an alternative to a swap would be to use short-term forward contracts. These would have to be rolled over on a frequent basis due to their shorter term; however, they would provide more flexibility and would not lock in Kilgore for more than a year, or even less if shorter-term contracts were utilized. However, this created a new form of uncertainty as rates on forwards several years into the contract would be unknown, and thus Kilgore could be locking in at either more advantageous or more disadvantageous rates in future hedges. There was also the concern that doing forwards or swaps would use up Kilgore's borrowing capacity at the bank. Having financial flexibility and borrowing capacity would be crucial until Kilgore got a handle on the cash flow implications. For this reason Cathy and her team explored the use of currency futures contracts. While these contracts had the advantage of being exchange traded, the maintenance of margin requirements would be another issue for Cathy's team to manage, to say nothing of the potential short-term implications of margin calls on cash flow concerns.

A third alternative was to use currency options. The advantage of options is that they would provide the most flexibility and would permit Kilgore to have windfall gains from advantageous movements in the Canadian dollar. This advantage, however, was offset by the fact that options incur an up-front cost—a cost that Rory argued would eat into the profitability of the contract. Belinda, a member of Cathy's team, had made some initial inquiries with Kilgore's bankers and calculated that the cost of three-month currency put options on the U.S. dollar would be approximately 1.3 percent of the notional amount of the contract.

A host of other issues remained to be examined as well. There were several operational issues such as who would be responsible for managing the hedges and choosing counterparties. There was also an issue of how any financial risk would be accounted for in the company's slowly developing commitment to an enterprise risk management framework.

It was near the end of the meeting when Steve asked if it was reasonable to not hedge at all and just "hope for the best." "After all," he added, "if things work out as they have been going, the contract should be quite profitable as it is. Why mess with something until it is broken?" That comment led to Cathy emphatically stating that "Hope is not a risk strategy!"

Therefore, there was a multitude of issues. The main concerns from Cathy's point of view were: (1) what products should be used to hedge the exchange rate risk, (2) whether the company should hedge the full exposure, (3) who should make the hedging decisions and take ultimate responsibility for them, (4) whether the company should use exchange-traded products or over-the-counter bank products, (5) how they should take into account the embedded options in the contract, and (6) how they should assess the effectiveness of the hedging that they were doing—what reports would they need to produce, and how would the analysis fit into an ERM framework? Cathy suspected that there were other issues, but these seemed to be the main issues that the discussions seemed to be coming back to.

Leaving the meeting, Cathy knew there were more loose ends than solutions. She needed to build a financial risk management process that was effective, easy to operate, and easy for everyone to understand. It also had to see the company through to the conclusion of the contract and any other long-term plans that Steve had for the company, and for himself. There was a lot riding on this, both for the company and for her career.

QUESTIONS

1. Assume that the management team has hired you to advise them on their overall risk profile and has asked you to prepare a SWOT analysis for their review and as input to the upcoming strategic planning session. What would you put into your analysis? Additionally, how does your analysis affect the risk management strategies that Kilgore might choose to utilize?

2. What are the main financial risk management issues that Cathy and the rest of the management team at Kilgore need to focus on?

3. What kind of a financial risk management strategy would you create to solve those issues?

4. What are the major opportunities and downside risks with the hedging framework that you suggest?
5. Besides hedging the Japanese manufacturer contract, how else might Kilgore effectively use financial risk management?
6. What factors need to be considered when integrating financial risk management into an enterprise risk management framework?

ABOUT THE CONTRIBUTORS

Rick Nason, PhD, CFA, has an extensive background in the capital markets and derivatives industry, having worked in equity derivatives and exotics, credit derivatives, and capital markets training in a senior capacity at several different global financial institutions. Rick is a founding partner of RSD Solutions, a risk management consultancy that specializes in financial risk management consulting and training for corporations, investment funds, and banks. Dr. Nason is also an Associate Professor of Finance at Dalhousie University in Halifax, Nova Scotia, where he teaches graduate classes in corporate finance, investments, enterprise risk management, and derivatives. He has been awarded several teaching awards as well as being selected MBA Professor of the Year several times. His research interests are in financial risk management, enterprise risk management, and complexity.

Rick has an MSc in physics from the University of Pittsburgh and an MBA and a PhD in finance from the Richard Ivey Business School at the University of Western Ontario. Additionally, he is a Chartered Financial Analyst charterholder. In his spare time he enjoys practicing risk management principles as he plays with his collection of pinball machines.

Stephen McPhie, CA, in his current position as partner of RSD Solutions Inc., advises businesses internationally on various aspects of financial strategy and risk mitigation. From 2000 to 2004, Stephen worked in London for Italy's largest bank. In the financial engineering group, he successfully created innovative cross-border financing structures that included private equity instruments with embedded derivatives. Previously he structured and distributed primary market debt and traded distressed and near-par debt in secondary markets.

Prior to 2000, Stephen held various positions in the United States, Canada, and the United Kingdom with a "big five" Canadian bank. His experience stretches from structuring and distributing leveraged and investment grade corporate transactions to relationship management, par and distressed secondary market trading, structured credit derivative products, workouts and credit and financial mandates, structuring and negotiating transactions (including leveraged, project finance, recapitalization of distressed situations, etc.), as well as negotiating complex legal documentation.

Stephen holds a BA in economics from Heriot-Watt University in Edinburgh, Scotland, and has qualified as a Chartered Accountant in both the United Kingdom and Canada. In this respect he worked for one of the large accounting firms carrying out assignments in the fields of audit, consultancy (including business valuations), and taxation.

CHAPTER 20

Implementing Risk Management within Middle Eastern Oil and Gas Companies

ALEXANDER LARSEN
Fellow, Institute of Risk Management (FIRM) and Honors Degree in Risk Management, Caledonian University, Glasgow, Scotland

T his case study is based on real-life examples of Middle Eastern oil and gas companies where risk management has been put into place. The case study is a consolidation of the various approaches and captures the challenges of implementing risk management in the Middle East. For the purposes of this case study, the name MECO has been chosen to represent the numerous companies used to gather this data. Risk management has not yet been fully implemented in any of these companies, and they have had varying degrees of success. This case study is by no means intended to present a successful risk management implementation or best practices. Instead, it is meant to show the challenges in implementing and sustaining a successful program and the types of things that can lead to a breakdown of risk management.

COMPANY BACKGROUND

MECO is a national oil company established in 1940 when a Middle Eastern government granted a concession to a Western company in preference to a rival bid from a variety of Middle Eastern oil companies. It is among the world's most valuable companies, with an estimated value of $5 trillion to $10 trillion (U.S. dollars). MECO has some of the largest proven crude oil reserves, and is one of the largest daily oil producers across more than 100 oil and gas fields in the Middle East.

Currently, MECO has an exclusive right to explore in key countries across the Middle East, although there has recently been a huge interest in entry to the countries by large international oil companies (IOCs). This interest comes despite the political unrest across the region and the constant threat of wars. Additionally, while in the past there has been little threat of IOCs receiving rights to explore, recently there has been pressure on MECO to improve efficiency, as it lags significantly behind the IOCs.

Despite having exclusive rights, there is also the concern about diminishing reserves, and therefore a key focus for the organization is exploration and finding new oil fields. This, alongside its strategic decision to expand through new ventures, from partnering with international oil companies to acquiring foreign companies, means that the organization is in a major state of change.

Being a government-run organization, one of its key objectives is to provide energy to the populations of the countries in which it operates. This is provided at no profit. Recently, there has been a boom in population alongside an increase in car ownership and country expansion plans, which have pushed MECO's profits down. The more oil required to be delivered to the countries it operates in, the less oil there is to sell. This is another reason for the decision to expand and explore.

ORGANIZATION CULTURE

The culture of MECO is very much driven by its geography, history, and employees. Like many organizations in the region, being essentially a public-sector company, it is a large employer of Middle Eastern nationals while also relying heavily on a large expat population of which the majority are Westerners.[1] This goes back to the organization's origins of being a Western company in the 1940s.

The company provides highly secure and lucrative employment in which benefits are vast, and most expats stay until retirement. It is not unusual to meet expats who have been with the company for decades. The same goes for the local Middle Eastern employees, who have often been educated by MECO and have continued their careers within the organization, never having experienced working anywhere other than at MECO.

In terms of career progression, it is very much judged on age and years at the company as opposed to merit, while the majority of very senior positions go to local Middle Eastern employees.

There is an aging workforce, with most employees having been with the company for over 20 years and being reluctant to change. Their view tends to be: "We have made a profit for 70 years, so why do we need risk management?" Due to a number of reasons during the late 1990s and early 2000s, including an oil price crash and regional instability due to the war in Iraq, MECO went through a period of being unable to recruit, and as a result, the organization now has an employee demographic of many young local workers and aging expat workers, with little in between. Due to the highly secure employment environment, there is often a lack of drive, innovation, and progress in terms of career development, and this can lead to serious change management issues.

LOCAL CULTURE

From a local culture perspective, not wanting to lose face is often an issue that comes up, and very often admitting to having risks in your workplace is considered a failure to do your job successfully. This being the case, it is not unusual to find that certain parts of the organization like to portray themselves as having no risks.

Another key factor tends to be the fact that nobody wants to be the bearer of bad news, which goes back to losing face. There have been instances where people turned up for a meeting but key individuals ended up not attending. No advanced warning was given by these key individuals, as it would have required them to "reject" the invitation, which is seen as negative.

Local culture is also very tribal, with a director having varying degrees of respect from employees or other directors based on their family ties. This can be a key area of opportunity for a risk management team trying to get buy-in for risk management if the team can capture the attention of the right directors. Tribalism also translates very often into the supply chain, where much of the supply chain is made up of regional players. While this can be advantageous in terms of having a good relationship with suppliers and allowing organizations to know who they are dealing with, it also opens up a huge risk of potential fraud.

There have been a few cases of fraud in Iraq and Kuwait that involved theft of oil through supply chains/relationships, or sabotage of foreign diesel shipments being delivered to project sites in order to ensure that organizations could get diesel only from local tribes.

It is important also to note that culturally, things move slowly and there is rarely a sense of urgency in getting work done; the locals prefer to put family, customs, and traditions first. What might seem like straightforward contract negotiations to more Western cultures will end up in long discussions and negotiations on various minor points of a deal over several long meetings. While this may seem counterproductive and unacceptable in Western organizations, it plays a key part in building up trust among business partners and allows for more flexibility and easier negotiations during later stages of a deal.

MECO STRUCTURE

The structure of MECO includes five business lines with about five administrative areas in each. Each administrative area then has divisions, and within these are departments.

For example, there may be an Operational Services business line that has Industrial Services as an administrative area. Within Industrial Services there may be a Marine division and an Aviation division, which both have fleets of either ships or airplanes being managed by various departments within their respective divisions. This provides an indication of the potential size in these divisions. For example, the Marine division and Aviation division are the size of some small to medium-sized companies that are in existence today.

MECO RISK MANAGEMENT BACKGROUND

Early in 2006, after concluding a study on enterprise risk management (ERM), the Management Committee requested that the ERM team pursue formal project risk management (PRM) as a pilot under the ERM effort within the project management department. Scoping of the pilot began in late 2006 with pilot completion in March 2008. Since 2006, the ERM team has also been following up with other parts of the organization, such as information technology (IT) on its development and implementation of risk management within its organization.

Both project management and IT put together policy and procedure documentation, which was signed off by their division heads, as well as setting up project teams within their departments. These teams included a full-time member and a few part-time members. Within both departments, a Risk Committee was set up that consisted of members from the division as well as department heads whose responsibility would be to escalate those risks that were deemed to be outside their control and to ensure that existing risks were being managed.

In both instances, the project teams eventually transitioned into risk management functions within each department and have now started looking at other aspects of risk such as business continuity and quantitative risk analysis.

The successful implementation of risk management within the project management and IT departments, which was reported in 2009, went a long way to convince the Management Committee to implement a companywide approach to ERM. This companywide approach would mirror the approaches taken in the two departments. In 2009, the CEO, after announcing himself as chief risk officer, instructed Internal Audit to champion ERM with the specific remit of identifying the company's top risks from a bottom-up approach but without the use of consultants.[2] Once work had been completed, it was expected that the risk management project team would come back to the Management Committee to report what the top 10 risks were.

In early 2010, Internal Audit put together an ERM project team made up of one full-time member and four part-time members (all with the title "auditor"). By the end of 2011, they had recruited a second full-time member, also under the title "auditor," while the part-time members ceased to work with the team.[3]

The team was tasked with identifying the top risks facing the company from a bottom-up approach. The project leader did acknowledge that there should be some sort of framework in place and, despite not being part of the remit, he asked the team to consider a Risk Framework that could be suggested briefly to the Management Committee at the same time as the presentation of the top 10 risks. Assuming Management Committee agreement, this Risk Framework could then be implemented at a later date as part of a second phase.

It is important to note that in the Middle East it is commonplace to see risk management sitting within Internal Audit. This is mainly due to Internal Audit being among the first to be exposed to the concept of risk management as well as the fact that the major auditing firms see risk as a way to secure more business with their clients and will sell risk management as an auditing function. Approaches that would be frowned upon by these firms in Europe, Asia, or North America are widely accepted in the Middle East. This is also a major topic of argument between risk managers and auditing firms at ERM conferences across the region.

RISK MANAGEMENT PRACTICES WITHIN MECO

Information Technology

The risk management program has been in place for the past four years and has been driven by the vice president, who heads up Administrative Area 3 (see Exhibit 20.1) and sees the value in risk management. Each IT department identifies risk, and this forms part of the IT division's risk register. This is then reported up to the administrative area through the IT Risk Committee and eventually to the vice president. This is the most advanced administrative area in MECO with regard to risk

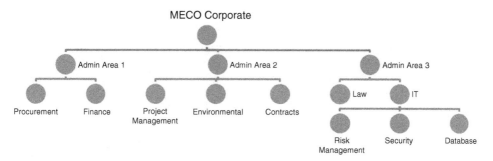

Exhibit 20.1 MECO Corporate Organization Chart

management; it has been improving its risk management capabilities consistently over the years, and continues to make improvements to the program.

Other divisions within Administrative Area 3, such as Law, have not yet started a risk management program. However, due to the success of IT's risk management, the vice president has requested that other divisions take a lead from IT. IT will then work as consultants alongside the risk management project team and will be involved in setting it up throughout the administrative area.

IT has a Steering Committee, which oversees the risk to the division and escalates risks where appropriate (e.g., where they have no control of the risk or a decision needs to be made at a higher level). They ensure there is documentation in place as well as appropriate reporting lines.

The biggest risk that IT has is that of a severe cyber attack. Operations are linked to the main servers, which means that if the main IT system is down, that could affect operations, leading to a shutdown of facilities. This risk was identified and IT security was put in force in order to manage this risk. However, despite best efforts, there are about 150 hacking incidents a day, and not all of them are successfully stopped.

IT has 10 dedicated staff members, including their business continuity planning team, which is very strong for a division's risk function and shows the support that the program has within Administrative Area 3. The risk management project team is hopeful that once all divisions within the administrative area have risk management in place, other administrative areas will follow suit and replicate their success.

Project Management

Project management was one of the pilot exercises for ERM within MECO. Risk management was introduced as a requirement for projects within the team, and Activity Risk Holder (ARH) was purchased as a result. ARH is a risk management software tool that allows risks and actions to be captured across an organization and projects.

Risks have been identified and assessed across a large number of projects over the past couple of years, and extensive documentation has been developed to support the process. This has mainly been built, developed, and managed by one project risk manager. This manager has worked hard to build a substantial database of risks that the organization can use as lessons learned for future projects, as well as a decision making support function for project and investment decisions. Unfortunately, due to key elements not being in place, the risk management drive has been lost and the process has essentially been reduced to nothing.

The failures have come as a result of:

- Lack of active management support
- Lack of resourcing
- Lack of corporate Risk Framework that allows key project risks to be escalated
- Lack of key performance indicators (KPIs), risk appetite, or tolerances set at corporate levels

Finance

Finance risk management involves risk financing. Currently, the department identifies risks and assets of an insurable nature and makes sure that all insurances are in place. They have a captive insurance company and manage limits and exposures. There is a desire to be more aligned to an overarching ERM process in which to identify further insurable risks as well as provide support for risk financing needs of the company. The key challenge to making the risk management function more effectively is that there is no risk appetite or tolerance set at a corporate level.

Environmental Protection Department

Environmental protection plays a key part in managing risk within the organization. It is divided into three main functions:

1. Environmental
2. Occupational health
3. Community health

Environmental protection deals with ensuring compliance to regulations, improving performance, and exceeding standards. Using a cradle-to-grave approach, it is involved at the start of projects or any potential use of new land. It has already been involved in moving the physical sites of major projects due to environmental issues. Environmental protection looks at site selection and considers wastewater, offshore versus onshore, emissions, and so on. It focuses on audit and monitoring.

If there is a need or a focus on, for example, old infrastructure, then it will identify project management as a key stakeholder and involve that department for certain improvements. This is reported into the environmental master plan, which covers these specific issues and has assigned budgets. Any gaps that need to be filled will be undertaken within this instrument.

Environmental protection monitors oil spills, and any oil spill is considered unacceptable. An oil spill is any spill of oil that is not part of normal operations (e.g., sweeping oil off a rig into the ocean is an oil spill).

The department has already identified aging pipelines as the major cause of spills, and all aging pipelines will be replaced. It has independent reporting lines and authority. During a crisis it acts as a resource in an advisory capacity.

Change in regulation is managed through formal channels. MECO acts as an adviser to the ministries nationally for potential regulation, balancing the public's needs with MECO's needs. Environmental protection provides input into all national environmental council suggestions.

Internationally, MECO has full-time employees working with ministries to support them when in meetings at the United Nations and so on. The Ministry of Petroleum usually attends.

Environmental protection uses a 3 × 3 matrix for effort and impact but does not capture risks in a traditional risk register.

Law

The law department currently has 25 or 26 members of staff within MECO. In most other major organizations, however, there can be hundreds of legal staff. There is an employee expansion initiative that will see an increase in legal staff of 50 percent over the next year.

Law gets involved with joint ventures, subsidiaries, government projects, and supporting due diligence. It plays a key part in contracts, as all contracts must be signed off by the law department.

The key functions are:

- Reviewing of contracts
- Setting up of contracts for joint ventures and so on
- In-country litigation and claims
- Out-of-country litigation and claims
- Antitrust (price fixing, etc.)
- Contract disputes
- Medical malpractice
- Tax and regulation
- Captives management
- Conflicts of interest/business ethics
- Patent filing and prosecution, mainly in the United States
- Boundary issues
- Mergers and acquisitions
- Aviation
- Corporate secretarial support for board, joint ventures, and so on

CORPORATE RISK EXERCISE

Risk Management Information Gathering Exercise (January 2010 to June 2011)

MECO undertook an extensive risk management information gathering exercise in order to provide the Management Committee with the key corporate risks. The risk management team had requested a workshop approach to the meeting in order to share the risks and get involvement from the Management Committee. However, this was rejected and a one-hour presentation was scheduled instead.

The ERM team met with the administrative areas' representatives. The team:

- Went over the history of ERM and outlined the purpose and key definitions
- Clarified the data collection form
- Consolidated this input to business line level, as appropriate, once input was received from all administrative areas and their divisions

The team had further discussion with compliance functions and key organizations. This step was necessary to help consolidate and prioritize business line risks to arrive at corporate-level risks. The team also integrated corporate planning input, which included particulars of internal and external risks as well as risks gathered from various publications. All this information made up the content of the Corporate Risk Register, which was used to derive MECO's risk profile.

The template used can be seen in Exhibit 20.2.

This is the template that was designed to collect the administrative area's and its divisions' risks. To ensure consistency of understanding, the team clarified each data entry column in a two-page document.

The key was to have the administrative area provide a risk number and a risk description; probability (in percentage terms); a source of the risk (internal, external, or shared); whether or not controls exist, and how effective these are (highly, partially, barely); and the risk priority (listing from 1 being the top risk, followed by 2, 3, and 4 for subsequent risks).

Exhibit 20.3 provides an example of the information received by the ERM team from the business.

In this example, the risk, its cause, and its impact are all clear. Using the risk description and data in the remaining columns, the team analyzed the data in such a way that it helped them consolidate and prioritize the risks, to arrive at the relevant business line level and later at corporate level.

Consolidation

Receiving more than 400 risks from the administrative areas, consolidation was undertaken at a business line level to arrive at about 100 risks. This list was shared with compliance functions and corporate planning as well as considering various published resources and surveys to come to a final 10 risks. These risks were to be

#	Risk Description	Probability (%)	Source	Controls Exist?	How effective are the Existing Controls?	Risk Priority

	Probability
Issue (already existing)	100%
Probable	>80%
Quite Possible	60–80%
Might Happen	30–50%
Unlikely	10–30%
Almost Impossible	<10%

Exhibit 20.2   MECO Corporate Risk Register Template

#	Risk Description	Probability (%)	Source	Controls Exist?	Effectiveness of Controls	Risk Priority
	Sudden or compounded failure of aging offshore trunk lines can impact meeting field production requirements. Some of the older offshore lines are telescoped and therefore cannot be intelligently scraped to detect actual condition and justify replacement.	>80	Internal + Between Orgs.	Y	Barely effective	1

Exhibit 20.3   Example of Risk Information Reviewed by the ERM Team

presented to the Management Committee in an hour-long presentation for consideration and confirmation as being the company's top risks. The approach can be seen in Exhibit 20.4.

Risk Framework

While the top risks had been collected, consolidated, and reviewed by 2011, work also began in early 2011 to put together a proposed Risk Framework. This had not been part of the team's initial remit; however, it was felt that having a one-hour presentation with the Management Committee was too good an opportunity to pass up. By presenting this element to the Management Committee alongside the top risks as a way to ensure that an ongoing process of identifying risks was in place, this would add value to the presentation.

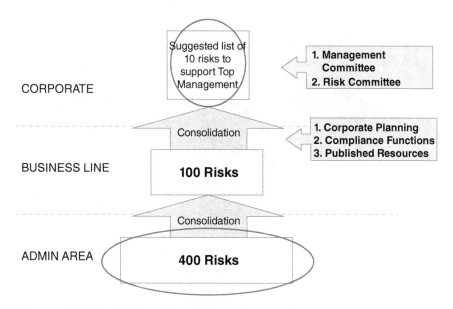

Exhibit 20.4   Risk Analysis and Consolidation Approach

Risk Management Approach

The risk management approach that the risk management project team put together considered such things as which standards to adopt and how risk management would flow through the organization (ISO 31000 was the eventual decision due to the high regard for ISO in the Gulf region, which would support implementation of risk management in the long run).

The key documents that were drafted were risk policy, Risk Committee, risk maturity model, risk procedure, risk training material, and risk maturity matrix.

Risk Policy

The risk policy included key sections such as:

- Background and purpose
- Objectives
- Scope
- Definitions
- Policy statement
- Risk philosophy

A traffic light system had essentially been suggested within the framework in the form of a 5 × 5 risk matrix that would help identify the organization's key risks. The matrix is shaded to indicate high, medium, and low importance. See Exhibit 20.5 for the risk matrix. Although this is a good system to use, the organization's risk tolerance and appetite had not been reviewed or set.

In order to set a risk tolerance, there needs to be a top-level decision as to what should be managed and what should not. Some interviews and a short workshop to assess and set the risk appetite and various tolerance levels were therefore discussed among the risk project team, which led into further discussions relating to having a Risk Committee.

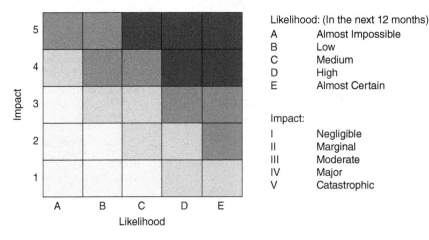

Likelihood: (In the next 12 months)

A   Almost Impossible
B   Low
C   Medium
D   High
E   Almost Certain

Impact:

I   Negligible
II   Marginal
III   Moderate
IV   Major
V   Catastrophic

Exhibit 20.5   Risk Matrix

Internal Audit had already noted to the Management Committee in previous meetings that it was difficult to meet with the Management Committee and that in order to implement risk management the team would need access to an over-arching body that could make decisions on behalf of the Management Committee. The risk management team could then, along with a Risk Committee, set the tolerance level for the organization as well as approve and make changes to any risk documentation that was being developed.

While other more scientific methods of setting a risk tolerance and appetite were available, they would have required more time and the use of consultants, which had already been ruled out by the Management Committee.

Risk Committee

The risk management team was keen to establish a Risk Committee. The team understood the importance of the Risk Committee in supporting the implementation of the Risk Framework should the Management Committee agree to implement it.

The Risk Committee would be the link between the corporate risk register and the business lines and would act as a filter for the Management Committee. Risks from the business line risk registers could feed into the Risk Committee for consideration toward the corporate risk register. Equally, any major project risks or joint venture (JV)/partner risks could feed through the Risk Committee, too.

Risk Maturity

The team agreed that in order to progress with risk management, consideration needed to be given as to where they were now and where they wanted to be in terms of risk maturity. Additional work was therefore undertaken to create a risk maturity model specific to MECO, which can be seen in Exhibit 20.6.

Risk Procedure

The risk procedure essentially expanded on the risk policy and gave a much more detailed account of the process of risk management, such as the traffic light system mentioned earlier in Exhibit 20.5, which was called a risk matrix.

The procedure also came with attachments such as: reporting structure, Risk Committee charter, assessment criteria (which expanded upon the 5 × 5 matrix and quantified it to an extent), example risk register, and example action plan.

Risk Training Material

The risk management team had been providing various training to the organization for some time, and it was agreed that something more formal should be put in place. First, training presentations were gathered from around MECO and consolidated into one agreed training presentation. Second, the team started the process of making it align with the Institute of Risk Management (IRM), which has a strong presence in the region as well as in Europe. The idea was to create training that would provide delegates with a certificate of attendance from the IRM to make it more attractive and beneficial. There were also tiers of training to be provided depending on the audience (managers, general staff, project managers, and risk coordinators).

Requirements to Meet Various Levels of Maturity

	Level 1: Undeveloped	Level 2: Formalized	Level 3: Established	Level 4: Embedded	Level 5: Optimized
Maturity Level Definitions	No structured approach for identifying and managing risks.	Policies and processes being established.	RM is implemented into routine business processes.	A proactive approach to the management of risks exists at all levels of the operating company.	Continuous improvement and full range and cycle of program activities being accomplished.
Risk Management Element		To become "Formalized," the following must be achieved:	To become "Established," the following must be achieved:	To become "Embedded," the following must be achieved:	To become "Optimized," the following must be achieved:
Governance and Infrastructure	1.1.1 A Risk Management Plan does not exist for the organization/project. 1.1.2 Responsibility for risk management (RM) has not been established. 1.1.3 No provision for RM activity in the budget. 1.1.4 No review of the effectiveness of any RM activity. 1.1.5 No improvement process for RM. 1.1.6 No Risk Policy in place which is signed and approved by Management Committee (MC).	2.1.1 Risk reviews are scheduled for each business line. 2.1.2 Accountability and authority for RM is formalized. 2.1.3 Benefits of RM have been communicated by EBOD. 2.1.4 An ERM department has been established. Roles and responsibilities are clear with specific areas of responsibilities assigned (i.e., Business Continuity, Joint Ventures, Operations). Some overlapping and shared responsibilities are made clear (i.e., Corporate Risk Register information gathering and consolidation, etc.).	3.1.1 Documented methodology for RM within Admin Area plans and activity in place. 3.1.2 The benefits of RM have been communicated. 3.1.3 A risk committee has been established with a cross organizational remit. 3.1.4 Risk coordinators have the skills, training, and resources to deliver on RM expectations. 3.1.5 MC formally receives updates on RM effectiveness. 3.1.6 RM aligned and coordinated with related areas of activity (e.g., HSSE, insurance, crisis management, key projects, etc.). 3.1.7 Risk Management Information System (RMIS) that allows consolidation and interrogation of risks across the organization in place.	4.1.1 The RM and Policies and Procedures conform with and are referenced by other local management processes, for example, a Project Management Plan. 4.1.2 A formal RM analysis is required on all projects/organizations as part of the initial estimation/approval process. 4.1.3 The RM process is fully integrated with all business processes, for example, Strategic Planning (business plan) and Budgeting. 4.1.4 MC & RM committee receive formal annual reports on the effectiveness of the RM framework, usually delivered by Internal Audit or a third party. This is based on set review criteria aligned to the RM policy and RM plan. 4.1.5 Risk Department has independent reporting lines. 4.1.6 Formal RM information system in place, which stores RM data centrally, used to develop shared risk and control.	5.1.1 Risk information forms a key input to decision-making processes and capital allocation across the Operating Company. 5.1.2 Improvements are formally monitored over time. Where requirements for improvement are identified, these are reported to the Operating Company Executive Management Committee as part of independent assurance activity and monitored. 5.1.3 The risk framework is formally examined in the event of significant change or when a loss occurs.
Identification and Prioritization	1.2.1 Risks are not formally captured across the organization. 1.2.2 Assessment (if performed) may not use a scoring scheme or may use inconsistent variables. 1.2.3 No defined measure of risk appetite.	2.2.1 Alternative methods for risk identification are considered when planning Risk Identification sessions. 2.2.2 The sources of knowledge to be used during risk identification are clearly identified (i.e., lessons learned logs, keywords, hazard identification prompt lists, and external functions/experts). 2.2.3 All business lines have a Risk Register which informs the Corporate Risk Reg ster. 2.2.4 Corporate Risk Register in place.	3.2.1 Risks are categorized. 3.2.2 Risk owners are allocated for each risk. 3.2.4 Risk maps are used to illustrate assessment results. 3.2.5 Risks are centrally consolidated and challenge provided where appropriate. 3.2.6 Emerging risks are formally considered and evaluated. 3.2.7 All Admin Areas have a risk register which informs the Business Line Risk Register. 3.2.8 Risk Appetite is defined.	4.2.1 A team based approach is used to identify risks. 4.2.2 Risk identification exercises conducted outside regular schedule (in event of major changes). 4.2.3 All employees know who to report an emerging risk to, should one become apparent. 4.2.4 Risks are assessed in a quantified approach. 4.2.5 Opportunities are identified as part of the Risk Identification process and the risks of not pursuing opportunities are captured.	5.2.1 A risk assessment process is in place (developed and documented) that considers the relative riskiness of different options when making management decisions. 5.2.2 Risk quantification takes into account the impact on other parts of the organization. 5.2.3 Key risk indicators (KRI) are developed for each risk.

Risk Treatment	1.3.1 Any risk identified is unlikely to have treatment specified, funded or tracked to completion.	2.3.1 All key risks have associated action plans. 2.3.2 Control effectiveness is formally assessed.	3.3.1 Risk Treatment is planned and monitored. 3.3.2 Assessment of effectiveness of proposed treatment is performed for all key risks (e.g., cost-benefit analysis, Delphi style workshop, etc.). 3.3.3 Business Continuity Management implementation in place and working with ERM department.	4.3.1 The project/organization has specific financial provision to cover contingency (fallback) plans and risk treatment strategies. 4.3.2 MC understand contingency (fallback) actions for Key Risks. 4.3.3 The allocation of funds for risk treatment is aligned with management priorities and decisions. 4.3.5 Cross business treatment plans are developed and coordinated where applicable.	5.3.1 An effective "three lines of defense" model is in place and fully integrated with all business processes ensuring that those responsible for taking risk are supported/enabled to manage. 5.3.2 The risk treatment process if fully integrated with the Operating Company's management processes. 5.3.3 The allocation of funds for risk-treatment actions is in alignment with management priorities and decisions.
Reporting and Monitoring	1.4.1 There is no formal process for key risk reviews. 1.4.2 There is no formal risk escalation procedures/ processes in place. 1.4.3 There is no organizational-wide communication on RM.	2.4.1 Business Line Risk Reporting has been established. 2.4.2 The risk register is reviewed and updated in accordance with the RM Policy and Procedure. 2.4.3 There is a formal mechanism for escalating risk. 2.4.4 Each risk treatment action has a target completion date which is actively and routinely tracked. 2.4.5 Those individuals with RM responsibilities are regularly provided with RM communications.	3.4.1 There is a defined process to review and report risk status and KRIs, using standard reports, to key stakeholders up and down the organization. 3.4.2 Risk Dashboards in place. 3.4.3 Regular communication on "risk status" is distributed to key stakeholders and interested parties as defined in the RM Policy and Procedures. 3.4.3 Alignment between RM and internal audit process. 3.4.5 RM process and output informs annual internal audit plan (risk based audit).	4.4.1 RM is a standing agenda item in MC meetings and discussion is documented. 4.4.2 Risks and risk treatment actions are actively and routinely tracked and financial provisioning is adjusted as risks expire. 4.4.3 There is a formal RM communication plan that addresses both internal and external communication requirements. 4.4.4 Regular testing and documentation of crisis management plans aligned to key risks. 4.4.5 Management and the RM committee receive formal annual reports on the effectiveness of the FM framework, usually delivered by Internal Audit or a third party.	5.1.5 The risk monitoring and control system is fully integrated with the Operating Company's control systems, monitoring programs, cost management and time management processes. 5.1.2 Responsibilities for each element of the risk management process have been allocated and integrated into the performance evaluation processes.
Risk Culture	1.5.1 RM training has not been provided to any employee.	2.5.1 RM training is provided to those with responsibility for RM. 2.5.2 RM policies and procedures are formally documented. 2.5.3 RM is owned at entity level.	3.5.1 Tailored RM training is proactively provided to all individuals. 3.5.2 RM guidance (manuals, policies/procedures) readily available to all employees (e.g., intranet).	4.5.1 RM training, relevant to their role, is embedded in the personal development plans of relevant individuals. 4.5.2 RM performance indicators are included in personal goals. 4.5.3 Development of open, challenging, and learning-based risk culture.	5.5.1 The development and setting of business objectives is completely aligned with the application of the RM process. 5.5.2 RM communication is completely integrated with the organization's overall communication plan. 5.5.3 RM communication to external stakeholders is used to instill confidence in the robustness of the organization.

Exhibit 20.6   MECO Risk Maturity Model

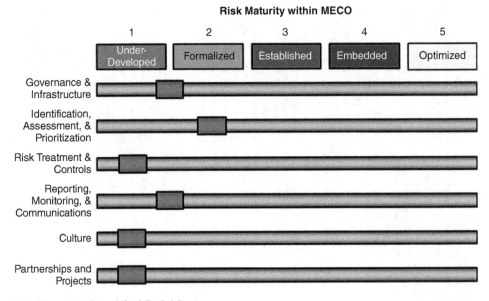

Exhibit 20.7 Simplified Risk Matrix

Risk Maturity Matrix

The risk maturity matrix was to be the key to the future success of risk management implementation. It would provide requirements and a road map to implementing risk management successfully throughout the organization based on the ISO 31000 model. It provided for a five-phase approach with clear and practical requirements to progression that any part of the organization could follow.

Based on the points within the matrix, a self-assessment was carried out in order to map out MECO's current maturity levels. These were presented in a simplified risk matrix in order to present the findings to the Management Committee, which can be found in Exhibit 20.7. The same methodology was used to measure and benchmark what maturity levels other oil and gas organizations had reached. This was mapped in a graphic that would be used to encourage top management to support ERM in order to reach similar maturity levels as competitors. The benchmark can be found in Exhibit 20.8.

Exhibits 20.9, 20.10., 20.11, and 20.12 provide lists of potential corporate risks that have been identified by other companies (Shell and BP) and organizations (E&Y and AON), which apply to the energy and chemical industries.

Management Committee Meeting, December 2011

The risk management team finally presented the top risks to the Management Committee, as well as their suggested way forward, in a one-hour meeting in December 2011. This was almost two years after the request by the Management Committee. As mentioned earlier, the risk management team had requested a workshop approach to the meeting in order to share the risks and get involvement

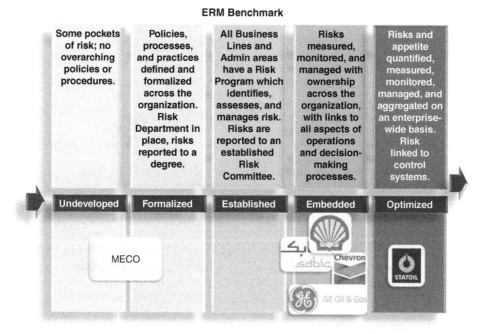

Exhibit 20.8 Maturity Level Benchmark

from the Management Committee. However, this was rejected and a one-hour presentation was scheduled instead.

The reactions were mixed, with many of the Management Committee members dismissing the risks as business issues and others questioning where they had come from (despite having signed off on them following the administrative areas' initial risks being sent to the risk management team).

The CEO remained positive and understood the need for a more corporate discussion around the identified risks. The group listened to the suggested approach and of having a Risk Committee. However, a majority opposed the idea of another

Exhibit 20.9 Benchmarks from AON Survey

1. Economic slowdown
2. Regulatory/Legislative changes
3. Business interruption
4. Commodity price risk
5. Supply chain failure
6. Exchange rate fluctuation
7. Increased competition
8. Failure to innovate
9. Environmental risk
10. Physical damage

Source: AON Global Chemical Business Survey 2011.

Exhibit 20.10   Benchmarks from E&Y Survey

1. Access to reserves (political constraints and competition)
2. Energy policies (regulation)
3. Cost containment
4. Worsening fiscal terms
5. HSE risks
6. Human capital deficit
7. New operational challenges (unfamiliar environments)
8. Climate change concerns
9. Price volatility
10. Competition from new technologies

Source: E&Y Global Oil & Gas Survey 2011.

committee being set up, and it was suggested that the risk management team use the Advisory Committee as a Risk Committee in order to progress their Risk Framework documentation and to review and filter the top risks before another meeting with the Management Committee.

The Advisory Committee is essentially a subcommittee of the Management Committee that vets upcoming agenda items and is made up of some Management Committee members.

Following the conclusion of the meeting, the risk management team was unable to get a time slot to see the Advisory Committee for over four months. Therefore, all documentation remained as drafts, and the risk information started to age with no formal process in place to identify and update risks.

Exhibit 20.11   Benchmarks from BP

1. Gulf of Mexico oil spill's continuing adverse impact on BP
2. The general macroeconomic outlook
3. Renew and reposition of BP portfolio (result of Gulf of Mexico impact on reputation)
4. Crude oil and gas prices' fluctuation
5. Climate change and carbon pricing
6. Sociopolitical risks where BP is operating
7. Competition and the need for continuous innovation
8. Poor investment decisions
9. Reserves replacement—inability to progress upstream in timely manner
10. Liquidity, financial capacity, and financial exposure
11. BP's insurance strategy
12. Ethical misconducts and noncompliance
13. Lack of BP full control over JVs and other contractual arrangements
14. Breach of digital infrastructure security causing serious damage to business operations
15. Ethical misconducts and noncompliance

Source: BP Corporate Risk Register.

Exhibit 20.12 Benchmarks from Shell

1. Change of China leadership
2. Change in the Middle East
3. Government protections in the countries we operate
4. Budget deficit in Europe and the United States
5. Cyber security
6. New product risk/reputation
7. Natural disasters
8. Democracy
9. Acquisitions
10. Divestment
11. Cost reduction/quality
12. Joint ventures
13. Entering in new countries

Source: Shell Corporate Risk Register.

Operational Excellence, June 2012 to December 2012

During the second part of 2012, a major initiative was put in place to implement Operational Excellence within the organization. The risk management team, still waiting for a meeting with the Advisory Committee, identified this as an opportunity to embed risk management without the need for authority or needing to convince each administrative area of the benefits.

Through relationship building and awareness of risk management, the risk management team managed to incorporate risk management into the Operational Excellence plan as being a key enabler. In other words, upon completion of the initiative in late 2013, and in order to meet its aspiration of Operational Excellence, MECO (all business lines and their administrative areas) would be asked to implement all key enablers of Operational Excellence, one of which, as stated, would be risk management. This would be a major initiative and would require a large number of consultants coming in to work on Operational Excellence implementation.

Previously, the risk management team had been seen as a team with a self-serving purpose who were trying to force new processes on the organization. Operational Excellence was therefore a huge opportunity for the risk management team, who hoped they would now be looked upon as a useful resource that would support the organization when it came to having to implement Operational Excellence requirements.

Risk Management Move to Corporate Planning, December 2012 to Present

By December 2012, over a year after the Management Committee meeting where the risk management team was instructed to use the Advisory Committee in order to progress risk management, a meeting had still not been set up. The CEO realized that risk management needed more authority and as a result instructed the Corporate Planning division, which was a major influencer in the organization and had a well-regarded vice president, to set up risk management as a function within that division.

Risk management would now form a part of the corporate planning structure with a manager and the two team members from the project team. The management would look to recruit up to three new members to the team, and the team's remit would be to set up an ERM framework, identify the top risks to the company, work on identifying risks to future investments, and form an integral part of the future corporate planning process.

Corporate Planning has a direct line to the CEO and has a large influence within the organization. This helped to ensure that within weeks of creating the function, meetings were set up for February 2013 with the Advisory Committee in order to review and confirm the top risks. Plans were already in place to fast-track the production of the Risk Framework documentation from their draft forms, with the risk management team having the authority to decide much of the approach.

One of the key areas of consideration going forward was implementation of a risk management information system (RMIS), and therefore the risk team started undertaking a RMIS study in order to identify appropriate software for the organization.

Moving the risk management team to an actual department meant that the team members would finally feel part of a real team. They would also have a proper remit and authority to undertake and implement risk management properly, while having much better access to decision-making authorities such as the Advisory Committee. Additionally, the fact that the CEO had made this decision meant that the Advisory Committee would probably fall in line more and support risk management.

Despite these positives, the risk management team would face challenges in terms of meeting the requirements of their remit based on their staffing numbers. Despite aspirations to recruit more members to the team, risk professionals are not easy to come by, and the fact that it takes six months to actually complete the recruiting process means that six months can easily become a year.

By early 2014, MECO was finally able to start filling roles, and it now has a team of 15 risk members at varying levels from analyst and business continuity roles up to manager positions. Another key decision was to allow consultants to support ERM implementation, and invitations to tender have now been sent out for millions of dollars' worth of consultancy business.

CONCLUSION

Risk management in MECO was a lengthy, drawn-out process for a number of reasons. The key reasons for the long process were a lack of a clearly defined scope, lack of authority, staffing limitations, slow corporate culture, and resistance to change. Risk management, had it been approached correctly, could have been successful much earlier. This is reflected in the IT and Project Management examples whereby success was dependent on staffing and buy-in from the top. Management needs to understand the benefits and be seen to support the process.

Within an organization such as MECO, support from the top is vital. Having a framework in place that was bought into by the CEO would have likely increased the chances of success. Additionally, the poor placement of the risk management team was another hindrance. This is all too often the case with risk management not being established as a department from the outset. Few risk professionals will be happy joining a newly formed risk management team or department that doesn't sit within a relevant and powerful division or have independent reporting lines.

Within MECO, the organization was asked to identify risk without having undertaken training, without a consistent framework or procedure to follow. Also the survey was not scientific in its approach.

Despite the positive move to the Corporate Planning division, the risk management team lost a staff member, who it took a year to replace. This has meant that many of the objectives set out for the team were not met and the organization had started losing faith in the department, setting it back yet again. This makes it a challenge for the newly established team of 15 to regain buy-in from lower levels of the organization despite finally getting support from top levels.

QUESTIONS

1. Prior to the Risk Management Information Gathering Exercise discussed earlier in the case, consider the challenges of the newly formed project team in undertaking Risk Management in such a situation.
2. (a) Discuss the challenges and how each of the departments might interact with and support Risk Management across the organization.
   (b) What are the major differences between IT and Project Management, considering they were both part of the initial Risk Management pilot? How might they have overcome this?
3. (a) What do you think were the major positives of the approach undertaken with regard to the risk management information gathering exercise?
   (b) What do you think were the challenges and pitfalls of gathering data in the way that they did?
4. What are the key challenges to the risk framework and risk approach proposed in 2011 by the risk management team?
5. Despite Operational Excellence providing the perfect platform to push Risk Management, discuss what the potential pitfalls may be.
6. Using the supporting documentation along with the case study information (Exhibits 20.9, 20.10, 20.11, and 20.12), provide a list of potential corporate risks that might have been identified by the project team.

NOTES

1. The word *expatriate* comes from the Latin words *ex* (i.e., out of) and *patria* (i.e., country or fatherland). An expat (i.e., expatriate) is a person who temporarily or permanently is residing in a country other than that of his or her upbringing.
2. *Remit* means the mandate, task(s), or area of activity officially assigned to an individual or organization.
3. It takes, on average, three to six months to hire a candidate once all interviews and contract negotiations have been undertaken, due to long visa requirement periods.

ABOUT THE CONTRIBUTOR

Alexander Larsen, Fellow, Institute of Risk Management (FIRM), holds a degree in risk management from Glasgow Caledonian University and has more than 10 years of experience within risk management across a wide range of sectors, including oil and gas, construction, utilities, finance, and the public sector. He has considerable expertise in training and working with organizations to develop, enhance, and embed their enterprise risk management (ERM), business continuity management (BCM), and partnership management processes.

Alexander spent the first half of his career in the United Kingdom working in senior risk consultancy roles with Marsh and Zurich before leaving to join Det Norske Veritas (DNV) in Malaysia and the United Arab Emirates with responsibility of developing their risk management services for the energy sector in the Middle East and Asia.

Since leaving DNV he has worked in the Middle East in a variety of roles. Prior to joining Lukoil, where he is currently Risk Manager for the West Qurna 2 Asset in Iraq, Alexander worked with a number of oil and gas companies, developing and implementing ERM frameworks and business continuity management within the Qatar Foundation.

CHAPTER 21

The Role of Root Cause Analysis in Public Safety ERM Programs

ANDREW BENT
Risk Manager

T his chapter provides an overview of how root cause analysis (RCA) techniques can be used by public safety and law enforcement agencies to support their enterprise risk management (ERM) programs. It provides an introduction to several of the more commonly used tools, and uses a series of case studies to illustrate how these can be applied in the public safety environment.

POLICING AND RISK

Public safety agencies (such as local police departments) have a long tradition of operational risk management—after all, almost everything they do has an enhanced level of risk associated with it. Police officers respond to situations where emotions are often running high, and where the threat of physical violence is never far from the surface. It is perhaps not surprising that conversations around risk often gravitate toward issues of officer and public safety, and rarely toward more mundane issues of business process or budget risk.[1]

In many ways, ERM is a natural fit for public safety agencies due to their risk-aware culture. One of the largest challenges in adopting ERM within a law enforcement agency is the need to redirect police officers' natural inclination to immediately solve the risk, rather than methodically analyzing it to understand its true nature. This is perhaps not surprising given the way most police officers are trained: observe a problem, evaluate the options, and then apply the best solution as rapidly as possible. Root cause analysis is one of the tools that can be used to overcome this hurdle, and it provides a means for law enforcement agencies to achieve even greater social returns on investment than would be otherwise possible.

Getting to the Root of the Problem

Root cause analysis has often been viewed as a tool best applied following significant or serious losses; it is typically applied to understand why risk events occurred, and to provide insight into future preventive actions. More recently, ERM practitioners have begun to recognize the value of using root cause analysis (RCA) tools and techniques as part of a proactive risk management approach. By understanding the root causes of their potential risks, organizations are better able to build strategies and plans that proactively address these risks and support the planned exploitation of opportunities.

Root cause analysis defines a loosely grouped collection of analytical tools, many of which have evolved from the fields of process safety and engineering. While the majority of these tools have traditionally been used to evaluate postevent losses, in many cases they are also capable of supporting proactive future risk planning. Both contexts will be discussed here in terms of how they can be used to support an enterprise risk management program, with the key being to remember that many of the approaches can be used in both reactive and proactive modes. Common RCA Tools lists 10 of the more common RCA tools in everyday use, with the first six of these discussed in the order they are listed.

Common RCA Tools

- Five whys analysis
- Cause and effect (Ishikawa) analysis
- Failure mode, effects, and criticality analysis (FMECA)
- Force field analysis
- Influence diagrams
- Concept fans
- Hazard and interoperability studies (HAZOP)
- Solution effects analysis
- Life cycle value analysis
- Hazard identification/environmental identification (HAZID/ENVID)

FIVE WHYS ANALYSIS

If you have spent any period of time around small children (generally those between the ages of three and eight years old), it is almost impossible to avoid the "why" game. The game starts with the child asking why something happened (or why the child isn't allowed to do something)—and is rapidly followed up by a barrage of further "why" questions until either the child's curiosity is satisfied or the exasperated adult gives up and throws out the infamous "Because I said so" answer so well known to most parents.

What is really happening during this game is that the child is employing one of the most effective and straightforward techniques available to gain meaningful insights into compounded situations. The asking of successive "why" questions enables the child to go beyond a simple sequential understanding of the situation, and develop a cause-and-effect-based understanding of how the situation got to its end point in the manner that it did.

To understand the effectiveness of this approach, consider the not-so uncommon policing situation related in Five Whys Analysis.

Five Whys Analysis

A police officer is dispatched to a disturbance outside a bar. On arrival, the officer discovers two males being restrained by security, and clear signs of a recent fight between the two men. The officer asks one of the men the following series of "why" questions:

Police Officer (PO):	"Why were you guys fighting?"
Subject:	"Because he called me [insert descriptive word]."
PO:	"Why did he call you that?"
Subject:	"Because I spilled a drink on him as I walked past."
PO:	"Why did you spill the drink on him?"
Subject:	"Because I tripped over his girlfriend's handbag that was sitting on the floor."
PO:	"Why did you not see the bag?"
Subject:	"Well, I … may have had a few drinks tonight … I guess."
PO:	"Why were you out drinking tonight?"
Subject:	"Well, um, I had a fight with my girlfriend at home so I decided to go drown my sorrows."

By asking a series of "why" questions, the officer is better able to understand what actually caused the fight to occur (the individual being emotionally distressed over the fight with his girlfriend), rather than the superficial reason (he got called a name because he spilled a drink—not an uncommon event in a busy bar). This would enable the officer to make better choices about how to deal with the situation, including deciding the level of intervention that is actually required. It could also provide insight into the individual's intent—a crucial element in successfully prosecuting many criminal code offenses.

While the technique is referred to as "five whys," there is no reason to deliberately extend (or restrict) the process to five questions. When there is no further viable answer to why an event occurred, it is likely that the root cause has been reached—irrespective of whether this takes three or 23 questions.

The Five Whys technique does have some limitations on its use. It is most useful in relatively simple situations that have a single, unbranched chain of events. If there are multiple possible "whys" identified at any level of the questioning process, it may be more useful to adopt one of the other techniques outlined next, to ensure that all the possible event chains are adequately captured and evaluated. It can also be highly subjective, and is typically restricted to the information known by (or available to) the questioner at the time. Consequently, the use of small groups that have a diversity of perspectives on the issue at hand can be helpful to overcome any inherent bias that individual participants may bring.

CAUSE AND EFFECT ANALYSIS[2]

The cause and effect analysis technique is applied by first identifying the issue or problem to be addressed, and writing it in a box on the right-hand side of the diagram. A series of branching lines are then drawn off a central line connected to this problem box. Each branching line is then headed by a single source type that represents a major source or cause of risk relevant to the problem. Commonly used source types include:

- Equipment—The role of equipment (general or specialized) on the problem, including the lack of equipment, as it impacts the problem
- Environment—The role of the physical or contextual environment as it impacts the problem
- Finance—The role of finance (or lack of finance) as it impacts the problem
- Materials—The role of nonequipment materials (including the lack of materials) on the problem, including the quality of the materials used
- Measurement—The role of data such as performance or quality metrics as they impact the problem, including the ability to identify impacts through the data
- People—The role of people as they impact the problem, including issues such as capacity, capability, and culture
- Process—The role of organizational or individual processes as they impact the problem, including the lack of, or overabundance of, effective processes

Not all problems will include all of these source types, and some problems may be better defined using other major cause headings. Irrespective of this, the purpose is to identify as wide a range of potential sources of risk as possible in order to develop a wide-ranging understanding of the problem. Once the major sources of risk have been identified, it is possible to use techniques such as brainstorming or five whys analysis to identify root causes that contribute to the problem that relate to each of the headings.

Example: Cause and Effect Analysis on Homelessness and the Criminal Justice System

In the North American law enforcement community, homelessness is often a major source of problems. Homeless people tend to be dramatically overrepresented both as victims and as perpetrators of crime. Issues of homelessness are often underscored by health, financial, and environmental conditions that make finding effective solutions a major challenge. Applying a simplistic five whys approach would likely lead to major risk factors being ignored or overlooked, which in turn could lead to the development of ineffective or inefficient solutions.

In applying the cause and effect analysis approach to this problem, some police agencies have been able to not only define their own role in addressing homelessness, but also better link in with the social and health agencies that have an important role to play in the solution.

Let's consider how a police agency might deal with this problem using the cause and effect approach.

Step 1: Define the Problem

By brainstorming, we might settle on this problem definition, which is presented from the perspective of the police agency: "Homeless individuals are overrepresented as both victims and perpetrators within the criminal justice system."

Step 2: Identify the Major Causes

In considering these issues, we may choose to use the following major headings:

- People—What role do homeless people themselves, and the employees of social and justice agencies, have in the overrepresentation of homeless people in the criminal justice system?
- Process—What processes used by police and justice and social agencies impact (both positively and negatively) the overrepresentation of homeless people in the criminal justice system?
- Measurement—What data do we have available (or is missing) that could help tell us why homeless people are overrepresented in the criminal justice system?
- Materials—What physical resources are available (or are missing) to help address the overrepresentation of homeless people in the criminal justice system?
- Finance—What and how are financial resources used (or could be used) to address the issue of homelessness as it impacts the criminal justice system?

Step 3: Identify the Subcauses of Risk

By brainstorming, followed by the use of a structured five whys approach, we could come up with a diagram that looked a little like Exhibit 21.1.

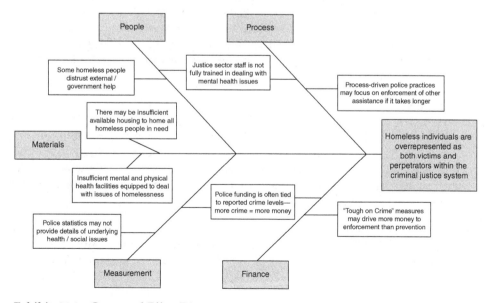

Exhibit 21.1 Cause and Effect Diagram

While this diagram represents a very light touch on the very important issues that impact homelessness, it could be significantly expanded by considering each major source in turn. It is also important to note that some root causes may be driven by two or more factors. In Exhibit 21.3, for example, the way that crime is reported is seen to be intimately tied to how police agencies are funded. Therefore, by changing the method of data collection (perhaps to include prevention metrics), it may be possible to develop a funding model that better reflects the full range of police responsibilities. Understanding not only the risks but also these interconnections is necessary to come up with a truly effective solution.

FAILURE MODE, EFFECTS, AND CRITICALITY ANALYSIS[3]

While failure mode, effects, and criticality analysis (FMECA) was originally developed to consider engineering process risks, it can also be applied to any form of process—even if the process deals exclusively with intangible or people-based risks. Before we consider how to apply this technique to a so-called soft process, it is perhaps most useful to look at an example that comes from a traditional engineering context so that we can understand the analytical process.

FMECA Example 1: Engineering Process[4]

A large milk factory has a unit that is designed to pasteurize milk prior to bottling. Pasteurization is a process that heats milk to a specific temperature (typically 71.7°C/161°F) for a period of approximately 15 to 30 seconds. It is used to reduce the level of contamination from microorganisms that naturally occur in raw milk products. This process enables milk to be stored for a period of several weeks without spoiling if it is adequately refrigerated. The basic process sees raw milk forced between a series of heated plates, with the heat from the plates being transferred into the milk at a specific rate to achieve the desired pasteurization temperature. The plates themselves are heated either by forcing heated water or steam through the interior of the plates, or by running heated liquids through a parallel path that runs counter to the flow of the milk.

Step 1: Identify Failure Modes
The first step is to identify the potential ways that the system could fail. These are typically described very simply by identifying the way that the failure could occur. While this can be done directly, it may also include inputs from other types of analysis, such as HAZOP or fault tree analysis (not discussed in this chapter). For our milk pasteurization example, some of the potential failure modes are identified in the second column of Exhibit 21.2.

Step 2: Identify the Potential Effects
Once we have identified our potential modes of failure, we can identify the effects of those failures. These can be both local failures as well as systemwide impacts. As part of this analysis, we also need to consider the potential causes of the failure. For our milk pasteurization example, we might identify the effects for our failure modes from step 1, as shown in Exhibit 21.3.

Exhibit 21.2 Failure Modes—Example 1

Part: Heat transfer unit

Function: Transfer of heat to milk products in order to achieve pasteurization

Item	Failure Mode	Local Effect	System Effect	Potential Cause	Current Control	O	S	D	RPN	Recommended Action
1	Heating water too cold									
2	Heating water too hot									
3	No heating water flow									
4	Heating water in milk flow									
5	Structural rupture									

Exhibit 21.3 Failure Modes and Effects—Example 1

Part: Heat transfer unit

Function: Transfer of heat to milk products in order to achieve pasteurization

Item	Failure Mode	Local Effect	System Effect	Potential Cause	Current Control	O	S	D	RPN	Recommended Action
1	Heating water too cold	Plates do not get hot enough	Pasteurization is not achieved	Heating unit temperature controls inoperable						
2	Heating water too hot	Plates get too hot	Milk is spoiled when protein is denatured	Heating unit temperature controls inoperable						
3	No heating water flow	Plates do not heat at all	Pasteurization is not achieved	Water pump is inoperable						
4	Heating water in milk flow	Milk flow is contaminated	Milk product has to be dumped	Leak in seals between plates						
5	Structural rupture	Loss of milk product and heating water	Milk product is lost/has to be dumped	Heating plates are not strong enough						

Step 3: Identify the Criticality of the Failure

Once we have identified our potential modes of failure and the effects these might have on our process, we need to consider how critical these effects might be to our objective (in this case, the pasteurization of milk). This step provides us with a good understanding not only of our risks, but also of those risks we may want to address first. To complete this step, we need to consider what existing controls we already have in place, as well as:

- The likelihood of occurrence (O) of the effect
- The severity (S) of the effect if it were to occur
- The probability of detection (D)—how likely we are to know that the effect has occurred

Each of these factors is usually given a score from 1 to 10 (or any other relevant scale), with the higher scores representing greater levels of risk. Once each element is scored, they are summed to produce an overall risk score, which is represented by the risk priority number (RPN). While the absolute number produced is less important than the difference between the numbers for each effect, it can also be a useful way of aligning your risk treatment plan with your organizational risk appetite or tolerance levels. Once the RPN analysis is completed, the final step is to identify what corrective actions you might need to take to address the risk.

For our milk pasteurization example, we might make an assessment based on our failure modes and effects from the first two steps, as shown in Exhibit 21.4.

We can see from our example that if the milk gets too hot the factory will have to dump it as unfit for consumption. We can probably address this risk relatively easily by installing a centrally monitored temperature gauge (rather than relying on periodic physical checks), which will also let us monitor the high temperature condition.

The engineering example has shown how we would apply this technique to a hard or physical process. Now we will look at how we can apply the same technique to a soft process encountered in the law enforcement environment.

FMECA Example 2: Operational Tactics Review Process

Like most organizations, police agencies have a number of predetermined processes that they use regularly to achieve their objectives. Also like most organizations, police agencies need to review their processes periodically to make sure they are still effective. This might occur as part of a regular review cycle, or may be brought about due to the manifestation of a risk that the process was not able to effectively deal with. In this example, we consider the process that an agency uses to deploy its uniformed patrol officers in a geographic area. Many North American police agencies deploy their uniformed officers based on the number of calls for service located in a geographic space (either a neighborhood or a collection of neighborhoods), and use metrics such as the time taken to respond to a call to define how many officers they need to meet these predetermined standards.

Step 1: Identify Failure Modes

For our patrol deployment example, some of the potential failure modes we might see are identified in the second column of Exhibit 21.5.

Exhibit 21.4 Failure Mode, Effects, and Criticality Analysis—Example 1

Part: Heat transfer unit

Function: Transfer of heat to milk products in order to achieve pasteurization

Item	Failure Mode	Local Effect	System Effect	Potential Cause	Current Control	O	S	D	RPN	Recommended Action
1	Heating water too cold	Plates do not get hot enough	Pasteurization is not achieved	Heating unit temperature controls inoperable	Local temperature gauge, monitored hourly	6	6	5	180	Install centrally monitored temperature gauge with low temperature alarm
2	Heating water too hot	Plates get too hot	Milk is spoiled when protein is denatured	Heating unit temperature controls inoperable	Local temperature gauge, monitored hourly	6	8	5	240	Install centrally monitored temperature gauge with high temperature alarm
3	No heating water flow	Plates do not heat at all	Pasteurization is not achieved	Water pump is inoperable	Water pressure gauge mounted to pump	4	6	5	120	Install low flow alarm on inlet pipe from pump to heating unit
4	Heating water in milk flow	Milk flow is contaminated	Milk product has to be dumped	Leak in seals between plates	Physical observation of leakage	3	10	3	90	Institute seal replacement schedule as part of maintenance program
5	Structural rupture	Loss of milk product and heating water	Milk product is lost/has to be dumped	Water and/or milk overpressurized; heating plates are not strong enough	Plates designed to withstand double normal pressures	2	10	8	160	Install pressure sensors and alarms on milk and heating water inlet pipes

Exhibit 21.5 Failure Modes—Example 2

Process: Patrol deployment model

Function: To provide police response to community calls for service in line with community and agency expectations

Item	Failure Mode	Local Effect	System Effect	Potential Cause	Current Control	O	S	D	RPN	Recommended Action
1	Response too slow									
2	Response too fast									
3	No response provided									
4	Wrong response provided									
5	Too much response provided									

Step 2: Identify the Potential Effects
Considering our potential failure modes, we can see that the crux of the issue is going to be matching the expected response (based on community and agency expectations) with the resources required to provide that response. Stepping through our effects analysis, we can identify what the impacts of getting it wrong might look like, as shown in Exhibit 21.6.

Step 3: Identify the Criticality of the Failure
Using the same approach as was outlined in the first example, we need to consider what existing controls we already have in place, as well as:

- The likelihood of occurrence (O) of the effect
- The severity (S) of the effect if it were to occur
- The probability of detection (D)—how likely we are to know that the effect has occurred

To score these elements (and ultimately develop our RPN) we may be able to use existing data sources to determine how often each of the failure modes has occurred in the past. Police agencies tend to keep a range of detailed records on what calls they have dispatched their officers to attend, as well as the time it took for them to arrive and deal with the situation. Where more quantitative data of this type is available, it may be possible to determine very accurately what each level of our O, S, and D scales represents. By applying a consistent approach of this type, it is likely that more confidence would be placed on the results by key decision makers.

For our patrol response example, we might make an assessment based on our failure modes and effects from the first two steps, as shown in Exhibit 21.7.

In this case, we can see how a process can be examined using the FMECA technique, with this analysis used to identify not only how it might perform compared to expectations, but also how any modes of failure errors could be reduced or corrected. Coupling this approach with a technique such as six sigma can be used to drive down the level of errors, as well as increase the overall performance of the process or system.

FORCE FIELD ANALYSIS

A common challenge when dealing with process issues is developing an understanding of how the interplay between factors impacts the overall risk situation. This can be particularly true when dealing with soft processes where human emotions, insecurities, judgments, and interests play a prominent role in determining the success or failure of an initiative.

Force field analysis is a technique used to identify those forces (or factors) that tend to support the status quo (which are known as restraining forces) as well as those forces that tend to support movement away from the status quo (which are known as driving forces). This approach can be used both to analyze those instances where you want to retain the status quo, as well as to provide insights into how you can deliberately move away from the status quo by manipulating either the restraining or the driving forces.

Exhibit 21.6 Failure Modes and Effects—Example 2

Process: Patrol deployment model										
Function: To provide police response to community calls for service in line with community and agency expectations										
Item	Failure Mode	Local Effect	System Effect	Potential Cause	Current Control	O	S	D	RPN	Recommended Action
1	Response too slow	Increased level of victimization or injury to callers	Increased cost/loss to society to deal with more serious crimes	Insufficient number of officers available to respond						
2	Response too fast	Increased number of officers required to provide response	Increased cost to community to provide policing services	Too many officers available compared to call volume						
3	No response provided	Increased level of victimization or injury to callers	Reduced confidence and trust in police agency and justice system	Insufficient or no officers available to respond to calls for service						
4	Wrong response provided	Reduced ability to effectively respond to situation	Decreased efficiency of policing delivery with increased costs	Poor alignment between needs of call and resources dispatched						
5	Too much response provided	Specialist or other resources not available to respond to other calls for service	Reduced effectiveness of overall agency response to all crime in community	Poor alignment between needs of call and resources dispatched						

Exhibit 21.7 Failure Mode, Effects, and Criticality Analysis—Example 2

Process: Patrol deployment model										
Function: To provide police response to community calls for service in line with community and agency expectations										
Item	Failure Mode	Local Effect	System Effect	Potential Cause	Current Control	O	S	D	RPN	Recommended Action
1	Response too slow	Increased level of victimization or injury to callers	Increased cost/loss to society to deal with more serious crimes	Insufficient number of officers available to respond	Periodic review of response time data	7	7	4	196	Increase number of officers assigned to geographic area with too slow response time; move from areas with too fast response time
2	Response too fast	Increased number of officers required to provide response	Increased cost to community to provide policing services	Too many officers available compared to call volume	Periodic review of response time data	4	6	4	96	Reduce number of officers assigned to geographic area with too fast response time, move to areas with too slow response time
3	No response provided	Increased level of victimization or injury to callers	Reduced confidence and trust in police agency and justice system	Insufficient or no officers available to respond to calls for service	Call-in/ rerouting dispatch protocol for when certain thresholds met	2	9	4	72	Implement more regular monitoring of calls by supervisors to trigger earlier call-in/reroute protocol
4	Wrong response provided	Reduced ability to effectively respond to situation	Decreased efficiency of policing delivery with increased costs	Poor alignment between needs of call and resources dispatched	Dispatch protocol listing resources required for type of call	6	4	7	168	Require supervisors to observe resource deployment, note instances of wrong deployment, update dispatch protocol
5	Too much response provided	Specialist or other resources are not available to respond to other calls for service	Reduced effectiveness of overall agency response to all crime in community	Poor alignment between needs of call and resources dispatched	Dispatch protocol listing resources required for type of call	5	4	7	140	Institute on-scene command structure to ensure unneeded resources are released for redeployment elsewhere as soon as possible, update dispatch protocol

Exhibit 21.8   Force Field Analysis

Driving Forces ⟶	Status Quo	⟵ Restraining Forces
Known criminals subject to monitoring conditions as part of parole terms	Increased crime levels within a community	Known criminal elements move into community
Strong community league group committed to maintaining standards		Reduced patrol presence in community
Police resources available to redeploy into community from other areas		Economic slowdown impacted businesses in area, leading to increased number of empty premises, homes
Availability of citywide funding for local business owners to bridge through economic slowdown		New low-cost liquor store opened up in community
Liquor licensing laws include review provisions for new premises		

In a law enforcement context, we might want to consider why crime is rising in a particular neighborhood. The status quo in this case would be the increased crime level in the community, as this represents the problem or condition that we want to move away from. In considering this problem, we would want to consider what factors might be able to drive down the crime rate (the driving forces), as well as those factors that might restrain this decrease (the restraining forces).

Shown diagrammatically, this analysis could be presented as shown in Exhibit 21.8.

Using this example, it may be possible for the police along with the local community to address those factors responsible for increased crime levels by matching the restraining forces with the driving forces. This could be achieved through activities such as increasing visible police patrols, increasing the number of parole checks to ensure compliance, and reviewing the effect of the new liquor store by examining the geospatial distribution of crimes that occur around the store. This information could then be used to limit the effect of the restraining forces (for example, by tightening liquor sale conditions), and even help to convert them into driving forces for change through community-based partnerships.[5]

INFLUENCE DIAGRAMS

The purpose of influence diagrams is to identify graphically those forces that could help or hinder a particular initiative, or where there is a need to understand the ability of a community to influence a particular problem. There are two general approaches to this technique: issues based and personality based. The technique will work equally well for either approach; however, it is important when trying to identify key personality influencers that this is done with a degree of discretion and with a clear understanding of how effective an individual's influence really is on the other people involved.

Problem Statement: Crime levels are rising in a specific neighbourhood

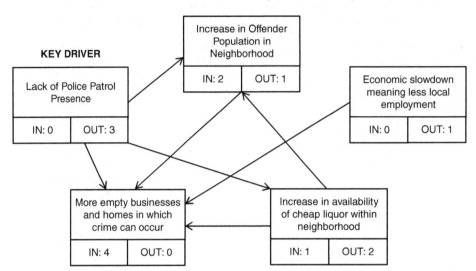

Exhibit 21.9   Influence Diagram for Rising Community Crime Levels

To demonstrate the technique, it is perhaps most useful to take an issues-based approach. The first step is developing a coherent statement of the problem to be addressed, which should then be recorded where it can be readily referenced by the analytical team. Once this is done, the issues (or forces) that impact the problem should be brainstormed, and placed in boxes laid out in a circular pattern. Once these are arranged, the group should consider each force in turn, and determine what other forces the force influences or impacts. This is shown by simply drawing a pointed line from the force to those other forces it may impact. Once this is completed for each force, the total number of lines in and out of each box should be tallied. The force with the most "out" lines (i.e., it impacts the greatest number of other forces) is likely to be the key driver or influencer on the problem. The force with the most "in" lines (i.e., it is impacted by the greatest number of other forces) is likely to be the key outcome that needs to be changed.

Using the same example from the force field analysis description, we could develop the influence diagram shown in Exhibit 21.9.

However, police agencies, like all other members of the public service, are impacted by issues of budget, finance, stewardship, and governance. With the 30 largest municipal police agencies in Canada now collectively employing nearly 32,000 officers (and approximately a further 12,000 civilian staff), policing can easily become a big business for many communities to manage.

As scrutiny of public spending has increased, policing has not been immune from criticism; in fact, its large budgets are often seen as an easy target, especially as crime rates continue to fall.

Under these pressures, many police agencies have begun to adopt those business processes now common in the private sector, including enterprise risk management (ERM).

Comparing RCA Tools

One of the key drawbacks of the five whys approach is that most problems are not explained by a single causal factor. In applying the technique, it is common to discover that there are multiple answers to a single question. By focusing on only one answer, it is possible that a root cause will be discovered that only provides a partial understanding of the problem. Cause and effect analysis (sometimes called Ishikawa analysis or fish-bone analysis) provides a means of plotting these multiple root causes in a way that allows the analyst to truly understand all the sources of risk, as well as the interdependencies among the causal factors.

Once the causes and their effects are fully mapped out, it would be possible to identify the key drivers of risks that impact the problem. Using techniques such as Pareto analysis (where 20 percent of the effort should deliver 80 percent of the results),[6] it would be possible to prioritize the issues and then make informed choices about which risks, and in which order, the agency would choose to address in dealing with the problem.

Failure mode, effects, and criticality analysis (FMECA) is a process that was developed by, and used extensively in, process-driven and engineering industries. It is an extension of the failure mode and effects analysis (FMEA) technique, which is designed to identify the inherent or root causes of risk associated with a process or system. By adding in an analysis of how critical these risks are, risk owners are able to identify those high-consequence and/or high-likelihood risks that they should address as a matter of priority.

Considering our influence diagram, we can see that the lack of police patrol presence impacts the greatest number of other forces. This conceptually makes sense given what criminology tells us about preventive policing. Where there is a lack of obvious police presence, individuals feel less inhibited about conducting activities that they would otherwise hide or not carry out, compared to how they would act in higher-scrutiny places. Equally, we can also see that the more empty homes and businesses there are in a neighborhood, the more safe places there are for crime to occur.

In this case, the most effective solution is likely to be an increase in visible policing in the neighborhood (something that the police can control), coupled with a community revitalization effort to fill the empty houses and businesses (most likely led by the community itself) in order to remove or reduce the number of places where criminals feel comfortable operating.

Combining the force field analysis and influence diagram techniques is often helpful, as it enables a fuller understanding of the factors in play to be developed. It also helps to develop an understanding of how and where existing pressures can be leveraged to achieve the desired outcome.

CONCEPT FANS

Concept fans are a pseudo-form of root cause analysis (RCA), and can perhaps be more appropriately viewed as a means of organizing the outputs of other RCA techniques. The concept fan technique can be used as a simple method of organizing the output of brainstorming activities, or in a more structured way to guide the development of thinking about a problem or a goal.

One way this technique can be used is as an effective means of examining the risks that surround a strategic objective or goal. Once the goal has been defined (using whatever strategic or RCA planning process makes sense for the organization), it is a straightforward matter of first identifying the potential sources of risk that could impact it, and then following these sources down to the specific risks that would arise from them.

In a law enforcement context, an agency may develop a strategic goal of reducing the level of reported property crime within its jurisdiction by 5 percent within one year. It would then need to consider what types of risks could impact its ability to achieve that goal. The agency may identify the following general sources of risks that might have an influence on its ability to be successful:

- Financial risk
- Human resources (HR) risk
- Information or data risk
- External influence (EI) (environmental) risk

At this point it is sufficient to simply identify these high-level sources of risk. The next step would then take each of these strategic sources of risk, and break them down even further into the specific risks and opportunities that would affect their objective for practical purposes. This might result in a list that looks like the one shown in Exhibit 21.10.

Exhibit 21.10   Concept Fan Example Table

Strategic Source	Specific Source of Risk or Opportunity
Financial risk	Insufficient funds to pay for extra enforcement and prevention activities
	Inability to move funds from other programs to support extra enforcement or prevention activities
	Processes in place to deal with fine-based revenue
	Freedom to reallocate funding within defined streams to support specific programs
Human resources risk	Insufficient flexibility in shift schedule to surge extra resources into higher-crime/higher-opportunity areas
	Not enough resources (total) to support specific crime reduction initiatives
	Contract with local Police Association allows for reallocation of resources at the request of the agency
Information or data risk	No or limited access to crime metadata to support effective targeting of neighborhoods or people
	Inaccurate data available to planning staff
	Specific crime data is able to be plotted geographically to identify localized crime hot spots
External influence risk	Limited public support for certain crime prevention techniques (such as stop and frisk)
	Greater public support for targeted, community-based crime reduction/prevention techniques

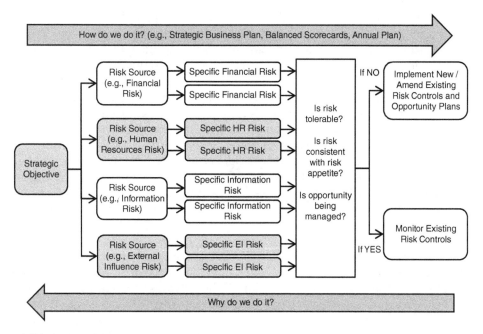

Exhibit 21.11 Concept Fan Example

By recognizing not only the risks but also the opportunities (which could be identified from the use of techniques such as force field analysis or influence diagrams), an agency would be able to better understand not only where its potential risks could come from, but also where there may be opportunities for leveraging existing strengths. Putting these elements together, the whole concept fan approach is shown in Exhibit 21.11.

CASE STUDY EXAMPLE: TACKLING VIOLENT CRIME

The following case study is based in a fictional North American city, but represents very real approaches used by various police agencies to tackle issues similar to those that are presented here.

Case Facts: General Background

Oil City is a sprawling North American city, with a population of nearly one million people. It is the main service town for a nearby oil and gas field, with many itinerant workers traveling between the city and the oil patch. As an energy-centric town, the local economy rides the waves of oil price fluctuations, with boom times drawing an influx of workers to the city who often spend money as quickly as they earn it. When the latest oil bubble bursts, these same workers often become stranded in the city and become dependent on local aid agencies to survive.

The population is increasingly multicultural, although the members of many immigrant groups feel increasingly isolated due to reasons of language, culture, and social status. First Nations people are drawn to the city from surrounding reserves in search of employment, but often struggle to find their place in a community that does not necessarily reflect their more traditional values. The city has brutally cold winters, and relatively short, dry summers that spawn regular tornados, making life difficult year-round for those forced to live rough.

Like most North American cities, Oil City has seen a gradual decline in its reported crime rates since peaking in the late 1970s and early 1980s. While crime has gone down across the board, the incidence of violent crime (crimes involving the use, or threatened use, of force against a person) has slowly been climbing over the past decade.

Specific Issue

In the first six months of the year the number of homicides committed in Oil City exceeded the total number of deaths for the whole previous year. At the current rate, the city is on track to more than double the previous year's rate, and may even triple it. On average, one person was murdered approximately every six days, and in one particularly bad week, three people were killed in the space of less than 72 hours. Both local and national media have picked up on the trend, with the city being dubbed the "National Murder Capital." The City Council and Police Board are both demanding action from the newly appointed Chief of Police, who has been in the job less than a month.

The specific facts available are:

- Of the 26 deaths in the first half of the year, 18 victims were homeless at the time or had been homeless within the previous three months.
- Of these 26 deaths, 22 had identified suspects, 12 of whom were homeless at the time of their alleged offending or had been homeless within the previous three months.
- Of the 26 victims and 22 identified suspects, 39 (81 percent) had consumed alcohol and/or narcotic drugs within six hours immediately before the fatal incident.
- Of the 39 victims and suspects who had consumed alcohol or narcotics within six hours of the fatal incident, 30 were impaired to a level that would have put them over the legal limit to drive.
- Seventeen deaths were the result of stab injuries caused by knives or other bladed weapons. Six deaths were the result of beatings, including those that involved the use of objects located at or near the scene. Two of the deaths were the result of gunshot wounds. In the final case the victim was deliberately run down by a vehicle.
- Each of the 30 homeless (or recently homeless) victims and suspects had been referred to or sought services from an average of 4.7 different health and social agencies in the previous six months.
- The victims of these crimes had an average of 13.2 previous convictions for petty offenses such as vagrancy, being drunk in a public place, or aggressive panhandling.

- The identified suspects in these crimes had an average of 9.6 previous convictions for violent offenses, and had spent an average of 3.75 years incarcerated for those offenses.

Developing the Approach

The Chief of Police was under huge pressure to act, and act quickly. However, knowing that a knee-jerk crackdown would not achieve sustainable long-term results, the Chief instead decided that a rapid risk assessment should be used to identify the root causes of the problem. Luckily, the Police Department had an enterprise risk manager who was able to help out.

The ERM manager was called in to a meeting with the Chief of Police, the criminal operations officer, and the head of strategic planning, and was set the following two tasks:

1. Identify the techniques that will be the most effective in identifying the root cause of the current surge in homicides in Oil City.
2. Choose the best approach, and justify selection of that approach.

Solution 1

The ERM manager went away and thought about the problem. It seemed that the issue wasn't just about the number of homicides; it was also about the amount of violence being committed in the lead-ups to those homicides. In reviewing the crime statistics (outlined previously), it was also apparent that there were close links to issues of drug and alcohol dependency and homelessness in play that were likely affecting the number of homicides occurring in the city.

Given the multidimensional nature of the problem, the five options the ERM manager seriously considered for root cause analysis were:

1. Cause and effect (Ishikawa) diagrams
2. Failure mode, effects, and criticality analysis (FMECA)
3. Force field analysis
4. Influence diagrams
5. Concept fans

The ERM manager did not consider five whys as an appropriate analytical tool for this problem, as it would be likely to oversimplify the issues and miss critical details that would probably be necessary to support the development of an effective response strategy. Similarly, techniques such as HAZOP (an inductive RCA technique) and HAZID (hazard identification) were unlikely by themselves to present useful insights into the range of soft issues being assessed.

The ERM manager settled on a multistage approach to the analysis. This approach acknowledged that there was a need to better understand the underlying causes of the risks. This knowledge was then used to break out each piece to better understand the "why" of the root cause. To achieve this, the ERM manager recommended that the Police Service:

- Start by developing a cause and effect diagram to identify and group the broad issues of risk.
- Use an FMECA model to evaluate the components of the cause and effect diagram to gain a deeper understanding of the root causes of risk and to identify potential risk treatments.

Understanding the Issues

After presenting the recommendations and rationale to the Chief of Police, the ERM manager was given approval to start developing the cause and effect diagram. In order to make this as robust as possible, the ERM manager called together a brainstorming group from across the operations, intelligence, community support, and leadership streams of the department. The first challenge they faced was to develop the problem definition.

Solution 2

The overall problem definition used to frame the cause and effect analysis was relatively straightforward to develop using a standard brainstorming approach:

What are the factors driving an increase in violent crime in Oil City?

The group quickly saw the advantage of using the following criteria to find the major causes and effects, equipment, environment, finance, materials, measurement, people, and processes. All of these sources were seen to be relevant (at least initially).

While these first challenges were overcome relatively easily, once the group started to identify the subsources of risk, they quickly came up against their next hurdle: How could they accurately (and defensibly) populate the subsources of risk?

Solution 3

The main issue the group faced was one of not only having to identify the subsources of risk, but also being able to defend them from internal and external review (and potential criticism). To overcome this issue, the ERM manager suggested that the following two RCA tools be used in series:

1. Force field analysis—used to identify key restraining and driving forces for change
2. Five whys analysis—used to follow each key restraining or driving force through to its root cause

As a result of the ERM manager's suggestion, the group developed the (partial) force field analysis diagram shown in Exhibit 21.12.

Once the team had completed the force field analysis, they considered each of the restraining forces in turn using the five whys approach. Exhibit 21.13 outlines the results for two of these restraining factors.

It is important to note that there were a number of equally important answers to the third "why" question. In order to capture each of these separate answers, the analysis team would have followed each of the pathways to its logical conclusion by repeating the five whys process for each strand.

Exhibit 21.12   Force Field Analysis

Driving Forces ⟶	Status Quo	⟵ Restraining Forces
Significant number of skilled social assistance agencies available to assist police	Levels of reported violent crime double the 10-year moving average	Social assistance agencies compete with each other for funding and donations, which are often based on occupancy/throughput
Ability to implement new liquor licensing regimes, placing limits on single bottle "big beer" sales		Ready community access to high-strength, low-cost alcohol (including single bottle "big beers")
Police resources able to be redeployed into problem communities from other areas		Cultural acceptance of individuals carrying edged weapons among homeless, disadvantaged communities
Existing legislation provides police powers to search, arrest for concealed weapons		Reluctance of prosecutors to pursue charges for carrying concealed weapon
Well-structured strategic management and initiative management capability within the Police Department		Reluctance of some police leaders to commit resources to crime prevention if there are no arrests to be made
		No coherent organizational coordination of crime prevention or violence reduction initiatives

Exhibit 21.13 Five Whys Analysis

Restraining Factor	Cultural acceptance of individuals carrying edged weapons among homeless, disadvantaged communities	Reluctance of prosecutors to pursue charges for carrying concealed weapon
Why #1	Homeless, disadvantaged community members feel that they need to protect themselves from harm	Prosecutors view the charges to be a lot of work for minimal punishment to the offender
Why #2	Members of the homeless and disadvantaged communities feel that police don't protect them to the same level as other communities	Prosecutors often have to return to the arresting police officer repeatedly for additional information that has not been provided in the original charge report
Why #3	Previous police interaction with victims from the homeless, disadvantaged communities has often been adversarial and not resulting in positive outcomes for the reporters/victims	Police officers use a generic charge report to file the arrest report, and it does not specify all the information necessary to sustain a concealed weapons charge
Why #4	Police members are not trained to recognize or relate to the specific physical, mental, and addiction issues more common among members of these communities that may impact how they are able to report crimes to the police	The Police Department records management system has not been configured with a specific concealed weapons charge report format
Why #5	Police officers are trained to respond to a call, deal with the issue as quickly as possible, and then move on to the next call	The Police Department IT group has never been asked to create a specific concealed weapons charge report with mandatory data fields

Once the analysis team had completed their force field and five whys analysis, they were able to develop a comprehensive cause and effect diagram. Exhibit 21.14 includes two or three examples for each subsource of risk; however, in practice the total diagram would have been far larger.

The completed cause and effect diagram provided a touch point for the remainder of the risk management and strategy development processes. It provided the analysis team with detailed information on the root causes of the risks, including

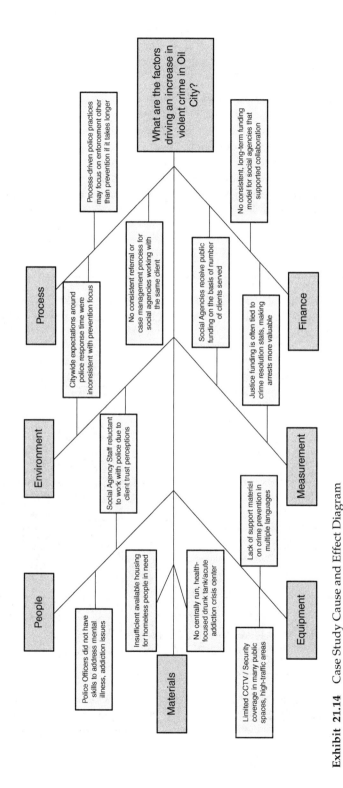

Exhibit 21.14 Case Study Cause and Effect Diagram

Reprinted with permission from *RIMS Strategic Risk Management Implementation Guide*. Copyright 2012 Risk and Insurance Management Society, Inc. All rights reserved.

the many behaviorally based risks they saw in their environment, as well as providing several logical starting points for developing risk treatments.

THE FMECA PROCESS

Once the analytical team started to look through the cause and effect diagram, they realized that one of the common themes related to the relationships among the different social assistance agencies that worked with the homeless and disadvantaged communities. It appeared that these agencies competed with each other to gain clients, as this enabled them to secure more public funding. In practice this meant that the faster they could turn a client around as "treated" or "helped," the faster they could obtain another new client—and thereby obtain more funding. How could the analysis team look at this issue using an FMECA approach?

Solution 4

The team produced the following FMECA table after looking at this issue. They defined the scope of the problem process as being the Social Assistance Agency Funding Model.

Process: Social Assistance Agency Funding Model										
Function: To provide public funding support to social assistance agencies that provide service to the homeless and disadvantaged of Oil City										
Item	Failure Mode	Local Effect	System Effect	Potential Cause	Current Control	O	S	D	RPN	Recommended Action
1	Funding based on output, not outcome	Increased pressure to cut time per client to move on to next client	Reduced effectiveness of response, increased cost to repeat assistance	Funding model focused on volume	Periodic funding body audits of client numbers (no quality check)	9	7	7	441	Rework funding model to focus on long-term outcomes rather than short-term volumes; provide a level of base funding independent of client numbers
2	No funding for collaborative programming	No incentive for agencies to work together	Increased cost to system to fund multiple similar/same programs	Funding model based on agency outputs rather than shared outcomes	Nil	10	5	10	500	Rework funding model to focus on shared outcomes, joint funding models for shared programming
3	No funding for specialist support services	Agencies providing single, highly specialized services are not publicly funded	Access to these services is severely limited, or on user-pays basis	Lack of recognition of need for particular services	Periodic reviews of programs that are eligible for funding	6	4	7	168	Identify current specialist skill gaps; push funding body to review funding model for these skills

It is important to remember that almost all of these actions would have fallen to other agencies to carry out—but by identifying the issue, the Police Department was better able to manage its own exposure to the effects of these nonowned risks.

Bringing It All Together

By the time the analysis team had completed the FMECA process for all of its risk sources and subsources, it was able to provide the organization with an exceptionally detailed and very comprehensive understanding of how these risks could affect (or already were affecting) the achievement of the department's goal to reduce the level of violent crime in Oil City.

The final step in the process was developing a single comprehensive risk treatment plan, which allocated both accountabilities and resources to those organizational leaders best suited to dealing with the risk. This risk treatment plan took the recommended actions from the various FMECA analyses, and combined them into one single source of truth for the department's violence reduction strategy. The RPN score from the FMECA was also used to help prioritize the initiatives, with the highest levels of risk generally being accorded a higher level of priority for treatment.

In order to align with the Police Department's existing strategy and business planning model (including its quarterly reporting cycle), the ERM manager also worked with the head of strategy planning to group risk treatments together to form overarching strategic initiatives.

Solution 5

The risk treatments identified in the FMECA analysis were:

- Rework funding model to focus on long-term outcomes rather than short-term volumes.
- Provide a level of base funding independent of client numbers.
- Rework funding model to focus on shared outcomes.
- Develop joint funding models for shared programming.
- Identify current specialist skill gaps and then push funding body to review funding model for these skills.

An overarching initiative that covered all of these risk treatments might look like this:

Initiative Name: Social Assistance Agency Funding Model Advocacy
Initiative Owner: Deputy Chief of Police, Community Support Services
Initiative Description: In order to encourage more effective collaboration between agencies, increase access to services, and reduce duplication of services among social assistance agencies, the Oil City Police Department will adopt an advocacy position on these issues, and use this position to intervene with the public health funding bodies with respect to the current social agency funding model.

Initiative Deliverables:

- Formation of joint funding model working group with Oil City Police Department and social assistance agency representatives

- Development of outcome-based funding model document that provides for joint funding, critical specialist skills funding, and dependable base funding independent of client numbers
- Consultation of proposed funding model among social assistance agencies
- Development of social assistance agency funding model position paper, supported by social assistance agency representatives
- Establishment of negotiations with public health funding body on proposed model

Available Resources:

- Deputy Chief of Police, Community Support Services (5 percent)
- Officer in Charge, Strategic Planning (10 percent)
- Officer in Charge, Community Outreach Programs (75 percent)
- Communications Adviser (10 percent)

CONCLUSION

Progressive public safety agencies are well placed to leverage their existing risk-aware culture to support an ERM approach. By adopting a range of root cause analysis techniques, these agencies are able to identify the underlying causes of community safety issues, and then develop strategies and partnerships that allow them to address these situations more effectively. In doing so, they are able to apply their resources more effectively, and also ensure that other parties to the problem are doing their part to manage the risk. Because public safety is a shared responsibility between the police and the public, the use of root cause analysis techniques provides public safety agencies the ability to reframe the conversation both internally and externally, and ensure that they are applying their resources in the most effective and efficient way possible.

QUESTIONS

1. Identify an emerging crime issue in your community using data available from sources such as local newspapers, online police reporting, and so forth. Frame the situation, and then identify the restraining and driving forces that may be impacting the issue.
2. Using your force field analysis, develop a cause and effect diagram for the situation.
3. Either using a FMECA approach or some other appropriate RCA tool, identify five risk treatment actions you would recommend to the local Chief of Police to address the issue.

NOTES

1. M. Burczycka, "Police Resources in Canada," Catalogue no. 85-225-X, Statistics Canada, Ottawa, 2013. For a discussion of crime rates in Canada, see "Indicators of Wellbeing

in Canada: Security—Crime Rates," at www4.hrsdc.gc.ca/.3ndic.1t.4r@-eng.jsp?iid=57 (last modified November 7, 2013).

2. For further detail on cause and effect analysis, see page 56 (B17) of IEC/ISO 31010, "Risk Management—Risk Assessment Techniques." See K. Ishikawa, *Guide to Quality Control*, for a detailed explanation of this technique.

3. For further detail on failure mode, effects, and criticality analysis, see page 46 (B13) of IEC/ISO 31010, "Risk Management—Risk Assessment Techniques."

4. It is not necessary to be an engineer to follow this example—it is sufficient to understand the way the FMECA process is applied, and accept that the answers provided are accurate.

5. For a fuller description of this phenomenon, see George Kelling and Catherine Coles, *Fixing Broken Windows: Restoring Order and Reducing Crime in Our Communities*.

6. Pareto analysis is a technique used to identify those courses of action or options that are likely to deliver the greatest benefit. It is based on the theory of diminishing returns, and can be referred to as the 80/20 rule, where 80 percent of the value is seen to be delivered through the use of 20 percent of the available resources. See, for example, Suzanne Turner's description in *Tools for Success: A Manager's Guide*, where the technique is referred to as "vital few analysis."

REFERENCES

Burczycka, M. 2013. "Police Resources in Canada." Catalogue no. 85-225-X, Statistics Canada, Ottawa.

Human Resources and Skills Development Canada. 2013. "Indicators of Wellbeing in Canada: Security—Crime Rates." www4.hrsdc.gc.ca/.3ndic.1t.4r@-eng.jsp?iid=57 (accessed November 7, 2013).

Ishikawa, K. 1985. *Guide to Quality Control*. 2nd Rev. Ed. Tokyo: Asian Productivity Organization.

ISO 31000:2009. "Risk Management—Principles and Guidelines." Geneva: International Organization for Standardization.

ISO/IEC 31010:2009. "Risk Management—Risk Assessment Techniques." Geneva: International Organization for Standardization.

Kelling, George, and Catherine Coles. 1996. *Fixing Broken Windows: Restoring Order and Reducing Crime in Our Communities*. New York: Free Press.

Turner, Suzanne. 2003. *Tools for Success: A Manager's Guide*. Berkshire, UK: McGraw-Hill Professional.

ABOUT THE CONTRIBUTOR

Andrew Bent is a practicing risk manager with a large Canadian integrated energy company. He was previously in charge of enterprise risk management for one of Canada's largest municipal police services. He holds a master's degree in strategic studies, as well as ARM-E, ARM-P, CRMA, CCSA, and CFE designations.

CHAPTER 22

JAA Inc.—A Case Study in Creating Value from Uncertainty

Best Practices in Managing Risk

JULIAN DU PLESSIS
Head of Internal Audit, AVBOB Mutual Assurance Society

ARNOLD SCHANFIELD
Principal, Schanfield Risk Management Advisors LLC

ALPASLAN MENEVSE
Risk Officer, Sekerbank T.A.S., Turkey

T his case study describes how enterprise risk management (ERM) was implemented at a fictitious company, JAA Inc. It provides extensive detail as to the governance structure, the processes, and the various tools used. The case is built on the principles/guidance of ISO 31000[1] and the implementation guidance created by HB 436.[2] The key players in this case are the heads of Internal Audit and Risk Management. It is interesting to see what they have done in the five years expended to implement ERM. We offer special thanks and appreciation to Grant Purdy from Broadleaf International in Australia for his continued support, dedication, and help provided to our efforts.

SETTING THE CONTEXT

It was a beautiful Wednesday afternoon in Chicago. Matt Damison, the chief internal auditor (CIA), and Frank Gillespie, the chief risk officer (CRO), were having lunch in JAA's cafeteria and reminiscing about the times at JAA when the company's performance was much lower than the current state. Only five years earlier, in 2008, the company had embarked on a comprehensive enterprise risk management (ERM) program. Both Matt and Frank, together with executive management and the board, had been actively involved in this initiative. At that time, JAA was also undergoing various regulatory audits, and employee morale was quite poor. The company has now been able to satisfactorily address these issues, and in fact has won numerous awards and been written about in various journals for its risk management program. JAA has progressed from being considered risk management novices to one of being leaders in the field of effective risk management, having accomplished this in less than four years but still recognizing that improvements need to be made. Matt and Frank have just received a phone call from the *Wall Street Journal* press. They agreed to be interviewed to explain the genesis of JAA's ERM implementation undertaken five years previously and how as a company it has since flourished. Senior and executive management have encouraged Matt and Frank to conduct such an interview to highlight the company's achievements.

Business Background

In 1972, JAA commenced operations as a private company founded by three brothers (Emile, Robert, and Frank Bergand) in Chicago, Illinois. In 1988 the brothers decided to take the company public and launched an initial public offering (IPO), as market conditions at that time were quite favorable and the brothers wished to reap financial benefits (i.e., cash out) after years of hard work. The brothers remained with the company and served in executive roles until they retired in 2003. JAA is listed on major stock exchanges, is headquartered in Chicago, and has a December 31 year-end. The financial statements appear in Appendix A.

The company has three operating segments:

1. A U.S. wholesale business
2. A U.S. retail business
3. An international business (wholesale and retail)

The aforementioned segments reflect the way the business is managed and performance is evaluated. The wholesale business focuses on the sale of undecorated apparel products to distributors in the United States and internationally. The international wholesale operating segments also produce apparel products that satisfy the preferences of those customers that favor a more local traditional style, to stay sufficiently competitive in those markets. This was determined from a risk workshop that identified the loyalty factor of international customers as a major business opportunity.

The company operates 57 retail stores in 10 different countries:

- North America—United States (28)
- South America—Argentina and Brazil (7)
- Asia—China, South Korea, and Japan (11)
- Australia (4)
- Europe—Switzerland and Turkey (4)
- Africa—South Africa (3)

The retail stores cater directly to the consumer, and most such stores are situated in major shopping malls using leased space. The stores target middle-aged men and women. Retail store customers represent quite a sophisticated group of shoppers. The stores compete on the basis of location, merchandise availability, price, and customer service. Retail sales are promoted via major newspapers and online media. JAA's major competitors are McCory, Bertang, and Keramtor.

The wholesale customer base comprises 100 key distributors. The split between retail and wholesale is 40 percent/60 percent, respectively. Competition at both the retail and wholesale levels is fierce and has necessitated that the company out-source part of its manufacturing to lower-cost countries. Key product cost competition is from China, Bangladesh, and Vietnam.

The apparel business/industry is characterized by rapid movements in fashion, changing consumer demand, and significant competitive pressures. JAA has emphasized quality merchandise at an affordable price. Wholesale customers are secured through a lean, but stellar, sales force established in the major cities around the globe (45 major cities). No one single distributor exceeds 5 percent of the company's sales. JAA also has an online catalog operation, whose critical success factors are website availability and design, advertising response times, and social media recognition.

The Bergand brothers are now the largest company shareholders, owning some 22 percent of the stock. There are a couple of large institutional investors that collectively own an additional 12 percent of the outstanding shares.

The executive and senior management teams comprise:

- President and CEO Michael Menorix
- Chief Financial Officer Jillian Verdiger
- VP of Marketing and Sales Mary Mordensti
- VP of Production Boris Dentiger
- VP of Human Resources Francine Tanserki
- Chief Internal Auditor Matt Damison
- Chief Risk Officer Frank Gillespie
- VP of Legal and Compliance Michael Perstay

JAA has its core U.S. manufacturing in a 360,000-square-foot facility, which also contains the corporate/executive offices and warehousing/distribution. The company also has two small satellite manufacturing facilities in Tampa, Florida, and Los Angeles, California, on company-owned properties. JAA has outsourced 25 percent of production in various agreements with third parties in Turkey, China, and South Africa. The company's apparel product line initially focused on men's coats, but over a period of time expanded to include a full line of men's clothing inclusive of pants, shirts, and coats. In 1999, an upscale line of women's clothing was added to the product portfolio.

The company purchases all fabric from 50 key suppliers, having trimmed its supplier base from 400 over the past five years. All suppliers are ISO 9000 certified and, as such, are subject to rigorous reviews prior to becoming JAA's suppliers. JAA uses state-of-the-art technology to enhance marketplace competitiveness.

The company has been fortunate in attracting high-caliber employees. It has had minimal turnover over the past three years, and it provides a generous compensation and incentive package to its employees. It is not subject to any collective bargaining agreements but to various environmental regulations in the United States and overseas. One other key area JAA is heavily focused on, and in strong compliance with, is monitoring compliance at third-party manufacturing facilities overseas.

Effective management of risk was recognized by the current management team as being critical to JAA's success. Thus the company sought individuals who were experienced in this field for key leadership positions in Internal Audit and Risk Management, as well as for the key board positions. When the current heads of Internal Audit and Risk Management joined the company in 2008, JAA had sustained six years of losses. JAA's creditworthiness is currently BBB as rated by the major rating agencies, having improved from junk status to this rating within four years.

Initial Steps: Strategic Planning and Business Objectives

JAA's management recognized in 2008 that there were concerns with the annual strategic planning process because the board members typically did not attend such meetings. This impeded their ability to address the key strategic questions JAA faced, and did not create an environment that could generate fresh insights. Typically, the focus on short-term performance was failing to identify risks that threatened long-term objectives. Such short-term thinking also neglected to think about untapped business opportunities.

JAA decided to discard the annual process and replace it with a much more intense form of strategic engagement with management and the board. They are now devoting extra time at each board meeting to pressure-test the strategy in view of its progress and changes in critical variables. There is a strong communication process of this new strategy throughout the organization to both the internal and external stakeholders. JAA prides itself in doing this well under President Michael Menorix's leadership. Management knows who the stakeholders are and their needs and has established different communication channels with them as appropriate, including webinars, phone conference calls, town hall meetings, written media, and so on.

JAA's management is aware of the many pitfalls of strategic planning and has recognized the need to view risk and strategy as two sides of the same coin because it knows that the two are linked. The company aims to increase shareholder value and to address the needs of the other stakeholders through successful pursuit of the following strategic objectives:

- Maintaining market leadership
- Sustaining technology leadership
- Strengthening global presence
- Delivering quality service
- Being seen as a leader in compliance with all laws and regulations

Establishing the Governance System

JAA has developed an excellent governance system by using many different metrics as described later. The Governance Framework is depicted in Exhibit 22.1. The board consists of external directors, including Sally Hendrix, who serves as chair of the Audit Committee. The Audit Committee members have served for periods

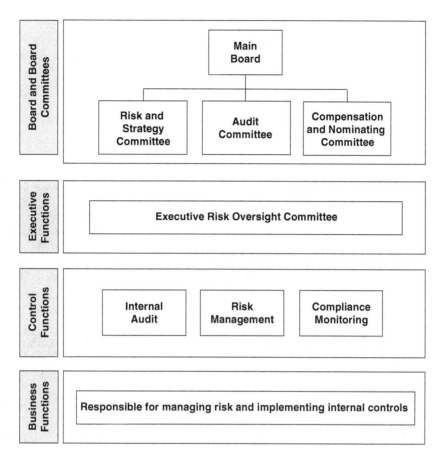

Exhibit 22.1   Governance Framework

ranging from two to seven years. All committee members, in addition to their professional qualifications and experience, are well versed in risk management. They have all attended formal training in this subject matter at leading risk organizations and have received training by both the Internal Audit and Risk Management groups of JAA as well.

The company's risk governance framework illustrates the governance arrangements for the board, management, independent control functions, and ongoing business operations that exercise governance over risk.

JAA's board is responsible for the governance processes that it requires management to execute. The company understands that effective oversight by its board and senior management is critical to the overall governance effort. It protects its shareholders and other stakeholders by ensuring sustainability of the business through achievement of superior performance. The board provides leadership to JAA by understanding and accepting its responsibilities for the adoption of strategic plans, monitoring of operational performance and management, determining the philosophy and effectiveness of the approach for managing risk (including internal controls for managing the day-to-day operations), and compliance with all relevant laws and regulations.

The directors of JAA Inc. have applied the principles of discipline, transparency, independence, accountability, responsibility, fairness, and social responsibility to ensure that sound governance is practiced consistently throughout the company. Being listed on the New York Stock Exchange and subjected to its listing requirements emanating from the Securities Exchange Act, the company requires:

- An independent board of directors with a majority of nonexecutive directors (NEDs)
- An Audit Committee
- Compensation and Nominating Committees
- That board members must gain approval prior to undertaking any other board assignments and in no event can any board member serve on more than three other boards
- Attendance of at least 75 percent of board meetings and its subcommittees annually
- Strong continuing education in various areas, including risk management, governance, and internal control
- Presence and functioning of an Executive Risk Oversight Committee (EROC)
- Presence and functioning of a Risk and Strategy Committee (RSC)

JAA continually seeks to improve its knowledge of international frameworks and standards to augment its governance processes. As such, it has incorporated best practices from South Africa (King III),[3] Canada (Criteria of Control),[4] United Kingdom (Combined Code,[5] Risk Management Consultation Draft—FRC[6]), and Australia (ASX and HB 436[7]) to update its risk management and governance frameworks.

The board of directors has delegated certain functions to the various committees. The board is kept up to date on:

- Business performance relative to strategy, budgets, business plans, risk criteria, capital adequacy and preservation, and earnings volatility
- Noncompliance with board policies, regulations, statutes, and accounting policies
- Significant breakdowns in operations, unsatisfactory financial performance, noncompliance with laws and regulations, ineffective management supervision and monitoring, internal controls or process failure, and organizational system or structure failure
- Effectiveness of the corporate governance process
- Corrective actions implemented in respect of these

Specific responsibilities of different committees are discussed next in the following subsections, namely Compensation Committee, Risk and Strategy Committee, and Executive Risk Oversight Committee.

The Compensation Committee

- Reviews and approves remuneration policy throughout the business
- Ensures that the remuneration policies adopted do not result in excessive risk taking

- Ensures that the compensation plans and compensation awarded to senior management are based on the achievement of objectives as a result of managing risks effectively
- Designs and approves the principles to be used in the performance agreements of management to ensure that key performance indicators (KPIs) of management encourage prudent risk taking and the management thereof

The Risk and Strategy Committee

- Sets and reviews JAA's risk criteria
- Oversees the risks to which the company is exposed, and monitors the activities of the Executive Risk Oversight Committee (EROC)
- Approves the risk management policy on behalf of the board
- Reviews the design, completeness, and effectiveness of the risk management framework to ensure that changes and updates to risk management are performed in accordance with processes approved by the board as documented in the risk management policy and that oversight of it is effective
- Ensures that infrastructure, resources, and systems exist to adequately oversee and monitor JAA's risks (this is done to ensure that risk taking is consistent with the risk criteria set by the board; at all times the board is aware of the comprehensiveness, accuracy, and status of the risk attitude)
- Reviews the effectiveness of risk reporting (including timeliness and events that could impact business objectives and the company's risk profile)
- Ensures that all strategic transactions undergo appropriate review and due diligence before submission to the board, particular focus being accorded to the risk criteria
- Reviews and challenges capital and liquidity stress testing

The Executive Risk Oversight Committee (EROC)

- Scrutinizes and challenges the risks identified to which the company is exposed and evaluates the assessment of these risks
- Assists the board in defining JAA's risk criteria that align with the objectives and strategies of the organization and monitors that risks are managed within the risk criteria
- Establishes the risk management policy
- Ensures that the framework for managing risk continues to remain effective
- Ensures that the necessary resources are allocated to manage risk
- Determines that the risk management performance indicators are aligned with KPIs of management performance of the organization
- Ensures and monitors legal and regulatory compliance
- Reviews results of stress and scenario testing for JAA's strategic objectives and attainment of them
- Assigns accountabilities and responsibilities at appropriate levels within the organization
- Reports on how managing risk is performed to provide assurance to stakeholders

Business Operations

In addition to the oversight functions (described next), JAA has embedded risk management into underlying business operations. For example, a risk management policy (see Appendix B) has been implemented across the company to support the effective implementation of risk management. A risk management framework, supported by various risk policies, has been implemented to provide guidance to all employees on how to address organizational components, such as business and strategy planning, budgeting, and performance management and reporting, as well as human resources, compliance, and information security. Heads of departments are responsible for the maintenance of the risk registers, which include treatment actions. All risks in this register are further consolidated and reported to the EROC with possible treatment options.

Oversight Functions

The company's independent oversight functions, namely the Risk Management department, the Legal department, the Compliance department, and the Internal Audit department, provide the required assurance. These functions report periodically to the board and its committees as appropriate.

Risk Management Department

The Risk Management department has a unique advisory role to all management levels as well as to the board while managing risks. Also, the department reviews and challenges the outcome and results of risk assessment activities performed by management and the resulting risk registers produced that include the risks that constitute the risk profile of JAA.

Legal Department

The Legal department is responsible for providing advice to the company, its divisions, and its employees on matters of law and legal protection by:

- Representing the company in all meetings, conferences, and public forums
- Preparation of protocols, claims, and court counterclaims
- Representation of the company in court
- Protection of the company's rights and interests in judicial settings
- Creation of legal documentation requirements

Compliance Department

The Compliance department helps in the following areas:

- Regulatory risk management—keeping company activities in strict compliance with current legislation
- Compliance monitoring—evaluating and measuring the state of compliance across the organization
- Investigations—managing investigations into wrongdoing and anything that increases regulatory-related risks

Internal Audit Department

The Internal Audit (IA) function is best in class. Matt Damison, who has 20 years of relevant internal audit and risk management experience, joined JAA in 2008 with strong academic and professional certifications. He belongs to several leading professional organizations such as the Institute of Risk Management in London, the Conference Board of Canada, and the Risk Management Institute of Australia. He also speaks and writes extensively on this subject matter.

Matt reports directly to the Audit Committee chair, Sally Hendrix, with dotted-line daily responsibilities to the chief executive officer, Michael Menorix. Matt meets with the Audit Committee on a periodic basis. He also attends the key meetings in the strategic planning process.

This is a summary of what he has done during this five-year period:

- The department adopted a comprehensive risk-based approach to the audit plan. All audit projects are derived from this risk-based plan. Special requests by management that are external to the risk assessment performed by management are reviewed very carefully, especially if the requests do not appear to address issues that are generating any new risks. Audits are thus focused on the company's highest risks or on the highest risks that are now reduced to within the stated risk criteria through management actions. Comprehensive reviews of every business/operational process are not performed, because such processes include areas of lower risks.
- Several senior-level personnel in the company formerly worked in the Internal Audit function, and Internal Audit has a track record of promoting high-quality performers to line management positions. The function has a solid track record with minimal turnover to outside the organization.
- The Internal Audit group consistently demonstrates how it has contributed to the success of the company by linking all commentaries on its accomplishments to the company's strategic objectives.
- Internal Audit annually evaluates risk management, and issues an opinion on it according to the 11 risk management principles stated in ISO 31000. This year, it has completed its third such review, focusing on:
  - The design of the risk management framework, including such things as assignment of responsibilities and accountabilities, context of the company, communication with the stakeholders, and mandate and commitment by the board
  - The implementation of the risk management framework
  - The risk process implementation, culminating in the generation of the risk register
  - Monitoring and review
  - Continuous improvement

External Auditors

Matt has also been successful in helping the company reinvent its relationship with the external auditor in the following areas:

- Prior to the heads of Internal Audit and Risk Management joining the company, the external audit process left much to be desired. Specifically, JAA never received a well-written management letter; if it received any letter at all, it was written quite superficially and was received by the company nine months subsequent to year-end. There was extensive overlap in some of the areas covered by external and internal audit. There were, as well, some key areas missed in the external audit that created surprises for the company.

- As a result of the foregoing, the following changes were implemented, creating many positive effects for the risk management framework:
  - The external auditors were invited to sit in on the key strategic planning sessions of the company.
  - There were ongoing meetings between the head of Internal Audit and the principal partner on the external audit team.
  - The external audit team compiled and wrote a comprehensive management letter with special emphasis on root cause analysis (meaning that they understood the root causes of specific problems). They ensured as well that all such comments were addressed by management of JAA and did not appear in the following year's management letter comments.
  - The external auditors, in performing their planning work for the current year's audit, began to utilize the existing risk management framework and process at the company, as created by the risk management function. This was to ensure that all parties' efforts were clearly aligned.
  - The internal auditors, in assessing effectiveness of the risk management framework at the end of the year, summarized as well the contributions to it by the external auditors.
  - The internal auditors did not act as surrogates for the external auditors, meaning that no internal audit time was expended in performing external audit work to reduce cost of the external audit.

Evolution of Risk Management

When initially appointed to their positions in 2008, the current heads of Internal Audit and Risk Management met with the CEO, as well as with the rest of the executive management team. After a number of discussions, it was decided to implement enterprise risk management (ERM) throughout the company so that JAA could achieve its business objectives, unlike the prior six financial years when performance was generally poor. As the CRO, Frank Gillespie was the key person who facilitated the risk management program with a team of three professionals reporting to him. The risk management team determined that the source of the problems in the company over the past several years stemmed from:

- Weak commitment to each of the business objectives
- Poor internal communications
- Absence of initiative taking
- Inconsistencies in internal reporting
- Unclear organization roles and responsibilities
- Failure to adequately monitor the international brand licenses and copyrights
- Failure to provide a safe working environment

These issues further served to demotivate the existing workforce, which in turn had the compounding effect of creating an environment where employees became hesitant to undertake new projects. Ultimately, this caused JAA to fall behind its competitors.

As the team scoured the marketplace in 2008, they noted that ISO 31000: 2009[8] was in draft stage, but its predecessor, AS/NZS 4360:2004, existed together with the accompanying HB 436 handbook. They decided to launch their risk management efforts using these guides.

After performing a detailed gap analysis of the existing risk management framework, Frank prepared the training curricula for all company employees. At the senior management level, he rolled out leadership and soft skill coaching courses. For the lower levels of management, he introduced training in communications, body language, and project management. In addition, for both groups, he introduced personnel conflict resolution, negotiations, presentation skills, and human behavior/bias training workshops. To create a teamlike environment and a great atmosphere between the different layers of management, Frank organized group hobby sessions such as photography, cooking, and several weekend hiking events. These served to repair impaired lines of communication, which in turn helped to reinvent JAA's new corporate culture.

Having performed a few cycles of workshops with senior management, Frank suggested that they needed to prepare a risk management policy with the information gathered from all key executives. The risk management policy became the foundation for the company's risk management framework. Frank also created standard risk management terminology to ensure that everyone gained a common understanding of risk management words and phrases. This was incorporated into the risk management policy.

INTRODUCTION OF ISO 31000 AND HB 436 TO THE COMPANY

After three years of diligent efforts in implementing this framework, benefits materialized through greater profits, revenue growth, shareholder value improvement, and individual performance. In 2009, when ISO 31000 became the international risk management standard, the company adopted it through its entire business. ISO 31000 represented an opportunity to create effective risk management within JAA as this was merely an upgrade of AS/NZS 4360.

Frank's group performed a new gap analysis while upgrading to ISO 31000 to determine what additional changes needed to be made in JAA's current risk management principles, framework, and process. JAA adopted ISO 31000 in two phases. The initial phase was at the business level since it was critical to incorporate this into the decision making processes of the company. The second phase was at the strategic level, which also included monitoring of the initial phase. The company made extensive use of the HB 436 handbook to help with the implementation process.

Defining the Context of JAA

The internal and external context of the company was clearly defined by the ERM team (see Exhibit 22.2). The objectives, stakeholders, and current business environment were compiled to ascertain strengths, weaknesses, opportunities, and threats facing the company. The team identified the following stakeholders of the

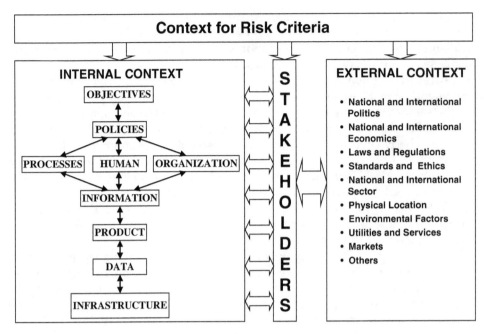

Exhibit 22.2 Using Context for Risk Criteria

company: shareholders, board members, employees, media, third-party outsourcing vendors, the World Trade Organization, regulatory agencies, stock exchanges, the Internal Revenue Service (IRS), environmentalists, suppliers, customers, labor unions, and immigration authorities.

The risk management policy in Appendix B is its third version in an effort to keep up to date with the latest developments and/or evolution in respect to risk management best practices, as well as how the business is supposed to operate. The latest update was performed during 2011 to address the principal elements of ISO 31000. The company also conducted an impact analysis using worst-case scenarios to set an operational baseline, and this further helped to formulate the risk criteria and JAA's attitude toward risks.

Defining Risk Criteria

JAA undertook the following six-step process to establish risk criteria at the company.

First, it selected each of the five strategic objectives and articulated its position on expected outcomes and how it would measure such outcomes.

The five objectives were:

1. Maintaining market leadership
2. Sustaining technology leadership
3. Strengthening global presence
4. Delivering quality service
5. Being seen as a leader in compliance with all laws and regulations

For example, the expected outcomes for "being seen as a leader in compliance with all laws and regulations" are minimal injury to employees, zero fatalities, not facing prosecutions and enforcement actions, and minimizing the cost of any cleanup. It decided to measure such outcomes by people impact, legal actions, and duration and cost of any cleanup.

Second, it developed scales for each consequence type using ordinal measurement with the low end representing tolerable or insignificant deviations from the expected values and the high end representing very high consequences that may be retained only by board approval. Such consequences are demonstrated in Exhibit 22.3 for quantitative consequences and in Exhibit 22.4 for qualitative consequences.

Third, it decided how likelihood would be expressed, and chose ranges from rare to very often with their associated probabilities, as can be seen in Exhibit 22.5a.

Fourth, it developed a table to derive the level of risk, and this can be seen in Exhibit 22.5b. The company opted to express the level of risk as a distribution instead of a point level so that different levels of impact could be expressed with the corresponding likelihood.

Fifth, it decided how the level of risk would be expressed by using a scale consisting of four levels from high to low, based on the combination of impact and likelihood mentioned before. With this table, for each risk, a treatment method is determined by multiplying the likelihood (probability) with impact level. Bow tie analysis[9] is being used to map objectives and the events or consequences.

Finally, it decided on the rules for evaluating a risk, and such rules are listed in the upcoming "Risk Attitude" exhibit, and in Appendix B, "Risk Management Policy."

Bringing Everything Together

At the initial stage with individual participants at a risk identification and assessment workshop, the CRO did not intervene, even though he believed that there was some bias in the opinions being expressed. As the sessions continued, interaction among the different participants resulted in a diminution of the biases. At the conclusion of each workshop, all the risks were prioritized according to group consensus. Communication among the team members and the great facilitation by the CRO helped to reduce the biases. A set of risk criteria[10] was developed (depicted in Exhibits 22.3, 22.4, and 22.5), which was used to guide strategic business decisions with respect to the apparent risks.

A new communication channel was established with the EROC and the risk owners, who met and continue to meet quarterly. This structure helped JAA establish a sound and trusted medium for the exchange of ideas, thus reducing misunderstandings. The meeting agenda usually included ongoing projects, new perceptions of risk, and changes in the context and alignment of the current risk profile with the organization's risk management policy and the risk attitude. The EROC demonstrated executive management's commitment to managing risk, and helped to establish a risk consciousness and risk culture within JAA.

The need for an increased awareness of sustainability among stakeholders was one area of concern, and as such it was one of the new projects undertaken by JAA. The company added new policies and a few application projects to increase public awareness. These projects also helped to increase the brand value.

Exhibit 22.3   Consequence Scales for Quantifiable Effect

Objective Type	Measure	Scenario	Metric for Impact or Consequence				
			5—Very High	4—High	3—Moderate	2—Low	1—Very Low
Financial	Sales growth	Quarterly sales expectations	> +25% < −25%	> +15% < −15%	> +10% < −10%	> +7% < −7%	> +4% < −4%
	Brand value	Market price volatility	> +25% < −25%	> +15% < −15%	> +10% < −10%	> +7% < −7%	> +4% < −4%
Reputation	Public relations	Media coverage value (+/−)	> $10M	> $7M	> $4M	> $2M	> $1M
			International media coverage	National media coverage	Local media coverage	Within the sector	Partial sector
	Employee commitment	Key personnel turnover	15%	10%	5%	3%	1.5%
Regulatory	Local licenses	Regulatory fines	> $1M	> $700,000	> $500,000	> $300,000	> $100,000
	Legal	Contract liabilities	> $10M	> $7M	> $4M	> $2M	> $1M
Customers	Quality perception	Customer satisfaction	> 80%	> 60%	> 40%	> 20%	> 5%
	Retail customer growth	New customers and retention	> 15%	> 10%	> 5%	> 3%	> 1.5%
	Retail branches	Branch performance	> +25% < −25%	> +15% < −15%	> +10% < −10%	> +7% < −7%	> +4% < −4%
Sustainability Business	Business continuity	Disruptions	> 3 days	> 2 days	> 1 day	> half day	> 1 hour
	Markets	Order delivery delays	> 5 days	> 3 days	> 1 day	> half day	> 1 hour
	Technology	Project delivery delays	> 3 months	> 2 months	> 1 month	> 15 days	> 1 week
Safety and Environment	Work safety	Incidents	1 casualty	> 1 major wound	> 1 minor wound	Minor wound	Local physical damage only

Exhibit 22.4 Consequence Scales for Nonquantifiable Effect

Rating	Financial	Reputation	Regulatory	Customer	Sustainability	Safety	Environment
Massive	Available financial resources affected highly so that revisions of business plans needed	Organization assets that represent value to company brand and market credibility severely affected	Market existence and/or ability to generate business severely affected	Performance or quality severely affected	Business flow severely affected	Multiple fatalities or irreversible disability to many individuals	Natural resources severely affected
Major	Available financial resources affected remarkably so that revisions of some of the elements of business plans needed	Organization assets that represent value to company brand and/or market credibility significantly affected	Market existence and/or ability to generate business significantly affected	Performance or quality significantly affected	Business flow significantly affected	Fatality and/or irreversible disability to one or many individuals/persons	Natural resources significantly affected
Moderate	Available financial resources affected noticeably so that revisions of a few of the elements of business plans needed	Organization assets that represent value to company brand and/or market credibility noticeably affected	Market existence and/or ability to generate business noticeably affected	Performance or quality noticeably affected	Business flow noticeably affected	Moderate irreversible injury or impairment to one or more persons	Natural resources noticeably affected
Minor	Financial resources affected at manageable level so that changes stay within the budget limit	Limited effect on brand value or market credibility	Effect stays limited and does not cause long-term business change	Effect can be considered manageable with little resources	Effect stays in expected regions and manageable with current assets	Hospitalization required; largely reversible injury to one or more persons	Visible local effect
Insignificant	Adjustments can be made with short-term arrangements of funds	Manageable with daily operations	Manageable with simple adjustments	Manageable with local resources	Manageable with local resources and current assets	Reversible injury requiring hospital treatment	Can be treated with current assets

Exhibit 22.5a   Likelihood/Probability Scales and Risk Levels

Likelihood	Probability	Possible Example Event
5—Very often	More than 10 times or once in 0–5% of the target time period	Contract liabilities are violated 12 times in 3 years
4—Often	5–10 times or once in 5–25% of the target time period	Imitation of JAA products is observed 9 times in 5 years
3—Even	3–5 times or once in 25–50% of the target time period	M&A is observed with outsourced contractors 3 times in 5 years
2—Few	1–3 times or once in 50–75% of the target time period	Dye technology is changed once in 5 years
1—Rare	1–2 times or once in 75–100% of the target time period	Environmental pollution is caused once in 10 years

Exhibit 22.5b   Defining Risk Levels

Risk Level	Quantitative Level	Qualitative Level
High	More than $10M or >1.5% of the net sales	Frequent occurrence and high or very high impact or above
Medium–high	$5–10M or 0.75–1.5% of the net sales	All between high and medium
Medium	$1–5M or 0.15–0.75% of the net sales	Few occurrences and low impact
Low	Less than $1M or < 0.15% of the net sales	All below medium

These projects later fostered a corporate culture of "learning to give." The company has also encouraged its employees to get involved in volunteer projects. JAA started to use natural dye colors wherever possible on the fabrics in the manufacturing process, which was greatly welcomed by its customers. Also, the company's credit rating increased one notch with the last rating revision. This in turn has helped the company access cheaper and longer-term loans.

The communication infrastructure is now robust. The Internet phone network is set up with regional sales functions for easy access to customer needs and resolving issues. Low-cost and high-availability web meetings were enabled with this project. An "I suggest" project, which helps the workforce describe innovative ideas about their jobs, has now been implemented with web-based software. Suggestions are reviewed and evaluated by risk and control owners. Prizes are provided for those whose suggestions are implemented. The project is also helpful to the company's efforts at enhancing the whistle-blower hotline.

During the risk workshops, it was identified that one of the root causes for a risk at the company was the potential for significant age gaps between the senior management and other personnel. Additionally, during the prior five years, most of the key personnel had left the company. Therefore, the company adopted new human resources performance and competence criteria so that highly qualified personnel could be retained. With these treatments, previously high-level risks and weaknesses have been reduced to low levels and JAA has enabled a forward-looking and proactive management approach to be put in place.

Moving Forward: Overseeing Strategy and Risks

To ensure that risks were adequately considered during the strategic planning process, JAA nominated its board-level Risk Oversight Committee to also be its Strategy Oversight Committee and named it the Risk and Strategy Committee (RSC). However, to ensure there is day-to-day monitoring of risks and controls and timely implementation of risk treatment plans to achieve strategic goals, JAA established an Executive Risk Oversight Committee (EROC) chaired by the CEO. The board believed this would reflect the corporate commitment of senior management to play an active role in day-to-day decision making and set the tone across the company that risk management is central to corporate culture.

Nonexecutive oversight of strategy and risk is the responsibility of the RSC, which regularly scrutinizes and exercises independent judgment over the most significant risks and effectiveness of the treatment plans and controls across the business. Discussions with the CRO and the heads of other oversight functions are also conducted without executive management being present. The nonexecutive directors (NEDs) are a step removed from the daily operations of the business, enabling them to assess and challenge the risk treatment plans. The complete board of JAA is responsible for overseeing achievement of strategy and the long-term goals of JAA through the risk governance structures it has established and maintained.

Looking to the Future: JAA's Management of Uncertainty

The successful turnaround in the fortunes of JAA is evidenced by its financial performance (see Appendix A) achieved through meeting its strategic objectives. JAA successfully seized opportunities emanating from the uncertainties impacting on those objectives. What follows is a comprehensive discussion on how JAA went about responding to the risks comprising its risk profile. The risk profile of the company appears in Exhibit 22.6a with a related risk map in Exhibit 22.6b. They clearly indicate how the risks of JAA have been changing due to its successful treatment of risks (i.e., emerging and current). The perceptions or flat trends exist because the treatment plans are a work in progress. As the treatment results are achieved, relative levels of risk will decrease as the benefits emerge for the objectives. The risks comprising the risk profile of the organization and the risk treatments selected to manage them are discussed next.

European Union (EU) Anti-Dumping Regulation Changes

Because of the latest data from the World Trade Organization (WTO), JAA noted that there is increased market penetration from Eastern markets to EU markets. Also, complaints from local manufacturers have commenced. The EU Parliament may start to investigate anti-dumping measures against Asian countries in the textile industry, which could very well result in increased tariffs. If this scenario is realized, this will strengthen global presence and help to maintain market leadership, two of the strategic objectives of JAA. This will also have an impact on production costs, satisfying new quotas, and logistics. If the net effect is negative, JAA may need to change its business model, which could create additional hardships on the company. To avoid this situation, the maturity level of markets in the Middle East and South Africa needs to be evaluated for both logistics and

Exhibit 22.6a   Current Risk Profile

Risk Source	2013 Perception	2014 Forecast	Trend
EU Anti-Dumping regulation changes	Medium	High	↑
Outsourcing and supplier contract management: Quality and delivery assurance	Medium	Medium	↓
Competitors' marketing strategies	Medium–high	High	↗
Imports: National FITs for trade discrimination	Medium–high	Medium–high	↘
Cost variability and management	Medium	Medium	↙
Local trade laws and regulations	Medium	Medium	↔
New fabric production and dye technologies	Medium	Medium–high	↙
Reaching target customers in new locations (countries)	Medium	Medium	↔
Environmental sensitivity of creditors	Medium	Medium–high	↗
Imitation of JAA's products	Medium–high	Medium	↘

Trends: ↑: Impact is increasing, ↗: Both impact and likelihood increasing, ↘: Impact decreasing but likelihood increasing, ↔: Same from the last assessment, ↙: Both likelihood and impact decreasing.

production sites as alternatives. This step will help to ensure preservation of competitive advantage and the ability to identify new markets.

Outsourcing and Supplier Contract Management: Quality and Delivery Assurance

The latest trends demonstrate that there will be high volatility caused by mergers and acquisitions among outsourced suppliers. The agreed standards of service-level agreements (SLA) may be degraded, which could cause delivery delays and quality issues because of laid-off workers who are more experienced and certified but more costly. This kind of situation may impact JAA's objective of strengthening its global presence. Therefore, it decided to maintain a database of potential suppliers and set up procedures for sample production lots with them so that it can respond in a timely fashion and shift outsourcing arrangements to limit delays and maintain product quality.

Competitors' Marketing Strategies

JAA noted that there has been an increase in new entries to the sector with aggressive marketing strategies, which may affect its objective of maintaining market leadership. The quality of its products and customer satisfaction have become increasingly important. To have timely and more comprehensive information, a new customer survey for both current satisfaction and future expectations will be needed among both customers and local retail partners. This will provide JAA with the information and ability to act promptly. If JAA fails to obtain adequate information on competition, then this could result in faulty strategy setting at JAA with severe consequences.

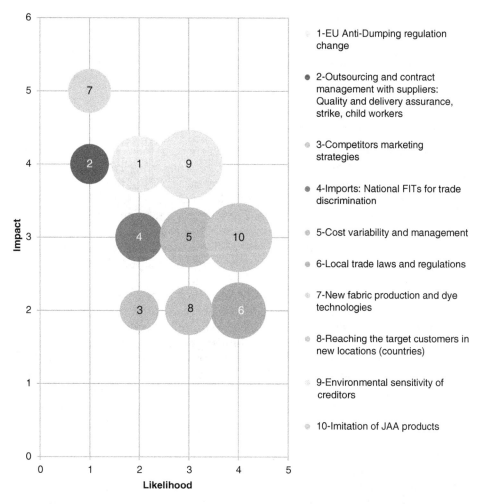

Exhibit 22.6b   Risk Map

Likelihood and Impact Matrix: Sizes of the bubbles are proportional to the relative interdependency of risk sources. The bigger the bubble, the greater the effect on other risk sources.

Imports: National Feed-In Tariffs for Trade Discrimination

Market sentiment has become more sensitive. Local producers in the countries in which JAA operates have become increasingly sensitive to price changes. It has been decided to monitor closely the price levels in these countries. Any changes in national feed-in tariffs (FITs) will have an effect in either direction, which will also affect all of JAA's objectives.

Cost Variability and Management

Because of social movements and environmental issues in some of the countries, the working conditions may be affected severely, which in turn may impact JAA's sales and production costs as well as business continuity. The risk treatment decided for reaching new markets and contractors will help to decrease the cost volatility in the long run. In the short term, risk acceptance criteria will be reduced and hedging will be required for short positions of the foreign exchange portfolio above the agreed risk criteria. In the long run, the cost parameters will be monitored continuously. According to the monitoring results, moving of production lines to different countries will be reevaluated (see Exhibit 22.7).

Exhibit 22.7 Risk Attitude

All negative risks must reside in a low region, and all positive risks must remain at least at a medium level. Exceptions must be decided according to Executive Risk Oversight Committee (EROC) approval and authorization levels. Specific limits and tolerances are set within the risk criteria to enhance risk management treatments. Each specific attitude is set consistently with the risk scales established as per Exhibit 22.3 or Exhibit 22.4. Exceeding the maximum or falling below the minimum is considered a risk indicator. Hence this must be immediately evaluated by the risk owner.

Human resources personnel turnover rate: Maximum 2 percent of the sector median. Maximum compensation can be two times the minimum compensation at the same level in the responsibility level. If the performance parameters do not match higher compensation, then it must be decided by the Compensation Committee whether or not to continue with this policy.

Business continuity: Maximum allowable total business disruption is three days in severe conditions (i.e., disasters) for operating centers.

Health and safety: Maximum of one occurrence in a three-year period. No employee or nonemployee deaths are acceptable. Maximum is one minor event per year.

Legal: No delays accepted in reporting and replying to official letters. Contract failures must strictly reside at low levels.

Concentration: No one single customer can exceed 5 percent of JAA's sales.

Customer satisfaction: Maximum yearly returned products 1 percent, and maximum yearly replaced products 1 percent of prior year's sales.

Market risk: Nonhedged foreign exchange portfolio balance can be a maximum 30 percent of the aggregate total open positions.

Local Trade Laws and Regulations

Compliance with local laws and regulations is one of JAA's strategic objectives. Therefore, a chief compliance officer position was established to bolster the compliance department and to improve its monitoring and assessment capability.

One of the most important risk sources is the potential U.S. and European Union Free Trade Agreement. It will highly impact JAA's business and result in new opportunities and threats. The non-EU operations may be affected negatively, whereas EU operations will benefit from this agreement. The compliance department will use its contacts and sources to proactively acquire information about the details of the agreement. This will ensure a precise risk assessment as to how these developments may benefit JAA or the threat they may pose for its EU operations.

New Fabric Production and Dye Technologies

JAA has the ability to reduce costs and demonstrate market leadership among competitors through the efficient deployment of technology. It decided to engage in several research projects with universities that have a high reputation in these areas to stay ahead of competitors, as stated in the company's objectives. Also, this will be done to ensure that disruptive entrants to its market can be dissuaded due to the technological advantages JAA enjoys and the cost other companies would incur to enter and compete in its market.

Reaching Target Customers in New Locations

Being unable to reach target customers in new locations is considered a major risk because it would affect the market share of JAA in the future. Since the treatment of this risk would affect some other consequences that would arise from other risks, it has a special priority because of this dependency. A special markets research team was established to gather detailed information about potential new markets and customers. This team will be responsible for the extraction of information about the cultural and behavioral expectations in the targeted countries.

Environmental Sensitivity of Creditors

There is a high interest from creditors of JAA concerning the environmental effect of production/chemical usage and treatment actions. Even though special agreements exist in the SLAs with our contractors, any failure to comply will severely degrade the credibility and the reputation of the company. Therefore all the outsourcing arrangements allow JAA to receive monitoring reports from the external and internal auditors of its business partners to ensure that governance processes and controls are effective and their operations efficient. They also allow the company to initiate its own assessments if these aforementioned assurances cannot be provided.

Imitation of JAA's Products

Given the high quality and international acceptance of JAA's products, it noted that several attempts have been initiated to copy the brand with inferior products. A market research team will also be responsible to detect such illegal activities and report as necessary, with action to be taken accordingly.

Each risk is reassessed whenever significant new information is collected from any item in the context, as well as on the feedback from the results of treatments. Risk levels are not changed until results from the treatments are validated.

APPENDIX A: JAA INC. FINANCIAL STATEMENTS

JAA Inc.
Balance Sheet
Period Ended: December 31, 2013
Consolidated Balance Sheets
(amounts and shares in thousands, except per share amounts)

	Years ended December 31,	
	2013	2012
Assets		
Current Assets		
Cash	$ 28,242	$ 12,853
Trade accounts receivable, net of allowances of $2,085 and		
$2,195 at December 31, 2013 and 2012, respectively	18,631	14,962
Prepaid expenses and other current assets	11,248	7,631
Inventories, net	153,438	164,229
Restricted cash	1,997	733
Income taxes receivable and prepaid income taxes	149	530
Deferred income taxes, net of valuation allowance of $12,760		
and $12,003 at December 31, 2012 and 2011, respectively	317	494
Total current assets	214,022	201,432
Property and equipment, net	89,778	87,438
Deferred income taxes, net of valuation allowance of $64,818		
and $61,770 at December 31, 2013 and 2012, respectively	961	1,529
Other assets, net	38,586	33,783
Total assets	343,347	324,182
Liabilities and stockholders' equity		
Current liabilities		
Revolving credit facilities and current portion of long-term debt	64,375	80,556
Accounts payable	43,425	33,920
Accrued expenses and other current liabilities	34,181	41,516
Income taxes payable	3,945	2,137
Deferred income tax liability, current	1,594	296
Current portion of capital lease obligations	3,705	1,903
Total current liabilities	151,225	160,328
Long-term debt, net of unamortized discount of $27,929 and		
$20,183 at December 31, 2012 and 2011, respectively	97,445	107,012
Capital lease obligations, net of current portion	4,371	3,844
Deferred tax liability	583	262
Deferred rent, net of current portion	30,706	24,706
Other long-term liabilities	17,695	10,695
Total liabilities	302,025	306,847

JAA Inc.
Balance Sheet
Period Ended: December 31, 2013
Commitments and Contingencies

Stockholders' Equity	$	$
Preferred stock, $0.0001 par value per share, authorized 1,000 shares; none issued	—	—
Common stock, $0.0001 par value per share, authorized 230,000 shares; 110,111 shares issued and 107,181 shares outstanding at December 31, 2013, and 108,870 shares issued and 105,588 shares outstanding at December 31, 2012	2013	2012
Additional paid-in capital	6,786	6,786
Accumulated other comprehensive loss	(2,725)	(3,356)
Accumulated profit	39,407	16,051
Less: Treasury stock, 304 shares at cost	(2,157)	(2,157)
Total stockholders' equity	41,322	17,335
Total liabilities and stockholders' equity	343,347	324,182

JAA Inc.
Income Statement
Period Ended: Dec. 31, 2013
JAA, Inc. and Subsidiaries
Consolidated Statements of Operations and Comprehensive Gain
(Amounts and shares in thousands, except per share amounts)

	Years Ended December 31,	
	2013	2012
Net sales	$779,534	$694,559
Cost of sales	384,783	359,927
Gross profit	394,751	334,632
Selling expenses	239,625	217,447
General and administrative expenses (including related party charges of $1,090 and $912 for the years ended December 31, 2013 and 2012, respectively)	120,625	97,327
Income (loss) from operations	34,501	19,858
Interest expense	859	1,283
Foreign currency transaction loss (gain)	775	(1,235)
Other expense (income)	4,384	(904)
Gain before income taxes	28,483	20,714
Income tax provision	5,127	3,729
Net gain	$ 23,356	$ 16,985
Basic and diluted earnings per share	$ 0.21	$ 0.15
Weighted average basic and diluted shares outstanding	105,980	105,980
Net gain (from above)	$ 23,356	$ 16,985
Other comprehensive (loss) income item:		
Foreign currency translation, net of tax	631	631
Comprehensive gain	$ 23,987	$ 17,616
Number of common shares issued	110,111	108,870

APPENDIX B: RISK MANAGEMENT POLICY

Purpose

Risk management is considered critical to the company and as such it is viewed as a lifetime strategic project for JAA. JAA continuously monitors and reviews its risk management framework in view of the 11 principles of ISO 31000 and puts great effort into achieving outstanding results through the ongoing learning process.

JAA encourages transparent communications and making decisions with the best available information. It also motivates its employees to clearly understand the business and be proactive in detecting opportunities and threats.

All personnel are expected and encouraged to understand this culture and thus be instrumental in being part of JAA's decision making process. Utilization of uniform terminology is considered a crucial component for building and maintaining the desired culture throughout the company.

This document has been accepted and signed by the board of directors as an indication that there is a common understanding of how the company will manage its risks. The target audience of this policy is the entire organization comprising both the internal and external stakeholders. Each employee is required to understand, manage, monitor, and act according to the policies, principles, and methodology stated in this document. The Risk and Strategy Committee (RSC) approves and oversees the risk management policy and monitors the effect of risk management on the organization. The RSC is assisted by the Executive Risk Oversight Committee (EROC) with the oversight and monitoring of the risks impacting JAA.

Scope

This document supplies overarching principles and a framework for JAA for effective risk management. Each business unit is responsible for taking the necessary actions for treatment within the risk criteria. Each business unit is required to use the policies and the methodology that follow to design its processes and procedures.

Objectives of Risk Management

The only purpose of risk management is to accomplish our business objectives, as that is what we are accountable for to the stakeholders of the company. Each employee has a vested interest to ensure that this happens to the best of his or her abilities and in a way that is consistent with his or her job descriptions. All risks must be understood and all key decisions must factor into such understanding before an action is taken. JAA acknowledges that increasing personal capabilities will also increase organization capabilities. Therefore, maximum prudent effort is expected from each employee in the decision making process to prioritize organization resources so that JAA's objectives are attained at all levels.

Terminology

Risk: Effect of uncertainty on objectives.
Risk criteria: Terms of reference against which the significance of a risk is evaluated.

Risk management: A discipline for managing uncertainty.

Risk monitoring: Continuous checking, supervising, critically observing, or determining the status in order to identify change from the performance level required or expected.

Risk register: A dynamic record that is maintained to monitor and review risks continuously. It is not intended to be used as a static document, and it represents one of the critical outputs of the risk management process.

Risk treatment: Process to modify risk.

Stakeholder: Entity that affects, is affected by, or perceives that it can be affected by a decision of the organization. Each stakeholder's needs and expectations have to be addressed explicitly in the risk management process. In addition, a robust communication process needs to be established with all stakeholders.

Risk Oversight Principles

The board acknowledges that it will not always be able to manage all of the risks the company faces within the set risk criteria. Consequently, a set of high-level principles that set the overarching boundaries for how the company will manage its risks effectively is in place, so that the strategic objectives can be achieved:

- The board will adopt measures to ensure a low level of volatility in revenues and earnings.
- The board will promote orderly business operations to guard against a loss of confidence in the company by all stakeholders, including shareholders, customers, suppliers, and regulatory agencies.
- The board will adopt measures to minimize regulation-related risks.
- The board will review any changes to the existing risk profile caused by the introduction of any new significant projects.
- The board will monitor business and strategic performance via reporting of key performance indicators. The risk criteria statements will provide a basis for strategic evaluation and assessment of new strategic directions.

A discussion of JAA's business strategy must include an analysis of the uncertainties impacting objectives of that strategy. This will provide JAA with an opportunity to improve the likelihood of strategic success by thinking about risks proactively.

Roles and Responsibilities

The board of directors (BOD) is accountable to ensure that the organization manages all risks. The BOD fulfills this duty by establishing the RSC, as well as an EROC for the governance process. The BOD evaluates the structure and effectiveness of the RSC and EROC yearly.

The chief risk officer (CRO) is an adviser to all committees. He or she is responsible for facilitating risk workshops and providing support to establish training curricula. He or she collaborates between the risk oversight and other risk management groups.

Risk Management Methodology

JAA uses the ISO 31000 Risk Management Standard and HB 436 to organize its risk management activities. The BOD oversees risk management through its established committees and delegates authority to management where needed. This mandate and commitment function is executed by the EROC. Risk policies adopted for the organization must be consistent with the ISO 31000 principles.

In the objective setting process, as part of business strategy, there must be an alignment with SMART criteria (i.e., specific, measurable, attainable, relevant, and timely). All company personnel need to understand the company's internal and external context. Risk assessment consists of event identification, risk analysis, and risk evaluation.

Scenario analysis and strengths, weaknesses, opportunities, and threats (SWOT) analysis are conducted to identify, analyze, and evaluate the risks. Surveys are conducted monthly to detect any changes in perception. Risk sources stated in the context are always included in threat and benefit analyses. Risk workshops are facilitated by the risk management department to identify, analyze, and evaluate JAA's risks.

All identified major risks are reported to the EROC, which in turn is responsible for the implementation and monitoring of risk treatment plans. Treatment plans include measurement and monitoring activities together with performance and success criteria. All risks are subjected to three different scenarios for what-if analysis. Each scenario set is divided into four categories as worst case, current conditions, best case, and most expected case, and is analyzed accordingly. The RSC oversees execution of the risk treatment plans.

Monitor and Review: At each fiscal year-end, monthly impacts of consequences are statistically combined and mapped to risk levels in the risk criteria to verify whether the previous predictions occurred. If there are any identified gaps and/or significant errors, the root cause of these gaps needs to be identified and results communicated to stakeholders to ensure that these can be included in the next assessment.

General Risk Management Policies

General risk management policies apply to the entire company. Policies provide high-level guidelines for managing risks within JAA. Commitment to comply with the general policies is a company-wide requirement. The following are key risk policies:

- *Corporate ethics policy.* Corporate ethics rules are monitored and maintained by the Audit Committee. Ethics are included in each training seminar and such seminars need to be taken periodically.
- *Customer satisfaction and retention policy.* Internal and external customer expectations are periodically monitored and communicated in a timely fashion to ensure that service levels are achieved for operational objectives.
- *Ownership policy.* No information, data, process, report, or asset can exist without having an owner attached to it. Change of ownership can be initiated only upon approval of a designated internal stakeholder. Ownership

is assigned according to priority criteria of "most used by," "first created by," and "most impacted by."

- *Training policy.* Each item in this policy statement must be included in the company's training program. Corporate culture can be established and maintained only by providing timely and sufficient training to each employee. No employee can be assigned responsibilities without adequate measurement of his or her competencies.

- *Information systems policy.* Objectives at all levels (strategic, tactical, and operational) should be mapped down to the infrastructure level. (see Exhibit 22.2). Context definition should be monitored and reviewed at least yearly and whenever a major event occurs. All risk owners must be cognizant of their dependency on other areas of the business. Integrity, consistency, and accessibility objectives are set by business lines, and information technology (IT) hardware and software architectures are designed to ensure the achievement of such objectives.

- *Access rights policy.* Access rights should be provided according to each employee's responsibility level. Access rights should not be changed without approval of a senior manager. All access rights need to be consistent with the authorization levels in Exhibit 22.8. No conflict of interest and segregation of duties issues are permitted to exist.

- *Human resources policy.* Background screening and training are required for all employees. Compensation is evaluated and performance is monitored by the Compensation Committee. Compensation must be proportional to responsibilities and should not motivate unnecessary and inconsistent risk taking as compared with JAA's risk criteria. Especially, performance measures will include and reflect a fair amount of collaborative and teamwork performance as well as individual performance to prevent destructive competition. Any contrary action will be considered a failure to comply with the corporate policies and will be treated according to company laws and regulations.

- *Outsourcing and contract management policy.* Outsourcing is used whenever it is beneficial for the organization to do so. A comprehensive risk assessment must be conducted and results must be communicated among internal stakeholders before establishing any outsourcing engagement. Service-level agreements (SLAs) are determined according to business needs and set within the tolerance levels of the objectives. Monitoring of SLAs is the responsibility of the owner of the business line signing the contract. Dependency on a single outsource agreement must be avoided by establishing alternate sources.

- *Business continuity policy.* Impact analysis is conducted yearly to assess the impact level of disruption to all business units. Service-level agreements are based on this impact analysis and must be signed by all parties. IT departments use this impact analysis to determine parameters for service levels. Each employee must have a designated backup coordinator.

- *Conflict of interest policy.* Conflicts of interest must be avoided. Special emphasis needs to be given to those areas sensitive to public perceptions. Corporate ethics is included in each training curriculum to establish enhanced awareness at JAA.

Exhibit 22.8   Authorization Levels for Risk Acceptance or Retaining of Risk

All management level personnel are to be assigned an authorization level by the board of directors (BOD). Purchases and borrowings must be performed in accordance with the levels of authority.

Risk attitudes are defined with risk criteria, and different risk attitudes may be assigned to specific risks in specific circumstances. Risk criteria are established by the RSC to evaluate the significance of risks and to distinguish the possible risk levels. For qualitative risk types, high-level risks can be accepted and retained only by the BOD; medium-level risks can be accepted and retained by the RSC; low-level risks can be accepted and retained by the EROC. The business lines are responsible for the implementation of the treatment of risks to align with risk criteria for the risks they own and need to manage.

For quantifiable risks, the following authorization levels are/should be applied:

Level A: Signature authority up to $10 million; $10 million to $50 million needs a second signature, and any level above this must be signed by the board of directors as well.

Level B: $1 million to $10 million

Level C: $500,000 to $1 million

Level D: Up to $500,000

Level E: No spending authorization

The BOD has a Level A authority, C-level executives have Level B authority, department heads have Level C authority, line managers have Level D authority, and all other personnel have Level E authority.

- *Segregation of duties policy.* Critical processes as defined by business lines are subject to design criteria of the "four eyes principle."[11] A commencer of any process should not have the capability to terminate it, and a second person should review and approve it.
- *Internal communications policy.* The company should establish specific communication channels. Stakeholders must be informed prior to any major changes being made. Communication response times should be created and compliance levels should be measured to ensure quality.
- *Public relations and external communications policy.* Corporate brand and reputation are our most critical assets. Therefore, maximum effort should exist to protect and increase their value. External communications must be carried out by trained and authorized personnel. All media and external relations need to be monitored by the public relations department. Any communications outside the company must be properly authorized.
- *Patents, trademarks, and copyrights policy.* Any type of innovation that would have an effect on corporate objectives is strongly encouraged and rewarded

proportionally to its contribution to effectiveness or efficiency throughout the organization. Patent rights belong to JAA. Appropriate permission and rights can be granted with the approval of JAA.

- *Sustainability and environmental protection policy.* Maximum effort must be provided to preserving the environment and the resources in each project to enable achievement of business objectives. Carbon emissions must be reduced as a priority throughout the business. Green sources of energy must be utilized if available. Energy backups must contain solar cells in production locations where at least moderate seismic rates are recorded.
- *Insurance policy.* Insurance needs are decided upon after evaluating the current risk profile. Market research must be conducted annually to identify the best total value, which is not necessarily the lowest rate.
- *Market risk policy.* Fluctuations in market prices and exchange rates affect the valuation and cost of JAA's products. Therefore, JAA's ability to compete in the marketplace may change accordingly. Close monitoring of costs is required throughout the entire business. Exchange rate risks above the limit of accepted amounts in export contracts must be hedged by futures contracts to ensure cost/profit stability. Market risk attitude was provided in Exhibit 22.7. Also, key risk indicators must be accepted and reviewed periodically for effectiveness. Liquidity risks need to be managed by the financial control and accounting departments. Liquidity figures are updated monthly and projected for the fiscal year. This document is reviewed yearly and updated as necessary by the EROC. The Internal Audit department is responsible for assessing the adequacy and alignment with this policy document of the applications and procedures throughout the organization.

PART A – QUESTIONS

1. How high do you assess the knowledge level of the business strategy throughout the company by the average employee? Is it your assessment that there is a robust understanding of JAA's business strategy? Support your position with examples.
2. As you are aware, effective implementation of ISO 31000 involves effective design and implementation of a risk management framework and effective implementation of the risk management processes. This will be verified by incorporation of 11 key principles. Find an example in the case for each of the 11 principles in action.
3. Why is it important that the company be able to identify JAA's major stakeholders? How should a company identify its stakeholders? What is meant by the concept that stakeholders select the company instead of the company selects the stakeholders?
4. What characteristics do you see in the board of directors that lend themselves to a strong tone at the top and a culture that fully embraces risk management?
5. If you compare the internal audit department at JAA to several that you know of currently in the marketplace, what are some of the major differences that you see at JAA that obviously have contributed to superior performance? What is unique and refreshing about the approach to the external audit as compared to what you have seen in industry?
6. What is your opinion of the risk (event) identification techniques in place at JAA? How do you think that the company evolved to using such techniques?
7. What is the linkage at JAA between the strategic objectives, context, stakeholders, and risk criteria? Support your comments with specific examples of the link in these four areas.

8. Why is it important that risk criteria be created as per JAA? Do you think it is possible for any reasonable risk treatment plan to be in place without creation of such criteria?
9. Review the risk management policy in Appendix B and describe the kinds of things that constitute a best-in-class policy.
10. What other types of general or specific polices can you describe to manage risks?
11. Why is it that "tone at the top" and a strong risk culture are critical components for a company's success, such as what you see at JAA?

PART B – QUESTIONS

1. If the internal audit department did not report directly to the Audit Committee, but to the CFO, what kind of issues would this raise in your mind? Is this something that you would support? Can you cite specific examples?
2. Is it important that internal audit annually reviews the company's risk management function? What advice would you provide to a head of internal audit that was not performing such a review? Have you seen any examples where internal audit has conducted such reviews and if not, why do you think this to be the case?
3. In many companies, it is typical for internal audit to itself perform a risk assessment which it will use for audit planning and execution purposes. Do you have any thoughts on what you see as the pitfalls in this? What is the ideal situation in a company?
4. Is it appropriate that internal audit provides an opinion on the integrity of work performed by the external auditors, as in the JAA case, and what do you see as pitfalls where internal audit does not do this? Should internal audit be asked to opine on the performance by the external auditors, when in fact not too long ago external auditors were the ones providing an opinion on internal audit performance?
5. What specific characteristics differentiate this external audit function from those you have seen over the past several years? How do you envision external audit fitting into JAA's overall risk management system?
6. If JAA was not using ISO 31000 and HB 436, but instead was using the COSO ERM framework and as well the new COSO internal controls framework, what challenges do you think the company would face in trying to roll out a credible program? Do you think they could be as successful? Support your opinion.
7. Would you consider using alternative internal control frameworks and if so, which ones?
8. Suppose the board decided that they did not need to monitor the risks at all and that this could be delegated down to the CEO. What problems do you see occurring in future?
9. Evaluate the different risk identification and analysis methods being used by JAA, and compare to other methods you are aware of that are not being used. Support your opinion on this subject matter.
10. Suppose that JAA did not have a formal system of risk management using ISO 31000. Do you think it is possible that they could still be doing an excellent job at managing their business risks? Please support your opinion in this regard.
11. How would the board measure the success of their risk management?
12. How would the Compensation Committee use risk management in their reward and compensation process of the company?

NOTES

1. ISO 31000:2009, "Risk Management—Principles and Guidelines," was issued by the International Organization for Standardization (ISO) and provides principles, framework, and a process for managing risk. It can be used by any organization regardless

of its size, activity, or sector. Using ISO 31000 can help organizations increase the likelihood of achieving objectives, improve the identification of opportunities and threats, and effectively allocate and use resources for risk treatment.

2. HB 436.SA/SNZ HB 436:2013, "Risk Management Guidelines: Companion to AS/NZS ISO 31000:2009."

3. The Institute of Directors in Southern Africa (IoDSA) formally introduced the King Code of Governance Principles and the King Report on Governance (King III) in September 2009. Like its 56 commonwealth peers, King III has been written in accordance with the "comply or explain" principle based approach of governance, but specifically the "apply or explain" regime. This regime is unique in the Netherlands and now in South Africa. While this approach remains a hotly debated issue globally, the King III Committee continues to believe it should be a nonlegislative code on principles and practices.

4. In 1995, the Criteria of Control Board of the Canadian Institute of Chartered Accountants (CICA) had written this guidance for people who are responsible for or concerned about control in organizations. Conceptually, it was considered a leader in thinking about control but was later abandoned by the CICA and ultimately overtaken in popularity by COSO's Internal Control Framework.

5. The UK Corporate Governance Code (formerly the Combined Code) sets out standards of good practice in relation to board leadership and effectiveness, remuneration, accountability, and relations with shareholders. The latest edition was issued in September 2012.

6. In November 2013, the Financial Reporting Council issued its Risk Management, Internal Control and the Going Concern Basis of Accounting Consultation on Draft Guidance to the directors of companies applying the UK Corporate Governance Code, and associated changes to the code.

7. "Risk Management Guidelines: Companion to AS/NZS 4360:2004." The Risk Management Guidelines companion to the AS/NZS ISO 31000:2009 handbook provides guidance for establishing and implementing effective risk management processes in any organization.

8. See note 1.

9. The use of bow tie analysis is described in ISO 31010 "Risk Management—Risk Assessment Techniques."

10. See ISO 31000:2009 section 5.3.5 for additional detail on risk criteria.

11. The "four eyes principle" refers to having two people view each transaction so that one checks on the other.

REFERENCES

AS/NZS 4360:2004, "Risk Management."

Canadian Standards Association. 1997. Q850-97 "Risk Management: Guideline for Decision-Makers."

COSO Internal Control Framework. 1992/1994. "Committee of Sponsoring Organizations of the Treadway Commission."

COSO Internal Control Framework. 2013. "Committee of Sponsoring Organizations of the Treadway Commission."

Financial Reporting Council. "Consultation Draft on Risk Management, Internal Control and the Going Concern Basis of Accounting."

Fraser, John, and Betty J. Simkins, eds. 2010. *Enterprise Risk Management: Today's Leading Research and Best Practices for Tomorrow's Executives.* Hoboken, NJ: John Wiley & Sons.

HB 436:2004, "Implementation Guidelines to AS/NZS 4360:2004."

HB 436:2013, "Implementation Guidelines to ISO 31000 Risk Management."

ISO 31000:2009, "Risk Management Framework."

ISO 31010:2009, "Risk Management—Risk Assessment Techniques."

ISO Guide 73:2009.

"King III Report on Corporate Governance." 2009.

Purdy, Grant. 2011. "Risk Appetite: Is Using This Concept Worth the Risk?" Broadleaf Capital International, Risk Post, NZ Society for Risk Management, September.

ABOUT THE CONTRIBUTORS

Julian du Plessis has more than eight years' financial sector experience. He is the Head of Internal Audit at AVBOB Mutual Assurance Society, a long-term insurer in the life and savings business. He joined AVBOB during 2011 as its Governance Officer. He previously worked at FirstRand Bank, one of the largest banking institutions in South Africa, as a senior risk manager starting out in the Group ERM department focusing on strategic risk management. Julian is a South African chartered accountant, and completed his professional training at Pricewaterhouse-Coopers. Julian has an MPhil (business management) master's degree obtained from the University of Johannesburg (2011), a B Compt Honors accounting degree from the University of South Africa (2000), and a B Admin (international politics) degree majoring in economics and political science from the University of Pretoria (1994).

Arnold Schanfield is a Principal with Schanfield Risk Management Advisors LLC. He is an internal audit and risk professional with diversified industry expertise, including consumer products, higher education, life sciences, manufacturing, not for profit, retail, trading companies, and higher education. He specializes in risk management implementations and has leveraged his prior experiences in internal audit, public accounting, and governance to the risk management discipline. Arnold holds an undergraduate degree (BSC) from Loyola College in Montreal and a graduate degree in public accountancy from McGill University in Montreal. In addition, he holds certifications of certified public accountant and certified internal auditor in the United States as well as a Chartered Accountant from Canada. Arnold has a passion for the risk management discipline and has used his experiences to develop seminar and training material that has been delivered to numerous companies. In addition, he comments and speaks frequently on risk management–related matters.

Alpaslan Menevse is currently the Risk Officer at Sekerbank T.A.S., which has in excess of 310 branches in Turkey. He has 28 years of experience in information systems, both as an academic and as a practitioner. In the early years of his career, he joined work groups as a team member of Business Process Management (BPM) in the manufacturing industry. During his academic career, as a computer and aeronautics engineer he was involved in several Information and Communication Technology (ICT) projects and completed his master's thesis in EUCLID RTP 11.3 artificial intelligence project of F-16 fighter jet simulator development, where he modeled pilot behaviors of risk assessments in BVR (beyond visual range) flight. He also led different sizes of local area network (LAN) and wide area network (WAN) projects during 1995–2004, specializing in business continuity and disaster recovery management.

He is a silver member of Information Systems Audit and Control Association (ISACA) and holds Certified Information Systems Auditor (CISA) and Certified in Risk and Information Systems Control (CRISC) certificates where he was one of the members of the review work group of the CRISC 2011 manual, which is the first book published in this area. He joined Sekerbank as the Internal IS Auditor and started working with AS/NZS 4360 in 2007. He is responsible for implementing ISO 31000 throughout the organization. He has a special interest in human behaviors and the human side of change management. Additionally, he is a member of the ISO 31000 TC 262 Technical Committee, United Nations Economic Commission for Europe (UNECE) - Risk Management Group (GRM) and also the chairman of the Turkish Standards Institute TS ISO 31000 MTC 132 Risk Management National Mirror Technical Committee.

Note: Authors of this case study manage the group on LinkedIn titled "Risk Management: Creating Value From Uncertainty." Any questions or comments can be forwarded either personally or as a discussion topic.

Website: http://lnkd.in/djN94XJ.

CHAPTER 23

Control Complacency
Rogue Trading at Société Générale

STEVE LINDO
Principal, SRL Advisory Services

T his case study is divided into two parts. Part One seeks to bring alive the circumstances leading up to the June 2010 public trial involving Société Générale, the French banking group, and Jérôme Kerviel, the equities trader whose positions caused Société Générale to lose €4.9 billion (U.S.$7.2 billion) in January 2008. Part One concludes with an exercise in which the reader is asked to form his or her own opinion on who was to blame for the losses, based on the information contained in Part One. Part Two reveals the actual outcome of the trial and offers additional study materials for the reader. A Classroom Guide, available separately to instructors wishing to facilitate interactive discussion of the case study in a classroom setting, identifies key risk management lessons from the case study and provides a session plan.

PART ONE: KERVIEL'S TRIAL—A MEDIA CIRCUS

On Tuesday, June 8, 2010, the criminal trial of 33-year-old Jérôme Kerviel began in Paris's Palais de Justice. The charges against him were forgery, abuse of trust, and illegal use of computers, brought by the Paris public prosecutor. Since the date he was charged, January 28, 2008, Kerviel had been free on bail and preparing his defense.

Despite the long time lapse between the January 2008 events that had caused Société Générale's losses and the commencement of the trial, media attention was at a fever pitch because of Kerviel's claims that he was a scapegoat for high-risk trading practices that were condoned by Société Générale when they were profitable. Kerviel released an autobiographical book presenting his version of the events shortly before the trial.

Société Générale, on the other hand, maintained from its earliest public communications the posture that Kerviel was a rogue trader who single-handedly developed methods to conduct unauthorized trading without being detected and used them to take massive trading positions that ultimately backfired when markets turned against him. Société Générale also sought to mitigate the damage to its reputation, due to the apparent facility with which Kerviel conducted his

Exhibit 23.1   Sample of News Headlines at the Time of Kerviel's Trial

Headline	Source and Date
Rogue Trader Says Ex-Bosses Encouraged Him	Reuters (June 8, 2010)
French Trader Stays Silent as Trials Begin amid Media Scrum	*The Guardian* (June 8, 2010)
$62 Billion of Suspect Trades Exposed Lack of Oversight	CBC (June 8, 2010)
Kerviel Gets Day in Court, SocGen Too	*Wall Street Journal* (June 7, 2010)
Kerviel's Trial—The World of Finance Takes a Hard Look at Itself (translation)	*L'Express* (June 25, 2010)
Rogue Trader Denounces "Banking Orgy" in Book	*Agence France Presse* (May 4, 2010)

unauthorized trading, by publishing in May 2008, a detailed examination of the operational and managerial circumstances that had allowed Kerviel's unauthorized trading to occur and the remedial actions it was taking to prevent recurrence. Société Générale stated from the outset its intention to hold the individuals accountable whom it considered responsible for the unauthorized trading, and took the first step by filing a civil lawsuit against Kerviel on January 24, 2008.

By June 2010, global financial markets were slowly recovering from the 2008 crisis, but memories of Société Générale's trading losses remained especially vivid because, at the time of their announcement in January 2008, the incident seemed to confirm investors' worst fears that banks in general were taking massive amounts of risk far beyond their traditional lines of business. Exhibit 23.1 shows selected news headlines published at the time of Kerviel's trial, which illustrate this loss of public confidence in banks' risk management discipline.

Société Générale—The Rise of Trading

In the years 1999 through 2006, Société Générale's net income increased 164 percent, from €2 billion annually to €5.2 billion. Though its retail and investment management businesses both prospered during this period, the main driver of Société Générale's higher profitability was its Corporate and Investment Banking (CIB) division, whose net income increased 230 percent, from €708 million annually to €2.3 billion. Within the CIB, the largest contributors to this profit growth were fixed income, foreign exchange (FX), equities, and commodities trading, which together accounted for 77 percent of CIB's net business revenues in 2006.

These results followed a strategic shift in business focus engineered by Daniel Bouton, who was appointed Société Générale's CEO in 1993 and became chairman and CEO in 1999. Bouton was not himself a trader or an investment banker, but a product of the French financial establishment. His early career was spent in government service with the French Finance Ministry. Like most leading public officials and executives of French financial institutions, he was a graduate of the École Nationale d'Administration, France's elite college of public administration.

Among France's top banks, Société Générale was not alone in pursuing growth in the early 2000s through expansion of its trading and capital markets business. Its larger rival, BNP Paribas, adopted the same strategy, as did major banks in other countries such as the United Kingdom, Germany, Switzerland, and the United States. For many of these banks, this strategy backfired when their fixed income desks became deeply involved in structuring, selling, and trading credit derivatives and debt securities backed by U.S. residential mortgages, and consequently were unable to avoid massive write-downs and funding crises when global credit markets seized up in the second half of 2008. Though Société Générale suffered some losses from its fixed income activities, the flaws in its expansion into trading truly came to light in the rogue equities trading incident that is the subject of this case study.

From Business to Retail to Investment Banking, from Private to Public to State Ownership

Société Générale was founded as a private bank by a group of industrialists in 1864, with the intention of providing finance for industry and commerce. Its early years were marked by a modest expansion of commercial lending activity and banking locations, but little interest in deposit taking or retail banking services. However, it demonstrated resilience in adverse times, such as France's economic slump in the 1880s. The turn of the century marked the beginning of several new directions, as Société Générale opened up its capital, actively sought to capture deposits, and launched itself into retail lending. It also established its international presence, principally in London and New York. After the upheavals of World War I, Société Générale rapidly expanded its domestic branch network, domestic lending, and deposit taking, as well as its shareholder base, surpassing Crédit Lyonnais in the mid-1920s to become France's leading bank.

The next phase in Société Générale's development was dictated by external events as France passed through the 1930s economic downturn, World War II, and the postwar rebuilding effort. In 1945, France's three largest commercial banks were nationalized, putting Société Générale into state ownership for the next 42 years. While economic policy prerogatives constrained the bank's domestic activities during the recovery years, the postwar revival of international trade presented new opportunities for overseas expansion. The next 30 years were transformative for the banking industry in general and for Société Générale in particular. ATMs and credit cards reinvented the economics of retail banking, and the breakdown of the Chinese wall between investment and commercial banking opened up securities underwriting and trading business to commercial banks. Société Générale successfully took advantage of these changes and, in 1987, became the first of France's nationalized banks to be reprivatized.

During the 1990s, the bank's primary strategy was to expand its share of the domestic banking market, which was undergoing a phase of consolidation. In 1997, it met with initial success by acquiring Credit du Nord, but in 1999 suffered a big disappointment when its friendly merger with Banque Paribas was snatched away by a hostile bid from Banque Nationale de Paris (BNP). As a consequence, Société Générale refocused its growth strategy in the 2000s on three pillars: international retail banking, investment management, and capital markets. The first pillar led to a string of retail banking acquisitions in former Soviet Union countries and Africa. The second pillar resulted in the establishment of a global platform of investor services, including fund management, mutual funds, and securities processing.

The third pillar was entrusted to its newly formed Corporate and Investment Banking (CIB) division, intended to achieve prominence in the markets for debt and equity securities and derivatives.

CIB Gets a Boost from Trading Talent

In 1997, Société Générale's CIB contributed just €151 million to the group's net income of €933 million, barely 16 percent. Then, in 1998 the CIB recorded a loss of €67 million as global markets suffered from the liquidity and volatility backlash from Russia's debt default and the collapse of Long Term Capital Management (LTCM). In 1999, shortly after Daniel Bouton was elected chairman of Société Générale in addition to his role as CEO, the CIB received a boost from the promotion of Jean-Pierre Mustier from head of international equity options trading to head of fixed income, FX, commodities, and derivatives. Over the previous 10 years since joining Société Générale, Mustier, aged 38, had gained high internal recognition for building a profitable equity derivatives trading business. CIB's earnings over the next four years proved Mustier's mettle. In 1999, CIB's net income jumped to €708 million, 35 percent of Société Générale's worldwide net income, and over the next three years CIB accounted for 36 percent of Société Générale's €6.2 billion cumulative net income, amounting to €2.3 billion. Mustier's contribution to this impressive performance earned him promotion to the position of CIB's global head and membership in Société Générale's Executive Committee.

Now all under Mustier's leadership, Société Générale's CIB began to deliver ever-higher profits. In 2003, its net income rose to €1.1 billion, which was 46 percent of the group total, followed by €1.4 billion in 2004, €1.8 billion in 2005, and €2.3 billion in 2006. Consistent with Mustier's demonstrated abilities, CIB derived a higher proportion of its revenues from trading than previously. In 2000, trading had accounted for 23 percent of CIB revenues. During the next six years, the percentage averaged 30 percent. This performance was made possible by a rapid expansion in the number of traders CIB deployed and the markets in which they were active. However, as the investigation into Kerviel's unauthorized trading later revealed, this growth in activity was not accompanied by a corresponding reinforcement of CIB's infrastructure and controls.

Société Générale Group Snapshot, December 2006

As 2006 turned into 2007, Société Générale's business performance appeared to be riding the crest of a wave. Compared to 2005, net income for 2006 increased 18.6 percent to €5.2 billion, net banking income increased faster than operating expenses (16 percent versus 12 percent), and all business units delivered higher returns. In 2006, Société Générale raised €2.4 billion of new capital, and Standard & Poor's and Fitch raised their long-term debt ratings from AA– to AA. Over the preceding seven years, the number of Société Générale's retail customers had increased 2.4 times, the assets under management by its wealth management business had increased 2.8 times, and the number of Société Générale employees had increased 1.9 times worldwide. As of December 31, 2006, Société Générale's

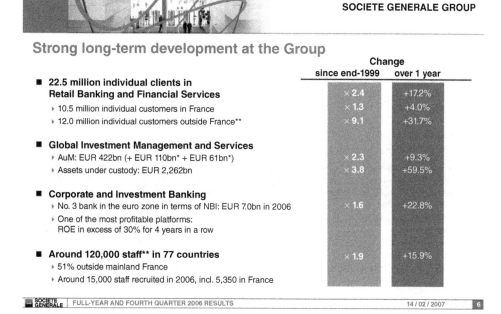

Exhibit 23.2 Highlights of Société Générale's 2006 Performance
* GIMS' AuM do not include EUR 110bn of assets held by customers of the French Networks (investable assets exceeding EUR 150,000) or EUR 61bn of assets managed by Lyxor AM, whose results are consolidated in the Equity & Advisory business line (EUR 61bn).
** Excluding Rosbank (Russia).
Source: Société Générale.

total group assets amounted to €869 billion, its risk-weighted assets amounted to €285 billion, and its shareholders' equity amounted to €22.3 billion. Selected 2006 group performance highlights published in Société Générale's annual shareholder filing are shown in Exhibit 23.2.

Measured by 2006 net investment banking income, Société Générale's CIB ranked #3 in the Euro-zone. Compared to 2005, its net income increased by 27 percent to €2.3 billion, bolstered by trading revenue that increased 37.5 percent and worldwide front office head count, which increased by 490 (+11 percent). The CIB reported that its fixed income desk had been ranked #2 in corporate eurobond issuance and its equity derivatives business named global equity derivatives house of the year by the International Financing Review. Forecasting continued capital markets growth for 2007–2010, the CIB's leadership saw no subprime mortgage clouds on the horizon, while its 2006 provisions for credit and trading losses declined from their 2005 level. Selected 2006 CIB performance highlights published in Société Générale's annual shareholder filing are shown in Exhibit 23.3.

For a more complete picture of Société Générale's financial profile, see its 2006 and 2007 income statements and balance sheets, presented later in this chapter.

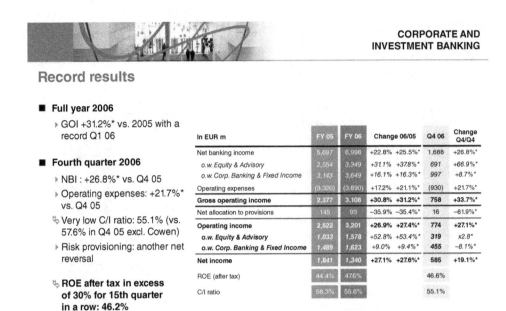

Record results

■ **Full year 2006**

  ▸ GOI +31.2%* vs. 2005 with a
record Q1 06

■ **Fourth quarter 2006**

  ▸ NBI : +26.8%* vs. Q4 05

  ▸ Operating expenses: +21.7%*
vs. Q4 05

  🌿 Very low C/I ratio: 55.1% (vs.
57.6% in Q4 05 excl. Cowen)

  ▸ Risk provisioning: another net
reversal

  🌿 **ROE after tax in excess
of 30% for 15th quarter
in a row: 46.2%**

In EUR m	FY 05	FY 06	Change 06/05		Q4 06	Change Q4/Q4
Net banking income	5,697	6,998	+22.8%	+25.5%*	1,688	+26.8%*
o.w. Equity & Advisory	2,554	3,349	+31.1%	+378%*	691	+66.9%*
o.w. Corp. Banking & Fixed Income	3,143	3,649	+16.1%	+16.3%*	997	+8.7%*
Operating expenses	(3,320)	(3,890)	+17.2%	+21.1%*	(930)	+21.7%*
Gross operating income	2,377	3,108	+30.8%	+31.2%*	758	+33.7%*
Net allocation to provisions	145	93	−35.9%	−35.4%*	16	−61.9%*
Operating income	2,522	3,201	+26.9%	+27.4%*	774	+27.1%*
o.w. Equity & Advisory	1,033	1,578	+52.8%	+53.4%*	319	x2.8*
o.w. Corp. Banking & Fixed Income	1,489	1,623	+9.0%	+9.4%*	455	−8.1%*
Net income	1,841	1,340	+27.1%	+27.6%*	585	+19.1%*
ROE (after tax)	44.4%	47.6%			46.6%	
C/I ratio	58.3%	55.6%			55.1%	

Exhibit 23.3   Highlights of CIB's 2006 Performance
* When adjusted for changes in Group structure and at constant exchange rates.
Source: Société Générale.

Jérôme Kerviel, an Ambitious Outsider

Hidden behind the rosy outlook depicted in Société Générale's 2006 financial results were two fires smoldering in its CIB. One, exposure to U.S. subprime residential mortgage-backed securities (MBSs), was about to spread like wildfire throughout the world's financial sector and engulf several larger and more ambitious banks than Société Générale. The other, unauthorized speculative trading in European equity markets, was about to drive a huge hole through Société Générale's reputation and profits at the hands of a single trader, Jérôme Kerviel.

Kerviel's position in Société Générale's CIB was unlikely to be noticed. He was one of seven traders in the Delta One Listed Products (DLP) team, a part of the Equity Finance section in the Equity Arbitrage group of the CIB's Global Equities & Derivative Solutions (GEDS) business unit. At the end of 2006, the CIB had almost 5,000 front office personnel worldwide. GEDS itself had a head count of over 1,300. GEDS's proprietary trading activities comprised two groups—volatility and arbitrage. As these names imply, GEDS's volatility traders were charged with profiting from directional trading positions, while the arbitrage traders looked to profit from long/short combinations of offsetting positions by capturing mispricing between assets with similar market sensitivity. A common feature of arbitrage trading is that price differentials are typically very small, which requires large notional amounts of offsetting trades in order to capture meaningful profits.

Kerviel joined Société Générale in August 2000 at age 23 to do modeling and process automation in CIB's middle office. In July 2002, he was promoted to trader assistant in CIB's Delta One Equity Derivatives product team, responsible for position valuations, price reserves, and risk analysis. In March 2004, he was appointed junior trader for the purpose of proprietary arbitrage trading in listed equity derivative products, including stock futures, indexes, exchange-traded funds (ETFs), and customized equity options such as turbo warrants.

Though inconspicuous in Société Générale's big picture, Kerviel's career progression was quite an impressive achievement considering his modest origins. He grew up in a small town on the coast of Brittany, and obtained a bachelor's degree in finance in 1999 at the University of Nantes, a provincial town in western France, and a master's degree in financial markets organization and control in 2000 at the University of Lyon. Just as executive positions in France's leading financial institutions were considered reserved for the alumni of elite colleges such as the École Nationale d'Administration that Daniel Bouton had attended, so high-earning trading positions were also considered to be the preserve of graduates from France's top 23 business schools known as *grandes écoles*, like Jean-Pierre Mustier.

At First a Few Side Bets, Then Massive Speculation

Kerviel began experimenting with directional positions during his first year as a Delta One trader, creating small index futures and cash equity positions that he closed out before the end of each day. Although these trades were unrelated to Kerviel's arbitrage trading assignment, his supervising manager monitored and discussed them and allowed Kerviel to continue. In 2005, Kerviel became bolder, venturing into overnight trades. Initially, it seems that this progression was also tolerated because of the small amounts, but a €10 million overnight cash equity position drew his manager's concern in July 2005. Kerviel's next move took him over the line into fraudulent activity. In order to continue taking overnight directional positions without arousing management concerns, he began to create fictitious trades to offset them in DLP's books. This practice continued in sporadic fashion and in relatively small amounts through the end of 2006, peaking at €140 million in August, unnoticed by Kerviel's manager or any of DLP's middle or back office personnel. Meanwhile, in the other sector where trouble was brewing for Société Générale, the first signs of distress were emerging in the U.S. residential mortgage finance market, as several subprime lenders started to report high delinquencies and the U.S. home construction index tumbled.

In January 2007, Kerviel's manager left Société Générale to take another job. For the next two months, Kerviel was effectively unsupervised. Finally, in April 2007, a new manager was assigned to Kerviel's DLP team, but this one had no prior trading experience and received no orientation on his critical duties. Meanwhile, in the European equity markets where Kerviel traded, the accelerating U.S. residential mortgage meltdown had not yet had any impact, but the opportunity to bet on a stock market correction proved irresistible. By January 24, Kerviel's directional short position in European equity index futures had reached €850 million. During February, Kerviel increased his short position to €2.6 billion (U.S.$3.4 billion), and by the end of March it had risen to €5.5 billion. As news from the U.S. residential mortgage market continued to deteriorate in June and two Bear

Stearns collateralized debt obligation (CDO) funds collapsed, Kerviel became even bolder. By July 19, his short equity index position hit a peak of €30 billion. So far in 2007, Kerviel's accumulated mark-to-market loss was €2.2 billion, which was hidden in the fictitious forwards that he entered into GEDS's transaction system.

The forward counterparties Kerviel selected were either "pending," Société Générale affiliates, or genuine but unsuspecting counterparties. To avoid detection, Kerviel assigned deferred start dates to these forwards, for which GEDS's internal policies did not require formal counterparty confirmations until the start date, which he could manipulate by canceling and reentering new fictitious trades. The sheer volume of this trading was not completely unnoticed. In fact, 41 queries about transaction anomalies, accounting discrepancies, and broker commissions were raised by Société Générale's back office during the period from June 2006 to January 2008, but in each case they were satisfied by Kerviel's trade amendments, cancellations, and explanations. A summary of the queries is shown in Exhibit 23.4.

During the next four weeks, Kerviel's massive stock market bet finally paid off, as stocks around the world fell 8 percent. His short equity futures positions erased their losses and began to show profits, allowing Kerviel to gradually unwind them and accumulate €750 million in profits, which he concealed in fictitious counterparty trades and provisions. In November, stocks began to recover and Kerviel reversed his strategy by building a €30 billion portfolio of unauthorized long equity futures positions matched by fictitious offsetting trades, which he liquidated in December with a further €750 million in profits. Again, the volume of Kerviel's activity attracted notice, this time in the form of an alert from Eurex about a large (€1.2 billion) purchase of equity index futures by DLP in November, which Kerviel's manager failed to follow up.

Exhibit 23.4   Internal Queries Raised about Kerviel's Fictitious or Unauthorized Trades, 2006–2008

Dates	No. of Queries	Focus of Query	Source Department
June 2006	1	Pricing discrepancies	GEDS Operations
Dec. 2006 to June 2007	5	Earnings discrepancies	CIB Accounting
Jan. to Oct. 2007	9	Unidentified counterparty or broker	GEDS Operations
Jan. to Nov. 2007	7	Unexplained balance sheet variations	CIB Accounting
Jan. 2007 to Jan. 2008	3	Trade entry errors	GEDS Operations
Feb. 2007	1	Trade settlement discrepancy	GEDS Operations
March to Oct. 2007	12	P&L and provision discrepancies, high notional amount of transactions	GEDS Operations, CIB Accounting
June to Aug. 2007	2	Reconciliation differences	GEDS Operations
Dec. 2007	1	High broker commissions	DLP trading management

Source: "Mission Green" report, General Inspection Services, Société Générale.

As 2007 came to a close on December 31, Kerviel was careful to close out all his unauthorized trades, ending with a €1.5 billion profit hidden in fictitious forwards with Société Générale affiliates. This was his prize for having held unauthorized directional positions in European stock indexes, in a volume equal to the bank's entire capital, during two prolonged periods of the year. Meanwhile, elsewhere in Société Générale, concerns were mounting that CIB's exposure to U.S. subprime mortgage-backed securities could prove very costly. The first admission of its troubles occurred in October 2007 when CIB's fixed income, currencies, and commodities business unit took a €230 million write-down in its U.S. residential mortgage-related assets. Even though European equity markets ended the year close to their levels before the July correction, Société Générale's year-end share price was still down 37 percent from its May 2007 peak.

Discovery, Damage Control, and Retribution

As soon as 2008's equity markets opened, Kerviel resumed his unauthorized directional trading, confident in his ability to keep calling market movements correctly and hiding his profits. Convinced that the European stock markets would extend their November rally into 2008, he began a series of unauthorized equity index futures purchases that reached a new peak of €49 billion on January 18, offsetting these positions with fictitious trades as before. However, unconnected to this even bolder move, his strategy was about to unravel because of an administrative, not operational, slip. In the first days of 2008, Kerviel changed the counterparty of the fictitious trades concealing his €1.5 billion 2007 profits from a Société Générale affiliate to an unsuspecting third-party counterparty. During 2007, he had made this kind of change many times without tripping any alarms. On this occasion, however, the counterparty he selected did not have a collateral agreement in place with Société Générale, which triggered a massive overage in the counterparty's credit value at risk (CVaR) limit.

Caught by surprise when queried by Société Générale's group risk management department, which was responsible for monitoring counterparty exposures, Kerviel decided to cancel the fictitious trades and create a provision in order to keep his 2007 profits out of sight. Without any signs of concern over this incident, Kerviel calculated an amount for the provision that would leave €15 million of his undisclosed profits to be accounted for in DLP's 2007 yearbook-end trading results and assure him of a high ranking among DLP's traders. Seemingly in the clear again, Kerviel did not know that a second trip wire was about to end his long and eventful trading journey. The query that unraveled his strategy did not come from risk management or operations, but from financial reporting.

January 15 marked the first consolidation of Société Générale's 2007 year-end financial reporting, which included regulatory capital. It also coincided with another slump in global equity prices, triggered by fears that U.S. and international banks were more exposed to subprime mortgage losses than previously disclosed. As Société Générale's preliminary risk-weighted asset (RWA) numbers began to be checked, the massive counterparty exposure that had triggered risk management's CVaR inquiry showed up in the bank's RWA numbers. When queried, Kerviel explained that the trades had been canceled, but the financial reporting group was not satisfied with his explanation. A flurry of e-mails and phone calls took place over the next two days between financial reporting and the DLP middle office and back office, during which Kerviel insisted that the trades had been canceled but gave no satisfactory explanation. Finally, a meeting took place where Kerviel discovered that the outsize RWA number was the result of his fictitious counterparty not having a collateral agreement in place; he thereupon changed his explanation, claiming that the wrong counterparty had been entered for the forwards and identifying another counterparty as the correct one. The meeting ended with Kerviel promising to provide documentary evidence of the replacement counterparty's agreement to the trades.

However, the financial reporting team were skeptical of Kerviel's new explanation and decided to escalate the incident to GEDS's senior management, given the very large size of the transactions. The next day, Friday, January 18, Kerviel modified the trades and sent e-mails that appeared to confirm that the forwards had been agreed with the replacement counterparty. Still concerned, representatives of financial reporting, DLP operations, and GEDS's senior management met at the end of the day and decided to independently confirm the existence of the forwards with the replacement counterparty the next morning, which was Saturday, January 19. Meanwhile, the week's close of business brought more gloom to Société Générale's stock price, which dropped another 8.2 percent as the French central bank announced that Société Générale and another major French bank would have to further write down the valuation of their U.S. assets. On Saturday, January 19, within hours of the fictitious nature of his December 2007 trades being revealed by the counterparty's negative confirmation response, Kerviel divulged the full extent of his €49 billion directional equity index positions, which was immediately communicated to Société Générale's executive management. A summary of the queries, conversations, and meetings that resulted in discovery of Kerviel's unauthorized trading is shown in Exhibit 23.5.

Sunday, January 20, began a series of four days of unthinkable consequences for Société Générale. After being advised of the known facts and extent of Kerviel's unauthorized trading, Bouton notified Société Générale's board and offered his resignation, which was declined and he was told to take charge of controlling the damage. The following day, Bouton obtained an unprecedented permission from France's Financial Markets Authority (Autorité des Marchés Financiers, AMF) to secretly unwind Kerviel's directional equity index position over the next three days before making a public announcement about Société Générale's unauthorized positions. As GEDS's traders set to work, no matter how discreetly they executed their sales, Société Générale inevitably suffered heavy losses due to the size of its positions and the equity markets' bearish trend. By close of business on January 23, all of Société Générale's unauthorized equity index positions were gone and a €6.4 billion loss was recorded, equivalent to 13 percent of the notional value of the positions that Kerviel had created just weeks earlier. Recognizing the damage that such a huge loss could have on market confidence in Société Générale's solvency, Bouton used the time before publicly announcing the losses to secure commitments to raise €5.5 billion of new capital. He also briefed the French, European, and U.S. monetary authorities ahead of the public announcement. On January 24, Bouton held a press conference and issued a letter to Société Générale's clients briefly describing the incident and declaring it to be under control. The letter also stated that Société Générale's capital was to be replenished by the new equity issuance.

Exhibit 23.5 Sequence of Queries, Conversations, and Meetings Resulting in Discovery of Kerviel's Unauthorized Trading

Date	Parties Involved	Issue	Outcome
Jan. 8, 2008	• Société Générale Risk Management • GEDS middle office • Kerviel	Exposure (CVaR) over limit for fictitious counterparty	Issue closed—trades canceled by Kerviel.
Jan. 15, 2008	• CIB Regulatory Reporting (CIB-RR) • GEDS middle office	Very high RWA and Cooke ratio for fictitious counterparty	CIB-RR sought clarification of Kerviel's previous explanations and trade cancellations.
Jan. 16, 2008	• CIB Regulatory Reporting • GEDS middle office • Kerviel	Correct financial reporting of very large trades, clarification of trader's explanations	Not convinced by further telephone explanations, CIB-RR scheduled meeting with Kerviel for January 17.
Jan. 17, 2008	• CIB Regulatory Reporting • GEDS middle office • Kerviel	Correct financial reporting of very large trades, clarification of trader's explanations	Kerviel advised that the wrong counterparty was entered for the trades and would be corrected. CIB-RR requested supporting documentation.
Jan. 18, 2008	• CIB Regulatory Reporting (CIB-RR) • GEDS Trading Management (GEDS-TM) • Kerviel	Trade cancellations, counterparty substitution, unconvincing trader explanations	CIB-RR briefed GEDS-TM, who spoke with Kerviel and received the same unsatisfactory explanations. Kerviel canceled and reentered the fictitious trades with the replacement counterparty and sent CIB-RR a falsified confirmation. CIB-RR and GEDS-TM met in the evening and decided to seek direct confirmation from the replacement counterparty.
Jan. 19, 2008	• CIB Regulatory Reporting • GEDS Trading Management (GEDS-TM) • Kerviel • Société Générale Executive Management	Proof of fictitious transactions, discovery of unauthorized trading positions	Confronted by proof of his fictitious transactions, Kerviel revealed the nature and extent of his past and current unauthorized trading positions that were offset by fictitious trades.

Source: "Mission Green" report, General Inspection Services, Société Générale.

In a subsequent interview he disclosed that Société Générale would take a further €2 billion write-down in its U.S. residential mortgage exposures for 2007 year-end. Bouton's revelations were generally greeted by astonishment that a financial institution of Société Générale's standing could have failed to prevent such egregious risk taking by a single individual.

In the following days, Société Générale filed a civil lawsuit against Kerviel, and Paris's public prosecutor filed criminal charges against Kerviel. Société Générale's board formed a special committee to investigate the incident, which commissioned an internal audit report and a diagnostic review of GEDS's internal control environment by Pricewaterhouse Coopers (PwC). The internal audit team's preliminary findings were published on February 21, its final report, and PwC's findings published on May 20. On April 17, Bouton relinquished his role as CEO but remained chairman for another year. On May 30, Mustier relinquished his position as global head of CIB. Several months later, Mustier was reassigned to head Société Générale's investment management business, but resigned from Société Générale a year later.

Postmortem

During the spring and summer of 2008, further details released about Société Générale's unauthorized trading losses continued to tarnish its reputation, while the outlook for banking as a whole darkened significantly, as delinquencies in U.S. residential mortgages spread losses and fear across the entire sector. The New York investment bank Bear Stearns ran out of funds in March 2008 and had to be rescued by JPMorgan Chase. IndyMac Bank failed in July, and Fannie Mae and Freddie Mac were put into receivership in September, closely followed by the bankruptcy of Lehman Brothers, rescue of Merrill Lynch by Bank of America, and the Federal Reserve's bailout of American International Group (AIG).

Meanwhile, the internal and external investigations into how Société Générale's management and control environment allowed Kerviel to conduct his unauthorized trading for so long and in such large amounts revealed an extraordinary range of failings. This was so much that the French Banking Commission (Commission Bancaire, CB) fined Société Générale €4 million in July 2008, an insignificant sum relative to the magnitude of Société Générale's trading losses, but close to the CB's legal maximum.

The principal findings of the internal and external investigations were as follows.

Managerial Supervision

GEDS's trading management had primary responsibility for continuously monitoring its trading positions; performing daily analysis of the coherence of risks, earnings, and positions; and ensuring that all transactions complied with the department's policies and limits. However, there was no explicit requirement to monitor cash movements. Société Générale's systems provided trading management with a series of transaction, profit and loss (P&L), and cash flow reports and, during 2005–2006, monitoring appears to have been done in a desultory manner by Kerviel's trading manager. However, after this manager's departure in January 2007, Kerviel's trading activity received no monitoring at all. Trading management was also tasked with responding to internal and external alerts and queries about the positions under their responsibility. In Kerviel's case these were rare; however, an alert from Eurex about a large transaction in November 2007 related to Kerviel's unauthorized directional positions was never followed up. PwC noted in particular that the rigor of DLP's front office oversight diminished as trading volume increased, allowing unauthorized activities such as day trading, P&L smoothing, and position transfers between traders to proliferate.

Control Environment

The primary control framework in which Kerviel operated had a number of serious deficiencies:

- There were no limits on notional transaction volumes or cash movements.
- Trade cancellations, modifications, deferred start dates, and provisions were not subject to exception treatment.
- There was inadequate separation of duties between DLP's front office and middle office: Kerviel was able to modify and cancel trades at will in GEDS's transaction system and create provisions that concealed his unauthorized profits.
- Policies and procedures for escalation of concerns were either unclear or nonexistent.
- There was no policy dictating minimum consecutive days of vacation.

The secondary control framework supporting DLP also had serious deficiencies.

- GEDS's back office support for DLP was separated into four different operations groups, which did not communicate with each other and whose procedures required them to raise and resolve but not to question trade-related queries.
- Société Générale's counterparty risk management group was required to raise and resolve exposure issues but not to validate the cause or solution. This group raised 20 queries that they considered resolved by Kerviel's explanations and amendments.
- Société Générale's market risk management performed a risk reporting and advisory role, but did not exercise trading oversight; consequently they were not involved in monitoring the alerts and unusual activity created by Kerviel's unauthorized positions and fictitious offsetting trades.
- During 2006 and 2007, GEDS's back office was chronically understaffed due to high employee turnover, while DLP's trading volume doubled, its range of traded products multiplied, and the number of traders increased from four to 23.

System Reliability

GEDS's transaction systems also had serious deficiencies:

- Faulty security protocols allowed Kerviel to continue to access and change system records after he was promoted from the middle office to the front office.

- Chronic accuracy, reliability, and timeliness problems predisposed operations and risk personnel to expect system errors to be the cause of processing exceptions, not suspicious activity.
- Daily reports of cash movements from margins and broker commissions were aggregated across portfolios, hindering identification of the unusual levels of activity created by Kerviel's unauthorized trades.

Risk-Sensitive Culture

The investigations also identified cultural deficiencies, specifically citing that DLP's trading oversight and control personnel were not trained or instructed to be alert for fraud and were slow and lax in responding to and resolving queries.

Action Plan
PwC reviewed and endorsed Société Générale's two-part remedial action plan, consisting of a series of immediate fixes and longer-term structural changes. The key elements of this action plan were:

- Immediate strengthening of GEDS's front office supervision across all equities, fixed income, derivatives, and commodities trading desks, by means of heightened awareness of responsibilities, introduction, and use of formal monitoring tools
- Immediate strengthening of GEDS's middle and back office controls by means of remedying controls found to be missing or ineffective
- Immediate strengthening of system access controls and information technology (IT) security
- Immediate strengthening of governance by specifying roles, responsibilities, and escalation protocols across all relevant positions
- A four-part transformation strategy to improve GEDS's control infrastructure, culture, and IT security, consisting of:
  1. More control-sensitive operations processes
  2. Creation of a cross-divisional operational surveillance program designed to identify and rectify anomalous situations and chronic conditions that could be symptomatic of or conducive to fraud
  3. Long-term IT security improvement plan
  4. Professional ethics and accountability education program for traders and their support staff
- Formation of two committees tasked with ensuring implementation of these four initiatives

Who Was to Blame?

The two years between publication of the two investigative reports into Kerviel's unauthorized trading and his trial were tumultuous for U.S. and European banks. A steady succession of huge asset write-downs, government bailouts, liquidity lifelines, and arranged takeovers of once-proud banks and insurance companies took place. Stock and housing prices tumbled, unemployment soared, and the U.S. and European economies slipped into recession. After multilateral government stabilization measures began to take effect, lawsuits began to emerge alleging dishonest lending and securitization practices. As Kerviel's June 8, 2010, trial date neared, Société Générale kept a low profile. Kerviel, on the other hand, sought to publicize his assertion that Société Générale unofficially endorsed his directional trading, with the publication of a book entitled *The Spiral: Memoirs of a Trader*.

Exercise

Now begins the interactive portion of this case study. The preceding narrative and exhibits have presented key facts that were publicly known at the beginning of Kerviel's trial. Whether or not the information they provide is conclusive one way or another is up to the reader to decide. In a real trial, prosecution and defense attorneys methodically lay out their respective evidence and arguments. To facilitate the reader's assessment of both arguments in this case study, a blank Critical Questions table is provided in Exhibit 23.6. The purpose of this table is for the

Exhibit 23.6 Critical Questions and Answers—Worksheet

Question	Answer Implying Guilty	Answer Implying Not Guilty
1		
2		
3		
4		
5		
6		
7		
8		
9		
10		
11		
12		
13		
14		
15		

reader to list critical questions that the trial judges should have asked in order to determine the truth behind each party's claims, and then to identify answers that would incriminate ("Guilty") or exonerate ("Not Guilty") Kerviel. Once this exercise has been completed, the reader may turn to Part Two.

PART TWO: OUTCOME AND LESSONS LEARNED

Part Two of this case study reveals the outcome of the trial and its consequences, provides a prepared list of critical questions on page 487 to compare with those compiled by the reader at the end of Part One (Exhibit 23.6) and additional learning materials in the form of: (1) a list of the reference materials used to compile this case study, (2) Société Générale's full-year 2006 and 2007 financial statements (Exhibits 23.7), and (3) a chronology of events leading up to, during, and after the period in which Kerviel's unauthorized trading took place (Exhibit 23.8).

SUMMARY INCOME STATEMENT OF SOCIETE GENERALE

(On millions of errors at December 31)	2007					2006			
	France	07/06 (%)	International	07/06 (%)	Societe Generale	07/06 (%)	France	International	Societe Generale
Net banking income	9,062	4,8	(292)	(111.8)	8,770	(21.2)	8,646	2,480	11,126
Operating experses	(5,539)	(4.0)	(1,224)	(4.5)	(6,763)	(4.1)	(5,773)	(1,281)	(7,054)
Gross operating income	3,623	22.6	(1,516)	(226.5)	2,007	(50.7)	2,873	1,199	4,072
Cost of risk	(96)	(1,300.0)	(40)	(229.8)	(136)	(450.4)	8	31	39
Operating income	3,427	18.9	(1,556)	(226.8)	1,871	(54.5)	2,881	1,230	4,111
Net income from long-term investments	229	(44.3)	(183)	NS	46	(88.9)	411	3	414
Operating income before tax	3,656	11.0	1,739	(241.1)	1,917	(57.6)	3,292	1,233	4,526
Exceptional items	(4,801)	NS	-	NS	(4,801)	NS	-	-	-
Income tax	1,473	(918.3)	459	(251.9)	1,932	(500.7)	(180)	(302)	(482)
Net allocation to regulatory provisions	(9)	(10.0)	-	NS	(9)	(10.0)	(10)	-	(10)
Net Income	319	(89.7)	(1,280)	(237.5)	(961)	(123.8)	3,102	931	4,033

Societe Generale net income for the 2007 financial year came out at EUR-961 million, down 123.8% on 2006. The breakdown of results for Societe Generale in France and abroad is given in the above table.

The principal changes in the income statement were as follows:

- Societe Generale was directly impacted by the effects of the US subprime mortgage crisis, leading to gross operating income down from 2006 to EUR 2,007 million:
- net banking income amounted to EUR 8,770 million, down sharply on 2006, due to the consequences of this crisis on the Corporate and Investment Banking arm. The solid commercial performance generated by this activity was thus erased by trading activities, owing to write down and losses:
  - EUR -1,250 million on unhedged super senior CDO tranches:
  - EUR -947 million on counterparty risk exposure to US monolines:
  - EUR -325 million on the RMBS trading portfolio.

  Retail Banking in France remained on a steady growth trend, in terms of both individual customers and business customers. Customer acquisition (+126,000 sight accounts in 2007) went hand in hand with the overall increase in customer savings. At the same time, outstanding loans to business customers remained on an uptrend in 2007.

- management fees totaled EUR 6,763 million, down from 2006, mainly due to the change in variable costs recorded by Corporate and Investment Banking, a direct reflection of the situation in 2007. Retail Banking in France expanded in 2008 with the opening of over 50 new branches:

- net income from long-term investments came out at EUR 46 million in 2007. This breaks down into EUR + 131 million in income from the disposal of subsidiary shares (of which a net capital gain of EUR +93 million from the exchange of Euronext shares for NYSE shares and the subsequent sale of the new entity's shares) and EUR −89 million stemming from the write-back of provisions for other shares in consolidated subsidiaries:

- exceptional items include the loss before income taxes of the unwinding of the directional positions on unauthorized and concealed trading activities discovered on January 19 and 20, 2008:

- the EUR 9 million allocation to provisions for banking risks corresponds to an allocation to an investment provision, in accordance with article 237 bis AII of the French Tax Code. A provision of EUR 10 million had been booked at December 31, 2006.

Exhibit 23.7   Société Générale's 2006 and 2007 Summary Income Statement

SUMMARY BALANCE SHEET OF SOCIETE GENERALE

ASSETS

(in billions of euros at December 31)	2007	2006	Change
Interbank and money market assets	137.5	114.2	23.3
Customer loans	225.5	186.9	38.6
Securities	411.0	392.8	18.2
- of which securities purchased under resale agreements	72.2	104.4	(32.2)
Other assets	247.7	173.3	74.4
- of which option premiums	179.7	133.7	46.0
Long term tangible and intangible assets	1.5	1.2	0.3
Total assets	**1,023.2**	**868.4**	**154.8**

LIABILITIES AND SHAREHOLDERS' EQUITY

(in billions of euros at December 31)	2007	2006	Change
Interbank and money market liabilities[1]	367.3	316.5	50.8
Customer deposits	229.2	187.2	42.0
Bonds and subordinated debt[2]	20.6	16.7	3.9
Securities	120.0	144.4	(24.4)
- of which securities sold under repurchase agreements	72.0	64.2	7.9
Other liabilities and provisions	266.6	181.3	85.3
- of which option premiums	185.9	136.9	49.0
Shareholders' equity	19.5	22.3	(2.8)
Total liabilities	**1,023.2**	**868.4**	**154.8**

(1) Including negotiable debt instruments
(2) Including undated subordinated capital notes

At December 31, 2007, Societe Generale Parent Company's total assets and liabilities amounted to EUR 1,023.2 billion, up 17,82% on December 31, 2006, a figure that is roughly equivalent to the improvement observed at December 31, 2006. The development of Societe Generale's activities are reflected in the key figures on the balance sheet:

- The increase in outstanding loans (20.7%), which came out at EUR 225.5 billion at December 31, 2007, was derived mainly from the rise in short-term loans (EUR _ 14.3 billion), mortgage loans (EUR + 6.2 billion) and equipment loans (EUR + 3.4 billion);

Source: Page 10 of Societe General Parent Company 2007 financial statements

Exhibit 23.7 *(Continued)*

Exhibit 23.8 Chronology of Events

Date	Internal/ External	Description
1991	Internal	Daniel Bouton joined Société Générale (SG) as EVP, after serving in a number of different positions in the French Finance Ministry, including that of Budget Director, from 1988 to 1991, Chief of Staff of Alain Juppe, Deputy Minister in charge of the budget from 1986 to 1988, in the Budget Department from 1977 to 1986, and in the Finance Inspectorate from 1973 to 1976.
1993	Internal	Bouton appointed CEO of SG Group.
Nov. 1997	Internal	Bouton appointed chairman and co-CEO of SG Group.
1999	External	SG's proposed friendly merger with Banque Paribas torn apart by hostile bid for both banks from BNP. SG escaped but Paribas succumbed, leaving SG's growth strategy in disarray.
1999	Internal	Jean-Pierre Mustier promoted from head of CIB equity options trading in SG's Corporate and Investment Banking (CIB) to head of fixed income, FX, commodities, and derivatives.
Aug. 2000	Internal	Jerome Kerviel (JK) hired to do modeling and process automation in CIB's middle office, aged 23.
July 2002	Internal	JK promoted to trader assistant in SG's Delta One equity derivatives product team, responsible for valuations, provisions, and risk analysis.
May 2003	Internal	Daniel Bouton appointed CEO of SG bank.
2003	Internal	Mustier promoted to head of CIB, beginning a period of aggressive and successful expansion in securities underwriting, derivatives, and proprietary trading. Over the next five years, CIB's glamor and earnings eroded SG's traditional control-oriented, retail banking culture.
March 2004	Internal	JK promoted to junior trader in Delta One Listed Products (DLP) team.
June 2005	External	A handful of U.S. investment banks set up short residential mortgages positions, even as their own and other banks' fixed income desks continue to source, warehouse, structure, and distribute subprime mortgages and MBSs.
July 2005	Internal	First unauthorized trades by JK, offset by fictitious trades with counterparties either SG subsidiaries, unidentified/pending, or third parties. JK's fictitious trades had deferred start dates, which did not require immediate confirmation.
Jan.–Dec. 2006	Internal	JK continued sporadic unauthorized trading, with insignificant gains or losses.
May 2006	External	First cutbacks and failures among U.S. subprime mortgage lenders; Merrill Lynch, unable to sell super-senior tranches of new subprime CDOs, set up a buy-and-hold trading desk. Some investment banks started producing CDOs designed to fail, so they could buy and profit from the investors' credit protection.

Exhibit 23.8 (*Continued*)

Date	Internal/ External	Description
Aug. 2006	Internal	JK's unauthorized trading volume moved up a notch to €140 million (U.S.$179 million) in equity index futures.
Sep. 2006	External	U.S. residential housing construction index down 40 percent year-over-year. Some investment banks began reducing their securitization activities and limiting their exposures to U.S. residential mortgages.
Jan. 2007	Internal	JK's immediate CIB trading manager left SG and was not replaced until April by another CIB manager who had no prior experience of trading management and received no detailed direction on his responsibilities until November 2007.
Feb. 2007	External	Trickle of losses and failures in U.S. subprime lending sector turned into a flood—Ownit, American Freedom Mortgage, Network USA, HSBC, Accredited, New Century, DR Horton, Countrywide.
Feb.–March 2007	Internal	Anticipating a stock market crash, JK progressively built up unauthorized short equity index futures positions amounting to €5.5 billion (U.S.$7.3 billion), masking the directionality of these trades with fictitious offsetting trades.
April–June 2007	Internal	JK further increased his unauthorized short equity index futures positions amounting to €30 billion with a cumulative P&L of €2.2 billion (U.S.$3 billion). Between February and June, 39 instances of discrepancies in settlement details, accounting entries, and broker commissions were flagged by SG's controllers, but deflected by JK's trade amendments, cancellations, and explanations.
May 4, 2007	External	SG's stock hit its peak of €140.55 per share.
June 2007	External	Bear Stearns halted redemptions in two CDO hedge funds, which immediately become insolvent.
July 2007	External	Equity markets slumped.
July 2007	Internal	JK unwound substantially all of his short equity index futures positions in the last week of July, having erased all of his losses.
Aug. 2007	External	Onset of credit crunch as traces of subprime MBSs in bank portfolios around the world set off a counterparty exposure panic that caused interbank and repo markets to freeze up. Investors everywhere started liquidating other assets in order to take refuge in U.S. Treasuries. The U.S. Federal Reserve made the first of many liquidity interventions, followed by the European Central Bank (ECB).
Sep. 2007	External	First month of negative U.S. job growth since August 2003.
Sep.–Nov. 2007	Internal	JK's remaining short equity index futures positions accumulated €750 million of profits before he unwound them in November 2007 when equity markets began to recover.
Oct. 2007	Internal	First effects of financial sector crisis on CIB revenues: €230 million write-down in SG's U.S. residential mortgage-related assets.

(*continued*)

Exhibit 23.8 *(Continued)*

Date	Internal/ External	Description
Oct. 24, 2007	External	Merrill Lynch announced Q3-07 loss of U.S.$5.5 billion, later revised to U.S.$8.4 billion.
Nov. 2007	Internal	JK built a €30 billion portfolio of unauthorized long equity futures positions matched by fictitious offsetting trades. An alert from Eurex about a large (€1.2 billion) purchase of equity index futures went unheeded.
Dec. 2007	Internal	JK liquidated his unauthorized portfolio of long equity futures positions, concealing the resulting €1.5 billion of profits in fictitious forward trades with an SG affiliate.
Dec. 2007	External	SG's market capitalization down 23 percent since June 2007 on fears that its exposure to U.S. subprime mortgages was much greater than disclosed.
Jan. 2–10, 2008	Internal	On January 2 JK switched his December 2007 fictitious forward counterparties from the SG subsidiary to a third party, unaware that the third-party counterparty he chose did not have a collateral agreement with SG, thus causing a huge CVaR exposure to show up in risk reports. *Note:* This issue did not occur in early 2007 when JK's unauthorized trades were losing money and SG's risk reports showed negative counterparty credit exposure to fictitious third parties. When the massive CVaR exposure was queried, JK canceled the fictitious forwards and instructed his (24-year-old) trading assistant to create a valuation provision of €1.485 billion to conceal the bulk of his 2007 gains, resulting in €15 million reported year-end trading profits versus actual trading profits of €1.5 billion.
Jan. 2–18, 2008	Internal	JK rebuilt a €49 billion portfolio of unauthorized long equity index futures positions with fictitious offsetting trades.
Jan. 14–17, 2008	Internal	The fictitious CVaR exposure disappeared from SG's daily counterparty credit risk reports but was still queried for 2007 year-end RWA and Cooke ratio reporting. JK met with SG's financial reporting group and explained that the counterparty he recorded for the forwards was incorrect and should have been a different third party (with a collateral agreement).
Jan. 15, 2008	External	Global slump in equity markets triggered by fears that U.S. and international banks were more exposed to subprime mortgage losses than disclosed.
Jan. 18, 2008	External	SG's stock dropped another 8.2 percent as Banque de France announced that SG and another major French bank would have to write down the valuation of their U.S. assets.

Exhibit 23.8 *(Continued)*

Date	Internal/ External	Description
Jan. 18, 2008	Internal	SG's financial reporting group escalated their concerns about JK's unusual transactions and explanations to CIB senior management. Meanwhile, JK canceled the fictitious December 2007 forwards, reentered them with the replacement counterparty, and falsified a confirmation document from the replacement counterparty. JK's supervisors decided to call the replacement counterparty to verify the existence of JK's forwards.
Jan. 19, 2008	Internal	SG's replacement counterparty advised that the forwards recorded by JK did not exist.
Jan. 19, 2008	Internal	JK's current portfolio of unauthorized long equity index futures positions with fictitious offsetting trades was discovered, amounting to €49 billion, equivalent to 181 percent of SG's capital of €27 billion, and already €2 billion underwater.
Jan. 20, 2008	Internal	SG's chairman and CEO Daniel Bouton tendered his resignation, which was rejected by the board and SG's union leaders, who insisted that he stay to resolve the rogue trading problem.
Jan. 21, 2008	External	European equity markets suffered further heavy declines (–6 percent). Bouton received approval from SG's regulator, Autorité des Marchés Financiers (AMF), to withhold disclosure of SG's unauthorized equity index portfolio for three days so that it could be liquidated without panicking already nervous equity markets.
Jan. 21–23, 2008	Internal	JK's €49 billion portfolio of unauthorized long equity index positions was liquidated, crystallizing losses of €6.4 billion.
Jan. 23, 2008	External	Bouton briefed France's President, Economy Minister, the ECB president, and chairman of the U.S. Federal Reserve on the origin and extent of SG's rogue trading losses.
Jan. 24, 2008	External	SG filed a civil lawsuit against JK for fraud.
Jan. 24, 2008	Internal	An investigation by SG's General Inspection Services (internal audit) was commissioned by the Executive Committee of the board to: (1) determine the exact nature and methods used by JK to conduct his unauthorized transactions, (2) verify the accuracy of the positions and subsequent losses, (3) investigate JK's motives and the role of any possible accomplices, (4) identify the cause of and responsibility for the internal control breakdowns, (5) verify the nonexistence of similar practices anywhere else in CIB.

(continued)

Exhibit 23.8 *(Continued)*

Date	Internal/ External	Description
Jan. 24, 2008	External	Trading in SG's shares was temporarily suspended as Bouton issued a public letter and newspaper interview describing the origin and extent of the losses and remedial actions being taken, including legal action against JK, separation of employees responsible for supervision and control of the department where JK's unauthorized trading occurred, and raising €5.5 billion of new capital.
Jan. 25, 2008	External	Police raided JK's apartment and SG's offices to seize JK's computer records.
Jan. 26, 2008	External	JK voluntarily surrendered to the police and was held in custody.
Jan. 28, 2008	External	JK was charged by the Paris prosecutor with forgery, abuse of trust, and illegal use of computers, and was released on bail.
Jan. 30, 2008	Internal	Independent board committee formed to investigate JK's unauthorized trading. Operational review of the circumstances and control failings commissioned from PwC.
Feb. 21, 2008	Internal	SG announced a Q4-07 loss of €3.4 billion, due to JK's unauthorized trading and increased its December 2007 write-downs on U.S. residential mortgage-related exposures to €2.3 billion.
Feb. 21, 2008	Internal	Preliminary findings of investigation by SG's General Inspection Services (internal audit function) published.
Feb.–March 2008	External	A steady stream of public sparring took place between senior SG, banking, and government officials regarding a possible takeover bid for SG and Bouton's responsibility for SG's rogue trading scandal.
March 16, 2008	External	Bear Stearns rescued by JPMorgan Chase with U.S.$30 billion New York Fed backstop.
April 2008	Internal	Bouton resigned as CEO, but remained as SG chairman.
May 13, 2008		SG announced another €596 million write-down to its U.S. residential mortgage-related exposures and completion of its €5.5 billion new equity raising.

Exhibit 23.8 (*Continued*)

Date	Internal/ External	Description
May 20, 2008	Internal	The investigation report by SG's General Inspection Services entitled "Mission Green" was presented to SG's board of directors. Key findings: (1) JK's unauthorized trading progressed through five stages—(i) intraday directional trades, (ii) overnight directional positions, (iii) disguising overnight directional positions with fictitious offsetting trades (947 instances), (iv) concealing gains from unauthorized directional positions with fictitious loss-making buy-sell trades (115 instances), and (v) concealing gains from unauthorized directional positions with valuation provisions (9 instances); (2) in 2007 JK built and liquidated two €30 billion unauthorized portfolios of equity index futures, concealed by fictitious offsetting trades, which generated net profits of €1.5 billion, and between January 2 and 18, 2008, he built a €49 billion portfolio of unauthorized equity index futures with fictitious offsetting trades, which was liquidated by the bank at a loss of €6.4 billion; (3) JK's 2007 incentive compensation would have been based on his reported 2007 trading P&L of €25 million, which resulted from €3 million in legitimate gains from his turbo warrant trading plus €22 million in gains generated by his unauthorized trades less €1.475 billion gains from his unauthorized trades concealed by his fictitious trades and provisions (*Note:* The seven valuation provisions and almost 15 percent of the fictitious trades were entered by JK's trading assistant); (4) the two factors that most contributed to SG's prolonged failure to detect JK's unauthorized and fictitious trading were: (i) ineffective trading management oversight represented by tolerance of intraday trading; disinterest in reconciling JK's profits, margin, and cash movements to his authorized trading activity; indifference to system and counterparty alerts; and, from April 2007, lack of trading oversight experience; and (ii) control procedures that were focused on reporting rather than investigating anomalies, were fragmented among different control groups, and had no triggers for deferred start dates, values, counterparties, trade modifications and cancellations, or mandatory vacation periods; (5) no other evidence was uncovered of similar fraudulent activities in SG's CIB. *Note:* The report contained no attribution of responsibility to SG's Risk Management, whose role as a second line of defense in managing trading risk was not clearly specified in SG's policies or procedures.

(*continued*)

Exhibit 23.8   (*Continued*)

Date	Internal/ External	Description
May 21, 2008	Internal	PwC delivered its diagnostic review of SG's unauthorized trading losses and remedial action plan. PwC endorsed the GIS report's findings and added several more: (1) There were no clear policies or procedures for escalation of queries; (2) trading oversight and control personnel were not trained or instructed to be alert for fraud; (3) trading oversight and control personnel were slow to respond to and lax in resolution of queries; (4) the rigor of DLP's front office oversight diminished as trading volume increased, allowing unauthorized activities such as day trading, P&L smoothing, and position transfers between traders to proliferate; and (5) trading oversight policy omitted to require monitoring of cash movements. PwC also endorsed SG's two-part action plan, consisting of a series of immediate fixes and longer-term structural changes, specifically: (1) immediate strengthening of GEDS's front office supervision across all equities, fixed income, derivatives, and commodities trading desks by means of heightened awareness of responsibilities, along with introduction and use of monitoring tools; (2) immediate strengthening of GEDS's middle and back office controls by means of remedying controls found to be missing or ineffective; (3) immediate strengthening of system access controls and IT security; (4) immediate strengthening of governance by specifying roles, responsibilities, and escalation protocols across all relevant positions; (5) a four-part transformation strategy to improve GEDS's control infrastructure, culture, and IT security, consisting of: (a) more control-sensitive operations processes; (b) creation of a cross-divisional operational surveillance program designed to identify and rectify anomalous situations and chronic conditions that could be symptomatic of or conducive to fraud; (c) long-term IT security improvement plan; (d) professional ethics and accountability education program for traders and their support staff; and (6) formation of two committees tasked with ensuring implementation of these initiatives.
May 30, 2008	Internal	Mustier resigned as CIB head and voluntarily surrendered his bonuses for 2007 and 2008; however, he remained with SG.
June 20, 2008	External	The French Banking Commission (Comission Bancaire, CB) interviewed SG officers in the course of investigating JK's unauthorized trading.
July 2, 2008	External	JK switched legal counsel to a more aggressive firm.

Exhibit 23.8 (*Continued*)

Date	Internal/ External	Description
July 4, 2008	External	The CB found that SG violated banking regulations by not having adequate financial controls, and imposed a fine of €4 million, close to its maximum allowable penalty. The CB's key observations were: (1) poor supervision, (2) monitoring staff inattentive to fraud, (3) deficiencies in IT systems, and (4) inadequate limits and policies.
July 11, 2008	External	IndyMac Bank placed into receivership.
Aug, 1, 2008	External	JK's trading assistant was indicted on a relatively minor charge of complicity.
Aug. 5, 2008	Internal	SG announced year-to-date losses and write-downs on exotic credit derivatives of €789 million.
Sep. 7, 2008	External	Fannie Mae and Freddie Mac placed into receivership.
Sep. 14–18, 2008	External	Merrill Lynch sold to Bank of America, Lehman Brothers filed for bankruptcy, AIG downgraded and rescued by New York Fed with a U.S.$85 billion borrowing line, money market mutual fund Reserve Primary Fund suffered such catastrophic losses on its asset-backed commercial paper holdings that its net asset value "broke the buck," and commercial paper market seized up.
Sep. 19–29, 2008	External	U.S.$700 billion "take-it-or-leave-it" Paulson rescue plan voted down by Congress, Washington Mutual seized by FDIC and its banking assets sold to JPMorgan Chase, Wachovia seized by FDIC, and sale of banking assets to Citigroup negotiated.
Sep. 2008	Internal	Mustier appointed CEO of SG's investment management business with €350 billion assets under management.
Nov. 3, 2008	Internal	SG announced a further of €370 million of losses and write-downs on exotic credit derivatives and €754 million of write-downs on its U.S. residential mortgage monoline insurance, provided mainly by AIG.
Nov. 1–30, 2008	External	Fed provided emergency US$ liquidity to foreign banks (most notably Depfa and Dexia), negotiated Troubled Asset Relief Program (TARP) equity stakes in second wave of U.S. banks, rescued Citigroup with another U.S.$20 billion of capital on top of U.S.$25 billion already injected, pledged U.S.$600 billion to buy MBSs guaranteed by Fannie Mae and Freddie Mac.
Dec. 2008	External	U.S. economy officially declared in recession since December 2007.
Feb. 18, 2009	Internal	SG announced its full-year 2008 results, which included €792 million losses and write-downs on exotic credit derivatives, €1.0 billion write-downs on its U.S. residential mortgage monoline insurance, and €1.2 billion losses and write-downs on its European asset-backed security (ABS) underwriting and distribution business. These losses were partially offset by €2.2 billion of mark-to-market gains on credit default swaps held for portfolio protection.

(*continued*)

Exhibit 23.8 *(Continued)*

Date	Internal/ External	Description
May 2009	Internal	Daniel Bouton ended his tenure as chairman of SG Group.
May 2009	External	France's economy declared officially in recession since Q3-08.
Aug. 2009	External	France's recession officially declared ended Q2-09.
Aug. 2009	Internal	Mustier resigned from SG Group.
2010	External	Regulatory and investor lawsuits emerged, aimed at deceptive residential mortgage securitization practices, flawed mortgage foreclosure practices, and misrepresentation of mortgage borrowers' creditworthiness.
May 2010	External	Publication of JK's memoir *L'Engrenage: Mémoires d'un Trader (The Spiral: Memories of a Trader)*.
June 8, 2010	External	JK's trial commenced.
Sep. 2010	External	U.S. recession declared officially ended as of June 2009.
Oct. 5, 2010	External	JK was convicted of the charges, sentenced to five years in prison with two years suspended, and ordered (symbolically) to repay SG's €4.9 billion in losses. JK filed an appeal and remained free pending its hearing.
2011	External	Markets became anxious over EU banks' exposure to peripheral EU countries.
2012	External	U.S. banks able to repurchase TARP stakes with new stock issuance.
Oct. 23, 2012	External	JK's appeal denied and his conviction upheld.
July 4, 2013	External	Paris employment tribunal denied JK's request to void his dismissal, levy a €4.9 billion fine on SG, and form an inquiry to question the justification of his conviction.

What Actually Happened

Kerviel's criminal trial lasted three weeks, during which the defense attorneys reinforced Kerviel's claims that his managers at Société Générale were well aware of the nature and scale of his trading and encouraged him to continue, so long as he made profits. They highlighted that Kerviel did not derive any personal profit from his unauthorized trades. Société Générale's attorneys, acting as co-plaintiff, acknowledged the failings in supervision and control described in the internal audit and PwC reports published in 2008, but rebutted any suggestion that the bank knowingly allowed Kerviel to conduct the unauthorized trading that resulted in its massive loss. Both parties had to wait another three months for the verdict, which caused a new uproar when it was announced on October 5, 2010. The three-judge panel found Kerviel guilty of all three charges—abuse of trust, forgery, and computer access abuse—and sentenced him to five years in prison with two suspended, ordering him to compensate Société Générale €4.9 billion (U.S.$7.1 billion) for its losses. No penalties or reprimands were directed at Société Générale at all. Kerviel's attorneys immediately filed an appeal, while the severity of the sentence and Société Générale's complete exoneration reignited media speculation that France's financial establishment had colluded to label Kerviel as a scapegoat.

Kerviel's appeal took another two years to be heard, but the result did not go in his favor. On October 24, 2012, the appeals judge upheld the trial verdict and sentence. However, Kerviel did not immediately go to jail or pay any of the compensation to Société Générale, whose amount was clearly symbolic. In fact, he disappeared from public view after the appeal and only briefly reappeared in July 2013, to ask a Paris employment tribunal for his January 2008 dismissal by Société Générale to be overturned and an independent inquiry constituted to investigate the circumstances surrounding it. However, the tribunal rejected his request, leaving Kerviel to seek other options to delay or escape his sentence.

QUESTIONS

1. Could other DLP traders have manipulated GEDS's transaction systems like Kerviel did?
2. Was it typical for middle office employees to be promoted to the front office?
3. When Kerviel worked in the middle office, did he show any unusual aptitude for manipulating the transaction systems?
4. Did DLP have any rules or disincentives designed to deter traders like Kerviel from undertaking unauthorized trading?
5. Why did Kerviel make such huge bets when he did not derive any personal benefit from the profits?
6. Had there been any previous instances or notifications of deficiencies in DLP's controls?
7. Was Société Générale prudent in assigning sole responsibility for market risk oversight to trading management?
8. Did GEDS make effective use of market risk management?
9. Why did financial reporting catch the fraud, not trading management, operations, or risk management?
10. Had there been any previous instances or notifications of deficiencies in DLP's transaction systems?
11. Why did operations employees fail to validate the explanations or escalate any of the many queries relating to Kerviel's unauthorized trades?
12. Did Société Générale omit any information at the trial that might have exonerated Kerviel?
13. Did the Paris prosecutor have sufficient grounds for criminal charges against Kerviel?
14. Did Société Générale sufficiently admit its responsibility for the losses?
15. Was Société Générale so focused on achieving growth on many fronts that it neglected to invest in sufficiently robust systems and internal controls?

REFERENCES

MarketWatch. 2008. "Text of Daniel Bouton's Letter to Customers and Shareholders Disclosing Société Générale's Trading Losses." January 24. www.marketwatch .com/story/letter-from-societe-general-ceo-to-customers-and-shareholders.

Société Générale. 2008. "General Inspection Department 'Mission Green' Summary Report." May 20. www.societegenerale.com/sites/default/files/documents/Green_VA.pdf.

Société Générale. 2008. "Report of the Special Board Committee Investigating the Trading Losses." May 23. www.societegenerale.com/sites/default/files/documents/ rapportcomitespecialmai2008.pdf.

PricewaterhouseCoopers. 2008. "Summary of Diagnostic Review and Analysis of the Action Plan." May 23. www.societegenerale.com/sites/default/files/documents/pricewatercooper.pdf.

Société Générale. "Annual Reports 1999–2007." www.investor.socgen.com/phoenix.zhtml?c=69575&p=irol-results.

Kerviel, Jérôme. 2010. *L'engrenage: Mémoires d'un trader (The Spiral: Memories of a Trader)*. Paris: Flammarion; pap. ed., J'Ai Lu, 2011.

ABOUT THE CONTRIBUTOR

Steve Lindo is a financial risk manager with more than 30 years' experience managing risks in asset/liability management (ALM), funding, international fixed income, and alternative asset portfolios. His current role is Principal of SRL Advisory Services, an independent consulting firm specializing in risk governance, culture and education, risk strategy, measurement, and regulatory expertise, in the United States and internationally. His career includes U.S. and international risk management positions with Fifth Third Bancorp, GMAC Financial Services (now Ally Financial), Cargill Inc.'s proprietary financial trading group (today operating as Black River Investments and Carval Investors), First National Bank of Chicago (now part of JPMorgan Chase), and Lloyds TSB Bank. During 2008–2010, he undertook a two-year engagement as CEO of the Professional Risk Managers' International Association (PRMIA), a nonprofit member organization with more than 75,000 members in 198 countries. He has a BA and an MA from Oxford University and speaks fluent French, German, Spanish, and Portuguese.

CHAPTER 24

The Role of VaR in Enterprise Risk Management

Calculating Value at Risk for Portfolios Held by the Vane Mallory Investment Bank

ALLISSA A. LEE
Assistant Professor of Finance, Georgia Southern University

BETTY J. SIMKINS
Williams Companies Chair of Business and Professor of Finance, Oklahoma State University

You have to risk going too far to discover just how far you can really go.
—Jim Rohn, adapted from T. S. Eliot

Vane Mallory is a large investment bank headquartered in New York. The firm is multifaceted, conducting normal investment banking activities such as underwriting and providing advising and brokerage services to its clients, but also trading on its own account through its trading desk.

You are a senior risk analyst at Vane Mallory investment bank. This is a new position for you and part of your responsibilities includes providing the value at risk (VaR) estimates to the chief risk officer (CRO) of the company, Christian Cross. You are responsible for reporting on two different portfolios:

1. A commodity portfolio that contains energy commodity assets.
2. An equity portfolio that contains stocks of firms based in the United States.

In your previous positions, you were not responsible for this calculation, and it is a relatively foreign concept to you. Accordingly, your boss, the chief risk officer, has given you a few days to acquaint yourself with the idea of VaR so you are prepared to calculate it accurately and efficiently. You did some research and talked to some of your colleagues, and found out quite a bit about VaR. A summary of your findings is included next.

RISK AND VALUE AT RISK OVERVIEW

There are many definitions of risk, but most relate to the possibility of an unexpected outcome. Risk is an inherent part of life for individuals, businesses, and corporations alike. Investment banks are no different, especially given the degree of innovation they have undertaken through the years. As regulations and markets change, profits can potentially decline. Consequently, other avenues must be discovered or created from which revenue can be generated. This process of financial innovation is fraught with risk. From the creation of mortgage-backed securities (MBSs) and collateralized mortgage obligations (CMOs), investment banks have been at the forefront of financial innovation. There are many types of risk, including market, credit, liquidity, operational, and legal risk.

There are various ways to measure risk. Risk is commonly thought of as volatility, which is measured by standard deviation. However, standard deviation is unconcerned with the direction of movement. Naturally, investors are not really worried about movement to the upside; it is the downside movement that is important. A measure of risk that focuses on downside movement is VaR. VaR is a key element of a firm's enterprise risk management (ERM) strategy. One aspect of ERM involves the likelihood and magnitude of impact of events or circumstances to the firm's objective, including both risks and opportunities. The concept of VaR encompasses this quite well and is an integral part of risk management.

Value at Risk

Risk metrics traditionally included valuation, sensitivity analysis, scenario analysis, and maybe even Monte Carlo simulations. VaR goes further: it blends the price-yield relationship with the likelihood of a market movement that is unfavorable. Correlation and leverage are taken into consideration, and a summary measure of portfolio risk is expressed in a single probabilistic statement (Jorion 2001, p. 27).

VaR was initially developed to measure market risk and has many applications, including risk management and measurement, financial control and reporting, and the computation of regulatory capital requirements. Investors can use VaR to analyze, with a given level of confidence, what is the worst-case scenario or how much they may lose in a given time period. Formally, "VaR described the quantile of the projected distribution of gains and losses over the target horizon. If c is the selected confidence level, VaR corresponds to the $1 - c$ lower-tail level" (Jorion, p. 22).[1] Intuitively, "VaR summarizes the worst loss over a target horizon with a given level of confidence" (p. 22).

History, Characteristics, and Assumptions of VaR

Value at risk is a risk management tool developed by Till Guldimann at J.P. Morgan in the 1980s. It was developed as a result of discussions surrounding the importance of "value risks" or "earnings risks." The parties determined that value risks were of greater consequence, and VaR was born.

VaR is applicable to many different assets, including stocks, bonds, and derivatives as well as single assets or portfolios of assets. There are several methods that can be used to calculate VaR, including (1) the historical method (nonparametric delta normal), which uses past data; (2) the parametric method, which only requires the mean and standard deviation to be used;[2] or (3) the Monte Carlo method, which uses future or forecasted data. Additionally, either percentage VaR or dollar VaR can be obtained, depending on the preferred output result. It is important to note that back-testing is extremely important with this technique. VaR is only an estimated worst-case scenario, and actual losses may surpass VaR. A loss that exceeds VaR is termed a "VaR break." VaR is rooted in the statistical and probabilistic foundations of portfolio theory. There is no one VaR value. In fact, there are multiple VaRs, depending on the circumstances and inputs.

There are five primary underlying assumptions for VaR. They are as follows:

1. *Stationarity.* A 1 percent fluctuation in returns is equally likely to occur at any point in time.
2. *Random walk of intertemporal unpredictability.* Day-to-day fluctuations in returns are independent.
3. *Nonnegativity.*[3] Financial assets with limited liability cannot attain negative values.
4. *Time consistency.* All single-period assumptions hold over the multiperiod time horizon.
5. *Distributional.* Daily return fluctuations follow a normal distribution with a mean of zero and a standard deviation of 100 bp[4] (Allen, Boudoukh, and Saunders 2004, 8–9).

With respect to the assumptions, the most obvious flaw is with the distributional assumption. Stock returns, in particular, have repeatedly been shown to not follow a normal distribution historically. However, using log returns can compensate for this issue.

Advantages and Criticisms of VaR

Like any measure, value at risk has pros and cons. There are several advantages to using VaR as a risk management measure. First, it provides a measure of total risk that is fairly easy to understand and explain. Second, as previously mentioned, it can measure the risk of many types of securities, including stocks, bonds, commodities, foreign exchange, and off-balance-sheet derivative assets like futures, forwards, swaps, and options. Also, VaR possesses very nice portfolio applications. It translates the concept of portfolio volatility into a dollar value and can be useful for monitoring and controlling risk inside a portfolio. Last, comparisons can be made between a portfolio and a market portfolio.[5]

No measure is perfect, though, and several criticisms of VaR exist; all measures have shortcomings that must be taken into consideration. Critics such as Nassim Taleb (1997) have professed the following: (1) VaR is somewhat of an untested model, ignoring 2,500 years of experience, and claims to estimate risks of "rare events," which is virtually impossible; (2) using VaR could provide a false sense of security that could lead to excessive risk taking and use of leverage; and (3) VaR ignores the tails and focuses on risks near the center of the distribution that are more manageable. This last criticism was suggested by David Einhorn (2008).

Additionally, many misuse VaR and its implications, which can be dangerous. VaR is not a worst-case scenario or a maximum tolerable loss. In fact, losses can be incurred multiple times per year that surpass the one-day 1 percent VaR. The main concern of risk management should be on what happens when a loss is incurred that is greater than VaR, not on VaR itself. Further, assuming that a loss will be less than a multiple of VaR (even two to three times) is dangerous. Last, VaRs should not be reported unless they are back-tested.[6]

Calculating Value at Risk

There are five basic steps to calculating value at risk. They are as follows:

1. Find the market value of the asset or portfolio.

2. Calculate the variability of the risk factors.

3. Establish the time horizon (or holding period).

4. Establish the level of confidence (e.g. 99 percent, 95 percent)

5. Report the value at risk estimate using the following equation and incorporating the values estimated in steps 1 to 4.

The dollar value at risk equation is as follows (see note 7):

$$VaR_\alpha^\$ = \text{AssetMktValue} \times \text{Variability} \times \text{NormDistFactor} \sqrt{\dfrac{\text{Holding period}}{\text{Trading days per year}}}^{7}$$

Additionally, there is another presentation of the dollar VaR equation that utilizes slightly different inputs (see note 8):

$$VaR_\alpha^\$ = \text{AssetMktValue} \times [1 - \exp(z_\alpha \times \sigma + \mu)]^{8}$$

As mentioned previously, percentage VaR can also be calculated. The steps are similar to those for the dollar VaR, with a few differences:

- Obtain the periodic log returns and then calculate the average log return.
- Calculate the volatility of the log returns. The variance can be found using VARP in Microsoft Excel and then taking the square root to find the standard deviation. Alternatively, STDEVP in Microsoft Excel can be used to find the standard deviation directly. Note: Both the VARP and STDEVP functions utilize the population version of the formula.

- Calculate VaR using the following equation once the desired confidence level has been selected.

The percentage VaR equation is:

$$VaR_\alpha^\% = z_\alpha \sigma$$

The equations just presented are for individual assets. A similar approach can be used for portfolios of multiple assets. Simply return to theories surrounding portfolios by finding the weighted average portfolio return, and obtain the volatility of the portfolio. Matrix applications are quite helpful in calculating portfolio volatility utilizing the concept of covariance. The portfolio VaR equation is:

$$VaR_\alpha^\$ = z_\alpha \sigma_p \times \text{PortfolioValue}$$

The standard deviation of the portfolio can be computed using percentage weights or dollar values of each asset within the portfolio. The end results are identical with either approach.

Confidence levels are self-selected in the VaR model. Obviously, choosing higher confidence levels will yield more precise VaR estimates; however, lower confidence levels provide estimated VaRs that are broader and more informative. Exhibit 24.1 contains several different confidence levels as well as the associated normal distribution factor or z value.

Dollar VaR: One-Asset Example

The mark-to-market value of the investment is $85 million. The standard deviation (variability) of the asset is 20 percent. Using a holding period of seven business days and a confidence level of 99 percent, what is the value at risk for this investment?

$$VaR_{1\%}^\$ = \$85 \text{ million} \times 0.20 \times 2.33 \sqrt{\frac{7}{252}} = \$6,601,666.67$$

Exhibit 24.1   Various Confidence Levels and Associated Alphas as Well as the z Value or Normal Distribution Factor Utilized in VaR Calculations

Confidence Level	Alpha (α)	z Value or Normal Distribution Factor
99.9%	0.10%	±3.09
99.5%	0.50%	±2.58
99.0%	1.00%	±2.33
97.5%	2.50%	±1.96
95.0%	5.00%	±1.65
90.0%	10.00%	±1.23

The interpretation: You are 99 percent confident that the loss will not exceed about $6.6 million.

Percentage VaR: One-Asset Example

Using the following information for stock XYZ, calculate VaR at the 95 percent level. Note: A short horizon is used for illustrative purposes only. A longer horizon should be used for actual calculations.

Date	Adjusted Closing Price	Periodic ROR
Dec. 9	$714.84	
Dec. 10	$718.42	0.50%
Dec. 11	$699.20	–2.71%
Dec. 12	$699.35	0.02%
Dec. 13	$694.05	–0.76%
Dec. 14	$689.96	–0.59%

First, the periodic rate of return (ROR) is found by taking the natural logarithm of the daily return. Next, the average daily periodic ROR is obtained by finding the simple average. It is –0.7085 percent. Third, the volatility must be calculated. This can be obtained by taking the square root of the variance (VARP in MS Excel) or by calculating the standard deviation directly (STDEVP in MS Excel). The variance is 0.0001, and the standard deviation is 1.0974 percent. Using the confidence level provided, VaR can be calculated. The normal distribution factor for the 95 percent level is 1.65.

$$VaR^{\%}_{5\%} = (1.65)\,1.0974\% = 1.8108\%$$

The interpretation: You are 95 percent confident that the worst loss will not exceed about 1.81 percent.

Exhibit 24.2 illustrates the distribution of VaR with 99 percent and 90 percent confidence levels as well. VaR at the 99 percent level is 2.56 percent, and it is 1.35 percent at the 90 percent confidence level.

YOUR TASK: CALCULATING PORTFOLIO VaR FOR VANE MALLORY

As noted previously, your boss tasked you with reporting VaR for several of the firm's portfolios. The CRO wants all portfolio VaRs reported at both the 90 percent and 99 percent confidence levels to gather as much information as possible about potential losses.

Christian Cross, the CRO of Vane Mallory, asked you to report on two portfolios. Each portfolio is equally weighted and contains five assets. One portfolio is comprised of energy commodities. The second portfolio you are responsible for monitoring contains equities. Information about the portfolios is provided next.

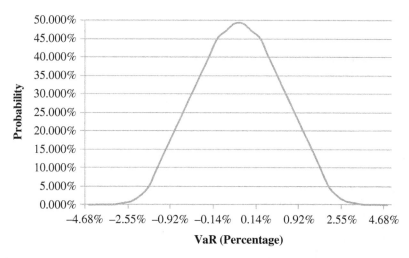

Exhibit 24.2 Potential Percentage VaR Losses (Gains) Based on the Various Confidence Levels or Probabilities

Portfolio 1: Energy Commodities

The firm holds a portfolio comprised of five different energy commodities: West Texas Intermediate (WTI) crude oil, Brent crude oil, natural gas, propane, and jet fuel. The firm invests equally in each asset. The current value of the portfolio is $50 million. Five years of monthly spot prices are used to determine the VaR inputs. All data were obtained from the U.S. Energy Information Administration, a division of the U.S. Department of Energy, for the period of 2008 to 2012.

The use of matrix applications in Microsoft Excel is convenient when analyzing portfolios. The expected return of the portfolio is 0.1484 percent, and the volatility (standard deviation) is 7.6366 percent. The covariance matrix and other important information are included in Exhibit 24.3. At the 90 percent and 99 percent confidence levels, the VaRs are approximately $4,696,515 and $8,896,649, respectively. The calculations are as follows:

$$VaR_{10\%}^{\$} = 1.23 \times \$50 \text{ million} \times 7.6366\% = \$4,696,515$$

$$VaR_{1\%}^{\$} = 2.33 \times \$50 \text{ million} \times 7.6366\% = \$8,896,650$$

Portfolio 2: Equities

This portfolio is comprised of the following equities (ticker): Alcoa, Inc. (AA), Citigroup, Inc. (C), Cisco Systems, Inc. (CSCO), Pfizer, Inc. (PFE), and Anadarko Petroleum Corporation (APC). The current value of the portfolio is $50 million, with $10 million invested in each company. One year (252 days) of asset returns are used in construction of VaR components. All asset prices were obtained from Yahoo! Finance for the period of May 22, 2012, through May 24, 2013.

Exhibit 24.3   The Covariance Matrix as Well as the Expected Return and Standard Deviation for Each Portfolio

Panel A: Energy Commodities
Covariance Matrix

	WTI	Brent Crude	NatGas	Propane	Jet Fuel
WTI	0.0094	0.0081	0.0011	0.0066	0.0074
Brent Crude	0.0081	0.0083	0.0012	0.0070	0.0074
Nat Gas	0.0011	0.0012	0.0123	0.0019	0.0016
Propane	0.0066	0.0070	0.0019	0.0099	0.0067
Jet Fuel	0.0074	0.0074	0.0016	0.0067	0.0080
Expected Return (Portfolio):					0.0015
Standard Deviation (Portfolio):					0.0764

Panel B: Equities
Covariance Matrix

	AA	C	CSCO	PFE	APC
AA	0.0002	0.0002	0.0001	0.0000	0.0002
C	0.0002	0.0004	0.0001	0.0001	0.0002
CSCO	0.0001	0.0001	0.0003	0.0000	0.0001
PFE	0.0000	0.0001	0.0000	0.0001	0.0000
APC	0.0002	0.0002	0.0001	0.0000	0.0003
Expected Return (Portfolio):					0.0014
Standard Deviation (Portfolio):					0.0119

Using matrix applications in Microsoft Excel, the expected return of the portfolio is 0.1440 percent, and the standard deviation is 1.1893 percent. The covariance matrix and associated calculations are provided in Exhibit 24.3, as a point of reference.

At the 90 percent confidence level, the VaR of the equity portfolio is approximately $731,409, while at the 99 percent confidence level the VaR is approximately $1,385,514. The calculations are:

$$VaR_{10\%}^{\$} = 1.23 \times \$50\,\text{million} \times 1.1893\% = \$731,409$$

$$VaR_{1\%}^{\$} = 2.33 \times \$50\,\text{million} \times 1.1893\% = \$1,385,514$$

The table presented in Exhibit 24.4 includes data for Apple (AAPL) and Hypercom (HYC). Question 7 will use the information in Exhibit 24.4 to have the reader conduct similar VaR calculations, using Apple Computer and Hypercom as the equities analyzed.

Exhibit 24.4   Data for Apple (AAPL) and Hypercom (HYC)

Date	AAPL Adj. Close	AAPL Periodic ROR	Date	HYC Adj. Close	HYC Periodic ROR
31-Dec	$322.56		30-Sep	$3.10	
3-Jan	$329.57	2.15%	1-Oct	$2.97	−4.28%
4-Jan	$331.29	0.52%	2-Oct	$2.90	−2.39%
5-Jan	$334.00	0.81%	5-Oct	$2.98	2.72%
6-Jan	$333.73	−0.08%	6-Oct	$3.07	2.98%
7-Jan	$336.12	0.71%	7-Oct	$3.11	1.29%
10-Jan	$342.45	1.87%	8-Oct	$3.04	−2.28%
11-Jan	$341.64	−0.24%	9-Oct	$3.04	0.00%
12-Jan	$344.42	0.81%	12-Oct	$3.07	0.98%
13-Jan	$345.68	0.37%	13-Oct	$3.13	1.94%
14-Jan	$348.48	0.81%	14-Oct	$3.14	0.32%
Average		0.7729%	15-Oct	$3.09	−1.61%
Variance		0.0051%	16-Oct	$3.04	−1.63%
Volatility		0.7125%	19-Oct	$3.02	−0.66%
			20-Oct	$2.94	−2.68%
			21-Oct	$2.99	1.69%
			22-Oct	$3.01	0.67%
			23-Oct	$3.27	8.28%
			26-Oct	$3.11	−5.02%
			27-Oct	$3.02	−2.94%
			28-Oct	$3.00	−0.66%
			29-Oct	$3.00	0.00%
			30-Oct	$2.85	−5.13%
			Average		−0.3822%
			Variance		0.0882%
			Volatility		2.9704%

CONCLUSION

Value at risk possesses many attractive features that can be useful when applied appropriately. Of course, understanding the limitations of VaR is essential, and such factors must be incorporated when applicable. VaR should never be thought of as a worst-case scenario, but should be considered carefully and used in conjunction with a broad-ranging risk management program. Till Guldimann, head of J.P. Morgan Global Research, stated: "RiskMetrics isn't a substitute for good management, experience, and judgment. It's a toolbox, not a black box" (Jorion 2001, p. 29).

QUESTIONS

1. Actual losses _____ the calculated level of VaR can occur:
   (a) greater than
   (b) less than
   (c) equal to

    (d) both b and c
    (e) all of the above

2. VaR is:
    (a) an exact science that yields exact estimates.
    (b) an educated estimate of market risk.
    (c) a risk management tool.
    (d) the variability of a portfolio.
    (e) both b and c.

3. Back-testing VaR is:
    (a) not relevant. All of the underlying assumptions are correct and hold in reality. Similar assumptions are used in most financial models.
    (b) extremely important. There are many underlying assumptions, which may or may not hold in reality.
    (c) a waste of time. It's just a guess after all.

4. Which assumption underlying VaR is the most important yet most questionable?
    (a) Distributional
    (b) Nonnegativity
    (c) Random walk
    (d) Stationarity
    (e) Time consistency

5. You may have noticed that VaR is reported as a positive number. What would a negative VaR suggest?
    (a) VaR is undefined.
    (b) Losses could be really, really bad.
    (c) There is a high likelihood of making a profit.

6. Assume a portfolio is currently worth $250 million. If the portfolio has volatility of 12 percent and a holding period of 15 business days, what is the VaR estimate with 97.5 percent confidence? Now assume the portfolio has volatility of 35 percent, what is the VaR estimate? Interpret the results. Discuss the difference in the estimates obtained.

7. See Exhibit 24.4, which contains the daily adjusted closing prices for Apple, Inc. (AAPL) in 2009 as well as the periodic daily log returns. Calculate the daily 1 and 5 percentage VaR for Apple and interpret the results.

8. Exhibit 24.4 reports the daily adjusted closing prices and periodic daily log returns for Hypercom Corp (HYC) in 2009. Calculate the 0.1 and 2.5 percentage VaR for HYC.

9. Calculate the monthly VaR at the 99 percent and 90 percent confidence level for various market segments given below. These are average value weighted returns obtained from http://mba.tuck.dartmouth.edu/pages/faculty/ken.french/data_library.html. The data include monthly returns from July 1926 through December 2010. Assume a current portfolio value of $100,000.

Industry	Consumer	Manufacturing	High Tech	Health	Other
Mean	0.0099	0.0098	0.0093	0.0107	0.0090
St. Dev VaR	0.0539	0.0558	0.0569	0.0575	0.0656

10. Discuss the VaR amounts obtained in question 9. Be sure to include the pros and cons of using a 90 percent versus a 99 percent confidence level.

11. What happens when markets are behaving irrationally? Do VaR estimates hold up in these types of circumstances?

NOTES

1. Alternatively, some sources will use z as the confidence level instead of c. The approaches are identical; it is simply a notational difference.
2. The parametric method for calculating VaR is commonly used, and the only variables needed to do the calculation are the estimated mean and standard deviation of the portfolio. This method assumes that returns from portfolios are normally distributed.
3. *Note:* Derivatives can violate this assumption.
4. Here, bp represents the common abbreviation of basis points. A basis point is 1/100th of a percent.
5. Most portfolios are compared against a benchmark, with the most common benchmarks being the market portfolio, such as an index for the overall market performance in a country. For example, in the United States, the common market portfolios are the Dow Jones Industrial Average (DJIA) and the Standard & Poor's 500 index.
6. The purpose of back-testing is to estimate the performance of a strategy as if it had been employed during a past period. Detailed historical data are needed to implement this procedure. VaR must be used with care, and that is why back-testing is highly recommended.
7. The number of trading days per year is 252.
8. Here and throughout the remainder of this chapter, σ represents volatility (variability), which is proxied by standard deviation, and μ is the mean or expected mean return. Additionally, z is the z_α value or normal distribution factor. Exp represents the exponential function.

REFERENCES

Allen, Linda, Jacob Boudoukh, and Anthony Saunders. 2004. "Introduction to value at risk (VaR)." In *Understanding Market, Credit, and Operational Risk: The Value at Risk Approach.* Oxford, UK: Blackwell Publishing.

Einhorn, David. 2008. "Private Profits and Socialized Risk." *Global Association of Risk Professionals Risk Review* (June/July). www.garpdigitallibrary.org/download/GRR/2012.pdf.

Jorion, Philippe. 2001. *Value at Risk.* 2nd ed. New York: McGraw-Hill.

Taleb, Nassim. 1997. "The World According to Nassim Taleb." *Derivatives Strategy*, December/January. http://derivativesstrategy.com/magazine/archive/1997/1296qa.asp.

ABOUT THE CONTRIBUTORS

Allissa A. Lee, PhD, is an Assistant Professor of Finance in the College of Business Administration at Georgia Southern University. Previously she was a visiting assistant professor of finance in the Spears School of Business at Oklahoma State University and the McCoy College of Business Administration at Texas State University–San Marcos. Dr. Lee has contributed to several academic publications, including in the *Journal of Banking and Finance,* and has presented at various academic conferences. Her research interests are varied and include mergers and acquisitions, banking, real estate, corporate issues, and journal citations. She earned her PhD in finance from Oklahoma State University. Before returning to academia, Allissa worked in the mortgage industry for MidFirst Bank.

Betty J. Simkins, PhD, is Williams Companies Chair of Business and Professor of Finance at Oklahoma State University. Betty received her PhD from Case Western Reserve University. She has had more than 50 publications in academic finance journals. She has won awards for her teaching, research, and outreach, including the top awards at Oklahoma State University: the Regents Distinguished Research Award and the Outreach Excellence Award. Her primary areas of research are risk management, energy finance, and corporate governance. She serves on the editorial boards of nine academic journals, including the *Journal of Banking and Finance*; is past co-editor of the *Journal of Applied Finance*; and is past president of the Eastern Finance Association. She also serves on the Executive Advisory Committee of the Conference Board of Canada's Strategic Risk Council. In addition to this book, she has published two others: *Energy Finance and Economics: Analysis and Valuation, Risk Management and the Future of Energy* and *Enterprise Risk Management: Today's Leading Research and Best Practices for Tomorrow's Executives.* Prior to entering academia, she worked in the corporate world for ConocoPhillips and Williams Companies. She conducts executive education courses for companies globally.

CHAPTER 25

Uses of Efficient Frontier Analysis in Strategic Risk Management

A Technical Examination

WARD CHING
Vice President, Risk Management Operations, Safeway Inc.

LOREN NICKEL, FCAS, CFA, MAAA
Regional Director and Actuary, Aon Global Risk Consulting

O ver the past 25 years, the use of advanced quantitative financial and behavioral analysis has received increasing attention in an attempt to better understand and predict the performance impact on hazard risk portfolios. The limitations of single discipline modeling and decision making, which can lead to misreading of financial and performance risks across broad operational categories, were highlighted by the collapse of the financial markets in mid-2007. The need to answer broader risk questions has motivated the risk management industry (i.e., insurance, actuarial, finance, audit, and operations) to recalibrate and redirect core analytical protocols toward a more integrated approach.

The effort to take advantage of complex data techniques was, in part, stimulated by the evolving risk management framework integration into what is now being modestly referred to as enterprise risk management (ERM) or strategic risk management (SRM).[1]

Within the 2013 Risk and Insurance Management Society (RIMS) SRM Implementation Guide, the concept of strategic risk management is defined as a "business discipline that drives the deliberations and actions surrounding business-related uncertainties, while uncovering untapped opportunities reflected in an organization's strategy and execution."

What distinguishes this definition from previous descriptions of enterprise-wide risk management (ERM) approaches is the effort to sustainably deliver a robust fact-based *strategic dialogue* across the entire organization. This new strategic dialogue requires an analytical framework that is dynamic and encompasses all areas of an enterprise. In this chapter, we demonstrate how the use of efficient frontier analysis (EFA), and many of its derivative techniques, provides a robust portfolio approach to hazard, operational, market, and reputational risk domains.

STRATEGIC RISK MANAGEMENT FRAMEWORK EXAMINED

One of the most important ways SRM is beneficial for an organization is its ability to create opportunities for interaction and risk discovery (sometimes called "risk sensing") across organizational boundaries. This has not always been the case with previous ERM frameworks, where conceptual frameworks were overly formalized and yielded very narrow risk estimates. For most active SRM practitioners, this has proven not to be the case. Even in the area of insurance, where dialogues around risk estimates of frequency and severity are common, the effort to cross internal organizational boundaries has sometimes been met with significant resistance or dismissal.

An illustration of the SRM approach as described by RIMS is shown in Exhibit 25.1.

While first impressions might suggest that the SRM framework is a closed system, in actuality it is a continuous cycle with a robust opportunity for various parts of an organization to recognize and examine risk profiles within the context of a strategy setting, with the focus toward establishing the trade-off between risk transfer and risk assumption.

Moreover, the notion of risk appetite and risk tolerance combined with scenario and stress testing speaks to a more comprehensive analytical framework.[2] The intent of this framework is to drive a different set of "analytically informed" discussions among decision makers who may also be asking whether the risk profile of the organization constitutes a competitive opportunity.

As Fox and Merrifield point out:

> Strategic risk management focuses on the risks that may impede *or* accelerate the organization's strategic objectives for creating value, whether that value is

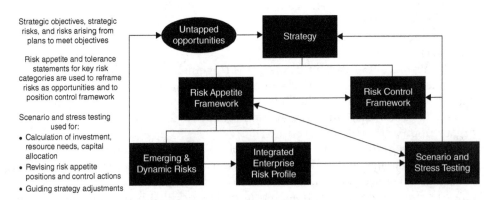

Exhibit 25.1 Strategic Risk Management Diagram

Source: RIMS Strategic Risk Management Implementation Guide 2012.

expressed as market share, profit, service provision, donor levels, social impact, or other benefit. Strategic risk management serves as a source of competitive advantage for decision making in two aspects: risk to the objectives themselves and risks arising from the plans to meet the objectives. While many organizations include risks to the objectives themselves, little consideration generally is given to the risks arising from the plans to meet the objectives, nor to the additional opportunities evolving from the underlying strategy and from emerging and dynamic risks. When addressed early and linked to the control framework, strategic adjustments can be made relatively quickly.

Fox and Merrifield, RIMS Strategic Risk Management Implementation
Guide, 2013

The fundamental difference between traditional risk assessment and SRM is the conscious effort to define *advantage* or *exploitable* risk profiles that can be used to sustainably differentiate or distinguish the organization in a competitively noisy environment.

MODERN PORTFOLIO THEORY AS A FOUNDATION FOR EFFICIENT FRONTIER ANALYSIS

Modern portfolio theory (MPT) is a mathematical method developed in the early 1950s and built out through the mid-1970s as a theory of finance that focuses on the maximization of portfolio return while minimizing the risk for a given amount or level of expected return, by specifically choosing the proportions of various assets contained in the portfolio. For the most part, MPT consists of a number of mathematical formulations that simulate and identify the impact of a risk-adjusted strategy investment diversification where the portfolio risk profile is collectively lower in value or volatility than any one asset.

In general, MPT models asset returns as a normally distributed function and recognizes risk as the standard deviation of return where the portfolio is viewed as the weighted combination of assets. Thus, the return of a given portfolio is considered the weighted combination of the asset return streams (Markowitz 1952).

Expected return is characterized as:

$$E(R_p) = \sum w_i E(R_i)$$

where R_p is the return on the portfolio, R_i is the return on the asset i, and w_i is the weighting of the asset i, which represents the asset i in the overall portfolio.

The operational concept behind MPT is that the assets in an investment portfolio should not be selected individually but should consider how their relative prices and values change across the portfolio. For many, this speaks to the relative trade-offs between calculated risk and expected return. Therefore, MPT would argue that assets and investments with higher expected returns attract higher measurable levels of risk. If the objective is to maximize the highest possible return on a portfolio of performing assets, MPT provides a way to describe and select those assets and investments that fit the return demand.

From an SRM perspective, within any operating organization there exists a series of hazard, operational, market, human capital, and reputational risks. These risks, while generally identified and mitigated separately, in fact exist in an integrated operational space—a risk portfolio. The essential questions that MPT can attempt to answer are:

- What is the economic value of an organization's material risk profile when characterized as a financial portfolio?
- How can the economic and operational volatility of an organization's risk profile be characterized dynamically and intertemporally?
- Are an organization's risk mitigation strategies and methods efficiently matching an organization's risk profile?
- If an organization changes its operations in a material way, what impact can be visualized across the organization's risk portfolio?
- Given the financial and operational activities of an organization, can an efficient[3] risk profile be determined? What trade-offs might be required to achieve an efficient risk profile? Efficiency could be defined as maximizing the contractual financial return relative to the expected utility of risk transferred to a third party. If the trade is equal—in other words, the price of the transference effectively matches the economic dynamics of the risk—then the trade may be considered efficient for both parties.
- If risk retention and risk transfer are considered two independent variables in an organization's risk profile distribution, how can the value of risk retention and risk transfer be maximized throughout an organization's insurance purchasing approach?

The approach to answering these questions is found with a number of mathematical techniques within MPT, notably efficient frontier analysis (EFA), dynamic financial analysis (DFA), capital asset pricing modeling (CAPM), or some other behavioral economic analysis of choice under conditions of information uncertainty. For the purpose of this chapter and its case study, we focus on the use of EFA within an insurance purchasing context.

It is important, however, to point out that some assumptions contained within the original MPT framework have been controversial and have generated a lively even-sided debate within the academic and practitioner literature base.[4]

The key assumptions include:

- The owners of portfolios are exclusively interested in the optimization problem.
- Asset returns are jointly normally distributed and random.
- Expected correlations between assets are fixed and constant without a time frame—in effect, forever.
- All parties to the use or exploitation of the portfolio always maximize economic utility regardless of other information, expectations, or considerations.
- All parties to the portfolio are considered rational and risk-averse.
- All parties to the portfolio performance have consistent, timely, and the same information at all points in time.

- All parties have the ability to accurately conceptualize and calculate the possible distribution of returns to the portfolio, and these calculations, in fact, match the actual returns of the portfolio.
- The performance of the portfolio is free of tax or transaction costs, and there is no transactional or postreturn friction.
- All parties to the portfolio are considered price takers, and their behaviors and choices do not influence the price market for the portfolio.
- Like the transactional or postreturn friction assumption, capital to invest in the portfolio is free and without an encumbering interest rate.
- A priori risk volatility can be conceptualized, calculated, and known in advance of the portfolio's construction, including asset/investment selection. Also, the portfolio's risk volatility is constant except when significant or material changes to the asset/investment distribution are made.[5]

For many, the primary criticism of the MPT model and many of its derivative subanalytics is that the assumptions are overly restrictive and do not adequately model real-world markets. Critics view MPT output and/or results as mathematical predictions about the future because many of the risk distributions, return calculations, and hypothesized correlations contained in the MPT approach are found in expected values. Since expected values are themselves statistical distributions, they may be inaccurate due to misspecification or may be subject to the influences of mitigating market information or circumstances.

Nonetheless, MPT and the use of EFA represent powerful ways to generate insight into portfolio performance and the prospective individual portfolio component efficiencies, which is a key step in implementing a strategic risk management philosophy.

PRACTICAL APPLICATIONS OF RISK MEASUREMENT FOR INSURANCE

Now we begin our journey through the practical application of risk theory applied to insurance risk and portfolios. The purpose of the process is to optimize insurance placements and risk limits for a relevant organization. We will start with a basic understanding of terminology, knowledge, and skills needed for a proper analysis, and then dive into the details and calculations necessary for a robust study. In the end, we will establish that this process can transcend insurance and be used in alternative risk transfer, noninsurance settings.

For the purposes of working through a real-life example, we need to establish insurance equivalents for the portfolio theory formulas. What follows is a list of definitions that we will use throughout this chapter and the equivalent portfolio theory definition.

From the previous section, we bring forth the standard portfolio theory formulas for the optimal return and optimal variance using the capital asset line:

$$E(r_c) = r_f + y[E(r_p) - r_f]$$
$$\sigma_p = w_A^2 \sigma_A^2 + w_B^2 \sigma_B^2 + 2w_A w_B \sigma_A \sigma_B \rho_{AB}$$

Expected risk spend $= E(rs_p)$ replaces expected return $E(r_p)$.

Here the expected risk spend on an insurance portfolio, $E(rs_p)$, replaces the expected return on an asset, $E(r_p)$. The expected risk spend is defined as the expected losses *not* transferred in the insurance contract plus the costs of the insurance contract. The expected risk spend is based on the insurance contract at hand, and will differ (often significantly) based on different contracts analyzed as part of the analysis.

> The risk-free rate is replaced by an insurance portfolio with no risk transfer (i.e., an uninsured risk line/portfolio).

The intent here is to set the steady state at no insurance purchase and determine if insurance will actually lower the risk to the organization. If it does, then insurance should be purchased. If it does not, insurance should not be purchased. In other words, on the capital market line for a given level of risk, you want to buy a portfolio with the highest level of return, but here you want to put together a risk portfolio with the lowest level of losses outside of the insurance contract for a given level of risk. By minimizing the losses, you are maximizing your return.

Visually, in our insurance example, you want to pick the bottom of the portfolio efficient frontier and not the one on the capital asset line as in typical portfolio theory.

Tail value at risk of loss = $TVaR_L$ replaces standard deviation of assets A, B, C ...

Tail value at risk, also known as *tail conditional expectation* (TCE) or conditional tail expectation (CTE), is a risk measure associated with the more general value at risk. It quantifies the expected value of the loss given that an event outside a given probability level has occurred.[6]

Modern Portfolio Theory (MPT)

Given a portfolio of A, one would prefer B, C, or D as compared to A as shown in Exhibit 25.2.

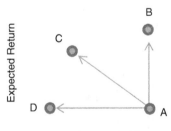

Exhibit 25.2 MPT Portfolio Preference

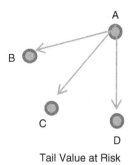

Tail Value at Risk

Exhibit 25.3 Efficient Frontier Framework Portfolio Preference

Efficient Frontier Insurance Framework

As for MPT, given a portfolio of A, one would prefer B, C, or D as compared to A as shown in Exhibit 25.3. However, notice that the preferred portfolios are now *below* the stated portfolio, as the preference here is to *lower* the expected losses and premium dollars spent.

The replacement of the typical finance standard deviation is an important one. In most financial textbooks (and practical usage), the standard deviation is most often from a normal distribution. In our example, we may use any multivariate distribution that is applicable, but for practicality we have chosen closed-form log-normal/Pareto distributions, which are typically used in insurance. We have also made another significant variation in the use of the tail value at risk (TVaR) instead of the standard deviation. The intent of this replacement is that most insurance contracts are low-probability contracts, so the standard deviation does not completely describe the use or intent of the contract. By using the tail value at risk, we can focus on the main use of the insurance contract and allow for multiple distribution functions, which will better describe the underlying distribution for its intended use.

The given probability of the TVaR calculation is up to the user. We have selected a probability level of 95 percent, meaning that the worst 5 percent of outcomes are averaged to produce the TVaR figure at 95 percent.

The next complexity of selecting a TVaR calculation means that one will almost always be required to run a simulation model to determine the statistic. Only the most simplistic applications will allow for a closed-form expression of the measure of volatility. Therefore, we have chosen to use Monte Carlo simulation for our application of the efficient frontier for insurance portfolios.

The added benefit of using a simulation model is that we are now free to use multivariate distributions, complex correlations, copulas, and other transformations that may be too complex for most formulaic calculations. It is also important to note that most insurance portfolios contain more than seven to 10 different contracts/risks; so modeling is often a required component for any portfolio analysis.

We certainly do not want to gloss over the correlation concerns with insurance contracts, as there are many. It is becoming more common to use copulas (and different versions of copulas formulas—for example, a Gaussian copula or a Gumbel copula[7]) to measure more complex correlations. The choice and use of correlations are critical elements of a proper model and should be reviewed with statisticians or actuaries versed in their use.[8] For our purposes, we have assumed no correlations, for the simplicity of the calculations and translation of the results into knowledge.

It should be noted that TVaR is a simple method to allocate capital for insurance risk. The TVaR demonstrates the level of risk for a given insurance line or contract. Capital can thus be allocated based on that level of risk. Capital allocation theory is beyond the scope of this chapter, as there are many other variations upon this theme for allocating capital. It should be noted that the next step beyond the portfolio optimization is capital allocation.

One immediate question with the introduction of the TVaR as a risk measure is: "What is the right level of risk?" Or in simpler terms: "What is the largest loss I am willing to take?" Management should make a conscious decision on the level of risk to take through a formal enterprise risk management program. Risk setting is a critical step in any efficient frontier analysis and should not be overlooked. For our purposes, we have assumed that the organization will seek to minimize risk and minimize the annual costs to the budget (i.e., uninsured losses and insurance costs).

With some liberties taken in the usage of financial theory in the development of our risk transfer methods, we can now build a framework to analyze risk and optimize risk transfer spends (i.e., like insurance). The framework is intended for financial professionals versed in financial theory and its applications. With proper application, many organizations across the world could more efficiently allocate their risk spends and reduce the risk to their balance sheets.

SAMPLE CASE STUDY

Let's start with a practical example of a large corporation with three basic insurance risks: earthquake exposure to buildings, workers' compensation insurance, and general liability insurance.

Earthquake risk is defined as the potential for loss to buildings and property from a large earthquake as well as business interruption following the event. For our sample company, management has chosen to insure earthquake risk with a policy that covers $25 million in business and personal property with a 5 percent per occurrence retention. Earthquake sprinkler leakage is not covered.

For workers' compensation, management has chosen to buy a retention policy with a $1 million per occurrence retention, with no upper limitation, as it is a statutorily unlimited coverage.

The general liability coverage is represented by a $25 million per occurrence limit and a $250,000 per occurrence retention.

Now that we have the insurance coverage, we can assume the risk of loss for each of the three lines of coverage follows basic loss distributions as follows:

1. *Earthquake (EQ).* Loss frequency has a Poisson distribution with mean $\lambda = 0.1$, and severity has a Pareto distribution with parameter $\theta = 5,000,000$, $\alpha = 50,000,000$.

Exhibit 25.4 Mean Retained Losses by Line

	Retention	Limit	Current
EQ	5%	$25,000,000	$2,500,501
WC	$1,000,000	Statutory	$3,163,992
GL	$250,000	$25,000,000	$1,597,373
Portfolio			**$7,261,866**

2. *Workers' compensation (WC)*. Loss frequency has a Poisson distribution with mean $\lambda = 50$, and severity has a lognormal distribution with parameters $\mu = 10$, $\sigma = 1.5$.
3. *General liability (GL)*. Loss frequency has a Poisson distribution with mean $\lambda = 10$, and severity has a lognormal distribution with parameters $\mu = 12$, $\sigma = 1.0$.

Notice that because the retentions are rather large, we are more focused on the tail portion of the loss distributions. We have decided not to use correlations for this example, to allow the reader to more easily follow and replicate the figures. In reality, correlations would be a key input into the model and would help determine the optimal risk transfer structures.

Exhibit 25.4 is a brief summary of the expected losses for the insurance policy and to the corporation below retentions and above insurance limits. The intent of this exhibit is to show the risk profile of the corporation using the assumed distributions listed earlier.

Note that there are many methods for fitting proper distributions and selecting the parameters to ensure good fits of historical data. Curve fitting is well beyond the scope of this chapter, and we will let the reader peruse other sources for details on loss distribution fitting.

With the knowledge of the current risk profile, we can now seek to optimize the portfolio and the insurance purchase by selecting different insurance options for our portfolio. By "options" we mean to choose different risk transfer contracts that can be used to modify the risk profile of the corporation. This can be done by taking a mathematical approach (using increments off of the current program) or by selecting common insurance contract terms known in the insurance marketplace. Exhibit 25.5 lists the options using the two different methods.

As one can see, there is almost an unlimited amount of options in the mathematical approach. The possibilities are only limited by your computing power.

Exhibit 25.5 Portfolio Options under the Mathematical Approach

	Option #1	Option #2	Option #3	Option #4	Option #5
EQ	5% retention $20M limit	5% retention $30M limit	5% retention $40M limit	5% retention $50M limit	10% retention $25M limit
WC	$250K retention Statutory limit	$500K retention Statutory limit	$2M retention Statutory limit	$3M retention Statutory limit	$4M retention Statutory limit
GL	$500K retention $25M limit	$1M retention $25M limit	$2M retention $25M limit	$3M retention $25M limit	$500K retention $30M limit

Exhibit 25.6 Portfolio Options under the Coverage Availability Approach

	Option #1	Option #2	Option #3	Option #4	Option #5
EQ	5% retention $20M limit	5% retention **$50M limit**	5% retention **$75M limit**	5% retention **$100M limit**	10% retention $25M limit
WC	$250K retention Statutory limit	$500K retention Statutory limit	$2M retention Statutory limit	**$5M retention** Statutory limit	**$10M retention** Statutory limit
GL	$500K retention $25M limit	**$2M retention** $25M limit	**$5M retention** $25M limit	**$10M retention** $25M limit	**$500K retention** $30M limit

It should also be noted that the selections for the different options are based on simple increments from the current values. These options may not be available in the insurance marketplace. This is somewhat intentional, as the goal is to find the optimal mathematical solution and then find the insurance option that gets closest to that optimal solution. The coverage availability approach is shown in Exhibit 25.6.

You will notice a subtle change in Exhibit 25.6, as indicated by the bolded options. The difference here is that we have selected options that can be knowingly purchased in the insurance marketplace. For more historical reasons than anything else, insurance risk transfer has been based around round numbers for retentions and limits. By using these options, we are guaranteeing (assuming the entity is insurable) viable options for the corporation.

Now the mathematicians can begin their number crunching. Using the options for Exhibit 25.5, we can determine the expected risk spend (expected losses to the corporation, which are the losses below the retention and above the limits) and the tail value at risk (TVaR) for each option, and then plot them on a graph. We have done this for each line described earlier and combined all the lines in a portfolio. We have assumed no correlations in the portfolio, to keep the mathematics and logic easier for the reader to follow.

To obtain Exhibits 25.7 to 25.10, we have run a simulation model using a Monte Carlo simulator. There are various software programs that provide the capability to simulate losses by using different distributions. Readers may wish to try the parameters within their own software to follow along.

Exhibit 25.10 provides the assumed insurance premiums for each of the mathematical options. In reality, we would work with insurance brokers to obtain insurance quotes for each of the options to arrive at a true market price for each option. The option exists to use an actuarial estimate of premium, which is not preferred. The reason an actuarial estimate of premium is not preferred is that the market does not always follow actuarial estimates and can often fall to other vagaries of market pricing (underwriting judgment, capital constraints, class restrictions, premium goals, etc.). Therefore, we recommend using different quotes provided by insurance brokers for each option. Given insurance premiums are presented in Exhibit 25.11.

Now with the options plotted (using our modeled losses, TVaR, and insurance premiums), we have created an efficient frontier and can determine the best option for a given level of risk. Ideally, we would select more than five options, and the options would be more complex. The beauty of the process is that it can be as simple

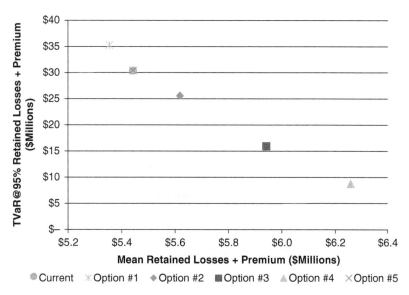

Exhibit 25.7 Earthquake Modeled Options

or complex as one desires. The process is flexible so as to handle different risk measures (not just TVaR) and can optimize different costs of risk (losses, insurance spend, internal costs, etc.).

It is also important to have an enterprise understanding of our risk appetite and tolerance. By having a formal statement of risk appetite, we can use that knowledge in the proper selection of the options in our efficient frontier.

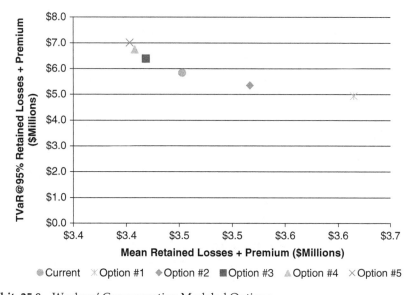

Exhibit 25.8 Workers' Compensation Modeled Options

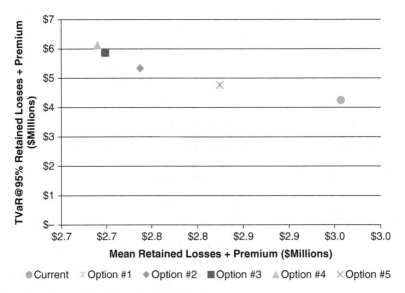

Exhibit 25.9   General Liability Modeled Options

Case Study General Findings

Using the same charts as previously, we can make a few judgments about the options presented. For this example, let's assume the company does not want to lose more than $20 million in a fiscal period. This would be considered its risk appetite and is roughly equivalent to maximizing utility for a corporation. By

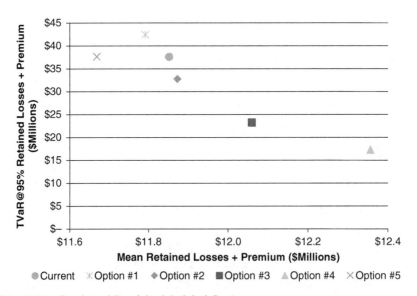

Exhibit 25.10   Combined Portfolio Modeled Options

Exhibit 25.11 Given Insurance Premiums

	Current	Option #1	Option #2	Option #3	Option #4	Option #5
EQ	$2,941,765	$2,353,412	$3,618,371	$4,942,165	$6,008,556	$2,941,765
WC	$ 288,796	$1,098,994	$ 607,957	$ 116,861	$ 64,051	$ 40,630
GL	$1,359,385	$ 696,302	$ 261,277	$ 68,436	$ 26,041	$ 696,302

selecting a program that puts the $20 million or more at risk, there is potential for breaching that corporate goal.

Note that the models assume that insurance is recoverable for the risk analyzed. This may not always be the case, so it is important to review coverage and ensure that the model is reflective of the coverage provided and that the insurance carrier's ability to pay is also reviewed.

The numbers and options have been chosen to reflect realistic scenarios. The results are typical of what we see in the insurance and corporate landscape.

Findings on the earthquake simulation are (see Exhibit 25.12):

- We have a wide variety of options and a wide variety of risk levels.
- The slope of the efficient frontier is very steep as a result.
- The options all lie close to the frontier, resulting in many efficient options.
- If the organization is using a risk appetite for *only* earthquake risks, then it would look at the efficient frontier below the $20 million tail value at risk level. (Options #3 and #4 qualify.)

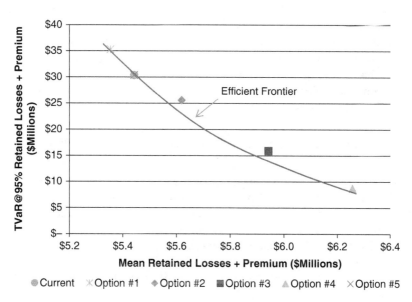

Exhibit 25.12 Efficient Frontier on Earthquake Options

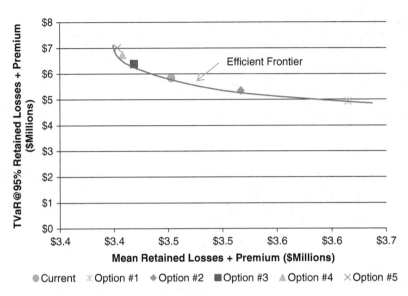

Exhibit 25.13   Efficient Frontier on Workers' Compensation Options

Findings on the workers' compensation simulation are (see Exhibit 25.13):

- We have a similar wide variety of options, but a much tighter range of risk levels.
- The slope of the efficient frontier is very shallow as a result.
- The options all lie close to the frontier, resulting in many efficient options.
- If the organization is using a risk appetite for *only* workers' compensation, then it would look at the efficient frontier below the $20 million tail value at risk level. All options qualify.
- Because workers' compensation risks are relatively stable, the model has only modest differences between options and all options are reasonable.
- To change the options to give a greater range of results, one could be more extreme on the options (assuming the insurance market is willing to provide such options to the corporation).

Findings on the general liability simulation are (see Exhibit 25.14):

- We have a similar wide variety of options, and a modest range of risk levels.
- The slope of the efficient frontier is shallow as a result.
- The options all lie close to the frontier, resulting in many efficient options.
- If the organization is using a risk appetite for *only* general liability, then it would look at the efficient frontier below the $20 million tail value at risk level. (All options qualify.)
- Similarly to workers' compensation, different options can be substituted here for a wider range of outcomes.

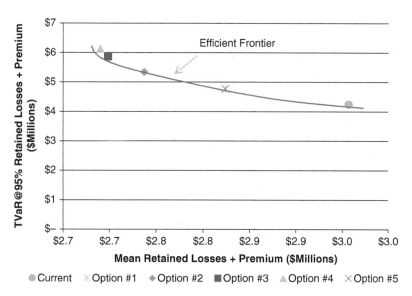

Exhibit 25.14   Efficient Frontier on General Liability Options

The portfolio shown in Exhibit 25.15 is simply the annual events for all three lines added together, again with no correlation assumptions (i.e., independence). Portfolio option #1 is the sum of each of the respective lines Option #1, with no aggregate insurance limitations assumed. The framework certainly allows for aggregations and correlations; we have not provided them here for simplicity.

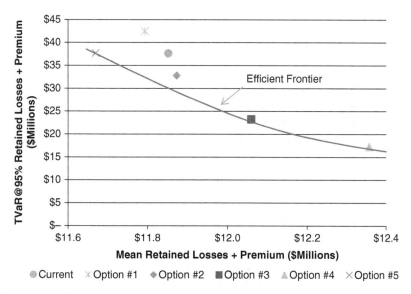

Exhibit 25.15   Efficient Frontier on the Combined Portfolio Options

Findings on the portfolio simulation are (see Exhibit 25.15):

- The portfolios no longer follow the efficient frontier, as some of the options lie considerably above the efficient frontier line.
- The slope of the efficient frontier is somewhat steep, and follows the risks that contribute to the portfolio (earthquake in this instance is driving the steep curve).
- If the organization is using a risk appetite for the entire portfolio, then it would look at the efficient frontier below the $20 million tail value at risk level. (Only option #4 qualifies.)

We can now see how the efficient frontier insurance framework utilizes the information provided, combines a complex set of insurance structures, and uses a risk appetite to select the best portfolio option. This framework facilitates a company's ability to make fact-based decisions, using real-time information. The organization no longer has to wonder if it is getting the best deal or if there were other options that might have provided a better bang for its buck.

INTENDED USES FOR OUR APPROACH

It is important to note that this framework, as all others, has limitations in its use. The intended purpose for this framework is to help large corporate organizations with their risk management process and portfolio management. The framework is robust enough to handle both insurance risk and noninsurance risk. It is best used within an established enterprise risk management discipline.

The following is a brief description of the benefits of an ERM strategy and how our framework fits within those benefits, which is important for understanding the full potential of its use. We have referenced James Lam's (2003) benefits, as they are excellent.

The four benefits to risk management as defined by James Lam[9] are:

1. Managing risk is management's job.
2. Managing risk can reduce earnings volatility.
3. Managing risk can maximize shareholders' value.
4. Risk management promotes job and financial security.

In item 1, Lam indicates that management has access to critical information about the business and therefore has a duty to use it to manage risk. We agree wholeheartedly with his assessment, and our process is intended to improve senior leaders' understanding of risk and give them more transparency in managing costs.

In item 2, Lam indicates that top-tier companies better manage their earnings volatility through risk management activities. Too often firms do not consider risk management or relegate it to small, back-room activities. This often overlooks the value that can be had by minimizing volatility on major risks to the organization.

By taking a more in-depth look at the portfolio of risk through the efficient frontier and making more data-driven decisions, volatility can be reduced.

In item 3, Lam indicates that firms can increase their shareholders' values by 20 to 30 percent or more by identifying opportunities for risk management and business optimization through a risk-based program.[10] This goes beyond just managing volatility and extends to a better-performing business model with more accurate information spread across the organization. Using risk-based measures is a critical element of any risk measurement department. Components like the efficient frontier require wide distribution and use; otherwise they are not getting the full attention they deserve.

For the real company this framework was modeled after, the efficient frontier was sent directly to the business leaders and they became owners of the risks for their particular areas of influence. They had to learn the language of risk and through a diverse corporate program are now using the risk assessments as part of their daily routines, leading to a better understanding of risk for the business leaders and more accurate information for the risk management team.

When implementing this framework at different companies, we often hear something to the effect of "What's in it for me?," which really gets down to job and financial security for individuals, as noted in item 4. A truly robust framework should allow for better risk taking, as the guidelines have been set and approved by management. With a data-first strategy there should be less concern over losing your job, as long as the risk is within the tolerances set by management. Thus, when a calculated risk does happen, the organization is ready to respond. All too often, the opposite is true and a surprise event leads to the ouster of a senior leader. We believe that our framework will help provide senior leaders with the information they need to take calculated risks and therefore preserve their livelihoods, regardless of their golden parachutes.

It is inherently assumed that the lines of insurance or risk transfer can be modeled appropriately. This is certainly not an insignificant assumption, as data limitations, information asymmetry, internal disputes, and plain modeling foibles can easily derail the best intentions of the framework.

To combat these issues, it is always important to stress test any model, back-test the model if possible, involve different business leaders to vet the results of the model, and use independent experts to question and test the assumptions in the model. Any model is only as good as its creators, so it is advised to hire the best and then "trust but verify."

MODERN PORTFOLIO CONCERNS CONTAINED IN THE FRAMEWORK

There are several modern portfolio shortcomings that we should address in relevance to our framework, represented in these MPT assumptions:[11]

- Asset returns are (jointly) normally distributed random variables.
- Correlations between assets are fixed and constant forever.
- All investors have access to the same information at the same time.

- All securities can be divided into parcels of any size.
- Risk and volatility of an asset are known in advance and are constant.

To address the first point, we have already discussed our use of nonnormal distributions and feel the framework is robust enough to handle any variation of distributions that a modeler feels is appropriate. In postmodern portfolio management, the use of normal distributions has also been relaxed for similar reasons, so this is not as much of a concern as originally stated.

Correlations are clearly not constant or fixed, and once more, they are hard to measure without good historical data. The modeler will often make assumptions around correlations and use copulas to simulate different relationships between correlations at different points of a distribution. It is clear that, again, modern computing power has allowed us to use correlations in a much different way than in the past. Unfortunately, the flexibility is not always a good thing. As correlations are often a modeler's assumption, the use and selection of them should be highly scrutinized.

In insurance, the market is very far from what one would call efficient. On stock exchanges there are clearinghouses and information services to provide an up-to-date information exchange. And even then, the market is not truly efficient. In insurance, pricing different contracts is dealt serious information asymmetry and is fraught with poor information, as the data and pricing start with an actuary in a corporate insurance company, then are translated by an underwriter, and then are ignored by sales professionals (only slight exaggerations involved). This lack of an efficient market is what makes our risk framework so critical. Without it, the insurance buyer has little chance of getting the best deal.

Our framework does have an issue with the ability to fractionalize options and to get the insurance market to respond to all potential mathematical pricing options. This can happen for a variety of reasons: internal restrictions, lack of proper information, risk limits, reinsurance requirements, and so on. The framework can, however, lead insurance markets to *more* optimal insurance contracts. So even if an option is not technically available, the closest option available in the marketplace can be substituted in similar fashion.

In insurance, especially for large corporations, the party who controls the information can hold a competitive advantage. Both parties to a transaction (corporation and insurance company) have pieces of the puzzle in determining the true risk exposure for the corporation. The insurance company has a significantly larger database of similar risks, and the corporation has very specific data to its risk profile and a much better understanding of how its risk profile is changing. All of this means that the underlying risk is clearly not constant and is difficult to predict. Thankfully, to optimize a risk portfolio one does not require perfect information, only relative accuracy and reasonable assumptions on information that is not available.

In our framework, we are not fully constrained by the limitation of modern portfolio theory, as we are not developing a theory, but rather a practical modeling application. We also have use of greater computer power than ever before, which allows the relaxation of many of the constraints presented earlier in this chapter. We believe that we have addressed the major concerns of modern portfolio theory and its application to insurance, but we will leave that conclusion fully up to the reader.

CONSIDERATION OF BEHAVIORAL CONCERNS IN STRUCTURE

A commonly stated concern with the efficient frontier theory is that is breaks down due to behavioral concerns with the market participants. The participants do not always maximize utility, information is not always readily available, and people do not always make decisions based solely on mean and standard deviations of returns.[12] Because of these concerns, it is necessary to discuss the behavioral implications for our framework.

We start with the definition of common behavioral errors associated with information processing and then move on to the types of informational errors.

Definition: "Information processing—errors in information processing can lead investors to misestimate the true probabilities of possible events or associated rates of return."[13]

The different types of informational processing errors are:

- Forecasting errors
- Overconfidence
- Conservatism
- Sample size neglect and representativeness[14]

People often have problems forecasting the future. The most typical concern is using the most recent information to forecast the future. As risk professionals, we see this every day as everyone thinks that the most recent years of information reflect the best and most reliable information. In reality, forecasting is much more complex than that. In our model, we rely on forecasting techniques, but concentrate on methods that use a minimum of five years of information and often 10 years or more of information if it is available. This reduces any forecasting errors and relies on data methods, which are more consistent than human forecasts.

Overconfidence is another common behavioral trait that is difficult to overcome. People often believe they forecast better than they actually do and are often unwilling to recognize that blind spot. This is where a robust process and using several independent experts can reduce the bias that comes from overconfidence. Any one person can have his or her own biases, even experts. So involving a team of experts and a process to reduce the bias is critical to getting a more accurate estimate of risk.

Sometimes a process or framework can be too slow to react to new information. A slow response often occurs in insurance where there is an unrecognized change in a company's risk profile. The client history and the industry data are naturally slow to reflect trends, and large volumes of data are required to finally identify new information. This phenomenon is the counterbalance to being too fast to react. The conservatism bias is best handled by involving business experts in the process to question and comment on changes in the business and to get a common understanding on how those changes are reflected in the modeling work.

Sample size bias is usually pretty well handled by expert modelers. They understand that small sample sizes are less credible than large ones and therefore provide less usable information within a forecast. This can be difficult to communicate, however, so it should be noted that communication of the biases of sample size neglect and representativeness is just as important as realizing them.

We next consider behavioral biases. It has been stated that "Behavioral biases largely affect how investors frame questions of risk versus return, and therefore make risk-return trade-offs."[15]

The main types of behavioral biases are:

- Framing
- Mental accounting
- Regret avoidance
- Prospect theory[16]

Framing is the way a question is posed about risk. The question can be posed as "Will you lose $50 million under a worst-case scenario?" or be posed as "Will you stand to make $5 million on the expected basis under the same scenario?" Different questions can lead to different responses, even in seemingly rational people. The way we approach framing is to include the positive and the negative, as well as several other scenarios to provide a range of responses. This can be information overload at first, but after the framework is understood, it provides key information to avoid the framing bias.

Oftentimes people segregate risks based on a particular belief or internal structure within an organization, saying it is fine to take risk in this particular area but not in another one. This is called mental accounting. Organizations are plagued with mental accounting as different divisions; regions, locations, and management all create some level of mental accounting for an organization. The only way to minimize this bias is to have the C-level executives dictate the level of risk they want to adhere to as an organization; otherwise the line-level managers will all view risk through their own lenses. Consultants can often point out this bias within a company, but a company that is not already aware of this bias can fail to use any risk framework appropriately.

Another large corporate risk is regret avoidance. This is the phenomenon that losing a bet on a scenario with long odds is more painful than losing the same amount on a game with a better expected outcome. This is illustrated in the saying "No one ever got fired by hiring IBM." Large corporations have different cultures and approaches to this bias. Some companies in Silicon Valley make an extra effort to avoid this bias and to create a risk-taking culture. Either way, this is a concern for our analysis. Any option we present, no matter how risk reducing to the organization, will look suboptimal to the current one based on our behavioral biases.

Prospect theory does not apply as well in a corporate environment as in a personal one. In prospect theory the change in wealth from one's current wealth is what is important, not the absolute wealth. For an organization, each employee has his or her own "wealth" and access to company funds. Many are limited in this area, and any change in wealth for the company is not often felt by the employee. There is a disengagement from the wealth of the corporation. This does not mean there is a certain level of bias in the corporation.

As we have shown, there are several behavioral considerations to make in any risk framework. We have tried to comment on how we address those concerns, but are sure there are many other successful ways to handle these biases. The key consideration here is to be aware of the biases and to make sure the organization addresses these issues as part of its enterprise risk management program.

QUESTIONS

1. How does efficient frontier analysis differ from other forms of complex risk assessment techniques?
2. What limitations might an analyst encounter through the use of efficient frontier analysis?
3. How can efficient frontier analysis results be communicated and utilized with nonmathematical decision makers?

ACKNOWLEDGMENTS

Special recognition is given to the following editors of this chapter:

Jillian Hagan, FCAS
Virginia Jones, ACAS
Betty Simkins, PhD

NOTES

1. "RIMS Strategic Risk Management Implementation Guide," 2013.
2. "Details of Risk Appetite and Tolerance," www.theirm.org/publications/documents/IRM_Risk_Appetite_Consultation_Paper_Final_Web.pdf.
3. We have defined *efficient* to mean the maximum return on investment for keeping risk or transferring risk to a third party.
4. Milan Vaclavik and Josef Jablonsky, "Revisions of Modern Portfolio Theory Optimization Model," 2011.
5. Jerry A. Miccolis and Marina Goodman, "Next Generation Investment Risk Management: Putting the 'Modern' Back in Modern Portfolio Theory," *Journal of Financial Planning*, January 2012.
6. Ibid.
7. Ibid. Bodie, Zvi, Alex Kane, and Alan Marcus. *Investments*. 8th edition. New York: McGraw-Hill.
8. For reference, a good article on copulas is available on the CAS website: www.casact.org/library/studynotes/feldblum-dependency2013.pdf.
9. James Lam, "Enterprise Risk Management from Controls to Incentives," 6–9.
10. Ibid., 8.
11. Miccolis and Goodman, "Next Generation Investment Risk Management," 2012.
12. www.investopedia.com/articles/investing/041213/modern-portfolio-theory-vs-behavioral-finance.asp.
13. Zvi Bodie, Alex Kane, and Alan Markus, *Investments*, 8th ed. (New York: McGraw-Hill, 2008), 385.
14. Ibid., 386.
15. Ibid., 387.
16. Ibid., 387–388.

REFERENCES

Bodie, Zvi, Alex Kane, and Alan Marcus. 2008. *Investments*. 8th edition. New York: McGraw-Hill.

"RIMS Strategic Risk Management Implementation Guide." 2013.

"Managed Futures—Reducing Portfolio Volatility, A Look into the Top 3 Managed Futures Accounts Worldwide." 2011. Emanagedfutures.com, March 19.

Markowitz, H. M. 1952. "Portfolio Selection." *Journal of Finance* 7:1, 77–91.

Markowitz, H. M. 1959. *Portfolio Selection: Efficient Diversification of Investments*. New York: John Wiley & Sons, reprinted by Yale University Press, 1970.

Merton, Robert. 1972. "An Analytical Derivation of the Efficient Frontier." *Journal of Financial and Quantitative Analysis* 7, September.

Miccolis, Jerry A., and Marina Goodman. 2012. "Next Generation Investment Risk Management: Putting the Modern Back in Modern Portfolio Theory." *Journal of Financial Planning*, January.

Lam, James. 2003. *Enterprise Risk Management from Controls to Incentives*. Hoboken, NJ: John Wiley & Sons.

Taleb, Nassim Nicholas. 2007. *The Black Swan: The Impact of the Highly Improbable*. New York: Random House.

Vaclavik, Milan, and Josef Jablonsky. 2011. "Revisions of Modern Portfolio Theory Optimization Model."

ABOUT THE CONTRIBUTORS

Ward Ching is Vice President, Risk Management Operations, at Safeway Inc., located in Pleasanton, California. His responsibilities include enterprise risk management, integrated risk finance, hazard loss control, environmental compliance, property risk control/engineering, and a variety of retail, distribution, and manufacturing risk management initiatives, including Safeway's Culture of Safety. Prior to joining Safeway, he was a principal at Towers Perrin and a managing director at Marsh. He completed his undergraduate and graduate degrees in international relations and economics at the University of Southern California, and has taught and written extensively on the subjects of international relations, game theoretical applications in foreign policy, and enterprise risk management.

Loren Nickel, FCAS, CFA, MAAA, is the Regional Director and Actuary for the Northwest Region (Seattle, San Francisco, and Los Angeles) and National Leader for Operational Risk for Aon Global Risk Consulting. He is responsible for providing clients with actuarial support as well as a variety of financial and tailored risk services. His work includes pricing, reserving, profitability studies, retention studies, dynamic financial analysis, and captive analysis for all major lines of insurance. He provides professional actuarial opinions as well as a variety of innovative risk solutions.

PART V

Mini-Cases on ERM and Risk

CHAPTER 26

Bim Consultants Inc.

JOHN R.S. FRASER
Senior Vice President, Internal Audit, and former Chief Risk Officer, Hydro One
Networks Inc.

Bim Consultants Inc. is a medium-sized consulting firm. It is a corporation with 30 partners who own most of the shares. It has 10 offices across Canada with 3,000 staff, and has been in business for 30 years. Senior staff also own shares and participate in an annual bonus scheme. Salaries are generally on the low side, but bonuses in good years can be quite high. The balance sheet is sound (see Exhibit 26.1).

The company has always prided itself on its customer focus. "Customers are number one" has been the mantra from the chairman, Mr. Smooth, for many years. Recently, however, revenue has been stagnant, and the younger partners are getting restless, wondering if the older partners have lost their edge and whether changes are needed to return to the glory days of large bonuses.

At a recent strategic planning meeting of the major partners, the decision was made to continue focusing on customers as number one, but also to explore how to increase revenue from within the existing clientele and to explore what additional services could be provided to enrich the client experience (and revenues). It was agreed that the strength of the firm was in its blue-chip client base and that this high-quality reputation was worth preserving. Some discussions were also held around the idea of selling a minority share of the company at a large multiple, if such a deal was identified. Bim Consultants' profit and loss and retained earnings are provided in Exhibit 26.2.

Earlier this week, the chairman received a call from the president of the Canadian subsidiary of a U.S.–owned competitor, Bravado International, saying that Bravado was pulling out of Canada and would consider an offer to sell the subsidiary to Bim Consultants Inc. The Bravado subsidiary had 12 offices across Canada and just over 3,500 staff, but had often drawn on its U.S. resources when required for large engagements.

Exhibit 26.1   Bim Consultants Balance Sheet

Bim Consultants Inc.
Summary Balance Sheet
As of December 31, 2014

	2014	2013
Year ended December 31 (Canadian dollars in millions)	$	$
Current Assets		
Cash and Short-Term Investments	12	7
Accounts Receivable	175	168
	187	175
Current Liabilities		
Accounts Payable	34	27
Short-Term Loans	100	110
	134	137
Working Capital	53	38
Fixed Assets		
Leasehold Improvements	196	178
Furniture and Equipment	100	94
Less Accumulated Depreciation & Amortization	(153)	(128)
	143	144
Net Assets	196	181
Share Capital		
Common Shares	100	100
Retained Earnings	96	81
	196	181

The chairman called an executive meeting and pointed out that making such a purchase would double sales, catapult Bim Consulting into the number one position in major markets in Canada, and provide a strong marketing thrust into previously untapped midtier markets. Based primarily on the persuasiveness of the chairman, the executive committee approved proceeding with the negotiations.

The president of the Bravado subsidiary cautioned Mr. Smooth that it was imperative not to have word of the negotiations leak out, as this could lead to a loss of key staff and possibly clients. Accordingly, he urged Mr. Smooth not to do the normal due diligence in the subsidiary's offices but to review the necessary records and meet with select senior executives of Bravado at an off-site location. This process seemed to work well, and the Bravado executives were well prepared and very likable. All the information checked out, and the way seemed clear to do a deal.

Exhibit 26.2 Bim Consultants Profit and Loss and Retained Earnings

Bim Consultants Inc.
Summary Profit and Loss and Retained Earnings
For the Year Ended December 31, 2014

	2014 $	2013 $
Year ended December 31 (Canadian dollars in millions)		
Revenue	300	290
Expenses		
Salaries	220	207
Other	20	18
Net Profit before Income Tax	60	65
Income Tax Provision	27	29
Net Income after Tax	33	36
Retained Earnings—Beginning of Year	81	65
	114	101
Dividends	18	20
Retained Earnings—End of Year	96	81

QUESTIONS

1. What is your assessment of the situation?
2. What advice would you provide to the board of Bim Consultants?
3. What pitfalls should they be concerned with?

ABOUT THE CONTRIBUTOR

John R.S. Fraser is the Senior Vice President, Internal Audit, and former Chief Risk Officer of Hydro One Networks Inc., one of North America's largest electricity transmission and distribution companies. He is a Fellow of the Ontario Institute of Chartered Accountants, a Fellow of the Association of Chartered Certified Accountants (UK), a Certified Internal Auditor, and a Certified Information Systems Auditor. He has more than 30 years' experience in the risk and control field, mostly in the financial services sector, including areas such as finance, fraud, derivatives, safety, environment, computers, and operations. In addition to this book, he also served as editor on *Enterprise Risk Management: Today's Leading Research and Best Practices for Tomorrow's Executives* (John Wiley & Sons, 2010).

CHAPTER 27

Nerds Galore

ROB QUAIL, BASc
Director, Enterprise Risk Management, Hydro One Networks Inc.

Nerds Galore (NG) is a Canadian service company with 1,000 employees working out of offices in 12 Canadian cities; the head office is in Edmonton, Alberta. NG provides full-service information technology (IT) support to small and medium-sized Canadian businesses, including help desk, on-site troubleshooting, security, network setup and support, backup services, wireless networks, hardware and software procurement, and website design and hosting solutions.

Nerds Galore was formed in 2000 in the garage of its founder, Jeeves Stobes. NG has enjoyed strong growth in its segment and has an excellent reputation with its customers. In the beginning, NG focused on a particular customer subsegment, small start-up businesses, especially on low-tech businesses such as boutique services. Lately its strategy has shifted more to midsize customers (which have deeper pockets and less chance of going broke) with more sophisticated technology needs.

Recently there have been problems for NG.

There has been steady decline in customer satisfaction, as shown in Exhibit 27.1.

Following a thorough investigation and follow-up with many of NG's key customers, the Executive Team has concluded that the main cause of this has been high internal staff turnover, leading to gaps in customer services and service continuity.

Indeed, staff retention has been an issue, as shown in Exhibit 27.2.

To continue to provide strong customer service, it is critical that team members are competent in the latest technology, and yet turnover has approached 20 percent in three recent years. This is a particular problem for NG because of its high focus on customer service; new staff receive extensive and costly training in NG's customer service and cross-selling approaches. The company's pay package is competitive but not at the very top; instead NG uses its reputation for excellent customer relationship and staff development to attract motivated staff. Note that it's well known that one of NG's competitors was recently raided by a large systems integration firm and lost most of its network management technical staff in a single quarter. NG has been having a particularly difficult time retaining staff in the larger urban centers and other technology hubs in Canada where there are more competitors and the competitors generally pay more.

Despite the fact that customer satisfaction has been declining, the Executive Team did note that revenue numbers have not suffered; in fact, they have

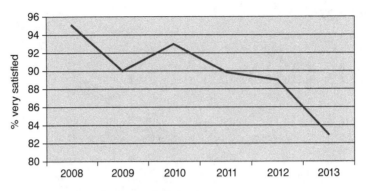

Exhibit 27.1   Nerds Galore Customer Satisfaction

continued to climb year over year, as shown in Exhibit 27.3. It was concluded that this lack of a drop in revenues is due to two factors:

1. Many current customers have multiyear contracts with Nerds Galore.
2. Very small businesses that have made up the bulk of NG's customer base are generally tolerant of minor service hitches and less focused on optimal technology performance.

Recently, the company suffered a major shock when one of its employees was killed in a head-on car crash while rushing to a customer site during a snowstorm in Rimouski, Quebec. The employee who was killed was a well-known and much admired member of the team, and many staff thought at the time that NG's Executive Team didn't respond properly to this event. In fact, the *Globe and Mail* ran a story on workplace tragedy and its impact on morale and used Nerds Galore as a case study on how *not* to manage sudden trauma, and, while the company's customers didn't seem to notice, NG did experience a sudden jump in staff departures and some difficulty in recruiting replacements.

Also, there is a sense that staff efficiency is not what it should be; in particular, scheduling technicians for on-site technical work has been a problem. Small business customers tend to have diverse and unique technology needs, and finding specialists who can work in multiple areas such as network support and voice over

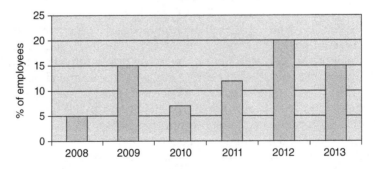

Exhibit 27.2   Nerds Galore Employee Turnover

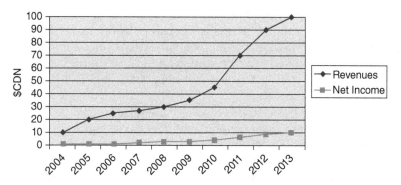

Exhibit 27.3 Nerds Galore Financial Performance

Internet Protocol (VoIP) while working with a single customer is difficult; most of the propeller-heads (as NG affectionately terms its technicians) are specialists in a few areas, and the company has found that its specialists are spending a lot of time behind the wheel traveling from site to site dealing with point solutions to individual technical problems. NG's founder and CEO, Jeeves Stobes, freely admits that the company's own internal technology has not really kept pace with the growth of the company. NG lacks a customer/account management program and relies on whiteboards and e-mail managed by the company's small core of four senior work schedulers (long-service employees who work out of a war room in Edmonton and know the company's customers and staff well) to schedule employees to customer sites. In addition, while the company has placed a premium on developing staff, this has been through informal mentoring and apprenticeships rather than formal development based on identified customer needs, and this approach has been difficult to sustain given the scrambles created by sudden staff departures.

As shown in Exhibit 27.4, CEO Stobes has set targets of 15 percent revenue growth year over year (which is close to recent rates of growth) and a net income target of 15 percent of annual revenues, which will be a stretch (recent years have yielded margins of 8 to 10 percent). Stobes has set a target of 95 percent customer satisfaction going forward.

Exhibit 27.4 Strategic Targets

	Actual	Targets				
	2013	2014	2015	2016	2017	2018
Revenues ($M) (target is 15% year-over-year growth)	100	115	132	152	175	201
Net Income ($M) (target is 15% of revenues)	10	17	20	23	26	30
Customer Satisfaction (% "very satisfied") (target is 95%)	83	95	95	95	95	95
Staff levels	1,000	1,100	1,200	1,300	1,400	1,500

Gil Bates, NG's vice president of human resources (HR), recently recruited from the competitor Propell-O-Rama, is concerned about not only the employee turnover rates but HR management in general. He has come forward with a five-point strategy for improved HR management, but has encountered stiff resistance from the rest of the Executive Team. The strategy is:

1. *Attract the best talent.* Do this by offering a positive and flexible work environment with flexible hours and a work-at-home culture.
2. *Retain good people.* Do this by offering employee recognition programs, providing multiskilling/cross-training (which will have the added benefit of greater customer satisfaction), and ensuring that compensation stays at or near the 75th percentile of competitors or comparators.
3. *Manage talent.* Put in place a formal talent management program so that high-potential employees are identified, developed, and mentored.
4. *Optimize the use of people.* Do this by purchasing and implementing a fully integrated customer management and workforce management tool, to allow greater scheduling and tracking of employee effort on customer accounts.
5. *Rely on outsourcers* to handle overflow of business requests that have highly volatile work volumes, or in areas where retaining internal capability and know-how is prohibitively expensive.

At a management discussion, it was agreed that the Executive Team would meet for a risk workshop to explore the following HR-related risks and to help the exectives evaluate the situation and decide on whether to invest in Bates's strategy:

- Inability to recruit people with needed skills
- Loss of staff with key internal knowledge
- Uncompetitive labor productivity
- Increased departures of skilled technical staff
- Loss of key business know-how

QUESTIONS

1. This is a relatively brief case study, yet the problems faced are quite complex. In your workshop, how did you handle uncertainty in the information you have been given and how does this translate into real-world workshops where not all the answers can necessarily be given at the table?
2. What were some of the risk sources that emerged repeatedly in evaluating the risks? How is this helpful?
3. How would this risk assessment aid in the decision on whether or not to proceed with the new HR strategy?

ABOUT THE CONTRIBUTOR

Rob Quail, BASc, is Director of Enterprise Risk Management at Hydro One Networks Inc. Rob has had a leadership role in enterprise risk management (ERM) at Hydro One since 2000, and developed much of Hydro One's pioneering ERM methodology. He has successfully applied ERM techniques to a diverse range of business problems and decisions, including annual business and investment planning; major transformational, infrastructure, customer, and technology projects, as well as acquisitions, partnerships, divestitures, downsizing, and outsourcing. Rob was a contributing author to *Enterprise Risk Management: Today's Leading Research and Best Practices for Tomorrow's Executives*, edited by John Fraser and Betty J. Simkins (John Wiley & Sons, 2010), and is guest lecturer for the Schulich School of Business Masters Certificate in Business Performance and Risk Management program at York University, Toronto. He is a popular speaker at risk management conferences, and performs as a musician in clubs in the Toronto area in his spare time. He is an industrial engineering graduate of the University of Toronto.

CHAPTER 28

The Reluctant General Counsel

NORMAN D. MARKS, CPA, CRMA
Fellow of the Open Compliance and Ethics Group, and Honorary Fellow of the
Institute of Risk Management

Business Software Corporation (BSC) is a global software company headquartered in the Silicon Valley of California, with annual revenues of over $1 billion. It is listed on major North American stock exchanges. The head of the Internal Audit function, Jason Garnelas, has been asked by the board to lead the establishment of an enterprise risk management (ERM) function. Top management, led by the chief executive officer (CEO), John Black, and the chief financial officer (CFO), Jim Toll, have indicated their support for this important initiative. The plan is for Jason to run the program for the first year, at which point management and the board will consider whether it is necessary and appropriate to hire a full-time risk officer.

Jason is grateful for the support of both the board and top management, because it is unusual for an entrepreneurial technology company to recognize the value of risk management and dedicate both time and resources to its implementation. In fact, at a meeting of the executive leadership, John Black explains that he holds his direct reports individually and collectively responsible for the management of risks to the business. He sees the role of the risk officer, currently Jason Garnelas on a part-time basis, as a facilitator to the leadership team. Jason will lead the development of a framework and process, and will facilitate the identification, assessment, and treatment of risk, but all decisions are a management responsibility.

Jason holds a series of one-on-one meetings with each of the CEO's and CFO's direct reports to understand, with them, the more significant risks to the organization. Most of them engage actively and with energy into the discussions, as they can see that the process will contribute to their and the company's success. Due to their travels, Jason is initially unable to meet with the executive vice president (EVP) of development (responsible for all the software developers) and the general counsel. But he is able to develop a preliminary list and assessment of the more significant areas.

The preliminary assessment is reviewed with the executive leadership team, and the CEO expresses his appreciation for the work that has been performed, but he is concerned that several of his direct reports identified the same areas of risk with significantly different evaluations of both potential impact and likelihood. He decides to assign each area of risk to individual executives who will own them and be responsible not only for monitoring the risk levels and assessing the potential impact and likelihood, but also for ensuring that actions are taken as and when necessary to bring the risk levels in line with acceptable limits established by the CEO and the board.

As everybody leaves the meeting, Jason chats briefly with the EVP of development and the general counsel, George French. The EVP quickly agrees to meet later in the week for an hour to review the risks in his assigned areas. But the general counsel asks Jason to step into his office.

The general counsel tells Jason that while he agrees that a risk management program is fine in theory, he has strong reservations. His concerns fall into two general areas.

First, the company, like every technology company, is routinely engaged in multiple lawsuits. Some lawsuits, particularly those concerned with the protection of intellectual property, involve potential settlements in the hundreds of millions of dollars—both in favor of and against BSC. These lawsuits have been identified as areas of risk that should be addressed by the new risk management program, but any formal assessment is discoverable by the opposition attorneys and could be used against BSC both in negotiations and at trial.

George understands that Jason needs his and his team's input to identify the potential impact of both favorable and adverse results to current and future lawsuits, and the likelihood of those results. But, because of the risk to the company that would be created by a formal risk assessment of the lawsuits, he has decided he cannot participate.

Second, BSC is listed on some U.S. exchanges and is subject to all U.S. Securities and Exchange Commission (SEC) filing requirements. The quarterly and annual filings have to include a discussion of the significant risks facing the organization.

The general counsel is concerned that BSC's competitors could gain an unnecessary advantage from a risk management program. His reading of the SEC rules is that the discussion in the filings has to be consistent with any formal discussion of risks by management and the board. So, if the internal discussion is too detailed and includes specific likelihood and potential effects for each risk area, that would lead to excessive and unnecessary disclosures to the company's disadvantage.

George believes that participation by the legal department will constitute formal risk discussions. Discussion of risk by the rest of the management team is a normal part of running the business, but when he and his team join the discussion it raises risk management from informal discussions to a formal process that should influence the risk disclosures in the company's SEC filings.

George tells Jason that he commends him for the initiative but cannot support it by contributing legal advice to the risk assessment and evaluation process. That should be the responsibility of the executive leadership team, with Jason's assistance. The involvement of the legal department represents, itself, too great a risk.

QUESTIONS

1. What are Jason's options? Can he accept a risk management program that does not involve the legal department?

2. Do you agree with George's arguments? Are they valid?
3. How would you proceed, if you were the risk officer?

ABOUT THE CONTRIBUTOR

Norman D. Marks, CPA, CRMA has been the chief audit executive of major global corporations for more than 20 years, and is one of the most highly regarded thought leaders in the global professions of internal auditing and risk management. He has been profiled as an innovative and successful internal auditing leader, and is a Fellow of the Open Compliance and Ethics Group and an Honorary Fellow of the Institute of Risk Management. Norman has been a motivational keynote speaker at conferences around the world and across the United States. In addition, he is a prolific blogger about internal audit, risk management, governance, and compliance.

CHAPTER 29

Transforming Risk Management at Akawini Copper

GRANT PURDY
Associate Director, Broadleaf Capital International

T his case study describes how the approach to managing risk can be transformed and enhanced in a company. The case study is based on a hypothetical mining company, Akawini Copper, that has recently been acquired by an international concern, United Minerals. Akawini has a rudimentary approach to risk management (RM) that must be improved if the new owners are to realize the level of return claimed in the business case that was used to justify the acquisition. Akawini owns a single mine and concentrate plant approximately 50 kilometers from the coast. It ships the concentrate using trucks to a nearby port for export. The company earns revenue of $774 million a year from the sale of concentrate and employs a total of 1,500 people at the mine site and port.

THE ACQUISITION AND DUE DILIGENCE

United Minerals has developed and implemented a framework for managing risk based on ISO 31000 (ISO 2009). In particular, this has enabled it to properly integrate the risk management process into its approach to making decisions on major projects and investment decisions and also into the way it develops, plans, and executes projects.

   During due diligence prior to the acquisition, the risk management team for United Minerals reviewed the current approach to risk management at Akawini and, from a cursory examination of documents, was able to determine that the approach was very limited and was unlikely to yield much real value. The team found, for example, that:

- A process for formal risk assessment was applied only to what were described as "business risks." This occurred only once a year as part of a risk review that updated the current risk register so that it could be reported to an Audit Committee.

- There was a different process applied for safety risks that actually did not consider risks as such but generated a risk rating using a matrix system only for hazards.
- No systematic process for assessing and treating risks was used in support of major decisions. In particular, project management did not include any form of explicit risk management process.
- The Akawini risk manager mostly dealt with insurance matters and asked the company's external audit provider to offer a facilitator for the annual risk review.
- The annual internal audit plan did not seem to be based on the outcomes of the risk assessment and did not focus on assuring many of the critical controls.
- The risk criteria systems used for both "business risks" and "safety risks" covered only detrimental consequences and seemed to be based on five levels of consequences and consequence types that were not associated in any meaningful way with the company's objectives.
- Both systems used the term *probability* to estimate likelihood and did not consider the frequency or return period for consequences.
- In both systems, risks were analyzed incorrectly by combining the likelihood of an event with what was described as "the plausible worse-case consequences." This produced many "extreme" risks, which were then being discounted by managers as implausible.
- Once risk registers were created on spreadsheets, they were kept on separate personal computers and were rarely considered until the next yearly review. Any risk treatment actions decided on were not followed up or closed out.
- Critical controls were not identified and were not assigned to individuals for ongoing monitoring and periodic review.
- There was no coherent process that defined and captured learnings from successes and failures.

The risk management team signaled its concerns to the acquisition team, and the need for improvement of Akawini Copper's approach to risk management to bring it into line with ISO 31000:2009. Then, the United Minerals framework was placed on the transformation plan and given a high priority.

THE TRANSFORMATION PROCESS

Once the acquisition had been completed, the risk management team followed the stepwise process in Exhibit 29.1 to transform the approach to risk management at Akawini.

The starting point was a structured analysis of Akawini's current approach to managing risks, to identify where changes had to be made and then to assign a priority to particular tasks. This was conducted in two parts:

1. A full desk-based review of Akawini's risk management documentation
2. A complementary set of interviews with Akawini management

The second activity was particularly important because it was the experience of the United Mineral risk management team that it was vital to observe and review

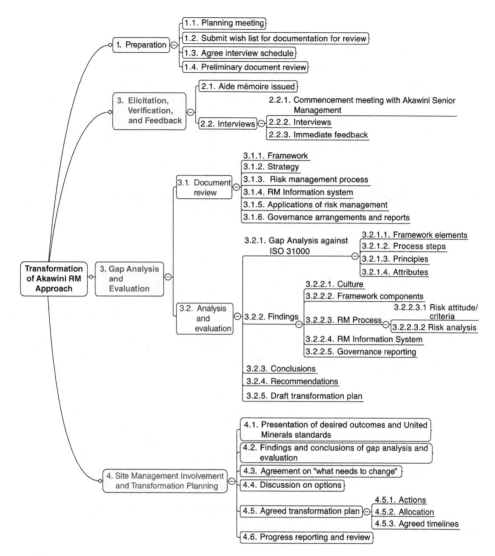

Exhibit 29.1 Risk Management Transformation Process Steps

how risk management takes place in practice. This was particularly true if there might be any discontinuity of practice across Akawini or inconsistent processes and systems. It was also important to test out Akawini management's perceptions of the current approach to risk management to see if it was currently viewed as effective and if managers perceived it as likely to satisfy their future needs.

The risk management team conducted a series of structured interviews with senior management from Akawini so that the team could draw objective conclusions on:

- The suitability of the current approach to manage risk associated with an organization of the size and complexity of Akawini, its risk profile,[1] and its risk attitude[2]

- The drivers of that attitude, based on what were recognized as the key success factors and growth objectives for the organization
- The perceived usefulness of the current risk management process and its degree of integration into key decision-making processes
- The strengths and limitations of the other risk-type specific approaches to risk management that coexisted in the company[3]—specifically, whether the tools and methods currently being used were capable of providing Akawini with a current, correct, and comprehensive understanding of its risks and informing it whether the risks were within its risk criteria[4]
- The level of understanding of senior management about aspects of the risk management culture
- An outline of the perceived risk profile of Akawini and whether this varied from that reported to the board in the past

Questions asked included:

- What is your definition of risk? How, in your view, do risk and its management relate to the company's objectives?
- What is the purpose of risk assessment? How often should risk assessment take place? What triggers it in your area?
- As a practical matter, how do you gain assurance that the critical controls that your part of the company relies on are in place, are effective, and work when required?

The risk management team members consolidated their findings and compared them with the elements of the existing United Minerals risk management framework and the requirements of ISO 31000. They particularly mapped what they found by comparing it with the principles for effective risk management in Clause 3 and the attributes in Annex A of the Standard.

GAINING SENIOR MANAGEMENT OWNERSHIP FOR TRANSFORMATION

For effective management, it was regarded as critical that senior management at Akawini appreciated and could comment on and contribute to the findings and conclusion of the review so that this would lead to ownership of the transformation plan. The risk management team therefore presented its findings and recommendations at a meeting with senior managers that covered:

- Fundamentals of risk and best practice risk management
- Overall findings and assessment of the benchmarking review
- Suggested improvements and enhancement strategies
- Draft enhancement plan

The risk management team elicited feedback and acceptance of the conditions it found and prompted a discussion on the desired situation. In this way the team helped managers identify what needed to change. The diagram of the desired

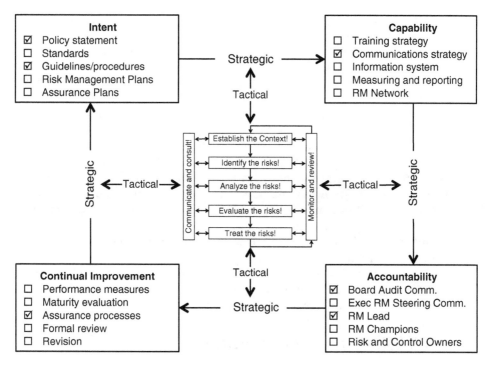

Exhibit 29.2   Desired Framework Architecture

☑ Indicates that the element is present and effective, ☐ means that it is not present or is ineffective.

framework architecture given in Figure 29.2 was used to demonstrate the strengths and weaknesses in the current approach.

To demonstrate the desired outcomes, the risk management team explained that the primary purpose of risk management in United Minerals was to act in a dynamic fashion to support decisions and that the company framework had been designed to ensure that:

- Assumptions and preconceptions were properly challenged before decisions could be made.
- Appropriate actions were then taken to reduce the uncertainty that objectives would be achieved.
- Early warnings were provided if key controls were not in place or were not fully effective, so that preemptive action could be taken.
- The organization learned in a systematic way from its successes and failures, at a fundamental level so that learnings would lead to lasting changes.

To help the organization as a whole improve its ability to manage risk, the company had adopted 10 performance requirements that it called its "standards." These were, in outline:

1. The risk management process will be integrated into all key decision making processes.

2. The risk management process will be integrated into strategic, business, and project planning processes.
3. Key controls will be identified and allocated to owners for monitoring.
4. After every major decision, event, or change or at the conclusion of all plans, the organization will learn lessons from successes and failures using root cause analysis.
5. The same, consistent methodology will be used for analyzing risks and for evaluating control effectiveness.
6. The significance of risks will be evaluated using one set of risk criteria.
7. Viable options for treating risks will always be considered, and those options will be implemented where there is a net benefit to the business.
8. Accountability for managing risk will be allocated in a manner that is fully consistent with the management of the business and with the delegations of authority system.
9. Only one database system will be used to hold and manage all forms of risk management information.
10. Sites will plan how they will implement these standards and will report on the progress with this implementation and the effectiveness of risk management as part of the company's governance processes.

THE TRANSFORMATION PLAN

The Akawini management team was then encouraged to discuss and compare options and to suggest major actions for the enhancement plan. The actions were allocated to members of the management team, and completion dates were agreed. These agreements were recorded and became the risk management plan that described the transformation process for managing risk at the sites. The management team was also asked to commit on a review and reporting process for the transformation plan.

QUESTIONS

1. If you were conducting interviews of the Akawini management team so that you could draw objective conclusions for the review described in the chapter, what questions would you ask?
2. What would you expect to see in the first year risk management transformation plan? What would be the typical tasks?
3. You have been asked to advise the Akawini management team on how they should promote and monitor the transformation of risk management in their business. What performance measures would you recommend they use so that they can monitor progress and performance?

NOTES

1. A risk profile is a description of a set of risks. In this case, it is that which represents the major risks the company faces.
2. The term *risk attitude* (defined as the organization's approach to assess and eventually pursue, retain, take, or turn away from risk) is used in ISO 31000 rather than the term *risk*

appetite for two reasons—it is a wider term (risk appetite is defined in ISO Guide 73 as the amount and type of risk that an organization is willing to pursue or retain) and also translates better into some other languages, a necessary consideration in the drafting of ISO 31000.

3. These are the outcome tests for effective risk management given in Annex A of ISO 31000.

4. Risk criteria provide both the means to determine and express the magnitude of risk, and to judge its significance against predetermined levels of concern. They comprise internal procedural rules selected by the organization for analyzing and then evaluating the significance of risk, and are also used when selecting between potential risk treatments.

REFERENCE

ISO. 2009. International Standard ISO 31000:2009, "Risk Management—Principles and Guidelines." Geneva, Switzerland: International Organization for Standardization.

ABOUT THE CONTRIBUTOR

Grant Purdy is Associate Director, Broadleaf Capital International. He has specialized in the practical application of risk management for more than 38 years, working across a wide range of industries and in more than 25 countries. He works with many types of organizations, helping them develop and enhance ways to manage risk in support of the decisions they make. This involves mentoring, training, and giving advice, predominantly to senior managers and boards. Grant is an accomplished trainer and speaker and has had more than 100 papers, books, and articles published. He has been a member of the Standards Australia and Standards New Zealand Joint Technical Committee on Risk Management for more than 12 years and was its chair for seven. He is coauthor of the 2004 version of AS/NZS 4360 and also of AS/NZS 5050, a standard for managing disruption-related risk, and has also written many other risk management handbooks and guides. He was the nominated expert for Australia on the working group that prepared ISO 31000 and Guide 73 and subsequently head of delegation for Australia on ISO PC 262, Risk Management.

CHAPTER 30

Alleged Corruption at Chessfield

Corporate Governance and the Risk Oversight Role of the Board of Directors

RICHARD LEBLANC
Associate Professor of Law, Governance, and Ethics at York University

T he police and the regulator contacted the author early in the author's governance review process. When the author attended his first meeting with the chairman of the board of directors for Chessfield Inc. and the regulator, the regulator mentioned the word *corruption* explicitly. Now the New York Police Department was also investigating the conduct of some of Chessfield's directors, by interviewing them and collecting evidence. The author's role was to conduct a thorough governance review, with a specific focus on risk management, and report his findings and recommendations to the regulator and board of directors. Chessfield is a fictional company; however, this case is based in part on actual situations that have been modified and disguised.

CHESSFIELD INC. AND ITS BOARD OF DIRECTORS

Chessfield is a well-known American company in the sports and entertainment industry. It is headquartered in New York, and is led and governed by an outspoken and successful CEO and a blue-chip board of directors. Several directors are household names and have been on the board for many years, knowing each other in social and professional circles. One director had been on the board for 28 years, the second-longest-serving director had been on the board for 24 years, and so on. The shortest-serving director's tenure was seven years. It was an all-male board, known fondly among a few directors as "the good ol' boys."

Governance and decision making were informal, and almost always by consensus. By externally viewing Chessfield, it would be difficult to glean that it had any governance shortcomings whatsoever. It had a majority of directors who were current or former CEOs, a separate chair, and other independent directors from prestigious New York professional services firms. It had three committees that were all composed of independent directors. The size of the board was

10 members. Chessfield appeared to comply at least in letter with all applicable governance regulations in place at the time.

WHISTLE-BLOWER COMPLAINT

A credible and anonymous whistle-blowing complaint had recently reached the regulator, from a possible former director or officer.

Chessfield was not a publicly traded company, but was in an industry that was highly regulated, given the potential for misuse of information and cash receipts, as well as the potential for harm (of patrons) and for organized crime.

The regulator had concerns about the compensation awarded to the CEO being approximately four times that of comparable industry peers, and potentially creating an incentive for undue risk taking; the apparent lack of internal controls over material risks, including operational risks; and possible impropriety by certain directors in using their positions for self-gain.

MESSAGE FROM THE CEO REQUESTING TO MEET THE AUTHOR

Chessfield's CEO e-mailed the author when the author was in Dallas, Texas, at a conference, asking for a meeting within 24 hours if possible. At that meeting in New York, with the CEO and Chessfield's legal counsel, the author was told that the company had just been put under regulatory investigation.

The author was asked whether he could assist by reviewing Chessfield's overall governance, and, in particular, risk management and compliance practices. The board chair had recommended the author to the regulator because the author had assessed a previous board on which the chair served at the time, and the author was independent.

The author agreed to conduct the governance review of Chessfield for a mutually agreed fee under two conditions. He made it clear to the board chair, CEO, and general counsel that:

1. He would be entitled to any document or access to any personnel he requested.
2. He must have a direct reporting line to the regulator, including separate meetings without the presence of any director or officer.

All parties agreed, including the regulator. The author was to have separate meetings with both the regulator and the New York Police Department official conducting the investigation.

GOVERNANCE DOCUMENTS, INTERVIEWS, AND ON-SITE OBSERVATION REQUESTED BY THE AUTHOR

As a starting point, the author asked for the following: any and all governance documents, including recent board minutes and meeting materials, bylaws, relevant correspondence, board and committee charters, risk registers, compensation plans, and financial statements (in no particular order).

The author, as part of his methodology and data collection, would also interview each director, each member of senior management, the internal audit function, and possibly other assurance staff. The author would also tour Chessfield's facilities and have access to the cash room[1] so he could see operations firsthand. All requests were acceded to, and the author began his work. This work took about 30 days on a part-time basis, and a report was generated to the board and endorsed by the regulator.

Document Review

It soon became apparent that governance documentation at Chessfield was minimal. The board did not have guidelines; committees did not have charters; position descriptions for board leadership roles, directors, and the CEO did not exist; and meeting agendas and minutes were very sparse, with the average meeting agenda being one page with key headings only. There was no documented, board-approved strategic plan or risk appetite framework. Indeed, many material risks were not reported to the board at all.

Documentation for key board decisions, including evidence of review, reporting, assurance, due diligence, and deliberation, appeared to be either lacking meaningful content or nonexistent.

Interview Data

Many noncompensation committee directors neither knew nor approved what or how the CEO and the former CEO (who was also on the board as the longest-serving director) were paid. The nonexecutive board chair had a consulting stream paid to him by Chessfield, which certain other directors did not know about. The internal auditor was junior, inexperienced, and unqualified; had operational and revenue generation responsibilities; and had little exposure to, or oversight by, the audit committee. Audit committee members did not possess adequate financial literacy or relevant qualifications. The compensation committee chair rarely attended meetings in person for health reasons, and did not possess compensation expertise. His tenure as committee chair exceeded 11 years. He was a former service provider (now retired) of a large New York law firm.

CEO COMPENSATION ISSUE

There was little correspondence evidencing the basis on which total compensation was awarded to the CEO. There was a spreadsheet with a password that was provided to the author by the CEO's assistant. When the author interviewed the chair of the compensation committee about the lack of either supporting documentation or independent assurance by a compensation consultant, the compensation committee chair told the author that the compensation committee was composed of experienced businessmen who were of the view that the CEO's compensation was appropriate given the CEO's performance.

The author was not provided with any CEO goals and objectives, key performance indicators, or trigger and target requirements for short-term or long-term incentives to be awarded or to vest. The foregoing items were asked for but, to the author's knowledge, did not exist. The compensation committee chair had friendships and social relationships with a number of directors, including the CEO. The basis for the quantum of compensation awarded to the CEO (1) relative to peers or (2) relative to company performance was not explicit.

The board chair and compensation committee chair said to the author that the regulator did not have the business judgment to opine on the quantum of CEO compensation. The author responded by saying that (1) the quantum of total compensation was very high compared to industry peers of a similar size and complexity, but, more importantly and particularly given this fact, (2) there should be a visible, diligent process to employ such business judgment of directors and to explicitly link pay to performance, which appeared to be what was lacking in any event.

RISK MANAGEMENT

There were very few explicit risk management protocols or systems to identify and mitigate material risks, including operational risk in particular. In the cash room, the controls were all manual (i.e., paper, with greater capability for management override or weaker controls, it would appear), as information technology was not used. Risk identification and assessment were not documented explicitly. There was no risk function reporting directly to the board or to a committee. Indeed, there was no risk function.

There was little evidence that internal controls over operational and compliance risks were designed and/or effective, regularly tested by the internal audit function, and reported to the board or a committee. A number of directors appeared blindingly ignorant of their obligation to oversee risk management.

SELF-DEALING ISSUE

There was not a conflict of interest policy that applied to directors. Board guidelines did not exist to address confidentiality, the use of corporate opportunity, the treatment of inside information, related-party transactions, or identifying and adequately addressing perceived conflicts of interest. The author was unable to ascertain self-dealing, but robust policies and controls did not exist to deter, detect, monitor, or enforce anticorruption, in any event.

Board Composition

As mentioned previously, several directors were long-serving. Independent directors were selected originally (and to the author's observation, still) on the basis of personal knowledge and prior working relationships. All directors, however, were believed to comply with formal independence standards in place. There was little if any documentation of such independence, of the expertise directors possessed, or of collective expertise that the board needed.

Preparation of the Author's Report and Communication with the Regulator

Given the foregoing, the author prepared 43 recommendations for the review of the regulator and the board of directors.

The regulator endorsed the 43 recommendations that the author provided, with minor modifications and with two additional recommendations to establish a compliance committee of the board and to have a board-approved strategic plan, which the regulator suggested and which the author incorporated into his report. There were 45 recommendations in the author's final report, which he was now to present to the board of directors of Chessfield. The report was 14 pages long.

CHESSFIELD BOARD MEETING TO DISCUSS THE AUTHOR'S RECOMMENDATIONS

The author was invited to present his report and 45 recommendations to the full board of directors of Chessfield Inc. in New York City at 10 A.M. on a Friday morning in December. This was a special board meeting, and the author's report was the only item on the agenda.

The author had 15 minutes to present a summary of his recommendations. (*Note:* The board had a full week prior to the board meeting to read the author's report.) There was to be a 45-minute period of dialogue and questions and answers, after which the author would leave the room and the board would discuss the report in closed session.

The author was told by the general counsel that the regulator had requested to the chair of the board that the board approve a resolution adopting the author's report in whole, supported by a commitment to implement the recommendations within the time frame prescribed in the report. The chairman of the board was to telephone the regulator shortly after the meeting to report whether this requested approval had occurred. (The regulator had told the chair early in the process that Chessfield was close to having its license to operate revoked because of the governance and risk shortcomings.)

When the author was invited into the boardroom, he saw that it was very formal. There were portraits of past directors on the walls, large mahogany chairs, and dark wood. The author did not observe any use of technology, such as laptops or tablet computers, which is typical in most boardrooms now.

At the board meeting, the author presented 45 recommendations based on his review and discussions with the regulator. A time frame for each recommendation was set out (up to eight months, eight to 12 months, and 12 to 18 months) within the report, along with independent validation and reporting back to the regulator, to ensure execution of the recommendations.

TWO CONTENTIOUS RECOMMENDATIONS

Directors accepted all of the recommendations initially except for two, which were: (1) that the three longest-serving directors (28, 24, and 23 years, respectively) resign, and (2) that a woman be selected for directorship and serve on the compensation committee in particular.

As far as the three longest-serving directors resigning was concerned, one director (28-year tenure) had, during the data collection phase, invited the author to his estate in Boston prior to the final report to tell the author how important the board was to him, and how he should be allowed to continue to serve so long as he is able. The author indicated politely that regulators are moving toward term limits of nine or 10 years to guard against entrenchment and compromising of independence over time. The author said that one of his recommendations was not only that he and two other directors should resign, but also that term limits be in place at 15 years for all incumbent directors and nine years for all new directors.

Recommending a Woman to Serve on the Board

The second issue was more contentious and surfaced at the board meeting itself. It was the author's recommendation that a woman be added to the board.

One director remarked, "Dr. Leblanc, you want us to put a *lady* on the board?" (Emphasis in original remark.) Another director remarked, "Perhaps we can have a lady in a wheelchair who is a lesbian." Many of the directors laughed at this comment.

The author indicated that evidence existed that CEO turnover is more sensitive to stock return performance in firms with a greater proportion of women; that women are more likely to join committees that perform monitoring-performing tasks; and that male directors have fewer attendance problems, the greater the number of women on the board.[2] The author also indicated that the regulator had agreed to all of his recommendations, including this one, and that there was a need for the skill set of compensation and information technology literacy on the board, given prior concerns and the transformation of the industry.

CONCLUSION

This case concluded one month after the author's presentation to the board, when the regulator asked the author to black-line, with suggested improvements, forthcoming regulations to apply to all companies under the regulator's purview, adopting many of the recommendations the author had provided for Chessfield.

QUESTIONS

1. What is your assessment of the situation at Chessfield?
2. What recommendations would you provide to the regulator?
3. What is your opinion of the governance regulation of Chessfield? In what ways should governance regulation improve, given the above?
4. What are the learnings and broader implications of this case?

NOTES

1. Part of this company's business operation involved receiving cash directly from consumers, which was assembled, tallied, and reconciled in what is known in the industry as the "cash room."
2. R. B. Adams and D. Ferreira, "Women in the Boardroom and Their Impact on Governance and Performance," *Journal of Financial Economics* 94 (2009): 291–309.

REFERENCES

Adams, R. B., and D. Ferreira. 2009. "Women in the Boardroom and Their Impact on Governance and Performance." *Journal of Financial Economics* 94, 291–309.

Basel Committee on Banking Supervision. 2010. "Principles for Enhancing Corporate Governance." *Bank for International Settlements Communications*, October.

Canadian Securities Administrators. 2008. "Request for Comment: Proposed Repeal and Replacement of NP 58-201 Corporate Governance Guidelines, NI 58-101 Disclosure of Corporate Governance Practices, and NI 52-110 Audit Committees and Companion Policy 52-110CP Audit Committees, 31 OSCB 12158."

Canadian Securities Administrators. 2010. "Staff Notice 58-306 2010 Corporate Governance Disclosure Compliance Review," December.

Caplan, G. R., and A. A. Markus. 2009. "Independent Boards, but Ineffective Directors." *Corporate Board*, March/April, 1–4.

Carter, D. A., F. D'Souza, B. J. Simkins, and W. G. Simpson. 2010. "The Diversity of Corporate Board Committees and Financial Performance." *Corporate Governance: An International Review* 18:5 (September), 396–414.

Carter, D. A., B. J. Simkins, and W. G. Simpson. 2003. "Corporate Governance, Board Diversity, and Firm Value." *Financial Review* 38, 33–53.

Elson, C. F., and C. K. Ferrere. 2012. "Executive Superstars, Peer Groups and Over-Compensation—Cause, Effect and Solution," August 7. Available on SSRN website at http://irrcinstitute.org/pdf/Executive-Superstars-Peer-Benchmarking-Study.pdf.

Financial Reporting Council. 2011. "Guidance on Board Effectiveness." *Financial Reporting Council Limited*, March.

Financial Reporting Council. 2012. "The UK Corporate Governance Code," September. Available online at www.frc.org.uk/Our-Work/Publications/Corporate-Governance/UK-Corporate-Governance-Code-September-2012.pdf.

Fraser, J., and B. J. Simkins, eds. 2010. *Enterprise Risk Management: Today's Leading Research and Best Practices for Tomorrow's Executives*. Hoboken, NJ: John Wiley & Sons.

Group of 30. 2012. "Toward Effective Governance of Financial Institutions." Washington, DC, 1–96.

House Committee on Financial Services. 2010. "Dodd-Frank Wall Street Reform and Consumer Protection Act." H.R. 4173, June 25.

Institute of Chartered Secretaries and Administrators. 2009. "Boardroom Behaviours—A Report Prepared for Sir David Walker by the Institute of Chartered Secretaries and Administrators." *Report*, June.

Institute of Corporate Directors. 2006. "ICD Key Competencies for Director Effectiveness." Competency list issued, Toronto.

Leblanc, Richard. 2011. "A Fact-Based Approach to Boardroom Diversity." *Director Journal, Institute of Corporate Directors* 154, March: 6–8.

Leblanc, Richard. 2012. "Discussion Notes for: OSC Dialogue." Toronto, October 30.

Leblanc, Richard. 2013. "Forty Proposals to Strengthen the Public Company Board of Directors' Role in Value Creation, Management Accountability to the Board, and Board Accountability to Shareholders." *International Journal of Disclosure and Governance* 10:4, 1–16.

Leblanc, Richard. 2013. "Review of the Regulatory Guideline for [a Regulator], Black-Lined Report," March 19.

Leblanc, Richard, 2013. "Review of the Regulatory Standard for [a Regulator], Black-Lined Report," March 6.

Leblanc, Richard, et al. 2012. "General Commentary on European Union Corporate Governance Proposals." *International Journal of Disclosure and Governance* 9:1, 1–35.

Leblanc, Richard, and James Gillies. *Inside the Boardroom: How Boards Really Work and the Coming Revolution in Corporate Governance*. Toronto: John Wiley & Sons, 2005.

Leblanc, Richard, and Katharina Pick. 2011. "Separation of Chair and CEO Roles: Importance of Industry Knowledge, Leadership Skills & Attention to Board Process." *Director Notes: Conference Board.* New York, August.

Lorsch, Jay, ed. 2012. *The Future of Corporate Boards.* Boston: Harvard Business Review Press.

Monks, R. A. G., and N. Minow. 2011. *Corporate Governance.* 5th ed. Chichester, UK: John Wiley & Sons.

National Association of Corporate Directors. 2010. "Template for Disclosure of Director Skills and Attributes," August. Resources@nacdonline.org.

National Commission on the Causes of the Financial and Economic Crisis in the United States. 2011. "The Financial Crisis Inquiry Report." U.S. Government Printing Office. Washington, DC, January.

Neill, D., and V. Dulewicz. 2010. "Inside the 'Black Box': The Performance of Boards of Directors of Unlisted Companies." *Corporate Governance: An International Review* 10:3, 293–306.

Trautman, Lawrence J. 2012. "The Matrix: The Board's Responsibility for Director Selection and Recruitment." *Florida State University Business Review* 11, 1–66. Available at http://papers.ssrn.com/sol3/papers.cfm?abstract_id=1998489.

U.S. Senate Permanent Subcommittee on Investigations. 2011. "Wall Street and the Financial Crisis: Anatomy of a Financial Collapse." U.S. Government Printing Office. Washington, DC, April 13.

Useem, M. 2006. "How Well-Run Boards Make Decisions." *Harvard Business Review* 84:11, 130–138.

ABOUT THE CONTRIBUTOR

Richard Leblanc is a governance lawyer, certified management consultant, and Associate Professor of Law, Governance & Ethics at York University. He holds a PhD focusing on board of director effectiveness. He has published in leading academic and practitioner journals, has advised regulators on corporate governance guidelines, and, as part of his external professional activities, has served as an external board evaluator and governance adviser for Australian Securities Exchange (ASX), London Stock Exchange (LSE), New York Stock Exchange (NYSE), NASDAQ, New Zealand Stock Exchange (NZX), and Toronto Stock Exchange (TSX) listed companies, as well as in an expert witness capacity in litigation concerning corporate governance reforms.

CHAPTER 31

Operational Risk Management Case Study

Bon Boulangerie

DIANA DEL BEL BELLUZ
President, Risk Wise Inc.

B on Boulangerie is a bakery business located in Oakville, Ontario. When the owner, Ray Pane, purchased the business three years ago, it consisted of a single site with baking facilities and a retail store and café. Based on market research with the bakery's retail and café clientele, Ray began to change and expand the product offerings to increase the volume of sales and margins. He also began a new line of business, wholesaling to local restaurants and high-end grocery stores within a 20-kilometer radius of the bakery.

Based on the success over the past three years (see Exhibit 31.1), Ray has made a strategic decision to expand his wholesale business, with the goal of tripling profits over the next three years (see Exhibit 31.2). He expects to accomplish this by: (1) covering a larger territory (i.e., expanding to a 120 km radius) for wholesaling to local restaurants and independent grocery stores across the entire Greater Toronto Area, and (2) introducing a new business line, white label products that he can supply to major supermarket chains.

To realize this strategy, Ray has leased and outfitted a separate baking facility to be primarily dedicated to supplying the wholesale business. Ray also hired a full-time vice president of sales and marketing (see Exhibit 31.3 for a summary of the Bon Boulangerie management team) to take over from him on the wholesale side. Finally, he purchased a second previously owned delivery truck and hired a full-time distribution manager.

Growth in the first three years is attributable to enhancement of product offerings and continual drive to find efficiencies in operations. In year 4, the new baking facility will open. It is expected that it will take several years to add new wholesale customers and wholesale products. Therefore, there will be unutilized capacity in the new facility. It is anticipated that expanding the wholesale business will, at least initially, require an increased level of product development, marketing, sales, and distribution.

Exhibit 31.1 Financials for Past Three Years

(all figures in $000's)	(Actuals)		
	Year 3	Year 2	Year 1
Income			
Café	300	273	246
Retail Bakery	718	624	562
Wholesale—Restaurants	410	234	0
Wholesale—Other Retailers	359	312	0
Total Revenue	**1,786**	**1,443**	**807**
Operating Expenses			
Cost of Inventories Sold	1,349	1,090	610
Marketing, General, and Administrative	361	291	163
Total Expenses	**1,710**	**1,381**	**773**
Net Income	**76**	**62**	**35**

Exhibit 31.2 Projections for Next Three Years

(all figures in $000's)	(Projections)		
	Year 6	Year 5	Year 4
Income			
Café	348	331	315
Retail Bakery	831	791	753
Wholesale—Restaurants	960	768	614
Wholesale—Other Retailers	4,306	2,153	1,076
Total Revenue	**6,444**	**4,043**	**2,759**
Operating Expenses			
Cost of Inventories Sold	4,926	3,105	2,175
Marketing, General, and Administrative	1,301	816	557
Total Expenses	**6,227**	**3,921**	**2,732**
Net Income	**217**	**121**	**27**

Exhibit 31.3 The Bon Boulangerie Team

- **Ray Pane**, President and CEO. After a successful legal career, Ray decided to pursue his dream of being an entrepreneur. He has a passion for fine food and is committed to providing his customers with high-quality, wholesome, and artisanal products.
- **Janice Sweet**, Manager, Accounting. Janice is a Chartered Professional Accountant who came to Bon Boulangerie with five years' experience in several finance roles at a furniture retailer. She joined Bon Boulangerie halfway through its third year of business. She is the company's

first in-house accountant. Prior to her joining, the accounting was done by an external bookkeeper on a contract basis. Janice has begun to introduce more systematic accounting processes. She is also working with Ray to develop more forward-looking reporting, including projections and forecasts of revenues and costs.

- **Joe Silkwood**, Vice President, Sales and Marketing. Joe was hired near the end of year 3 when Ray decided to expand the wholesale business. Joe is a classic salesman; he's outgoing and optimistic. He has nearly 10 years' experience in the grocery business.

- **Rick Kneader**, Manager, Baking Operations. Ray hired Rick as the head baker for the retail bakery at the beginning of year 1. Rick is a true artisan who successfully developed the new products that have been responsible for the increases in sales in the café and retail bakery in its first three years of business. He also runs a tight ship and has managed costs well, despite shifting to products with higher-cost ingredients. With the opening of the new commercial baking facility in year 4, Ray has received a promotion to Manager of Baking Operations for both the retail and the commercial facilities. He will now spend less time working with his hands and more time overseeing junior bakers while managing the expenses at the commercial baking facility.

- **Mohammed Sharif**, Manager, Distribution. Mohammed has been hired by Ray to manage distribution to the expanding roster of wholesale customers—both restaurants and other retailers. He has worked in the trucking field for 15 years. He will expand and supervise the existing team of drivers who were hired in year 2 to distribute product to wholesale customers. Ray has also made it clear that he expects Mohammed to find efficiencies and reduce shipping costs.

- **Jelena Zarinovic**, Manager, Retail Operations. Jelena has been with the company since it started. In fact, she worked for the previous owners. She is the only full-time retail sales employee. She is friendly and adored by customers and the many part-time sales associates. However, she is less interested in paperwork and is finding it challenging to learn the new accounting procedures that Janice is implementing.

QUESTIONS

Answer the following questions to identify the key operational risks that Ray and his team need to address. Note, additional information on the principles and steps of operational risk management (including a worked example) are available in Chapter 16, "Operational Risk Management," of the book *Enterprise Risk Management: Today's Leading Research and Best Practices for Tomorrow's Executives* (John Wiley & Sons, 2010).

1. How does Ray's strategic objective translate to the operational level, that is, what is his key operational objective(s) for the wholesale business line?
2. What performance drivers, that is, the internal capabilities (e.g., people, processes, and systems), and external factors need to be present to achieve operational success?

3. What are the risk factors that drive the uncertainty around achieving operational objectives?
4. Which risk drivers are most likely to impact operational objectives?
5. How large of an impact might those key risk factors have? Hint: Use scenario analysis to explore the full range of potential outcomes.
6. Based on your analysis, what are the "significant few" factors on which Ray should focus his attention to manage the operational risks associated with the new facility?
7. What underlying assumptions underpin your analysis and conclusions?

ABOUT THE CONTRIBUTOR

Diana Del Bel Belluz is the President and Founder of Risk Wise Inc., a risk management consulting firm that provides advice and support to executive leadership teams and boards who want to achieve more effective, proactive, and strategic management and oversight of risk. Her forte is helping leaders to solve the people issues associated with bringing enterprise risk management (ERM) to life in their organizations. Diana advances the practice of ERM through her thought leadership as an educator, conference organizer, speaker, and author of ERM resources, including numerous articles, book chapters, and the *Risk Management Made Simple* Advisory, a quarterly publication of ERM implementation tips and resources available at www.riskwise.ca. She also wrote Chapter 16, "Operational Risk Management," of the book *Enterprise Risk Management: Today's Leading Research and Best Practices for Tomorrow's Executives*, edited by John Fraser and Betty J. Simkins (John Wiley & Sons, 2010). She holds bachelor's and master's degrees in systems design engineering from the University of Waterloo and is a professional engineer.

PART VI

Other Case Studies

CHAPTER 32

Constructive Dialogue and ERM

Lessons from the Financial Crisis

THOMAS H. STANTON
Fellow, Center for Advanced Governmental Studies at Johns Hopkins University

T he financial crisis caused immense harm. Millions of people lost their homes to foreclosure and many more lost employment and, as the stock market dropped, their retirement and investment savings. The financial and economic carnage caused by the crisis has led to increased emphasis on enterprise risk management (ERM), in the sense of identifying and addressing risks that can prevent accomplishment of a company's mission or objectives.

ERM played little role in risk management of financial institutions before and during the financial crisis. In a 2005 report on the state of ERM, Anette Mikes found that "enterprise risk management remains a rather elusive and under-specified concept."[1] Many large, complex financial firms, such as Citigroup and American International Group (AIG), lacked even an enterprise-wide view of risks, which is a precondition but different from ERM. Parts of those firms continued to build their exposures to subprime mortgages and other risky financial products while other parts tried to shed those risks before the crisis broke.

To understand risk management at large, complex financial firms before the crisis, one must look for critical elements of ERM, but generally not for ERM itself. This chapter focuses on one critical element, *constructive dialogue*, which includes (1) processes for eliciting risk-related information that flows to the top of the organization where it can be addressed in decision making, and (2) full, candid, and respectful discussions of risk/reward trade-offs. The financial crisis demonstrated how constructive dialogue was essential to promote sound decision making at a time when the expanding housing and credit bubbles had lulled many financial firms into complacency.

As a staff member of the U.S. Financial Crisis Inquiry Commission (FCIC), I had the opportunity to interview CEOs, risk officers, traders, bankers, regulators, and policy makers to try to understand the difference between financial firms that successfully navigated the crisis and those that did not. FCIC interviews took place in 2010 while people, still in shock at the destruction caused by failures of financial firms and their regulators, were generally eager to tell their sides of the story. The

FCIC also had access to thousands of internal documents that helped to inform our questions and establish patterns of prudent or imprudent decision making at various firms and regulators.[2]

When the FCIC published its final report,[3] I built on its work and wrote a book, *Why Some Firms Thrive While Others Fail: Governance and Management Lessons from the Crisis* (Oxford University Press, 2012). The book examines a dozen large financial firms, four that navigated the crisis successfully and eight that failed in the sense that they went out of business, were acquired on disadvantageous terms, or required government aid to stay afloat. The book asks a simple question: What were key differences in governance and management (including risk management) that distinguished the two groups of firms?

CONSTRUCTIVE DIALOGUE: THE ESSENTIAL DIFFERENCE BETWEEN FIRMS THAT NAVIGATED THE CRISIS AND THOSE THAT FAILED

One single factor distinguished the two groups: Firms that successfully navigated the crisis built a process of constructive dialogue into their decision making. When making major decisions, successful companies brought together proponents in the firm who favored a revenue-generating activity and those such as risk officers who worried about its possible disadvantages and downsides. The CEO or another senior manager encouraged a respectful exchange of views between these perspectives to gain a better understanding of the risk/reward trade-offs of the activity. These were the firms that successfully avoided exposure to unacceptable volumes of subprime mortgages and other risky products before the crisis or that shed or mitigated their exposures in a timely manner before taking major losses.

Successful firms had cultures that welcomed input from those concerned about risk. In the felicitous phrase of organizational development specialist, Jack Rosenblum, they recognized that "feedback is a gift." By encouraging constructive dialogue between those seeking increased profits and those concerned about risks, company leaders elicited information and obtained a more robust understanding of the contours of decisions than they otherwise would have had. Perhaps my favorite example comes from an official of a successful firm who told me, "The CEO often asks my opinion on major issues," and then added, "but he asks 200 other people their opinions, too." When he made a decision, that CEO had a strong sense of the risks and rewards that it entailed.

When there was still time before the financial crisis finally broke in 2008, information flow and constructive dialogue were essential to allow a firm to avoid, shed, or hedge its exposure to toxic assets (i.e., those that looked to be safe but in fact contained major embedded risk). Classic toxic assets were AAA-rated private-label mortgage securities that appeared to give financial firms both safety and higher yield than the usual safe assets. While toxic assets were risky investments for any firm, they proved fatal for highly leveraged firms that lacked the balance sheet strength to absorb the losses.[4]

SUCCESSFUL FIRMS: JPMORGAN CHASE, GOLDMAN SACHS, WELLS FARGO, AND TD BANK

While ERM was not developed to the point that it is today, the elements of information flow and constructive dialogue were the essential distinguishing features between successful firms and those that failed. My book identifies four firms that successfully navigated the crisis: JPMorgan Chase, Goldman Sachs, Wells Fargo, and Toronto Dominion Bank (TD Bank). Each distinguished itself in operational competence and intelligent discipline, but with different approaches. JPMorgan Chase's story is of preparing the company to be strong enough to take advantage of long-term opportunities. Goldman's is of firmwide systems and capacity to react quickly to changes in the environment. Wells Fargo is a company with a strong culture of customer focus and restraint. And TD Bank provides the simple lesson: If you don't understand it, don't invest in it.

Constructive dialogue was built into the cultures of these firms. The first important element was an emphasis on ensuring that information flowed to parts of the organization that needed it. As one JPMorgan Chase executive put it, "Jamie [Dimon] and I like to get the bad news out to where everybody can see it ... to get the dead cat on the table."[5] Goldman Sachs maintained a "culture of over-communication; multiple formal and informal forums for risk discussions coupled with a constant flow of risk reports."[6] Dan Sparks, formerly head of the Goldman mortgage desk, told FCIC staff that he reported bad news to the firm's top management because "Part of my job was to be sure people I reported to knew what they needed to know."[7] The Wells Fargo Vision and Values Statement emphasizes risk awareness as a part of the company's culture:

> We want compliance and risk management to be part of our culture, an extension of our code of ethics. Everyone shapes the risk culture of our company. We encourage all team members to identify and bring risk forward. We should thank them for doing so, not penalize them. Ben Franklin was right: An ounce of prevention is worth a pound of cure.[8]

TD Bank's CEO, Edmund Clark, wanted to hear negative news fast:

> I'm constantly saying to people: "Bring forward the bad news; the good news will surface soon enough. What I want to hear about is what's going wrong. Let's deal with it." ... It's about no surprises. Any number of problems we've had to deal with could have been solved if the person had only let us know early on. ... In fact [employees] joke that I'm only happy when the world's falling apart and that I'm a total pain when everything is going well.[9]

The second important part of effective constructive dialogue is that managers need to have a forum where they can conduct open and respectful but possibly intense debates about what the information actually means. This part of constructive dialogue has been a feature of well-run banks for a long time. Banks use a credit committee to deliberate about whether to make particular loans. Loan officers bring information about a proposed large loan to the committee. There, under the watchful eye of a senior manager, the loan officer presents the case to make the loan, followed by the underwriting department's presentation about risks that the loan involves. If the dialogue goes well, the result might be a synthesis between the two views. Instead of simply making a yes-or-no decision, the credit committee might decide to ask for more protection, such as an added guarantee or a shorter term, or more collateral, as a way to allow the transaction to go forward. The final result often can be a higher-quality decision than either the loan officer or the underwriter would make by themselves.

JPMorgan Chase

At JPMorgan Chase, constructive dialogue at the top management level helped protect the company from taking major losses in the financial crisis. The 15-member operating committee is a diverse group "of longtime loyalists, J.P. Morgan veterans, and outside hires." They meet monthly for intense debate about developments in the company and in the markets it serves.

> The group is generally loud and unsubtle ..., the atmosphere is variously described by the participants as "Italian family dinners" or "the Roman forum—all that's missing is the togas." Dimon will throw out a comment like "Who had that dumb idea?" and be greeted with a chorus of "That was your dumb idea, Jamie!" "At my first meeting, I was shocked," says Bill Daley, 60, the head of corporate responsibility and a former Secretary of Commerce. "People were challenging Jamie, debating him, telling him he was wrong. It was like nothing I'd seen in a Bill Clinton cabinet meeting, or anything I'd ever seen in business."[10]

A similar atmosphere prevailed at monthly meetings of top management of each of JPMorgan Chase's major operating units:

> To make it on Dimon's team you must be able to withstand the boss's withering interrogations and defend your positions just as vigorously. And you have to live with a free-form management style in which Dimon often ignores the formal chain of command and calls managers up and down the line to gather information.[11]

As one participant told *Fortune* in 2008, Dimon was tough but open to feedback. "He understands the details completely, he loves to debate and disagree, yet he'll let you do it ... [a]s long as you know what's in Appendix 3 of your report as well as he does."

In October 2006 at one of the monthly reviews, the part of JPMorgan Chase's retail operations that serviced mortgages reported a significant increase in delinquencies by subprime mortgage borrowers. Data confirmed that the trend was widespread in the subprime market and that competitors' subprime holdings were performing even worse. Other parts of the company also reported indicators that mortgage securities were increasingly troubled. Putting all of this together, Dimon issued an order to all parts of the company to shed its exposure to subprime mortgages. JPMorgan Chase took losses that were modest compared to its major competitors.

As Northwestern University Professor Russell Walker concludes:

In the case of JPMorgan, it was the retail banking division that shared data with the investment bank on the escalations in mortgage delinquencies. This sharing of data across business lines allowed Mr. Dimon and his corporate team to change strategy on the investment side. For many organizations, sharing information that challenges accepted norms or questions conventional wisdom is not welcomed. Other banks could have done the same as JPMorgan, but the practice of communicating risks and data across business lines was absent. The lesson, of course, is that an enterprise must be willing to communicate about risk, especially when things are going well and the risk has yet to be realized.[12]

Goldman Sachs

Goldman Sachs has built constructive dialogue into the firm's daily processes. The firm uses mark-to-market accounting to assess the value of each trader's positions. The firm maintains a parallel structure so that a controller supervises each trader's position and marks it to market each evening. This information helps manage trading positions through devices such as internal pricing to ensure that assets do not remain on the balance sheet for too long. The information from each position is rolled up through the organization to the CFO, who obtains a timely firmwide view of positions and exposures. Goldman CFO David Viniar told the FCIC that there may be disagreements between a controller and a trader, and in such cases the controller's view is likely to prevail.

The firm reported that "Dan Sparks, then head of the mortgage department, [told] senior members of the firm in an email on December 5, 2006, that the 'Subprime market [was] getting hit hard.... At this point we are down $20mm today.' For senior management, the emergence of a pattern of losses, even relatively modest losses, in a business of the firm will typically raise a red flag."[13]

The immediate result, Sparks explained to the FCIC, was that he suddenly received visits from senior Goldman officials who before had never bothered to learn the details of his operations. CFO Viniar convened a meeting to try to understand what was happening. Goldman's senior management decided, in Viniar's phrasing, "[t]o get closer to home" with respect to the mortgage market. In other words, in its combination of long and short positions, the firm would begin taking a more cautious and more neutral stance. It would reduce its holdings of mortgages and mortgage-related securities and buy expensive insurance protection against further losses, even at the cost of profits forgone on what had looked like an attractive position in mortgages.[14]

In January and February 2007 Goldman hedged its exposure to the mortgage market. The firm then closed down mortgage warehouse facilities, moved its mortgage inventory more quickly, and reduced its exposure yet further by taking on more hedges and laying off its mortgage positions. The end result was that Goldman avoided taking the substantial losses it would have suffered if it had not reacted so promptly to signs of problems.

In one area, Goldman was slow to recognize emerging risk: This concerned the firm's reputation. When FCIC staff asked a Goldman risk officer who was responsible for reputational risk, the answer came back that everyone was responsible; the company had not organized to deal with reputational risk. In early 2011 the firm published a response to its problems with reputational risk, including a new committee structure for reporting potential conflicts and a code of conduct. Goldman stated that this would be integrated not only into processes of the firm, but also into its culture:

> The firm's culture has been the cornerstone of our performance for decades.... We must renew our commitment to our Business Principles—and above all, to client service and a constant focus on the reputational consequences of every action we take. In particular, our approach must be: not just "can we" undertake a given business activity, but "should we."[15]

In 2011, Goldman separated its reporting of business segments so as to distinguish investing on behalf of clients from the firm's proprietary trading on its own account, an area of public controversy that had been subject to some reputational risk in the aftermath of the financial crisis.

Wells Fargo

Wells Fargo protected itself in the financial crisis because of a strong company culture with several important elements: (1) a general conservatism that precluded simply following the market with new products and services, or even acquisitions, until these had been tested within the firm for consistency with the company's culture and values; (2) an emphasis on developing relationships with customers rather than simply viewing sales of products and services as transactions; and (3) a decentralized structure that made heads of business units responsible for the risks of their activities.

These cultural attributes helped Wells Fargo to weather the crisis more successfully than many of its peers. The focus on the customer meant that it refrained from offering the most risky mortgage products. Richard Kovacevich, then chairman of the Wells Fargo board and past CEO, told the Stanford Graduate School of Business in 2009 that the bank "did not offer any no-doc option, negative-amortization loans, to subprime borrowers. These exotic subprime mortgage loans were not only economically unsound, they were not appropriate for many borrowers. We lost 4 percent market share in our mortgage business for three years between 2005 and 2007, $160 billion in originations in 2006 alone."[16]

Wells Fargo supported this customer-centric approach with its core business strategy, which was to be able to cross-sell financial products to its existing customers. Again Richard Kovacevich:

> Consistent, organic revenue growth through cross-selling is probably Wells Fargo's most distinctive skill. Our average retail household has 5.9 products, and over one in four has over eight products. These are, by far, the highest cross-sell ratios in the industry and about twice the industry average.

The logic was that if customers lost money on a risky financial product, then they would not turn to Wells Fargo for the many other financial products and services they would purchase from a trusted source.

Wells Fargo also had a management style that sought to promote constructive dialogue. Kovacevich rejected hierarchical control as an effective means to promote performance. Instead, as CEO he had seen his job as:

> to select the best people to run [individual Wells business lines] and ... groups, let them do it, coach them so they learn even faster, and assure we have a strong internal check-and-balance audit process that verifies that they are adhering to the principles and the policies that we've agreed upon.
>
> People at the top should, above all, be leaders.... At Wells Fargo, we believe personal leadership is the key to success. We believe the answer to every problem, issue, or opportunity in our company is already known by some person or team in the company. The leader only has to find that person, listen, and help effect the change. By the way, the people with the best answers are not always the people with the most stripes. True leaders do not demand loyalty; they create it. They use conflict among diverse points of view to enable the team to reach new insights. They exert influence by reinforcing values.

John Stumpf, Richard Kovacevich's successor as CEO, told the FCIC, "We believe at the company that risk is best managed as close to the customer as possible with strong oversight from independent bodies within the company."[17] Part of the process of checks and balances was what Michael Loughlin, the Wells Fargo chief risk officer (CRO), called "[providing] effective challenge." He offered the FCIC several examples of how oversight from his office helped detect risk shortcomings in major business units and led to remediation and, in some cases, changes in business unit management.[18]

The result of the Wells Fargo culture and processes was that the company refrained from taking major losses and came through the financial crisis with greater strength than before. Wells Fargo doubled in size and, through its acquisition of Wachovia, which had failed in the crisis, became a national company.

Toronto Dominion Bank (TD Bank)

TD Bank is the only bank in our sample that appears to have maintained a working ERM framework before the crisis. The 2007 TD Annual Report presents the Enterprise Risk Framework and "the major categories of risk to which we are exposed, and how they are interrelated." The report defines ERM in appropriate terms:

> This framework outlines appropriate risk oversight processes and the consistent communication and reporting of key risks that could hinder the achievement of our business objectives and strategies.[19]

Among other elements of the framework,

> The corporate Risk Management function, headed by the Chief Risk Officer, is responsible for setting enterprise-level policies and practices that reflect the risk tolerance of the Bank, including clear protocols for the escalation of risk events and issues. The Risk Management Department monitors and reports on discrete business and enterprise-level risks that could have a significant impact.[20]

TD Bank provides a useful lesson about the need to surface anomalous facts, investigate them, and make a disciplined decision. While the FCIC did not interview people from TD Bank, the company's annual reports and other public information tell the story. In the early 2000s, Toronto Dominion Bank had had an active international business in structured products. Then, with little explanation, CEO Edmund Clark announced in the company's 2005 annual report, "We … made the difficult business decision to exit our global structured products business.… While the short-term economic cost to the Bank is regrettable, I am pleased that we have taken the steps we have and that we can continue to focus on growing our businesses for the future to deliver long-term shareholder value."[21] The company reported taking significant losses as it unwound its positions in 2005 and 2006.

How did CEO Clark make the decision both to avoid exposure to the U.S. subprime market and to shed the firm's exposure to structured mortgage products and derivatives? "I'm an old-school banker," Clark told a reporter in May 2008. "I don't think you should do something you don't understand, hoping there's somebody at the bottom of the organization who does."[22]

Clark said he spent several hours a week meeting with experts to understand the financial products being traded by the bank's wholesale banking unit. "The whole thing didn't make common sense to me," Clark said. "You're going to get all your money back, or you're going to get none of your money back. I said, 'Wow! if this ever went against us, we could take some serious losses here.'"[23]

Clark recalled that stock analysts at the time wrote that he was an "idiot" for taking his long-term perspective.[24] Yet, as the crisis hit, the company could report that it held no exposure to U.S. subprime mortgages, no direct exposure to third-party asset-backed commercial paper except for exposure of its mutual funds and asset management group, and no direct lending exposure to hedge funds, with only nominal trading exposure.[25] Because TD Bank came through the crisis intact, it was able to begin systematic expansion from its Canadian base into the U.S. market. By 2013, through a series of acquisitions, TD Bank had become one of the 10 largest U.S. banks, with branches extending along the East Coast from Maine to Florida.

FIRMS THAT FAILED TO NAVIGATE THE CRISIS

By contrast to the examples of financial firms that successfully navigated the crisis, those that failed lacked constructive dialogue in their cultures. I met with one CRO who explained her dilemma: If she kept raising concerns with management, she would become a pain in management's neck; but if she didn't raise concerns, she would be known as the CRO at an institution that blew itself up. She left the firm in 2006 and the firm failed in 2008.

A distinguishing characteristic of unsuccessful firms was their pursuit of short-term growth without appropriate regard for the risks involved. In 2005–2007 both Fannie Mae and Freddie Mac decided to take on more risk and increase exposure to the subprime mortgage market just as home prices were peaking. Other firms that decided similarly around the same time included Lehman Brothers, Washington Mutual (WaMu), and Countrywide.

Many of the firms that took excessive risk at the wrong time did have chief risk officers (CROs). Sometimes, the chief risk officer reported to the head of a business unit rather than to a committee of the board of directors or at least to the CEO. This muted the CRO's ability to assess risk or make recommendations that top management would hear. Some of the firms that failed either fired the CRO (Freddie Mac) or moved the CRO to a less important position at the company (Lehman) or layered the CRO far down in the company and ignored his input (Countrywide). In one major case, the corporate CRO simply lacked access to information at a part of the firm that was taking excessive risk (AIG). At many firms, ERM specialist Stephen Hiemstra explains, risk management was a compliance exercise rather than a rigorous undertaking.[26]

Firms that came to grief in the crisis lacked both (1) a proper flow of information from inside the organization to the top, and (2) forums for constructive dialogue, so that sound decisions could include consideration of risks as well as potential rewards.[27] Classic was the experience of a Fannie Mae official who told the FCIC that his unit produced pricing models showing that Fannie Mae was not appropriately pricing the mortgages that it purchased. The official recounted that the executive vice president to whom he reported asked, "Can you show me why you think you're right and everyone else is wrong?"[28]

Citigroup CEO Charles Prince, only partly in jest, characterized Citigroup as not having one good culture but five or six good cultures. Prince told the FCIC about his frustration at the inability of Citigroup's business lines to communicate with one another. In an e-mail in October 2007, he wrote about Citi's "[i]ncredible lack of coordination. We really need to break down the silos!"[29] An inability to communicate effectively across organizational lines meant that a firm lacked an enterprise-wide view of risks. A 2008 UBS report to shareholders on the firm's losses similarly notes the absence of strategic coordination at that institution. While the various risk functions relating to market risk, credit risk, and financial risk came together to assess individual transactions, "[i]t does not appear that these functions sought systematically to operate in a strategically connected manner."[30]

The CEOs of both Citigroup and AIG told the FCIC that until sometime in 2007 they were completely unaware of the financial products that almost took their firms down.[31] In part this resulted from the immense size and organizational complexity of these firms. Citigroup had 350,000 employees and nearly 2,500 subsidiaries, and AIG, much smaller than other large, complex financial institutions,[32] consisted of 223 companies that operated in 130 countries with a total of 116,000 employees.[33]

Another problem was the CEO or other powerful top manager who simply refused to take feedback. The FCIC heard repeated statements that pressure from chief officers to increase market share was a problem, for example at Moody's Investors Service, which came under pressure to please issuers with its ratings, and numerous financial institutions, including AIG Financial Products, Lehman, Countrywide, and WaMu. As a European supervisor told staff in an interview, "The best guys in the banks are often the arrogant ones."

The financial crisis was not the first time that executives followed success with serious lapses in judgment. Some years before the crisis, Professor Sydney Finkelstein of Dartmouth College's Tuck School of Business pointed to a pattern:

> Want to know one of the best generic warning signs you can look for? How about success, lots of it! . . . Few companies evaluate why business is working (often

defaulting the credit to "the CEO is a genius"). But without really understanding why success is happening, it's difficult to see why it might not. You have to be able to identify when things need adjustments. Otherwise you wake up one morning, and it looks like everything went bad overnight. But it didn't—it's a slow process that can often be seen if you look.[34]

This observation helps to relate the credit bubble to governance and risk management: In years when house prices were appreciating and the economy displayed apparent moderation, financial firms grew and reaped generous returns, regardless of whether they had the people and systems and processes in place to ensure effective risk management. The problem was exacerbated as financial firms consolidated and became larger and more complex. CEOs of firms that made substantial profits during the credit bubble too frequently came to believe in their ability to make decisions without soliciting constructive dialogue to inform themselves.

One consequence of this attitude was the diminished role of the risk function at many firms. The FCIC placed on the public record an Oliver Wyman report from early 2008 that describes "Gaps in Risk Management" at Bear Stearns, which failed shortly thereafter. Of relevance here in a long list of shortcomings was the observation that Bear Stearns had a "[l]ack of mandate for the Risk Policy Committee" and a "[l]ack of institutional stature for [the] Risk Management Group." The report bolsters the latter observation by stating, "Risk managers [are] not positioned to challenge front-office decisions."[35]

Clifford Rossi, who held senior risk management and credit positions at Citigroup, Washington Mutual (WaMu), Countrywide, Freddie Mac, and Fannie Mae, observed what he calls "risk dysfunction" at a number of firms. Each of these symptoms relates to the inability of risk managers to bring information to top levels of the company and to engage in a process of constructive dialogue when the company makes major decisions:

- Low morale and self-esteem among risk managers;
- Openly derisive comments and attitudes toward risk staff;
- High turnover in risk functions: voluntary and involuntary;
- Increasingly combative and aggressive posture toward risk management;
- Lack of stature of risk management; and
- Risk management viewed as a cost center.[36]

Based on his experience, Mr. Rossi contends that, to do their work, risk officers need "air cover" from senior officers and the board of a company (and, I would add, from regulators).

JPMORGAN CHASE AFTER THE CRISIS: THE PERILS OF HUBRIS

The problem of too much success also beset JPMorgan Chase, despite (or perhaps because of) its emergence from the financial crisis as a complex financial institution with $2.3 trillion in assets. In 2012, JPMorgan Chase unexpectedly lost $6.2 billion on operations of its London office. When news accounts broke, CEO Dimon dismissed them on an analysts call as "a tempest in a teapot." Two weeks later losses accelerated significantly, and only then did top management request an independent review of positions of the London office.

In early 2013 the company published findings of the internal task force investigating the losses. Of relevance here, the task force found that the company failed to allow negative messages to rise to top management and failed to engage in timely constructive dialogue to understand the contours of the problem:

- "A number of … employees … became aware of concerns about aspects of the trading strategies at various points throughout the first quarter. However, those concerns failed to be properly considered or escalated, and as a result, opportunities to more closely examine the flawed trading strategies and risks … were missed. . . .
- "These concerns were not fully explored. At best, insufficient inquiry was made into them and, at worst, certain of them were deliberately obscured from or not disclosed to [London] management or senior Firm management. Although in some instances, limited steps were taken to raise these issues, as noted above, no one pressed to ensure that the concerns were fully considered and satisfactorily resolved. . . .
- "[The London office's] Risk Management lacked the personnel and structure necessary to properly risk-manage the Synthetic Credit Portfolio, and as a result, it failed to serve as a meaningful check on the activities of the [office's] management and traders. This occurred through failures of risk managers (and others) both within and outside of [the office]. . . .
- "As Chief Executive Officer, Mr. Dimon could appropriately rely upon senior managers who directly reported to him to escalate significant issues and concerns. However, he could have better tested his reliance on what he was told. This Report demonstrates that more should have been done regarding the risks, risk controls and personnel associated with [the London office's] activities, and Mr. Dimon bears some responsibility for that."[37]

The JPMorgan Chase board of directors issued its own report, emphasizing that it could not make sound decisions without access to good information:

> The ability of the Board or its committees to perform their oversight responsibilities depends to a substantial extent on the relevant information being provided to them on a timely basis. . . . Because the risks posed by the positions in the [London office] were not timely elevated to the Risk Policy Committee as they should have been or to the Board, the Board and the Risk Policy Committee were not provided the opportunity to directly address them.[38]

The company responded to these losses in a way that would seem to banish current hubris from its risk management and decision making processes. Top management accepted resignations from several high-ranking officers, including the chief investment officer to whom the London office reported and the firmwide chief risk officer, and terminated or accepted resignations from a number of employees of the London office. The board of directors, while expressing confidence in how he ultimately responded to the crisis, cut Mr. Dimon's 2012 compensation by 50 percent.

CONCLUSION

The JPMorgan Chase example is instructive. Past success doesn't always predict success in the future. Not only is constructive dialogue an essential part of a company's culture, but it also must be continually nurtured by top management to ensure that it endures. If it is not embedded in the company's culture, constructive dialogue tends to be displaced by the drive for revenues, profits, market share, and the substantial personal remuneration that these bring for top officials of large, complex financial institutions and their most profitable units.

This leads to one final conclusion with respect to large, complex financial institutions, or other large, complex firms that require high-quality decision making to protect the public from major harm: Better decision making is essential in today's increasingly complicated world. Ultimately, if constructive dialogue is not part of a company's culture, then the company's regulators will need to insist on it. The crisis and its immense costs suggest that companies should change their approach and try to listen to their supervisors and consider the merits of supervisory feedback. While regulators may not have the depth of expertise or access to detailed information available to managers in a large financial institution, feedback from supervisors can sometimes help to improve decisions merely by posing the right questions and pursuing the answers. In the end, constructive dialogue from a regulator may be the only way for overbearing top company managers to receive the feedback that they need in order to make better decisions and to protect the public's health, safety, and economic well-being.[39]

QUESTIONS

1. What are the preconditions for conducting constructive dialogue in an organization?
2. Is effective risk management possible without constructive dialogue?
3. What are the forces that tend to undermine effective risk management in an organization?
4. Given its obvious value in helping an organization to understand the major risks that could prevent it from accomplishing its mission and objectives, why was the financial sector, including a risk-sensitive organization such as Goldman Sachs, so slow in adopting ERM?
5. If you are a bank examiner, what are the signals you would find that would show that a bank is engaging in good risk management?
6. If you are a bank examiner, what are the signals you would find that would show that a bank is failing to engage in good risk management?

NOTES

1. Anette Mikes, "Enterprise Risk Management in Action," London School of Economics and Political Science, Discussion Paper No. 35, August 2005.
2. The FCIC placed numerous interview records and documents on the public record. They are available at the FCIC permanent website, at http://fcic.law.stanford.edu/resource.

3. Available for downloading at http://fcic.law.stanford.edu/report.
4. The financial crisis broke in two waves. First, firms started taking losses on assets that they had considered to be safe (especially AAA-rated private-label mortgage securities). Second, when firms realized they didn't understand the assets on their balance sheets or, by extension, on the balance sheets of their counterparties, the market panicked and withdrew liquidity from counterparties it considered potentially troubled because of too many toxic assets on the counterparties' books. It was the panic that allowed a relatively small volume of toxic assets to precipitate the financial crisis and its consequences. See Thomas H. Stanton, *Why Some Firms Thrive While Others Fail: Governance and Management Lessons from the Crisis* (Oxford University Press, 2012), Chapter 2, "Dynamics of the Financial Crisis."
5. Shawn Tully, "Jamie Dimon's Swat Team: How J.P. Morgan's CEO and His Crew Are Helping the Big Bank Beat the Credit Crunch," *Fortune*, September 2, 2008, http://money.cnn.com/2008/08/29/news/companies/tully_dimon.fortune/index.htm, accessed February 14, 2013.
6. "Risk Management at Goldman Sachs," February 20, 2007. Materials provided to the Senate Permanent Subcommittee on Investigations.
7. FCIC interview with Dan Sparks, Goldman Sachs, June 16, 2010.
8. Available at https://www.wellsfargo.com/pdf/invest relations/VisionandValues04.pdf.
9. Edmund Clark, "Corporate Transparency and Corporate Accountability—Today's Table Stakes for Senior Executives," remarks to the Executive Women's Alliance Conference, Vancouver, July 12, 2004.
10. Tully, "Jamie Dimon's Swat Team."
11. Ibid.
12. Russell Walker, "Fortune Favours the Well-Prepared," *Financial Times*, January 29, 2009.
13. Goldman Sachs, "Goldman Sachs: Risk Management and the Residential Mortgage Market," April 23, 2010, 5. Materials provided to the Senate Permanent Subcommittee on Investigations.
14. Jenny Anderson and Landon Thomas Jr., "Goldman Sachs Rakes In Profit in Credit Crisis," *New York Times*, November 19, 2007.
15. Goldman Sachs, "Report of the Business Standards Committee: Executive Summary," January 2011.
16. Richard Kovacevich, "What I've Learned Since Business School," 2009. Video available at www.youtube.com/watch?v=XTh4ELp2VDc.
17. FCIC interview with John G. Stumpf, chairman and CEO, Wells Fargo, September 23, 2010.
18. FCIC interview with Michael Loughlin, chief risk officer, Wells Fargo, November 23, 2010.
19. TD Bank Financial Group, "152nd Annual Report 2007," 60–61.
20. Ibid.
21. W. Edmund Clark, "President and CEO's Message," TD Bank Financial Group 2005 Annual Article, 2006, 6.
22. Bloomberg, "The Bank That Said 'No' to Subprime Debt," *Sydney Morning Herald*, May 27, 2008. Available at www.smh.com.au/business/the-bank-that-said-no-to-subprime-debt-20080527-2ihd.html.
23. Ibid.
24. TD Bank Financial Group, National Bank 2010 Financial Services Conference, presentation, March 30, 2010.
25. TD Bank Financial Group, "Investor Presentation, September 2007," Slide no. 15.
26. Stephen W. Hiemstra, "An Enterprise Risk Management View of Financial Supervision," *Enterprise Risk Management Institute International*, October 2007.

27. This also applies to nonfinancial firms. My book assesses decision making and costly mistakes such as the BP Gulf oil spill, fatalities at the Massey Mining Company, and hospital medical errors. Failures at nonfinancial firms show the same patterns of overbearing or distracted CEOs or others (e.g., doctors) who make poor decisions without obtaining feedback, and cultures that emphasize production without adequate consideration of risk.

28. Financial Crisis Inquiry Commission, "Final Report of the Financial Crisis Inquiry Commission," 2011, 181–182.

29. Financial Crisis Inquiry Commission, "Interview of Charles O. Prince," transcript, March 17, 2010, 37 and 41, respectively, available on the FCIC permanent website.

30. UBS AG, "Shareholder Report on UBS's Write-Downs," April 18, 2008, 40.

31. Financial Crisis Inquiry Commission, "Interview of Charles O. Prince," March 17, 2010, 73–74; and Financial Crisis Inquiry Commission, "Official Transcript, Hearing on 'The Role of Derivatives in the Financial Crisis,'" June 30, 2010, 151; both available on the FCIC permanent website.

32. Richard Herring and Jacopo Carmassi, "The Corporate Structure of International Financial Conglomerates: Complexity and Its Implications for Safety & Soundness." In Allen N. Berger, Phillip Molyneux, and John Wilson, eds. *The Oxford Handbook of Banking*, 2009, Chapter 8. "Among the 16 international financial conglomerates identified by regulators as large, complex financial institutions (LCFIs), each has several hundred majority-owned subsidiaries and 8 have more than 1,000 subsidiaries."

    On the other hand, FCIC staff learned in interviews with federal regulators that many of these subsidiaries and affiliates were small institutions, acquired in a process of accretion, that had little financial significance.

33. Government Accountability Office, "Troubled Asset Relief Program, Status of Government Assistance Provided to AIG," September 2009, 5; AIG, Form 10-K for 2008, 7.

34. Sydney Finkelstein, *Why Smart Executives Fail, and What You Can Learn from Their Mistakes* (New York: Portfolio, 2003), 251–252.

35. Bear Stearns, "Management Committee: Risk Governance Diagnostic; Recommendations and Case for Economic Capital Development," February 5, 2008. Available on the permanent FCIC website.

36. Clifford Rossi, "Removing Barriers to Pathological Risk Behavior: The Art of Effective Communication," Association of Federal Enterprise Risk Management Summit, September 18, 2012.

37. "Report of JPMorgan Chase & Co. Management Task Force Regarding 2012 CIO Losses," January 16, 2013.

38. "Report of the Review Committee of the Board of Directors of JPMorgan Chase & Co. Relating to the Board's Oversight Function with Respect to Risk Management," January 15, 2013.

39. See, e.g., Thomas H. Stanton, "Listening to Regulators Can Keep Your Bank out of Trouble," *American Banker*, August 20, 2012; and Thomas H. Stanton, comment to the Federal Reserve Board on the proposed rulemaking on "Enhanced Prudential Standards and Early Remediation Requirements for Covered Companies. www.federalreserve .gov/SECRS/2012/February/20120215/R-1438/R-1438_021312_105398_555068728868 _1.pdf.

ABOUT THE CONTRIBUTOR

Thomas H. Stanton is a Fellow of the Center for Advanced Governmental Studies at Johns Hopkins University, President-Elect of the Association of Federal

Enterprise Risk Management (AFERM), a former director of the National Academy of Public Administration, and a former member of the federal Senior Executive Service. His publications include two books on government-sponsored enterprises (GSEs), including *A State of Risk: Will Government-Sponsored Enterprises Be the Next Financial Crisis?* (HarperCollins, 1991), and two edited books on government organization and management. His two recent books are *Why Some Firms Thrive While Others Fail: Governance and Management Lessons from the Crisis* (Oxford University Press, 2012) and *Managing Risk and Performance: A Guide for Government Decision Makers*, co-editor with Douglas Webster (John Wiley & Sons, 2014). Mr. Stanton's B.A. degree is from the University of California at Davis, M.A. from Yale University, and J.D. from the Harvard Law School.

CHAPTER 33

Challenges and Obstacles of ERM Implementation in Poland

ZBIGNIEW KRYSIAK, PHD
Associate Professor of Finance, Warsaw School of Economics, Poland

SŁAWOMIR PIJANOWSKI, PHD
President, POLRISK Risk Management Association, Poland

This research is about the status of enterprise risk management (ERM) implementation in Poland's companies. We analyze the challenges and obstacles to a more mature stage of ERM rather than a compliance- or governance-driven one. Poland, after the transition into the free market economy in 1989, became open to the knowledge and transfer of the best practices from around the world. Since 1995, with the publication of AS/NZS 4360 and COSO II in 2004, as well as easy access via the Internet, it seems that theoretically there should not be a delay in implementing modern risk management (RM) processes in Poland. While there is contact with authors and thought leaders taking part in the creation of various ERM standards, and with some professionals implementing ERM in various companies, barriers still exist. These barriers are due to geographical distances, language differences, budget constraints, a lack of awareness, or other business priorities. We (the authors) first heard about AS/NZS 4360 in 2004 while looking for inspiration from various standards to improve risk assessment methodologies for our companies. In 2004, the aforementioned standards were translated into Polish and published in the Polish Ministry of Finance's *Orange Book Risk Management—Principles and Concepts*. A similar publication had also been done earlier by the UK Ministry of Treasury, and another handbook of risk management for the audit department, which included descriptions of some risk management tools and standards. Later, in 2005 and 2006, the Ministry of Finance also led a project implementing ERM in selected units of public administration as a pilot phase.

Managers in Poland were becoming familiar with ERM concepts mainly by educating themselves. In 2006, the POLRISK Risk Management Association[1] was established, and later became a member of the Federation of European Risk Management Associations (FERMA).[2] Under POLRISK, ERM has been popularized in a more structured way by its first founding members and other officers. Since 2006, ERM experts from around the world have begun to come to Poland as speakers in the annual conferences organized by POLRISK.

There are many people involved with Poland's ERM efforts.[3] We have the honor to be two of them. For example, late in 2009, Slawomir Pijanowski, on behalf of POLRISK, with the support of Kevin W. Knight, AM, initiated the preparation for adoption of ISO 31000 in Poland. In 2011, Mr. Pijanowski, as representative of both POLRISK and the Polish Committee for Standardization, joined ISO/PC 262, contributing to the elaboration of ISO 31004. It is, however, difficult to demonstrate the benefits of ERM in Poland, because there are few good examples of ERM implementation in domestic companies. Additionally, there are few CEOs or independent parties who have observed how ERM adds value. This state of ERM implementation provides the motivation for our case study. This case study examines the reasons, challenges, and obstacles of ERM implementation and will help us reach the right conclusions.

METHODOLOGY TO DIAGNOSE THE STATUS OF ERM IMPLEMENTATION

The sources used in this article come from:

- Research performed by the authors on approximately 100 companies in 2006 and with 300 managers in 2010.
- The POLRISK Risk Management Association, with 100 members, at various workshops, conferences, seminars, and training courses where ERM has been challenged, questioned, and openly discussed.
- Participation in the creation of an ERM program in the telecommunications industry.
- Exchanging practical knowledge, experience, or training about ERM among the Polish practitioners (various managerial positions, CEOs, boards, experts, and specialists) of the following industries: telecommunications, energy, logistics (road, post, railway industry), oil and gas, consulting, insurance, banks, hospitals, and construction.

We would like to share our observations by pointing out areas of weakness, as well as the challenges of demonstrating ERM's value per se for boards, managers, and operational employees. There are 3,000 companies in Poland with more than 250 employees that would potentially benefit from ERM implementation. Assuming that ERM is justified for companies with at least 250 employees, then our studies deal with about 10 to 20 percent of such companies in Poland. The research includes only private companies, excluding the financial industry (i.e., insurers, banks, investment funds, etc.), and not public administration.

We use the following three definitions of ERM:

1. Enterprise risk management can be defined as an integrated approach to credit risk, market risk, operational risk, business risk, and economic capital management. This includes risk control, mitigation, and risk transfer to maximize the value of the company (Lam 2003).
2. In ISO 31000, risk management is defined as coordinated activities to direct and control an organization with regard to risk (ISO Guide 73:2009, definition 2.1).

3. Enterprise risk management is a process, effected by the entity's board of directors, management, and other personnel, applied in the strategy setting and across the enterprise, designed to identify potential events that may affect the entity, and manage risk to be within the risk appetite, to provide reasonable assurance regarding the achievement of entity objectives (COSO II, 2004 definition).

An important issue at the top of the risk management activities is value creation. What creates a company's value are vision, strategy, knowledge on how to commercialize ideas, innovation, implementation, managers' and employees' attitudes, and decisions influencing specific value sources and drivers. To create shareholder value, a company has to take on the right risks, retain them, and manage them within its boundaries. The major risk management activities here are as follows (Antikarov 2012):

- Identify the strategic risks associated with each strategic alternative and select the strategy with the best risk/reward characteristics.
- Build and apply strategic flexibility/agility to take advantage of new strategic opportunities and protect against materialized strategic risks.
- Build and apply operational flexibility and resilience to manage ongoing business environment volatility.
- Build and apply financial flexibility allowing the company to survive, execute its strategy, and not transfer ownership during periods of financial distress.
- Build full risk assessment into the performance evaluation of existing businesses and the corresponding rewards and compensation of management and employees.
- Build full risk assessment into the evaluation, ranking, and selection of new investment projects.

In Exhibit 33.1, we display the general framework of the methodology we use for the analysis of the case study. We will present the status of ERM implementation in Poland relating to the four stages of risk management maturity described by Purdy (2010): increasing levels of maturity for (1) management of specific risks, (2) the approach to risk driven by governance, (3) risk management driven by the changes within the organization, and (4) the integrated approach. In the applied methodology, the characteristics proposed by Antikarov (2012) fit more or less to Purdy's "Integrated" stage 4 shown in Exhibit 33.1. Exhibit 33.2 displays the main components of risk management proposed by ISO 31000.

MAIN ISSUES IN POLAND'S ERM IMPLEMENTATION

There are many issues faced by companies in Poland in the process of ERM implementation. The main systemic natural obstacles are:

- There has been little attention paid to ERM among nonfinancial sectors, although the level of interest has slowly increased since 2004, approaching the highest interest around 2009 to 2011.

	Risk Specific	Governance Driven	Change Driven	Integrated
Efficiency of Risk Management Process (Returns/Effort)	Different types of processes for different types of risk. Risk categorization is largely consequence based. Attempts to integrate measurement. Negative perception of risk. Terms *hazards*, *risk*, and *threats* are used interchangeably. Risk is seen as harm, loss, and detriment. RM is closely linked to insurance.	Risk is motivated by reporting. High-level risk assessment is stipulated by reporting requirements, normally only once or twice a year. Risk measures vary according to types of risk. Risks are seen as events—mostly with negative consequences. There are inconsistent approaches for managing different types of risk.	Risk is associated with management of change. RM processes are separate but are invoked by decision-making process. Risk is driven by performance-based standard. Risk is seen as effect of uncertainty on objectives. Uniform system for analysis of most types of risk.	Risk is implicit in all decision making. RM processes are integrated into key organizational processes. RM is integral to the system of management. RM is culturally driven by performance standard. Risk is seen as effect of uncertainty on objectives. Effective RM leads to resilience and agility.
	Degree of Integration of Risk Management, Extent of Accountability			
	Stage 1	Stage 2	Stage 3	Stage 4

Exhibit 33.1 Risk Maturity Levels Used in Methodology.
Source: G. Purdy, "How Good Is Our Risk Management? How Boards Should Find Out," Risk Watch, Conference Board of Canada, December 2010.

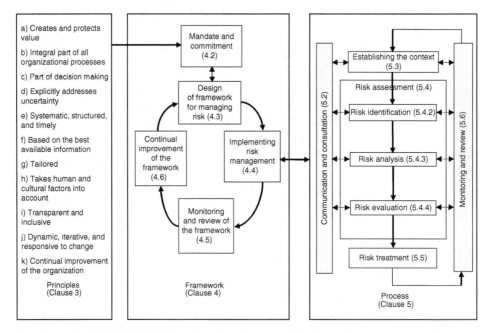

Exhibit 33.2 ISO 31000:2009 Relationships between Principles, Framework, and Process
Source: ISO 31000:2009.

- There are few domestic companies that can be used as examples of good ERM and as a benchmark for the Polish business community. In other words, there are few examples that can be used as good references regarding risk management matters such as financial results, reports, management discussion and analysis (MD&A), and communication of risk within the investor relations process.

- There has been a relatively short time for gathering experience from companies on ISO 31000 implementation; only two years have passed since the publication in March 2012 of PN-ISO 31000:2012, Risk Management— Principles and Guidelines. The Polish Committee for Standardization reports that there is interest in ISO 31000, but there are common misunderstandings of what ISO 31000 really is. One of the examples is in using the term *risk mitigation* instead of *modification* or *treatment*. Also, there is no guidance on ISO 31000 in the Polish language. These translation issues are delaying adoption of various guidelines because all those activities need sponsorships for funding. The same holds for risk management books; some of the classics, such as works by James Lam, are not translated into Polish, and this is blocking widespread practical knowledge on ERM. Any meaningful guidance remains within the advisory services industry, with no guarantee that risk management is done coherently or correctly with the approach prescribed by ISO 31000. In contrast, Australia and New Zealand have had more than 17 years of experience with standards of risk management, and there are many publicly available guidelines being applied by public and private companies in those countries, creating stronger fundamentals there as compared to in Poland. That is what we can call the "experience gap."

- There are very few domestic experts in Poland who have had the opportunity to implement ERM as a real change management process instead of a governance-driven one. There are few companies interested in building the value of the company through effective risk management. However, there are some ERM implementations in Poland in logistics, energy, oil, gas, telecommunication, mining, insurance, and the public sector. Risk management becomes a more important topic due to investors' requirements in the construction industry and the European Union directives for the railway industry.

- The POLRISK Risk Management Association needs further development in order to become a strong, recognizable body for legislative initiatives related to governance and risk management for the good of the business community. In Polish enterprises there is a need for building the risk manager profession, which would have to be built almost from scratch. The issue of the scope of duties of a risk manager is often discussed in the European forum because a risk manager's responsibilities are perceived differently from country to country. In the FERMA bylaws the responsibilities of the risk manager are not addressed, but FERMA is considering covering that issue in the requirements for the certification of risk managers. This all presents big challenges to the harmonization of educational programs with expected skills for risk managers in European countries. When this is done, it will be

a big step in the promotion of the profession and risk management itself in Poland and elsewhere in Europe.
- MBA programs and higher education in Poland do not include enough enterprise-wide risk management topics. There are one or two exceptions of postgraduate studies including ERM standards. One way to promote ERM is to integrate ERM studies with strategic management and value-based risk management courses and executive MBA programs.
- The tradition of risk management became broken under the various socialist economic systems between 1945 and 1991. For example, there are at present only a few captive insurance companies in Poland. Before World War II, there were around 300 captives and mutual insurance companies. The use of such risk management techniques by many organizations was an important part of the culture then relating to managing risk. Risk managers in international companies are now managing captives together with coordinating ERM. We are in the process of rebuilding the number of captives and that culture. The POLRISK Risk Management Association also supports this process.

Apart from the aforementioned systemic issues in Poland, there is also confusion among proponents of ERM in Poland about what are regarded as weaknesses of the ERM concept itself, concerning the tools, models, terminology, publicly available materials, and articles. Examples of concerns are:

- In most of the cases, the risk matrix or heat map does not show the efficiency of controls.[4]
- There is also a lack of references to or use of historical data or simulation as justification for the respective risk level to support decision making. Greater use of actual data is considered necessary to assure a high quality of risk management.
- There seem to be two schools of holistic risk management currently struggling with each other on the pros and cons of the setting of risk appetite or concepts like inherent and residual risk.

Due to a lack of understanding by those involved and the apparent confusion over the foregoing concepts, these differences do not help the followers of ERM, because in many cases, they are not able to clearly and in a convincing way explain or translate those different concepts into decision making processes and value creation. Problems arise if executives who are trying to properly understand ERM are asked to explain why the concept of risk appetite is needed. Executives, managers, and directors expect a clear message about whether this exercise with ERM can increase performance, reduce costs, optimize margins, or make good decisions on current resources and capital allocation. All of these issues, both at the international level and at the local level, only confirm that ERM as a concept itself still is not stabilized or is not ready to be used. As a result, managers we have spoken with indicate that they are not going to implement ERM because of these problems.

Risk management terminology, principles, frameworks, and processes in Poland are orientated primarily toward either internal controls or governance.

Some companies are making efforts to influence value via risk management. ERM is viewed by managers in Poland as an optimizing activity in achieving objectives and therefore is perceived as integrally related to strategic management. The major question stated by practitioners in Poland is: "What is the real added value of ERM?" The partial answer to that question can be obtained by referring to the meaning of good performance or good execution of strategy and goal achievement. In Exhibit 33.3 we offer an answer in the form of comparative statements of good practices of the execution and performance of the strategy applied from classic books on the topic. ERM is frequently commented on by Chartered Institute of Management Accountants (CIMA)-designated experts, CEOs, CFOs, financial controllers, and other top managers as something they are already doing, which they perceive as:

- Strategy development and its execution by risk management
- An idea that is perhaps worthy to apply and utilizes various risk criteria focused on efficiency and performance or risk controlling as part of business controlling

Using three of the best books on strategy execution (Kaplan and Norton, Bossidy and Charan, Welch) and one on performance (Peters and Waterman), we put together the comparative statements indicating some ideas and sources of ERM principles being used in management mainstream practice and literature. Since many Polish executives refer to these books, ERM must be shown in the light of which practices should be part of a company's management framework, as is also recommended in ISO 31000. Exhibit 33.3 shows the relationship between ERM concepts and strategy execution and performance.

From these comparisons, there are important conclusions that may be applied to the case study of ERM in Poland. Suboptimal efficiency of management may result from the fact that ERM is a missing link between strategic management (SM) and value-based management (VBM). Selling ERM in isolation from strategy and value-based management creates a risk of unsuccessful ERM implementation. Selling the triple package of SM, ERM, and VBM together and creating the adequate educational program increase the chance that the value proposition related to ERM will be accepted by the boards of directors at enterprises in Poland.

Moreover, in the view of Polish CFOs and CEOs, a properly defined strategy is in fact a reflection of a new or updated arrangement of a company's capital and assets/resources allocation. Therefore, the risk management function must be close to strategy and produce a strategic portfolio of initiatives, programs, projects, and processes. Thus the reporting line of the risk management department should always be where decisions are made on capital and resources allocation—that is, in the strategy department or in CFO-managed business units such as value-based financial controlling and budgeting (i.e., operating expense [opex] and capital expenditure [capex]). If these functions were supported by various tools applied for risk assessment, monitoring, and modeling, then most of the CEOs and CFOs would be interested in applying such approaches into their daily management practice.

Exhibit 33.3 Comparative Statements of Good Practices in Strategy Execution and Performance

Robert S. Kaplan and David P. Norton, *The Execution Premium* (2008)	Jack Welch, *Winning* (2005)	Larry Bossidy and Ram Charan, *Execution* (2002)	Tom Peters and R. H. Waterman Jr., *In Search of Excellence* (1982)
Management system linking strategy to operations: 1. Develop the strategy (strategic analysis, SWOT, risk assessment of strategy, how best to compete). Here we should know at least the type of strategy and related risk. Risk taking is related to type of strategy and its flexibility in Michael Raynor's (2007) sense: low cost, differentiation, diversification. 2. Plan the strategy (strategy maps—links with risks. How we measure our plan: setting objectives—basis for risk assessment of the objectives, stress testing of assumptions, strategic project, programs, portfolios, initiatives, who will lead execution of strategy?) Establish the context. Here is a place for risk limits, (appetite) tolerances against targets in strategic plan.	Strategy is a game, vital, dynamic. No scientific approach to strategy is needed; overloading strategy with science is unproductive. Jack Welch defining strategy as "allocation of resources"; "strategy is what remains after removing big words related to it." "Strategy is making choices on how to be competitive. (As for strategy, you should think less and act more. In other words, this is again about execution.) Strategy is simple—you choose general destination and pursue it with your best effort." Forget about scenarios, plans, whole-year research and 100-page reports, recommendations, and so on. To be number one or two in each industry—to reach this goal you have to repair/restructure, sell, or close the companies."	Execution: Three core processes of execution of any business: 1. Strategy process—link people and operations. Strategy review. 2. Operations process—link strategy and people. 3. People process—link strategy and operations. Three blocks of execution: 1. Seven essential behaviors of leaders: Know your people and your business. Insist on realism. Set clear goals and priorities. Follow through. Reward the doers. Expand people's capabilities. Know yourself. 2. Framework for cultural change—operationalizing culture: Behaviors are beliefs turned into action (principle a) reward performance (compare Lam [2003]—"Pay for the performance you want"), allow robust dialogue. Behaviors deliver the results. Social software of execution, leaders get the behaviors they exhibit and tolerate.	• A bias for action, active decision making—"getting on with it." • Close to the customer—learning from the people served by the business. • Autonomy and entrepreneurship—fostering innovation and nurturing "champions." • Productivity through people—treating rank-and-file employees as a source of quality. • Hands-on, value-driven—management philosophy that guides everyday practice—management showing its commitment. • Stick to the knitting—stay with the business that you know. • Simple form, lean staff—some of the best companies have minimal HQ staff.

584

3. Align the organization (it is in fact "design of risk management framework" and "establish the context" phases of risk management process in ISO 31000).
4. Plan operations (and include risk management plan).
5. Monitor and learn (is our strategy working? it isn't too late?). These questions should be asked first at the "develop the strategy" phase (will our strategy work? are assumptions credible? is our strategy feasible?). Similar to monitor and review in ISO 31000.
6. Test and adapt (that is, what should result from "monitoring and review" phase). (Continuous improvement in ISO 31000—part of framework.) What is missing? Principle (d) from ISO 31000—RM explicitly addresses uncertainty.

Three stages of strategy execution:
1. Elaborate big idea—Big Hairy Audacious Goals (BHAGs) for business, smart, realistic, feasible, relatively quick way of generating competitive advantage.
2. Assign right people to right tasks to successes with implementation of idea. (We could say to the right risk management framework and pay key attention to "establish the context phase" as in ISO 31000.)
3. Continuously with persistence seek best methods of implementation of idea, adapt it, improve it—in company or outside of it. (Continuous improvement in ISO 31000—part of framework.) What is missing? Principle (d) from ISO 31000—RM explicitly addresses uncertainty.

3. The job leader should not delegate—having the right people in the right place.
All of the above are risk management framework activities as in ISO 31000 if looked at from a risk perspective and implementation of the process. We see also the risk management principles "add value, include human and cultural factors." What is missing? Principle (d) explicitly addresses uncertainty.

- Simultaneous loose-tight properties—autonomy in shop-floor activities plus centralized values.
 (All of the above can be seen in principles of risk management and framework scope and have to be a tailored in establishing the context in risk management process and framework level.)
 What is missing? Principle (d) from ISO 31000—RM explicitly addresses uncertainty.

Source: Author's research, S. Pijanowski.

BOARD PERCEPTION OF ERM: "WE HAVE TO CHANGE THE WAY WE RUN THE BUSINESS, BECAUSE LACK OF ERM CREATES INEFFICIENT MANAGEMENT"

In program and project management terms, ERM is, in fact, change management or an organizational change project or program. So the board, ideally, should be the first catalyst for change, instead of any lower level of management. Our experience shows that an attempt by middle-level managers to convince board members about ERM is not effective and can create, to some extent, a misunderstanding, as we show next. The critical thing here is to see who the messenger is. It should be the CEO who raises the need, or it could be the board of directors, or the audit committee in a supervisory board representing the interests of owners or key stakeholders. As for any conviction, this may happen first informally in terms of bilateral talks between one board member and an "$n-1$" manager ("n" means board level). Then if there is trust and proper understanding by the board member, the senior executive may be able to explain ERM to the board member and have him or her promote the idea at the board level. A misperception of ERM by boards in Poland, especially in highly regulated industries such as energy, mining, or telecommunications, can be summed up in one simple sentence: "I won't sign anywhere formally that I know about any risks and that I continue managing the company, or a functional area, despite the identified risk."

Let us examine examples of how ERM concepts might be communicated and how the board may misunderstand what is intended:

- Telling the board how it should manage risk, as, of course, it is highly probable that such a message will be rejected. The board believes that it is already hired to oversee the management of the organization, including its risks, and to achieve appropriate results. If there is a better system than what is applied now, we have to be ready to show how much the financial results will change by using it.
- Saying to the board that the current motivational system should be changed to include rewards not only for performance but also for risk treatment methods that should lead to better performance.
- Saying to the board that management should identify which of the top management staff are the primary risk owners for each major risk. The directors already feel that they are responsible for the results or performance, so the nomination of a risk owner is perceived to some extent as a redundant activity. If responsibility has already been assigned for performance, what else needs to be done?
- Saying to the board that the current decision-making process could be better if risk assessment techniques were used to support decision making. This could be interpreted as saying, "I could tell you, as an ERM follower, how to make better decisions." This could be risky.
- Saying that current coordination processes of various parts of company are not optimal (e.g., that higher costs are being incurred from having separate

insurance for individual areas of the organization), and that some solutions optimize costs but generate other risks.
- Saying that the current strategy execution could be better and also the budgeting process (including capital allocation).
- Saying that one risk champion will overview what other top management staff are doing.
- Telling the board that they have to commit to what they are already obliged to do by signing off on the policy of risk management.
- Telling the board to change the managerial information and reporting to include risk profiles and risk assessments.
- Telling the board to change the culture, or even the corporate identity, in order to allow mistakes and failures and thereby to learn from the past, and to openly speak about risks. Would this mean the board should tolerate staff making mistakes twice or tolerate incompetence among the staff?

These examples of the challenges of communicating with boards when seeking to implement ERM are based on what we have experienced in practice. If someone presenting ERM concepts communicates them in the wrong way to the board, such as: "I know better," "You manage inefficiently," "You could do it better," "I would like to criticize how you manage the company," or "You are not competent," thus giving the message that the board is managing the company poorly because it does not have ERM in place, this is highly risky. Therefore, good preparation and use of properly worded arguments are critical to avoid such perceptions, regardless of whether the messenger is a consultant or an "$n - 1$" director or manager. When anyone who is suggesting using ERM is on a lower level than the executive board, all of the foregoing questions arise and can be mental blocks. Let us see now in more detail who in Poland is usually getting management to buy in.

WHO IS GETTING MANAGEMENT BUY-IN FOR ERM?

The ERM implementation activities in Poland are mainly driven from the following sources:

- Governance stimulation, such as a supervisory board (board of directors) recommendation, governance (stock exchange), or audit good practices committees. For public administration units, the Public Finance Act states that there is an obligation to include risk management as part of managerial supervision.
- POLRISK Risk Management Association, since the beginning of its existence
- Internationally operated brokers in Poland.
- Risk management consulting companies.
- The companies themselves or head offices of international companies that are operating as subsidiaries or affiliates in Poland.

Our survey of 100 POLRISK members showed that a lot of interest in ERM in Poland is generated by various specialists or senior experts related to business continuity management, information technology (IT), physical security, operational risk, project risk management, internal audit or internal supervision from commercial and public sector, internal control, and legal attorney, but rarely pure insurance managers. Some board members or directors showed interest, but not many. Professional consultants who participated in POLRISK discussion panels or workshops told us that they had problems with communication and explaining ERM concepts to the boards.

We decided to explore the challenges of communicating with boards, and after discussions with executives it appeared that the key aspect is the context in which ERM is presented. We have identified that problems with executive communication are related to two main personality profiles in business. The first is that it is difficult or almost impossible to be both a good manager and an expert in the subject matter simultaneously. Why? The main difference is how decisions are made: The expert needs almost a 99 percent certainty to give a recommendation on a specific solution, system, or expertise. In turn, the manager operates and makes decisions with more uncertainty involved—it does not matter if there is a 60 percent certainty or an 80 percent certainty. The point is that this substantial difference requires the development of different skills.

The decision of an individual to pursue or develop a career toward being a highly skilled executive or an effective manager means resignation from being an expert, which means in turn also abandoning the expert's mentality and way of making decisions. And when in corporate reality those two mentalities meet on boards, audit committees, or any executive meetings, those differences arise and are reflected in attitudes, wording, and beliefs. For managers, the uncertainty of making decisions is normal—they may even pursue it. Experts, however, when talking about uncertainty while presenting ERM, use terms like "mitigate" or "avoid" risk in a different context. They are not decision makers, so they do not understand that anyone who makes important business decisions accepts that there are regulators, audits, internal competitors, and the like who may second-guess the decisions of any given manager.

Therefore, the pure concept of documenting all assumptions, risk analysis, and consequences of decisions seems to be ERM utopia, as no manager would like to deliver any formal evidence or proof for potential corporate enemies or competitors that the decision was made despite high risk—because this may later be easily judged as incompetence and could be used to terminate the manager's contract immediately. So, paradoxically, not documenting everything is in fact the behavior of good personal risk management. This we know from several very experienced managers we interviewed. Why are we saying this? The reason is that ERM buy-in is often promoted (we assume this is the case not only in Poland) by experts or consultants rather than by pure managers—and hence problems with communication, mentality, and business justification arise. The manager is bold, risk taking, and brave by nature, whereas the expert is more risk averse, cautious, circumspect, and risk avoiding by nature.

This is a paradox. ERM is often suggested and promoted by experts who do not like to take risks and are not making important decisions. Successful ERM has been driven by CFOs or CEOs who are passionate about ERM—we directly know that this is the case. So perhaps awakening a passion for risk management in CEOs or CFOs is the right way to go. When we include the differences in experience of both groups of professionals, it is very hard to find a common understanding even on an interpersonal level, excluding knowledge of risk management itself.

SPECIFIC CHALLENGES AND OBSTACLES OBSERVED IN RISK MANAGEMENT

In this section, we describe key issues within the risk management domain that we identified during our study, obtained during interviews with managers, and gathered on specific topics (for example, risk appetite) from various risk management experts.

Terminology

Authors of both scientific and business literature seem to exhibit little discipline for using the same terminology about risk consistently. Terms such as information, noise, uncertainty, risk, ambiguity, threat, hazard, opportunity, vulnerability, exposure, consequence, and strengths are examples of where we observe a lack of precision in definitions. What we observe (not only in Poland) is mixing the meaning of threat with risk, showing risk as the opposite of opportunity, instead of threat and opportunity. This issue directly influences practitioners' perceptions and approaches to ERM. Another example is the hypothesis of informational efficiency of a capital market, which has a lot to do with investors' risk management and their evaluation of companies. The efficient market hypothesis (EMH) does not have a precise definition of what information is (see Pijanowski 2005–2006), and that is why the hypothesis is called unsolvable, but when we define parameters of information and uncertainty, it can be solved in a convincing way.

Moreover, we have observed that the current inconsistencies and ambiguity regarding the term *risk appetite* cause directors not to buy into the ERM concept because it cannot be properly explained or justified by its followers.

Principles

If we look at the implementation of ERM in Poland, we see that risk is not part of key managerial decisions, despite a risk management policy being formally agreed upon. The only decision regarded as relating to risk is to comply with the law (i.e., "We have to do it, so we must do it"). We know several cases where one consulting company corrected the other consulting company's frameworks. Our conclusion is that ERM is often sold in isolation from strategy and value-based management.

Risk Management Frameworks

Our experience shows that ERM processes in Poland—mainly frameworks, policies, procedures, and methodologies—are mainly governance driven. There are of course some exceptions, and in the energy sector it has been identified that there is a company that makes an effort to increase its value through effective risk management.

Writing a risk management policy is relatively easy. Typically, the policy is combined with a risk assessment methodology. The main framework that is used in Poland is COSO 2004—almost always fully used by the public sector. We can say that it is an auditor-based view of risk management. Some companies use the MoR (Management of Risk) Framework (UK Office of Government Commerce), some became interested in ISO 31000, some frameworks were developed and delivered by consulting companies, and some were elaborations of the company's own framework as based on various aspects from the different frameworks just mentioned.

Risk Owners

After the relatively easy part—writing some documents—the execution phase starts. What are the typical challenges during the execution phase? In an ERM implementation in which we participated, confirming the risk owners was one of the first challenges, as business managers perceived being a risk owner as an unfavorable label in the company. For example, a billing process owner did not understand that he should be a risk owner since he managed the budget and had targets and goals related to the billing process. The billing process owner did not want to be a risk owner for political reasons—he did not like to be associated with IT billing systems problems, and he postulated that the head of IT should also be a risk owner. This is an example of a typical silo-based approach. For middle- or high-level managers, being a risk owner looks like a dangerous role. Finally, after discussions that confirmed that he had the budget to influence the process and by referring to the risk management policy, he had to agree, but he was not happy with the new responsibility. So perhaps it is better to call the role a risk management leader, risk coordinator, or risk manager, rather than a risk owner.

Organizational Placement of ERM

Another topic that we explored was the organizational arrangement of where the risk management function or department should be placed. Our research showed that typically the function either was within the internal audit department, the internal supervision department, or the insurance department, or was a direct report to the CFO. The way it appeared was as though one was chasing people to get them to perform risk management (legal, internal control, insurance, etc.). Almost nobody wanted to be responsible for ERM, as it was treated as a new scope of responsibilities with compensation remaining at the same level.

The Influence of the Size of Organizations

We observed that the nature of risk management frameworks in medium-sized companies could be different than for larger companies. Board members of medium-sized companies told us that silo-based thinking was not an issue in many medium-sized companies as there are simply no silos. Executives also asked, "What is the business case for risk management in medium-sized companies?"

When we explored the matter in more detail, it was evident to us that integration was not the main issue; instead the lack of managerial information on margin or profitability of various projects and contracts was really the issue, as well as what to write in tender offers about how the company manages risk of customer demands (for example, investors expect it from vendors in the construction industry) and vendor credibility before making decisions. We have to be aware not to provide arguments on ERM benefits like integration of various risk treatment activities in medium-sized companies, as they may not be as applicable for those companies as for big companies.

Risk Management Process

Risk identification is one of the key steps of the risk management process. We explored how people describe risk and found that a lot are confusing threat with risk or mixing up other risk terminology. When we looked into how people describe risk, we found that the risk description being used in companies is not a real risk description at all. There are a lot of risk registers with no risk information but rather only threat or vulnerability descriptions that are understandable only to the person who wrote them (almost 95 percent of the cases we checked). People are rating risks without explaining why, or without justification of what supports making decisions and what does not. The Statement of Context[5] is not present, which would help readers to understand why specific risk criteria have been set. Almost nobody is aware that the Statement of Context is one of the deliverables of the "establish the context" phase of the risk management process in ISO 31000.

The reason for this is that there is no proper guidance on how to describe risk properly in the absence of risk management implementation guidelines. Due to this lack of more detailed guidance, despite being interested in ISO 31000, corporate representatives have problems with understanding it, resulting in a poor opinion of the ISO 31000 standard in Poland. Unfortunately, ISO TR 31004, produced by the ISO/PC and the ISO/TC 262 Working Group in its final version, does not fulfill this requirement; therefore, we will have to elaborate on it on our own with the support of international experts who really know ISO 31000 and how it should be implemented.

If we have no good guidance on risk management and there are no volunteers to take responsibility for promoting ERM, we will have to create the right profession and professionals to deal with risk. When we looked into the formal professions registry of the Social Policy and Labor Ministry in Poland for job position lists that include *risk* in the name, we found only *underwriter*—being translated as a risk management specialist and an appraiser of a company's risk. That leads us to the conclusion that is the title of the next section—we have to build the chief risk officer (CRO)/risk manager profession from scratch.

WE HAVE TO BUILD THE CHIEF RISK OFFICER/RISK MANAGER PROFESSION FROM SCRATCH

In 2009, the POLRISK Risk Management Association board asked its office assistant to contact 253 companies by phone, including 77 percent associated with the

Polish Association of Listed Companies on the Warsaw Stock Exchange (WSE), to inquire about whether they had a risk manager who potentially could join the association. We wanted to diagnose the awareness and needs related to risk management in Poland, primarily among listed companies on the WSE. The results of these phone interviews are as follows. Thirty-three (13 percent) of the companies did not want any further contact. The main reasons were that they were not interested because they did not have risk managers, they were not interested at all, they received from their head office a strategy already written and ready to implement ("We receive strategy out of the box"), they were just tired of receiving various training offers, and the like. In a few cases it was mentioned that "Risk management is outsourced." The most interesting example from a global company was: "Risk management is at the discretion of the head office." Only 11 companies out of 253 (4.3 percent) declared potential interest in joining the POLRISK Risk Management Association.

This is perhaps not fully representative research on the perception of risk management in Poland, but it shows, together with other surveys, that we have to build the risk manager profession in Poland from scratch. Of course, this conclusion does not apply to financial risk managers holding the PRM (Professional Risk Manager—Professional Risk Managers' International Association [PRMIA]) designation or the FRM (Financial Risk Manager—Global Association of Risk Professionals [GARP]) designation. More than 1,000 people in the financial industry are similarly certified in Poland.

After the intensive telephone interviews, we changed the strategy of increasing the POLRISK membership. POLRISK, after two years of pilot risk management courses, confirmed that there was an interest in risk management professional development, and now it is updating the program scope of knowledge necessary for risk managers and chief risk officers, who will be expected to present a holistic big picture of the company's risks. Fortunately, we will also join with the FERMA certification of risk managers projects like the other European associations that are members of FERMA.

When we showed one example of a mature ERM implementation in North America, one of the Polish managers told us that ERM promoted by middle-level managers looks like "a cry for help" for those who would like to be recognized at the board level. Many risk management group discussions on LinkedIn only confirm that statement. This is the most radical but real opinion on ERM we have ever heard. Again, this was a lesson for us; we, as a community, have to be well prepared to know what specifics strictly belong to ERM and how it can be integrated with strategic and value-based management.

WHAT NUMBERS SAY ABOUT ERM MATURITY

One of our surveys showed that about 2 percent of the companies were willing to implement ERM in 2006, and this increased to around 12 percent in 2010. However, most of the companies that have implemented ERM have fewer than 250 employees. Only 2 percent of companies with more than 250 employees had implemented ERM by 2010. This shows that Polish companies are still at the beginning of the ERM journey.

The survey in 2006 was based on the information obtained from about 100 companies and in 2010 the information was collected from about 300 managers. The ERM implementation was divided into six stages, where stage 0 means no ERM and stage 5 means ERM is an integrated system. The characteristics of all stages are described as follows:

- No functions, organizational structure, and analytical tools are in place to be available for ERM, and there are no plans to implement ERM. (**Phase 0: No ERM**)
- There are some initial preparations toward ERM implementation. (**Phase 1: ERM Introduction**)
- There exist selected tools and instruments in the analytical area applied for ERM. (**Phase 2: ERM Analytical Tools and Instruments**)
- There are some functions, processes, procedures, and tools implemented for ERM. (**Phase 3: ERM Functions, Processes, and Tools**)
- There is a mature infrastructure applied to risk management, but an integrated ERM system doesn't exist, which would be heading toward the holistic approach. There are plans to develop existing infrastructure toward an integrated ERM system. (**Phase 4: ERM Mature but No Integrated System**)
- There is an integrated system of ERM. (**Phase 5: ERM Integrated System**)

In Exhibit 33.4, we display in graphic mode the stages of ERM implementation in Poland and their major characteristics.

Exhibit 33.5 reflects the advancement of ERM within the companies in Poland in 2006. About 42 percent of the enterprises were not applying any type of ERM, and none of them had an ERM integrated system. Only 2 percent of the enterprises had mature ERM systems, 23 percent were in the introductory phase, 8 percent had

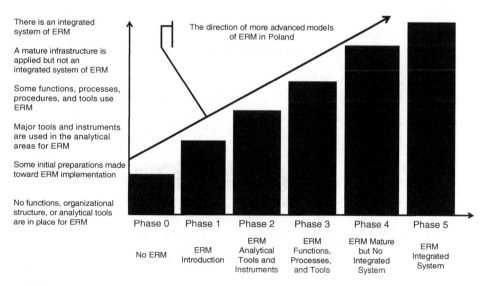

Exhibit 33.4   Stages of ERM Development

Source: Author research, Z. Krysiak.

What is the stage of the ERM development? : 2006

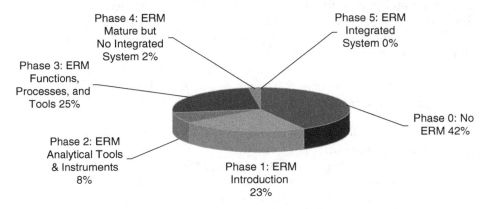

Exhibit 33.5 Stages of ERM Development in 2006 in Poland
Source: Author research, Z. Krysiak.

available analytical tools, and 25 percent implemented ERM functions, processes, and tools.

Exhibit 33.6 reveals the advancement in ERM within the companies in Poland in 2010. We observed that from 2006 until 2010 there was significant progress in the advancement of ERM implementation. An integrated ERM system was present in 12 percent of the companies versus 0 percent in 2006. We observed as well that in 2010 more enterprises (4 percent) had switched to mature ERM, compared to the 2 percent in 2006. In 2010, about 40 percent of the companies still were not engaged in ERM, which is very close to that observed in 2006 (42 percent). The advancement in ERM was made basically by the group of companies that in 2006 had started the process.

What is the stage of the ERM development? : 2010

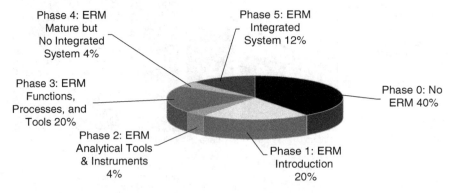

Exhibit 33.6 Stages of ERM Development in 2010 in Poland
Source: Author research, Z. Krysiak.

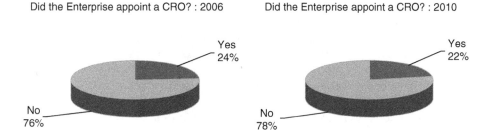

Exhibit 33.7   Appointment of CROs in Polish Companies
Source: Author research, Z. Krysiak.

RISK MANAGEMENT FRAMEWORK—ACCOUNTABILITY

In Exhibit 33.7, we show how many Polish companies have appointed a CRO. The responsibility for leading the risk functions in the company, as measured by appointing a CRO, was reported by 24 percent of companies in 2006, and 22 percent of companies in 2010. Approximately 80 percent of the companies did not see this as an important issue. In later research (i.e., the Polish Edition of the Aon Global Risk Management Survey), the existence of a risk management department or a CRO was reported as 29 percent in 2011 and 25 percent in 2013.

In Exhibit 33.8, we show who was appointed with the CRO responsibility. For 2010, the CRO function was performed in about 81 percent of the cases by financial directors versus 43 percent in 2006. This shows that the responsibility of a CRO is moving to a more appropriate level, and that enterprises are recognizing the importance of ERM. The same scope of research in the Polish Edition of the Aon Global Risk Management Survey showed that if there is no risk management department in companies operating in Poland, then the CEO and CFO are the key job positions responsible for ERM; that is: CEO in 2009, 30 percent of answers; in

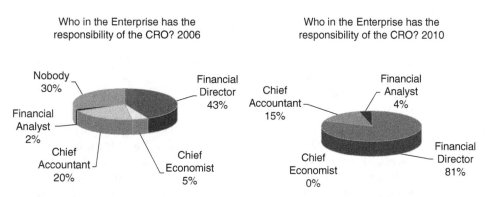

Exhibit 33.8   Functional Managers Charged with the Responsibility of the CRO in Enterprises in Poland
Source: Author research, Z. Krysiak.

2011, 39 percent; and in 2013, 34 percent; and CFO in 2009, 30 percent; in 2011, 52 percent; and in 2013, 31 percent. These results were different than in the Global Edition of Aon's survey; that is, the CFO was the key role in 35 percent of the cases versus 25 percent for the CEO in 2013. In turn, if companies have a risk management department in Poland, the role of the CFO is a leader both in the Polish Edition and the Global Edition of the Aon survey. The question "To whom does the Risk Management Department report?" was that RM reports to the CFO/treasury as follows: in 2009, 45 percent; in 2011, 42 percent; and in 2013, 51 percent.

IMPACT OF THE RISK ASSESSMENT TOOLS ON THE PERFORMANCE OF THE COMPANIES

The quality of risk management depends very much on the tools, analytical models, and resources available at the enterprise. This area was included in the research to find out how different risk and value measures and metrics are quantified, modeled, and used in the decision-making process during the creation and updating of the strategic planning and also the shaping of the overall ERM process. This study was based on approximately 100 companies in Poland operating in different businesses in several geographical markets, including international and global markets, and of different sizes. The criteria to diagnose the quality of risk management were:

- Type of methods used for the company valuation
- Application of discounted cash flow (DCF) analysis for project appraisal
- Utilization of Monte Carlo simulation
- Evaluation of investment projects supported with the real option method
- Assessment of the enterprise's default risk in both the short term and the long term
- Comparison of the dynamics in company value and its risk
- Estimation of the enterprise's losses due to risk realization
- Analysis study on the adequacy of the company's capital against the estimated risk
- Credit, market, and operational risk analysis
- Monitoring of the risk profile from different specific perspectives
- CRO functions and responsibilities
- Organizational and human resources dedicated to ERM
- Stage of the development of ERM within the enterprise
- Types of financial instruments and the scope of their applications to ERM

Based on these criteria, we evaluated the frequency and the quality of the practice of all issues related to the criteria. The evaluation led to our rating of the risk management quality in the enterprises. The rating was designed to be an integrated measure to differentiate the quality of risk management among the enterprises. This rating was related to the financial results to reveal the impact of ERM on company value. Proving a positive relationship between the rating of risk management and the enterprise value would provide a very attractive measure for the partial assessment of the risk management quality and the maturity of ERM.

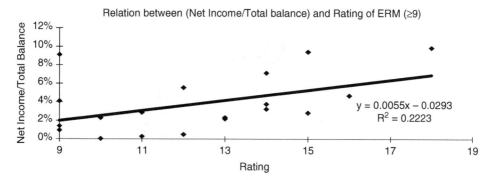

Exhibit 33.9   Relationship between Net Income/Total Balance Ratio and Rating of ERM (Rating ≥9)

Source: Author research, Z. Krysiak.

The relationship between the financial results and the rating of the risk management quality is displayed in Exhibit 33.9. The financial results are reflected by the ratio of net income to total balance. The regression in Exhibit 33.9 relates to the enterprises with high ratings equal to or over 9. We can draw the conclusion that high ratings showing good quality of risk management have a positive impact on the financial results. From the statistical point of view this correlation is not very strong, but as a practical matter it can be interpreted as positive. The improvement in the quality of risk management in the future can be observed in an increasing value of R^2. The high deviations of the financial results for the enterprises with the same ratings mean that the tools, models, instruments, and other technical resources in the process of ERM are applied in various companies with different final effects.

In contrast, Exhibit 33.10 shows no relationship between financial results and the rating of risk management quality for the enterprises with ratings below 9. Additionally, Exhibit 33.10 shows that the deviations of the financial results for the

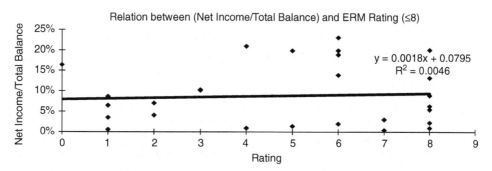

Exhibit 33.10   Relationship between Net Income/Total Balance Ratio and Rating of ERM (Rating ≤8)

Source: Author research, Z. Krysiak.

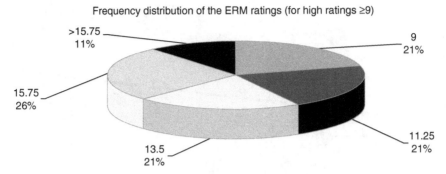

Frequency distribution of the ERM ratings (for high ratings ≥9)

Exhibit 33.11   Frequency Distribution of ERM Ratings for High Ratings ≥9
Source: Author research, Z. Krysiak.

same ratings are very high, which indicates that low ratings reveal a low quality of risk management.

In Exhibit 33.11 we show the frequency distribution of ERM ratings equal to or over 9. Exhibit 33.11 also demonstrates that the enterprises are in different stages of ERM implementation. The progress in the implementation of ERM tools for the companies with high ratings is quite evenly spread out. There are about 21 percent of the companies in each group with ratings of 9, 11.25, and 13.5. The rating of 15.75 was assigned to 26 percent of the studied companies, and 11 percent received ratings over 15.75.

The study of the more detailed financial reports for the companies with the high ratings, which was performed for the five years preceding the case study, indicates that the financial results of different types (i.e., from profit and loss, balance sheet, and cash flow statements) reveal increasing trends and low volatility over time. The enterprises with high ratings show consistency between the goals stated in the strategy and the execution of the strategy. The companies operating in international markets, and those with foreign shareholders, usually achieved high ratings. Based on the outcomes shown in Exhibits 33.9 and 33.10, we can draw the very rough conclusion that the criteria used for the evaluation of the quality of risk management in this case study are useful to obtain a good diagnosis.

CAPITAL ALLOCATION: A FREQUENTLY MISSED PART OF THE ERM FRAMEWORK AND RISK TREATMENT

One of the key issues in ERM is the allocation of capital based on the identified risks. The capital at risk or capital on risk (CoR) in financial institutions is called the economic capital and is estimated based on the value at risk approach (Jorion 2007). This capital should play an important role in protecting the enterprise against the default risk. The allocation of the capital for risk, based on the quantification of the potential risk impact, may be called a risk budgeting process. The ability to assess the capital based on risk may be perceived as a kind of maturity in the evolution of ERM. One of the important standards of ERM in supporting the development

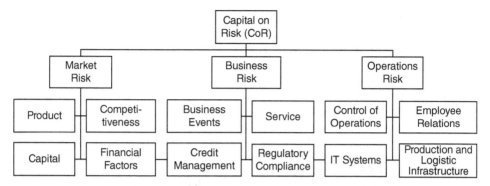

Exhibit 33.12   Examples of Main Risk Sources to Be Covered by Capital on Risk
Source: Author research, Z. Krysiak.

of the strategy is the identification of the most important risks (e.g., the top 10) out of the dozens or hundreds inherent with the enterprise's activities. From that perspective, the identification of risks and the quality of the budgeting process impact the accuracy of the estimated capital required.

The study of the risk profiles within the enterprises in Poland involved 36 types of different risks. These risks have been characterized by measures like the probability of risky events, the exposure from risky events, and the level of control over risk drivers or risk sources. Exhibit 33.12 displays the classification of the studied risks. At the bottom there are 12 subgroups of risk. Each subgroup was further subdivided into three detailed risks, so that we finally obtained 36 specific risks.

The study was performed at the end of 2010 by obtaining information from approximately 300 managers from different types of companies. We think that the only approach to modeling of the economic capital underestimates its value because models do not consider decision-maker perceptions about the risks. We assumed that managers as the decision makers have appropriate business understanding and that they provide substantial information about risk characteristics regarding all business processes. The collection of the data from the managers across the different businesses and functional areas of activity demonstrated an adequate knowledge about the risky events, the importance of particular types of risks, relationships between the risk outcomes, and the level of risk control. Based on this research, we determined the expected average risk impact across industries in Poland and the value of the economic capital.

Exhibit 33.13 shows the 10 most important risks and the level of control assigned to each risk. The level of control of 5 would be the highest control, while 0 would mean that no control is in place. The most important risks within the top 10 perceived by managers in Poland are shareholder and stakeholder relations, cost structure, and solvency and cash flow. At the very bottom of that list are investment projects' strategy, business continuity and downtime, and fraud, theft, reliability, quality.

The research confirms also how an important part of the risk management process in ISO 31000 is communication and consultation with stakeholders. We have to implement very efficient controls here, such as high managerial competencies

Exhibit 33.13 Top 10 Risks in Enterprises in Poland in Respect to Level of Risk Control

Top Risks	Level of Risk Control
Shareholder and stakeholder relations	3.80
Cost structure	3.76
Solvency and cash flow	3.53
Quality of products and services	3.47
Products and services offered	3.47
Credit capacity and creditworthiness	3.44
Liquidity of funding sources	3.44
Investment projects' strategy	3.40
Business continuity and downtime	3.36
Fraud, theft, reliability, quality	3.36

Source: Author research, Z. Krysiak.

and communication skills in order to properly manage board perceptions (see the 10 key points listed earlier in the section titled "Board Perception of ERM."

The assessment of the probability of risks, exposures, and level of controls was used to calculate expected losses, as presented in Exhibit 33.14, which afterward served to calculate the capital on risk. Based on the data obtained from the study, the expected value of the capital on risk should be three to five times that of the net income (NI).

This implies that by increasing the equity by the value of capital on risk, which should be invested in liquid and risk-free assets, the return on equity (ROE) would be reduced. Assuming that current ROE equals 20 percent, return on risk-free assets equals 5 percent, and there is no change in the net income, then the increase of the equity to between three and fives times NI would drop the ROE down to between 14.5 percent and 12.5 percent, respectively. The other consequence of that is the change in the structure of the capital, which potentially could lead to the increase in the weighted average cost of capital. The risk inherent in the enterprise

Exhibit 33.14 Top 10 Risks in Enterprises in Poland in Respect to Expected Losses

Top Risks	Value of Expected Losses in Relation to Net Income
Cost structure	0.14
Management of malfunctions	0.14
Business continuity and downtime	0.13
Liquidity of funding sources	0.12
Account receivables	0.12
Fraud, theft, reliability, quality	0.12
Solvency and cash flow	0.12
Shareholder and stakeholder relations	0.11
Management and responsibilities	0.11
Products and services offered	0.10

Source: Author research, Z. Krysiak.

is not cheap. This example shows that, on one hand, an enterprise pays approximately one-quarter of ROE, but on the other hand, this expense could save the enterprise in case one or more risk events materialize.

CONCLUSION

If we want to change our companies to be risk-based managed companies, ERM must be sold as an integral part of a triple package: value-based management, strategic management, and strategy execution, with ERM as an important link between these. Critical changes in the positioning of ERM as part of such a package are necessary to move from governance-driven phases to being change driven (or the integrated phase of risk management maturity).

The top 10 risks identified by our research show that, from a framework perspective, key risks are correlated with management and stakeholder expectations and perceptions. This confirms that the communication and consultation process is a critical part of the risk management process defined in ISO 31000, and it must be performed by highly skilled managers or other professionals with little tolerance for mistakes.

Experts and managers need to use consistent and easy-to-understand risk-related terminology across all stages of the risk management process to facilitate proper and efficient communication. The simpler, the better. People have problems with differentiating data from information, hence the problem of mixing risk information with threat data or opportunity data instead of considering information on both threat and opportunity. It is important for communication to express that risk is a relationship between potential causes and effects, and these two may never be totally separated. Risk management is a never-ending learning experience and reminds us to keep terminology and language consistent throughout, as to the principles, framework, and risk management process being integrated with strategy planning, execution, and value-based management and controls.

Exhibit 33.15 shows the results from our experience, business practice, and research. ERM in Poland is mainly driven by governance concerns, which apply to around 12 to 20 percent of 3,000 companies with over 250 employees. As for branches interested in holistic risk management (such as energy, gas and oil, construction, logistics, insurance, telecommunications, pharmaceuticals, chemicals, mining, public administration, aviation, and legal companies), this is a good basis for change. Because a public finance act and obligation include risk management as part of managerial supervision, risk awareness will be communicated to around 40 percent of the working population in Poland, as many people work in public administration. Taking into account the obstacles and challenges we have in Poland, there is much good news. It would be worth further research to observe how Poland progresses in relation to other countries. That would give us all, as an international community, the ability to observe how well ERM is progressing, worldwide or not. There is already some research in this area—for example, Aon's Risk Maturity Index.

We must be aware of the weaknesses of risk management in the context of human attitudes. The perception of top executives and boards is that risk still has negative connotations in many languages and cultures and it is a natural barrier. Not everyone is keen to talk about risk; people like to concentrate on successes and

Exhibit 33.15   ERM Maturity Level in Poland's Nonfinancial Industry

	Stage 1	Stage 2	Stage 3	Stage 4
Terminology	Risk specific Never-ending challenge			
Principles	Risk specific	Governance driven		
Framework	Risk specific	Governance driven		
Process	Risk specific	Governance driven	Change driven A few companies	Integrated A few companies on the way, POLRISK members, energy industry

Source: Authors' research.

opportunities. Also, managers may resist talking about risk in order not to be perceived as incompetent professionals. They assume that if they are professionally good at something, they should not be generating risks.

Medium-sized firms may need less integration of strategic management with risk management due to the lack of silos in those companies, as "the left hand knows what the right hand is doing." What they need is up-to-date and online information, reports on how the business is performing, and what is the margin level. They need a reasonable risk management tool kit and supervision of margins.

A strong risk management profession with a defined scope of knowledge is necessary to promote risk management. The natural reporting line for a risk manager within an organization structure should be to the CFO or higher, and be aligned with the value-based controlling and strategy department or unit. Those departments should be working in integrated ways so that proper capital and asset resource allocation is made toward identified risk levels and cost/benefit analysis with integrated risk treatment options across the company.

A strong risk management association is also necessary to promote best practices in risk management and the gathering community of risk management professionals. In 2013, POLRISK changed its mission to the creation of value from effective risk management integrated with strategic management and value-based management. The promotion of ERM as a concept is no longer sufficient; there must be demonstrated value creation for a company arising out of it. The ERM journey continues.

QUESTIONS

1. List and describe the challenges of implementing ERM in Poland.
2. The quality of risk management depends on many criteria. Discuss the criteria that can be used.
3. What were the main drivers for ERM implementation in Poland?

NOTES

1. More information on the POLRISK Risk Management Association can be found at the association's website: www.polrisk.pl.
2. More information on the Federation of European Risk Management Associations can be found at www.ferma.eu.
3. We would like to mention and honor here all the people we know, but we are aware that this would be an imperfect and incomplete list. However, we are sure that on such a list there are at least POLRISK founding members; former presidents Rafal Rudnicki and Tomasz Miazek; current POLRISK board members Ewa Szpakowska, Hanna Gołaś, and Jerzy Podlewski; and all active previous and current POLRISK members.
4. The need for evaluating the quality and extent of risk treatments, including controls, is essential, and the techniques for including this in risk assessments are described in *Enterprise Risk Management: Today's Leading Research and Best Practices for Tomorrow's Executives*, edited by John Fraser and Betty J. Simkins (Hoboken, NJ: John Wiley & Sons, 2010), on pages 162, 163, 166, 173, and 174.
5. The Statement of Context is an output from the "Establishing the context (5.3)" stage of the risk management process (Clause 5 Process in ISO 31000:2009 standard).

REFERENCES

Antikarov, V. 2012. "Enterprise Risk Management for Non-Financial Companies—From Risk Control and Compliance to Creating Shareholder Value." ERM, Society of Actuaries Monograph M–AS12–1, Chicago. www.soa.org/Library/Monographs/Other-Monographs/2012/April/2012-Enterprise-Risk-Management-Symposium/.

Bossidy, L., and R. Charan, with C. Burck. 2002. *Execution: The Discipline of Getting Things Done*. New York: Crown Business.

Copeland, T., and V. Antikarov. 2003. *Real Options*. New York: Texere.

Fraser, John, and Betty J. Simkins, eds. 2010. *Enterprise Risk Management: Today's Leading Research and Best Practices for Tomorrow's Executives*. Robert W. Kolb Series in Finance. Hoboken, NJ: John Wiley & Sons.

Jorion, Philippe. 2007. *Value at Risk: The New Benchmark for Managing Financial Risk*. New York: McGraw-Hill.

Kaplan, R. S., and D. P. Norton. 2008. *The Execution Premium: Linking Strategy to Operations for Competitive Advantage*. Boston: Harvard Business School Publishing.

Krysiak, Z. 2011. "Strong Risk Management Culture as a Major Factor at Modern Organization" (Polish title, *Silna kultura zarządzania ryzykiem jako cecha nowoczesnej organizacji*). *e-Mentor* 2:39, s. 24–31.

Krysiak, Z. 2013. "The Value of the Operational Risk in the Holistic Approach" (Polish title, *Wartość ryzyka operacyjnego banku w ujęciu holistycznym*). *Bezpieczny Bank* 1:50, s. 112–129.

Lam, James. 2003. *Enterprise Risk Management: From Incentives to Control*. Hoboken, NJ: John Wiley & Sons.

Monahan, Gregory. 2008. *Enterprise Risk Management—A Methodology for Achieving Strategic Objectives*. Hoboken, NJ: John Wiley & Sons.

Pagach, Donald, and Richard Warr. 2011. "The Characteristics of Firms That Hire Chief Risk Officers." *Journal of Risk and Insurance* 78:1, 185–211.

Peters, T., and R. H. Waterman Jr. 1982. *In Search of Excellence: Lessons from America's Best-Run Companies*. New York: Harper & Row; Profile Books, 2004.

Pijanowski, S. P. 2005–2006. "Is the Polish Stock Market Weak Form Efficient?" *International Journal of Banking and Finance* 3/4 (Special Issue), 33–62. (Journal of North Malaysia University.) The eight papers in this special issue were selected after blind peer review as the top papers among 144 papers submitted for publication. http://epublications.bond.edu.au/cgi/viewcontent.cgi?article=1041&context=ijbf.

Purdy, G. 2010. "How Good Is Our Risk Management? How Boards Should Find Out." *Risk Watch*, The Conference Board of Canada, December, 9–11.

Purdy, G. 2013. "Most Effective and Efficient Way of Managing Risk." Workshop material for POLRISK Risk Management Association, Warsaw, May 9.

Rappaport, A. 1998. *Creating Shareholder Value: A Guide for Managers and Investors*. New York: Free Press.

Raynor, M. E. 2007. *The Strategy Paradox*. Warsaw: Studio EMKA.

Shimpi, P. 1999. *Integrating Corporate Risk Management*. New York: Texere.

Shimpi, P. 2005. "Enterprise Risk Management from Compliance to Value." *Financial Executive* 21:6, 52–55.

Welch, Jack, with Suzy Welch. 2005. *Winning*. New York: HarperBusiness.

Wiklund, D., and B. Rabkin. 2009. "The Balance Sheet Perspective of Enterprise Risk Management." *Financial Executive* 25:2, 54–58.

ABOUT THE CONTRIBUTORS

Zbigniew Krysiak, PhD, is an Associate Professor of Finance at the Warsaw School of Economics in Warsaw, Poland. He gained a doctor of philosophy degree in economics from Warsaw School of Economics for his research into the application of options in default risk assessment and company valuation. He holds an MBA (master's degree in banking and financial engineering) from the University of Toulouse, France. He was a visiting professor at Pepperdine University in Los Angeles and Northeastern Illinois University in Chicago. Currently, he is teaching students at Northeastern Illinois University on financial engineering in business applications. He is the author or coauthor of more than 100 publications, intended both for practitioners and for the academic community, concerning finance, risk management, financial engineering, and banking.

Dr. Krysiak has about 25 years' experience in business, working for European and American nonfinancial and financial enterprises. The functions he has held include: management board member of Bank Guarantee Fund, managing director of the Property Finance division and adviser to the president at PKO Bank, vice president of the management board at Intelligo Bank, vice president at AIG Bank, financial manager at PepsiCo in Poland, and member of the supervisory board at the insurance company TU Europa. He was a member of the European Banking Industry Committee (EBIC), and a member of the Mortgage Funding Expert Group (MFEG) at the European Commission. He is a member of the Scientific Committee of the Warsaw Stock Exchange in Poland.

Sławomir Pijanowski, PhD, is President of the POLRISK Risk Management Association in Poland, where he is responsible for development of good risk management practices for the Polish market. He is a member of the Technical Committee No. 6 Management Systems at the Polish Committee for Standardization, a member of ISO/TC 262 Committee, where he was one of four task leaders elaborating on the first draft of the ISO 31004 standard, Risk Management—Guidance for the Implementation. He is coauthor of *Risk Management for Sustainable Business*, published by the Polish Ministry of the Economy. He initiated and completed the project of adoption of the ISO 31000:2009 standard into Polish PN-ISO 31000:2012, Risk Management—Principles and Guidelines.

Dr. Pijanowski has had long-term experience in the areas of change management, organizational transformation, strategic-level program and project management, business continuity, IT security, banking, and business systems implementations. He was coauthor of the methodology of one of the first Polish implementations of ERM in a leading telecommunications company in Poland. He verified the quality of the risk registers of the Orange Technological Partnership in UEFA EURO 2012 Football Championships in Poland. He acted as an external expert for the National Foresight Program "Poland 2020" in the following research fields: safety, information technology (IT), and information and communications technology (ICT). His PhD is from the Poznań University of Economics, department of investment and capital markets, where he also graduated from the Faculty of Management with a specialty in capital investments and financial strategies of enterprises.

CHAPTER 34

Turning Crisis into Opportunity

Building an ERM Program at General Motors

MARC S. ROBINSON
Assistant Director, Enterprise Risk Management, GM

LISA M. SMITH
Assistant Director, Enterprise Risk Management, GM

BRIAN D. THELEN
General Auditor, GM

T his case study chronicles the ground-up implementation of enterprise risk management (ERM) at General Motors Company (GM), starting in 2010 through the first four years of implementation. Discussion topics include lessons learned during implementation and some of the unique approaches, tools, and techniques that GM has employed. Examples of senior management reporting are also included.

> I think risk management is an element of all good executive management teams and boards. It will ensure viability in downturns and high-risk periods. I think if that is done not only within the automotive industry, but on a global and specifically on a national scale, economies will be in better shape because it is additive. If everybody is doing their job in assessing and understanding risk, the ultimate outcome will be much more positive for our national economy and society, and it is incumbent that corporate leadership understands that responsibility.
> —*Daniel F. Akerson, Chairman and Chief Executive Officer,*
> *General Motors, October 2012*

BACKGROUND AND IMPLEMENTATION

The enterprise risk management (ERM) program at General Motors was founded in late 2010 at the direction of GM's then newly appointed chief executive officer (CEO), Daniel F. Akerson, who sought to leverage the program as another means to achieve a competitive advantage in the industry. Having gone through bankruptcy in 2009 as a new board member, Akerson felt that a more robust risk management program would help guide the organization around the drivers of killer risks[1] going forward. His goal was to help the company ensure that it was prepared, agile, and fast to respond in an ever-changing world. Perhaps most importantly, Akerson wanted an ERM program that would focus not only on risks but on opportunities as well.

A chief risk officer (CRO) was selected and appointed from within, and the Finance and Risk Policy Committee of the board of directors was chartered to oversee risk management as well as financial strategies and policies. In support of the program, a senior manager and director joined the team. Risk officers were also identified and aligned to all direct reports of the CEO; this helped to ensure that all aspects of the business were covered. The CEO is the ultimate chief risk officer, and his direct reports are the ultimate risk owners. Members of the risk officer team were carefully selected by senior leadership based on their strong business experience, financial acumen, and most of all their ability to lead in the identification and discussion of risk in an objective and transparent manner. These representatives were expected to actively participate in the evolving ERM program while still handling their existing responsibilities.

In 2011, the general auditor and CRO roles were combined, and in support of this change, the Audit Committee assumed oversight of risk management. The Finance and Risk Policy Committee continued its focus on financial policy and decision making.

GENERAL MOTORS' APPROACH TO ENTERPRISE RISK MANAGEMENT

The ERM process was built with GM's vision in mind: to design, build, and sell the world's best vehicles (see Exhibit 34.1). The process itself was geared toward the identification and management of key (potential "killer") risks. The ERM team assisted line management in developing a list of top company risks, identifying risk owners, assisting management in the development of risk mitigation plans in conjunction with the management teams, providing ongoing monitoring, and reporting results to senior management and the board.

The scope of GM's initial ERM program intentionally did not fit the typical ERM definition of an all-encompassing, holistic approach. As a bottom-up implementation, senior leadership wanted ERM to focus on those elements of risk and opportunity that were most important to the company. We at GM have since enhanced our program with additional high-impact features, which are detailed later in this chapter.

Overall, however, our approach was to move away from the typical ERM view, which focuses on "what can go wrong." We took a more actionable view of "what can go right," placing emphasis on both opportunities and risks, to ensure that we were leveraging our ERM program to be well-positioned in the industry.

Lessons Learned: Identifying Risks

A critical success factor that has been a part of our program since inception has been to continually seek out several views, including views from sources outside the company, of risks that the industry and company may face. In addition to regular meetings with our risk officers, we conducted a number of focus groups and

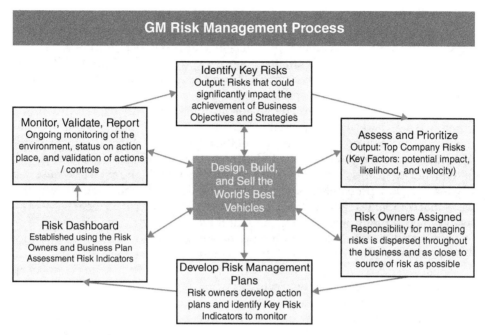

Exhibit 34.1   GM Risk Management Process

workshops to gain insight into potential blind spots that may exist, and to capture various views on emerging risks. To solicit this information, we reached out to deep thinkers and those with broad business experience both within and outside of our organization and sought input across demographic groups, including Generation Ys or recent college graduates and young professionals.

The careful attention devoted to capturing several perspectives from various demographics, both inside and outside of the organization, has led to some great successes and has consistently influenced the composition of our top risks list. Our commitment to seeking out diverse views has helped us to avoid confirmation bias,[2] and helped us to ensure that we are not seeing our world through rose-colored glasses.

Lessons Learned: Developing Top Risks Lists and Reporting to Senior Management

There is a tendency to underestimate risks. If you go back and look at the problems we ran into over the last four to five years, everybody knew there was a housing bubble there. Everybody knew the banks and others were stretched out. But rather than face up to the fact that you had this huge risk and understand what the consequences were of the risk materializing, it was relatively easy to say, "Well, it is a low-probability risk, so let's go on—things look good." It may be a low-probability event, but those low-probability events have a way of materializing, and therefore we need to better understand what happens.

—*Mustafa Mohatarem, Chief Economist, General Motors, October 2012*

While we understand the value of assessing probability and impact for risks, we have made additional improvements to our process for ranking and prioritizing risks. In the past, we facilitated meetings at which our risk officers were asked to score proposed risks individually along defined impact and probability scales. The output of the session was a typical "heat map" with risks that were ranked or plotted based on probability and impact scores.

However, we quickly learned that not only was this a very tedious process, but it injected a great deal of subjectivity since many of the participants did not really have specific knowledge of these parts of the business. We have also learned from various world events, such as the Fukushima disaster in Japan, that there may be a tendency to dismiss risks with the potential for very high impact because they have a very low probability of occurring. These low-probability events are often risks that companies cannot afford to miss. As we looked back on what has worked well or needed improvement, we thought there was a better way to provide our board and other stakeholders with more meaningful and actionable information. This prompted us to make a number of changes to improve the program.

First, we gave the responsibility for assessing the probability and impact ratings related to risk to the senior executives who were assigned the primary responsibility for overseeing the risks, since they were uniquely positioned to provide the most accurate assessment. We stopped the practice of asking risk officers to vote on impact and likelihood levels. Instead, when developing (or refreshing) the top risks list, we employed a real-time, web-based pairwise comparison[3] tool to assist in prioritizing the risks in relation to each other. When developing our top risks, we briefed participants (risk officers) with precise risk descriptions to help enable their decisions when voting on each risk pair. Once we completed the various pairing sequences, the tool generated our preliminary risks list. This preliminary list was then subjected to various sense checks[4] prior to delivering a proposed top risks list to our senior management or board.

Second, we moved away from using a ranked top risks list altogether. Too much time was being spent on whether a risk should be number 3 or number 5, for example, when the choice did not at all affect how the ERM team or management would address the risk. We moved instead to a three-tiered approach (Exhibit 34.2), which more broadly separated risks by their relative importance. We did not limit ourselves to any predefined number of risks in any given tier; we looked for natural breaks in terms of concurrence on what is a top risk (often looking at the pairwise scoring) versus what is more of an emerging risk.

Third, we focused on using three measures—the levels of inherent, current, and residual risk—as indicators of where the organization currently viewed the effect of its mitigation activity and where the level of risk was expected to be upon completion of the mitigation plans. We created a five-point scale with definitions surrounding the ratings for inherent and residual risks (see Exhibit 34.3), and asked the respective risk officers to provide these assessments in consultation with their Executive Committee members (GM senior leaders reporting directly to the CEO) using the ERM risk template. While just a minor modification to the previous ERM risk template, this assessment of current and expected future risk levels quickly became a focal point for senior management and the board committees when presented. With current and future risk levels now documented, we were able to provide the board with better insight into the status and projected movement of our

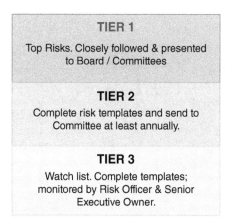

TIER 1

Top Risks. Closely followed & presented to Board / Committees

TIER 2

Complete risk templates and send to Committee at least annually.

TIER 3

Watch list. Complete templates; monitored by Risk Officer & Senior Executive Owner.

Exhibit 34.2   Three-Tiered Approach

top risks (see Exhibit 34.4). We continued to provide the standard heat map of risks, but the new chart provided the type of forward-looking insight and status that heat maps do not provide. The new chart has been very well received and we continue to utilize it.

Lessons Learned: Understanding Corporate Culture

The ERM implementation at General Motors has enjoyed great success for several reasons: There has been excellent support from the CEO and senior management; we have a strong, knowledgeable, and highly engaged ERM team and risk officer organization that touches every part of the business; and we have been able to garner proactive involvement through understanding and properly leveraging corporate culture.

We recognized early on that we would need to ensure that the ERM environment at General Motors was an open forum where people could share freely. In fact, the importance of objectivity and transparency cannot be understated in terms of the success of any ERM program. Perhaps it is attributable to human nature, but we found in the past that people had a tendency to identify a problem and keep it to themselves while they tried to resolve or address it, rather than putting it on the table for discussion. As this was not the culture that we wanted in the ERM program, we reduced the probability that this would occur by selecting the right people to lead by example.

We looked for several specific traits when selecting our risk officers:

- High potential executives and leaders
- Strong business experience and good financial acumen, including strong technical expertise in the region/function of responsibility
- Superior communication skills; unafraid to speak up and discuss issues openly
- Big picture thinkers

Inherent Risk Scale

Rating	Definition
1 – Minimal	Minimal level of business risk.
2 – Low	The inherent risk could at most result in an impact under USD $X or produce a relatively minor impact on the company's ability to meet strategic goals or execute its priority initiatives.
3 – Moderate	The inherent risk could at most allow financial exposure up to USD $X, or have a moderate negative impact on the company's ability to meet strategic goals or execute priority initiatives.
4 – Significant	The inherent risk could result in significant negative consequences as measured by either: Financial impact of USD $X; Important impediments to achieving strategic business initiatives; Corporate, brand or reputational risk. Senior management attention is required to support risk mitigation plans as well as reduce impediments.
5 – Critical	Potential for catastrophic, negative impact if financial, strategic or reputational risk is not properly managed. Financial exposure could exceed USD $X. Senior management and Board attention to these risks is needed.

Residual Risk Scale

Rating	Definition
1 – Acceptable	The implemented mitigation plans provide assurance that the amount of residual risk is minimal and within the company's risk tolerance (if defined).
2 – Low	The residual risk could at most result in an impact under USD $X or produce a relatively minor impact on the company's ability to meet strategic goals or execute its priority initiatives.
3 – Moderate	The residual risk that remains once mitigation plans have been implemented could at most allow exposure up to USD $X, or have a moderate impact on the company's ability to meet strategic goals or execute priority initiatives.
4 – Significant	While mitigation plans are in place the level of residual risk status could still result in significant negative consequences as follows: Financial impact of USD $X; Important impediments to achieving strategic business initiatives still exist; or significant corporate, brand or reputational risk still exists. Senior management attention is required to support risk mitigation plans as well as reduce impediments.
5 – Critical	Mitigation plans are either not yet in place or cannot reduce the amount of residual risk to a reasonable level. Potential for catastrophic, negative impact if financial, strategic or reputational risk not properly managed. Financial exposure could exceed USD $X. Senior management and Board attention to these risks is needed.

Exhibit 34.3 Five-Point Scale

- The ability to reach across the organization and provide outstanding support to the top-line executive they represent

To the extent that we had any concerns regarding the ability of participants to be objective and transparent, we were able to largely avoid these issues by seeking out and selecting the right risk officer team members. The team has been highly engaged, and we are beginning to see evidence of this culture spreading through their various areas of accountability. We are now at the point where our services are often on a "pull" rather than "push" basis, which has been very rewarding to achieve.

My role as a risk officer is to look across the product development enterprise, and identify risks which are systemic that we may already be addressing, but I am taking a look to make sure that the risk is sufficiently addressed. Or, in the case of where it is a new technology or a new risk, working with the owner to take a look from a strategic perspective. What can they do more? What can they do better in terms of addressing the risk? Are they engaging all of the cross-functional groups? Do they really understand the societal impacts of the technology they are putting in place? As engineers, we tend to think about $F = MA$,[5] but this is about expanding the scope a little bit more so that we take it at a holistic level.

The ERM program gets quite a bit of support from senior leadership. We regularly review the status of our projects with leadership and we also seek advice and guidance from them on where they see risks in the enterprise that we might not otherwise be addressing in our regular channels.
— *Katherine Johnson, Director, Global Product Development,*
General Motors, October 2012

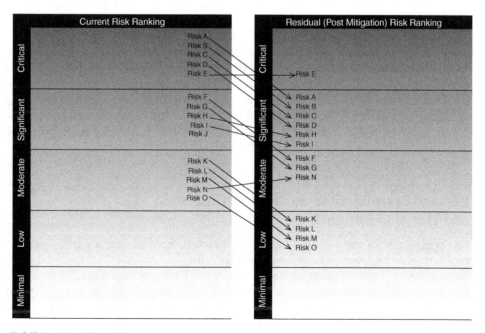

Exhibit 34.4   Heat Map

We also understood that our risk officers came from various functional and regional positions, and would not necessarily be experts in risk management. As a result, we created an orientation/training for risk officers that was very well received. Once the first two individuals were given the orientation we did not have to contact anyone else to take it, as word quickly spread because it was seen as value-added and good use of their time. Risk officers contacted us to ask for the orientation, and this positively impacted the engagement of our program participants.

It was during these orientations that we learned more about various micro cultures in the company. One of the slides in the orientation talked about various risk management techniques: to avoid, accept, reduce, or transfer risk. Early on, as we explained the slide to one risk officer—that there are many ways to deal with risk—he had an insightful comment: "You know, I am really glad that you are implementing this program. Some think that risk is bad and you have to eliminate it 100 percent."

The orientation sessions provided an environment for healthy discussions about risk being ubiquitous and therefore always a part of doing business. We stressed that the intention of this program was to *manage* risk, not attempt to eliminate all risk. To reinforce this, we discussed different ways to deal with identified risks, including accepting them. Going forward, we verbally included these points with every risk officer orientation. This was another means for us to support the transparency and objectivity we sought—people would not feel comfortable talking about risks openly if they thought there was a corporate culture that mandated all risk was to be eliminated.

Our orientation session also included discussions about our risk templates (see Exhibit 34.5). While companies, including General Motors, seem to embrace the use of red-yellow-green-colored charts, the problem of course is that the use of red is often associated with a failure or poor result. We were concerned, given the prior comments, that people might not adequately assess their risks if they believed the point of the program was to make everything green on the charts. At one of our risk officer meetings, a risk officer presented a chart showing a key risk that was rated with an orange color, both before *and* after mitigation efforts. We took time in the meeting to point this out—that some risks "are what they are"—and there is only so much we can do to be prepared. The point is not to get the risk to be rated green, but to assess it *accurately* for what it is, and to ensure that we are prepared and doing everything we reasonably can to deal with it.

Lessons Learned: Strategic Risk Mitigation and Decision Support

The central philosophy of GM's ERM approach is that the responsibility for risk mitigation and opportunity seizing rests with the operational leaders of the company. No staff can or should address all the varied risks of the company; they lack the awareness, expertise, manpower, and authority. But ERM can provide—and has at GM even at this early stage—enormous value beyond the core and critical functions of risk identification and risk education. This is essential to have enterprise *risk* management rather than enterprise *list* management. GM's ERM is able to

Risk Title
Executive Owner:

Risk Definition	Assessment	
[insert approved risk scenario]	Inhernet Risk (<u>before</u> any actions) Current Level of Residual Risk Residual Risk	4 – Siqnificant 2 – Managed 2 – Low

Key Events That Trigger Risk Exposure	Description of Residual Risk
1. Insert Event 2. Insert Event 3. Insert Event 4. Insert Event 5. Insert Event	• Financial: • Strategic: • Reputation: • Other:

Risk Mitigation Actions	Responsibility	Completed / Due Date
1. Insert Improvement Opportunity	Name	Date
2. Insert Improvement Opportunity	Name	Date
3. Insert Improvement Opportunity	Name	Date
4. Insert Improvement Opportunity	Name	Date
5. Insert Improvement Opportunity	Name	Date

Key Risk Indicators	Related Risks / Additional Comments
Insert Key Risk Indicators	Insert Related Risks / Additional Comments

Once Implemented, will risk mitigation actions reduce exposure to an acceptable level? YES / NO

Exhibit 34.5 Risk Template

provide this value because of a combination of a unique perspective and expertise in a set of analysis, facilitation, and decision-support tools of particular relevance to risk mitigation and opportunity seizing.

Through the risk identification process, ERM staff is exposed to the entire range of global functions and issues, along with internal assessments of corporate strengths and weaknesses, in a way that is typically limited to senior management. Risk identification also requires engaging with internal and external thought leaders and experts to think through emerging risks and blind spots to create an information base similar to a partner at a strategy consulting firm. The assignment to focus on risk and opportunity, with a corporate perspective and without operational responsibilities, gives a frame of mind and freedom for strategic thinking that is often helpful to decision makers.

At GM, the unique perspective within ERM is made more valuable with a set of tools that helps decision makers better understand and evaluate issues involving external risks and opportunities, and thereby improve their decisions. Any list of top risks will have both internal risks—typically involving execution or compliance—and external risks, whether from shocks, predictable events, evolutionary changes, or actions from outside actors like competitors, current or potential partners, dealers, suppliers, governments, or unions. Internal execution risks are usually managed with special focus from operating units, while compliance risks are typically addressed by education and controls monitored by specialized staffs such as security, information technology, human resources, legal, tax, and audit.

External risks, on the other hand, are more difficult for operating leaders to evaluate and react to appropriately. There is a natural human tendency to think that tomorrow's external environment will be like today's, only better. Operating leaders tend to focus on their own strategies, worldviews, and "day jobs," failing to fully consider external players and uncertain events.

Even in a negotiation, the tendency to focus on the company's perspective can be a problem. Of course, the negotiating team is aware of the other party at the table—whether a union, supplier, or potential partner. But even experienced negotiating teams can benefit from thinking through systematically what is truly important to both sides and how to improve negotiating leverage and to frame issues. However, the biggest blind spots for negotiators usually relate to parties *not* at the table or to the *aftermath* of a deal. For example, GM often engages in bargaining with its labor unions while those unions are simultaneously bargaining with other companies in the industry. Understanding the perspective and issues in those parallel negotiations can be important to the outcome at GM, particularly since there is often an expectation that the pattern established with one company will apply to others. Union locals or subgroups can also have powerful effects on the final outcome. In other contexts, predicting possible rejection by regulators may lead to a different strategy on a merger or acquisition deal, or understanding legislative risk might alter a corporate initiative. Identifying stresses and differences in interests in advance can lead to favorable restructuring of a joint venture or early resolution of an underlying issue.

GM's ERM staff has adapted a set of tools designed to improve decisions in complex, multiplayer situations or issues. The approach usually involves organizing workshops with cross-functional leaders and subject matter experts, facilitated by ERM staff. When the issue or event is known—such as a major current negotiation or an announced change in fuel economy regulations 10 years in the future—the workshop focuses on answering three questions:

1. Who else can affect the outcome? (Players)
2. What can GM and others do? (Options)
3. What do GM and the other players want? (Preferences)

The importance of thinking through these questions systematically can be shown in a mistake from GM's past. Like other auto companies, GM relies on independently owned dealers to sell its vehicles. In the late 1990s, some GM executives saw the potential for significant strategic benefits from having a few company-owned dealers, such as an unfiltered exposure to shoppers and a chance to test new marketing and retailing concepts. Though it was recognized that dealers would oppose the idea and that it would be illegal in some states, extensive planning proceeded and a major initiative—GM Retail Holdings—was announced. Within days of the announcement, GM quickly realized this was a poor decision, and within months GM's CEO went to the annual dealer association conference to announce the termination of the initiative and to apologize for it.

What happened to cause such an unfortunate outcome? First, the leaders of the initiative misread GM's preferences. They thought that GM valued the potential benefits of the company-owned dealers more than they would regret an adverse dealer reaction. When the angry reaction came forcefully through many channels to numerous executives, it turned out that the assessment was wrong. Second, some options controlled by the dealers were not well understood. When dealers started pulling or threatening to pull some of those levers, GM recognized the decision's downside potential. Third, the executives forgot a player—state legislatures. Legislation was introduced in several states (where GM Retail Holdings was considering the placement of dealerships) that would make company-owned stores illegal competition for the independent dealers, and it seemed likely that the legislation would pass. If you miss preferences, options, and/or a player, your strategy, negotiation, or initiative can fail.

GAME THEORY

When GM's actions will have an impact on what the others do (see Exhibit 34.6), a form of game theory can help avoid misunderstandings. Using game theory,[6] the team can put themselves into the shoes of each player and ask whether they want each option to be taken (including options they do not control) and how important that option is relative to others on the list. With these assessments, it is possible to identify a natural outcome[7]—where momentum will lead the issue—as well as a danger outcome[8] and a target outcome[9] for GM. The information gathered is so rich that it can guide both strategy and tactics. Because there is a tight logical connection between the recommendations and the inputs provided by participants, decisions are often changed based on the analyses.

Since the combined knowledge of the participants about the external players and their options is usually strong, the predictions of their behavior are remarkably accurate. Even when there is disagreement or uncertainty about what other players want, the analysis can identify robust strategies or narrow the areas where additional information is needed. GM used to have a Defense Operations unit that once developed a design for a military vehicle that the designers thought could displace the Humvee[10] used by the U.S. Army. At the time, GM had recently acquired the Hummer brand (since discontinued), which sold a civilian version of the Humvee, so this idea generated significant controversy. Game theory analysis showed that the right actions for GM depended heavily on the preferences of the Army, with disagreement about what they were. GM leaders decided to ask the Army, inviting key generals to hear about the Defense Operations concept. The generals made

Other players	Issue/event known	Issue/event uncertain
Other player(s) decisions important and affected by your actions	Game Theory	Scenario gaming or tabletop
Other player(s) decisions are important but independent	War gaming	Scenario planning

Exhibit 34.6 Game Theory

clear that they had no interest in switching from the Humvee, and further investment was avoided.

The high value that GM leaders attach to the predictions and insights that the game theory process generates is reflected in the more than 120 times the tool has been deployed since 1999. The issues have included negotiations of all types, competitive strategy, public policy strategy, crisis management, and new business development, and have covered every region and most functions. Speed and efficiency are also major attractions; a complex issue can be analyzed and action plans developed and approved in less than one week. When the Risk Management function was created, a natural home for these decision-making tools became obvious.

War Gaming and Scenario Planning

Even when GM decisions do not affect the decisions of other players—as often is the case with long-term product or technology strategies—it can be valuable to think through how other players will act, since that can give a more accurate and unbiased assessment of the risks and opportunities. War gaming workshops often start with known information on the strategies, strengths, weaknesses, and plans of key players. The key trend or issue that is the focus of the war game is explained; for example, there may be tighter fuel economy regulations scheduled to go into effect in some country in a few years. Then participants put themselves in the shoes of the other players and predict their responses to the trend or issue. Implications for GM's strategy and opportunities to mitigate risks are then identified.

When events are highly uncertain or even have low probability, like an economic crisis or oil shock, it can still add value to assess how external actors would respond if the event were to occur. This helps to stress test the contingency plans and can identify potential opportunities or risks to mitigate. By adding external players to the scenario planning, the need to bring in additional functions becomes apparent. If and when the event occurs, the action or crisis team will have a broader perspective and connection to important expertise, and information will be easier to access. The ERM staff can facilitate this type of contingency planning and the cross-organization connections through the risk officer network.

Thinking through how an event can spread or become a crisis makes the organization more sensitive to signals and triggers for more intense planning and preparation. A tool that GM has used in contingency planning is "DefCon" level,[11] an idea borrowed from the U.S. Defense Department. When a risk with high impact but low likelihood is identified, it may not make sense to spend time and resources on detailed plans and preparations, particularly if there is likely to be significant notice or more urgent signals prior to the event. Instead, there can be a "plan to plan" with only preliminary analysis done at an early stage but commitment made for further analysis and action if particular indicators or signals are seen. The leadership group decides whether the event likelihood has reached a more serious DefCon level, triggering the appropriate preparations and actions.

External risks are difficult for any organization to understand and manage, particularly if the risks are only emerging or rare, or involve parties not at the table. By going beyond risk identification to helping decision makers achieve a 360 degree understanding of the external environment and players, ERM can aid good decision making. By using their unique perspective and a broad array of tools, ERM staff can frame the risks and opportunities and make actionable recommendations, thereby making the good decisions more likely and more robust.

LOOKING FORWARD

As we enter our third year of ERM, we have a number of initiatives under way to enhance the ERM program and better integrate it with other internal control efforts. First, we have worked with our internal audit leadership to ensure that the top company risks are being considered in their annual internal audit risk assessment, which drives the internal audit plan. These top risks will be one of many factors used to assess which processes, areas, and functions in the company should be considered for an internal audit.

We continue to look for ways to identify and assess emerging and blind spot risks and opportunities earlier and more comprehensively. In that regard, we intend to engage the corporate Intelligence Network—a cross-functional and informal group of people whose jobs require looking for societal, market, technology, and competitive trends relevant to GM around the world to supplement the knowledge and sources of the risk officer network and ERM team.

There is always room for improvement in the plans to mitigate risks and seize opportunities. Both the risk officer network and the ERM staff can be valuable resources to an individual risk officer or functional leader trying to analyze a risk, develop a plan, and check it for robustness. We intend to utilize these capabilities more fully and systematically, particularly for complex cross-functional and cross-regional issues.

While our initial ERM focus has been to identify and manage top risks, we also realize that this is only one part of a successful ERM program. With reasonable attention to the top risks now in place, we are ready to address oversight of the day-to-day operational controls. In this regard, we are in the process of developing an enhanced program for operational control self-assessment (CSA),[12] which is often cited as a fundamental and critical component of any successful ERM program. This program will begin with a joint risk assessment conducted across the organization in conjunction with internal audit.

GM implemented various versions of CSA over the years, but these processes waned over time and no longer fully support the business as intended, largely due to resources being redirected to support Sarbanes-Oxley resource requirements. There are many ways to achieve control self-assessment, and we recognize that typical programs are often criticized as not adding value because they lack substance or are simply check-the-box exercises. On the other hand, Sarbanes-Oxley at its core is intended to be a management self-assessment of controls over financial reporting despite having evolved into requiring very in-depth, time-consuming assessments.

There is a need to avoid either creating a burden on the organization to the point where the cost outweighs the benefits (which is how many businesses have viewed Sarbanes-Oxley) or creating a program that is low-cost but lacks any substantive value. Our goal in creating an improved CSA program is to strike a balance so that we are maximizing value to the organization and our shareholders by enhancing operational control assurance while spending resources wisely.

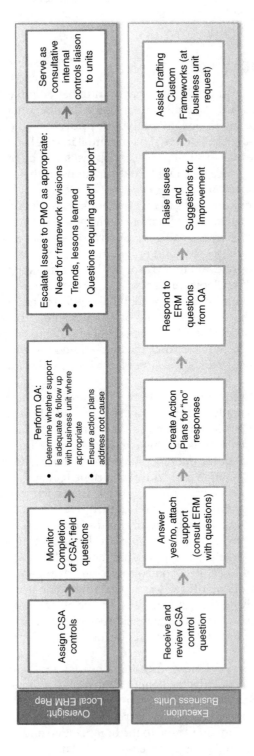

Exhibit 34.7 CSA Root Cause

The approach we have developed is a policy-based CSA that will start with asking business unit operations' line managers simple yes or no questions with regard to their compliance on specific policy requirements. However, we are taking this process a few steps further by requiring the managers to attach supporting evidence for their responses. To ensure that the supporting evidence is valid and sufficient, an ERM CSA representative will consult with the manager on control design and perform a quality assurance validation of the submission. The representative will also respond to any questions and assist in action plan development as needed. The ERM CSA representative will also review any action plans to correct self-identified deficiencies to make sure that the action plan addresses the root cause of the issue (see Exhibit 34.7).

We prefer this approach because it strengthens accountability at the operational level having frontline responsibility for internal controls. As a policy-based program, it drives behaviors that strengthen the company as a whole:

- Policy and process owners realize that they can leverage policies as a means to ensure results. If key risks are addressed in the policy, they will be assessed through CSA, and deficiencies will be uncovered and resolved by operating management.
- All business teams obtain a clear and consistent understanding of major activities and objectives of global or regional processes.
- CSA elevates the importance of up-to-date, accurate policies that address key risks.

Given that CSA is a global program, we expect that implementation will continue well into 2014.

CONCLUSION

We expect that the ERM tools we have implemented will improve GM's ability to identify, exploit, or mitigate, and communicate risk to senior leaders and the board of directors. We view this as a competitive advantage for General Motors that will enable us to react more quickly with improved and well-defined actions. We believe that an integrated risk management process (ERM, Sarbanes-Oxley, CSA, and consolidation of other compliance/assessment types of activities) will enable GM to utilize its compliance resources much more efficiently. Importantly, it will enable the company to have a consolidated, holistic view of risk and allow management and the board of directors to take comfort knowing that mitigation activities will be visible and tracked, and owners will be held accountable.

QUESTIONS

1. What are the pros and cons of having risk officers as part-time assignments within different functions and business units?
2. Can you think of a company whose strategy failed due to their failing to consider the actions of external players?
3. Do you think that companies need to experience a crisis to take risk seriously?

NOTES

1. Killer risks are those that would have a major effect on the short- or long-term profitability of the enterprise.
2. Confirmation bias is the tendency of people to favor information that confirms their beliefs.
3. Pairwise comparison is a method of ranking that compares a list two at a time. Earlier assessments are used to reduce the total number of comparisons.
4. Sense checks are a means of avoiding large errors by reviewing preliminary results with experts or management.
5. F = MA stands for the basic equation of mechanics: Force = Mass × Acceleration.
6. Game theory is a large topic. The tool described is a practical application that predicts actions based on assessments of the options and preferences in the situation or "game."
7. Natural outcome is a stable outcome (set of choices by the various players on the options they control) that will result if players do not behave strategically. It can be thought of as momentum.
8. Danger outcome is a stable outcome that is worse than the natural outcome from the perspective of the project sponsor; it can result if assessments are mistaken or players make errors.
9. Target outcome is a stable outcome that is the best potentially attainable by the company, given the options and preferences of the various players. It is better for the company than the natural outcome and mitigates the risk of the danger outcome.
10. Commonly known as the Humvee, the High Mobility Multipurpose Wheeled Vehicle (HMMWV) is a military transport used by the U.S. Army for many functions and produced by AM General.
11. DefCon is short for defense condition and is used by the U.S. military to describe the desired state of readiness. Wikipedia has a good description and history.
12. Control self-assessment is a technique that has managers review and certify the existence and quality of the controls around policies, procedures, and practices.

ABOUT THE CONTRIBUTORS

Marc Robinson is Assistant Director of Enterprise Risk Management at GM. He is an economist with over 25 years as an internal consultant at GM. He has also taught at UCLA, Stanford University, and the University of Michigan, and was Senior Staff Economist on the Council of Economic Advisers under President George H.W. Bush.

Lisa Smith, CRMA, CCSA, is Assistant Director of Enterprise Risk Management at GM. She has served in a variety of audit-related roles since joining GM in 2002, including the global implementation of ERM starting in 2010. She has an MBA from the University of Michigan and also serves as an instructor for the Institute of Internal Auditors.

Brian Thelen has been General Auditor at GM since 2011, and served as Chief Risk Officer through July 2014. Prior to that, he was Vice President of Audit Services at Delphi Corporation, Vice President of Internal Audit Services at Waste Management, and general auditor at American Standard. He started his career at Ernst & Young and has a CPA and an MBA.

CHAPTER 35

ERM at Malaysia's Media Company Astro

Quickly Implementing ERM and Using It to Assess the Risk-Adjusted Performance of a Portfolio of Acquired Foreign Companies

PATRICK ADAM K. ABDULLAH
Vice President, Enterprise Risk Management, Astro Overseas Limited

GHISLAIN GIROUX DUFORT
President, Baldwin Risk Strategies Inc.

T his case study focuses on the implementation and use of enterprise risk management (ERM) to screen proposed investments, assess the risk-adjusted performance of a portfolio of foreign investments, and make key investment decisions at Astro Overseas Limited, the company responsible for all international investments (subsidiaries and joint ventures) for Astro Holdings Sendirian Berhad (herein known as "Astro"). We start by providing some background information on Malaysia, on its corporate governance code and practices, and risk management practices at Astro. We then describe how Astro Overseas Limited uses ERM to assess and filter potential investments, and subsequently, how ERM is implemented at successful investments. Finally, we explain how Astro Overseas Limited combines information from the risk profile and financial performance of each investment, and reflects the performance on a dashboard together with all other investments in its portfolio to make better risk/return investment decisions.

MALAYSIA

Situated between 2 degrees and 7 degrees to the north of the equator, Malaysia is a diversely populated federal democracy of 29.3 million[1] Malays, Indians, Chinese, and many other ethnic groups[2] who speak Malay (the official language), English, various Chinese dialects, Tamil, Telugu, and Malayalam. Its major religions are Islam, Buddhism, Taoism, Hinduism, Christianity, and Sikhism. The life expectancy of its citizens ranges from 73 years (for men) to 77 years (for women), and the literacy rate is 89 percent.[3]

Exhibit 35.1　Map of Malaysia
Source: U.S. Central Intelligence Agency's *World Factbook.*

Geographically, Malaysia is almost as diverse as its culture (see Exhibit 35.1). Eleven states and two federal territories—Kuala Lumpur and Putrajaya—form Peninsular Malaysia, which is separated by the South China Sea from East Malaysia, where we find the states of Sabah and Sarawak on the island of Borneo and a third federal territory, the island of Labuan.

Malaysia's main industrial sectors are rubber and palm oil processing and manufacturing, light manufacturing industry, logging, and petroleum production and refining. Its main exports are electronic equipment, petroleum and liquefied natural gas, wood and wood products, and palm oil. The country's gross domestic product (GDP) per capita is equivalent to U.S. $8,800, and its currency is the ringgit (1 RM being equivalent to 0.3140 USD).[4]

The country's capital, Kuala Lumpur, is at the center of the Multimedia Super Corridor (MSC), Asia's equivalent of the United States' Silicon Valley. That is where we find the head office of our company, Astro Malaysia Holdings Berhad, more precisely located at the All Asia Broadcast Center, in Technology Park Malaysia.

The Astro Group

Established in 1996, the Astro Group is a leading and growing integrated consumer media and entertainment group present in Malaysia, Southeast Asia, and regional foreign markets, with operations in four key areas of business: pay TV, radio, publications, and digital media.[5] It has established partnerships in different countries with A&E, Google, Lionsgate, MSNBC, and other leading media companies. Through Celestial Pictures, Astro also owns and distributes the Shaw Library, the world's largest Chinese film library. It owns Adrep as well, a national radio airtime management and sales company operating in China.

The Astro Group is comprised of Astro Malaysia Holdings Berhad (AMH), which was listed in the main board of the Malaysian Stock Exchange in 2012, and Astro Overseas Limited (AOL) overlooking all international investments.

AMH focuses on Pay-TV, Radio, Publications, and Digital operations in Malaysia and has a customer base of over 4 million residential pay TV customers or approximately 56 percent penetration of Malaysian TV households. Astro Radio operates Malaysia's highest-rated stations across key languages.

AOL holds investments in a portfolio of companies involved in Pay-TV, radio, content aggregation, creation and distribution, digital and multimedia services, and includes companies in Australia, China, Hong Kong, India, Indonesia, Singapore, Vietnam, Saudi Arabia and the MENA region, United Kingdom, and North America (see Exhibit 35.2).

CORPORATE GOVERNANCE IN MALAYSIA

The 1997 Asian financial crisis exposed many weaknesses in the region and spurred multiple reforms, including a drive to improve corporate governance.[6] Malaysia introduced its first corporate governance code in 2000 and revised it in 2007. In 2011, its Securities Commission established a "Blueprint" to achieve excellence in corporate governance, and in 2012 delivered a new "comply or explain" code.[7] According to its risk management guidance, the board of directors should:

- Establish a sound framework to manage risks.
- Understand the principal risks of all aspects of the company's business.
- Recognize that business decisions involve the taking of appropriate risks.
- Achieve a proper balance between risks incurred and potential returns to shareholders.
- Ensure that there are systems in place that effectively monitor and manage these risks.
- Determine the company's level of risk tolerance and actively identify, assess, and monitor key business risks to safeguard shareholders' investments and the company's assets.
- Disclose in the annual report the main features of the company's risk management framework and internal controls system.

According to the 2013 ASEAN Corporate Governance Scorecard published jointly by the ASEAN Capital Markets Forum and the Asian Development Bank,[8] the performance of Malaysia's Top 100 companies (PLCs) in terms of conformity to recommended corporate governance principles and practices "is commendable and at the same time presents opportunities for more improvement." Among the areas for improvement identified by the report was the "lack of disclosure of key risks (other than financial risks)."

ENTERPRISE RISK MANAGEMENT AT ASTRO

In the aforementioned corporate governance context, Astro's listed vehicle, AMH states in its Annual Report 2013: "The Board is committed to applying and upholding high standards of corporate governance to safeguard and promote the interests

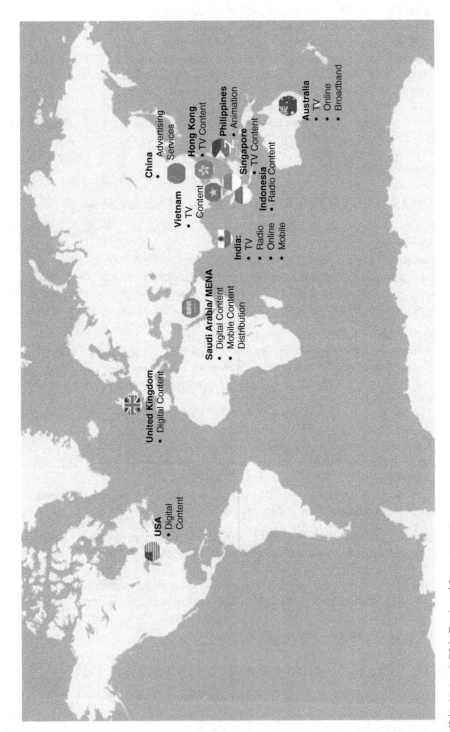

Exhibit 35.2 AOL's Regional Investments

of the shareholders and to enhance the long-term value of the Group. To this end, it has adopted the principles and recommendations set out in the Malaysian Code on Corporate Governance 2012."[9]

The annual report states that the board is charged with, among other responsibilities, the review and approval of changes to management and control structures, including ERM. "The Board is committed to the implementation of Group Risk Management (GRM) as an integral part of the Group's planning practices and business processes, encapsulating the continuous identification, assessment, monitoring, and reporting of risks at all levels, from projects, [to] operations to strategy. The Group Risk Management Framework, consistent with the Committee of Sponsoring Organizations (COSO) enterprise risk management framework, sets out the risk management governance and infrastructure, risk management processes and control responsibilities."[10]

The board of directors, through its Audit Committee, is assisted in these responsibilities by AMH's Group Risk Management Committee (GRMC). The GRMC meets at least quarterly, includes senior management from each business segment and unit, and is chaired by AMH's CEO. The CEO and CFO are accountable to the board of directors for the implementation of strategies, policies, and procedures to achieve an effective risk management framework.

Furthermore, Astro has linked senior executive pay to sound risk management up to the highest level of the organization: "Risk management has been identified as a key result area in the annual performance evaluation of the CEO and CFO."[11]

If the lack of disclosure of key risks (other than financial risks) by top Malaysian companies was noted in the 2013 Corporate Governance Scorecard mentioned earlier, it is not the case at Astro, which also follows the guidance of the Global Reporting Initiative Framework and discloses—in addition to financial risks—seven other key risks: market and competition; political, legal, and regulatory; services availability; procuring exclusive and compelling content; technology and innovation; people; and branding and reputation.

Astro is also committed to what is increasingly recognized as a key success factor of long-lasting ERM implementation: risk culture. "Risk awareness and control consciousness are integral in cultivating a good risk and governance culture among the Group employees. Risk and control briefings, online training, and a web portal are in place to facilitate the ease of reference and better understanding of the risk management framework and internal control procedures."[12]

Finally, to ensure consistent practices, Astro has adopted the concepts and terminology of the ISO 31000 International Standard (Risk Management—Principles and Guidelines, 2009) and the COSO process to ensure the ERM program is effectively implemented.

ASTRO OVERSEAS LIMITED

We now focus on the implementation and use of ERM to assess the risk-adjusted performance of a portfolio of foreign investments and to make key investment decisions at Astro Overseas Limited (AOL), the company responsible for all international investments (subsidiaries and joint ventures).

AOL's board of directors is very experienced and oversees the company's risk management framework. The board of AOL reiterates regularly that risk management is as important as maximizing profitability, and they should both be given equal weight in establishing investment performance benchmarks. AOL's objective is to achieve investment returns that are considered reasonable for markets in which it invests and the stage at which the investment is in its life cycle and risks for the investments. It looks at the long-term success of these investments, the risks of these companies over time and not necessarily to obtain short-term gain. While the board of directors is cognizant of ERM framework and methodology, they are also mindful that the approach to its implementation varies from one investment to another depending on the size and scale of each business. In this respect, influence of the investee company's board and audit committee plays an important role to ensure the process is successfully implemented. Senior management needs to fully understand and appreciate that although the process is a little provocative, it is value adding and has the potential to create a more robust business. Also, for investments which are smaller, resources and talent may be limited and there is a need for AOL to extend assistance to these investee companies to implement and manage the program until such time the investee company has adequate resources to do it on their own.

EVOLUTION OF ERM AT AOL

As we will soon see in detail, AOL has reached a level of maturity sufficient to work with the management of the investee companies to implement its ERM Framework. The evolution of AOL's ERM maturity over time is illustrated in Exhibit 35.3.

Exhibit 35.3   Evolution of AOL's Risk Management

REACTIVE	PROACTIVE	ADAPTIVE
DISASTER RECOVERY	BUSINESS CONTINUITY	ENTERPRISE RISK MANAGEMENT
What if something happens?	When our business is disrupted	How can we act for competitive gain?
• Actions are in response to what has just happened • Typical action plans are insurance, incident reporting, response plans	• Focus on response to continuity of services with the least amount of interruptions possible • Requires proactive collaboration of all units within the organization • Typical action plans are BCP plans, IT backup centers	• Shift from loss prevention to revenue protection and generation • Acting before people or assets are impacted • A culture of adapting and thriving in the face of complex changes while creating value

Respond	Recover	Continue Operations	Revenue Preservation	Pursue Opportunities

Like many companies, AOL's approach to risk management started in a reactive mode, with a basic ability to respond to negative events. It then progressed to being able to recover as quickly as possible from a potential interruption, and then moved on to a more proactive mode with business continuity planning (BCP)—being able to prepare to ensure the continuity of critical operations and business activities in almost any circumstance. Later on, AOL started to enter the adaptive mode, with a focus of the risk management function on revenue preservation.

Now well into the adaptive stage, AOL is able to use ERM for anticipating risks before they impact employees or assets, protecting revenue generation, gaining competitive advantage, and creating value by adapting to the complex and changing media business environments one finds while investing in foreign countries and cultures. This ability plays an important part in the screening of potential investments by AOL and contributes to AOL's profitable growth strategy through international expansion.

- AOL's investment strategy is to focus on businesses in the media and entertainment sector including platforms, distribution of content, and businesses closely related to AMH's core businesses, including media such as TV, radio, content creation and aggregation, Internet Protocol television (IPTV),[13] and advertising. A major challenge for AOL is implementing ERM across its investment portfolio where it does not have a majority position. Other key challenges in terms of risk management include: Implementing ERM consistently across all investments.
- Managing differences in terms of cultures and obtaining buy-in from management.
- Managing the expectations of board members.

ROLE OF ERM IN THE ACQUISITION PROCESS

Astro is growing through acquisitions and therefore has developed a method to systematically and efficiently screen investment opportunities. Exhibit 35.4 shows how AOL makes investment decisions through a layered investment risk funnel.

A first risk review of the opportunity pipeline is performed by the senior leadership team of AOL.

If that first hurdle is cleared, a second risk review is conducted. This review is led by the Business Development (BD) Team in conjunction with the ERM Team. As anyone who has ever been involved in mergers and acquisitions knows, a full risk assessment prior to an acquisition is almost impossible to carry out during the due diligence process, owing to the speed at which negotiations evolve and to their highly confidential nature. When in the process of making an investment, it is not the right time to be running risk workshops. This being said, AOL's ERM Team has established a number of key activities to be carried out during the preacquisition portion of the process, as we see in more detail in Exhibit 35.5. The result of this second risk review is either an approved investment proposal or a rejection of it.

A third risk review is performed by the BD Team during the negotiation period. After the negotiation, if the acquisition offer is accepted and the contract is signed, AOL's ERM Team enters the most important portion of the process, the

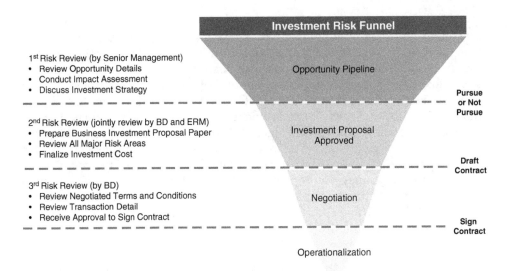

Exhibit 35.4   Making Key Investment Decisions

focus on implementing its ERM Framework: the operationalization phase, or the Monitor and Review panel of Exhibit 35.5.

During the Preacquisition portion of the process in Exhibit 35.5, the ERM Team uses a set of guidelines to determine a preliminary risk profile of each of the potential target companies. The word preliminary is important here. The initial evaluation will include issues related to political and regulatory risks,

The ERM Framework focuses on the "Monitor & Review" phase of AOL's value chain

Preacquisition	Monitor & Review	Postacquisition
• Guidelines to handle initial opportunities identified	• Definition of objectives for the investment	• Establish and monitor exit strategies triggers
• Detailed research to evaluate investment, including operations, business model, strategy, and growth plan	• Set targets and monitor achievement of financial and nonfinancial targets	• Escalation mechanism for management to inform Board and seek decision / guidance
• Identify key risks and mitigation plans	• Monitor achievements of the approved business plans and identify gaps	• Negotiation guidelines
• Consider funding structure, management returns, and exit strategy	• Develop effective and appropriate reporting mechanisms and dashboards	• Assessment of potential buyers
• Perform due diligence process	• Conduct strategy reviews	• Managing confidential information
• Obtain necessary Board approvals for go/no-go decisions	• Manage risks	

**Focus of the AOL
ERM Framework**

Exhibit 35.5   Overview of ERM's Role in AOL's Acquisition Process

partner management, skills, expertise and human resources, operational influence, the company's business model, its strategy, growth plans, operations, and cultural fit. From the initial assessment come the preliminary key risks and existing risk treatments or mitigation plans required for the potential target. Once this preliminary risk profile has been obtained, the BD Team will then identify the potential acquisition's funding structure, management fees, and return on investment, as well as exit strategy options. These analyses and scenarios are then put to the test or confirmed further. Finally, the preacquisition activities conclude with a "go/no-go" recommendation to the board of directors. If the board of directors approves the investment proposal, the approval will normally have recommendations and stipulated conditions that need to be met for the acquisition to proceed.

During the *monitor and review* phase, the ERM Team will further develop the preliminary risk profile using the strategic objectives approved by the board of the investee company as a starting point. Based on these objectives, the ERM Team will also use specific financial and nonfinancial targets set by management to undertake their assessments. The risk profile provides further evidence as to whether the current targets can be met under existing business conditions. It is then reasonable to assume that the strategic objectives, as well as the financial and nonfinancial targets, may be adjusted once the board of the investee company is fully apprised of the risks associated with the business. Designated directors from AOL who are on the board of the investee company will work with management to make the necessary adjustments. The adjustments made are normally to ensure that objectives are reasonable and adequately robust to meet set performance targets.

AOL's ERM function adopts a consistent methodology and has an established risk dashboard and reporting templates for all companies within its portfolio. It also has developed appropriate and effective mechanisms for its implementation and use. The initial risk-based strategy review is followed by regular annual reviews over the life of the investment. Finally, AOL's ERM function has oversight and regularly monitors the risk management process of the investee company.

The *postacquisition* stage is concerned with the execution of an appropriate exit/divestment strategy. In the preacquisition phase, potential exit strategies are identified. In the monitor and review step, these strategies are constantly reviewed and relevant triggers determined and tracked. These are indicators or metrics with thresholds set so as to trigger the consideration of exit strategy options and eventual execution of one of them—terminating the investment. The divestment process starts when the monitoring of triggers has resulted in the decision to execute an exit strategy. The ERM Team contributes to the escalation of the recommendation to divest, through management and to the board of directors of AOL, with a focus on the risk/return aspect of the recommendation. Once the decision has been obtained from the board, where required, the ERM function helps the divestiture team to set the negotiation guidelines, assess the risk profile of potential buyers, and manage sensitive confidential information until the divestiture is closed.

The Monitor and Review Step—Focus of AOL's ERM

As mentioned, the monitor and review step is focused on the effective implementation of AOL's ERM Framework. Once the investment has been made, AOL seeks to work with management to adopt and integrate AOL's ERM Framework quickly.

To that effect, AOL has instituted a number of key measures to ensure not only that ERM is implemented quickly and effectively, but in addition, it seeks to have the ERM framework adopted by the business for the long term. The key measures put in place to ensure those results are achieved include:

- A risk key performance indicator (KPI) (with an estimated weight of 10 percent tied to the compensation package) is assigned to the business heads of each investment to ensure that they are vigilant in managing their risks and implementing the necessary mitigation strategies.
- Risk management performance is monitored on a quarterly basis, after which a report card is developed outlining the areas of compliance and areas where gaps have been identified (i.e., the proportion of their risk management actions that are on target).
- Results are consolidated on an annual basis for review by the Remuneration Committee of the board of directors.
- To further inculcate the ERM culture, an "Introduction to ERM" course has been included as part of the core syllabus for induction training.

AOL is sufficiently experienced at implementing ERM that it rolls out its Framework using typically 60 person-days of its own ERM Team over a three- to four-month period. However, as mentioned earlier, the plan can only materialize if there is full support from the board and audit committee of the investee company, and there is management commitment in ensuring the program meets its objectives.

Shortly after AOL has completed the investment, AOL's ERM Team identifies two or three persons from the investee company who will be trained into AOL's ERM approach and brought on board as soon as the implementation project starts. We will collectively refer to them as the Joint ERM Team (JET). The overall ERM implementation process is illustrated in Exhibit 35.6. It will culminate in the investee company having an up-to-date risk profile consisting of a risk map, a risk register, and details for each risk identified (causes, treatments, controls, action plans, and steps required to complete each action plan).

This process is performed in three steps: Planning, Rollout, and Sustainability.

At the *Planning* step, the JET starts the stakeholder management activity, first engaging with the investee company's senior management team (SMT) to explain the process, reach mutual understanding, and obtain buy-in. A risk champion is determined among the SMT members. This senior executive will be the sponsor of the ERM implementation process. A Risk Committee, which also constitutes the ERM steering committee during the implementation stage, is also formed. It will include the CFO, other senior executives, and their direct reports.

Then, the implementation project plan is devised, including its scope, time line, the project team membership, and delegation structure (number "1" in Exhibit 35.6).

As mentioned earlier, the *Rollout* step is performed in three phases over the aforementioned three- to four-month period, using most of the 60 person-days of AOL's ERM Team.

Phase I uses approximately 30 person-days of AOL's ERM Team and starts with awareness training sessions. The JET enters into the information gathering activity

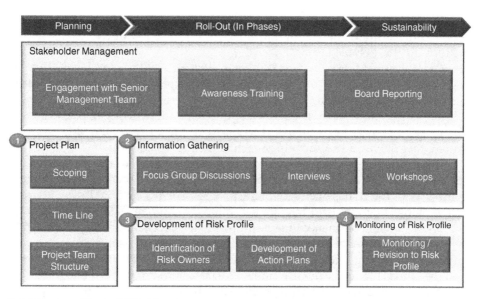

Exhibit 35.6 Typical ERM Implementation Process for Operating Entities

(number "2" in Exhibit 35.6), organizing the first risk workshop with the SMT. This part of Phase I uses a top-down approach. The JET members discuss the industry and business challenges of the company with the SMT. The workshop will produce a laundry list of risks, and they ask the SMT, as an initial assessment, to rank them simply, using their best judgment, as low, medium, or high.

This is then followed by the interviews stage. They may interview up to one-third of the organization (for example, 100 out of a total of 300 employees) from the bottom up. Based on the company's objectives, they ask participants what their objectives and targets are, what may impede them from meeting their objectives (these become their risks), their causes, and the risk treatments and/or controls that are already in place. The JET also uses the high-level risk list from the SMT workshop to prompt and facilitate discussions if necessary. The AOL ERM Team calls this the Level 1, or ground level, risk identification. At this level, risks are neither screened nor validated (they are not yet what they call "sanitized").

Then, the JET interviews Level 2 managers, who are the direct supervisors of Level 1 interviewees. As with the previous stage, they perform first a zero-based risk identification discussion with Level 2 managers. This is followed by discussions on the list of risks and causes as identified during the Level 1 analysis/results. The JET looks for agreements and disagreements and tries to balance them out.

Based on Level 1 and Level 2 results, the JET "sanitizes" the risks and causes, which means that they regroup some risks and eliminate others that seem out of place based on the JET's business judgment and experience in risk management. They then bring the "sanitized" and prioritized risk list to the company's SMT. At this point, the risk register is constituted of only a one-dimensional rating (low, medium, or high), together with the causes of risks and treatments and controls in place.

This is the end of Phase I, and the AOL ERM Team gives the investee company a period to consider, analyze, and think about both the top-down risk list and the bottom-up one, before starting Phase II.

Phase II uses approximately 20 person-days of AOL's ERM Team. Combining the top-down and bottom-up results, the JET typically finds that 75 percent of the risks are common and 25 percent may be different. The JET and SMT reconcile them through what AOL calls a "dispute/validation" workshop. The investee company's risk register is then agreed to. Next, the JET asks the SMT to assign, among themselves, a risk owner for each of the identified risks.

Depending on the nature and size of the business, there may be between 10 to 20 risks for each investee company. Those risks are managed by the investee company, and AOL has oversight of the process. The JET and SMT use the overall rating of low, medium, and high to determine the company's top 10 risks.

The JET then commences the risk profile development activity (number "3" in Exhibit 35.6). The team members discuss each risk with its owner individually. During the meeting, they address the risk's causes, its probability of occurrence, and the impact (or "consequence" in ISO 31000 terminology) if it materializes, taking into consideration the existing risk treatments and controls already in place as the case may be. To identify the root causes of the risk, the team drills down to a reasonable depth. This process requires judgment and experience. As an indication, they may go as far back as three years in terms of data history, but not much more, as they find that drilling further down tends to bring diminishing returns compared to the expense and effort involved. The JET and risk owner also look at the strength of each of the controls in place, asking themselves: "Is it sufficient or not?" In other words, they use a binary decision method. If the JET and risk owner find that control is lacking, the JET works with the risk owner to determine what should be done and to establish action plans to treat the risk accordingly. This is the end of Phase II.

The JET populates the risk profile, including the risk map, and sends them back to risk owners with their action plans. Following the end of this phase, the JET and risk owners enter a two-week period of follow-up and challenges. The JET encourages risk owners to think outside the box while also considering the costs of their existing treatments, controls, and key action plans.

Phase III uses approximately 10 person-days of AOL's ERM Team. This phase starts with a third SMT risk workshop. The company's risk profile, including the risk map and the key risk action plans, are reviewed collectively and challenged. Again, this is a validation workshop. The validation process allows the SMT, for instance, to ensure that one action plan does not duplicate or contradict another action plan or existing treatment and/or control. Once the key risk action plans have been validated by the SMT, the JET meets again with risk owners individually to revise those action plans and reassess their cost/benefit analyses as required. The JET returns to the SMT with the risk map and action plans, including their cost/benefit analyses. The SMT provides final validation of the risk profile, including risk map, action plans, costs or budgets needed, and the time line to implement the action plans.

Finally, the *Sustainability* step is performed on a continuous basis (number "4" in Exhibit 35.6). It consists of monitoring the risk profile of the investee company and reporting it to the board (see Exhibit 35.7).

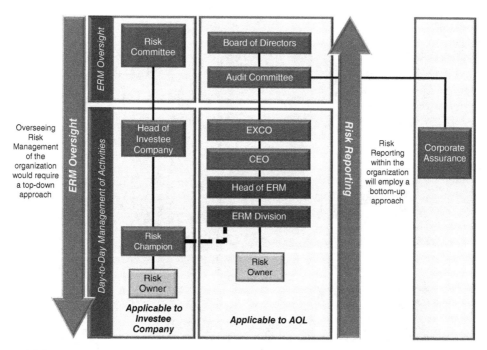

Exhibit 35.7 Reporting and Monitoring Structure

The risk owners selected by the investee company will then implement key action plans by project-managing the deliverables. The action plans are broken down into key action steps and target dates for completion. The ERM Framework (see Exhibit 35.8) is handed over to the local ERM Team, which consists of the local members of the JET and must include at least two persons who have been trained by AOL's ERM Team.

The Vice President of Enterprise Risk Management (VPERM) of AOL's ERM Team, serves as a liaison between the operating company's ERM Team and the SMT to ensure that everyone is on the same page in understanding what is expected in terms of risk management. AOL's VPERM undertakes reviews with the investee company (and all other companies in the portfolio) every six months by meeting and discussing with the CEO, the SMT, and the local ERM team, to monitor the risk management process at a high level.

In between those reviews, there are monthly meetings and a comprehensive formal quarterly review by a representative of the AOL's ERM Team, the local ERM team, and the risk owners to monitor the execution of the action plans, revisions required for the risk profile, and reporting on risks.

Once action plans for a risk have been completed, they become treatments or controls. The ERM team monitors the effectiveness of these controls and if they are working effectively, it contributes to the establishment of the risk's trend in ranking—stable, up, or down—as part of the regular reporting process.

Emerging risks are also considered regularly. Once a key emerging risk has been identified and considered significant, an assessment process similar to the rollout described earlier, including phases I, II, and III, is performed for that risk.

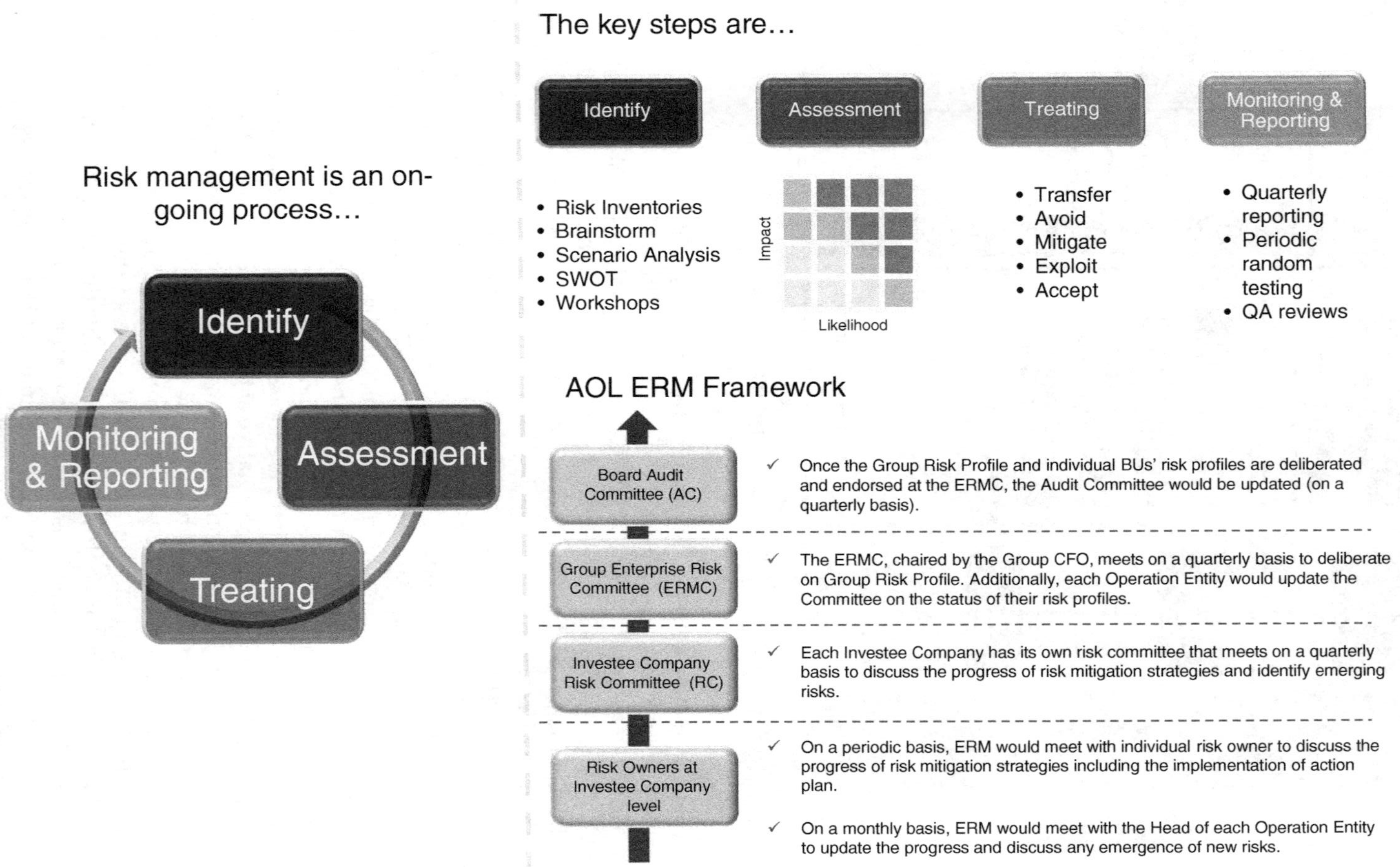

The key steps are…

Identify
- Risk Inventories
- Brainstorm
- Scenario Analysis
- SWOT
- Workshops

Assessment

Impact / Likelihood

Treating
- Transfer
- Avoid
- Mitigate
- Exploit
- Accept

Monitoring & Reporting
- Quarterly reporting
- Periodic random testing
- QA reviews

AOL ERM Framework

Board Audit Committee (AC)

✓ Once the Group Risk Profile and individual BUs' risk profiles are deliberated and endorsed at the ERMC, the Audit Committee would be updated (on a quarterly basis).

Group Enterprise Risk Committee (ERMC)

✓ The ERMC, chaired by the Group CFO, meets on a quarterly basis to deliberate on Group Risk Profile. Additionally, each Operation Entity would update the Committee on the status of their risk profiles.

Investee Company Risk Committee (RC)

✓ Each Investee Company has its own risk committee that meets on a quarterly basis to discuss the progress of risk mitigation strategies and identify emerging risks.

Risk Owners at Investee Company level

✓ On a periodic basis, ERM would meet with individual risk owner to discuss the progress of risk mitigation strategies including the implementation of action plan.

✓ On a monthly basis, ERM would meet with the Head of each Operation Entity to update the progress and discuss any emergence of new risks.

Risk management is an on-going process…

Identify → Assessment → Treating → Monitoring & Reporting

Exhibit 35.8   AOL's Risk Management Process

RISK PROFILE: RISK MAP AND ACTION PLANS

As explained earlier, the investee company's risk profile includes its risk map and set of assessments and action plans for each key risk. As shown in Exhibit 35.8, AOL's risk map is represented using a 4 × 4 matrix of impact versus likelihood/probability, with scales ranging from 1 to 4, "4" representing the highest probability or impact. When two risks are symmetrically placed in the matrix vis-à-vis its diagonal, for instance, one with ratings of probability "2" and impact "3" and the other with ratings of probability "3" and impact "2," a higher priority is given to the risk with the higher impact.

Exhibit 35.9 illustrates how AOL tracks its summary risk profile on risk maps, identifying the inherent or gross risk rating (the level of risk that would prevail in the absence of treatments), the residual or net risk rating (the actual level of risk given the existing treatments in place), and the target risk rating (the appetite for that risk, which will be achieved through the execution of the key action plans).

To give these concepts more concrete meaning, consider a hypothetical investee company of AOL, Trex Radio, operating in the Socialist Republic of Vietnam. To simplify matters, let's assume it focuses on six key risks, as displayed on the summary risk map of Exhibit 35.10, where risks are displayed on a net basis (residual risks).

As can be seen from Exhibit 35.10, AOL uses a numbering system whereby the first number represents the likelihood (or probability), and the second one the potential impact if the risk materializes. This map shows simply the existing risks, but as the legend at the bottom of the chart indicates, AOL can also highlight existing risks that have been redefined and/or reranked, as well as new/emerging risks.

For illustration purposes only, Exhibit 35.11 shows what this means concretely for one hypothetical yet realistic key risk, that of R2, the ability to develop creative and compelling content.

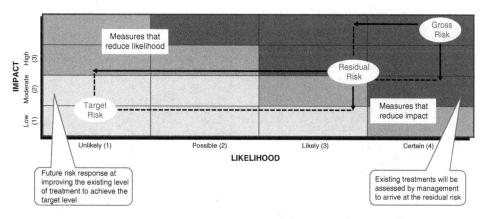

- Inherent / Gross Risk Rating – risks that exist before considering the effectiveness of existing controls
- Residual / Net Risk Rating – risks taking existing controls into consideration
- Target Risk Rating – management's desired risk level

Exhibit 35.9 Risk Map Displaying Inherent/Gross, Residual/Net, and Target Risk Ratings

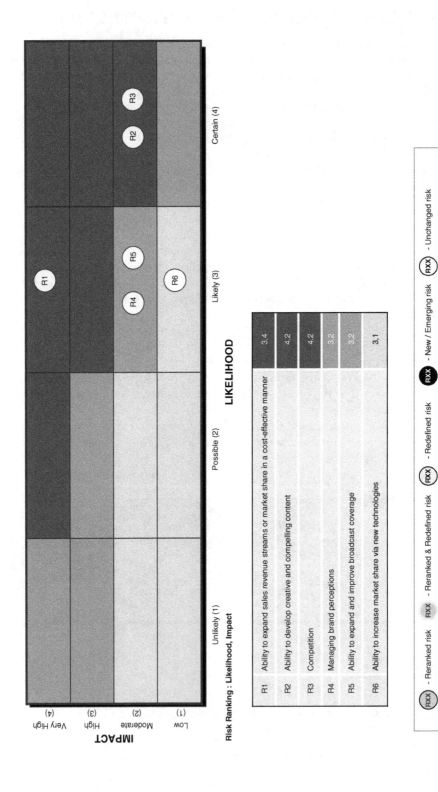

Exhibit 35.10 Risk Map of Trex Radio, Vietnam, a Hypothetical AOL Investee Company

Risk R2	Ability to develop creative and compelling content	Risk Ranking	Gross	Nett	Target
			4,3	4,2	2,2

Risk Explanation	Content is key for increasing listenership. Therefore, it is essential to fulfil the demand by establishing / acquiring quality production of compelling content and procuring exclusive content rights to differentiate ourselves from the competitors including management of brand perception.

Consequences	• Loss of listenership • Loss of advertising revenue

Risk Owner	Jason Hewitt

Potential Causes	Controls	Key Action Plans
Changing listeners' trends and preferences	Various forms of market research are regularly conducted to identify listenership trends and preferences such as: • Listener Advisory Board (biannually) • Auditorium Music Testing (minimum annually) • Perceptual studies on DJ personalities • Music research • AC Nielsen media survey (twice yearly) Use of Xrater (online survey) to track changing listener habits apart from existing research, which is available. Trex Radio nurtures own talent by informal mentoring / coaching by respective superiors in selected departments.	• Quarterly review of breakfast benchmarks • Biannually conduct breakfast show and breakfast talent perceptual review • Continuation of breakfast show producer training • Key shift producers to be migrated into employment contracts and away from vendor relationship • Introduce a KPI for producers to track the increase in audience listenership by 100% from current standing through direct engagement over radio, social media, mobile apps, and phone listenership • Review pay and reward for breakfast shift producers • Identify and develop one shift, which could be used to replace key breakfast shift on core stations.

Exhibit 35.11 Detail of Risk Profile—R2

This example considers a typical key risk that any media company faces, which is the ability to develop creative and compelling content that attracts and retains a target audience. In this illustration, we consider the radio programming of the hypothetical Vietnam subsidiary, Trex Radio. To better understand the following considerations, the reader should note that the key radio period for listenership in Vietnam is the morning breakfast time period.

As can be seen from the Risk Explanation section, Trex Radio needs to acquire/develop and protect unique quality content that will differentiate itself from the competition and sustain or increase listenership and advertising revenues. One of the potential causes that may put this ability at risk has been identified as "Changing listeners' trends and preferences" that would not be matched by the company. Without any risk treatment, Trex Radio has determined that the gross risk rating is "4,3," which means probability 4, impact 3, which lies in the "red zone" (upper right area in chart).

The existing treatments/controls are also explained: Trex Radio commissions traditional market research and online surveys, and it nurtures its own talent to differentiate itself. With these treatments in place, the current net risk rating is "4,2," which means that the existing treatments do not reduce the probability that the risk will occur, but will reduce its impact if it does occur—yet not sufficiently to move it from the "red zone."

The appetite for that risk, the target risk rating, is "2,2" (which would bring the risk in the "green zone," lower left area in chart). Some key action plans have been identified and selected to bring the probability down two notches, and they

Risk R5	Ability to expand and improve broadcast coverage				
No	Detailed Action Plan	Action by	Target date	Status	Remarks
1	Finalize the Vietnam Telecom contract and complete upgrade of antennas and transmitters for the key markets in the next 10 years, and focus on improving transmission quality of the existing transmission.	Trex			
	a) Liaise with General Counsel on contract matters and finalize it.	Trex / Vietnam Telecom	Apr 2012	☑	Completed
	b) Obtain signatures from both parties	Trex / Vietnam Telecom	May 2012	●	Draft contract completed and agreed. Pending review and sign-off by Vietnam Telecom
	c) Vietnam Telecom orders antennas and transmitters from supplier	Trex / Vietnam Telecom	June 2012	●	As per schedule
	d) Commence installation of antennas and transmitters	Trex / Vietnam Telecom	Dec 2012	●	As per schedule
	e) Carry out system and transmission test	Trex / Vietnam Telecom	Aug 2013	●	As per schedule
	f) Commissioning and handover	Trex / Vietnam Telecom	Oct 2013	●	As per schedule

Exhibit 35.12   Detailed Action Plan—R5

are listed in the exhibit. One of them is: "Key shift producers to be migrated into employment contracts and away from vendor relationship." How would this action reduce the probability of the risk that changing listeners' preferences creates a mismatch between their needs and the company's programming? The answer is that by enticing key shift producers to become employees as opposed to freelancers (for instance, by revising their pay and reward upward—see next key action in the list of the exhibit), the company will be in a better position than its competitors to quickly anticipate the programming changes necessary to keep in line with potential shifts in its audience's needs. Also, another action plan geared toward increasing emotional attachment of the producers to the station is: "Introduce a KPI for producers to track the increase in audience listenership by 100 percent from current standing through direct engagement over radio, social media, mobile apps, and phone listenership." This action plan is geared toward building loyalty, and producers are rewarded accordingly for meeting the set targets.

Of course, all of these treatments and action plans have a cost. As explained previously, a cost/benefit analysis of these actions must be performed and a budget justified and approved.

Exhibit 35.12 illustrates a hypothetical yet realistic action plan for another typical risk for a radio company, Trex Radio's R5 risk: the ability to expand and improve broadcast coverage.

As explained previously, action plans are broken down into key action steps featuring "Action by," "Target date," "Status," and "Remarks" columns. In this case, key action number 1 to reduce the risk R5 (ability to expand and improve broadcast coverage) is to contract the telecom company Vietnam Telecom to upgrade and improve Trex Radio's transmission in key markets for 10 years. It has been broken down into six action steps, from a) Liaise with General Counsel to f) Commissioning and handover. The Status column has four possible states: (1) a check mark when the action step has been completed, (2) a green circle when it is on target, (3) a yellow circle when it is at risk of delay, and (4) a red circle when it is overdue. This is to ensure that the agreed action plan is project-managed and delivered on a timely basis. *Note:* Since the exhibit is printed in grayscale, green appears as the lightest shade in the exhibit, yellow as the middle shade, and red as the darkest shade.

THE INVESTMENT PERFORMANCE DASHBOARD

As is appropriate for a book on ERM cases, we have focused much of the chapter on AOL's ERM Framework. But since our goal is to show how it is used in practice to make risk-based investment decisions on a portfolio of foreign investee companies, we now turn our attention to the investment side of the equation. Exhibit 35.13 illustrates AOL's formula to build its investment performance dashboard.

The investment performance dashboard is a matrix that allows comparing the operating entities in the portfolio to one another using their current investment value on one axis and their total investment performance score (TIPS) on the other (see Exhibit 35.13). The former is obtained through recognized valuation methodologies such as the discounted cash flow (DCF) method, while the latter is the sum of two risk scores: the qualitative investment risk score and the quantitative financial risk score.

The qualitative investment risk score is obtained by using the risk map of the top 10 risks of the investee company. AOL's approach to obtain this score is to multiply the probability by the impact for each of the top 10 risks and to add them up. A lower score means a safer investment with a lower risk profile (safer from an investment standpoint). The maximum score possible is $10 \times 4 \times 4 = 160$.

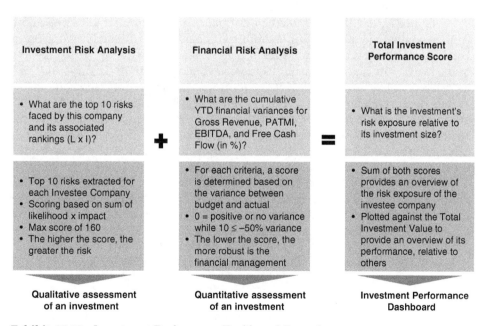

Exhibit 35.13 Investment Performance Dashboard Formula

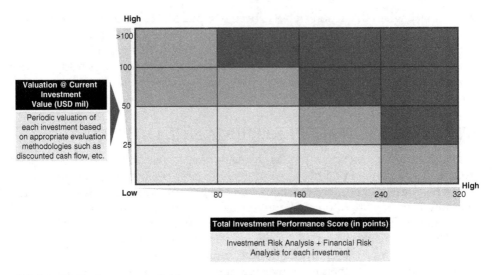

Exhibit 35.14   Investment Performance Dashboard

The quantitative financial risk score is obtained by looking at the deviations from the plan of four financial metrics: gross revenue; profit after tax and minority interests (PATMI); earnings before interest, taxes, depreciation, and amortization (EBITDA); and free cash flow. For each metric, a score is derived from the variance between its budgeted amount and the actual number realized. The score can range from 0 (when there is a positive variance or no variance) to 10 (when the variance is –50 percent). A lower score is indicative of a more robust financial management and means a safer investment from a financial point of view.

As stated earlier, the investment performance dashboard (Exhibit 35.14) allows AOL to compare its portfolio of operating companies based on their value on the vertical axis and their total investment performance score on the horizontal axis. In the matrix, the higher the value of the investment, the more sensitive AOL is to its risk score. Investments of low value (bottom row) are in the green zone as long as they don't reach the 240 TIPS point. Conversely, investments of USD 50 million or more are never in the green zone and require a regular monitoring of their risk score—from both an ERM and a financial variance point of view. *Note:* Since the exhibit is printed in grayscale, yellow appears as the lightest shade in the exhibit, green as the middle shade, and red as the darkest shade.

Exhibit 35.14 places the hypothetical AOL investee company, Trex Radio (investee company B1 in the chart), alongside eight others on the investment performance dashboard for comparison purposes. We can see that Trex Radio is in the green zone and that AOL would probably track more closely other subsidiaries such as B9 (TV Manila), B4 (Channel 2 HK), and B5 (IPTV Dubai).

As the legend states, the color-coding of the dashboard is based on:

- The value of AOL's investment
- The financial performance and risk management of the investee company
- The effectiveness and timeliness of key risk action plans

The green zone (the lightest shade of gray) represents investee companies where the potential impact on AOL is low due to the size of the investment and/or there are adequate controls in terms of risk management and financial performance. The yellow zone (the middle shade) indicates a medium potential impact due to the investment's size and/or deficiencies in management (e.g., not meeting targets or delays in completion of plans). The red zone (darkest shade) indicates a need for urgent attention because of a high potential impact due to the size of the investment and/or performance is far below expectations—the company cannot produce results and suffers major delays in the completion of action plans.

Of course, these are simplified guidelines that need to be filtered through sound business acumen. A large investment that performs impeccably might not require urgent attention but consistent monitoring and review, while a smaller one that performs poorly may fall in the red zone instead of the yellow one. These guidelines have proved useful over time in assisting with the management of AOL's portfolio of investee companies.

AOL tracks its portfolio's investment performance dashboard on a quarterly basis (see Exhibit 35.15). Exhibit 35.16 displays a hypothetical variation from one quarter to the next. AOL's ERM Team is able to explain the variations in terms of either the valuation of the investment, the financial risk variance, or the investment risk score. It should be noted that a reduction in value of the investment is considered positive insofar as it is voluntary, for instance, when AOL sells a portion of its participation. If the reduction in value happens without a change in AOL's stake in the company, further investigation is required to determine the risk associated with such a negative change and to make adequate investment recommendations to the board of directors, as will be shown in the next exhibit.

HELPING THE BOARD MAKE INVESTMENT DECISIONS

Exhibit 35.17 shows how AOL's ERM Framework ultimately assists its board of directors in making key investment decisions about its portfolio of foreign investee companies.

Horizontal movements in the investment performance dashboard represent a change in the performance score. On that front, an increase in the performance score requires more attention. But a decrease in the performance score (financial or risk scores) may also call for further analysis, because, as we know from the risk/return relationship, a reduction in the risk profile may also mean a corresponding decrease in profitability that, if sustained, would mean a relative stagnation in AOL's investment value in the future. Possible strategic decisions for that axis of the dashboard range from reviewing the business model, the strategies, or the financial processes, the capital required to sustain or grow the business or to simply divest it.

Vertical movements in the investment performance dashboard represent a change in investment value. As explained earlier, a reduction in value indicates a lower risk in the matrix as long as it is a result of selling a portion of the business. Otherwise, a decrease in valuation is obviously a negative sign. The possible actions are similar to those above: review with a view to maintain or to divest.

Valuation @ Current Investment Value (Nov '13)
(USD million)

>100
100
50
25

Total Investment Performance (Financial & Risk) Scores (in Points)

80 160 240 320

B2 B6 B7 B1 B8 B4 B3 B9 B5

Legend

xx Current Bubble

x.x Bubble positioning from the previous quarter

The impact to the Group is Low based on the amount invested *and / or* the financial performance and efforts to mitigate the risks for the investment are on track against set targets. Action Plans are effective to mitigate the risks and are completed on a timely basis.

The impact to the Group is Medium based on the amount invested *and / or* the financial performance and efforts to mitigate the risks for the investment are not meeting set targets. Action Plans implemented are not achieving the desired results and there are delays in completion.

The impact to the Group is High based on the amount invested *and / or* the financial performance and efforts to mitigate the risks for the investment are far below expected the targets set. Action Plans implemented cannot produce the desired results and there are major delays in completion. Urgent management focus is required.

Ref	Business Unit Name
B1	Trex Radio
B2	Radio India
B3	Channel 1 (HK)
B4	Channel 2 (HK)
B5	IPTV (Dubai)

Ref	Business Unit Name
B6	Radio Indonesia
B7	TV Indonesia
B8	TV Vietnam
B9	TV Manila

Exhibit 35.15 Investment Performance Dashboard Comparison

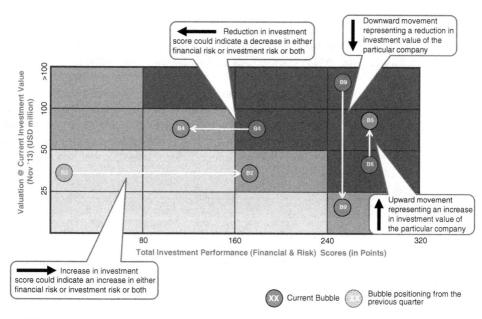

Exhibit 35.16 Investment Performance Dashboard—Quarterly Movements

Exhibit 35.17 Assisting the Board in Making Key Decisions

Movements	Description	Plausible Strategic Decisions
Increase in investment score	An indication that either the company has increased its risk exposure or is unable to achieve the budgeted financial targets.	- Review of business strategies. - Review of budget process. - Need for additional fund injection either via debt or equity. - Possible divestment due to unfavorable changes in the business / regulatory environment or other factors.
Decrease in investment score	An indication that either the company has decreased its risk exposure or achieved its budgeted financial targets. However, it is important to further analyze data to determine actual performance.	- Possible increase in investment stake due to good performance. - Review business model / practices and consider replicating success stories across other companies. - Could arise out of poor management of strategy implementation. Exit?
Increase in investment value	Depending on the method used for valuation, this is usually a positive indication that the company is doing well.	- Possible increase in investment stake. - Consideration for upside sale of the company.
Decrease in investment value	Depending on the method used for valuation, this usually means the company may not be able to break even.	- Possible divestment in investment stake. - Need for additional fund injection either via debt or equity.

CONCLUSION

This case study illustrates how a structured and diligent approach to ERM implementation, monitoring, and reporting can add value not only to the investee company adopting it, but also to the parent company having to make investment decisions for its portfolio of direct foreign investments. For this case study, we showed how the investment performance dashboard could allow a company to compare investment value to total investment risk score and compare profitability to overall risk. Without being fully quantitative, this approach brings the management of a portfolio of direct investments closer to the risk/return management of a portfolio of financial investments.

QUESTIONS

1. Identify some reasons why risk management practices might not take off and/or be embedded effectively in an investee company.
2. Who should participate in the ERM process to ensure successful implementation of this on-going program?
3. What should the CEO's role be for the successful implementation and on-going performance of an ERM process?
4. How will senior management benefit from supporting ERM implementation?
5. Does ERM require reporting to executive management? If so, what types of reports are most suitable for executive management?
6. What do you think is the best approach in ensuring a successful implementation of ERM? Please provide a few different elements.

NOTES

1. BBC News Asia-Pacific, May 23, 2013. www.bbc.co.uk/news/world-asia-pacific-15367879.
2. Tourism Malaysia, November 17, 2013. www.tourism.gov.my/en/my/WebPage/About-Malaysia.
3. National Geographic, November 18, 2013. www.travel.nationalgeographic.com/travel/countries/malaysia-facts.
4. *Financial Times*, November 18, 2013. www.ft.com/intl/markets/currencies.
5. Astro Malaysia Holdings Berhad's Annual Report 2013.
6. Ibid.; Corporate Governance on Asia, Asian Roundtable on Corporate Governance, OECD, 2011.
7. Malaysian Code on Corporate Governance 2012, Securities Commission Malaysia, March 2012.
8. "ASEAN Corporate Governance Scorecard, Country Reports and Assessments 2012–2013," Joint Initiative of the ASEAN Capital Markets Forum and the Asian Development Bank, Asian Development Bank, 2013.
9. Astro Malaysia Holdings Berhad's, "Go Beyond: Annual Report 2013," 48.
10. Ibid., 55.
11. Ibid., 55.
12. Ibid., 56.
13. Internet Protocol television is a system through which television services are delivered using the Internet Protocol suite over a packet-switched network such as the Internet, instead of being delivered through traditional terrestrial, satellite signal, and cable television formats.

REFERENCES

Asian Development Bank. 2013. "ASEAN Corporate Governance Scorecard, Country Reports and Assessments 2012–2013," Joint Initiative of the ASEAN Capital Markets Forum and the Asian Development Ban.

Astro Malaysia Holdings Berhad. 2013. "Go Beyond: Annual Report 2013."

Securities Commission Malaysia. 2012. Malaysian Code on Corporate Governance.

ABOUT THE CONTRIBUTORS

Patrick Adam Kanagaratnam Abdullah is the Vice President of Enterprise Risk Management (ERM) for Astro Overseas Limited (AOL). He specializes in the implementation of ERM practices across AOL's investments, which are located primarily in Asia Pacific. He has over 21 years of experience in safety and crisis management and 17 years in risk management that includes ERM and Business Continuity planning. He is also responsible for statutory compliance monitoring and reporting for AOL group of companies. He has a BSC (Hons) in Environmental Management from the Science University of Malaysia (USM). He also has an Accredited Safety Auditor Certification from Edith Cowan University, Western Australia. He represent Malaysia as a Board member of Pan-Asia Risk and Insurance Management Association (PARIMA) which has been set up to promote professionalism and a high and efficient standard of competence for risk management practices in Asia. When required, he also presents ERM and Business Continuity planning papers at conferences, and facilitates work group discussions on risk management practices.

Ghislain Giroux Dufort is President of Baldwin Risk Strategies Inc., a consulting firm advising boards of directors and management teams on risk governance and ERM. He has 25 years of experience in management, risk, international business, and consulting, including at Transcontinental, Willis, Hydro-Québec International, the Mathematical Research Center, and Export Development Canada. He headed an international business program and taught at the HEC Montreal Business School. He is a graduate of the London Financial Times Non-Executive Director Diploma, has an MBA from McGill University, and an M.Sc. in Applied Mathematics and a B.Sc. in Physics from the University of Montreal. He is a member of the Strategic Risk Council of the Conference Board of Canada, of the London-based Institute of Risk Management (including its Global Education Advisory Board and Panel of Judges for its Global Risk Awards), and of the Institute of Risk Management of South Africa. He writes on risk and participates in international risk conferences as chair and speaker.

About the Editors

John R.S. Fraser is the Senior Vice President, Internal Audit, and former Chief Risk Officer of Hydro One Networks Inc., Canada, one of North America's largest electricity transmission and distribution companies. He is a Fellow of the Institute of Chartered Accountants of Ontario, a Fellow of the Association of Chartered Certified Accountants (U.K.), a Certified Internal Auditor, and a Certified Information Systems Auditor. He has over 30 years of experience in the risk and control field, mostly in the financial services sector, including areas such as finance, fraud, derivatives, safety, environmental, computers and operations. He is a member of the Faculty at the Directors College for the Strategic Risk Oversight Program, and has developed and teaches a masters degree course entitled Enterprise Risk Management in the Masters in Financial Accountability Program at York University where he is an adjunct professor. He is a recognized authority on enterprise risk management (ERM) and has co-authored several academic papers on ERM. He is co-editor (with Betty Simkins) of a best-selling university text-book released in 2010, *Enterprise Risk Management: Today's Leading Research and Best Practices for Tomorrow's Executives.*

Betty J. Simkins, PhD, is Williams Companies Chair of Business and Professor of Finance at Oklahoma State University. Betty received her PhD from Case Western Reserve University. She has had more than 60 publications in academic and practitioner journals. She has won awards for her teaching, research, and outreach, including the top awards at Oklahoma States University: Regents Distinguished Teaching Award, Regents Distinguished Research Award, and Outreach Excellence Award. Her primary areas of research are risk management, energy finance, and corporate governance. Betty serves on the editorial boards of nine academic journals, including the *Journal of Banking and Finance*; is past coeditor of the *Journal of Applied Finance*; and is past president of the Eastern Finance Association. She also serves on the Executive Advisory Committee of the Conference Board of Canada's Strategic Risk Council. In addition to this book, she has published two others: *Energy Finance and Economics: Analysis and Valuation, Risk Management and the Future of Energy* and *Enterprise Risk Management: Today's Leading Research and Best Practices for Tomorrow's Executives* (co-edited with John Fraser). Prior to entering academia, she worked in the corporate world for ConocoPhillips and Williams Companies. She conducts executive education courses for companies globally.

Kristina Narvaez is the president and owner of ERM Strategies, LLC (www.erm strategies.com), which offers ERM research and training to organizations on various ERM-related topics. She graduated from the University of Utah in environmental risk management and then received her MBA from Westminster College. She is a two-time Spencer Education Foundation Graduate Scholar from the Risk and Insurance Management Society and has published more than 25 articles relating to enterprise risk management and board risk governance. She has given many presentations to various risk management associations on topics of ERM. She is an adjunct professor at Brigham Young University, teaching a business strategy course for undergraduates.

Index

CPSIA information can be obtained
at www.ICGtesting.com
Printed in the USA
BVHW010723080819

555158BV00045B/244/P

9 781118 691960